D1683736

THE MAGNIFICENT MUGHALS

THE MAGNIFICENT MUGHALS

Editor
ZEENUT ZIAD

Foreword by
MILO CLEVELAND BEACH

OXFORD
UNIVERSITY PRESS

OXFORD
UNIVERSITY PRESS

Great Clarendon Street, Oxford OX2 6DP

Oxford University Press is a department of the University of Oxford.
It furthers the University's objective of excellence in research, scholarship,
and education by publishing worldwide in

Oxford New York

Auckland Cape Town Dar es Salaam Hong Kong Karachi
Kuala Lumpur Madrid Melbourne Mexico City Nairobi
New Delhi Shanghai Taipei Toronto

with offices in

Argentina Austria Brazil Chile Czech Republic France Greece
Guatemala Hungary Italy Japan Poland Portugal Singapore
South Korea Switzerland Turkey Ukraine Vietnam

Oxford is a registered trade mark of Oxford University Press
in the UK and in certain other countries

© Oxford University Press 2002

The moral rights of the author have been asserted

First published 2002

All rights reserved. No part of this publication may be reproduced, translated,
stored in a retrieval system, or transmitted, in any form or by any means,
without the prior permission in writing of Oxford University Press.
Enquiries concerning reproduction should be sent to
Oxford University Press at the address below.

This book is sold subject to the condition that it shall not, by way
of trade or otherwise, be lent, re-sold, hired out or otherwise circulated
without the publisher's prior consent in any form of binding or cover
other than that in which it is published and without a similar condition
including this condition being imposed on the subsequent purchaser.

ISBN 978-0-19-579444-1

Second Impression 2007

Design by: **s+ndesign**

Cover: Badshahi Mosque, Lahore, Pakistan
Photograph by Pervez A. Khan, Fellow, Royal Geographical Society

Title Pages
SHAHJAHAN EXAMINING THE ROYAL SEAL.
by Abul Hasan ca. 1628.
Collection Prince and Princess Sadruddin Aga Khan (M. 140).

Frontispiece:
AN ALTERCATION IN THE BAZAAR.
From a copy of the *Kulliyat* of Sa'di ca. 1604.
Collection Prince and Princess Sadruddin Aga Khan, (Ms. 35, f. 19b).

Page viii
A SINNER'S PASSIONATE PLEA TO GOD.
From a copy of the *Kulliyat* of Sa'di ca. 1604.
Collection Prince and Princess Sadruddin Aga Khan, (Ms. 35, f. 107b).

Page x
THE MANUSCRIPT ATELIER.
From a copy of the *Akhlaq-i Nasiri ca.* 1590-95.
Collection Prince and Princess Sadruddin Aga Khan (Ms. 39, f. 196a).

Typeset in Granjon
Printed in Pakistan by
Nikmat Printers, Karachi.
Published by
Ameena Saiyid, Oxford University Press
No. 38, Sector 15, Korangi Industrial Area, PO Box 8214
Karachi-74900, Pakistan.

DEDICATED TO THE MEMORY

OF

MY FATHER

MAJOR-GENERAL SAHIBZADA ANIS AHMAD KHAN

WITH LOVE AND GRATITUDE

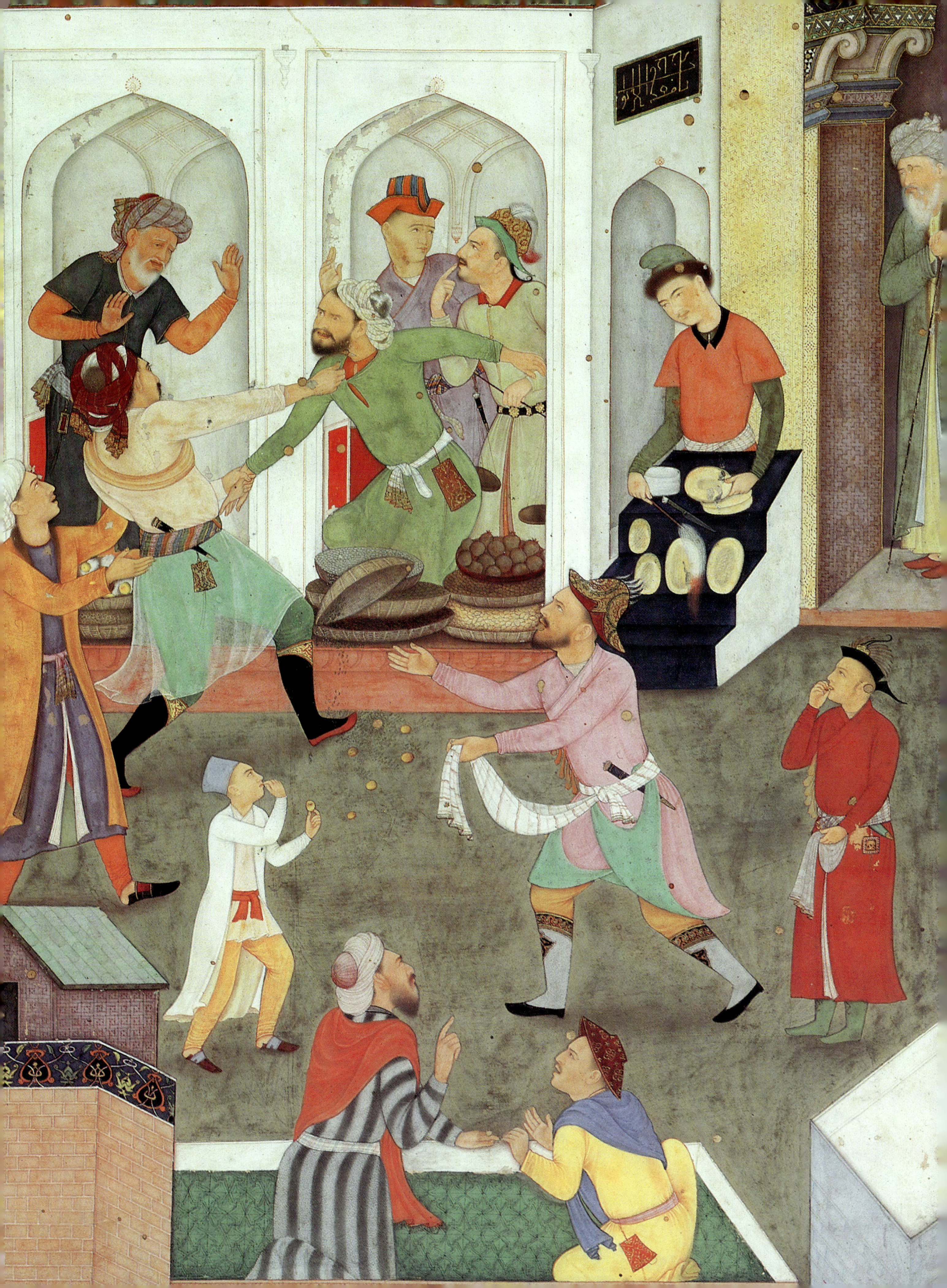

Contents

	FOREWORD by Milo Cleveland Beach	xi
	ACKNOWLEDGEMENTS	xvii
	INTRODUCTION by Zeenut Ziad	xviii
1	**THE MUGHAL EMPIRE** *John F. Richards*	1
2	**THE LIVES AND CONTRIBUTIONS OF MUGHAL WOMEN** *Ellison B. Findly*	25
3	**RELIGION** *Annemarie Schimmel*	59
4	**LITERATURE** *Wheeler M. Thackston*	83
5	**URDU LITERATURE** *Shamsur Rahman Faruqi*	113
6	**IMPERIAL MUGHAL PAINTING** *Joseph M. Dye III*	143
7	**ARCHITECTURE** *Catherine B. Asher*	183
8	**MUSIC AND DANCE** *Bonnie C. Wade*	229
9	**THE ECONOMY** *Irfan Habib*	269
10	**COINAGE AND MONETARY SYSTEM** *Aman ur Rahman and Waleed Ziad*	281

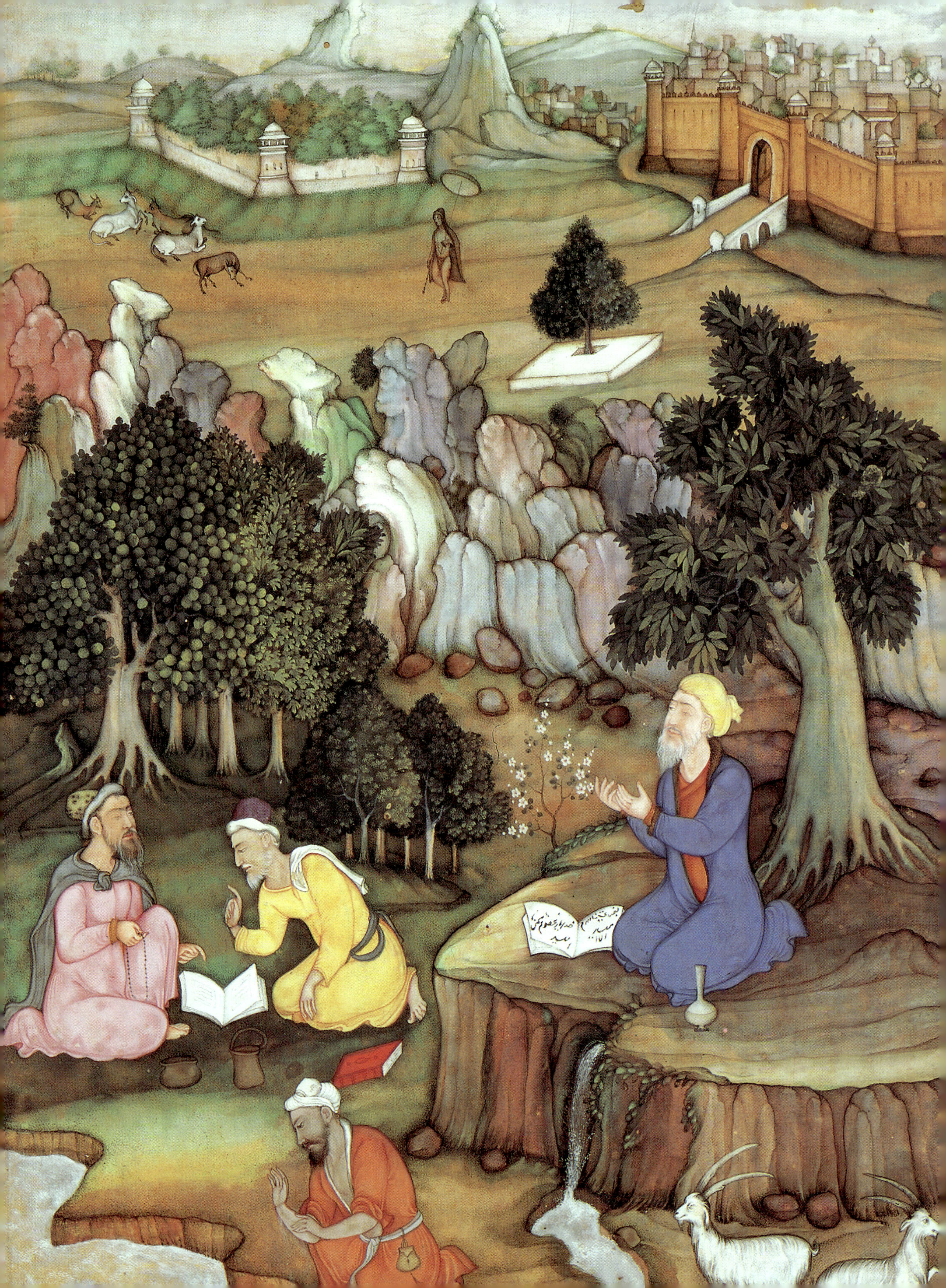

Contents

GENEALOGICAL CHART	302
CHRONOLOGY	304
CONTRIBUTORS	309

MAPS

1. The Mughal Empire, 1707	2
2. Major Architectural Sites and Cultural Centres in the Mughal Empire	182
3. Economic Map of the Mughal Empire, 1707	272

INDEX	311

ان باب حفظ کن و بانی تتبع آن وصایا میکند عمل تام شود

FOREWORD

Milo Cleveland Beach

For the casual visitor to Pakistan, India, or Bangladesh, the major monuments of the Mughal era are continually and easily encountered. Great fortress complexes dominate Lahore, Delhi, and Agra, while mosques, palaces, tombs (of which the Taj Mahal is only the most famous), bridges, caravanserais, and the remains of gardens animate landscapes across South Asia. Now among the most alluring destinations for travellers, it is only relatively recently that the world of the Mughals has become familiar to people living beyond the Subcontinent, and recognized as a particularly stimulating period in the world's history. Once simply a distant and fabled embodiment of wealth and power, it gave to English and European languages a term ('mogul') with exactly that connotation but with no initial awareness of its historical roots. The ease of modern travel, however, as well as contemporary photographic images and travel narratives, and an extraordinary series of exhibitions of Mughal art, have vastly expanded popular interest in the accomplishments of the empire established by the emperor Babur and his descendants.

The first major public exhibition anywhere devoted solely to Mughal art occurred in New York City in 1963. *The Art of Mughal India*, organized by Stuart Cary Welch for the Asia House Gallery, launched a series of presentations that continues today. A ground-breaking exhibition, it was one of the stimuli that provoked serious interest among a range of scholars at the time, resulting in the expansion of understanding that has led to this volume. But whereas in 1963 Mughal painting could be discussed in isolation, the essays in this book demonstrate over and over again the richer understanding that comes to any disciplinary interest with recognition of the wide range of inter-relationships within which it exists. Aman ur Rahman and Waleed Ziad, for example, write that:

> To the Mughals, coins were not merely a means of exchange, but also a powerful and efficient means of propaganda: a symbol of imperial grandeur carrying the seal of the emperor to every corner of the empire, a testament to the spread of his domain and unchallenged sovereignty. Mughal coins were characterized by superb calligraphy and high quality execution; each piece was an exceptional work of art. The innovations and features of the coins from Akbar's reign were numerous, and, served a political purpose remarkably well.

They also remind us that Abdus Samad, the Persian master painter who came to the Subcontinent from Iran to become head of the royal painting workshops under Akbar, was also appointed head of the imperial mint. While indicating a concern for aesthetics across seemingly unrelated operations of the empire, the authors further imply that study of the impact of the imagery on coins would be fruitful to both political and artistic understanding of the Mughals; coins of superb quality circulated widely, after all, whereas important paintings on paper stayed within the imperial and aristocratic collections.

Soon after it first became known in Europe, the term 'mogul',—an early transliteration of a designation more often today spelled 'Mughal', both being adaptations of 'Mongol'—came to embody the European imaginative invention of an exotic, decadent East, a phenomenon well studied by Edward Said and others. However, as Wheeler Thackston points out, the people we call Mughal (a designation they would have considered derogatory) termed themselves 'Timurids', in honour of the great Turko-Mongol conqueror Timur, from whom they were descended. This is only one way by which Europeans have misrepresented the dynasty. During the period of the British raj, not surprisingly, British and other European historians often compared the political and social world of the Mughals to European interests in a dismissive, negative manner. Such attitudes also provided the foundation for innumerable works of fiction and poetry, and theatrical extravaganzas ranging from John Dryden's *Aureng-zebe* (1675) to Edmond Autran's comic opera of 1877, *Le Grand Mogul*. Almost inevitably, such viewpoints encouraged non-Indian scholars to find value and justification for Mughal historical and artistic traditions in European terms. The catalogue for the 1963 exhibition, for example, stated in its introduction: 'The sixteenth century was an age of individualism. Humanism had triumphed, even in India. We know dozens of Mughal Old Masters by name and style, and we can speak of them as we do of Rembrandt or Durer.'

As more information was discovered about the emperors themselves, figures admittedly of extraordinary power and fascination, they became the central element of early studies. *The Art of Mughal India* further asserts: 'The emperors' varying moods found expression at the hands of their artists and craftsmen, who gave tangible form to their flights of fancy.' In keeping with European interest in individuals as the determinative forces of history, the emperors were equated with the artists and architects responsible for the shape and character of Mughal civilization, and often given credit for their achievements. The personal role of the emperor as patron was, of course, critically important in the development of Mughal arts and architecture, but in recent years certain facts have appeared that provide a more balanced understanding. Annemarie Schimmel writes:

> The fact that Akbar married a number of Rajput princesses and that he granted Amritsar as a fief to the Sikh leader Ramdas, had political rather than religious reasons, and his interest in the Jesuit fathers sprang from his insatiable curiosity. It seems that the 'un-Islamic' trends in Akbar's politics have also been exaggerated by the Jesuits who had hoped to win him over to Christianity.

In other words, previous interpretations of the sources and reasons for Akbar's decisions and accomplishments are now often under reconsideration. For example, European contact was a crucial ingredient in the stylistic mixture which produced a distinctively Mughal style of painting—this was recognized already in the official contemporary history of Akbar's reign. This interest had long been thought to have evolved only after Akbar's contact with Portuguese Jesuits in the 1570s and in response to his documented interest in Christianity—an interest the Jesuits believed would lead inevitably to conversion. New discoveries of European influenced images of even earlier date, however, indicate that imperial painters almost certainly had access to and learned new techniques from European prints before Akbar was known to have been aware of these images. In other words, indigenous painters, rather than European visitors, may have been substantially responsible for initially arousing Akbar's curiosity.

Studies of Mughal art have also been based on perceptions of strong differences in the direction of patronage under each of the artistically active emperors. However, closer analysis reveals that painting styles developed smoothly and logically during the transitional periods between imperial changeovers. For instance, the earliest examples of historical documentation through painting—one of the innovations usually attributed to Akbar's patronage—are actually found during the period of Humayun's rule, while the interest in acutely sensitive, highly individualized portraiture and technical refinement that has been used to define Jahangir's patronage (which it does), initially appeared in works made for Akbar at the end of his reign. Prince Salim, the future Jahangir, supported quite different stylistic interests at his rebel capital in Allahabad during the years before his accession. The style of imperial painting defined by the years of Jahangir's rule therefore evolves directly from developments initiated under his father's patronage in the imperial workshops—a group of artists and craftsmen (and traditions) which Jahangir inherited at his accession. It can therefore no longer be convincingly argued that paintings were simply illustrations of the interests and moods of whichever emperor was in power. Painting and painters had a momentum of their own that was as capable of determining, as of simply responding to, imperial interests: a phenomenon that needs greater study.

The creative atmosphere of the Mughal court was immensely cosmopolitan. '[The] educated elite…left Iran, generally for the Subcontinent, where opportunities were more promising …Poets…came to the Subcontinent in record numbers,' Wheeler Thackston notes. Both Annemarie Schimmel, through a virtual inventory of the religious movements of the time, and Bonnie Wade describe the international atmosphere in detail. Bonnie Wade not only notes the presence of musicians, performers, and instruments from very diverse cultural communities in South, Central, and West Asia, she defines the rapid change of musical and performance practice as individuals encountered and learned from traditions other than those in which they had themselves been trained—exactly what we see happening, for instance, in painting and architecture. Whether in the literary and visual arts, architecture, or music and performance, such encounters among creative individuals made at a court where a wide range of peoples and traditions were newly brought together, and where experimentation was encouraged, must have been at least as important to the evolution of the new and uniquely Mughal style as were the specific enthusiasms of the individual emperors.

It was the willingness to respect and incorporate aspects of the source traditions that distinguishes Mughal culture, and (not insignificantly) attests to its political astuteness. Even with coinage, after they note the need to provide a uniform currency throughout Akbar's increasingly far-flung empire, Rahman and Ziad continue: 'Occasionally…local currencies maintained some of their indigenous characteristics within the Mughal monetary framework, so that they would be acceptable to the population.' And, of course, that population would in turn feel itself a recognized and valued part of the imperial realms.

If Akbar formed and solidified the structures that empowered the empire, his son Jahangir provided polish and refinement. Rahman and Ziad write further:

> In addition to improvements in quality, Jahangir's creativity and artistic taste brought about a number of extraordinary monetary innovations. With such a well established and successful system in place, later Mughals did not deem it necessary to make any significant changes in monetary policy.

Other areas, too, later operated on the strong foundations built by Akbar, Jahangir, and Shahjahan. Towards the end of Aurangzeb's rule, however, imperial power began to wane, coinciding with increased religious conservatism. Joseph Dye notes the seeming decline of painting during Aurangzeb's reign when he writes, 'The fate of the imperial style after Aurangzeb's death in 1707 is a story that remains to be told.' And one hopes this observation will be stimulating to a new generation of scholars, for these later developments should now be seen as a fundamental change in the character of Mughal style rather than simply a phase of decadence—the traditional interpretation. As the excitement of the first contact by artists with alternative traditions, noted above, changed with time into familiarity, the stimulation provided by those first meetings was no longer possible. The Mughals were increasingly integrated into the cultural world of South Asia, and working methods and techniques had become comfortable, rather than stimulatingly novel. As with coinage, it was no longer innovation that provided incentives for artists, but the chance to maintain and refine the newly established traditions.

In Mughal studies, scholars have long concentrated on the period in which the emperors seemed most interesting individually, and in which innovation and change was most rapid. Art historians, for example, could focus on the unique qualities of individual painters, while the men depicted in portraits could be recognized and celebrated for their achievements. This answered the art historians' technique of comparing work by recognizably individual artists, and of determining how these men effected the sequential changes that defined a seemingly linear and historically consistent evolution of style. However, the Mughal interest in individuality found initially in Babur's memoirs—the first autobiography in the Muslim world—and ending with the conservatism of Aurangzeb, is not only distinctive within Indian and Muslim traditions, it was also effected only for a part of the period of Mughal rule. To pretend that we can understand all of Mughal culture by concentrating on this aspect alone and ignoring the character of the remaining years is very misleading.

There has been considerable neglect—perhaps especially in the field of the arts—of Mughal activity in the eighteenth and nineteenth century. S.R. Faruqi, however, attempts to redress this indifference and makes a bold claim in his essay:

> Culturally and spiritually, the eighteenth century was more vibrant than its predecessor.

Further, Catherine Asher remarks:

> As the Mughal empire diminished new powers emerged in their stead: in the east, north, and Deccan, Shia Muslim houses came to the fore, while elsewhere Rajput Hindus were able to assert their authority as never before…Architectural

production is rarely considered during these last 150 years; when buildings are discussed they are generally deemed to be decadent, as if political decline is reflected in architectural terms...In fact a good deal of innovation is seen in buildings produced under the later Mughals and in particular those built by the many new emerging powers.

While articulating the attitude of traditional scholars who have reduced the arts to simple illustrations of major historical events and imperial personalities, she notes the corresponding neglect of Mughal influence and activity away from the imperial centres. Faruqi, in turn, mentions the distaste which Urdu, or literary Hindi, first provoked among the intelligentsia in Delhi, where it was seen as an uncultured product of the provinces. Modern scholars are therefore not alone in their focus on the capital areas. For the study of the period from the eighteenth century onward, however, such a limitation is no longer appropriate. If the Mughals were an intrusive element that came into India from Central Asia in 1526, initially seeming distinctive from the cultures already existing within the Subcontinent, by the late seventeenth century they had so successfully influenced and been influenced by older South Asian cultures that, from that time, they are best considered simply one of the many seamlessly inter-related cultural traditions encountered in South Asia. In 1590, for example, Mughal painting and architecture were uniquely distinctive, quite different from the images or living spaces of Rajput Rajasthan (to take just one example). But a century later, there is little meaningful stylistic difference; it is often impossible to tell if a mid-eighteenth century painting is from the imperial workshops, or made for a raja in Rajasthan. This is not a sign of decline but rather of highly sensitive growth, and firm evidence of the degree to which the Mughals became thoroughly integrated into the land they had initially entered as strangers. (By contrast, of course, the British both arrived in and departed from South Asia as foreigners.)

However, whereas Mughal art in the century following Akbar's accession in 1556 is the most intensively studied of all South Asian artistic traditions, the contemporaneous arts of Hindu (meaning Rajput) India are among the most neglected—despite the fact that the best works are of a quality and originality as fine as any Mughal illustrations. In exploring this neglect, it is not unimportant that there was little interest by traditional Rajput patrons and artists in the Mughal concern for historical documentation, portraiture, or the use of style to express personal sensibilities—and thus little chance for European art historians to find, isolate, and laud those qualities. Given its character, Rajput art has drawn little serious and sustained attention from non-Indian scholars; they simply did not have the academic tools to explore its significance. And as Mughal art became increasingly indistinguishable from Rajput attitudes over time, European historians lost interest in that tradition as well.

John Richard's essay on Mughal history moves away from the viewpoints of colonial historians; he recognizes and highlights the positive achievements of the Mughals in South Asia, and thus provides a framework for the many new interpretations offered in this volume.

Irfan Habib's essay may best define the welcome new perspective. He begins his study of the economy of the Mughal empire by bringing us through the forests, across the fields and into the villages to meet the villagers and peasants—the sources of Mughal wealth. He then reminds us:

> The revenues that the Mughal emperor collected, drawing from lands reserved for the treasury—the so-called *khalisa sharifa*—and the princes and nobility collected, drawing from their *jagirs*, amounted to an enormous drain of wealth from the countryside.

Of course, matters were not, in fact, so simple:

> The royal and aristocratic demand for luxuries and craft products not only helped maintain large populations of local craftsmen, but also craftsmen working at towns in distant regions, specializing in particular goods. Even when the demand was for imported horses of high breeds...from Iran and Central Asia, this too indirectly assisted the Indian craft sector since the animals were paid for mainly through the export of Indian products, notably textiles.

Habib introduces his readers to the Mughal world through people long ignored, as does Ellison Findly. Her interest in Mughal women has meant that no longer can (or should) one move through Mughal buildings or look at Mughal paintings without being aware of what would have been happening out of sight. The activities in the women's sphere, she writes, were often crucially determinative to the historical scenes being enacted in public view: 'Mughal life centred, in its day to day regularity, around the doings of women,' and these women (who came from Muslim, Hindu, Jain, Zoroastrian, and even Christian families across South and West Asia) represented a broad diversity of ethnic traditions and expectations. This is an aspect little noticed until very recently, just as the evidence for musical practices had been ignored—despite the abundance of information available in even well-known, often published paintings—until Bonnie Wade realized the importance of these carefully documented details. Through his exploration of the Urdu *ghazal*, Faruqi dispels many myths about literary and social norms in the eighteenth century. He also counters the image of women created by modern Urdu writers:

… the beloved in the eighteenth-century *ghazal* is not the passive, hiding-behind-the-*purdah*, slightly tubercular, recoiling from the slightest physical contact, shrinking-violet type of girl much touted by modern writers as the optimal beloved in the *ghazal*. This image gained currency through modern 'classicist' poets like Hasrat Mohani (1875-1951), and attempts continue to be made to fit all *ghazals* to this image…

This is the first single volume in which such a wide variety of subjects relating to the Mughal world, and such a range of interpretations, has been explored. The new interests and directions celebrated by the writers of this volume are only possible because of the work of past scholars, of course, but they raise a new base of understanding upon which the future architecture of Mughal studies can continue to rise.

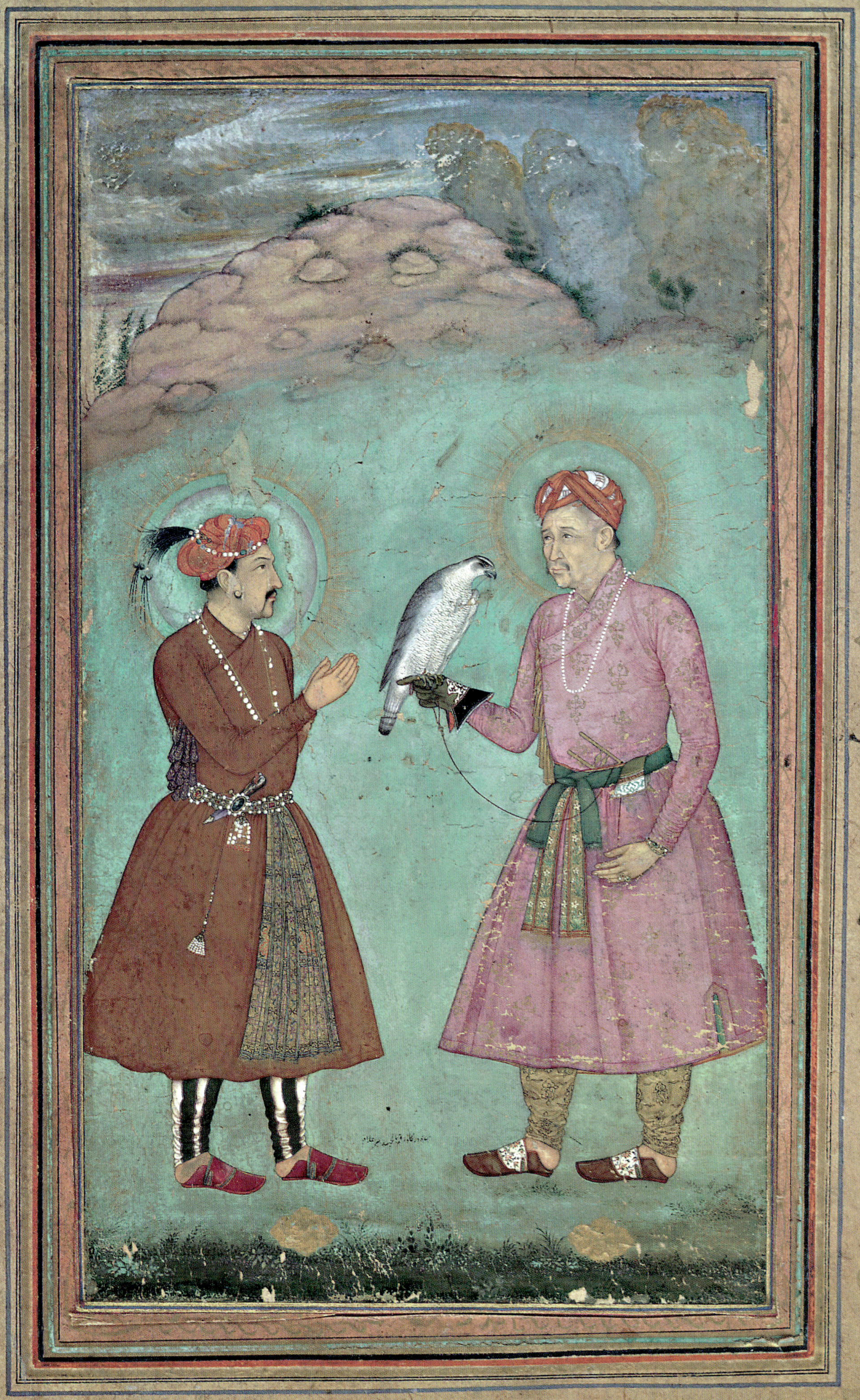

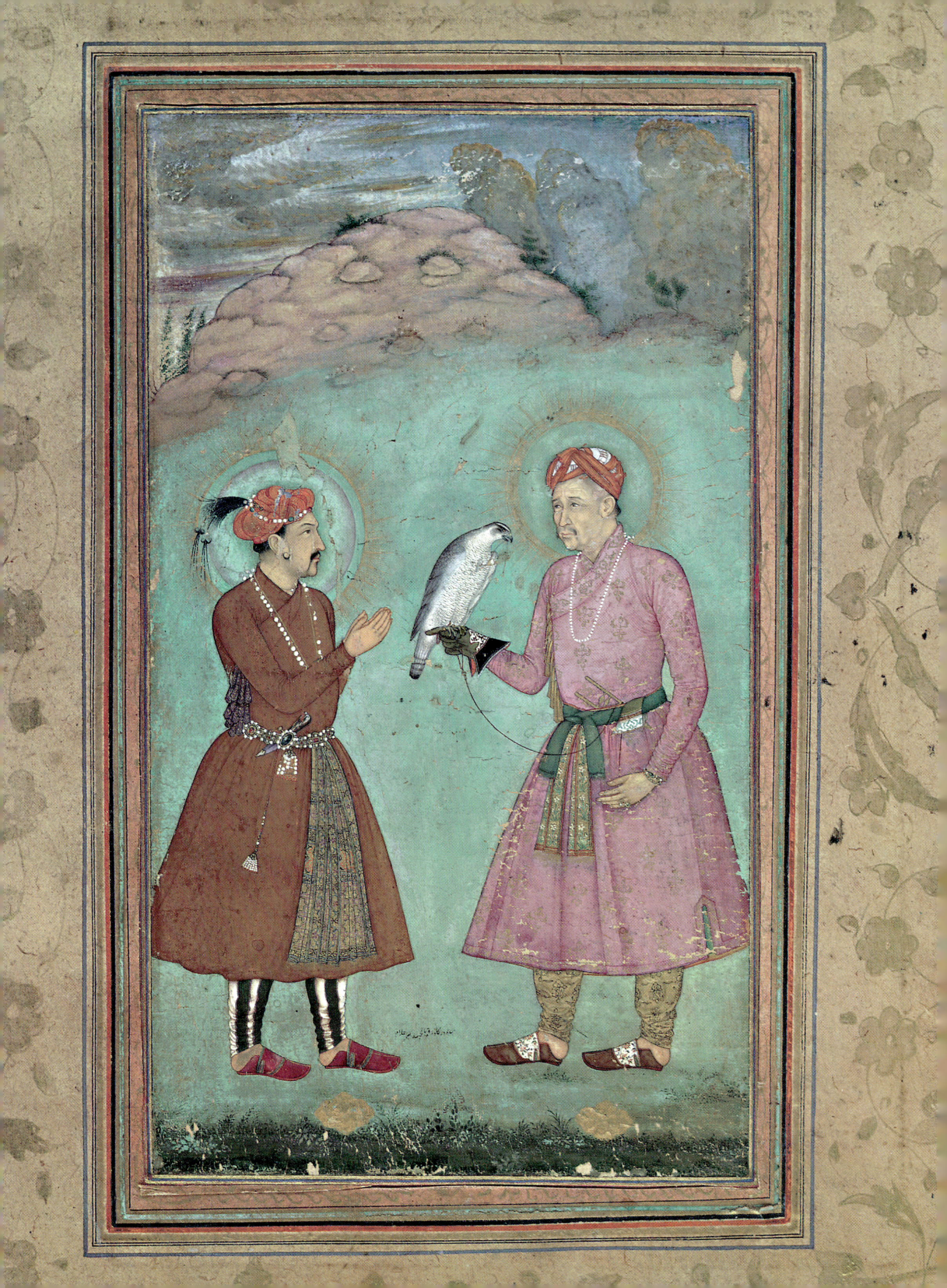

ACKNOWLEDGEMENTS

I must first express my profound gratitude to Milo Beach for his advice and support. This book would not have been possible without his help.

I gratefully acknowledge the generosity of the sponsors: Citibank, Jaffer Brothers Private Ltd. and Shell Pakistan Ltd. I am indebted, in particular, to Haamid Jaffer for his invaluable support. My sincere thanks also to Hassan Madani of Shell Pakistan Ltd. I am very grateful to Jagdish P. Goenka for his generosity in graciously permitting me to reproduce paintings from the great Goenka Collection. Prince and Princess Sadruddin Aga Khan generously provided transparencies from their Collection. They possess some of the finest examples of Mughal art in the world and therefore such beneficence in promoting scholarship is all the more exceptional. I commend the Prince and Princess and thank them sincerely. I am obliged to Hamid Akhund for kindly providing photographs.

I would like to acknowledge the permission given by the National Museum of Art of Romania to reproduce illustrations from a Mughal *murraqqa* (album) recently discovered by the curator of Oriental Art, Mircea Dunca-Moisin, in the National Library archives. The Mughal miniature seen on the opposite page, *Akbar and Jahangir,* is in a private collection. Previously the artist was unknown. I was fortunate to be able to attribute it to the renowned artist, Balchand, who began painting in the late Akbari period and reached maturity in Jahangir's reign.

Wheeler Thackston sustained me with help above and beyond the call of duty and Catherine Asher with her continuous encouragement. For their extremely pertinent comments and insights, I am deeply grateful to Syed Ali Jafari, Sabir Shafi Khan, and particularly to Mirza Hussain Khan, who also took on the burden of sharing his expertise in IT. My sincerest thanks to Munis Faruqui, Muhammad Umar Memon, Akbar Naqvi, and Unver Shafi who were very generous with their advice and time. Muhammad Umar Memon also very kindly permitted me to reproduce material from *The Annual of Urdu Studies*, of which he is the editor. Nadira Hussain brought her professionalism in graphic design, and untiring effort, to the difficult task of designing this book. I remain indebted to Shamsur Rahman Faruqi for contributing the chapter on Urdu literature despite serious health problems.

To my brother-in-law Zia Shafi Khan I owe an enormous debt for his unstinted efforts on behalf of this book. I am especially indebted for the support and suggestions of my brother Sahibzada Ajaz Anis and for the warm and untiring hospitality of my sister-in-law Tasneem at whose home I stayed for extended periods. The encouragement of my husband, Ziad Alahdad, provided the underpinning for this endeavour. In the end, my greatest debt is to my children, Homayra and Waleed, who have not only been my source of inspiration but an invaluable help at every step. It is for them and their generation that this book is intended.

INTRODUCTION

Zeenut Ziad

This volume has its origins in a highly successful lecture series organized by the Smithsonian Institution in Washington D.C. to introduce the Mughal legacy to the American public. Several eminent scholars were invited to discuss different aspects of the Mughal age. I had the pleasure of coordinating this course with invaluable support from Dr Milo Beach, Director of the Freer and Sackler Galleries of the Smithsonian Institution, and one of the world's leading authorities on Mughal art.

The enthusiastic response of the course participants led to the idea of compiling a book based on the lectures. While general histories of the Mughals and specialized books on individual subjects abound, no one authoritative volume covering major aspects of the Mughal legacy, elucidated by the foremost specialists, has been published. I hope this collection will fill the gap.

The research of the past few decades has considerably enriched and deepened our understanding of this period but the Mughal era is one that will be debated for years to come; there cannot be a 'last word' on the empire or on its protagonists. The traditional historiography of the Mughals has emphasized the sharp differences in policy between Akbar and Aurangzeb but it is necessary to balance the picture by recognizing the continuities as well[1]; the neglect of the post-Aurangzeb period has also to be rectified by highlighting the creative vigour of the later Mughal age. The true pleasure of approaching a period of such fascinating vitality is in exploring its strengths and weaknesses, in bringing out the paradoxes and contradictions and in avoiding simplistic interpretations. Appropriately, the essays in this volume represent different, and sometimes divergent, points of view and offer a variety of interpretations.[2] The aim is to present a broad view of the Mughal empire that will engender an appreciation of the political, economic, social, and cultural renewal the Mughals brought to the South Asian Subcontinent[3] and for the model of statecraft they gave to the world.

The Mughal age (1526-1858) has been described as 'one of the greatest periods of human achievement'.[4] This Indo-Muslim empire was the exemplar of a vibrant, culturally plural, multiethnic polity—the success of which modern states would do well to emulate. To understand this achievement in all its dimensions, it must be remembered that Mughal hegemony extended over 150 million people, predominantly non-Muslims (at that time the population of all Europe, excluding Russia, is estimated at 100 million). To govern this vast, heterogeneous population the Mughals devised a political system based on the principles of accommodation, local autonomy, alliance building, and respect for different traditions. In the process they harnessed the energies and strengths of this diversity and succeeded in establishing an effective and enduring state.

The first six emperors of this dynasty, often called the Great Mughals, continue to exercise a powerful fascination. In the pages of history one does not frequently encounter six consecutive generations of rulers each with an extraordinary, complex, and multifaceted personality. Albeit in varying degrees, each emperor was a humane individual with refined sensibilities. These were men of both style and substance. Even the emperor Humayun, sometimes sidelined by historians, exhibited, among other qualities, remarkable perseverance and tenacity in reclaiming his throne whilst Aurangzeb, frequently portrayed as harsh and unfeeling, could lament at the end of his life:

> I know not who I am, where I shall go, or what will happen to this sinner full of sins

It is universally acknowledged that this was a period in which diverse cultures were blended harmoniously and with incomparable refinement to produce one of the most artistically creative eras of world history. What is less well known, however, and has become evident through recent research, is that:

For nearly a hundred and seventy years (1556-1719) the Mughal empire remained a dynamic, centralized, complex organization...Mughal success was the product of hard-driving, active rulership exercised by extremely capable rulers who acted as their own chief executives. Military victory, territorial expansion, and centralized control rested upon the management skills and strategic vision of the emperors and their advisers.

It was an intrusive, centralizing system which unified the subcontinent...imposed an unprecedented level of public order...stimulated production and encouraged market growth. Few persons and communities, if any, were left untouched by this massive edifice.[5]

Unification, however, was not at the cost of a loss of identity or authority of the constituent parts; other historians underscore the multi-layered diffusion of power: 'While differences remain on the extent of centralization actually achieved, the Mughal empire is beginning to be viewed as a complex, nuanced and loose form of hegemony over a diverse, differentiated and dynamic economy and society.'[6]

Mughal rule expressed in a new form the unique character of the Subcontinent. Integrated South Asia asserted itself and for the first time became a major player on the world scene. This is all the more remarkable considering the tendency that existed in historic India to fragment into natural regions, and the circumscribed vision of the rulers of this collection of states. At its zenith Mughal India was the wealthiest and one of the most powerful empires in the world.

The Muslim Mughals originally brought with them strong egalitarian and democratic traditions from their Central Asian home. However, these proved unsustainable given the prevailing complex social conditions in India and the political imperatives of empire. In the Mughal system, wealth had to be earned, but it was, as everywhere else in the contemporaneous world, concentrated in a few hands—this was the age when the civilized world lived within carefully delineated class structures. The problem of social mobility in India was further compounded by the caste system that had been in place for nearly 3000 years; in Hindu kingdoms, participation in government was usually confined to a few upper castes. Yet even within this context the Mughal system was a meritocracy in every field of endeavour, where talent and learning could command magnificent rewards. Contrary to popular belief, the enormous wealth of the nobility was attained through ability and drive. Another view that has been challenged is the status of the peasantry: as Bose and Jalal point out, 'The picture of an emaciated and oppressed peasantry, mercilessly exploited by the emperor and his nobility, is being seriously altered in the light of new interpretations of the evidence'.[7]

An Indo-Muslim culture, built on 800 years of accommodation and assimilation between Hindus and Muslims, had already established many of the structures that the Mughals subsequently reformulated and refashioned to create a political system responsive to all, regardless of race and religion: 'Rarely has a political entity fostered such an open and receptive atmosphere towards influences from every possible provenance, and with such happy results'.[8] At the imperial court, the famed Mughal ethos evolved from the different traditions of South, Central, and West Asia, leavened with the royal family's exquisite taste. The Mughal sensibility was exceptional in the way it conjoined the cerebral and conceptual with the perceptual and sensual. The various influences became richer and deeper as they were transformed by the

---

1. For example: there is no doubt that the expansion of the nobility under Aurangzeb, particularly after 1681, brought about an increase of Hindus at all levels of the army, nobility and administration. Studies by M. Athar Ali (The Mughal Nobility under Aurangzeb, Oxford University Press, 1997, p. 31) indicate that among the mansabdars holding ranks above 500 zat the proportion of Hindus increased from 22 per cent under Akbar in 1595, to 32 per cent under Aurangzeb in the period 1679-1707.
2. The individual essays are discussed in the Foreword.
3. 'South Asia', as used throughout this book, refers to present-day India, Pakistan, and Bangladesh. It is this region that will be interchangeably referred to in this book as South Asia, the Subcontinent or India (undivided). Historically this vast region was known by its Persian name, Hindustan, and at various times in the Mughal period incorporated a large part of present-day Afghanistan.
4. Marshall G.S. Hodgson, *The Venture of Islam: Conscience and History in a World Civilization, Vol. 3, The Gunpowder Empires and Modern Times*, The University of Chicago Press, 1974, p. 4.
5. John F. Richards, *The Mughal Empire*, Cambridge University Press, 1995, pp. 1-2.
6. Sugata Bose and Ayesha Jalal, *Modern South Asia: History, Culture, Political Economy*, Sang-e-Meel Publications, Lahore, 1998, p. 36.
7. Bose and Jalal, p. 43.
8. Richard C. Foltz, *Mughal India and Central Asia*, Oxford University Press, Karachi, 1998, p. 77.

supremely creative Mughal vision. It was precisely because of its accessibility and intrinsic beauty that the Mughal aesthetic was absorbed so seamlessly by all peoples across the length and breadth of the Subcontinent. At the same time the Mughals stimulated and promoted the flowering of local traditions. The Mughals not only made Hindustan their home, they cherished it and adorned it with their best.

In the Mughal era, new and significant developments took place in many areas other than those addressed in this book, including administration, fiscal policy, trade, and military organization. The aesthetic sophistication of the Mughals too, manifested itself in every sphere of activity, and outstanding contributions were also made in fields as diverse as textiles, cuisine, etiquette, gardens, and jewellery[9]. These topics, unfortunately, could not be individually dealt with in a single volume.

* * *

The Mughals can rightfully claim a place both within the Subcontinent's history and the wider canvas of Muslim civilization. It is a unique fact of history that wherever Muslims spread—whether to Mali in West Africa, Spain in Europe, Anatolia, Central Asia or South East Asia—they catalyzed the indigenous cultures and created civilizations where artists and intellectuals of every faith and persuasion flourished, producing a rich tapestry of accomplishments.

The Mughals were heirs to this legacy. Akbar's inclusive attitude was rooted in Islam, particularly in the universalism practiced by the Sufis.[10] The Mughals, both men and women, were strongly influenced by and deeply imbued with the teachings of various Sufi traditions and that may indeed have been the fountainhead of their refined aesthetic and humane political and social vision. Beauty is exalted in the Sufi tradition because it is a facet of the transcendence of God. By surrounding oneself with beauty (see footnote 9), God can be experienced in every aspect of life: 'Islam throughout its history and within the depth and breadth of all its authentic manifestations, from architecture to the art of dress, has emphasized beauty and been inseparable from it'.[11] The Sufis, then,

actualize the spirit of Islam when they act on the Quranic message:

God loves those who do what is beautiful,[12]

Islam's assertion of the transcendent One God has its counterpoint in its stress on the essential equality, and by extension, fellowship, of humankind; consequently all humanity must be embraced when 'doing what is beautiful'. Rumi, the Sufi saint avidly read across the Mughal empire, exemplified this when he addressed humankind as follows:

> Come again, again!
> Come again, whoever you may be,
> Whether an infidel, a fireworshipper or a pagan;
> No matter whether you've broken your vows
>   a hundred times.
> Ours is not a door of despair.
> Just come as you are.

The essays in this volume reveal an often overlooked fact: not only was the pervasive atmosphere of tolerance and respect for other faiths a manifestation of Sufi influence, but the literature, music, architecture, art, and even dance of the Mughal era were inspired and influenced by Sufi thought.

The Sufi saints and teachers, in addition to spreading the humanistic message of Islam, were also a conduit for disseminating Mughal high culture and honing the sensibilities of the common man. At regular gatherings and on special occasions alike, people from all religions and walks of life, including the emperor, participated in events at the Sufi *khanqahs* (dwelling places), *dargahs* (shrines) and mosques. Perfectly proportioned, delicately embellished and radiating a sense of peace and harmony, these buildings embodied the 'beautiful'. Usually commissioned by the imperial family or nobility, they exemplified the best in architecture, in calligraphy and in arabesque and geometric design. The musical genre, *qawwali*, combining ecstatic music and devotional poetry, was an integral part of the gatherings at the *khanqahs* and *dargahs*. *Qawwali* belonged to the finest classical music tradition and, in fact, contributed significantly to the evolution of classical forms. Regional languages were also commonly employed in mystical verse and came into their own through the talents of the Sufis. *Qawwali* often inspired ecstatic dance, during which a respectful decorum was maintained by the other participants. Proper etiquette, an element of 'beautiful' conduct or *adab* (a word always implying beauty, refinement and subtlety), was essential in creating the ambiance of harmony and grace at these sittings. High culture filtered down through emulation as well. Whatever the means of dissemination, the people, particularly in the urban centres, were as justly proud of their reputation for culture, courtesy and sophistication as they were of their beautiful cities.

* * *

One of the discreditable deeds of British colonial rule and a grievous wrong done to the people of the Subcontinent, was that the Mughals were made the principal (but by no means, the only) target of a deliberate defamation of South Asian history. Despite the sad political record of the later emperors, such was the aura of the Mughal dynasty, that to the Indian people, it still symbolized India and its achievements continued to be held in the highest esteem. By demeaning a cherished heritage, the intention was to demean and destroy the self-esteem of the possessor of that heritage and thereby render him a more pliable object. In this the British succeeded.

There are still those in the Subcontinent who tend to pass hasty judgement on the Mughals. This may be for a variety of reasons: most have yet to outgrow the colonial-imposed mindset; some insist on drawing comparisons with a distant ideal; and then there are those who systematically nurture regional or communal prejudices and consciously deny their own roots or distort the past. Among the most unfortunate consequences of this denial and distortion have been a reductive communalism and an alienation from a precious heritage.

The history of Europe bears testimony to numerous instances of brutality and endless feuding. Yet Europeans do not reject this past; instead they cherish and preserve the good and the beautiful in their tradition for they sensibly believe, and have effectively demonstrated, that tradition is not the opposite of progress but is the *vehicle* for it. Finally, they have learned from their monumental mistakes and initiated the processes of reconciliation and integration on their continent.

An uplifting example is Spain. More than 500 years ago the Spanish Inquisition set about obliterating the human, material and intellectual evidence of Spain's Golden Age under eight centuries of Muslim rule. In one form or another the process continued into the twentieth century. And then a remarkable journey of rediscovery began. Today vestiges of the Muslim past are sign-posted and that glorious heritage is rightly celebrated. The essence of this renewal has been poignantly expressed by Antonio Gala, the renowned Spanish writer:

---

9. The dazzling Mughal jewels and jeweled objects in the collection of Sheikh Nasser al-Sabah of Kuwait were displayed at the British Museum during the summer of 2001, in a major exhibition entitled Treasury of the World: Jeweled Arts of India in the Age of the Mughals. The exhibition will later tour the USA. The remarkably diverse exhibits include utensils, weapons, jewelry, carved gems, harness fittings, elephant goad, and even flywhisks. It appears that no object was considered so mundane that it could not be bestowed with beauty or embellished with jewels. The richness of the pieces and the exquisite aesthetics and craftsmanship awed visitors and reviewers. In particular, it was the ability of Mughal artists to fashion pieces of unique beauty through the incorporation of many traditions that won lavish praise in reviews: 'Objects of hybrid design, unseen in the East or the West, came into existence, studded with stones of a magnificence equally undreamed of. Even armorers allowed themselves to be carried by the tidal wave of exoticism…Mogul artists seemed equally at ease with the shapes and motifs from every culture…The Mogul artists' aptitude at performing in every mode made them capable of merging conflicting influences into a new style' (Souren Melikian, Cultural Fusion in the Moguls' Age of Jewels, International Herald Tribune, 26-27 May 2001). Such aesthetic versatility could only flourish in 'an atmosphere of enlightened patronage, ecumenical openness, general curiosity and cultural excitement of the type that characterized the Mughal era at its most creative' (Manuel Keene with Salam Kaoukji, Treasury of the World: Jeweled Arts of India in the Age of the Mughals; The Al-Sabah Collection, Kuwait National Museum, Thames and Hudson Ltd., p. 142).
10. For the definition of Sufism see Glossary p. 82 in the Religion chapter.
11. Seyyed Hossein Nasr, *Islamic Art and Spirituality*, Oxford University Press, 1990, p. 200.
12. Nearly seventy verses in the Quran convey this message, for example: 2:195, 3:133-4, 4:125, 5:13, 6:151, 7:56, 10:26, 11:115, 13:18, 16:128, 32:6-7, 39:34, 40:64, 53:31. Also see Sachiko Murata and W.C. Chittick, *The Vision of Islam*, Paragon House, New York, 1994. Chapters 7 and 8.

History can be pendular, but it does not retrocede. Nevertheless, it exists. That is why I am irritated at the lack of understanding by some in regards to how much the presence of Islam in Spain has influenced the world, how its sudden appearance caused a transcendent and unalterable upset in our contexture and our development; …eight centuries of our cohabitation are not susceptible to being interpreted as having had the expulsion of Islam as its principal aim…most importantly: it is useless to fight against what is within us, against what we are; the Spanish culture without Islam would be inexplicable.[13]

Numerous generations in the Subcontinent have lived and are still living the Mughal legacy in diverse ways, often without even being aware of it as such. As the essays in this volume amply demonstrate, the Subcontinent's culture without the Mughals would be inexplicable.

---

13. *The Legacy of al-Andalus*, Preface by Antonio Gala, Bega Communicacion, p. 10.

I
THE MUGHAL EMPIRE
John F. Richards

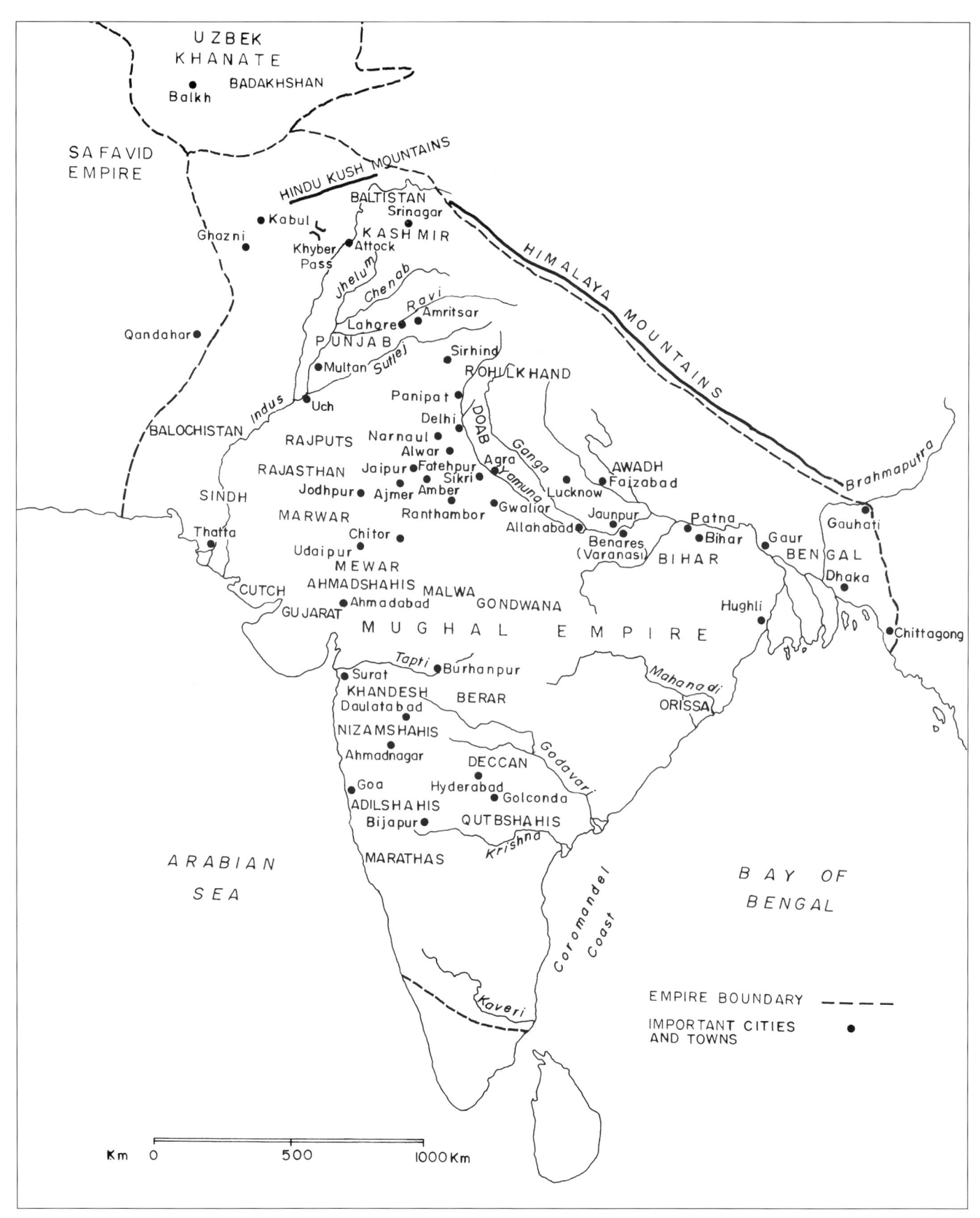

The Mughal Empire, 1707

VICTORIES AND CONQUESTS

The Mughal empire was one of the largest states in the early modern world. At its greatest extent in the early 1700s, the Mughal empire comprised virtually all the lands of the Subcontinent and demanded tax or tribute from as many as 150 million persons. The Ottoman empire's subjects at that date numbered twenty-four million or one-sixth that figure. Only the Ming emperor of China ruled over a similarly large population. Individual European states were small by comparison. The entire British Isles in 1700 had a population of just under six million or one-twenty-fifth that of Mughal India. Both in absolute size and in density, human populations in South Asia were among the highest in the pre-modern world. One systematic world population reconstruction puts the Subcontinent in 1700 at 165 million or nearly one-quarter the population of the globe (710 million). This was equivalent to that of China proper at 155 million and considerably greater than Europe, without Russia, at one hundred million.

Often overlooked is the sheer size and diversity of the lands that the Mughals ruled. The Subcontinent or South Asia, (4.5 m. sq. kms.), exceeds China proper (4.0 m. sq. kms.) and has somewhat less territory than Europe without Russia (4.8 m. sq. km.). Stretching from the mountains of the Hindu Kush in the northwest to the mouths of the Ganga and Brahmaputra rivers in the Bengal delta and from the Himalayan mountain ranges in the north to Sri Lanka lying just beyond the tip, the Subcontinent's climate, land forms and ecological systems are as diverse, if not more, as those in Europe or China. Human culture revealed a similar variability. To be sure the still-imposing heritage of Sanskrit language and civilization, the basic tenets and practices of Hinduism, the caste system and other cultural practices brought an overall unity to the region—just as similar institutions did in Europe. The Subcontinent was divided into fifteen or more distinctive linguistic-cultural regions like Bengal, Gujarat or Tamil Nadu. Each major region had its distinctive identity with its history and ethos, written language, dominant caste and ethnic groups, dominant religious practices, cultural markers including vernacular house styles, clothing styles and cuisine, political configuration, and even modes of cultivation and cropping patterns. Within each of the larger regions were smaller sub-regions—often refuge areas—where minority ethnic groups frequently spoke their own languages and maintained a distinctive relationship to their own physical environment.

Throughout its long history the Subcontinent, like Europe, was divided politically in a system of continuing inter-state conflict and negotiation. The largest states in South Asia tended to be regional. Often these regional polities were split up into varying numbers of sub-regional entities. Occasionally, an especially talented or aggressive ruler might add other kingdoms to his domain and his successors build up control over either much of North India as did the Guptas or much of South India as did the Colas. Unlike China, there was no continuing expectation and tradition of unified empire over all of India. Centralized empires that integrated the entire Subcontinent in a meaningful way for long periods had not been seen since the days of the Mauryas—if then.

The Mughal empire was the end product of a protracted nine hundred-year sequence of Muslim invasions and conquests in India. The Mughals did not bring Islam to the Subcontinent—they were the beneficiaries of this long interaction between civilizations and cultures. Since the seventh century, when Muslim armies from Seistan first clashed with those of Hindu/Buddhist rulers on the western borders of present-day Afghanistan, Muslim invaders from Central Asia and the Middle East confronted Indian border kingdoms. Slowly, over decades and centuries, these conquerors gained control of territory and pushed the military frontier east and south until, in the early 1200s they ruled the entire Indo-Gangetic plain. A century later, the strongest of these states, the Delhi Sultanate, sent armies south to defeat and expel regional Indian rulers in the Deccan and beyond. For a few decades a single Muslim ruler, the Sultan of Delhi, seemed ready to unify the entire Subcontinent under his domain. By 1400, however, political breakup occurred and Indo-Muslim domination over North India and the Deccan found expression in regional kingdoms once again. By this time Indo-Muslim rulers sat on the thrones of the Deccan kingdoms.

Successful military operations and state power created an Indian Muslim community in the Subcontinent that grew by immigration, natural increase, and conversion of Hindus to Islam. The majority communities remained Hindu, as conversions were limited in number. As the military frontier passed, within the framework of Muslim rule, Hindus and Muslims lived peacefully and developed accommodations that brought synthesis in a broader culture and society that transcended religious differences. Perhaps most important for the Mughals was the fact that the legitimacy of a Muslim political order in most of India, save in the extreme south, was firmly established. Generation after generation of Hindu warriors, priests, merchants, and peasants became accustomed to Muslim authority and found ways to prosper beneath it. The Mughals were the heirs to centuries of military victory and political socialization.

The Mughals also inherited from the Muslim world the techniques and the ambition of extended, centralized rule of empire. Islam was an expansive and conquering civilization where the ideal of caliphal rule that would unify the Muslim community was always present. The Delhi Sultans had shown the way. India could be unified. Zahiruddin Muhammad Babur, the Chaghatai Turkish prince whose victories in North India founded the Timurid/Mughal empire, reveals in his memoirs how thoroughly steeped, by his familial culture, he was in notions of sovereignty, conquest, and grand empire as a direct descendant of both Timur and Genghis Khan.

When in the early 1500s Babur, new ruler of Kabul in Afghanistan, contemplated expansion, he looked southeast to the Muslim-ruled North Indian plain with its rich agriculture, trade and industry, and enormous population. By this time, the most powerful Indo-Muslim ruling elites were in fact Afghans who had migrated into India to take advantage of the opportunities offered by the Delhi Sultanate. Afghan rulers controlled the mix of large and small Indo-Muslim kingdoms that stretched from the eastern border of Afghanistan across the plain to Bengal. The largest of these entities was the Lodi Sultanate of Delhi. At this time, a group of Hindu chiefs and their followers, the Rajputs, posed a possible threat to Muslim power in North India. The Rajputs had been pushed into the less productive semi-arid regions of Rajasthan, but in the course of the 1400s they had gradually built up a resurgent warrior society in a collection of decentralized kingdoms and nascent states.

Finally, in 1526 after a series of near-yearly raids from Kabul into the Lodi-controlled Punjab plain, Babur confronted the assembled army of Ibrahim Khan Lodi, Sultan of Delhi, at the battlefield of Panipat only a few miles west of Delhi itself. Babur's twelve thousand-man army, equipped with matchlocks and field artillery firearms, broke the cavalry charges of a far larger Lodi force without firearms. The death of Ibrahim Khan Lodi and dozens of his leading nobles in battle cleared the way for an unchallenged occupation of Delhi. Babur seized the royal palaces and treasure, ascended the throne at Delhi, and proclaimed Timurid rule over Lodi domains. Within a year, in 1527 Babur led his small army against eighty thousand Rajput cavalry and five hundred war elephants to the field of battle at Kanua. The Rajput forces, also lacking firearms, were put together by a confederacy of Rajput rulers headed by the most powerful Rajput king, Rana Sanga, the Rana of Mewar. Once again Babur won decisively. Rana Sanga and many other Rajput rulers and nobles died in the battle. The possibility of renewed Hindu Rajput power in North India died with them.

Much has been made of the Mughal adoption of firearms from the Ottoman example and their successful use in these early battles. It is likely that Babur's guns and matchlocks gave him the deciding edge at Panipat and Kanua. Over the next few decades, however, the use of cannon and matchlocks diffused steadily throughout the Subcontinent. The Portuguese, who had been sailing directly to India since the days of Vasco da Gama, brought knowledge of the new technique and enough examples of the guns themselves to allow them to be manufactured in India. Rulers of Indian regional kingdoms wasted little time in adopting the new weaponry. Thereafter the Mughals faced opponents similarly equipped. Subsequent Mughal victories and conquests did not occur because of any monopoly of firearms. However, the logistics and costs of using artillery and matchlocks probably favoured larger, more centralized state structures in the early modern period.

Far from a continuing triumph, the first three decades of Mughal rule in India unfolded a prolonged tale of loss, expulsion and exile and, finally, restoration for the dynasty. When in 1530, shortly after his victories, Babur died at Delhi his son Humayun (r.1530-40, 1555-56) succeeded to the throne. To the older territories in Afghanistan and Central Asia, Babur had added

Punjab, Delhi, and Bihar in North India. Under the Mughal tradition of appanage rule, Humayun conceded control of Badakhshan to Sulaiman, of Kabul to Kamran, and gave large districts in India to two of his other brothers to administer. Shortly thereafter his brother Kamran asserted fully independent control over Kabul and Punjab.

To Humayun, weakened by sibling rivalries, fell the task of defending and consolidating his father's conquests in North India against still-powerful and unsubdued Afghan commanders who controlled territories in the eastern Gangetic plain. Humayun made the strategic mistake of ignoring and underestimating this threat by attempting to conquer the Sultanate of Gujarat in a five-year series of campaigns. While Humayun led his armies to Gujarat, Sher Khan Sur, one of these Afghan commanders in southern Bihar, rapidly consolidated his power and became the leader of the continuing Afghan resistance to the Timurids. After winning a second major battle in 1540, Sher Khan sent Humayun fleeing as a royal refugee with only a few hundred followers toward western India. Sher Khan took the title Sher Shah Sur and proclaimed himself ruler of Hindustan. Eventually Humayun made his way east to Persia to the court of Shah Tahmasp the Safavid ruler. Here, after converting publicly to the Shia form of Islam, he obtained Safavid support to regain Kabul, then held by his brother Kamran, as an independent ruler. Finally, after eight years, in 1553, Humayun captured his brother and ascended the throne at Kabul.

In the five years before he died in 1545, Sher Shah Sur managed to bring the entire Indo-Gangetic plain from Punjab to Bengal under unitary and centralizing Afghan rule. However his son Islam Shah (r.1545-1553) failed to sustain his father's achievements and when Islam Shah died, the Sur domains split into four regional units. Humayun led a Mughal army into the Punjab plain and confronted Sikandar Shah Sur, ruler of that region in battle at Sirhind. A hard-fought battle ended in Mughal victory and the flight of Sikandar. Humayun then marched unopposed to Delhi and placed himself once again on the throne that he had lost. Humayun had little time to enjoy his victory. Within seven months, he met with a fatal accident and left a precarious holding to his thirteen-year-old son Jalaluddin Muhammad Akbar.

In 1556 Bairam Khan, a senior noble of Babur, assumed the role of protector and regent for the young Akbar. His first task was to defeat the remaining Sur princes and commanders to the east who were busily mobilizing armies. Between 1556 and 1558 Bairam Khan and his commanders fought two major battles against Sur armies and drove the Afghans back to Bengal. Mughal armies occupied Lahore and Multan in the Punjab and seized the fort at Ajmer on the border of Rajasthan, occupied Jaunpur in the eastern Gangetic valley, and after a prolonged siege took the fort of Gwalior, the strongest fort in North India. These swift campaigns gave the Mughals undisputed control of Hindustan, the heartland of North India, with Delhi as the capital city.

Asserting his independent rule in 1560, the young Akbar proved to be one of the most formidable military commanders and strategists that the Subcontinent has ever produced. Over the next forty-five years of his long reign, Akbar built up a magnificent army that defeated and neutralized Afghan resistance and conquered all of North India. This was a remarkable unbroken series of military triumphs. Mughal armies seized the kingdom of Malwa in 1561; stormed the great Afghan fortress at Chunar in eastern India in the same year; overran the kingdom of Garha-Katanga (Gondwana) in 1564; besieged and destroyed the greatest Rajput fortresses of Chitor and Ranthambor in 1568-69; invaded and conquered the kingdom of Gujarat in 1572 (and reconquered the kingdom against a nearly-successful rebellion of Gujarati nobles in 1573); invaded and annexed Afghan-held Bihar, Bengal, and Orissa in a hard-fought, two year campaign, 1574-76; marched to Kabul to depose Akbar's half-brother in 1581; subdued the Yusufzai and other Afghan tribes in the northwest to secure control of the overland caravan trade during the years 1585-1591; invaded and annexed Kashmir in 1585; and had invaded and seized the kingdom of Sindh in the lower Indus valley by 1593. Turning toward the south in the Deccan, Akbar invaded the Sultanate of Ahmadnagar and annexed the province of Berar before withdrawing in 1596; and finally, conquered and annexed the Sultanate of Khandesh along with another large chunk of the Sultanate of Ahmadnagar in 1601.

Akbar succeeded in unifying North India under a centralized regime more completely than had the Sultans of Delhi two hundred years before. Unlike the

Gate of Akbar's Tomb, Sikandra

Red Fort, interior, Delhi

Imperial chamber, Red Fort, Delhi

Gate of Red Fort (Palace fortress of Shahjahanabad), Delhi

Photos: Ziad Alahdad

Sultans of Delhi, however, Akbar did not direct an ideologically focused campaign fuelled, at least in part, by religious zeal as Delhi's commanders deposed non-Muslim rulers. Instead, most of Akbar's opponents were themselves Muslim and ruled with the help of Muslim elites.

Under Akbar, the Mughal empire distanced itself from orthodox Islam and no longer appealed solely to Muslims for its primary political support. Akbar, who was trying to build viable political institutions for a predominantly non-Muslim society, moved toward a broader, more flexible notion of the political community of early modern India. In his vision, the Islamic profession of faith was not to be the critical test for full political participation. His most dramatic measure to further this goal came in 1579, when he abolished collection of the burdensome *jizyah**, the capitation tax paid every year by non-Muslims as protected clients within the Muslim state. Following a precedent already established by previous Indo-Muslim regimes, Akbar recruited and promoted Hindus into the highest levels of the imperial elite.

Akbar's greatest success lay in his Rajput policy. Under these arrangements, Rajput rulers and their kinsmen and followers accepted appointment as Mughal nobles with high rank, pay, and perquisites. Rajput princesses married Akbar, entered his harem and established weighty kinship ties between the Rajputs and the Mughal dynasty. The rajas kept control over their own ancestral lands in Rajasthan as non-transferable holdings. Revenues from these lands were applied to their pay and allowances. The net effect was to protect the local position of each raja from internecine encroachment and to open up new areas of wealth, power and purpose within the imperial system. Akbar won the loyalties of tens of thousands of Rajput warriors, generation after generation by this generous policy.

Akbar and his advisers self-consciously created a new dynastic ideology that relied far less on appeals to Muslim beliefs and far more on the charismatic authority of the emperor and the Timurid house. In the latter half of Akbar's reign, Abul Fazl, his leading adviser began to build a larger ideological structure centred on the emperor. Abul Fazl developed a new legitimacy for Akbar that went beyond the usual claims of Timurid or Muslim kingship. In the immense chronicle called the *Akbarnama* Abul Fazl, using the imagery of light, asserted Akbar's divinely illumined right to rule lesser human beings. He portrayed Akbar as a superior being who existed closer to God than ordinary men and who was the recipient of a hidden light that radiated from his brow. It was this light transmitted through the generations of Timurid ancestors that validated Akbar's rule. This argument meshed with Akbar's own spiritual quest in which he moved away from the observances and, as some claim, the beliefs of conventional Islam. In the 1580s he began openly worshipping the sun every day with a set of rituals of his own devising. Simultaneously, he began to enlist selected nobles as his personal disciples who took an elaborate oath of personal devotion to the emperor and prostrated themselves before him in the manner of a Sufi disciple before his master. The rituals and oaths of discipleship persisted in the reign of Akbar's son Jahangir, but seem to have died out by the time of his grandson, Shahjahan, who did not share his forebears' mystic enthusiasms.

Mughal armies defeated confident capable rulers with wealth and large armies at their command whose claim to legitimacy was as great as that of the Timurids in India. Mughal campaigns and victories were hard-fought and bitterly contested. Nearly all Akbar's battles were bloody and desperately fought and his sieges lengthy and difficult.

How did Akbar win such an astonishing series of victories? At no time was it foreordained that he would forcefully unify North India. Most of the credit must be given to Akbar's extraordinary personal gifts as a ruler, organizer, and commander of men. He gathered trusted confidants around him whose abilities nearly matched his own. He was, however, his own strategist and executive officer who vigorously commanded his armies in the field. He kept admirable discipline, but rewarded initiative and spirit among his men. Akbar's organizational skills ensured that money, weapons, supplies, and transport were available to his campaigning armies. On campaign, Akbar's shrewd policies ensured that fair treatment and payment encouraged rural inhabitants and traders to keep his forces supplied and to provide intelligence. He was not unnecessarily cruel or horrific in his treatment of conquered peoples. Akbar's armies were a finely tuned war machine that steadily gained capacity and

---
* Editor's Note: For details see p. 82.

confidence. The armies in turn were supported by an efficiently run revenue system and state structure oriented toward expansion.

In part Akbar was favoured by fortune. He could have been killed at any time. He survived at least two assassination attempts and the dangers of campaigning, battle, and disease. He survived two internal revolts by dissident Mughal nobles. The first in the mid-1560s involved an ethnic group of Uzbek nobles. The second, in 1579-80 brought together nobles in the eastern provinces who protested against Akbar's centralizing measures and his liberal religious policies. The second revolt was far more serious since Mirza Muhammad Hakim, Akbar's half-brother who sat on the throne at Kabul, had offered his support to the insurgents in a bid to displace Akbar.

Akbar succeeded because he won. Each victorious battle and campaign, each kingdom annexed added further momentum to the Mughal cause. Akbar obtained treasure from loot and tribute that financed further expansion. His armies were always paid and never lacked for troops or commanders recruited from North India's plentiful military manpower. He deployed huge numbers of heavy cavalrymen, matchlockmen, pioneers, and large numbers of field and siege guns as well as war elephants. By the end of his reign, his opponents began to surrender on terms rather than resist to the bitter end. As the tally of his conquests rose, Akbar's public reputation soared. He, together with his best-known advisers and companions, became a figure of enormous popular interest. A genre of folk-tales, jokes and stories circulated about him and continue to be told today.

Territorial expansion, although not as successful or as rapid, continued after Akbar's death in 1605. The seventeenth century empire remained a war state anxious for conquest. Over the next century both symbolic and executive power remained firmly in the hands of Akbar's descendants: his son Jahangir (r.1605-1627); his grandson, Shahjahan (r.1628-1658) and his great-grandson, Aurangzeb (r.1658-1707). Each of the three engaged in aggressive campaigns aimed at extending the boundaries of the empire. Each emperor discovered that expansion to the north beyond the mountain borders of the Subcontinent was difficult and only possible with greater expense and determination than they were willing to expend. Beyond the Subcontinent's physical boundaries in the north lay extended supply lines, forbidding terrain, and thinly populated societies not overly impressed with Mughal power. The bounds of imperial power in the north coincided with the shift from South Asia to other world regions.

To the northeast successive Mughal armies faltered in bitter, water-borne campaigns up the Brahmaputra river against determined opposition from the equally aggressive Ahom State. Even after a massive effort in the 1660s under Aurangzeb, imperial rule could only be pushed northeast as far as Gauhati in Assam.

To the north, the Mughal emperors approached the forbidding northern passes of the Himalayas cautiously. They imposed firm tributary relationships on Kangra, Garhwal, and the other Rajput hill kingdoms of the foothills and even sent an army into Little Tibet or Baltistan. But the Mughals never attempted to take Nepal or to send armies beyond the Himalayas into Tibet proper.

To the northwest, in the 1640s Shahjahan invested heavily in a determined campaign to conquer the Central Asian kingdom of Balkh. The Timurids claimed these territories as part of their familial patrimony held by the hated Uzbeks. From Kabul Shahjahan sent a large expeditionary force to seize Balkh. After heavy casualties and enormous expense, the Mughal commanders discovered that they could not live off the sparse landscape nor could they supply their armies in the face of determined Uzbek resistance. Finally, the Mughals accepted a vague assertion of subordinate status by the Uzbeks and returned to Kabul in failure.

Further southwest lay the boundary between Safavid Iran and Mughal India. Here Qandahar, the great border fortress that controlled major caravan routes between India and Iran, had shifted back and forth between the empires. After it was retaken by the Safavids in 1648, Shahjahan sent three major expeditions within four years to besiege the fortress without success. Qandahar remained under Persian control for the remainder of the century. A wealthy, war-like and confident Safavid regime set the limits for Mughal expansion into Iran and the Middle East.

Unsurprisingly, perhaps, the Mughal emperors, Central Asian horsemen that they were, completely ignored and never (as far as we know) even discussed the possibility of building an ocean going navy and engaging in maritime expansion. From the ports of Gujarat, for example, a Mughal fleet could have occupied Yemen with its rich trading centres, imposed Mughal guardianship of the holy cities, and dominated the rich Indian ocean trading system. From the ports of Bengal, Mughal fleets could have captured control of Indian ports in the south, in Sri Lanka and even moved into Southeast Asia. Admittedly, to challenge the Portuguese and later northern European warships was a formidable task worthy of a new Akbar. Yet Mughal rulers and grandees, acting as individual investors, commissioned and operated large sea-going merchant vessels for trading purposes. For the Mughal state to build a navy was certainly not out of the question. Both funds and expertise could be readily obtained. In the end, however, expansion to the south into the Deccan beyond by land proved to be irresistible.

The three remaining Muslim Deccan Sultanates—Ahmadnagar, Bijapur and Golconda—wealthy, populous, and close-at-hand, were immediate targets. Under Akbar, sharply focused campaigns, critical battles and the death or flight of the ruler resulted promptly in occupation of new territories and annexation. Conquest in the Deccan, in contrast, was a decades-long frustrating process subject to negotiation, intrigue and even corruption among Mughal field commanders. In the case of Ahmadnagar, the loss of one battle did not mean surrender of the entire kingdom, but instead renewed defiance mounted from territories not occupied by the Mughals. A charismatic resistance figure, Malik Ambar, a *habshi*, or Abyssinian military slave-commander, created a new capital for Sultan Murtaza Nizam Shah (1599-1631) at Khadki (later Aurangabad) near the great hill-fort at Daulatabad. From this redoubt Malik Ambar directed a decades-long policy of alternately fighting and negotiating with the Mughals and with the Sultans of Bijapur and Golconda. After the deaths of Malik Ambar and Sultan Murtaza, however, power fell to Shahji Bhonsla, a prominent Maratha nobleman who placed a young Nizam Shahi prince on the throne of Ahmadnagar as his puppet.

In 1632 the emperor Shahjahan, himself a veteran of the Ahmadnagar campaigns and negotiations, organized a successful Mughal campaign that ended in the siege and capture of Daulatabad fort. The Nizam Shahi ruler became a Mughal captive in the state prison at Gwalior fort. Ahmadnagar became a province of the Mughal empire directly administered by an imperial governor.

Annexation of Ahmadnagar removed a buffer state and thrust Mughal boundaries directly adjacent to those of the two remaining Deccan Sultanates: the Adil Shah dynasty of Bijapur ruled the Marathi and Kannada-speaking portions of the western Deccan and the Qutb Shah dynasty of Golconda ruled the Telugu-speaking eastern Deccan. Shahjahan soon demanded that both monarchs formally submit to Mughal hegemony. They were to give up the two key symbols of independent rule by minting coins in the name of the Mughal emperor and having his name read in the Friday prayers. They were also to pay a large annual tribute and accept diplomatic officers from the emperor in residence at their courts. Golconda complied at once; Bijapur delayed. When Shahjahan sent three Mughal armies that laid waste the countryside and converged on his capital, the Sultan of Bijapur capitulated.

By 1635 Shahjahan had stabilized the southern frontier of the Mughal Empire without taking on the burden of direct rule. For the next half-century Bijapur and Golconda continued in a tributary relationship to the Mughals. After 1635, secure on their northern borders, both states aggressively consolidated power and added territory to the south that extended the Indo-Muslim power deep into the Tamil-speaking region of the extreme south. As their holdings and their wealth increased, the Adil Shahis and Qutb Shahis maneuvered to fend off an ongoing threat of Mughal annexation by intervening with bribes and diplomacy in Mughal court politics.

Cumulative imperial pressures undercut and weakened the power and reach of both rulers and contributed to perceived mismanagement and disorder in each kingdom. Weak rule in Bijapur permitted the growth of a determined Maratha resistance movement headed by a resourceful Maratha commander, Shivaji Bhonsla. Eventually, the threat of an alliance between the resurgent Marathas in the west and the Qutb Shahis in the east prompted Mughal action. The emperor Aurangzeb took personal command of massive imperial armies and brought them south into the Deccan. By 1685 he had attacked and captured the capital of Bijapur and in 1687 he directed the capture of Golconda fort after a lengthy siege. With their rulers deposed and made captive, each kingdom became a province in the Mughal empire. This left Aurangzeb free to stamp out the independent Maratha kingdom established by Shivaji Bhonsla when he crowned himself in 1674 at Puna. The capture and execution of Shambhaji Bhonsla, Shivaji's son and successor in 1689 seemingly closed this campaign. In a few bold strokes Aurangzeb had thrust Mughal borders south of present-day Madras. This was the last great extension of territory before the decline of the empire in the eighteenth century.

STABILITY AND PEACE

Mughal conquest and annexation of formerly independent kingdoms such as Ahmadnagar, although certainly a dramatic political change, does not appear to have caused severe hardship or dislocation for other than the defeated rulers and their most committed followers. Mughal officials retained the boundaries and internal administrative divisions of the conquered kingdom. The boundaries of the former kingdom defined a new Mughal province; its former provinces became Mughal districts and its former districts became Mughal subdistricts or *parganas*. Usually the former capital city, its fortress, and palaces became the provincial capital occupied by an imperial governor and his establishment. After capitulation, the Mughals did not engage in savage reprisals against their former enemies. (During most such wars imperial promises and money had already suborned the loyalties of many high-ranking nobles and officials of the former kingdom). They did not attempt to expel potentially troublesome populations and replace them by new migrants. Instead, the Mughals preferred a cautious approach in which changes would come over time as regulation, imperial governance, and tax systems tightened their hold and increased pressures upon local society.

The Mughal emperors offered new opportunities for lucrative imperial service to many of the defeated nobles and their kinsmen and followers and to many petty officials, soldiers, clerks, and other servants of the old regime. The local landed warrior-aristocracy became Mughal *zamindars* with the same duties and responsibilities for order and tax collection that they had held in the past. Important religious institutions and individual figures generally retained some form of state patronage after the conquest—and in some cases found increased largess.

Mughal conquest brought a new degree of peace, order, and stability. If nothing else, the threat of Mughal harassment and attack was removed. The possibility of military invasion by neighbouring states ended. By and large imperial subjects were not subjected to brutality and depredation by invading armies as they traversed the countryside. It is true that in some regions inclined toward resistance to centralized authority, the political transition provided an excuse for *zamindars* to withhold tax payments (the imperial definition of rebellion) and to resist new imperial officials. Mughal military governors (*faujdars*) massing heavy cavalry and musketeers usually dealt rapidly and forcefully with this type of resistance.

What were the reasons for this impressive stability? First, the monarchy itself evolved into a powerful, centralizing institution. From Babur (d. 1530) to Muhammad Shah (d. 1748), each member of the dynasty—well educated, highly trained—acted within a deeply internalized model of virtuous rulership. The Mughal princes received ample exposure to the notions of rule embedded in the Islamic tradition as modulated by Persian notions of monarchy and sovereignty. They were also strongly imbued with principles of appropriate royal behaviour from their familial tradition stretching back to Timur and his successors in Central Asia. When Akbar added to this mixture an ideology of divinely ordained legitimacy, the dynastic charisma of the Timurids gained enormous power and further constrained the actions of each ruler. The Mughal emperors, while sufficiently ruthless when they deemed it politically useful, ruled their dominions with a strong sense of responsibility for the welfare of their subjects. They were not the Oriental despots of European caricature. Simply put, the Mughal emperors believed that their dynasty had a divinely ordained mission to bring peace, order, and stability to the peoples and lands under their dominion and, as a corollary, to bring more lands and peoples under the imperial umbrella.

The Mughal emperors delegated sparingly to ministers. They themselves acted as chief executives of the empire. The Mughal emperor took advice from appointed ministers, but did not relinquish key decision making powers. They were deeply involved in every aspect of the empire and its governance and sensitive to

Gate of Lahore Fort, Pakistan
Photo: Pervez A. Khan, F.R.G.S.

the impact that their decisions made. They reacted decisively and quickly to threat of rebellion or insurrection. Each emperor (save Akbar) had ample experience of military command and imperial administration as a mature prince. The Timurid emperors had daily access to detailed information sent to the court by spies and reporters from every province in the empire. This inflow of information added to the emperor's already extensive knowledge of each region and locality of the empire. Whatever their personal pleasures and interests, these were hard-working monarchs acutely attuned to the political currents of their time.

The sitting Mughal ruler was the greatest celebrity and best-known personage of his time. He came under intense and unrelenting scrutiny. His appearance in daily public audience was essential to prevent speculation about his health and vigour. Imperial audiences (*durbars*) and processions were the much-discussed public spectacles of the time. News from court spread widely and rapidly throughout the empire. The latest news and speculations from the court and harem were staples of Mughal popular culture. Wealthy merchants, nobles posted on duty away from the throne, tributary rulers and chiefs, heads of religious orders, among others, sent paid agents to attend public audiences, to bribe imperial servants and to gather gossip and rumour about the emperor and his actions.

Second, Mughal dynamism depended upon a cadre of several hundred to a thousand or more omnicompetent imperial officers who were recruited, appointed, promoted, and posted by the emperor himself. The nobility consisted of a heterogeneous collection of men native to South Asia and foreign-born aristocrats. They were primarily Muslim, with a substantial admixture of Hindu, largely Rajput, officers. Nobles were available for posting in either civil or military roles throughout the empire at any time. They served as provincial governors, military intendants (*faujdars*), field army commanders, commanders of strategic forts, and as governors of important ports like Surat. When recalled to the imperial presence they attended daily court audiences and, on a rotating assignment, personally directed their troops in mounting guard around the emperor and his household. In theory, Mughal nobles were subject to unpredictable and relatively frequent transfer and reassignment. Until old age, death, or disgrace, they were bound firmly into the emperor's service. These officers carried out military and administrative tasks, as needed anywhere in the empire at any time. Higher-ranking officers received honourific titles specified by the emperor that changed as they progressed upward in their careers.

With some exceptions, Mughal officers were not feudal nobles with hereditary lands and titles. They were instead members of a service nobility deeply dependent upon the emperor for its lavish pay, status, and power. A minority of imperial officers possessed specialized technical skills in fiscal and revenue matters. All had at least a rudimentary exposure to the procedures and requirements of imperial rules and regulations. All imperial officers were skilled military commanders prepared at any time to lead men in battle. Mughal expansion relied upon the skills, energy, and at times sacrificial courage of this martial elite.

The salaries, perquisites, status, and tasks for each officer were determined by their personal rank (*zat*) denoted in a numerical ranking system. The numerical rank of each officer invariably appears in imperial documents whenever the title of the officer is given. Expressed in multiples of ten, officers, called *mansabdars* (rankholders) received ranks as high as 5000 *zat* or as low as 10 *zat*. Although technically *mansabdars*, officers holding ranks below 250 *zat* held little power or influence. Those holding ranks of 1000 *zat* or above were called nobles or *amirs*. The emperor personally specified each officer's rank by a shifting set of criteria based upon performance, personality, and political considerations. Far from a civil service or bureaucratic system of ranks, this was a highly personalized set of honourific rewards and, if necessary, punishments.

The emperor awarded a second numerical rank beside the personal or *zat* rank. Also based upon the 10 to 5000 decimal scale, trooper (*suwar*) rank specified the number of heavy cavalry troopers to be recruited, organized, and commanded by the officer in question. Generally trooper rank did not bear a fixed relationship to personal rank except that it usually did not exceed that number. Originally, under Akbar, who devised the system, trooper rank specified the number of cavalrymen on a one-to-one basis. By the mid-seventeenth century this had been reduced to a one-third ratio or below depending upon whether the officer was in the field or not. In the days of Shahjahan, for example, an *amir* ranked at 3000 personal and 1500 trooper was required to bring to imperial muster 500 fully-equipped heavy cavalrymen mounted upon approved horses and equipment. When certified that his troops had met imperial requirements at muster, the officer received a fixed sum per trooper in addition to his personal salary set by his *zat* rank.

Under the Mughal system the state paid military costs, but shifted the organizational burden of military management to its individual commanders while retaining strict quality controls. Higher-ranked *amirs* personally commanded a military contingent that accompanied him on every assignment. Each *mansabdar* usually mobilized his sons, brothers, uncles, and other close male relatives as well as family servants and slaves, followed by more distant kinsmen who shared lineage ties. To fill out his contingent, the *mansabdar* resorted to the military labour market in which could be found experienced and proficient soldiers available for hire. Often close relatives or favourites of the commander also obtained imperial appointments themselves to lesser ranks. They in turn recruited the requisite number of followers. This created a clustering effect by which a higher-ranking *amir* or nobleman brought the stipulated number of his own troops to the field and also had attached to him other lesser-ranked commanders with their followers.

In addition to soldiers, each noble employed numerous clerks and petty officials who, although armed, were not really warriors, but scribes. The day-to-day business of the empire relied upon the services of numerous clerks and petty officials who were expert in Persian and in the minute details and procedures of imperial administration. Often such men were employed directly in the imperial administration and given ranking as smaller *mansabdars*. Or, if they served a great noble, they might receive appointment from the emperor as a *mansabdar*. Others merely served in the retinues of greater and lesser *mansabdars* without such recognition. The quiet industry of these men engaged in clerical, accounting, and management tasks supplied the procedural binding that kept the Mughal empire functioning.

By and large these were men belonging to service families and lineages, some Muslim, some Hindu, who could claim a lengthy tradition of clerical service to Indo-Muslim rulers even before the arrival of the Mughals. Prominent among these were the Kayasths—a caste that while remaining Hindu in its beliefs and practice, had deeply assimilated the language, culture, and norms of the Muslim elites that its members served. Young boys in these service families received instruction from early childhood in Persian language and literature. They learned to write in Persian—especially the fast shorthand-like script called *shikast*. They learned the proper protocols for addressing letters and heading documents and the set format for various official forms as well as the phraseology involved in official business. They learned how to calculate intricate sums and mathematical problems, how to keep accounts and treasuries, how to obtain receipts and maintain records of fiscal and other transactions. They also learned the nuances of personal demeanour and deference required in various formal situations. And most importantly they absorbed the values of discretion, silence, and loyalty to their masters.

The emperor and each *mansabdar* were tightly linked by a personal connection. The authoritative nexus between emperor and higher-ranking officers was absolutely critical to the success of the empire. The emperor depended on the loyalty and, more importantly, the devoted submission, intellect, and energetic action of his *mansabdars*. Codified ritual practices for public appearances at court were an especially potent demonstration of this relationship. Court ritual with its solemnity and unchanging nature daily reaffirmed the emperor's authority and the reassuring stability of the empire. All serving nobles and higher-ranked *mansabdars* were obliged to attend daily public audiences if they were in the capital. Each member of the court audience played his assigned role—whether passive or active—for a wide range of ceremonies. Seated on his throne, whether in a palace or under the canvas of a great tent in the imperial encampment, the emperor issued proclamations and announced policies, rewarded and promoted successful officers, accepted young men as disciples and imperial officers (*mansabdars*), gave gifts and grants of land to pious men, punished criminals and traitors, received foreign deputations and defeated rulers, and listened to news and reports from throughout the empire.

Disarmed, stripped of their attendants, the highest nobles of the empire stood in rows fixed by rank before their seated sovereign. The higher an officer's rank, the closer he stood to the emperor. The close personal tie between emperor and noble was symbolized by gift exchanges. When approaching the emperor the officer extended a gift of gold coins or other precious objects and the emperor reciprocated with his own gift. A common reward consisted of partial or full robes of honour—beautifully embroidered and decorated with gold and silver thread—placed first upon the shoulders of the emperor and then draped over the recipient. In this way the master incorporated his servant's body to his own. Elaborate rules for polite behaviour and norms of exposure to Indo-Persian high culture chipped away at indiscreet behaviour and action by the emperors and their elite followers. At lesser levels, governors and nobles duplicated the style, if not the grandeur, of royal court audience. For example, provincial governors held similar daily public audiences that all imperial officers at their capital attended under similar rituals of discipline and submission.

In restricted or private court audiences also rigid rules of behaviour were in effect. And, even in more intimate settings of banquets with food, drink and music and dance, nobles were always constrained in their speech and behaviour toward the emperor and toward one another. Whether in Turkish, or increasingly in Persian, Mughal forms of address, humour, lines of poetry and modes of verbal exchange were stylized and refined. The body language of gestures, facial expressions, and manners was as punctilious and as important. Those who had not been assimilated to this Persianate high culture had a difficult time. From earliest infancy the Mughal emperors were trained in and imbued with the skills of this high culture. They acted as arbiters of appropriate behaviour. Normally bellicose men, accustomed to violence, curbed their impulses in the royal presence. Any violent acts on these occasions were punished immediately by armed guards who stood by.

Elite opinion and discourse in turn constrained royal decisions and behaviour. The imperial service nobility or *amirs* held individual and collective sensibilities and notions of proper policy and treatment that could not be breached without the risk of armed rebellion by powerful grandees who commanded their own armies. Systematic cruel and tyrannical behaviour toward the nobility was a costly option in this system. The emperor balanced his favours and preferential treatment between noble factions and ethnic groups to prevent political challenges to his authority. Mature imperial princes who held the highest ranks and status within the corps of nobles raised a continuing danger of revolt against their father, the emperor. Frequently major policy issues were expressed by constellations of nobles aligning themselves between two or more opposed princes of the blood.

Third, imperial political stability rested upon a firm contractual relationship between the empire and thousands of rural warrior-aristocrats, the *zamindars*, who possessed entrenched local power in every province of the empire. When Akbar began to build a newly centralized imperial administration, the North Indian countryside, in a configuration common to many Eurasian medieval and early modern societies, was studded with the forts and residences of local magnates who maintained a rustic aristocratic life-style. These *zamindars* directly managed and cultivated their lands with servants and slaves. They also claimed a hereditary right to extract a share of the harvest from the peasant communities living in a wider zone under their control. When forced to do so, these rural aristocrats disgorged a portion of that land revenue as tribute or tax to meet demands from the larger state. Depending upon the number of villages he controlled, each *zamindar* employed dozens to hundreds of armed retainers—for the most part infantry, not mounted cavalry—in his service. In most areas the *zamindars* were Hindus, but in a considerable minority they were Afghans or other Muslims who had carved out petty domains for themselves. Often *zamindars* shared caste identities and lineage ties with the village headmen and leading peasants in the villages under their control. Some *zamindari* houses derived their power from their founder's service to previous regimes that resulted in royal land grants. Others became dominant in a violent process of localized settlement and colonization at the expense of non-Hindu ethnic or tribal groups. In some localities Hindu monasteries or Muslim Sufi shrines acted as *zamindars*; in others, closer to towns or cities, the ruling state dealt directly with individual villages and their headmen without having to deal with intermediaries, but by far the greatest number of peasants were subordinate to *zamindars*.

By the sixteenth century Indo-Muslim regimes had succeeded in imposing state power over the *zamindars*. The Sultans sharply limited internecine warfare amongst the rural aristocracy. The state validated the holdings of rural aristocrats by issuing official documents written in Persian and the local language that fixed and recorded boundaries and specified the amounts of land revenue due and payable each year from those holdings. In each subdivision of a province, called a *pargana*, the ruler appointed a leading *zamindar* to serve as a headman or *chaudhuri* who was responsible for collecting the specified revenues from their fellows and sending these payments to the provincial capital. The rulers also identified Brahmin families or members of other literate castes to keep records of revenue assessments and collections for each *chaudhuri*. Both officers received percentages of the revenues paid, tax-free lands, and other perquisites for their services.

When the regime was strong, no individual or group of rural *zamindars* could long resist the military power of the centre. Wider combinations against the state were unlikely because over generations in subservient relationships to Indo-Muslim regimes, the *zamindars* were hindered by foreshortened political horizons. They did not expect to directly challenge Muslim rule or to evade its demands. The payments made by *zamindars* more often resembled tribute exacted from a subordinate ruler than taxes levied over a directly ruled area. The sums demanded were only loosely tied to the size and productive capacity of the peasant villages controlled by the *zamindar*. Instead they correlated with the distance and capacity for troublesome resistance of the local magnate in question. Payments could be erratic. In the confusion of a weakened regime or in times of foreign invasion, *zamindars* held back revenue payments until firm centralized authority was restored. Periodically some local magnates challenged state authority by going into rebellion and refusing to pay the revenue until a punitive expedition forced them back into compliance.

Under Akbar the Mughals devised systematic policies to penetrate and scrape away the tough carapace of rural society formed by the *zamindars*. A fixed goal of the imperial administration that never wavered over a century and a half was to convert its relationship with *zamindars* from one of political negotiations with subordinate rulers to that of uniform regulations imposed upon a quasi-official service class in the countryside. The *pargana* was no longer to be a miniature tributary kingdom, but a petty revenue and administrative unit existing at the convenience of the Mughal empire. Throughout the empire Akbar stationed military commanders (*faujdars*) heading contingents of heavy, mailed cavalry, and fort commanders stationed at virtually impregnable strongholds. Imperial officials circumscribed the military power of the *zamindars* by such measures as forbidding them to manufacture firearms.

More devastating was the imperial policy of establishing direct relationships with peasants and peasant communities within each *zamindar's* holdings. By this means imperial officials cracked open the hard cyst-like resistance of South Asian rural society to state power. Akbar's new revenue system devised early in his reign steadily undercut the powers of the rural aristocracy. By measuring cultivated lands in each village and by determining average prices and yields, imperial revenue officers set tax assessments on the basis of actual production by crop in each region of the empire. *Zamindars* received written contracts that specified their duties and allotted them a fixed percentage of the revenues assessed and collected. The emperor intervened freely in successions to the rulership of aristocratic holdings and appointed the most pliable candidates. Imperial officials selected and appointed *chaudhuris* and accountants at the village level as well as the subdistrict level. The contractual relationship between empire and *zamindar* only extended to the lifetime of its recipient. The imperial administration could, and occasionally did, dispossess *zamindars* who proved troublesome.

Most *zamindars*, however, found their diminished powers compensated by participation in a growing and prospering rural economy. Mughal-imposed peace and stability, growing urban and town populations, and rising industrial production intensified demand for cash crops. The new markets generated profits for cultivators and for the rural aristocracy of the empire. The agreed-upon share of tax revenues stipulated for *zamindars* became a form of property that could be mortgaged or even sold. Individuals unconnected to the rural aristocracy bought these rights as numerous surviving sale deeds attest.

THE ECONOMY

Europeans and Middle Easterners travelling in the Mughal empire invariably commented upon the enormous wealth of the emperor and his nobles. Visitors privileged to attend an imperial audience described the lavishness of the textiles and furnishings, the brilliance of the court dress worn by the emperor and his grandees with its intricate weaving and gold and silver brocade; the profusion of diamonds, rubies, emeralds, pearls, and other precious stones worn as ornamentation on clothes and weapons. They were impressed by the vast numbers of attendants at these occasions—all well dressed and equipped—and the order and discipline imposed. They remarked on the vast numbers of cavalrymen, musketeers, cannon, and war elephants maintained by the emperor and other notables of the empire. They listened to speculations and rumour about the size of the imperial treasuries and their storied holdings of coin, specie, and precious stones. They noticed that Mughal coins—the copper *dam* and the silver rupee—were not discounted from their nominal value, were not debased, and circulated in astounding numbers. The wealth and resources of even the greatest European and Middle Eastern rulers seemed to diminish by comparison.

From the Middle East religious scholars, Sufi saints, poets, painters, calligraphers, reciters of the Quran, and other specialists in the Islamic arts made the arduous journey to India to share in the Grand Mughal's largess. Every year military commanders, many of impeccable aristocratic backgrounds, travelled from Iran or other parts of the Middle East to seek service with the Great Mughal. Some were political fugitives, others adventurers, all sought a share of the fabled riches of Mughal India. Many found a welcome at the Mughal court and employment for themselves and their followers as imperial officers. Rarely did traffic go in the other direction. Mughal *amirs* were unlikely to migrate to Isfahan or to Istanbul to better their lot.

As military victories and conquests proceeded the Mughal empire gained new resources. From Akbar's conquest of Malwa in 1561 till the fall of Golconda in 1687, plunder from the vaults of defeated kings flowed into the Mughal treasury. With expansion came larger tax and tribute revenues levied on additional populations. The financial reserves of the Mughal emperors grew to several hundred million rupees in silver and gold coin as well as other forms of precious objects and jewelry. The emperors, unlike many other early modern rulers, did not have to borrow from private financiers to fund military campaigns or monumental building. Even such expenditures as those of Shahjahan (r.1628-1658) for construction of the palaces, fortresses, canals, and arcades of Shahjahanabad Delhi (now Old Delhi) or the costs of the Taj Mahal, that great mausoleum dedicated to his late wife, were met without strain from his treasuries. Moreover, several hundred grandees or *amirs* who shared in the imperial largess also built up vast hoards of coin and precious jewels and objects. Their liquid wealth formed part of the imperial reserves.

Mughal wealth rested on a carefully crafted imperial revenue system that tapped the productive capacities of tens of millions of South Asian peasant farmers. The Indian early modern economy's productive capacity was only equalled by that of China. That productivity rose throughout the seventeenth and on into the eighteenth century as peasant cultivators adopted more valuable crops, farmed their fields more intensively, cleared new fields from unused village margins, and migrated to settle, clear, and farm new tracts of land in forested regions.

Building upon the extended experience of earlier Indo-Muslim regimes, Akbar and his financial advisers devised a land revenue system that efficiently assessed and collected a considerable portion of the crops harvested by every peasant-cultivator in the empire. Under the regulation land tax system, Mughal revenue officials had access to survey data that recorded areas under cultivation for each peasant in each village. From these data they assessed taxes according to recorded prices and yields of crops grown in each locality. They insisted that taxes be collected in fixed instalments each year in imperial copper or silver coin—not produce. This requirement forced the sale of immense quantities of foodgrains and other crops in an ascending series of markets that brought food and supplies to the growing towns and cities of the regime. Mughal taxation does not seem to have hindered steady expansion of rural production. Cultivators cleared new lands, adopted new crops—especially New World plants like tobacco and maize—and responded to market incentives by growing a wide variety of cash crops such as cotton, poppy for opium, and sugarcane.

Salaried imperial officers collected taxes directly in lands denoted as imperial crown lands. These were not a fixed territory but rather a designation applied to some of the most productive tracts in the empire. Cash receipts from these lands moved directly into provincial treasuries and were at the disposal of the emperor. Collection of taxes from the majority of the population and lands of the empire fell to imperial *amirs* and *mansabdars* in an unusual decentralized system. Under the system of salary assignment (*jagirs*) nearly all save the lowest ranked imperial officers received their pay in the form of written documents that authorized them to collect the assessed taxes in named villages, groups of villages or even entire subdistricts that might contain up to a hundred or more villages. The assessed land and other revenues for the areas named in the *jagir* document matched the specified pay that the officer was entitled to receive for his personal and trooper rank. Armed with this authorization, the officer sent his agents to the areas to collect the revenues in instalments from village and *pargana* headmen. Imperial officers had no claim on particular lands that they might consider their home territories. Instead, revenue officials selected lands for *jagir* assignment from amongst a pool of available villages and territories that were temporarily unassigned. In practice, however, *mansabdars* tended to obtain salary assignments located in the provinces that they were currently serving.

Local revenue officials exerted tight control over the methods and the amounts collected by the agents of the assignment-holders (the *jagirdars*). This was not a tax farming system by which entrepreneurs bid for the right to collect assessed taxes over a specified region. Instead, the *jagir* system was a flexible and efficient system, closely monitored by the centre that shifted organizational responsibility for tax collection to the imperial officer corps. Each *mansabdar* was forced to employ clerks, agents, bookkeepers, and other staff to manage his fiscal affairs properly. The system also relied upon private agency in that officers frequently resorted to local moneylenders for loans in advance of collections and for remitting funds by means of bills of exchange rather than sending cash. In case of resistance or non-payment, the holder of a salary assignment could turn to the local military governor (*faujdar*) or provincial officials for forceful assistance in making his collection. If, however, the *jagirdar* employed excessive force or tried to collect more than he was due local *zamindars* hastened to complain to these same officials and asked for relief. Whether imperial supervision effectively restrained the *jagirdars* or whether in practice they were free to oppress the peasants within their holdings is a matter of scholarly dispute. What is certain is that the official revenue system put immense resources in the hands of nobles and higher-ranking *mansabdars* and depended upon their organizational skills for revenue collection.

Imperial prosperity also rested on the remarkable productivity of South Asia's export economy. As it had since antiquity, the Subcontinent maintained a favourable balance of trade in merchandise and services. Indian spices and dyes grown and processed as cash crops commanded a world market. Large diamonds of the highest clarity and purity from the fabled mines of Golconda far exceeded those of any other region in number and value during the seventeenth and eighteenth centuries. The Subcontinent's merchants assembled vast shipments of hand-woven Indian cotton and silk cloth to trade in the ports of the Persian Gulf, East Africa, and Southeast Asia. By 1500 the Portuguese had opened up direct trade relations between Europe and the Subcontinent under a state-run monopoly in order to trade in Indian pepper and precious stones. By 1600 the British, Dutch and later the French East India Companies further expanded this connection. High quality, relatively low-priced hand-woven, colourful South Asian cottons replaced linen and woolen cloths for both the lower and higher ends of the consumer market in Western Europe. By the 1680s the East India Companies sold tens of millions of yards of Indian cloth each year. These new markets stimulated production, increased employment, and injected profits into the Mughal economy.

Lacking a countervailing product that would sell in the South Asian market, European traders carried New World silver and gold coin and specie to pay for purchased cloth. By the latter 1600s they were carrying on average 34 tons of silver and a half-ton of gold each year to India. Since the Mughal emperors did not permit the circulation of foreign coin in their dominions, payment for cloth, pepper, and other exports had to be made in imperial coin. Imperial port officers forced all traders bringing in bullion and coin to take it directly to the nearby imperial mint for melting and conversion, after payment of the minting fee, to silver rupees and gold *muhrs*. Only then could they pay Indian brokers and traders receive payment for goods ordered. The impact of this new export trade made itself felt directly in four coastal textile producing regions: the areas surrounding Surat in Gujarat, that between Krishna and Godavari rivers in northern Coromandel, the southern Coromandel between Pulicat and Madras, and the Ganges delta forming a hinterland Hughli port in Bengal. In these areas demand for textiles reached deep into the countryside to employ rural weavers, spinners, washers, and dyers living in scattered villages.

The stream of precious metals pouring into the Subcontinent strengthened Mughal finances. The vast circulation of silver rupees was heavily dependent upon New World silver since South Asia had almost no domestic production. Customs duties on imports and mint fees offered ready profits. Land revenues rose as peasant cultivators shifted to higher-value cash crops like cotton, indigo, or mulberry (for silk production). The trade nexus between the Mughal empire and Europe benefited both sides—and not only the European consumer.

As in any society, Mughal prosperity and political stability did not mean that wealth was distributed equally—far from it. Travelers saw ample evidence of poverty in cities and the countryside. But it is doubtful that the poor were relatively more numerous or suffered more than those in similar circumstances in contemporary Europe or Asia. Over the long term Indian traders and merchants and other professional groups in the towns probably added to their wealth and security. So also did *zamindars* and leading peasants in the countryside. Even smaller peasants and their dependent labourers probably did reasonably well in ordinary circumstances. The land was far less crowded than it is today. Peasants could readily feed their livestock on grazing lands adjacent to each village. They added to their income in the form of hunted and gathered resources from marginal areas surrounding the villages. There were also opportunities for pioneers willing to clear new lands in areas like East Bengal or the foothills of the northern plains.

To be sure, if the monsoon failed and rains did not come in sufficient quantity harvests would suffer. Two to three drought years resulted in absolute shortages of foodgrains in the afflicted regions. The government could do little because draught and pack animals ate as much as they carried beyond a certain distance. Relief shipments of food were only possible by river and coastal transport. Under these conditions famine with its starvation, disease, and mortality afflicted South Asia just as it did every other early modern society.

CONCLUSION

Under the emperors Shahjahan and Aurangzeb the Mughal empire retreated from Akbar's inclusive political ideology and imperial culture. They responded to and encouraged an orthodox Muslim reaction in which prominent Sufi teachers from the Naqshbandi and other orders took a leading role. Concerned to guard the Sunni Muslim community in the Subcontinent from heresy and against the assimilative qualities of Hindu life and beliefs, they urged the Mughal emperors to look to the strict interpretations of the *shariah* and its obligations for pious rulers. For example, a group of *ulema* tried to circumvent the prohibition in the Quran against destroying places of worship by subscribing to an extremist view that new temples and churches could not be permitted nor could the repairs of existing structures. Aurangzeb tried to enforce this measure and even went so far as to destroy a number of newly-built temples during his reign. Changes in imperial attitudes were signalled especially by Aurangzeb's restoration of the *jizyah* or the capitation tax on non-Muslims in 1679, just a century after its removal by Akbar. New attitudes corroded the relationship between the emperor and many Rajputs. Aurangzeb's intervention in a succession dispute to the throne of Marwar after the death of Maharaja Jaswant Singh Rathor in 1578 flared up in Rajput defiance and a full-scale revolt in the kingdoms of Marwar and Mewar. For a brief time, the rebels joined forces with Aurangzeb's son Prince Akbar who had gone into rebellion against his father and his strict Muslim policies and anti-Rajput bias. In the end the revolt failed and Akbar went into exile to the Middle East.

One of the most vexing question in Mughal history lies in the interpretation of these new directions in Mughal policy and change in imperial culture. Did Aurangzeb act wisely to restore the essential Muslim nature of his dynasty's rule and of Indo-Muslim states in India after it was unwisely weakened by Akbar? Or, did Aurangzeb's embrace of the orthodox revival corrode the very practices and attitudes that had been among the most successful of Akbar's innovations and thus weaken the empire? These are not easy questions to resolve. It seems reasonably certain that Aurangzeb's relationship with non-Muslim nobles—whether long-standing servitors like the Rajputs, or newly recruited Marathas in the Deccan—were uneasy at best. Any damage to this absolutely vital link between emperor and significant numbers of nobles and high-ranking *mansabdars* probably did weaken the empire. Whether this was decisive in the later decline and breaking apart of the empire is difficult to determine.

Founded and built on the synergy of expansive conquest, added resources, and deepening administrative control, the Mughal empire lost that momentum after the Deccan conquests. An imperial elite accustomed to never-ending expansion and victory found it difficult to respond to the persisting Maratha rebellion in the south. Despite the capture and execution of Shambhaji in 1689, a Maratha king in exile encouraged the incessant raiding and plundering of Maratha military captains in the newly-annexed territories taken from Bijapur and Golconda. Imperial officials sent to the new lands had little time to establish their authority before they were beset by Maratha raids that disrupted rural productivity and challenged imperial rule. Aurangzeb's preoccupation with the Deccan crisis and his absence from the north between 1689 and his death in 1707 weakened the central administration of the empire. The Deccan wars were costly in men and resources drawn from the north and even more costly in the plummeting morale of Mughal *amirs* and *mansabdars* who found themselves, often with inadequate supplies and support, losing battles in protracted, wearisome campaigns.

During the later years of Aurangzeb's reign two linkages essential for Mughal centralized authority weakened. The ties of emotion and interest that bound the nobility to the monarch and the dynasty began to fray. So also did those contractual ties that linked the rural warrior aristocracies to the empire. For nobles and *zamindars* alike, the aim was to convert armed grandees or warrior aristocrats into dependable imperial servants. Imperial expansion was the impetus for a slow, steady socialization of both groups into a higher service nobility and a lower service rural aristocracy. These processes virtually came to a halt in the period between 1689 and 1720. Factional conflict and military defeats forced high-ranking nobles to look to their own survival as the emperor became less able to command respect and muster resources from the centre. In the countryside, the very economic success of the regime had put increasing resources of men and money in the hands of newly emboldened *zamindars*. The latter discovered that they could revert to older forms of internecine warfare to expand their holdings and evade the constraints of imperial regulations. Preoccupied with other matters, Aurangzeb and his advisers did not recognize and could not devise ways to cope with the steadily-growing confidence of the *zamindars*.

After Aurangzeb's death in 1707 the centralized structure of the empire broke apart. In the thirteen years between that event and the accession of Muhammad Shah in 1720, the empire suffered four, bitter, wracking wars of succession. The emperors no longer commanded the loyalty and devotion of the corps of *mansabdars*. Instead intense factional conflict between parties of nobles eroded the ties of emotion and interest between the emperor and his officers. The final denouement came when those same nobles, headed by two brothers (the Sayyid brothers) who had placed the emperor Farrukhsiyar on the throne in 1713, forcibly deposed and killed him in 1719. They put a young Timurid prince on the throne as a puppet ruler. These events were accompanied by fighting in the streets of Delhi by rival factions. Within a year another group of nobles defeated and killed the Sayyid brothers and placed Muhammad Shah on the Mughal throne.

Muhammad Shah presided over a loosely connected set of regional kingdoms rather than the centralized empire of Aurangzeb. The political crisis at the centre permitted governors in the provinces to become regional rulers. They made formal ritual statements of submission to the Mughal emperor and sent some monies to the centre, but were no longer subject to either transfer or to imperial command. Each provincial governor developed his own cadres of servants and supporters and paid them from the resources of his province. No longer could the emperor transfer *mansabdars* throughout the empire or assemble field armies from contingents mobilized from several provinces. Those finely tuned instruments of imperial control—the regulation revenue system and the *jagir* system—no longer functioned. Under these circumstances the Maratha rebels in the south consolidated their power under the Peshwas and slowly, but surely, seized control of entire Mughal provinces in western and southern India.

By the mid-1750s, Bengal, a regional Mughal successor state, proved vulnerable to a military intervention carried out by the English East India Company. In 1764 at the battle of Buxar in the eastern Gangetic plain, the combined forces of the Mughal emperor and the ruler of Awadh failed to recover Bengal. Before the British conquest of Bengal, imperial recovery might have occurred. It is possible that a new Timurid emperor could have emerged with the charismatic personality and military skills of his forbears to reassemble a new Mughal empire. Or, a Maratha leader who assumed the Mughal throne and its symbols of power might have rebuilt the empire. These are not entirely fanciful possibilities as the recovery of the Ottoman empire from its eighteenth century malaise testifies. Certainly the awe and respect felt by men of the eighteenth century for Mughal institutions and grandeur remained intact. Had the British been faced with a reviving Mughal empire in Bengal at mid-century, they would not have prevailed, but would have been forced to negotiate. The subsequent history of India might not have been that of direct colonial rule, but might have more closely resembled that of China under the Manchu dynasty subject to Western pressure, but not outright conquest.

Instead what the Mughals left as their legacy to the new conquerors of India was the example of successful political unification of the Subcontinent by centralized authoritarian rule supported by the Mughal land revenue system. To the world at large the Mughals left a sophisticated, graceful high culture whose artifacts—

from the gardens and iconography of the Taj Mahal to the music and albums of miniature painting—continue to appeal directly and powerfully to all who encounter them. ✦

BIBLIOGRAPHY

Akbar's India: Art from the Mughal City of Victory. New York, New York: Asia Society Gallery, 1985.

Abu al-Fazl ibn, Mubarak, and Henry Beveridge. *The Akbarnama of Abu-l-Fazl, Bibliotheca Indica; new series; no. 910.* Delhi: Rare Books, 1972.

Arasaratnam, Sinnappah, and Aniruddha Ray. *Masulipatnam and Cambay: a history of two port-towns, 1500-1800.* New Delhi: Munshiram Manoharlal Publishers, 1994.

Asher, Catherine B. 'Kacchavaha Pride and Prestige: The Temple Patronage of Raja Mana Simha'. In *Govindadeva: A Dialogue in Stone*, edited by Margaret Case. New Delhi: Indira Gandhi National Centre for the Arts, 1996.

Athar Ali, M. *The Mughal nobility under Aurangzeb.* Rev. ed. Delhi; New York: Oxford University Press, 1997.

Attman, Artur. *The bullion flow between Europe and the East, 1000-1750, Acta Regiae Societatis Scientiarum et Litterarum Gothoburgensis. Humaniora, 20.* Göteborg: Kungl. vetenskaps- och vitterhets-samhället, 1981.

Axelrod, Paul, and Michelle A. Fuerch. 'Flight of the Diety; Hindu Resistance in Portuguese Goa'. *Modern Asian Studies* 30 (1996): 387-421.

Babur, and Annette Susannah Beveridge. *The Bábar-Náma, being the autobiography of the Emperor Babar, the founder of the Moghul dynasty in India, E.J.W. Gibb memorial series v. 1.* Leyden, London: E.J. Brill; B. Quaritch, 1905.

Bailey, Gauvin Alexander. *The Jesuits and the Grand Mogul: Renaissance Art at the Imperial Court of India, 1580-1630. Vol. 2, Occasional Papers.* Washington, D.C.: Freer Gallery of Art, Arthur M. Sackler Gallery, Smithsonian Institution, 1998.

Baladouni, Vahé, Margaret Makepeace, and East India Company. *Armenian merchants of the seventeenth and early eighteenth centuries: English East India Company sources, Transactions of the American Philosophical Society; v. 88, pt. 5.* Philadelphia: American Philosophical Society, 1998.

Barret, Ward. 'World Bullion Flows, 1450-1800'. In *The Rise of Merchant Empires: Long-Distance Trade in the Early-Modern World, 1350-1750,* edited by James D. Tracey, pp. 224-254. Cambridge: Cambridge University Press, 1990.

Begley, W.E., Ziyaud-Din A. Desai, and Aga Khan Program for Islamic Architecture. *Taj Mahal: the illumined tomb: an anthology of seventeenth-century Mughal and European documentary sources.* Cambridge, Mass. Seattle, Wash.: Aga Khan Program for Islamic Architecture; Distributed by the University of Washington Press, 1989.

Blake, Stephen P. *Shahjahanabad: the sovereign city in Mughal India, 1639-1739, Cambridge South Asian studies; v. 49.* Cambridge [England]; New York: Cambridge University Press, 1991.

Boyajian, James C. *Portuguese Trade in Asia Under the Hapsburgs.* Baltimore: Johns Hopkins Press, 1993.

Burton, Audrey. *The Bukharans: a dynastic, diplomatic, and commercial history, 1550-1702.* New York: St. Martin's Press, 1997.

Case, Margaret H., ed. *Govindadeva: A Dialogue in Stone.* New Delhi: Indira Gandhi National Centre for the Arts, 1996.

Chandra, Satish. *The Indian Ocean: explorations in history, commerce, and politics.* New Delhi; Newbury Park Calif.: Sage Publications, 1987.

Chandra, Satish. *Medieval India: from Sultanat to the Mughals.* New Delhi: Har-Anand Publications, 1997.

Chandra, Satish. *Medieval India: society, the jagirdari crisis, and the village.* Delhi: Macmillan, 1982.

Chandra, Satish. *Mughal religious policies, the Rajputs and the Deccan.* New Delhi, New York: Vikas; dist. by Advent Books, 1993.

Chandra, Satish. *Parties and politics at the Mughal Court, 1707-1740.* 2nd ed. New Delhi: People's Pub. House, 1972.

Chandra, Satish, and Centre for Studies in Social Sciences. *The 18th century in India: its economy and the role of the Marathas, the Jats, the Sikhs, and the Afghans, Sakharam Ganesh Deuskar lectures on Indian history; 1982.* Calcutta: Published for Centre for Studies in Social Sciences, Calcutta by K.P. Bagchi & Co., 1986.

Chandra, Satish, Raghubir Singh, and G.D. Sharma. *Marwar under Jaswant Singh, (1658-1678) = Jodhpur hukumat ri Bahi.* Meerut: Meenakshi Prakashan, 1976.

Chatterjee, Anjali. *Bengal in the reign of Aurangzib, 1658-1707.* Calcutta: Progressive Publishers, 1967.

Chaudhuri, K.N. *Asia before Europe: economy and civilisation of the Indian Ocean from the rise of Islam to 1750.* Cambridge England; New York: Cambridge University Press, 1990.

Chaudhuri, K.N. *The English East India Company: the study of an early joint-stock company, 1600-1640.* New York: Reprints of Economic Classics, 1965.

Chaudhuri, K.N. *Trade and Civilization in the Indian Ocean: An Economic History from the Rise of Islam to 1750.* Cambridge: Cambridge University Press, 1985.

Chaudhuri, Susil. *Trade and commercial organization in Bengal, 1650-1720, with special reference to the English East India Company.* Calcutta: Firma K.L. Mukhopadhyay, 1975.

Dale, Stephen. 'The Islamic Frontier in Southwest India: the Shahid as a Cultural Ideal Among the Mappilas of Malabar'. *Modern Asian Studies* 11 (1977): 41-55.

Dale, Stephen. *Islamic Society on the South Asian Frontier: The Mappilas of Malabar 1498-1922.* Oxford: Clarendon Press, 1980.

Dale, Stephen F. 'Trade, Conversion and the Growth of the Islamic Community of Kerala, South India'. *Studia Islamica* 71 (1990): 155-175.

Das Gupta, Ashin. *Indian merchants and the decline of Surat: c. 1700-1750.* 1. Aufl. ed, *Beiträge zur Südasienforschung; Bd. 40.* Wiesbaden: Steiner, 1979.

Das Gupta, Ashin, and M.N. Pearson. *India and the Indian Ocean, 1500-1800.* Calcutta; New York: Oxford University Press, 1987.

Dutta, S.C. *The north-east and the Mughals, 1661-1714.* New Delhi: D.K. Publications, 1984.

Eaton, Richard. *The Rise of Islam and the Bengal Frontier 1204-1760.* Berkeley: University of California Press, 1993.

Farooqi, Naimur Rahman. *Mughal-Ottoman relations: a study of political & diplomatic relations between Mughal India and the Ottoman Empire, 1556-1748, IAD oriental (original) series; no. 32.* Delhi, India: Idarah-i Adabiyat-i Delli, 1989.

Foltz, Richard. 'The Central Asian Naqshbandi Connections of the Mughal Emperors'. *Journal of Islamic Studies* 7 (1996): 229-239.

Foltz, Richard. 'The Mughal Occupation of Balkh 1646-1647'. *Journal of Islamic Studies* 7 (1996): 49-61.

Gommans, Jos. 'The Silent Frontier of South Asia, c. A. D. 1100-1800'. *Journal of World History* 9 (1998): 1-24.

Gordon, Stewart. *The Marathas, 1600-1818, The New Cambridge History of India; II, 4.* Cambridge, England; New York: Cambridge University Press, 1993.

Gordon, Stewart. *Marathas, marauders, and state formation in eighteenth-century India.* Delhi; New York: Oxford University Press, 1994.

Gordon, Stewart Nelson. 'Old rights and new masters: Maratha conquest and control in eighteenth century Malwa'. University Microfilms International, 1980.

Goswamy, B.N., and J.S. Grewal. *The Mughal and Sikh rulers and the Vaishnavas of Pindori; a historical interpretation of 52 Persian documents.* [1st] ed. Simla: Indian Institute of Advanced Study, 1969.

Goswamy, B.N., and J.S. Grewal. *The Mughals and the Jogis of Jakhbar; some madad-i-maash and other documents.* [1st] ed. Simla: Indian Institute of Advanced Study, 1967.

Grewal, J.S. *In the by-lanes of history: some Persian documents from a Punjab town.* 1st ed. Simla: Indian Institute of Advanced Study, 1975.

Grewal, J.S., and Satjit Singh Bal. *Guru Gobind Singh: a biographical study.* Chandigarh: Dept. of History, Panjab University, 1967.

Guha, Sumit. 'An Indian Penal Regime: Maharashtra in the Eighteenth Century'. *Past and Present*, no. 147 (1995).

Gulbadan, and Annette S. Beveridge. *The History of Humayun (Humayun-nama), Oriental translation fund. New ser. I-XIII.* London: Printed and published under the patronage of the Royal Asiatic Society, 1902.

Gupta, Satya Prakash, and Aligarh Muslim University Centre of Advanced Study in History. *The agrarian system of eastern Rajasthan, c. 1650-c. 1750.* Delhi: Manohar, 1986.

Habib, Irfan. *The agrarian system of Mughal India, 1556-1707.* Bombay, New York: Published for the Dept. of History, Aligarh Muslim University by Asia Pub. House, 1963.

Habib, Irfan. *Akbar and his India.* Delhi: Oxford University Press, 1997.

Habib, Irfan. *An atlas of the Mughal Empire: political and economic maps with detailed notes, bibliography and index.* Aligarh. Delhi; New York: Centre of Advanced Study in History, Aligarh Muslim University; Oxford University Press, 1982.

Habib, Irfan. *Caste and money in Indian history, D.D. Kosambi memorial lectures; 1985.* Bombay: Dept. of History, University of Bombay, 1987.

Habib, Irfan. 'A Documentary History of the Gosains (Gosvamis) of the Caitanya Sect at Vrindavana'. In *Govindadeva: A Dialogue in Stone*, edited by Margaret Case. New Delhi: Indira Gandhi National Centre for the Arts, 1996.

Habib, Irfan. *Peasant and artisan resistance in Mughal India, McGill studies in international development no. 34.* Montreal, Quebec, Canada: Centre for Developing-Area Studies, McGill University, 1984.

Habib, Irfan, and North-Eastern Hill University. *Interpreting Indian history.* Shillong: North-Eastern Hill University Publications, 1988.

Hintze, Andrea. *The Mughal Empire and Its Decline: An Interpretation of the Sources of Social Power.* Aldershot: Ashgate Publishing Ltd., 1997.

Hussain, Mahmood, Abdul Rehman, James L. Wescoat, Smithsonian Institution, Pakistan. Dept. of Archaeology & Museums, and University of Engineering and Technology. *The Mughal garden: interpretation, conservation and implications.* Rawalpindi: Ferozsons, 1996.

Inayat, Khan, W.E. Begley, and Ziyaud-Din A. Desai. *The Shah Jahan nama of 'Inayat Khan: an abridged history of the Mughal Emperor Shah Jahan, compiled by his royal librarian: the nineteenth-century manuscript translation of A.R. Fuller (British Library, add. 30,777).* Delhi; New York: Oxford University Press, 1990.

Irvine, William. *The army of the Indian Moghuls: its organization and administration.* London: Luzac, 1903.

Irvine, William, and Jadunath Sarkar. *Later Mughals.* New Delhi: Oriental Books Reprint Corp.; exclusively distributed by Munshiram Manoharlal, Delhi, 1971.

Israel, Jonathan Irvine. *Dutch primacy in world trade, 1585-1740.* Oxford, England, New York: Clarendon Press; Oxford University Press, 1990.

Jackson, Peter A. *The Delhi Sultanate: a military and political history, Cambridge studies in Islamic civilization*. New York, NY: Cambridge University Press, 1999.

Jahangir, Alexander Rogers, and Henry Beveridge. *The Tuzuk-i-Jahangiri, or, Memoirs of Jahangir, Oriental translation fund. New series vol. XIX, XXII*. London: Royal Asiatic Society, 1909.

Karim, Abdul. *Murshid Quli Khan and his times, Asiatic Society of Pakistan no. 12*. Dacca: Asiatic Society of Pakistan, 1963.

Kausar, Sajjad, Michael Brand, and James L. Wescoat. *Shalamar garden Lahore: landscape, form & meaning. 1st ed., Museums & monuments series; no. 1*. Karachi, Pakistan: Dept. of Archaeology and Museums, Ministry of Culture, 1990.

Koch, Ebba. *Dara-Shikoh Shooting Nilgais: Hunt and Landscape in Mughal Painting*. Vol. 1, Occasional Papers. Washington, D.C.: Freer Gallery of Art; Arthur M. Sackler Gallery; Smithsonian Insitution, 1998.

Kolff, D.H.A. *Naukar, Rajput, and sepoy: the ethnohistory of the military labour market in Hindustan, 1450-1850, University of Cambridge oriental publications; no. 43*. Cambridge; New York: Cambridge University Press, 1990.

Kulkarni, A.R. *Maharashtra in the age of Shivaji*. 1st ed. Poona: Deshmukh, 1969.

Manucci, Niccolao, and William Irvine. *Storia do Mogor, or, Mogul India, 1653-1708, Indian texts series*. London: John Murray, 1907.

McLeod, W. H. *Guru Nanak and the Sikh religion*. Oxford: Clarendon Press, 1968.

McLeod, W. H. *Sikhism*. London; New York: Penguin Books, 1997.

McLeod, W. H. *The Sikhs of the Punjab*. Newcastle upon Tyne: Oriel, 1970.

Moosvi, Shireen. *The economy of the Mughal Empire, c. 1595: a statistical study*. Delhi; New York: Centre of Advanced Study in History, Aligarh Muslim University; Oxford University Press, 1987.

Mukherjee, Rita. 'The Story of Kasimbazar: Silk Merchants and Commerce in Eighteenth Century India'. *Review* 16 (1994): 499-554.

Mundy, Peter A., Richard Carnac Temple, and Lavinia Mary Anstey. *The travels of Peter Mundy, in Europe and Asia, 1608-1667, Works issued by the Hakluyt Society...2d ser no. 17, 35, 45-46, 55, 78*. Cambridge Eng.: Printed for the Hakluyt Society, 1907.

Mustaidd Khan, Muhammad Saqi, and Jadunath Sarkar. *Maasir-i-alamgiri: a history of the Emperor Aurangzib-Alamgir (reign 1658-1707 A.D.) of Saqi Mustad Khan*. 2nd ed. New Delhi: Oriental Books Reprint, 1986.

Naqvi, Hameeda Khatoon. *Mughal Hindustan, cities and industries, 1556-1803*. 2d ed. Karachi: National Book Foundation, 1974.

Naqvi, Hameeda Khatoon. *Urban centres and industries in upper India, 1556-1803*. Bombay, New York: Asia Pub. House, 1968.

Naqvi, Hameeda Khatoon. *Urbanisation and urban centres under the great Mughals, 1556-1707; an essay in interpretation*. Simla: Indian Institute of Advanced Study, 1971.

Nizami, Khaliq Ahmad. *Akbar & religion, IAD oriental (original) series; no. 33*. Delhi, India: Idarah-i-Adabiyat-i-Delli, 1989.

Pollock, Sheldon. 'Ramayana and Political Imagination in India'. *The Journal of Asian Studies* 52 (1993): 261-297.

Prakash, Om. *The Dutch East India Company and the economy of Bengal, 1630-1720*. Princeton, N.J.: Princeton University Press, 1985.

Prakash, Om. *Precious metals and commerce: the Dutch East India Company in the Indian Ocean trade, Collected studies series; CS443*. Aldershot, Hampshire, Great Britain; Brookfield, Vt., USA: Variorum, 1994.

Ray, B.C. *Orissa under the Mughals: from Akbar to Alivardi: a fascinating study of the socio-economic and cultural history of Orissa, Orissan studies project; no. 10*. Calcutta: Punthi Pustak, 1981.

Raychaudhuri, Tapan. *Bengal under Akbar and Jahangir; an introductory study in social history*. Delhi: Munshiram Manoharlal, 1969.

Raychaudhuri, Tapan. *Jan Company in Coromandel, 1605-1690; a study in the interrelations of European commerce and traditional economies, Verhandelingen van het Koninklijk Instituut voor Taal-Land- en Volkenkunde, deel 38*. 's-Gravenhage: M. Nijhoff, 1962.

Raychaudhuri, Tapan, and Irfan Habib. *The Cambridge economic history of India*. Cambridge, Eng.; New York: Cambridge University Press, 1982.

Riazul, Islam. 'A calendar of documents on Indo-Persian relations, 1500-1750'. Iranian Culture Foundation; Institute of Central & West Asian Studies, 1979.

Riazul, Islam. *Indo-Persian relations; a study of the political and diplomatic relations between the Mughul Empire and Iran, Sources of the history and geography of Iran no. 32*. Teheran, 1970.

Richards, John F. 'Early Modern India and World History'. *Journal of World History* 8 (1997): 197-209.

Richards, John F. *Kingship and authority in South Asia*. Delhi; New York: Oxford University Press, 1998.

Richards, John F. *Mughal administration in Golconda*. Oxford Eng.: Clarendon Press, 1975.

Richards, John F. *The Mughal Empire, The New Cambridge history of India; I, 5*. Cambridge; New York: Cambridge University Press, 1993.

Richards, John F. *Power, administration, and finance in Mughal India, Collected studies series; CS419*. Brookfield: Ashgate Pub. Co., 1993.

Richards, John F. 'The Seventeenth-Century Crisis in South Asia'. *Modern Asian Studies* 24 (1990): 625-638.

Richards, John F., and Joint Committee on South Asia. *The Imperial monetary system of Mughal India*. Delhi; New York: Oxford University Press, 1987.

Richards, John F., and Trustees of the E.J.W. Gibb Memorial. *Document forms for official orders of appointment in the Mughal Empire: translation, notes and text, 'E.J.W. Gibb memorial series'; New ser., 29.* Cambridge: Trustees of the E.J.W. Gibb Memorial, 1986.

Rizvi, Athar Abbas. *Muslim revivalist movements in northern India in the sixteenth and seventeenth centuries.* Agra: Agra University; Balkrishna Book Co., Lucknow, 1965.

Rizvi, Saiyid Athar Abbas. *Religious and intellectual history of the Muslims in Akbar's reign, with special reference to Abul Fazl, 1556-1605.* New Delhi: Munshiram Manoharlal Publishers, 1975.

Rizvi, Saiyid Athar Abbas, and Vincent John Adams Flynn. *Fathpur-Sikri.* Bombay: D.B. Taraporevala Sons, 1975.

Roy Choudhury, Makhan Lal. *The Din-i-Ilahi, or, The religion of Akbar.* Calcutta: University of Calcutta, 1941.

Sarkar, Jadunath. *History of Aurangzib, based on original sources.* Calcutta: M.C. Sarkar & Sons, 1919.

Sarkar, Jadunath. *The history of Bengal; Muslim period, 1200-1757.* Patna, India: Academica Asiatica, 1973.

Sarkar, Jadunath. *House of Shivaji: studies and documents of Maratha history: royal period.* 2nd ed. Calcutta: S.C. Sarkar & Sons, 1948.

Sarkar, Jadunath. *The India of Aurangzib: topography, statistics, and roads, compared with the India of Akbar.* Calcutta: Bose Bros., 1901.

Sarkar, Jadunath. *Shivaji and his times.* Bombay: Orient Longman, 1973.

Sarkar, Jadunath. *Studies in Aurangzib's reign (being Studies in Mughal India, First series).* Calcutta: M.C. Sarkar & Sons Ltd., 1933.

Sen, Geeti, and Mubarak, Abu al-Fazl ibn. *Paintings from the Akbar nama: a visual chronicle of Mughal India.* Varanasi, India: Lustre Press under arrangement with Rupa Calcutta, 1984.

Shahnavaz Khan, Awrangabadi, Baini Prashad, and Shahnavaz Abd al-Hayy ibn. *The Maathir-ul-umara: being biographies of the Muhammadan and Hindu officers of the Timurid sovereigns of India from 1500 to about 1780 A.D, Bibliotheca Indica; work no. 202.* Calcutta: Asiatic Society, 1941.

Siddiqi, Iqtidar Husain. *Afghan despotism in India, 1451-1555.* New Delhi: Indian Institute of Islamic Studies, 1966.

Siddiqi, Iqtidar Husain. *Mughal relations with the Indian ruling elite.* New Delhi: Munshiram Manoharlal, 1983.

Siddiqi, Iqtidar Husain. *Shershah Sur and his dynasty.* Jaipur: Publication Scheme Jaipur, India, 1995.

Siddiqi, Iqtidar Husain. *Some aspects of Afghan despotism in India.* Aligarh: Three Men Publication, 1969.

Singh, M.P. *Town, Market, Mint and Port in the Mughal Empire.* Delhi: Adam Publishers, 1985.

Streusand, Douglas E. *The formation of the Mughal Empire.* Delhi; New York: Oxford University Press, 1989.

Subrahmanyam, Sanjay, ed. *Money and the Market in India 1100-1700.* Delhi: Oxford University Press, 1994.

Subrahmanyam, Sanjay. *The Portuguese Empire in Asia 1500-1700: A Political and Economic History.* London and New York: Longman, 1993.

Tali'yar, Udiraj, and Jagadish Narayan Sarkar. *The military despatches of a seventeenth century Indian general; being an English translation of the Haft anjuman of Munshi Udairaj, alias Tale'yar Khan (Benares ms. 53 b-93b).* Calcutta,: Scientific Book Agency, 1969.

Tillotson, G.H.R. *The Rajput Palaces: The Development of an Architectural Style, 1450-1750.* New Haven: Yale University Press, 1987.

Tracy, James D. 'Asian Despotism? Mughal Government As Seen From the Dutch East India Company Factory in Surat'. *Journal of Early Modern History* 3 (1999): 256-284.

Tracy, James D., ed. *The Political Economy of Merchant Empires.* Cambridge: Cambridge University Press, 1991.

Tracy, James D., ed. *The Rise of Merchant Empires: Long-Distance Trade in the Early Modern World, 1350-1750.* Cambridge: Cambridge University Press, 1990.

Vaughn, Philippa. 'The Mughal Garden at Hasan Abdal: A Unique Surviving Example of a "Manzil" Bagh'. *South Asia Research* 15 (1995): 241-265.

Wescoat, James L., Joachim Wolschke-Bulmahn, Dumbarton Oaks, and Arthur M. Sackler Gallery (Smithsonian Institution). *Mughal gardens: sources, places, representations, and prospects.* Washington, D.C.: Dumbarton Oaks Research Library and Collection, 1996.

Wink, André. *Land and sovereignty in India: agrarian society and politics under the eighteenth-century Maratha svarajya, University of Cambridge oriental publications; no. 36.* Cambridge, Cambridgeshire; New York: Cambridge University Press, 1986.

Overleaf:
A PITCHED BATTLE IS FOUGHT.
Detail from a painting of one of Akbar's battles. Painted by Nur Muhammad in Bikaner. Mughal, end of the 16th century. Courtesy of the Goenka Collection.

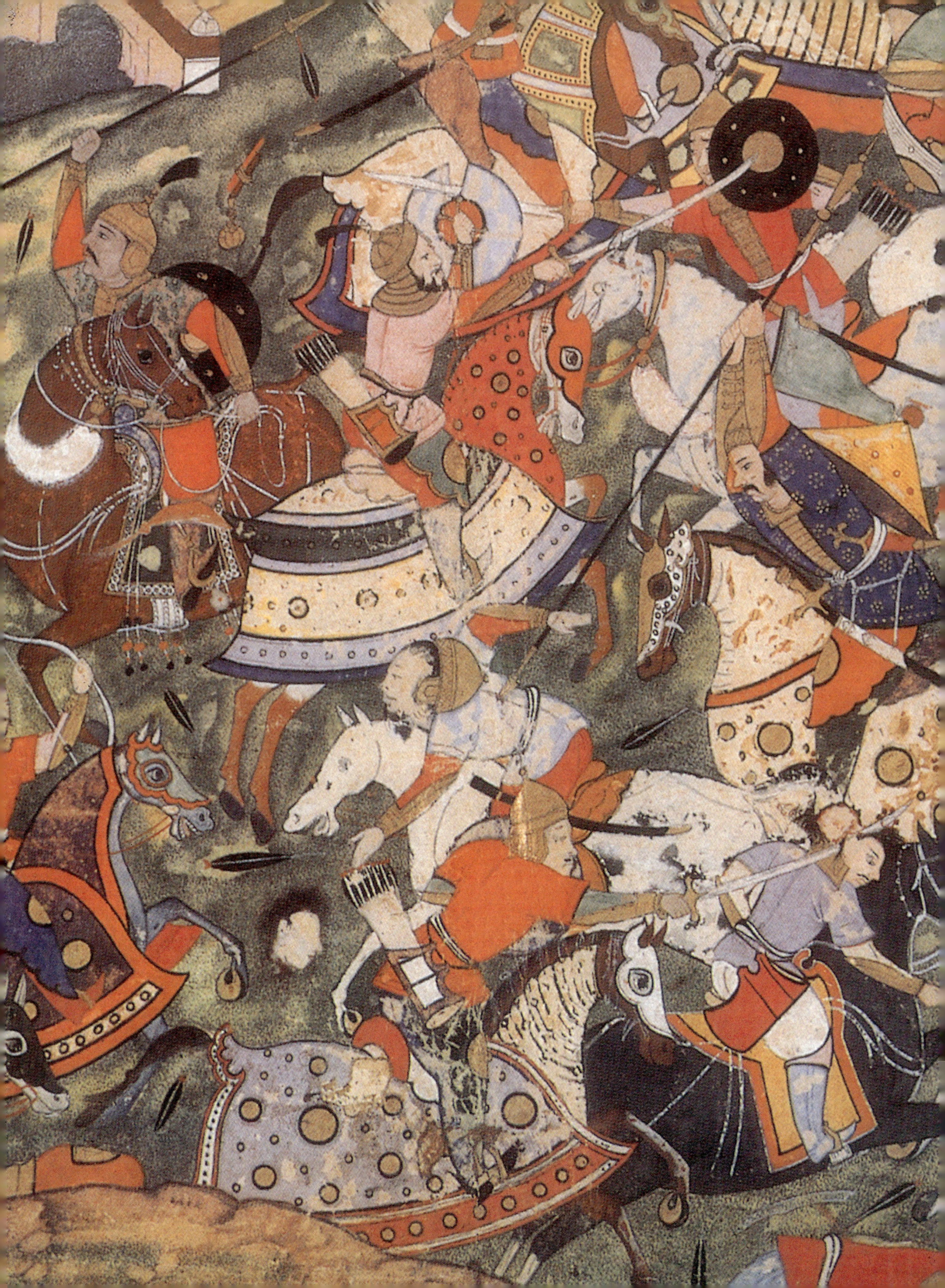

2
THE LIVES AND CONTRIBUTIONS OF MUGHAL WOMEN
Ellison B. Findly

Fig. 1: THE YOUNG AKBAR RECOGNIZES HIS MOTHER, from an *Akbarnama*, ca. 1604. Courtesy of the Freer Gallery of Art, Smithsonian Institution, Washington, D.C., 39.57. (Emperor Humayun is seated on the right)

From as early as the *Babur-Nama*, it is clear that the definitive institution in Mughal life was the family. Most of the imperial Mughal memoirs and historical accounts of individual reigns contain full genealogies which not only chart the expanded networks of family kinship structures, but also give rich accounts of personalities and individual relationships which served to cement the bonds in each successive generation of the Mughal dynasty. Family life in Mughal circles centred around a protected and circumscribed pattern of life within the imperial compounds, but its strength was most surely fortified by periodic festivals and rituals, the most important of which was marriage. Marriages forged links between families, and wedding feasts were grand affairs which celebrated and renewed the strength of diverse extended family ties.

At the centre of the familial nexus were Mughal women, who served as bridges connecting disparate lineages and affirming the alliances of powerful kingdoms. In Mughal memoirs, any description of a noble or administrative official comes complete with descriptions of all the women in his life as well as a full character assessment of each. Unlike the surrounding Hindu culture, in which daughters were neglected and sons apotheosized, Mughal culture celebrated, honoured, and protected its women and, when a daughter died, she was always described in the texts in glowing terms and with real sorrow. Mughal documents are fulsome in terms of gender in this respect: the births and deaths of all important women are mentioned in full detail. More than just an idealized elevation of women, however, Mughal life centred, in its day to day regularity, around the doings of women, for, as the Venetian Niccolao Manucci noted, 'all…[Mughals] are very fond of women, who are their principal relaxation and almost their only pleasure'.[1] Life in the women's apartments, the *zanana*, then, served as mainstay, sustenance and inspiration for all the activities of Mughal sovereign life.

Among Mughal women, the most significant from early times on were the elder women whose age, experience, wisdom, and lineal ascendancy placed them in a position of great respect and deference among both the other women and all the men of the palaces (*mahal*).[2] These elder women served as political advisers to the Mughal court, as supervisors of *zanana* life, and as surrogate caretakers of the vast array of palace offspring. Among these elder women the most revered were those who could be called 'mother' either by blood-line, milk-line (as wet-nurse or 'foster-mother'), or by formal or informal adoption. This is understandable as the position of a mother is pivotal in Islam. She commands the greatest respect and love, as is evident in the well-known Prophetic tradition: 'Paradise lies at the feet of mothers'. Mothers and grandmothers had the greatest influence in terms of giving advice or persuading to act, and it is one of the famous stories of Mughal succession that Akbar's mother Maryam Makani and then, more successfully, Salima Sultan Begum (his first-cousin, wife of Bairam Khan, and later, Akbar's own wife) worked to bring about a reconciliation between Salim and Akbar shortly before Akbar's death.[3] These efforts then became crucial in the accession of Salim/Jahangir to the Mughal throne in 1605.

The *Akbar Nama* tells another story of the love between sons and mothers, this one of the child Akbar who, when brought into the presence of a host of court women after being separated from his mother for a long time and, without her being marked out in any way, recognized her immediately and ran to her embrace (Fig. 1). Akbar, 'a very fortunate prince, and pious to his mother,' was also known for frequently shouldering her litter himself when she was on a journey and, 'commanding his greatest nobles to do the like,' would carry her himself from one side of the river to the other.[4]

Akbar's son Jahangir was also especially attached to his mother and, as the Rev. Edward Terry, chaplain to the first official English embassy in India, said, he 'not seldom would shew many expressions of duty and strong affections to his mother'.[5] In his own memoirs Jahangir often notes his attendance on his mother in her palace or a garden. He frequently held his lunar and solar birthday weighings at her house, from which the proceeds would be passed out among the

---
1. Manucci 2.319.
2. A.S. Beveridge in *Humayun-Nama*, p. 20.
3. See passages from the *Akbar Nama* in Elliot and Dowson 6.98-99, 108-109. The central position of mothers is also emphasized in the lives and sayings of Sufi saints. The high status of wet-nurses derives from the esteem in which Prophet Muhammad (PBUH) held his own wet-nurse Bibi Halima. See Schimmel, pp. 21, 89, 93.
4. Thomas Coryat in Foster, *Early Travels*, p. 278.
5. Terry, p. 389.

company of palace women (harem) and the poor of the kingdom.[6]

As Mughal culture evolved, however, the notably strong tie between mother and son became overshadowed by another idealized relationship, that between lover and beloved. As we will see, the focus on romantic love emerges more strongly in the reign of Jahangir, culminating under Shahjahan and, even though mothers are venerated throughout Mughal times, the power of the consort tie becomes increasingly significant. Early examples of romantic love include the *Babur-Nama*'s depiction of Babur's love for Mahim and Humayun's romantic attachment to Hamida Banu—relationships that had their revered precedent in Prophet Muhammad's (PBUH) ideal relationship with his wife Khadija.[7]

From early on in Mughal culture, the mother-son tie was symbolized in the imagery of the Virgin Mary and Jesus Christ, both of whom are deeply venerated in Islam.* Gulbadan, for example, describes the meeting between Babur's chief wife Mahim Begim and his son and heir Humayun, who had just been struck seriously ill, as follows:

> They met in Mathura. To her experienced eye he seemed ten times weaker and more alarmingly ill than she had heard he was. From Mathura the two, mother and son, like Jesus and Mary, set out for Agra.[8]

And in the *Akbar Nama*, the birth of Akbar from Hamida Banu (Maryam Makani) is characterized as if it were the immaculate birth of Jesus from his mother Mary.[9] Although this imagery can be found from the beginning, interest in the figures of Jesus and Mary becomes substantial only with the accessions of Akbar and Jahangir to the throne, when Portuguese Jesuit attempts to convert Mughals through gifts of European Christian art and promises of political and mercantile support were at their height. During this time, as Maclagan points out, the use of 'Mary' in the titles of the two most important mothers, Maryam Makani (of Akbar) and Maryam Zamani (of Jahangir), became significant. Although he says that both 'of these are titles suitable for a...[Muslim] Court, and...do not imply that the possessors of the titles bore the name of Mary or were Christians,'[10] against the background of a growing interest in, or even cult of, the Madonna they become especially noteworthy.

The Jesuits arrived at Akbar's court in the mid-to-late sixteenth century primarily for the purpose of proselytizing. They soon believed that the most efficient means to that end, at least among high ranking Mughals, was the presentation of gifts of trade coming into the Portuguese settlement in Goa. Akbar revelled in the images given to him of Jesus and the Madonna. Some of these were copies of paintings in Europe while others were originals—in fact, those in Akbar's possession were often said to be the best of their kind from Europe.[11] The Jesuit father Pierre Du Jarric notes that Akbar was often seen 'even wearing suspended from his neck by a gold chain, a reliquary, which had on one side of it an Agnus Dei, and on the other an image of our Lady'.[12] Once a very beautiful picture of the Madonna was brought from Goa and on seeing it, Akbar bowed his head, raised his hands to his face, and asked that the picture be put in his lodging high on the wall as it was 'unseemly that the picture of the Lady Mary should be below him'.[13]

Even as a prince, Akbar's son Salim fell under the powerful sway of the Madonna image. When the Jesuits arrived at court with pictures for Akbar and none for him, Salim would become angry and order copies made of Akbar's Madonnas for himself.[14] Salim was often seen praying before images of Mary, and frequently in public expressed his great devotion to both Mary and Jesus.[15] This devotion grew immeasurably after his reconciliation with Akbar, and it was at this time that people began to notice a large emerald engraved with a crucified Christ which he carried around on a gold chain.[16] Once he ascended the throne as Jahangir, he adorned many of his palace rooms and courtyard walls with images of Christ and the Virgin Mary (Fig. 2),[17] and Father Fernao Guerreiro notes 'that these sacred pictures, which fill the...[Muslims] with astonishment every time they look upon them, are thus publically displayed in this infidel King's chamber, which resembles the balcony...of a devout Catholic King rather than of a Muslim'.[18] Jahangir took care to be well versed in the doctrines of Mary and Jesus and used images of them on seals closing many official documents.[19]

The power of the mother-son relationship for the Mughals, epitomized in their fascination, and even identification, with the Mary-Jesus bond and set within the larger framework of celebratory views and treatment of women, is countered by a darker set of images given to us in both Mughal and European texts. Pieter van den Broecke, an official with the Dutch East India Company, for example, reports that Shaikh Qasim, who was appointed governor of Bengal in 1613 and who incited violence out of old hatreds, was removed from office soon thereafter and, fearful of reprisals, 'put to death all his mahel or women, so as not to be hampered by them (in his fight) or prevent their falling into the hands of his enemy'.[20] This slaughter of women for utilitarian reasons at moments of crisis, or for reasons of preserving family honour, seems to have occurred in more than isolated instances among surrounding Rajput contemporaries, for the *Padshahnama* reports that when 'pressed hard by the pursuers, Jajhar and Bikramajit put to death several women whose horses were worn out, and then turned on their pursuers.[21] Although, as Khafi Khan notes, women prisoners were often treated with great respect and courtesy by Muslim conquerors (as Ibrahim Lodi's mother was by Babur despite the fact that she tried to poison him),[22] Maratha conquerors, usually allied with the leader Shivaji, often attacked and mutilated even noble Mughal women during skirmishes: 'One of...[the Amir's] women was so cut about that her remains were collected in a basket which served for her coffin'.[23] Other reports of his show that Muslim armies were not immune from such cruelty, for followers of Abul Hasan captured and dishonoured women of all social backgrounds, and Mughal emperors themselves, from Jahangir's time onward, often treated wives of imperial dissidents quite harshly.[24]

Women of the protected Mughal palaces were certainly aware of such atrocities, as they were aware of the continued presence of Hindu women who became *suttees*, wives purified through death by fire on their husband's funeral pyre. The *Akbar Nama*'s description of the *suttee* focuses on the wife's courage before imminent death in the midst of her own grief for the loss of her husband, as well as on the honour bestowed on both families by her self-sacrifice. Only in passing, by saying that her commitment to the flame may be willing or unwilling, does Abul Fazl suggest the enormity of this second loss of life. Although Akbar appears to have opposed the practice of the *suttee*, he was somewhat ambivalent about interfering in Hindu customs.[25] Jahangir abhorred the burning of a *suttee*, as he did the practice of female infanticide, and forbade them under penalty of capital punishment.[26] Early Europeans in India were aware of the prevalence of *suttee*, describing in great detail both the dress and jewels of the honourable wife as well as the incendiary details of her death.[27] Although Peter Mundy of the English East India Company notes that 'since the Mogolls comeinge burninge is worne out of date',[28] the French physician François Bernier gives a lengthy description not only of the legal procedures a Hindu woman must have gone through in late Mughal times to become a *suttee* but story after story of widow-burning that he himself saw[29]—indicating quite clearly that the practice continued with some prevalence, and that detailed knowledge of each case was part of the common knowledge passed around in the marketplace and making its way quickly into the apartments of Mughal women.

It is likely then that the great range and number of women protected and cared for within the boundaries of Mughal imperial life were aware that theirs was a life of greater pleasure, greater opportunity, and indeed greater safety than that of the Hindu, and even Muslim, women

---

6. *Tuzuk-i Jahangiri* 1.131, 145-46, 148, 154-55, 239; 2.98. All references to the *Tuzuk* are from the translation of Alexander Rogers.
7. See Findly, *Nur Jahan*, pp. 213-214.
8. *Humayun-Nama*, p. 104. For more on the roots of this in the Islamic reverence for Mary and Jesus, see Schimmel, pp. 22-23, 55, 58, 94, 96.
   * Editor's Note: Also see p. 72 in Schimmel's chapter on Religion in this book.
9. *Akbar Nama* 1.178-183.
10. Maclagan, p. 158.
11. Du Jarric, pp. 19-20, 26, 66.
12. Du Jarric, p. 72.
13. Du Jarric, p. 110.
14. Du Jarric, pp. 66-67.
15. Du Jarric, p. 81.
16. Du Jarric, p. 190.
17. Finch in Foster, *Early Travels*, pp. 163, 184; Guerreiro, pp. 49, 63-64.
18. Guerreiro, p. 64.
19. Guerreiro, pp. 66-67, 78.
20. Van den Broecke, p. 51.
21. Elliot and Dowson 7.49-50.
22. Elliot and Dowson 7.260.
23. Elliot and Dowson 7.270-71.
24. Elliot and Dowson 7.320, 327.
25. *Akbar Nama* 3.594-5; Elliot and Dowson 6.68-69.
26. *Tuzuk-i Jahangiri* 2.181.
27. Finch in Foster, *Early Travels*, pp. 14, 16-17, 22; Withington in Foster, *Early Travels*, p. 219.
28. Mundy 2.179-180.
29. Bernier, pp. 306-314.

Fig. 2: Jahangir and Prince Khurram Feasted by Nur Jahan, from an album of Shahjahan, ca. 1617. Courtesy of the Freer Gallery of Art, Smithsonian Institution, Washington D.C., 07.258.

living beyond the palace walls. Here they were able to be immensely creative—and to develop a wide range of intellectual, technical, and social skills, for they had tutors in all subjects and were encouraged to build substantial monuments, to indulge in sports and hunting, to make charitable contributions, and to participate in business dealings. In all, the complexities of the *mahal* being what they were, the women within experienced their share of benefits and deprivations but, for the most part, enjoyed lives of safety, security, comfort, and repose.

PROFILES OF MUGHAL WOMEN

The company of women was, for Mughal men, a normal part of almost all their activities. Women were present not only at court functions and, behind the *jali* (the intricate lattice screen), at business dealings with domestic and foreign petitioners, but also during wars, on the hunt, and for most recreations and pilgrimages as well (Fig. 3). When travelling, women's camps were among the first to go up, and senior men routinely went to the dwellings of the great women during such times to check on their well-being. The constitution of the 'female townships' was vast and included mothers, foster-mothers, aunts, miscellaneous older women, wives, mistresses, concubines, daughters, granddaughters, nieces, women slaves, eunuchs, and a variety of other relatives, friends, staff, and visitors. In each generation of Mughal life, several of the women stand out memorably as individuals who by character and accomplishment strongly affected life at court and in the countryside. While not all can be mentioned here, the following are notable for their contributions:

---

30. *Babur-Nama*, p. 43. All references to the *Babur-Nama* are to the translation of Annette Susannah Beveridge, unless otherwise noted.
31. *Humayun-Nama*, p. 68.
32. A.S. Beveridge in *Babur-Nama*, p. xxviii; *Babur-Nama*, pp. 19, 21, 147-49, 157.
33. *Humayun-Nama*, p. 18; see also *Babur-Nama*, pp. 147, 84.
34. *Humayun-Nama*, pp. 37, 85, 117-129.
35. *Humayun-Nama*, p. 174.
36. On Babur's wives, see *Babur-Nama*, pp. 120, 135-36, 339, 344, 375, 711-714; *Humayun-Nama*, pp. 89-90.

Esan Daulat Begim. Wife of Yunus Chaghatai (Yunus Khan), Esan Daulat was the maternal grandmother of Babur. Born of nomad stock, she held firmly to values of steadfastness and bravery, and was Babur's main counsellor during his early struggle to hold Ferghana. Babur notes of her that few 'amongst women will have been my grandmother's equals for judgment and counsel; she was very wise and farsighted and most affairs of mine were carried through under her advice'.[30] Gulbadan relates the story of one of her 'defiant acts' when she had her maids attack, with a knife, the man to whom a captor had given her and, as sole rationale for the act, 'had observed that she was the wife of Yunus Khan'.[31]

Qutluqh Nigar Khanim. Daughter of Esan Daulat Begim and mother of Babur, she was born of a scholar's family and educated well, probably in Turkish and Persian and in all the necessities of domestic management. Babur had a tremendously strong bond with her, and she was with him on most of his guerrilla expeditions and during times when he was without a throne. She was a compassionate woman, visiting many others during their illnesses and, at such times, Babur worried incessantly for her health.[32]

Khanzada Begim. Babur's sister, older by five years, she was devoted to him throughout his life. At the surrender of Samarkand, she fell into the hands of Shaibani Khan and in time became his wife, a circumstance called by Gulbadan 'as having sacrificed herself in…[this her first] marriage to secure Babar's safety'.[33] She was later to marry again and to become a formidable power in Babur's harem, organizing the marriage feast for Babur's son Hindal and taking in as her charge Babur's grandson Akbar.[34] As Gulbadan notes, she 'was very fond of him [Akbar], and used to kiss his hands and feet, and say: "They are the very hands and feet of my brother the Emperor Babar, and he is like him altogether"'.[35] Khanzada, at the age of sixty-seven, was responsible for negotiating the surrender of Humayun's rebellious brother, Askari, making several trips between the warring brothers.

Mahim Begim. Babur's chief and favourite wife[36] and mother of Humayun, she held a very high place in the harems of Babur, Humayun, and Akbar. As the wife of Babur's greatest affection, she was allowed to promote Humayun and then Akbar with some energy and to become prominently involved, as Mughal sovereignty developed, in the political affairs of each.

Gulbadan Begum. Daughter of Babur and Dildar,[37] and step-sister of Humayun, she was a noted calligrapher and is most famous for writing her memoirs of Mughal life under the title of *Humayun-nama*, encouraged by her nephew Akbar. Adopted by Mahim Begim, at age two in 1525, along with her brother Hindal (in 1519), she knew great fatherly affection from Babur: 'I fell at his feet; he asked me many questions, and took me for a time in his arms, and then this insignificant person felt such happiness that greater could not be imagined'.[38] Her relationship with her adoptive mother—'Her Highness, My Lady'—was very strong and she grieved immensely at Mahim's death when she was only ten.[39] Gulbadan married her second cousin Khizr Khwaja Khan,[40] and was one of several women of the Mughal household to go on an extended pilgrimage to Mecca (1576-1582).[41] At her death in 1603, Akbar was greatly saddened, as he 'had much love for her, and from respect he supported her bier for some steps on his own shoulder'.[42]

Maryam Makani (Hamida Banu). Wife of Humayun[43] and mother of Akbar, she was a powerful force at the Mughal court, exhibiting great encouragement for the maintenance of family bonds and a clear hesitancy about the presence of foreigners. Her strong character was evident even as a young girl when she initially refused to marry Humayun.[44] When she was pregnant with Akbar, Hamida Banu's physical appearance foretold the greatness of the future emperor, as 'a strange light was perceptible from her bright brows. Often her divine countenance had, to observers, the appearance of mirrors such as fastened by tire women near the temples of secluded chaste ones'. Continued sightings of brilliant light from her forehead confirmed prophecies of Akbar's majesty,[45] drawing on the divine connections increasingly important to Mughal symbology. Hamida Banu loved Akbar immensely and grieved even over a tooth infection he incurred,[46] indicative of the intimate tie between the two, as Fig. 1 demonstrates.[47] Although she had Russian slaves in her service for a long time,[48] she was against the presence of foreign religions and, on her return from the long group pilgrimage to Mecca, protested against the presence of Portuguese Jesuits and other Christians at court.[49] Her death in 1604 affected Akbar greatly and he is said to have shaved his hair and moustache, thrown off his turban and all ornament, and put on clothes of mourning. He was the first to carry her body on his shoulder, with grieving courtiers helping out in turn as the cortege proceeded to Delhi.[50]

Maham Anaga. Chief wet-nurse to Akbar, she loved him immensely, and would willingly have sacrificed her life for him. She cooperated with Akbar in his desire to be rid of Bairam Khan and, on his behalf, undertook political negotiations and supported the maintenance of strong family ties, especially to his mother. Maham's son, Adham Khan, eventually turned against Akbar but she persevered in her allegiance to Akbar and in time brought Adham Khan before the emperor with his stolen booty. Maham wielded great power under Akbar until he was nineteen, but with power came arrogance and, when Akbar eventually exercised his imperial independence, Maham's influence quickly waned. She died in 1562, forty days after the death of her son. Among her accomplishments were the establishment of a *madrasa* or school in Delhi, expertise in arranging banquets, and success in marital negotiations.[51]

Salima Sultan Begum. Granddaughter of Babur through one of his daughters, she was married first to Bairam Khan and then to Akbar,[52] becoming his favourite wife.[53] She was one of the most highly educated women at court, and was a great reader and poet, writing under the pen name of *makhfi*. She accompanied Gulbadan and other women on the great pilgrimage to Mecca,[54] and her compassion and mediational skills played a large role in reconciling Akbar with Salim towards the end of Akbar's life. She died in 1613 and of her Jahangir states: 'She was adorned with all good qualities. In women this degree of skill and capacity is seldom found.'[55]

Ruqayya Sultan Begum. Another granddaughter of Babur through his son Hindal, she was the first wife of Akbar. Childless herself, she raised Khurram (Shahjahan) and served as patron and sponsor for Mihrunnisa (Nur Jahan) during the time between the death of the latter's first husband and her marriage to Jahangir in 1611.

Maryam Zamani (Jodha Bai). Daughter of a Hindu prince,[56] wife of Akbar, and mother of Jahangir (Fig. 4), she and Akbar were unable to produce an heir for some time. Journeying to the tomb of Khwaja Muinuddin Chishti, Akbar and his Hindu wife were on the lookout for the dwelling of a dervish named Shaikh Salim who lived on a hill near Sikri, one of the villages around Agra. Finding him, they were told that Akbar would have three sons, at which Akbar vowed to dedicate the first to the holy man. At the birth of his first son, Akbar called him Salim, and proceeded to build a grand and beautiful city, Fatehpur Sikri, in the vicinity of the dervish's home.[57] Maryam Zamani, as she would later be called, was a loyal, devoted, and beloved wife and mother, but she was most noted for her involvement in international trade, an effort encouraged by Jahangir for women of his harem. Maryam Zamani's most famous ship, the *Rahimi*, ran in international waters carrying a variety of goods, primarily cottons and indigo, and repeatedly had trouble with other powers on the open sea, notably the Portuguese.[58] The importance of her ventures, however, is not the details of the ship's history, but that Maryam Zamani was one of the earliest and most enterprising women to move into overseas trade. Her death in 1623 was noted in due course by Jahangir, but it did not receive the full lavish details given to other 'mothers' as her son was himself too far gone into opium and drink to give them.[59]

Bakhtunnisa. The half-sister of Akbar and wife of Khwaja Hasan of Badakhshan, she was appointed to the governorship of Kabul in the wake of the conspiracy and rebellion of her brother, Muhammad Hakim, the previous governor of Kabul. Under her rulership, the political situation stabilized and Akbar was able to avoid regional conflict brewing at the time.[60]

Shah Begum (Raj Kumari Man Bai). First wife of Jahangir and daughter of his maternal uncle Raja Bhagavandas of Amber, she was sister of Raja Man Singh and mother of Jahangir's first son, Khusrau.[61] Jahangir was betrothed to her when he was only fifteen years old and, according to the Shujauddins, she was the first of his eighteen wives.[62] On the birth of Khusrau, she was given the title Shah Begum and is most noted for the events surrounding her death. There had, for a long time, been serious tension between Jahangir and his eldest son Khusrau, because of efforts in certain quarters to elevate him to the throne in Jahangir's stead. Just after Jahangir's accession in 1606 Khusrau went into revolt. Khusrau's behaviour so humiliated Shah Begum that she took poison and died.[63] Of her Jahangir writes:

> When she could not endure the bad conduct of her son and brother towards me she became disgusted with life and died, thereby escaping the present grief and sorrow. In consequence of her death, from attachment I had for her, I passed some days without any kind of pleasure in life or existence.[64]

Jagat Gosain. Daughter of the Hindu prince, Mota Raja (the fat Raja) and second wife of Jahangir, she was the mother of his third son and eventual heir Khurram (Shahjahan).[65] According to legend, there was tremendous jealousy between her and Jahangir's last wife, Nur Jahan, and stories emerging several generations later focus on a courage with weapons greater than Nur Jahan's, a verbal dexterity greater than Nur Jahan's, and a love of colours brighter than those favoured by Nur Jahan. She was, unfortunately, almost completely eclipsed during her lifetime by the dominance in the *zanana* of this last and extremely

---

37. For a list of Babur's children, see *Akbar Nama* 1.279.
38. *Humayun-Nama*, p. 102.
39. *Humayun-Nama*, p. 116.
40. A.S. Beveridge in *Humayun-Nama*, p. 31.
41. *Akbar Nama* 3.205, 569; *Tabakat-i Akbari* in Elliot and Dowson, pp. 391-392.
42. *Akbar Nama* 3.1226.
43. *Akbar Nama* 1.364-365.
44. Misra, p. 114.
45. *Akbar Nama* 1.43-44; see van den Broecke, p. 7.
46. *Akbar Nama* 3.108.
47. See A.S. Beveridge in *Humayun-Nama*, p. 39.
48. Maclagan, p. 40.
49. *Humayun-Nama*, p. 75.
50. *Akbar Nama*, p. 1245; *Takmila-i Akbar-nama* in Elliot and Dowson 6.113; van den Broecke, p. 30.
51. Misra, pp. 25-29, 91-92, 97, 114-115.
52. A.S. Beveridge in *Humayun-Nama* p. 57; *Akbar Nama* 2.97.
53. Findly, *Nur Jahan*, p. 20.
54. A.S. Beveridge in *Humayun-Nama*, pp. 69-70; *Tabakat-i Akbari* in Elliot and Dowson, p. 427.
55. *Tuzuk-i Jahangiri* 1.232-233.
56. *Akbar Nama* 2.243.
57. *Akbar Nama* 2.502-509; *Tuzuk-i Jahangiri* 1.1-3.
58. See Findly, 'The Capture of Maryam-uz Zamani's Ship.'
59. *Tuzuk-i Jahangiri* 2.261.
60. Misra, p. 31.
61. For other wives that Jahangir mentions, see *Tuzuk-i Jahangiri* 1.144, 145, 160, 326; 2.159.
62. Shujauddin, pp. 93-98.
63. *Akbar Nama* 3.677-678; *Tabakat-i Akbari* in Elliot and Dowson 5.447.
64. *Tuzuk-i Jahangiri* 1.56; see *Takmila-i Akbar-nama* in Elliot and Dowson 6.112; *Waki'at-i Jahangiri* in Elliot and Dowson 6.294-295.
65. *Tuzuk-i Jahangiri* 1.19.

Fig. 3: BABUR VISITING THE BEGUMS AT HERAT IN 1506, from a *Baburnama*, ca. 1590. Courtesy of the British Library, London, Or. 3714, f. 256v.

charismatic wife.⁶⁶ On her death in 1619, Jahangir made a special effort to console their son Shahjahan.⁶⁷

Mother of Qutbuddin Khan Koka. A strong mother figure to Jahangir, she had nursed him with her own milk when he was an infant: she 'had given me her milk and was as a mother to me or even kinder than my own kind mother, and in whose lap I had been brought up from infancy'.⁶⁸ Her son became Jahangir's foster-brother. In Mughal culture this relationship was exceptionally strong. Jahangir's grief was great at Qutbuddin Khan Koka's death in 1607 at the hands of Nur Jahan's first husband, Sher Afgan,⁶⁹ alleviated only by the fact that his friend's mother had died a few months before and was thus spared this grief. At her death, Jahangir 'placed the feet of her corpse on my shoulders and carried her a part of the way (to her grave). Through extreme grief and sorrow I had no inclination for some days to eat, and I did not change my clothes'.⁷⁰

Nur Mahal; Nur Jahan (Mihrunnisa).⁷¹ Born in Qandahar as her parents, Itimaduddaula Ghiyas Beg and Asmat Begum, were on their way from Tehran to Akbar's court in Agra, she grew up in a well-placed and well-educated family increasingly connected to the Mughal court. Married to Ali Quli Beg Istajlu (later Sher Afgan), she had one daughter, Ladli. Sher Afgan was killed in a skirmish in Bengal in 1607, and Mihrunnisa and her daughter were brought back to Jahangir's court where they lived quietly for four years.⁷² In 1611, at the Nauroz or New Year's festival, an annual celebration with elaborate decorations, feasts, bazaars, and mock bartering,⁷³ Jahangir saw Mihrunnisa for the first time, fell in love with her (Fig. 5), and made her his eighteenth and last wife—marriage to widows being particularly encouraged in Islamic tradition; the Prophet's (PBUH) wife Khadija herself was previously widowed. Jahangir named her Nur Mahal or 'light of the palace' and in time Nur Jahan or 'light of the world.'⁷⁴

After Nur Jahan's marriage to Jahangir, the power structure at court began to change rapidly. The emperor repeatedly promoted Nur Jahan's father, Itimaduddaula, and a brother, Asif Khan, to positions of great prestige and influence and, in time, a *junta* or 'faction,' as Sir Thomas Roe the first official English ambassador to the Mughal court called it, developed.⁷⁵ This group, headed by Nur Jahan, was virtually in charge of all sovereign decisions and power,⁷⁶ although she continued to work together with Jahangir on such projects of mutual interest as gardens, monuments, and patronage of the arts.

Nur Jahan became the dominant member of the large company of women based in the *zanana* as well. She had charge of Shah Shuja, one of Shahjahan's sons,⁷⁷ and was often the only one successfully able to tend to Jahangir's frequent illnesses.⁷⁸ As van den Broecke notes: 'When all men had departed, the queen came out in all her splendour, undressed him and put him to sleep in a hanging bed, which was constantly rocked otherwise he got no sleep'.⁷⁹ While she was noted for her great charity to orphaned Hindu girls and to pilgrims at religious shrines,⁸⁰ she was also fond of luxury goods, and had an insatiable desire for gifts from domestic and international petitioners. Not only was she the recipient of much largess from her second husband, as well as of the entire estate of her father upon his death in early 1622,⁸¹ but she engaged extensively in domestic and international trade. Letters kept by the East India Company, for example, detail the myriad gifts brought to her by English merchants as well as specific luxury items she requested in trade.

During the time she held the reigns of power court officials and European visitors had much to say about the extent and nature of Nur Jahan's power and influence. According to Muhammad Hadi,

---

66. Shujauddin, pp. 94-95.
67. *Tuzuk-i Jahangiri* 2.84.
68. *Tuzuk-i Jahangiri* 1.84-85.
69. *Tuzuk-i Jahangiri* 1.113-115.
70. *Tuzuk-i Jahangiri* 1.85.
71. See Findly, *Nur Jahan*.
72. *Tatimma-i Waki'at-i Jahangiri* in Elliot and Dowson 6.397-398; Van den Broecke pp. 39-40; Mundy, p. 205.
73. Roe 1.142-144.
74. *Tatimma-i Waki'at-i Jahangiri* in Elliot and Dowson 6.398; *Ikbal-nama-i Jahangiri* in Elliot and Dowson 6.403-405; Coryat in Foster, *Early Travels*, p. 278; Van den Broecke, p. 42. See Schimmel, p. 21, 26, 27.
75. For example, *Tuzuk-i Jahangiri* 1.199-200, 202; *Tatimma-i Waki'at-i Jahangiri* in Elliot and Dowson 6.398.
76. Roe 1.118, 146; 2.281-283, 293-294, 310.
77. *Tuzuk-i Jahangiri* 2.45.
78. *Tuzuk-i Jahangiri* 1.266; 2.213-214.
79. Van den Broecke, p. 91.
80. *Tatimma-i Waki'at-i Jahangiri* in Elliot and Dowson 6.399; Coryat in Foster, *Early Travels*, pp. 279-280.
81. *Tuzuk-i Jahangiri* 2.221-222.

...by degrees she became, except in name, undisputed Sovereign of the Empire, and the King himself became a tool in her hands. He used to say that Nur Jahan Begam has been selected, and is wise enough to conduct the matters of State, and that he wanted only a bottle of wine and piece of meat to keep himself merry.[82]

Mutamad Khan added that it 'is impossible to describe the beauty and wisdom of the Queen. In any matter that was presented to her, if a difficulty arose, she immediately solved it. Whoever threw himself upon her protection was preserved from tyranny and oppression'.[83] In 1611, the year of her marriage to Jahangir, the English merchant William Hawkins was already aware that he needed to present special gifts to the King's 'new paramour'.[84] Roe discerned quickly that Nur Jahan 'wholly gouerneth' her husband, that his own greatest problem (and therefore his greatest fear) was drawing her anger down upon him, and that often the king himself had to fall 'downe and take...his Mistris by the feete to obtain her leaue' to do something.[85] Having fully 'yeeilded himself into the handes of a woman,' Jahangir was often undone by 'the false teares of womans bewitching flattery' and felt deeply any neglect he may have made of her.[86]

Writing of Nur Jahan's actions during the succession wars as Jahangir's health waned, van den Broecke describes her as a vicious and cunning woman, whose only purpose was to gain power for herself and her own and who, in the process, had ruined her husband's reputation; her means to power, he argued, was 'pretended love and sweet words, for which...[Jahangir] had to pay dearly'.[87] As Della Valle notes, not only was Jahangir's 'whole Empire...govern'd at this day by her counsel,' but she had 'cunningly remov'd out of the Haram...all the other Women who might give her any jealousie'.[88] Europeans entering India later were less critical of her reputation for ruthlessness and intrigue. Bernier says, for example, that her 'transcendent abilities rendered her competent to govern the Empire without the interference of her husband',[89] and Manucci describes Nur Jahan as 'a woman of great judgment and, of a verity, worthy to be a queen'.[90]

Shahjahan marks the death of the dowager queen Nur Jahan with a small note in his memoirs indicating that it would be useless to praise her upon her passing as she had already reached the height of fame. The range of Nur Jahan's contributions to Indian culture remain almost unparalleled by anyone else till today.

Asmat Begum. Wife of Itimaduddaula and mother of Nur Jahan, Asmat Begum is known chiefly for having invented rose perfume. According to Jahangir, she was making rose water one day and discovered that the scum which had formed on the top had a powerful and refreshing scent as if 'many red rosebuds had bloomed at once'.[91] He rewarded her generously for her creation.

Mumtaz Mahal (Arjumand Banu Begum). Daughter of Asif Khan, niece of Nur Jahan, and most beloved wife of Shahjahan, she was the inspiration for the building of the Taj Mahal. Married to Khurram in 1612,[92] she was a loyal and devoted wife and went with him almost everywhere he travelled. She bore him many children[93] and it was during the birth of their fourteenth, on 17 June 1631, that she died. Legendary in his grief, Shahjahan put on white clothes, remained secluded for a week, and for a long duration refused to listen to music and singing or to wear fine linen. Eventually his eyes grew weak from weeping and he took to wearing glasses, and even his beard turned white. Arjumand Banu's body was sent to Akbarabad for burial and in time she found final repose in the exquisite domed mausoleum built by her husband and known to the world as the Taj Mahal.[94]

Begum Sahib (Jahanara Begum). Eldest daughter of Shahjahan, she took over as head of the imperial household after the death of her mother.[95] She was known to be very beautiful, 'discreet, loving, generous, open-minded and charitable,' and was much beloved by her father; some Europeans have charged that the relationship was incestuous, but others of their contemporaries refute it.[96] Jahanara was the recipient of much largess and had many jewels,[97] and her generosity to religious causes was well-known. Her brother, Dara Shikoh, promised her she could marry, as other Mughal princesses had and would (including Akbar's sisters and daughter, Jahangir's daughter, Dara Shikoh's daughter, and Aurangzeb's daughters) but she remained unmarried. Traditionally, however, there was great concern over the marriage of a princess for it was problematic owing, first, to the difficulty of finding a suitable match and, second, to the possible threat to the throne posed by her in-laws. Europeans present circulated stories about Jahanara's many lovers and of the terrible fates befalling those men discovered in the *zanana* by Shahjahan,[98] but these narratives are held in suspicion. Jahanara was highly regarded as a mystic and it is said that her teacher Molla Shah (a saint of the Qadiri order) would have passed the mantle on to her, except that she was a woman. When Shahjahan died, Jahanara oversaw his burial herself.[99]

Raushanara Begum. Sister to Jahanara, she allied herself with her brother Aurangzeb to counterpoise the sibling alliance of Jahanara and Dara Shikoh.[100] Most of what we know about her comes from Manucci and consists primarily of his stories of her very promiscuous and hedonistic behaviour. We are told that unable, ultimately, to support her in this lifestyle, Aurangzeb, now on the throne, decided to act:

Already angered at the misconduct of his sister, Aurangzeb shortened her life by poison. Thus, in spite of all she had done to get her brother made king, she experienced herself his cruelty, dying swollen out like a hogshead, and leaving behind her the name of great lasciviousness.[101]

Udaipuri Begum. The beloved wife of Aurangzeb, she was 'a Georgian by race' and a former wife of Dara Shikoh. Her one unfortunate habit, however, was 'the habit of drinking spirits' to the point of frequent intoxication.[102] Because of this the other women of the *zanana*, jealous of Aurangzeb's affection for her, one day asked for her presence at court 'so that the conversation might take a more elevated tone'—knowing full well that at that particular time she was in a highly intoxicated state. When Aurangzeb saw the wildness of her behaviour, he was most distressed and 'turned in fury upon the doorkeepers who were bastinadoed for want of vigilance over the gates'[103]—though he never lost his great love for this wayward woman.

Zebunnisa. Eldest daughter of Aurangzeb, she was an active advocate of her brother Muhammad Akbar and, when he rebelled against his father, she continued a secret correspondence with him. When the letters were discovered, her property and yearly allowances were confiscated by her father, and she was sentenced to life imprisonment, dying in 1702. Like other daughters of Aurangzeb, particularly Zinatunnisa, Zebunnisa was trained in the serious study of religious doctrine and in matters of faith, and she was known as an excellent scholar in several academic areas and as a literary figure and patron of some renown. She sang well and composed songs and planted many of the gardens of her day.[104]

Zinatunnisa. Another daughter of Aurangzeb, she facilitated many things on her father's behalf, including the care of political prisoners at court and acting as mediator between the emperor and his sons. Like her sisters, she too was mystically inclined, and was known for her philanthropy and patronage of caravanserais.[105]

LIFE IN THE WOMEN'S APARTMENTS

Life in the *zanana* was as diverse, complex, and multi-layered as that of a small city. Ordinarily, there were several thousand women housed in the

---

82. *Tatimma-i Waki'at-i Jahangiri* in Elliot and Dowson 6.398-399.
83. *Ikbal-nama Jahangiri* in Elliot and Dowson 6.405.
84. Hawkins in Foster, *Early Travels*, p. 94; see p. 101.
85. Roe 1.111, 118, 267.
86. Roe 2.293, 281, 290n.
87. Van den Broecke, pp. 90, 91, 92.
88. DellaValle 1.53, 54.
89. Bernier, p. 275.
90. Manucci 1.157.
91. *Tuzuk-i Jahangiri* 1.270-271; 2.115; *Waki'at-i Jahangiri* in Elliot and Dowson 6.338.
92. *Tuzuk-i Jahangiri* 1.224-225; *Shah Jahan Nama*, p. 6. All references to *Shah Jahan Nama* are to the translation of A.R. Fuller.
93. *Shah Jahan Nama*, pp. 6-7, 10, 11, 38.
94. *Shah Jahan Nama*, pp. 70-71, 73-74, 83, 95.
95. *Shah Jahan Nama*, pp. 6, 71.
96. Bernier, p. 11; Manucci 1.208-209; Tavernier, p. 275. Much of such European travel literature can be treated as eye-witness accounts. However, since Europeans had no access to the *zanana* (except in very rare cases) their reports on events within the *zanana* are based on hearsay. Misattribution does occur—as in the case of Manucci incorrectly citing Nur Jahan, and not her mother, as the creator of rose perfume. In light of this, care must be taken with information from certain texts.
97. *Shah Jahan Nama*, pp. 432, 447; Tavernier, p. 275.
98. Bernier, pp. 12-14; Tavernier, p. 300. The problematic nature of this material, however, is discussed in Schimmel, pp. 50-51.
99. *Shah Jahan Nama*, pp. 564-565.
100. See Richards, p. 161.
101. Manucci 2.177; 1.230; 2.30-32.
102. Manucci 2.135-136, 100.
103. Manucci 2.99-100.
104. Misra, pp. 50, 51, 64n, 87, 90-91, 95, 113; Richards, pp. 182-184.
105. Misra, pp. 51, 52, 87, 110, 112; Richards, p. 231.

Fig. 4: THE BIRTH OF A PRINCE, from a *Jahangirnama*, ca. 1620. Attributed to Bishndas.
Francis Bartlett Donation of 1912 and Picture Fund, courtesy of the Museum of Fine Arts, Boston, 14.657.

various Mughal *mahals*,[106] including mothers, grandmothers, wives, sisters, daughters, aunts, and other female relatives. In addition, the number of 'service women' was very large, and included concubines, servants, slaves, female guards, spies, entertainers, soothsayers, and various visitors staying for indefinite lengths of time. By most accounts, life in the women's apartments was physically safe, financially secure, relatively stable politically, and replete with material luxuries, daily and seasonal entertainments, and the ups and downs of constant female companionship on a very large scale.

The most significant occasion whereby a woman entered the harem of a particular emperor was through marriage. Muslim marriages, according to Terry were 'solemnized with some pomp,' accompanied by music and merriment as the bride and groom travelled to the marriage location, then to 'return to the place of the married couple's abode, where (they say) if the parties be able they make some slight entertainment for them; immediately after which they all disperse, and the shew is over'.[107] Because the purpose of marriage was the procreation of children, especially sons, particular attention was focused on the couple's first intercourse and the public display of its success (Fig. 6).

Some traditional jurists have interpreted verse 4:3 of the Quran to mean that a man can have more than one wife, that is, up to four, but *only* on the condition that he treat them equally in all respects. Since it is almost impossible for men to fulfil this condition (as the Quran notes in verse 4:129), other scholars have concluded that the Quran clearly advocates monogamy as the general rule. However, many men were able to find loopholes. Mughal emperors, often married many more than four wives, and Christian visitors to India struggled morally with this practice.[108] In Maclagan's opinion, it was the Muslim permissibility of polygamy (and Christian commitment to monogamy) which was a lynchpin in Jahangir's final refusal to convert to Christianity;[109] added to this was Jahangir's problem with theological aspects of the divinity of Christ, a topic much debated at the Mughal court.[110] One reason cited for the presence of so many sexually eligible women, wives and otherwise, in the palaces, was the 'policy' noted by Terry that neither the emperor nor his nobles 'come near their wives or women, after they exceed the age of thirty years.'[111] Given the known practices of Mughal emperors, however, this statement is quite incorrect.

Under Akbar, marriage and its rules and objectives became the object of administrative discussion. Akbar argued strongly for the benefits of arranged marriages,[112] and noted the following as important considerations: no marriage should be made before puberty; both bride and groom must consent to the marriage and have the consent of their parents; no marriage should be made between near relatives; no excessively high dowries should be given; not everyone should marry more than one wife; both parties should be taxed according to their worth; and a 'master of marriages' (*tu'i-begi*) should scrutinize the circumstances of the couple.[113]

Women entered the imperial family, that is, were 'given' by their families to the emperor and princes, under several circumstances, the most prominent being the creation of a political alliance between the emperor and a local noble whose allegiance was deemed important.[114] Women were also exchanged in marriage for land, and there is some evidence for marriage by capture.[115] Although there were occasions early on when love marriages were made,[116] such as that between Humayun and Hamida Banu, it wasn't until later, under Jahangir and especially Shahjahan, when romantic love became an important ideal at court and exceptionally close marital ties were a familiar occurrence: for example, Jahangir and Nur Jahan, Shahjahan and Mumtaz Mahal, Dara Shikoh and Nadira Banu, and Aurangzeb and Dilras Banu Begum.

The diversity of the harem was evident in the wives of the emperor themselves. Akbar, for example, had wives of not only Muslim and Hindu backgrounds, but of Christian as well.[117] Critical of this intermarriage, Bernier says, 'although these Kings are *Mahometans*, they do not scruple to marry into heathen families, when

---

106. Manucci 1.188; 2.308, 320.
107. Terry, p. 285.
108. Terry, p. 286.
109. Maclagan, p. 69.
110. Findly, *Nur Jahan*, p. 202.
111. Terry, p. 387.
112. *Akbar Nama* 3.677-678.
113. *Ain-i Akbari*, pp. 287-288.
114. See *Babur-Nama*, p. 120; *Akbar Nama* 3.51-52.
115. *Babur-Nama*, pp. 125-126; 147, 184.
116. *Babur-Nama*, p. 64; Thackston, *Baburnama*, pp. 54, 212.
117. Maclagan, pp. 157-160.

such a measure may promote their interests, or when they may thus obtain a beautiful wife'.[118] Evidence of life in the *zanana* shows that the imperial court strove to preserve the ethnic and religious diversity brought into the community by each new wife, and there does not appear to have been any intolerance for the great variety of customs and religious practices which abounded in all corners.

Intermarriage was also a widespread feature of the burgeoning international culture in India just outside the Mughal palace walls. Male Europeans—of Portuguese, Dutch, and English descent—were all involved at high and low levels in relations with local women and, in time, an extensive system of categorization emerged based on place of birth of offspring, background of parents, legality of the parental relationship, and financial arrangements which surrounded it. The attempt to import native English women into India to marry English factors there, proved futile as many of the English wives became barren on Indian soil due, it was said, to the climate.[119]

Married life in the *zanana* carried some bit of struggle with it. Although divorce was rare, except in the cases of 'very cross-tempered' women,[120] and although the emperors of each and every generation spent enormous amounts of time with the women in the *zanana* (see Fig. 3), there was a good bit of competition among the women for the emperor's attention. Not only was there competition for the emperor's time and intimate presence, but also for the privilege of bearing his children and especially his first son and heir. Because all wives wanted to bear the emperor an heir, any pregnancy by a legitimate wife caused a great stir and, reports the French jeweller Jean-Baptiste Tavernier, 'when the Princesses in the imperial harem became aware that there is one among them with child, they immediately use all conceivable(!) methods to cause a miscarriage'.[121] Adoption, formal and informal, was fairly common by women in the 'mother' category and, while some adoptions were controversial, such as that by Babur's wife Mahim of another wife's (Dildar's) children, Hindal and Gulbadan, it was fairly routine for a child to be handed over to a woman in the *zanana* other than its natural mother, to be nurtured and raised. Children were also handed over to women other than their natural mothers in order to be suckled, and the use of wet-nurses within the palace walls was a very common practice (Fig. 7). Boy children who had been thus nursed by the same wet-nurse or 'foster-mother' became 'foster-brothers' and had a life-long bond between them equal to, and sometimes even greater than, that between natural blood brothers.

The structure of the harem was complex and intricately determined, ultimately, by the fact of the women's seclusion (*purdah*). 'Secluded behind the screen of chastity,'[122] high-placed Muslim women were kept separate from the commerce of public intercourse in order to preserve, say the texts, their honour and reputation.[123] The sequestering of women either behind a veil or screen was well known in traditional Indian Hindu culture and had, for centuries, been a prominent feature of upper class life. For Mughals in India, then, seclusion was enforced more strictly than in their original Central Asian home, and was a practice for the elite, not for ordinary women who were regularly seen about town. Noble women could, however, watch public goings-on from within the palaces,[124] and Roe has written of one such marvellous encounter:

> At one syde in a wyndow were his two Principall wifes, whose Curiositye made them breake litle holes in a grate of reede that hung before yt to gaze on mee. I saw first their fingers, and after laying their faces close nowe one eye, Now another; some tyme I could discerne the full proportion. They were indifferently white, black hayre smoothed vp; but if I had had no other light, ther diamondes and Pearles had sufficed to show them.[125]

No men were allowed entrance into the *zanana* except immediate relatives, for example, husbands and sons, unless special permission was given by the emperor. One such famous case is that of Nur Jahan's father, Itimaduddaula, whom Jahangir came to consider such an intimate friend that he honoured him in 1616 'by directing the ladies of the harem not to veil their faces from him'.[126]

The structure of the harem, as set up by Humayun at his accession, was established according to gradations and ranks that had at their heart a central valuation on seniority.[127] This emphasis on seniority was present from the very beginning, as when Babur's kinswomen arrived at his camp and he immediately went to pay his respects to the most elderly.[128] Again, Gulbadan relates of the time during Humayun's reign when she went about the royal camp and was shown her assigned tent placed precisely according to standard ranking order.[129] And she speaks often of presents coming into the women's palaces which were handed out in sequence and in value according to the prevailing gradations of women.[130] During Jahangir's reign senior women, often in the 'mother' category, routinely received preferential treatment during court entertainments and on travels, and at every proper moment the appropriate obeisance, prostration, and greeting was offered to those of highest rank.[131] Names and titles played a role in such ranking as well and Manucci notes that when ladies carried the title 'Begum' it indicated that they were of the imperial household. Moreover, individual titles bestowed on each woman by the emperor were designed 'to suit the persons receiving them'.[132]

The apartment assigned to each woman as well was based on rank, and foreign visitors to the court were often aware of which woman was assigned to which area.[133] Finch describes the lodgings for the emperor's women in the palace fortress at Lahore as having galleries and windows looking out over the river as well as into the court. Although the doors of the women's chambers were fastened on the outside, and not from within, the areas allotted to the *mahal* women were spacious. Windows had beautifully carved screen patterns, and walls often had inlaid mirrors, painted designs, carved sculptural reliefs, and paintings hung all around.[134] Running water was channelled through exterior courtyards to irrigate flower beds and orchards and in through interior rooms for cooling purposes—often flowing down wide stone panels carved in variegated patterns to bring the soothing sound and spray to the frequently parched surroundings. In addition, the areas available for women to use were so large that huge bazaars were often held to which traders from all over the empire were invited and gossip from the countryside could be exchanged.[135]

Within the *zanana* the doings of the women were reported regularly to the emperor through weekly accounts. As Manucci notes,

> These news-letters are commonly read in the King's presence by women of the *mahal* at about nine o'clock in the evening, so that by this means he knows what is going on in his kingdom. There are, in addition, spies who are also obliged to send in reports weekly about other important business, chiefly what the princes are doing, and this duty they perform through written statements.[136]

Women of the apartments also served as spies on other women and, 'by promises and deceit,' were able to extract information useful to the eunuchs guarding the *zanana* and ultimately to the emperor.[137] Outside visitors to the apartments were welcome but had to go through an elaborate presentation process by which messages were carried through various levels of servants; normally an appropriate length of time was levied on the guest's visit.[138]

The secluded compounds of women were kept secured by the posting of, frequently armed, women guards (*urdu begi*) at critical stations—Bibi Fatima was, for example, the famous chief armed woman of Humayun's harem.[139] In Akbar's time there were so many royal ladies (about 5000, each with separate apartments) that keeping order and proper administration was a major challenge, and palaces were divided into enclosed sections and faithful servants appointed as officers. The *daroghas*, for example, were virtuous matron women appointed as superintendents over each section, with one being selected for the duties of a writer.[140] Inside the harem, sections were guarded by vigilant and conscientious women, with the most

---

118. Bernier, p. 126.
119. Qaisar, pp. 13-14, 116-117.
120. *Babur-Nama*, pp. 267-268.
121. Tavernier, p. 313.
122. *Akbar Nama* 1.179.
123. Terry, p. 283.
124. Roe 1.21, 32, 106.
125. Roe 2.321.
126. *Tuzuk-i Jahangiri* 1.351.
127. *Humayun-Nama* in Elliot and Dowson 5.123.
128. *Babur-Nama*, pp. 301, 616.
129. *Humayun-Nama*, p. 67.
130. *Humayun-Nama*, p. 95.
131. *Tuzuk-i Jahangiri* 1.76, 92.
132. Manucci 2.311, 315.
133. DeLaet, pp. 39-41.
134. Finch in Foster, *Early Travels*, pp. 163-164, 186.
135. *Akbar Nama* 1.428.
136. Manucci 2.309.
137. Manucci 2.311-312.
138. *Ain-i Akbari*, p. 47.
139. *Humayun-Nama*, p. 40.
140. *Ain-i Akbari*, pp. 45-47.

Fig. 5: DALLIANCE ON A TERRACE, ca. 1600-1640. Courtesy of the Los Angeles County Museum of Art, from the Nasli and Alice Heeramaneck Collection, Museum Associates purchase. M.83.1.6.

trusted of them placed at the apartments of the emperor. Outside the inner enclosure, eunuchs acted as guards and, at some appropriate distance, faithful Rajputs did such duty, while beyond them were the porters of the gates. Moreover, on all four sides of the apartment complex were guards of nobles, troops, and Ahadis—independent horsemen given special training and under special financial arrangement with the emperor.[141] Thus, as Jahangir notes in his memoirs, the *zanana* was never left unprotected.[142]

The most critical member of this security team, however, was the eunuch whose job it was to keep strict guard over the women in the *zanana*. While eunuchs played an important role in palace life, some emperors such as Jahangir protested against large scale traffic in eunuchs. Through this traffic parents, often in Bengal (but later in other places as well), gave some of their sons 'to the governor in place of revenue…and every year some children are thus ruined and cut off from procreation'.[143] Despite Jahangir's desire to prohibit such practice, there was a clear need within Mughal administration for eunuchs and thus, all through the palaces of women, for example, were those who 'when they be very young…[had been] deprived of all that might after provoke jealousy…a soft tender people… that never come to have any hair on their faces'.[144] Because of their unique physical condition, eunuchs were allowed intimate physical proximity to women of all rank, and most women of stature had individual eunuchs assigned especially to them. Eunuchs knew the personal details of most love lives in the *zanana* and could touch and examine women's bodies without fault.[145] Eunuchs had access to all rooms and chambers and, for good or ill, had a real double loyalty: to the emperor for guarding and protecting the honour of the women in the harem, and to the women for facilitating illicit practices and relations. This was a particularly trying process in the case of a princess like Raushanara Begum, for example, 'who longed very much to get rid of the hindrances of the harem and [to be] able to indulge her libidinous propensities.'[146] Unfortunately, eunuchs who helped her overly much in patrolling information to and from the outside world were killed[147] and, in time, we are told, Aurangzeb became so disgusted with the failure of the system that he not only had the eunuchs killed but Raushanara Begum as well.[148] Eunuchs who themselves became entangled in love relations were looked down upon as well, and Bernier describes the case of one such poor man who fell in love with the sister of a scrivener and met an immediate and untimely end.[149]

The finances of the harem were a complex but orderly affair. The system under Akbar awarded very liberal allowances to women, exclusive of gifts, with women of the highest rank receiving 1610-1028 rupees per month and servants receiving either 51-20 or 40-2 rupees per month.[150]* Associated with the women's apartments was a writer who supervised the expenses of the harem and who kept an account of its cash and stores. Any woman could apply to one of the *tahwildars*, or harem cash-keepers, for amounts within the limits of her allowance and, upon request, a memo was then sent by the *tahwildar* to the writer and cash then came to the woman from the general treasurer. The procedure involved the writer's submitting a receipt for counter signature by the state ministers, it being stamped by a seal used only for harem monies, and, when payable, the monies were paid over 'by the cash-keeper of the General Treasury to the General *Tahwildar*, who on the order of the writer of the Harem, hands it over to the several Sub-*Tahwildars* for distribution among the servants of the seraglio'.[151] The writer's job also included making an estimate of total annual expenses of the *zanana* women. A good example of the generosity of this system is the allowance that was given by Shahjahan to the old dowager queen Nur Jahan living in Lahore after Jahangir died; this allowance of two lakh (200,000)

---

141. *Ain-i Akbari*, pp. 46-47, 259-260.
142. *Tuzuk-i Jahangiri* 1.73.
143. *Tuzuk-i Jahangiri* 1.150-151. Says Manucci (2.73) of this practice: '…all eunuchs, grandees as they may be, have no other than poor and miserable progenitors, who out of absolute hunger have sold their sons.'
144. Terry, p. 89; see also Finch in Foster, *Early Travels*, p. 18.
145. Manucci 1.192-193.
146. Manucci 2.60.
147. Manucci 2.31, 50-51.
148. Bernier, pp. 14, 132-133.
149. Bernier, p. 131.
150. For a discussion of copper, silver, and gold coins, and of the contemporary purchasing power of the rupee, see Moreland, pp. 51-53.
* Editor's Note: Also see the chapter on Coinage in this book, pp. 292-3.
151. *Ain-i Akbari*, p. 46; see also Manucci 2.308, 310, 350.

rupees per year was paid to her from Jahangir's death in 1627 until her own death in 1645.[152] However, the hightest allowance on record is the annual sum of ten lakh rupees given to Mumtaz Mahal by Shahjahan.

Money and material resources came to the women in the *zanana* in various other ways as well. One resource was revenue from land, given sometimes as a one-time-only gift by a family member or petitioner at court to a harem woman, and at others as an ongoing source of continued revenue.[153] Women also received numerous gifts of money, jewels, and clothes, ordinarily on special occasions of domestic festivals and homecomings but also just as a distinctive tribute to the honour in which they were held.[154] In addition, adventurous women earned revenues through domestic and international trade. Finally, women received resources and income through inheritance from a deceased relative,[155] the allocation of which was often in the hands of the emperor. The most famous case of a woman receiving such inheritance was that of Nur Jahan, who was given the entire estate of her father Itimaduddaula upon his death in 1621,[156] bypassing her brother Asif Khan. Generally, women managing large amounts of money and wealth had special officials (a *nazir* or *vakil*) who administered and supervised all of these incomes, properties, lands, and construction activities.

The use and expenditure of all these material resources fell primarily into three categories: the giving of gifts in return, the purchase of luxury items to be used by the women themselves, and gifts made in charity. Return gifts by harem women were often made at times of great festivity such as rites of passage (birth ceremonies and weddings) and occasions marking some special accomplishment, such as Nur Jahan's feasting of Khurram/Shahjahan upon his victorious return from the Deccan in 1617 (see Fig. 2).[157] Purchase of luxury items to be used by the women themselves was an almost daily activity, as buying from local shopkeepers and traders as well as international merchants at court kept mahal women in constant supply of clothes, jewellery, perfume, cosmetics, and a varied assortment of trinkets. One of the most extravagant women in this regard was the wife of a noble, Jafar Khan, active during Aurangzeb's reign, and Tavernier notes that 'she alone expends more than all the wives and daughters of the Emperor put together; it is on this account that her family is always in debt'.[158] Mughal women, finally, allocated their resources to charity, a religious obligation incumbent upon all those of Muslim, Hindu, and Christian background. Nur Jahan, for example, is said to 'have portioned [with dowries] about 500 girls in her lifetime, and thousands were grateful for her generosity'.[159] Other women as well gave not only to needy orphaned girls but to large groups of the poor and disenfranchised throughout the empire.

Most of the pastimes of the harem took place within the palace walls which secluded the women from direct participation in the outside world. These pastimes, for the most part, fell into three categories: women's daily toilet of cleaning and grooming themselves, their daily entertainments of games and amusements, and special occasions of regular seasonal festivity or family celebration. Women's daily toilet involved the use of a great number of luxury items, some procured locally and some available only through international trade. One of the most precious was perfume, and Akbar himself had perfumes made for the *mahal* women inside his own establishments, out of such things as amber, camphor, civet, musk, aloe, sandalwood, storax, calembic, frankincense, and bdellium.[160] Often perfumes were made from elixirs extracted from flowers, such as the rose perfume invented by Nur Jahan's mother, Asmat Begum.[161]

Women spent a great deal of their time on clothes and interior uses of textiles, and had at their disposal an extensive variety of materials, including cottons, silks, wools, mixtures, brocades, velvets, and satins—some made locally and many imported from Europe, the Middle East, and other parts of Asia.[162] Foreign travellers in India during Mughal times have left numerous descriptions of clothing and jewellery worn by Hindu and Muslim women who went out in public,[163] and report that in several secluded establishments women wore each outfit only once—to be buried after the first wearing, there to rot.[164] For the dress styles of Mughal women, however, our main evidence comes from miniature paintings where we can see the fairly rapid evolution from the modest, full covered styles worn by Mughal women up through Akbar's reign (see Figs. 1, 3, 7) to the more open, immodest, Hindu-inspired styles prevalent from Jahangir's time on (see Figs. 2, 5). Hindu influence on Mughal women's dress, in fact, prevailed despite attempts to curb its openness by Muslim clerics.[165]

For entertainment, women in the *zanana* had daily access to a prolific range of activities. Outside news was available primarily through visitors and the communication channels of the eunuchs, and such news provided fuel for much of the gossip passing through the chambers.[166] In addition, women spent their time on interior decoration of their quarters, on landscaping their gardens,[167] on embroidery,[168] on board games such as *chaupar* and *chandal mandal*,[169] on playing cards (*ganjafa*), and on study, reading books, writing, and verse-making.[170] Moreover, tutors were employed to educate women in subjects as diverse as astronomy, poetry, mysticism, and mathematics. Women were also interested in listening to music and watching dances performed by female troupes[171] (see Fig. 8), in falconry, in hunting (despite vows of non-violence taken by various emperors),[172] in playing polo, in watching fireworks,[173] and in hearing stories of magic and superstition.[174] These pastimes could take place in groups or individually, and the great spaces of most Mughal palace chambers allowed for as much or as little privacy as each woman desired.

The lives of *mahal* women, finally, were punctuated by the festivities of special occasions. Central in the range of festivities were weddings and birthday celebrations, the most important birthday observed being that of the emperor.[175] Jahangir's birthday, for example, was celebrated by both the solar and lunar calendars and often took place at the palace of his mother, Maryam Zamani.[176] The other major festival was that of Nauroz, or New Year, occurring in the early spring of each year and lasting for eighteen days. As described by Hawkins, the Mughal palaces were beautifully decorated to display the vast wealth of the emperor, with the central object being a richly ornamented tent in velvet, gold, and silver covering 'at the least two acres of ground, but so richly spread with silke and gold carpets and hangings in the principall places, rich as rich velvet imbroydered with gold, pearle, and precious stones can make it.' Private rooms were set aside for the most senior women so that they could see but not be seen. Days of feasting and gift-giving took place,[177] with one of the main events being a large bazaar. Many women attended this indoor market, at which female vendors from all over the country displayed their wares.

> The king cometh with the Sultana etts. weomen, himselfe playing the Broker. They all take what they like and have notes given them by those weomen that can write. They [the vendors] deliver the said Notes to their husbands and [who] are accordingly paid out of the kings treasurie. This they doe because the Kinges weomen are never suffered to goe abroad.[178]

In addition to the two regular festivities of the emperor's birthday and Nauroz, women in the *zanana* celebrated special occasions marking significant moments for the Mughal family. Feasts were given for sons heralding any honour they might have brought upon the empire, such as that given for Shahjahan in

---

152. *Badshahnama* in Elliot and Dowson 7.69-70.
153. See *Akbar Nama* 1.415; *Tuzuk-i Jahangiri* 1.342; Hawkins in Foster, *Early Travels*, p. 98.
154. See *Humayun-Nama*, p. 76; *Akbar Nama* 3.91; *Tuzuk-i Jahangiri* 1.130, 225, 401; *Shah Jahan Nama* pp. 22, 90, 532; Manucci 2.321, 322.
155. *Waki'at-i Jahangiri* in Elliot and Dowson 6.285.
156. *Tuzuk-i Jahangiri* 2.228.
157. *Tuzuk-i Jahangiri* 1.397; see also 2.190, 221, 260.
158. Tavernier, p. 310.
159. *Tatimma-i Waki'at-i Jahangiri* and *Ikbal-nama-i Jahangiri* in Elliot and Dowson pp. 399 and 405 respectively.
160. *Ain-i Akbari*, pp. 83-87.
161. *Tuzuk-i Jahangiri* 1.270-271.
162. *Ain-i Akbari*, p. 98.
163. Terry, pp. 204-205; Finch in Foster, *Early Travels*, p. 13; Finch in Foster, *Early Travels*, p. 22; Della Valle 1.44-45; Manucci 2.316-318.
164. Finch in Foster, *Early Travels*, p. 162.
165. Manucci 2.139.
166. *Humayun-Nama*, pp. 67, 197; Manucci 2.309.
167. *Humayun-Nama*, p. 179.
168. Findly, 'Nur Jahan's Embroidery Trade.'
169. *Humayun-Nama*, p. 178.
170. See *Humayun-Nama*, p. 57; Manucci 2.308; Tavernier, p. 299.
171. *Humayun-Nama*, pp. 94-96; Manucci 2.6; 312-314, 322-323.
172. *Tuzuk-i Jahangiri* 1.348, 369, 375; 2.35-36, 83, 105, 236; *Waki'at-i Jahangiri* in Elliot and Dowson 6.366; Findly, 'Jahangir's Vow of Non-Violence.' The most exceptional woman sharpshooter was Nur Jahan who, as reported in Jahangir's memoirs, outshone even the best marksman of the empire, Mirza Rustam, in her ability to hit and kill tigers with just one shot. *Tuzuk-i Jahangiri* 1.348, 363, 375, 402-403; 2.40, 104-105, 133.
173. Manucci 2.318.
174. *Humayun-Nama*, p. 167.
175. *Humayun-Nama*, pp. 117-129; *Tuzuk-i Jahangiri* 1.81; De Laet, p. 99-103.
176. *Tuzuk-i Jahangiri* 1.77-78, 145, 148, 155, 239; 2.214; Manucci 2.325; Tavernier, pp. 301-302.
177. Hawkins in Foster, *Early Travels*, pp. 117-118.
178. Mundy 2.237-238; see Coryat in Foster, *Early Travels*, p. 278; Du Jarric pp. 65-66; *Waki'at-i Jahangiri* in Elliot and Dowson 6.361.

Fig. 6: THE WEDDING NIGHT OF HAMIDA AND HUMAYUN, from a *masnavi* of Khwaja Kirmani, Baghdad, copied in 1396. Courtesy of the British Library, London, Add. 18113, f. 45v.

1617 celebrating his victories in the Deccan (see Fig. 2);[179] or to mark returns to health of emperors, as Nur Jahan hosted for Jahangir in 1621 when he recovered from a serious illness;[180] or celebrations were held to honour reunions with parents long absent, as by Mumtaz Mahal for her parents in 1628.[181] Finally, women of the harem occasionally went on picnics during good weather, when excursions out of the palace into the gardens and hills allowed them, for instance, to gather fresh fruit and to see an unusual waterfall.[182]

In all these festivities, food played a central role and not only were fresh fruits and vegetables brought in from orchards and gardens far afield, but cooks laboured long on new or complicated recipes to please increasingly discriminating palates. It was through the refined tastes of the royal family that the famous Mughal cuisine was created. The provision of meat for festivities often came directly from imperial hunts, but had to be coordinated with the vows of non-violence and vegetarianism taken by emperors such as Akbar and Jahangir. Women, however, did not seem to participate in such personal prohibitions and apparently ate meat freely, accordingly as it was available and sumptuously cooked. More notable however, was the consumption of alcohol and eventually opium. In the *Babur-Nama*, a male guest at a party was noted as saying 'I've never seen a woman drink…Invite her to the party',[183] but by Shahjahan's time drinking by women was *de rigueur*. Manucci describes what he understood to be Jahanara's habit as so thorough that she imported wine from Persia, Kabul, and Kashmir. Moreover, he says, 'the best liquor she drank was distilled in her own house. It was a most delicious spirit, made from wine and rose-water, flavoured with many costly spices and aromatic drugs.' She considered it so precious that she often gave it as gifts.[184] Although Muslim clerics forbade women from drinking and from taking *bhang*, opium, and other drugs, the women 'paid no heed to the orders…given…saying those orders did not apply to them, but to men only.'[185] Such accounts, and others by foreign travellers, however, contradict traditional, more restrained, accounts of Jahanara's behaviour. Mughal men, of course, had a history of overindulgence in alcohol and opium—many having died of its effects—and some women in the *zanana*, Aurangzeb's favourite wife Udaipuri Begum, for example, showed that this addiction was not limited by gender.

Religion played an important role in *zanana* life, and the diversity of backgrounds of the wives and concubines meant that religious tolerance was an important key to palace harmony. On the whole, there was no attempt to convert women coming into the apartments and, with the few exceptions of Christian wives, there seems not to have been a concern about the need for one persuasion over another.[186]* Aside from the celebrations of such holidays as the Persian New Year or Nauroz, the Islamic month of fasting or Ramadan, and the Hindu springtime extravaganza of Holi, two religious activities occupied harem women the most: charity and pilgrimages. Most women, whose personal purses allowed it, gave money and materials in cash and women like Gulbadan,[187] Haji Begim,[188] and Nur Jahan[189] were especially known for their generosity.

Pilgrimages were undertaken by Muslim and Hindu women alike and most considered it a duty[190] to make pilgrimages both to general religious sanctuaries such as Mecca as well as to shrines and tombs of particular importance to their own families. The most famous pilgrimage made by Mughal women was that undertaken to Mecca during Akbar's reign. The trip lasted from 1576 when the pilgrims left Gujarat to 1582 when they returned to Fatehpur Sikri, and the group included such prominent women as Gulbadan Begum and Salima Sultan Begum.[191] Other Mughal women went with smaller entourages to Mecca, and many

---

179. *Tuzuk-i Jahangiri* 1.380, 385, 395, 397.
180. *Tuzuk-i Jahangiri* 2.212-215.
181. *Shah Jahan Nama*, p. 21.
182. *Humayun-Nama*, pp. 43-44.
183. Thackston, *Baburnama*, p. 302.
184. Manucci 1.211.
185. Manucci 2.139.
186. See, however, the case of the sons of Prince Danyal through whose conversion to Christianity Portuguese wives would be introduced into the *zanana*. Maclagan, p. 72.
  * **Editor's Note: For details see p. 72 in Schimmel's chapter on Religion in this book.**
187. *Humayun-Nama*, p. 76.
188. *Akbar Nama* 3.38n; 3.107.
189. *Tatimma-i Waki'at-i Jahangiri* and *Ikbal-nama-i Jahangiri* in Elliot and Dowson 6.399 and 465 respectively; Coryat in Foster, *Early Travels*, p. 280.
190. *Humayun-Nama*, p. 69.
191. *Humayun-Nama*, pp. 58, 69-73; *Akbar Nama* 2.366-367; 3.2-5-210, 569-573.

routinely visited tombs of their dead parents or those of past emperors,[192] bringing offerings and circumambulating the base of the main building.

In spite of so many luxuries, illness was often a feature of life in the *zanana* although, as Manucci notes, there were tendencies to gloss over any sickness as being in tension with the general court affirmation of pleasure and ease:

> When these ladies chance to fall ill, they are carried away to a very pretty set of rooms in the palace, which they style the *bimar-khanah*, or house of the sick. There they are nursed and tended with all possible exactitude, and they only come forth either well or dead.[193]

Great care was taken when a woman fell ill and there was much celebration, as in the case of Nur Jahan and Jahanara, when she recovered.[194] Although most often the Muslim doctors attached to the court were able to treat any illnesses that befell *mahal* women, emperors were increasingly willing to allow foreign doctors entrance into the apartments to attend those whose illnesses were troublesome. In Shahjahan's reign, for example, a Dutch surgeon named Pitre de Lan, was allowed to bleed the 'young Queen and the Queen-dowager' as each put her arm out to him through a hole in the curtain.[195] Under Aurangzeb, Bernier was brought in to treat *mahal* women by having a Kashmiri shawl draped over his head and by being led to the women's apartments under the guidance of a eunuch who described in detail all that they passed.[196] Manucci knew of foreign physicians who came in to treat women and at times was himself part of such a visit:

> [The physician] stretches out his hand inside the curtain; they lay hold of it, kiss it, and softly bite it. Some, out of curiosity, apply it to their breast, which has happened to me several times; but I pretended not to notice, in order to conceal what was passing from the matrons and eunuchs then present, and not arouse their suspicions.[197]

When the men of the imperial family got sick, especially the emperor, the women of the *zanana* became particularly mindful and involved: letters from his mother and grandmother came to Babur when he was ill;[198] women worried obsessively when pimples broke out all over Salim's body;[199] and Jahangir eventually allowed no one else to nurse him except Nur Jahan who succeeded in bringing him around to health when others had failed.[200] Sickness, thus, called into play the familial, and especially the maternal, bonds already so strong in knitting together the Mughal dynastic network.

Finally, though secluded behind decoratively perforated screens from public view, *mahal* women were encouraged to travel from the beginning of Mughal times—even though this travel maintained the strict veiling and concealment needed for the preservation of family honour and reputation. Early on travel for women consisted primarily of accompanying male members on hunts[201] and military expeditions, or of going on religious pilgrimage. Although there were occasional excursions for women for pleasurable activities, like gathering fruit, in Babur and Humayun's reign,[202] travelling for pleasure by women was not really significant until Jahangir's reign when he not only spent considerably more time in the company of women but allowed them expanded sensual pursuits as well.[203] It was with the beginning of his regular trips to Kashmir in 1620, however, that Jahangir made an institutional commitment to incorporate the search for good and healthful climates, the building and use of gardens, and the expansion of leisure pursuits as important court activities.[204] While the almost annual trips to Kashmir from 1620-1627 had as one of their purposes the search for settings more conducive to Jahangir's good health, they were also expressly undertaken (probably each at the insistence of Nur Jahan) for the benefit of the women of the harem—as a relief from the heat, as a chance to taste good fruit, and as an opportunity to luxuriate in the beautiful surroundings of mountain trees and flowers. This new acknowledgment of the sensuality of women was in contrast to the restraint and modesty imposed on them in earlier Mughal reigns and was in part due to the great ascendancy of Nur Jahan and in part to the increasing influence of Hindu culture at court.

Although midway through the Mughal period women began to travel more and for their own purposes, women's travel remained very difficult and slow.[205] The need for a great number of tents and pavilions to accommodate the large groups of noble women, concubines, servants, and eunuchs and the often rough terrain the 'moving city' had to make its way over, especially on trips up into and down from mountainous destinations, rendered the trips very slow, and often separate groups of men would move on ahead more quickly.²⁰⁶ The slowness and frequent delays of women's trips also meant, however, that their groups could move at a more leisurely pace, thus making the trip itself a source of pleasure. Occasionally, under a different travel plan, women's baggage was sent on ahead and women would take a shorter route being able thus to move more quickly. In all cases of women's travel, however, there were enough provisions so that at night, during encampment, women would always be housed at the centre of the grounds for protection.²⁰⁷

Modes of travel for women varied, but the primary considerations in all of them were safety and concealment. While there is evidence from early Mughal times onward that women rode on horseback,²⁰⁸ the more frequent types of transportation included the following: palanquins or litters carried either by men, horses, elephants, or camels; carts or coaches drawn by oxen or horses; and cradles strapped to the sides of camels. Litters, or the small public enclosures carrying Mughal women were often 'pretty receptacles, surrounded with curtains'.²⁰⁹ 'They are gilt and painted and covered with magnificent silk nets of many colours, enriched with embroidery, fringes, and beautiful tassels.' Often slaves went before the women with peacock tails to brush away dust and flies, and it was impossible for any petitioner to get close enough to do business, as the retinue for high-born women, at least, was large, resplendently decorated, noisy with musicians and elephant bells, and exceedingly well-protected.²¹⁰ Routine travel by Mughal women thus reflected the safety and luxury of their lives in the *zanana*.

WOMEN'S CONTRIBUTIONS TO POLITICS AND TRADE

The safety and protection of the *zanana*, however, did not preclude Mughal women from direct and indirect involvement in public affairs, in particular in politics and trade. Against the background of the real power, political expertise, and wise rule of such Hindu queens as Rani Durgavati and Tara Bai,²¹¹ and of Muslim queens such as Razia Sultana, Chand Bibi Sultan and Haram Begim,²¹² Mughal women showed great ingenuity in the exercise of power. Akbar, for example, appointed his sister, the wife of Khwaja Hasan of Badakhshan, as governor of Kabul, which she successfully administered for three years.

Mughal women helped shape the political culture of their times in a number of ways. First, they worked behind the scenes in marriage negotiations, steering emperors and princes in directions that would be most beneficial as political alliances, and welcoming new wives and extended female family members into the complex culture of the women's apartments. Second, they corresponded by letters and by couriers (bearing gifts) with the noble wives of rulers of other countries and kingdoms, thus encouraging negotiations and solidifying contacts beneficial to the empire.²¹³ Moreover, women often accompanied the emperor on diplomatic missions, thereby strengthening the swaying power of such visits to other courts.²¹⁴ And *mahal* women often bestowed their own gifts on ambassadors

---

192. *Tuzuk-i Jahangiri* 1.110; 2.101.
193. Manucci 2.319.
194. *Tuzuk-i Jahangiri* 2.53; *Shah Jahan Nama*, pp. 317-320.
195. Tavernier 1.241-242.
196. Bernier, p. 267.
197. Manucci 2.329.
198. Thackston, *Baburnama*, p. 91.
199. *Akbar Nama* 3.288.
200. *Tuzuk-i Jahangiri* 1.266; 2.11-12, 35, 213-214; *Waki'at-i Jahangiri* in Elliot and Dowson 6.381; Manucci 1.168.
201. *Tuzuk-i Jahangiri* 1.129-130, 390; 2.73-74, 219.
202. *Humayun-Nama*, pp. 189, 196.
203. For example, *Tuzuk-i Jahangiri* 1.132, 241, 298; 2.68, 81; see Findly 'The Pleasure of Women.'
204. *Tuzuk-i Jahangiri* 2.81; see Findly, 'Nur Jahan and the Idea of Kashmir.'
205. *Babur-Nama*, p. 136; *Humayun-Nama*, p. 143; *Akbar Nama* 2.85-86; 3.823-824; *Tabakat-i Akbari* in Elliot and Dowson 5.457; *Tuzuk-i Jahangiri* 2.123.
206. Manucci 2.69.
207. *Ain-i Akbari*, pp. 47-49; Bernier, p. 361.
208. *Humayun-Nama*, pp. 169-170, 189.
209. Terry, pp. 144, 404-405; Roe 2.324; Tavernier, p. 224; Bernier, pp. 371-374; Manucci 1.212-213; 2.340. See especially chart no. 12 in Mundy (between pp. 179-180).
210. Bernier, pp. 371-374.
211. *Akbar Nama* in Elliot and Dowson 6.33, 93, 99; *Akbar Nama* (of Faizi Sirhindi) in Elliot and Dowson 6.118-122, 144; Van den Broecke, pp. 24, 27, 28; *Muntakhab-ul Lubab* in Elliot and Dowson 7.366-367.
212. *Akbar Nama* 3.212-214, 318-320. See Richards, p. 54.
213. *Tuzuk-i Jahangiri* 2.205.
214. *Ikbal-nama Jahangiri* in Elliot and Dowson 6.429.

The Magnificent Mughals

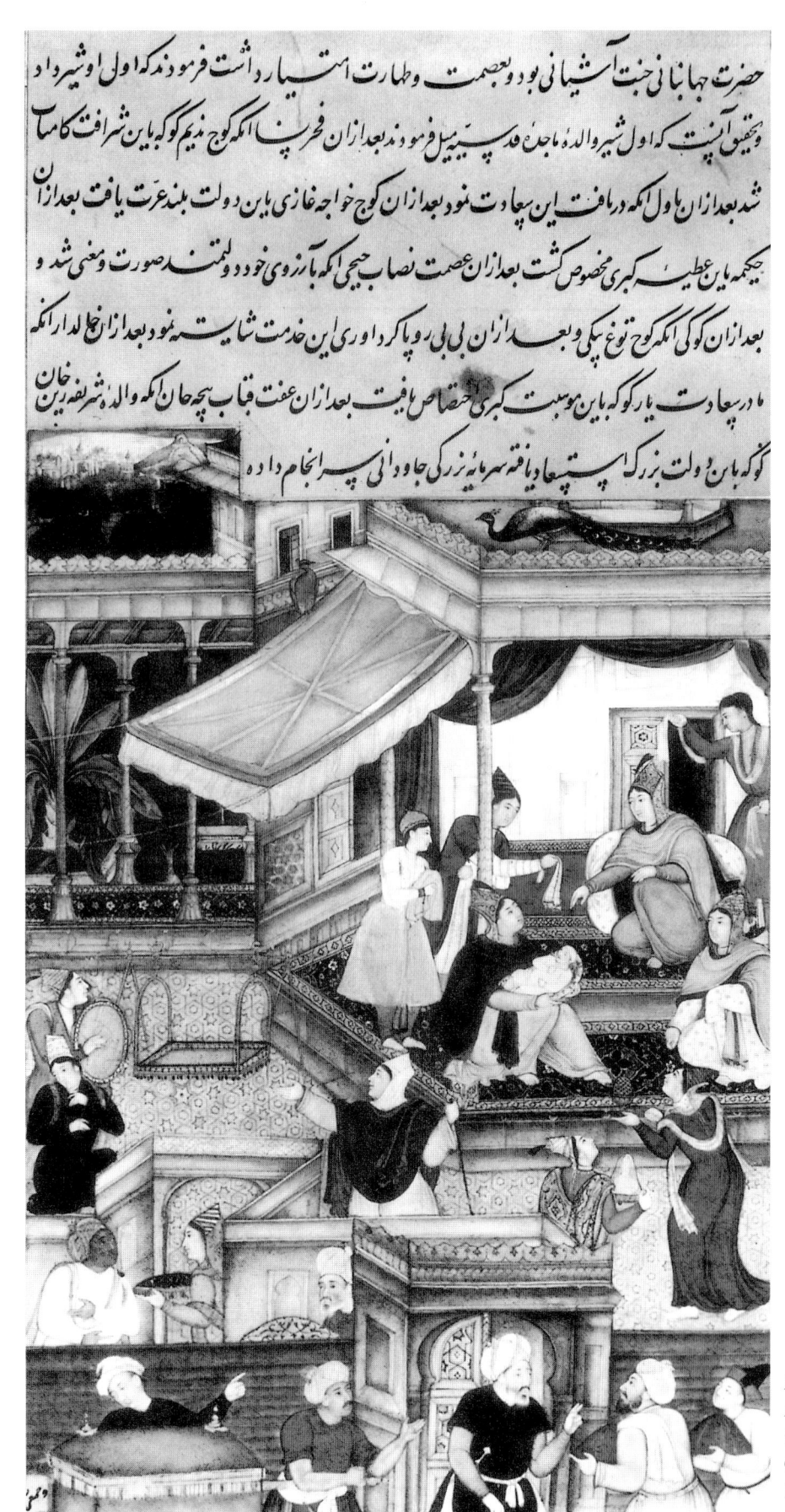

حضرت جہانبانی جنت آشیانی بودو بعصمت و طہارت استیار داشت فرمودند که اول او شیر داد
و تحقیق آنست که اول شیر والده ماجد سپید میل فرمودند بعد ازان فخر پن الکه که بدیم که باین شرافت کامل آ
شد بعد ازان با ول که در یافت این سعادت نمود بعد ازان خواجہ غازی باین دولت بلند عزت یافت بعد ازان
حکیمہ باین عطیہ کبری مخصوص کشت بعد ازان عصمت نصاب حجی که با آرزوی خود دولت صورت و معنی شد و
بعد ازان کوکی الکہ کوچ توغ بپی و بعد ازان بی بی روپا کرد و ری باین خدمت شایستہ نمود بعد ازان خال دار الکہ
مادر سعادت یار کو کہ باین موہبت کبری حصاص یافت بعد ازان عفت قباب بچہ جان الکہ والدہ شر تفقہ این خان
کو کہ باین دولت بزرگ استسعاد یافتہ سرمایہ بزرگی جاودانی سپر انجام دادہ

Fig. 7: THE INFANT AKBAR PLACED IN THE CARE OF HIS NURSES, from an *Akbarnama*, ca. 1603-04. Courtesy of the British Library, London. Or. 12988, f. 20v.

who came to the Mughal court and who made special visits to the thresholds of the *zanana*.²¹⁵

Third, Mughal women of high rank often had their own armies, of both foot- and mounted-soldiers, who could be called upon to respond to outlying skirmishes, support military endeavours of male relatives, or even engage in operations of their own initiative. Fourth, women at court had a pivotal role in the appointment and promotion of relatives and friends to positions of stature and financial responsibility. Again, the most noted example of this involvement in the shaping of court hierarchy was Nur Jahan whose family benefitted tremendously from her enhanced position as Jahangir's wife. Although they were well placed at court before her marriage to him in 1611, after that event her family members rose to truly monumental positions in the influence they had over the affairs of the empire.²¹⁶

The most important way women shaped Mughal politics, however, was by actual involvement, even entanglement, in political affairs at court. Benign involvement usually entailed acting as mediators and peacemakers,²¹⁷ as when Humayun's sister Masuma Sultan Begum petitioned the emperor about her husband's guilt and received from him an order of reconciliation.²¹⁸ The most famous example of such intercession by women in the role of peacemakers occurred, as mentioned earlier, at the end of Akbar's reign, when the intense efforts of Gulbadan Begum, Maryam Makani, and Salima Sultan Begum proved successful in bringing about a reconciliation between Akbar and Salim.²¹⁹ This struggle for the throne led, in a few years, to the open rebellion of Khusrau against his father, now the emperor, and although once again the women of the harem, including Jahangir's mother, tried to intercede on behalf of a reconciliation, this time they were not successful.²²⁰

Many Mughal women were strong-willed and forceful by nature and did not leave their political involvement simply at peacemaking, but became active participants in a wide range of political machinations. No woman in Mughal times, however, was more powerful or more influential than Nur Jahan, who upon her marriage in 1611 quickly moved into the sovereign vacuum left by her husband's addictions and virtually ruled the empire until his death in 1627. She is said to have had the entire management of the empire in her hands, such that few decisions were made without her involvement and that the course of political events was bound to her own self-interest in government affairs.

Nur Jahan's political power was institutionalized after her marriage to Jahangir in the formation of a ruling group made up of four individuals: Nur Jahan, her father Itimaduddaula, her brother Asif Khan, and her step-son Shahjahan. This faction, clearly dominated by Nur Jahan, inspired fear in local and foreign petitioners²²¹ who worried that any disfavour incurred with this group would be disastrous to their cause. Of Jahangir and Nur Jahan, Mundy notes, 'hee became her prisoner by marryeing her, for in his tyme shee in a manner ruled all in ruleing him, Coyninge money of her owne, buildinge and disposeinge as shee listed, puting out of the Kinges favour and receiveinge whome shee pleased'.²²²

The issue around which the faction united most centrally, according to sources, was the disenfranchisement of Jahangir's eldest son Khusrau. Out of favour already because of succession tensions in 1605 and his own rebellion in 1606, Khusrau was nevertheless a favourite of *mahal* women and a friend to the Christian foreigners at court. Without any interference by the faction, he may well have been reinstated as Jahangir's heir and succeeded to the throne in 1627. However, Shahjahan, the third son, had his own ambitions for the throne and joined by Nur Jahan, whose attempts to marry off her daughter Ladli to Khusrau had been rejected and by Asif Khan whose daughter was married to Shahjahan, the group had clear rationale for working against the good favour of Khusrau with his father. The faction worked first for the continued house arrest of Khusrau, and eventually persuaded Jahangir to entrust Khusrau into the hands of

---

215. *Shah Jahan Nama*, p. 499.
216. *Tuzuk-i Jahangiri* 1.260, 278; 2.80; Van den Broecke, pp. 65, 72.
217. *Babur-Nama*, p. 113.
218. *Akbar Nama* 1.330; see *Tabakat-i Akbari* in Elliot and Dowson 5.302, 392.
219. *Humayun-Nama*, p. 76; *Akbar Nama* 3.1222-1223; Du Jarric, p. 188; De Laet, p. 169; Van den Broecke, pp. 26-27.
220. *Tuzuk-i Jahangiri* 2.299.
221. Roe 1.118, 146.
222. Mundy 2.206.

his brother Shahjahan while the latter was in the Deccan. Few doubt that Khusrau's death in the south was anything but murder.[223]

In time Shahjahan himself rebelled against the dominance of Nur Jahan and, with the mediating power of Itimaduddaula gone after his death in 1622, the faction rapidly deteriorated. Nur Jahan maintained her own power at the helm, however, and now turned all her efforts to stymieing Shahjahan's quest for the throne. She persuaded Jahangir's fourth son to marry her daughter Ladli and worked hard, though eventually unsuccessfully, to undermine Shahjahan's support in various parts of the empire.[224] In rebellion, Shahjahan garnered the support of his father-in-law Asif Khan and an able military leader named Mahabat Khan—a coup that would eventually prevent Nur Jahan from realizing her goals. By the time of Jahangir's death in 1627, Shahjahan had become powerful enough to order the execution of all would-be contenders to the throne and to manoeuvre Nur Jahan into genteel exile in Lahore.[225]

Nur Jahan did, however, have one great moment of glory in the last years of her reign and this was her routing of the rebellion of Mahabat Khan. Seeking to avenge a slight against his new son-in-law, Mahabat Khan staged a surprise attack on Jahangir's river-side camp and took the emperor hostage. Still free, Nur Jahan's forces attacked Mahabat Khan's army: mounted on elephant back, with her granddaughter and her granddaughter's nurse together with her in the *hauda*, 'on account of her great bitterness [Nur Jahan] wanted to show her woman's courage to Mahabat Khan.'[226] Although her brother Asif Khan had early on fled to Attock, Nur Jahan fought on bravely across the river, distinguishing herself as a soldier, as she had done earlier as a marksman. She was eventually taken prisoner by Mahabat Khan's forces, however, but ultimately secretly recruited an army and planned an elaborate, and successful, escape.[227]

Nur Jahan's initiative and strength of will surfaced in another area beyond the *mahal* walls, that of domestic and international trade. Bequeathed enormous wealth by his father,[228] Jahangir and his court were able to engage in a great variety of mercantile activities needing large amounts of capital, and a good proportion of this wealth resided in the purses of the *mahal*.[229] Domestic trade involved large quantities of food items available only in certain parts of the country, local specialty textiles, and spices and mineral stuffs reflective of the Subcontinent's great geographical variety. International trade, however, was more specific: the Dutch in India were particularly interested in spices, and the English in cotton and silk cloths and in indigo dye.[230] To procure these, the English brought in their own textiles (broadcloths and wool), embroidered cloths,[231] quicksilver (mercury), sword blades, dogs, coaches, musical instruments, porcelain, ivory, gemstones, and some spices. The only items that really traded well in Mughal circles, however, were silver from East Asia and paintings, drawings, and engravings from Europe.

While women were certainly involved in determining what kinds and qualities of trade items were wanted at court from the very beginning of the Mughal period, it was under Akbar and especially under Jahangir that Mughal women were reported to have become especially active in domestic and international trade. Using monies from gifts and revenues from land, women like Nur Jahan traded in domestic items and, at critical points along mercantile roadways in lands she controlled, extracted taxes for the movements of all manner of goods. This use of personal resources to invest in trade items in order to get a return through their sale and through taxes was a considerable departure from the normal *mahal* activity of bestowing resources in charity and for the upkeep of religious establishments and mausoleums.

International trade, however, seems to have occupied more time than domestic trade for several Jahangiri figures, most notably for his mother Maryam Zamani and for Nur Jahan. Maryam Zamani ran ships in international shipping lanes which carried a variety of goods, but primarily cottons and indigo dyes. She often encountered trouble in the waters—having to pay exorbitantly high prices for a Portuguese *cartaz*, being chased by pirates seeking to steal her goods, and being the object of hijacking schemes for use as a pawn in putting pressure on Jahangir[232]—but survived most of them to continue doggedly in her trading efforts.

The most significant trading contact, however, was between Nur Jahan and the first English embassy which approached the Mughal court to set up official trading contracts. English seeking trade negotiations had been working the Mughal empire through their factory system from the earliest days of the seventeenth century. Their primary interest was in procuring indigo and cloth but they wanted, as a long-term goal, to negotiate contracts with the Mughal court which would place English merchants in preeminent place for securing goods. As Roe found out during his tenure in India (1615-1619), such a contract did not fit Mughal sensibilities concerning international relations or etiquettes, and Roe for his part blamed the faction, and especially Nur Jahan, for his failure. Roe first learned of the hindrances he would encounter when, on coming to the court in January of 1616, he could not be formally received until the queen, i.e., Nur Jahan, had inspected his official seal. Moreover, although Shahjahan was first assigned to be the protector of English interests in India, in due time Nur Jahan asked for this position, in which all English goods would be under her supervision.[233] It soon became clear to the English embassy that the only interest the Mughal court had in their presence was in procuring luxury items for its own use, and very quickly the embassy's role dwindled to one of bickering over gifts. Roe should have known this, for Hawkins wrote, as early as 1611, that 'there is no man that commeth to make petition who commeth emptie-handed,' and that he especially needed gifts for Nur Jahan: 'I sent my broker to seeke out for jewels fitting for the King's sister and new paramour...'[234] In hopes of a trading accord, Roe ordered a great variety of sumptuous gifts from England, most of which proved unsatisfactory: wools were too hot for wear in India, items of iron rusted on shipboard, wooden and leather goods rotted on the way over, rare animals arrived sick or dead, and one-time-only items like musical instruments, an English coach, and select pieces of furniture soon lost their luster. Wine, however, was well-received as were rare and unusual objects of art. Roe soon realized that his fortunes depended on procuring exactly what Nur Jahan wanted and received lists from her of desired items (such as beaver hats and embroidered pieces) which he specially commissioned:

> If the Queene must be presented (which I will not aduise too, and doe purpose, as well out of necessytye and Iudgment, to breake this Custome of daylye bribing) fine needle woorke toyes, fayre bone lace, cuttworke, and some handsome wrought wastcote, sweet bagges or Cabinetts, wilbe most Convenient...I would add any faire China Bedsteeds, or cabinetes or trunks of Japan are here rich presentes.[235]

Increasingly, presents were sent especially for Nur Jahan[236] and the Mughal court responded with gifts in kind of fresh fruits and women servants.[237]

The most popular gifts given by the English, as they had been in the case of the Portuguese Jesuits, were European paintings, prints, and drawings. Unlike the Portuguese who gave primarily religious paintings, the English brought and were asked to bring images of more secular subjects: portraits of royalty and nobles, pictures of Parliament and of gardens, and renderings of European mythological materials. While not all paintings were a uniform success—one of Venus and Satyr caused a stir over perceived racial indignities[238]— on the whole the Mughal court, and especially the royal couple much appreciated the images and had their own painters copy them in profusion.[239]

Even the artwork, however, did not turn the Mughal government toward the desired trading accords, and often Roe complained that his failure was due to his being so poorly set out. He once confessed, in fact, that '[I am] ashamed of my Prouision,' and that the presents he brought were uniformly despised.[240] In general, though, Roe accepted that differences in cultural etiquette and in trading needs were what really kept the two governments apart, and grew bitter about India as a successful trading environment: 'this is the dullest,

---

223. Roe 2.363-364, 404-407, 281-283, 293-294; Van den Broecke, pp. 52-54; De Laet, pp. 198-199; Tavernier, pp. 268-269.
224. *Tuzuk-i Jahangiri* 2.235-277, 289; *Waki'at-i Jahangiri* in Elliot and Dowson 6.383-386; Van den Broecke, p. 88; *Badshah-nama* in Elliot and Dowson 7.5-6, 137.
225. *Ikbal-nama-i Jahangiri* in Elliot and Dowson 6.435-438; *Shah Jahan Nama*, pp. 12-15; Tavernier, p. 270.
226. Van den Broecke, p. 76.
227. *Ikbal-nama-i Jahangiri* in Elliott and Dowson 6.420-428; Manucci 1.165; De Laet, pp. 222-233.
228. De Laet, p. 111; Van den Broecke, pp. 33-35.
229. De Laet, pp. 238, 240; see Manucci 1.199
230. Terry, pp. 107, 108, 110-112, 397.
231. See Findly, 'Nur Jahan's Embroidery Trade.'
232. Maclagan, p. 223; Finch in Foster, *Early Travels*, p. 129; Roe 2.421-425, 429, 480, 517.
233. Roe 1.109, 249, 186; 2.436, 444.
234. Hawkins in Foster, *Early Travels*, pp. 89, 94.
235. Roe 1.119; see 1.203; 2.288, 290n, 324, 347.
236. Roe 2.384, 386, 427, 437, 458.
237. Roe 1.170-174.
238. Roe 2.386-387.
239. Roe 1.254-256.
240. Roe 2.326; 1.97.

Fig. 8: SHAHJAHAN HONOURING PRINCE AURANGZEB AT HIS WEDDING, Agra, Diwan-i Khass, 19 May 1637. From a *Padshahnama*, folio 218B, attributed to Bhola, ca. 1640. The Royal Collection ©1998 Her Majesty Queen Elizabeth II

basest place that euer I saw, and maketh me weary of speaking of it'.²⁴¹ If he were to blame any one person in particular, however, it would be his 'protectresse' Nur Jahan who, while subverting what could have been national networks into purely personal ones, in fact brought in numerous items—embroidery and pictures of women²⁴²—which would influence generations of Indian craftspeople and artists in the years to come.

WOMEN'S CONTRIBUTIONS TO THE ARTS

According to legend and local tradition, Mughal women made tremendous contributions to the domestic arts. New creations in clothing and jewellery and cosmetics and bodily ornamentation almost certainly grew out of the daily experimentation *mahal* women engaged in as they tried out new items made available through international and domestic trade. New inventions in perfume, of course, were the institutional province of, probably male, perfume makers under emperors like Akbar,²⁴³ but women also experimented, as Asmat Begum did in developing rose perfume under Jahangir. Although teams of speciality cooks were responsible for most of the cooking and meal preparation, *mahal* women certainly made suggestions, and many recipes bequeathed to today's Mughal gourmets bear the names of individual women culinaires, such as Nur Jahan. The domestic arts of interior design and wall decoration were also certainly developed in large part by the women who lived within the *zanana* chambers, and rug design may have been patronized by women as is said to have been the case for Nur Jahan, whose earth tone favourites for rugs (ivories, golds, and browns) are reflected in the floors of the tomb she designed for her father Itimaduddaula.

Other specialized arts for women included embroidery and, again in the case of Nur Jahan, we have evidence of embroidery designs used by *mahal* women in the carved reliefs of the Itimaduddaula tomb;²⁴⁴ moreover, the exquisite cashmere (Kashmiri) shawl designs from later eras are directly attributable to the patronage of Nur Jahan and Jahangir. The English ambassador Roe was aware of the extensive role of embroidery in *mahal* culture and says: 'They imitate euery thing wee bring, and embroder now as well as wee'.²⁴⁵ Women wrote poetry as well, and those like Salima Sultan Begum, Nur Jahan, Jahanara, and Zebunnisa were, by tradition, composers of some renown. Many women 'had great acquaintance with words',²⁴⁶ and contests took place in the *zanana* pitting literary composers against one other. A few women of high stature were also involved in the minting of coins and, again, Nur Jahan is an excellent example of a woman issuing coins in her name from several locations, some bearing designs of the zodiac.²⁴⁷

Patronage was another way Mughal women could contribute to the arts, and it is clear that, in at least three areas, women's sponsorship of other artists helped shape the development of design and connoisseurship in their arts. In painting, for example, there are few actual references to women painters, but it is more certain that women patrons of artists and of painting studios had a tremendous influence on the direction of both the content and the style of the miniatures themselves. A good illustration of this is the increasing openness to depicting the pleasure and sensuality of women under Jahangir's reign, a trend normally attributed to Nur Jahan who was influenced by the values and patterns of Hindu art as well as by her own commitment to the expression of women's sensibilities.²⁴⁸ Music and dance performances in the *mahal* were also patronized by women, in part because it was not considered appropriate for them to take up these activities themselves, and in part because such performances provided entertainment. Such patronage, however, not only kept various music and dance styles alive but, in trying to please *mahal* women, the performers fine-tuned their performances on a regular basis.

The two most important artistic contributions of Mughal women, however, were in the patronage and actual design of selected buildings and gardens.* This happened in two ways: either women were given pre-existing sites to manage, care for, and develop out of

---

241. Roe 1.113; see also 1.56, 68, 73, 119, 120, 127; 2.460.
242. See Findly, 'Nur Jahan's Embroidery Trade' and 'The Pleasure of Women.'
243. *Ain-i Akbari*, pp. 78-93.
244. See Findly, 'Nur Jahan's Embroidery Trade'.
245. Roe 2.478.
246. *Babur-Nama*, p. 265.
247. Shujauddin, pp. 99-100.
248. See Findly, 'The Pleasure of Women.'
  * Editor's Note: see also Catherine Asher's chapter on Architecture in this book.

their own purses, or they built new sites of their own design, again financed from their own resources. Examples of the first type have been recorded for the reign, particularly, of Jahangir. He gave, for example, a garden in Agra left by Shah Quli Khan Mahram, who had no heirs, to Ruqayya Sultan Begum, as a mark of the great honour and esteem in which he held her.[249] The site of Ramsar was given over to Nur Jahan who held feasts and entertainments there.[250] And Nur Jahan remade Babur's old garden in Agra now called Nur Afshan.[251]

Sites actually designed and built by women were numerous as well. When in Kabul, Jahangir notes the garden made by Bika Begim, his father's grandmother; that made by Maryam Makani, his own grandmother; and that by Shahr Banu Begim, an aunt of Babur's.[252] In Barah, he notes a garden built by his mother Maryam Zamani[253] and a number of gardens and elaborated sites developed by Nur Jahan: Nur Manzil, Vernag, and Achval.[254] Buildings by women had an early history in Mughal times as well. Haji Begim, Humayun's widow, for example, contributed to the outstanding mausoleum built for her husband in Delhi. The many constructions designed and patronized by Nur Jahan include the marble inlaid tomb of her father Itimaduddaula in Agra, the Pather Masjid in Srinagar, and the Nur Mahal Sarai in the Punjab. This last was completed in late 1620 and its opening was celebrated with much entertainment and feasting.[255] Other rest-houses, palaces, wells, and gardens are said to have been built by her, according to several English travellers in the empire, for example, Mundy and Finch,[256] and late in her life her reputation as a patron and designer of sites grew increasingly wide-spread. Moreover, it was she who built the beautiful mausoleum for Jahangir in Lahore. In the next generation, the princess Jahanara acquired a number of properties and built several mosques and rest-houses on them and Aurangzeb's daughter, Zinatunnisa, was a builder of many caravansarais and of at least one tomb, her own, in Delhi,[257] thereby further substantiating the permanent artistic legacy of Mughal women.

---

249. *Tuzuk-i Jahangiri* 1.48.
250. *Tuzuk-i Jahangiri* 1.342-343.
251. *Tuzuk-i Jahangiri* 2.196-198.
252. *Tuzuk-i Jahangiri* 1.106.
253. *Tuzuk-i Jahangiri* 2.64.
254. *Tuzuk-i Jahangiri* 2.75-76, 142, 172-175; see also Bernier, pp. 413-414.
255. *Tuzuk-i Jahangiri* 2.192, 220; see also Mundy 2.78, 79n, 83.
256. Mundy 2.101, 214; Finch in Foster, *Early Travels*, p. 148.
257. *Shah Jahan Nama*, pp. 137, 206, 458; Manucci 1.212-213.

CONCLUSION

On the whole, life for women in the *zanana* was safe and secure and increasingly congenial to the many intellectual, economic, political, religious and artistic opportunities available to them. In this environment, women were able to make tremendous contributions not only to the life of the extended court but to the larger cultural milieu of the empire as well. In areas of politics, economics, trade, and social and religious life, the

LADY WITH A WINE CUP.
Late Mughal; ca. 1700. Courtesy of the Goenka Collection.

Mughal women's influence was strong and powerful. In other areas as well, especially in the patronage and development of the arts, Mughal women excelled, and innovations in gardens, architecture, painting, poetry, literature, embroidery, rugs, clothing, jewellery, perfume, and cooking by women were commonplace. The impact of these contributions is evident even today, and their careful transmission through the hands of craftsmen and by patrons of both oral and textual traditions has ensured that these contributions remain intricately woven in South Asian life.

Although focused, ultimately, around the needs and pursuits of the reigning emperor, the day-to-day experience of *mahal* women was governed in reality by the structures and individual personalities of the company of women themselves. Seclusion (*purdah*) meant not only that Mughal women were ostensibly set apart from public life, but that the public did (and now historians do) not have much access to them. Aside from one memoir (the *Humayun-Nama*), remnants of poetry, selected buildings and gardens, and suggestions of a few paintings and textile designs, there is only a little that can be said to be a *direct* expression of *mahal* women's experience. There are no real portraits of them, as artists were not allowed into the women's apartments, and any representation of individual women, whether visual or prose, was mediated by male recorders who reflected the character, actions, and feelings of Mughal women in ways that were often formulaic and idealized. With so little real information about the inner lives of *mahal* women, we are left to speculate about the degree of happiness, satisfaction, and fulfilment achieved by elite court women in this era. While we assume life in these chambers was on the whole very rewarding, the daily tensions, the unique individual propensities, and the private dreams are left unknown.

BIBLIOGRAPHY

Primary Sources

Ball, V., trans. and William Crooke, ed. *Travels in India by Jean-Baptiste Tavernier*. 2 vols. London: Oxford University Press, 1925.

Beveridge, Annette Susannah, trans. *Babur-Nama* (Memoirs of Babur). 1921. Rpt., Delhi: Low Price Publications, 1989.

Beveridge, Annette S., trans. *The History of Humayun (Humayun-Nama) by Gul-badan Begam (Princess Rose-Body)*. London: Royal Asiatic Society, 1902.

Beveridge, H. trans. *The Akbar Nama of Abu-l-Fazl*. 3 vols. 1902-1939. Rpt., Delhi: Low Price Publications, 1989.

Blochmann, H., trans. *The Ain-i Akbari, Abu'l-Fazl 'Allami*. 1871. 2nd ed., Rpt., Delhi, Aadiesh Book Depot, 1965.

Brock, Irving, trans. and Archibald Constable, ed. *Travels in the Mogul Empire, A.D. 1656-1668, by François Bernier*. 1891. Rpt., Delhi: S. Chand & Co., 1968.

Elliot, H.M., trans., and John Dowson, ed. *The History of India as Told by Its Own Historians: The Muhammadan Period*. Vols. 5, 6, 7. London, 1873, 1875, 1877. Rpt., New York, AMS Press, Inc., 1966.

Foster, William, ed. *Early Travels in India*, 1583-1619. Humphrey Milford: Oxford University Press, 1921.

Foster, William, ed. *The Embassy of Sir Thomas Roe to the Court of the Great Mogul, 1615-1619*. 2 vols. London: Hakluyt Society, 1899.

Fuller, A.R., trans., and W.E. Begley and Z.A. Desai, eds. *The Shah Jahan Nama of 'Inayat Khan*. Delhi: Oxford University Press, 1990.

Grey, Edward, ed. and G. Havers, trans. *The Travels of Pietro Della Valle*. 2 vols. London: Hakluyt Society, 1892.

Hoyland, J.S., trans. and S.N. Banerjee, annot. *The Empire of the Great Mogol; A Translation of De Laet's 'Description of India and Fragment of Indian History'*. 1928. Rpt., Delhi Idarah-i Adabiyat-i Delli, 1975.

Irvine, William, trans. *Storia do Mogor or Mogul India, 1653-1708, by Niccolao Manucci, Venetian*. 2 vols. London: 1907. Rpt., Calcutta: Editions Indian, 1965.

Maclagan, Edward. *The Jesuits and the Great Mogul*. London: Burns Oates & Washbourne Ltd., 1932.

Narain, Brij and Sri Ram Sharma, trans. and ed. *A Contemporary Dutch Chronicle of Mughal India (by Pieter van den Broecke)*. Calcutta: Susil Gupta (India) Limited, 1957.

Payne, C.H., trans. *Akbar and the Jesuits, An Account of the Jesuit Missions to the Court of Akbar by Father Pierre Du Jarric*. London: George Routledge & Sons, Ltd., 1926.

Payne, C.H., trans. *Jahangir and the Jesuits, With an Account of the Travels of Benedict of Goes and the Mission to Pegu, From the Relations of Father Fernao Guerreiro, S.J.* New York: Robert M. McBride & Company, 1930.

Rogers, Alexander, trans., and Henry Beveridge, ed. *The Tuzuk-i-Jahangiri, or Memoirs of Jahangir*. 2 vols. 1909-1914. Rpt., Delhi: Munshiram Manoharlal, 1968.

Temple, Richard Carnac, ed. *The Travels of Peter Mundy, in Europe and Asia, 1608-1667*. Vol. 2. London: Hakluyt Society, 1914.

Terry, Edward. *A Voyage to East-India*. London: J. Wilkie, W. Cater, S. Hayes, and E. Easton, 1777.

Thackston, Wheeler M., trans. *The Baburnama, Memoirs of Babur, Prince and Emperor.* New York, Oxford: Oxford University Press for Freer Gallery of Art & Arthur M. Sackler Gallery, Smithsonian Institution, Washington, D.C., 1996.

Tirmizi, S.A.I. *Mughal Documents, 1526-1627.* New Delhi: Ramesh Jain, Manohar Publications, 1989.

Secondary Sources

Chopra, Pran Nath. *Some Aspects of Society and Culture During the Mughal Age (1526-1707).* Agra: Shiva Lal Agarwala & Co. (P.) Ltd., n.d.

Findly, Ellison Banks. 'The Capture of Maryam-uz-Zamani's Ship: Mughal Women and European Traders,' *Journal of the American Oriental Society*, 108.2 (1988): 227-238.

Findly, Ellison Banks. 'Jahangir's Vow of Non-Violence,' *Journal of the American Oriental Society,* 107.2 (1987): 245-256.

Findly, Ellison Banks. 'Nur Jahan's Embroidery Trade and Flowers of the Taj Mahal,' *Asian Art and Culture*, 'Indian Textiles and Trade' issue, ed. by Ellison Banks Findly, Spring/Summer 1996: 6-25.

Findly, Ellison Banks. *Nur Jahan, Empress of Mughal India.* New York: Oxford University Press, 1993.

Findly, Ellison Banks. 'Nur Jahan and the Exercise of Power,' *Manushi*, 84 (September-October 1994): 14-21.

Findly, Ellison Banks. 'Nur Jahan and the Idea of Kashmir,' in B.K. Thapar commemorative volume, Archaeological Survey of India, New Delhi, n.d.

Findly, Ellison Banks. 'The Pleasure of Women: Nur Jahan and Mughal Painting,' *Asian Art*, 'Patronage by Women in Islamic Art' issue, ed. by Esin Atil, Spring 1993: 66-86.

Findly, Ellison Banks. 'Religious Resources for Secular Power,' in *Women and Religion*, volume, ed. Debra Campbell, *Colby Library Quarterly* 25.3 (Sept. 1989): 129-148.

Lal, K.S. *The Mughal Harem.* New Delhi: Aditya Prakashan, 1988.

Misra, Rekha. *Women in Mughal India (1526-1748 A.D.).* Delhi: Munshiram Manoharlal, 1967.

Moreland, W.H. *India at the Death of Akbar: An Economic Study.* Delhi: Atma Ram & Sons, 1962.

Pant, Chandra. *Nur Jahan and Her Family.* Allahabad: Dan Dewal Publishing House, 1978.

Qaisar, Ahsan Jan. *The Indian Response to European Technology and Culture (A.D. 1498-1707).* Delhi: Oxford University Press, 1982.

Richards, John F. *The Mughal Empire.* I.5 of *The New Cambridge History of India.* Cambridge University Press, 1993.

Schimmel, Annemarie. *My Soul is a Woman: The Feminine in Islam.* Trans. by Susan H. Ray. New York: The Continuum Publishing Company, 1997.

Shujauddin, Mohammad and Razia. *The Life and Times of Noor Jahan.* Lahore: The Caravan Book House, 1967.

3
RELIGION
Annemarie Schimmel

HOLY MEN IN A LANDSCAPE.
Hindu and Muslim holy men read and discuss. Mughal, second quarter of the 17th century or later.
Courtesy of the Goenka Collection.

RELIGIOUS POLICIES OF THE GREAT MUGHALS

Islam in the Subcontinent always displayed two faces which we might call, for want of a better term, the India-oriented, 'mystical,' inclusive one and the Mecca-oriented, 'prophetic,' exclusive one. These two trends are visible from early times and became more evident in the conflict between Akbar's ideals and those of the Naqshbandiyya at the beginning of the seventeenth century. They are then fully developed in the conflict between Dara Shikoh and Aurangzeb.

Of course, every Muslim is 'Mecca-oriented', turning toward the Kaaba in prayer; yet, the true meaning of this expression is that a representative of this trend found his ideal outside the Subcontinent and that he still felt, as Shah Waliullah once said, that 'he lives in exile,' even though his forefathers had emigrated to that region centuries before.

When the Mughals came to power in 1526 they took over many of the religious organizations established under the previous Turkish and Afghan dynasties which had ruled northern India from the turn of the millennium onwards, when Mahmud of Ghazna invaded the northwest of the Subcontinent not less than seventeen times. The study of the classical works of Islamic theology and, even more importantly, of jurisprudence was continued. Casual remarks in historical works mention the books or treatises studied under the early Mughals. The training of jurisconsults who were needed in the administration was one of the important aspects of religious education. The *madrasas* in Agra, Lahore, Delhi and other places in the expanding empire trained numerous scholars in the traditional fields, while the Sufi masters taught their disciples classical writings such as Rumi's *Masnavi* and, from the early fifteenth century, gave Ibn Arabi's works a central place in their lives.

The young seventeen-year-old conqueror of Sindh, Muhammad ibn Qasim (r. 711-715), had stated that the Hindus should be treated in the same way as the *ahl al-kitab* (see Glossary) in the central regions of the Muslim world; they had freedom of worship but had to pay the *jizyah*. At the time of Feroz Shah Tughluq (r.1351-1388), and even earlier, the *jizyah* was not levied on Brahmins. But besides the *jizyah*, an additional pilgrimage tax had been introduced by some Muslim rulers.

Iltutmish (r. 1211-1236) created the office of *Shaikh ul-Islam* to look after ecclesiastic affairs, the distribution of royal charities and the patronage of faqirs, dervishes, and religious mendicants. A century later Alauddin Khilji (d. 1316) created the office of *Sadr as-sudur*, the highest authority on the shariah and at the same time head of the central *waqf* administration.

During Babur's short reign little time remained for a change in the religious offices. Humayun largely followed the inherited practices. During the Sur interregnum the role of the leading religious dignitaries remained the same; in fact Makhdum ul-Mulk, a leading orthodox theologian appointed by Humayun, continued without qualms in the office of *Shaikh ul-Islam* even under Sher Shah Sur. After his return from Iran and before his sudden death in 1556, Humayun had no time to tackle the problems of religious administration.

With Akbar the period of changes begins. It would be wrong to call him 'a mystic who created an empire'; he had a living interest in religious questions but was certainly much more interested in the expansion and consolidation of his empire than in being a mystic in the true sense of the word. It is likely that millenary ideas were in the air, with the year 1000 of the Hijra (1591) approaching, and the dream of a king in whose realm members of all religions and civilizations could peacefully live together was certainly attractive for him and his advisers. To live under a sacred king seemed to be an ideal for the society of the second millennium of the Islamic era.

Akbar needed capable religious administrators in his early years and appointed Abdunnabi to the office of *Sadr as-sudur*; he was the grandson of the Chishti-Sabiri master Abdulquddus Gangohi, but had given up the mystical tradition of the family. However, relations between him and Makhdum ul-Mulk, who was in charge—among other offices—of all *farmans* (orders) of *madad-i maash* (pension), were anything but friendly. Finally, the emperor sent both of them together to perform the pilgrimage to Mecca (1577). This was a real punishment for both, and the two men died soon after their return in 1582. An enormous amount of wealth was found in Makhdum ul-Mulk's possession.

Akbar proved his intention of creating possibilities for a peaceful coexistence between the different religious groups of his empire, first by abolishing the *jizyah* in

1564; likewise, restrictions against the building of places of public worship were removed. In 1564 he performed his first pilgrimage on foot to Ajmer to visit the shrine of the Chishti saint, Muinuddin Chishti (d.1236) and continued these visits for fifteen years, endowing the shrine with precious gifts. His descendants followed his example for a long time. Akbar used to send money to Mecca to help the poor and the needy in the holy city and, in 1576, had desired to perform the Haj.

Akbar's first surviving son Salim, the later Jahangir, was born in 1569 in Sikri as a result of the prayers of the saint Salim Chishti. This event stimulated Akbar's religious interest. Out of gratitude he erected a sanctuary for the saint, around which the city of Fatehpur Sikri was built. In his new capital an *ibadatkhana* (house of worship) was erected in 1575. There the emperor could listen to the debates between theologians and representatives of the different schools of Islamic thought and practice as well as members of the other religions of the Subcontinent—Hindus, Jains, Zoroastrians and, from 1580 onwards, some Christians. The meetings were held on Thursdays and Fridays. Badauni has dramatically described the quarrels between the theologians, which annoyed the emperor and contributed to his aversion to the representatives of orthodoxy. The emperor turned more toward a mystical approach to religion, which was, after all, better suited to bring together the different people in his empire.

Akbar's change of interest (or rather, the strengthening of some ideals in his soul) can be traced to an experience during a royal hunt in early 1578. When he saw the hundreds of animals driven together in the *qamargah* (hunting enclosure) he was suddenly overcome by what we may call a mystical vision. He called off the hunt and began to adopt some new practices. He prohibited the killing of animals on certain days and abstained from wine and meat at fixed times; he even cut his hair, as the dervishes often do.

Shaikh Mubarak, renowned for his piety, became his trusted friend. His two sons, Abul Fazl and Faizi, soon belonged to the emperor's closest partisans: Faizi (d. 1595) excelled in literary pursuits while Abul Fazl was to become the emperor's chronicler until he was murdered on behalf of Jahangir in 1602.

In 1579, a year after the spiritual experience during the hunt, Akbar issued—with the help of Shaikh Mubarak—the so-called *mahzar*, a document wrongly called the 'infallibility decree'. It gave him the right to practice *ijtihad* and to interpret Muslim law in case the theologians failed to agree. Akbar's action was probably the result of his annoyance with the theological squabbles he had often witnessed in the *ibadatkhana*; for now he took away from the theologians the right to persecute those whose opinions differed from theirs.

The king was considered the *imam-i adil*, the just imam. That would mean that he was superior even to the *mujtahid*. In the eyes of some of his admirers he seemed to personify the *insan-i kamil*, the Perfect Man, as envisaged in the writings of many Sufis, especially of the Ibn Arabi school. It was also claimed that he carried in himself the *farr*, the light of kingship, a concept known from the ancient Persian tradition (*khwarena*). The idea of the 'royal fortune', a special power that is inherent in a true king and helps him to overcome seemingly insurmountable difficulties is a well known theme in the folk tradition of many countries. Hence his chronicler, Abul Fazl, ascribes to him all kinds of miraculous acts, including the production of rain at a time of intense heat. But Akbar also said in such a case:

> The Divine Goodness towards His servants is greater than that His mercy should depend upon appeals to Him, or upon our calling His Attention to the matter, or that we should teach Him graciousness! (*Akbarnama* III 148)

A number of religious scholars such as Abdunnabi the *Sadr as-sudur*, Makhdum ul-Mulk, the chief *qazi*, and others, signed the *mahzar* more or less unwillingly. The document had been drawn up by Shaikh Mubarak, but many pious Muslims were shocked since it seemed as if the ruler had assumed a role outside the realm of his authority.

Two years later, in 1581, the *Din-i Ilahi*, also called *Tauhid-i Ilahi*, was promulgated. It was an order or brotherhood rather than a new religion. For Muslims like Badauni the *Din-i Ilahi* seemed to mean that the emperor had willingly and wittingly left Islam and now posed as the founder of a new religion; that is, he had assumed, so to speak, a prophetic role. As the Prophet Muhammad (PBUH) is considered the 'Seal of Prophets', such a claim is tantamount to apostasy.

However, the beliefs and practices of the *Din-i Ilahi*

are nowhere expressly stated. One knows of the four degrees of devotion; for when the Sindhi ex-ruler Mirza Jani Beg was brought before Akbar as a prisoner he joined the small group and was asked whether he was willing to sacrifice, for the emperor, 1) his property 2) his life 3) his honour and 4) his faith. That means that the ritual of the initiation resembled to a certain extent the Sufi initiation, for the Sufi has also to promise that he will obey his master 'like the corpse in the hands of the undertaker', that is, without a will of his own. Absolute loyalty is his duty. Scholars have speculated whether or not the *Din-i Ilahi*, with its elements from various religious traditions (including a strong streak of mysticism), can be called a syncretistic religion supposed to embrace every religious current in the Subcontinent, and thus a substitute for Islam. But it is a fact that only a very small number of people (eighteen, according to one source, but clearly more) were admitted—Man Singh, Akbar's trusted Hindu general simply refused to enter the elite circle and not more than a handful of intellectuals seemed to have accepted it.

Akbar's motto was *Sulh-i Kul*, 'Peace with everyone', although this certainly did not apply to his continuing struggle against movements which seemed to disturb the security of his empire. Neither the power given to him in the *mahzar*, nor the *Din-i Ilahi*, left visible traces in the post-Akbar period. Yet, both of them were sufficient to lead many critics and admirers of Akbar, both in his own country as well as in Europe, to claim that he had given up Islam and was the founder of a new 'humanistic' religion.

To be sure, Akbar prayed in various places, including Christian churches, while he also continued to use some of the Divine Names known in Islam, as battle cries, such as *Ya Muin* (when he was close to Ajmer, the place devoted to Muinuddin Chishti) or *Ya Hu Ya Hadi* (The Guide) and suggested even to Badauni to call his newborn son Abdul Hadi (slave of The Guide). But Badauni, embittered and disappointed, claimed in his Chronicle that the emperor prohibited Muslim prayer, as well as the pilgrimage, that he exchanged learned mullahs for donkeys and that 'the mosques were as empty as the wine-houses in Ramadan'—and yet, we should not take all these complaints at face value. Badauni, too orthodox for Akbar's taste and hence not sufficiently rewarded, had to voice his anger and did it with the kind of exaggeration that is the result of disappointment. Akbar certainly continued to show reverence to things Islamic. He had sent his aunt Gulbadan and his wife Salima along with numerous ladies of the royal family for the pilgrimage to Mecca. On their return in 1582, one of their co-travellers brought back the relic of the *qadam rasul*, a footprint of the Prophet (PBUH), which Akbar went out of the city to welcome and pay homage to.

The fact that Akbar married a number of Rajput princesses and that he granted Amritsar as a fief to the Sikh leader Ramdas, had political rather than religious reasons, and his interest in the Jesuit fathers sprang from his insatiable curiosity. It seems that the 'un-Islamic' trends in Akbar's politics have also been exaggerated by the Jesuit fathers who had hoped to win him over to Christianity.

After Akbar's death (1605), Salim succeeded him despite his earlier falling out with his father. Akbar's two other sons, Murad and Danyal, had died from the misuse of alcohol and opium. Salim too was addicted to these vices and could be very cruel, yet he tried to continue some of Akbar's religious ideals after his accession. He had an intense veneration for saintly people, particularly the Qadiri saint Mian Mir in Lahore. The Hindu ascetic Gosain Jadrup of Ujjain was Jahangir's friend as well. Jahangir continued his father's visits to Ajmer. During the first year of his reign, however, he had to act against the Sikh *guru* Arjun who had sided in the struggle for succession with Jahangir's son. But the famous, just, Shia *qazi* Nurullah Shushtari of Lahore was executed in 1610 without major reason. Later, under the influence of Nur Jahan, whom Jahangir married in 1611, the Shia element grew stronger at court, which had repercussions on political decisions. But the emperor was more interested in natural sciences and fine arts than in politics and left politics, especially in the Deccan, to his able generals.

The situation did not change much under Shahjahan although he was slightly more orthodox than his father. He liked to think of himself as heir to King Solomon, as art works from his reign prove, implying that he wanted to rule justly. He did not reintroduce the *jizyah* but once more levied the pilgrimage tax, against which Brahmins from Benares protested. In 1642 the *Sadr as-sudur*, as the highest religious official, became a *mansabdar* with a personal rank (*zat*) of 4000, which points to the importance of his post. From that time it was ordered that Hindu places of worship should not be repaired or rebuilt, but the prohibition was apparently not too strict.*

The twofold character of Islam in the Subcontinent shows itself best in Shahjahan's two sons, Dara Shikoh the mystic and Aurangzeb the 'fundamentalist'. Dara Shikoh tried to implement the ideas of his great-grandfather Akbar while Aurangzeb wanted India to be a truly Muslim country and tried to maintain the distinctive features of Islam by protecting it against the admixture of Hindu elements—possibly under the influence of some followers of the Naqshbandi master, Ahmad Sirhindi, who had fought against Akbar's 'heresies'.

Aurangzeb, ruling for nearly fifty years after imprisoning his father and killing his brothers, reorganized the religious administration. The collection of *fatwas* issued during his rule, the *Fatwa-i-Alamgiri*, allows an insight into the methods of solving juridical and religious problems. In 1679, halfway through his reign, the *jizyah* was reintroduced (although a great number of irregular taxes were abolished), and the more cheerful aspects of life were rigidly controlled; the *muhtasib* (censor) had to look not only into the activities of the merchants and the quality of products in the bazaar but also into the use or rather misuse of alcohol—hence Christians had to live outside Delhi where they could make and drink their own wine.

Aurangzeb was fond of moderate Sufism. He visited holy men like Abdul Latif Burhanpuri who advised him to lead a virtuous life and protect the oppressed. But as much as he was interested in the mystical poetry of Jalaluddin Rumi (which moved him to tears) he apparently disliked the verse of Hafiz and had his *Divan* banned due to the frequent mention of wine (although both Humayun and Jahangir had used this *Divan* for prognostication). Music was frowned upon, and in 1696 Aurangzeb stopped the performance of the Shia Muharram rites and processions. Certainly with advancing age his attitude was hardening; hence his rule has been criticized by liberal Muslims and Western and Indian historians, while some historians in Pakistan tend to praise his *shariah*-bound rule and his justice. The majestic Badshahi mosque in Lahore reflects his ideals. Aurangzeb, who died in 1707 at the age of almost ninety years, reverted in one respect to the ancient traditions of the House of Timur: he did not want to be buried in a sumptuous mausoleum as his forefathers from Humayun to Shahjahan did, rather, he chose a simple tomb (similar to Babur's tomb in Kabul) in Khuldabad in the Deccan, close to the shrine of a Sufi master—a choice that shows an aspect of the emperor that is often overlooked. His personal life also had been remarkably simple. He did much for the diffusion of education, supported fine scholars and poets and himself wrote beautiful Persian prose.

After Aurangzeb's death the quick succession of powerless rulers did not allow for stable political development, let alone a new religious policy, but they distanced themselves from Aurangzeb's policy and in 1713 Farrukhsiyar abolished the *jizyah*. The rivalry between the Sunni and the Shia factions at court led to the disaster of Nadir Shah's pillaging Delhi in 1739, and to the foundation of the principality (later kingdom) of Awadh with its strong Shia bias. The British slowly but cleverly cemented their position and expanded their rule until the Mughal empire was incorporated into the British Crown after the Revolt of 1857. The last emperor, Bahadur Shah Zafar, a gentle, Sufi-minded man, a fine poet in Urdu, and a good calligrapher, died in Rangoon in exile in 1861.

THE MUGHALS AND SUFISM

Orthodox theology and jurisprudence certainly formed the basis of life and statecraft during Mughal times, but it seems that the influence of mystical currents and thoughts was even more important.

Sufis had settled in the Subcontinent as early as the eleventh century (Hujwiri, d. ca. 1071 in Lahore). Two centuries earlier the martyr-mystic Hallaj had wandered from Gujarat through Sindh and along the Silk Road, and his name remained alive through the ages. Lahore became the first centre of Persian-inspired Muslim culture in the Subcontinent. In the thirteenth century Sufi missionaries such as Muinuddin Chishti of Ajmer, Bakhtiyar Kaki of Mehrauli and others settled in India, as did the Suhrawardi saint, Bahauddin Zakariya of Multan. Sufis played the main role in the Islamization of the Subcontinent. The Chishtiyya remained for

---

* Editor's Note: For further elaboration see the Architecture chapter, pp. 204, 214-5.

centuries the most influential order; it spread rapidly due to the untiring activity of the saints, whose simple and unsophisticated preaching and practice of love of God and one's neighbour impressed many Hindus. The shrine of the Chishti saint Nizamuddin Auliya (d. 1325) is a religious centre in Delhi to this day visited by people of all religions. Ali-yi Hamadani (d. 1385) established the Kubrawiyya in Kashmir, and at the same time the Firdausiyya extended its activities to Bihar. The Shattariyya were important in central India, and the stern Naqshbandiyya gained momentum with the advent of the Mughals.

Babur was accustomed to showing reverence to the Sufis in his Central Asian homeland. His family had connections with the Naqshbandiyya and in his lively memoirs he tells some interesting stories about them. Babur's interest in Sufism led him to translate a treatise by the leading Naqshbandi saint of Central Asia, Khwaja Ahrar (d. 1490) into Turkish verse (*Risala-yi Walidiyya*) and he called himself in a verse 'the servant of the dervishes'. Later, members of the family of Khwaja Ahrar intermarried with the Mughals. In India, Babur turned his interest to the Chishti order, which thereafter remained closely associated with the dynasty. An outspoken interest in religious problems remained a continuing feature among both the men and women of the Mughal family.

Babur's son Humayun was a great believer in Sufi saints and during his exile in Iran he visited the mausoleums of several major saints such as Abdullah-i Ansari (d. 1089), Ala ad-daula Simnani and others. But his special master was Shah Phul or Buhlul, whose family claimed descent from the great Sufi poet Fariduddin Attar. Shah Phul was a specialist in incantations and exorcism; he was executed by Humayun's brother Hindal who disliked and feared his influence upon the then fugitive Humayun.

Shah Phul's brother Muhammad Ghaus Gwaliori (d. 1562) exerted a much greater influence, if not on the rulers, then upon the people. He composed his main work, the *Jawahir-i Khamsa*, 'Five Jewels,' in both Arabic and Persian; this is a combination of mystical, cosmological and magical teaching, difficult to disentangle by the un-initiated. The theologian Ali al-Muttaqi issued a *fatwa* against Muhammad Ghaus. However Tansen, the greatest musician at Akbar's court, was a devotee of Muhammad Ghaus, and it may well be that his beautiful mausoleum in Gwalior, with its intricate marble lattice work, was sponsored by Tansen, whose modest tomb is situated only a few steps from that of the mystic. Music was, after all, the best way to an understanding between Hinduism and Islam—and was therefore disliked by the strictly orthodox Muslims.

Akbar, it is told, liked to listen to the spiritual letters of the Bihari saint Sharafaddin Maneri (d. 1380) as well as to Maulana Rumi's poetry, but he was mainly attracted by the Chishti masters. The relations of the earlier northern Indian rulers with Nizamuddin Auliya of Delhi are well known, and his shrine remained the spiritual centre of Delhi which every official guest had to visit (such as the Ottoman captain Piri Reis in 1555). Akbar visited Muinuddin Chishti's shrine in Ajmer first in 1564, and continued his annual visits until 1579; from 1580 onward his son Danyal, born in Ajmer, replaced him. Akbar endowed the shrine with many precious objects, such as enormous candlesticks and the cauldrons from which visitors during the *urs* are fed. Jahangir also donated a silver railing and a cauldron to the shrine, as he tells in his memoirs (1613), and Princess Jahanara, Shahjahan's daughter, visited Ajmer after her recovery from terrible burns.

Since Akbar trusted in the Chishtis he also asked the Chishti master Salim of Sikri to pray for a son for him, and after the birth of Salim (named after the saint) in 1569 the emperor began to build the city of Fatehpur Sikri, not far from his then capital, Agra. He resided only fifteen years in this magnificent city of red sandstone in which Salim Chishti's shrine of white marble stands like a luminous pearl. In Fatehpur Sikri some of Akbar's ideals were realized; here the discussions with members of different religious groups took place and his own religious ideas were formulated. He left the city in 1585 to settle for a long period in Lahore. The enormous gateway of Fatehpur bears the inscription 'The world is a bridge; pass over it but do not build a house on it.' The superb calligraphy of this saying, which tradition ascribes to Jesus, was executed in 1601 by Mir Masum Nami, the Sindhi author, calligrapher, physician and diplomat, which shows that Fatehpur remained important for Akbar even after he had left it.

Visits by Akbar to other Sufi centres are mentioned; the tomb of the famous Sufi hero Salar Masud in

Bahraich is among them, as well as Pakpattan, where the Chishti Fariduddin Shakarganj (d. 1265) is buried. Yet, there was also a negative reaction to his predilections. His very positive attitude towards mystical movements aroused the aversion of the more rigid Muslims, as can be seen from Badauni's poisonous remarks. But even a Sufi master began to criticize Akbar's lenient attitude to 'pure' Islam. That was Ahmad Sirhindi, a disciple of Khwaja Baqibillah, the Naqshbandi.

Ahmad Sirhindi began his religious career with a treatise against the Shia—a topic that remained important in Mughal political life. Then the young writer, who was born into a Chishti-Sabiri family, began to counteract Akbar's ideas; his tolerance and his sympathy with Hindus and his, as it seemed, heretical ideas were not compatible with Ahmad's understanding of Islam. He wrote numerous (534!) letters to the leading figures of the empire to convince them of the danger hidden behind such devious movements and to call them back to the strict understanding of Prophetic traditions. These letters became an important means in the hands of reformers during the subsequent centuries and were translated into Turkish as well.

Ahmad Sirhindi developed daring ideas of his own and saw himself as the reformer, nay rather the renewer of Islam—hence his sobriquet *mujaddid*, the renewer who appears on the scene at the beginning of each century. Ahmad, however, is the *mujaddid-i alf-i thani*, the 'renewer of the second millennium of the Hijra.' With a daring cabalistic theory, he showed that the name 'Muhammad' in the course of the first millennium had changed into 'Ahmad,' and thus established a very special relationship between the Prophet (PBUH) and himself. Against Ibn Arabi's theory of *wahdat al wujud*, 'Unity of Being,' he emphasized the idea of *wahdat ash-shuhud*, 'Unity of the visionary experience', which means that the mystic experiences unification for a moment but realises that as a creature he can never be fully united with the Divine, and instead of saying 'Everything is He', he realizes that 'Everything is from Him'. Sirhindi's claims went too far, and it is not surprising that Jahangir, who became aware of the reformer's criticism of Mughal religious policy, had him imprisoned in 1619 in the fortress of Gwalior, where he underwent the spiritual experience of *jalal*, 'God's tremendous power'. Released after one year, and reinstated in Jahangir's favour, the *mujaddid* continued his preaching and writing until his death in 1624. His shrine in Sirhind is a place of pious visits, and even Iqbal went there in 1932. But some of his contemporaries, such as the great *muhaddith* (scholar of *hadith*) of Delhi, Abdul Haq, were critical of Sirhindi's far reaching claims.

One of these claims was that three of his descendants would be the *qayyum*, as he himself was; that is the highest rank in the spiritual hierarchy, superior even to that of the *qutb*, the 'axis', the leader of the entire Sufi hierarchy. It is a strange coincidence that shortly after the death of the last *qayyum*, Pir Muhammad Zubair in 1739, Nadir Shah plundered Delhi and returned to Iran with the unlimited wealth of the Mughals—as though the blessing power of the *qayyums* had indeed come to an end! However it is difficult to assess what role the *qayyums* really played between 1624 and 1739—the works written about them, such as the still unpublished *Raudat al-Qayyumiyya*, are filled with miracle stories and speak of the enormous respect the Mughal rulers had for them. But we deal here with hagiography rather than with history.

In one way the spiritual presence of the successors of the *mujaddid* remained strong: one of the disciples of the last *qayyum*, Muhammad Nasir Andalib of Delhi (d. 1758), became the founder of the *Tariqa Muhammadiyya*, a mystico-fundamentalist movement which was to develop into a military movement at the beginning of the nineteenth century, directed first against the Sikh, then against the British. Andalib's son, Mir Dard (d. 1785) however, became the first major Urdu poet to write mystical verse of great beauty; his major prose work *Ilm ul-Kitab* offers an interesting survey of his mystical experiences. Supported first by one of Aurangzeb's daughters, Dard later became a friend of the emperor Shah Alam II, 'Aftab', who had finally reached Delhi in 1770 after 'ruling' in exile from Allahabad and Lucknow. This poetically-minded ruler sometimes attended the musical sessions which Dard, contrary to the negative Naqshbandi attitude to music, arranged in his house.

Dard was not the only leading Naqshbandi in Delhi. The empire crumbled after the constant attacks of Iranians, Afghans, Marathas, and Sikhs, and the rulers looked for someone to cope with these difficulties on the spiritual level. That was Shah Waliullah, the son of one

MANUSCRIPT OF THE QURAN.
Naskh script with gold leaf. 17th century. Photo: Mohammed Ali Qadir. Courtesy of Mohatta Palace Museum, Karachi.
Qalam: The Arts of Calligraphy exhibition. NM 1965-182.

of the jurists who worked on the compilation of the *Fatawa-i Alamgiri*. He spent several years in Mecca and then returned to Delhi. Initiated into the four major Sufi orders he tried to prove that all of them were equal, as were the four orthodox *madhhab* (legal schools of Islam).

His main aim was to stimulate unity among the Muslims to resist the external and internal disorder. To him the main reason for the unfortunate situation of the Indian Muslims was their ignorance in religious matters. Therefore he translated the Quran into Persian, the language of the intelligentsia; later, two of his sons continued his work by translating the Holy Writ into Urdu. In his *Hujjat Allah al-baligha*, Shah Waliullah tried for the first time an analysis of the reasons for the plight of the Muslims, and this work is still being taught at Al-Azhar in Cairo, despite its very idiosyncratic Arabic style. One has to keep in mind that *Hujjat Allah* is the title usually given to the *Mahdi*, and Shah Waliullah claimed for himself another title usually connected with the *Mahdi*, that is, *Qaim az-zaman*. God, so he said, made him 'His vicegerent in blaming', that is, he is charged with blaming the Muslims for all their faults. On the one hand this entails attacks on the philosophers in the same way we find them in the writings of Sanai and Attar in the Middle Ages. On the other hand he is also averse to those so-called Sufis whom he, like his contemporary Dard, blames as *karamat-furushan*, 'miracle mongers', just as he speaks against visits to the shrines of men like Salar Masud and other legendary Sufis, which amounts, for him, to idolatry.

The Mughal government sought the assistance of the active theologians to solve the problems posed by the Sikhs and the Marathas. Strangely enough, the danger that was posed by the British, who after their victory in 1757 at Plassey, Bengal, insidiously and with great determination advanced westward, was apparently not realized. Shah Waliullah suggested asking the Afghans for help, but the helpers were worse than the enemy and Delhi was once more pillaged, its inhabitants massacred—events described by some contemporaneous poets who lamented the fate of 'Delhi, where now tears flow instead of the river.'

Shah Waliullah died in 1762, while another member of the Naqshbandiyya, Mazhar Jan-e Janan, was killed by a fanatic Shia in 1781—the shaikh, whose *tariqa* is still flourishing in India, had ridiculed a Muharram procession.

A few years later, Shah Alam II was blinded by a young Rohilla, and although the *shariah* requires that the rulers have no corporeal defects, he stayed in office under British protection until he died in 1806. A tendency to mystical thought among the aristocracy continued to the end of the Mughal empire in 1858.

The Naqshbandiyya played a very special role under the Mughals from the very beginning, as much as they contrast with the music-loving Chishtiyya. But another *tariqa* too became important—the Qadiriyya, first introduced in the Deccan, then in Uch in southern Punjab and the adjacent province of Sindh. The Qadiri saint, Mian Mir settled in Lahore where Jahangir was impressed by his piety. Through the emperor, his grandson Dara Shikoh had his first contacts with the saint. The young prince and his sister Jahanara, one year senior to him, became disciples of the saint to whom Dara Shikoh devoted a fine biography, *Sakinat al-Auliya*. After her mother Mumtaz Mahal's death in 1631, Princess Jahanara, then eighteen years of age, took over the duties of First Lady of the great Mughal empire, and yet she found time to pursue her interest in mystical thought and was initiated into the Qadiriyya by Mian Mir's successor Molla Shah Badakhshi, who thought her to be worthy of becoming his successor, 'if the rules of the *tariqa* would permit that'.

Despite her Qadiri affiliation, Jahanara remained faithful to the family tradition of visiting the sacred places of the Chishtiyya, such as Ajmer, where she went after recovering from her accident. After Aurangzeb's ascent to the throne and Dara Shikoh's execution in 1659, Jahanara devoted herself to the service of her imprisoned father. But she continued patronizing scholarly work, especially Sufi literature, so that a good number of commentaries to Rumi's *Masnavi* were composed during her days. When she died in 1689 she chose to be buried in Delhi in the courtyard of the shrine of Nizamuddin Auliya, in a modest open enclosure, while her brother is buried not far from that place, in Humayun's tomb. Although all Mughal ladies were highly educated, of special note is Aurangzeb's daughter Zebunnisa, a poet, who followed her aunt's example and chose the path of mysticism and scholarship and her equally well educated sister Zinatunnisa, famous for her charity.

Dara Shikoh had been interested in mystical thought and practice from his youth. He copied classical Sufi texts, such as a *masnavi* by Rumi's son Sultan Walad, and collected mystical sayings and stories; his only independent book is Mian Mir's biography, which also contains some pages on the saint's pious sister, Bibi Jamal. Dara Shikoh's poetry follows traditional patterns, but his line 'Paradise is where there is no mullah' has been quoted time and again. Following Akbar's attempts to create a *Majma al-bahrain*, the 'Mingling of the Two Oceans' (Quran 18:60), he discussed mystical terminology with the Hindu sage Baba Lal Das and thought that the *Upanishads* might be the 'book that is hidden' (Quran 56:78). In 1657 he published a translation of fifty *Upanishads*. Dara Shikoh had to pay for his undertaking with his life and the unusual people with whom he used to surround himself (such as Sarmad or the Hindu Brahmin) certainly added to the orthodox faction's aversion to him.

RELIGIONS OF THE MUGHAL EMPIRE

Hindus

Persian and Persianate literature often use the contrasts of 'Turk and Hindu', the Turk representing the radiant, strong but generally cruel, white beloved, and the lover, the dark-skinned, lowly, meek Hindu. To a certain extent, this poetical expression reflected social realities, especially after northern India had been conquered by Mahmud of Ghazna (d. 1030). However, the great scholar, Al-Biruni (d. 1048), who wrote the first objective account of India and Indian thought, showed Hindu social perceptions to be the opposite: for the Hindus the Muslims were *mlechha*, 'dirty', that is, their company was defiling.

As we mentioned, from the days of Muhammad ibn Qasim the Hindus and Buddhists were regarded and treated as *ahl al-kitab* and had to pay the *jizyah*; but Akbar, hoping for a reconciliation of the two major communities of his empire finally cancelled the *jizyah* in 1564. This action went together with Akbar's attempt to raise Hindus to high positions. The keeping of the revenue records had always been a domain of Hindus. They worked in the lower and middle echelons of the revenue departments; but it was under Akbar that a Hindu, Todar Mal, was appointed minister of finance for the first time. To understand the significance of this act one has to remember that an ultra-orthodox historian such as Barani (d. ca. 1360) had objected even to the possibility that a recent convert from Hinduism to Islam might occupy a responsible position in the administration; only people of pure Turkish extraction should be eligible. This attitude changed dramatically in Akbar's time: in 1594-5 we find eight Hindus among the twelve provincial finance ministers.

Akbar also made use of the military skill of leading Rajput rajas, most importantly of Raja Man Singh, about whose role in the fight against the Raushaniyya even the most outspoken Muslim writer, Badauni, admiringly quotes the verse: 'A Hindu wields the sword of Islam.'

Akbar's attempts to seek a reconciliation between Hinduism and Islam becomes clear from his numerous marriages with Rajput ladies—beginning with the mother of his future successor, Salim Jahangir. Thus he secured the help of their families. The ladies were allowed to continue their customs and their worship inside the palace.

Akbar was interested in making the contents of Hindu literature known to members of the Muslim elite. As early as the thirteenth century the Hathayoga treatise *Amrtakunda*, the 'Well of Immortality', had been translated into Arabic in Bengal, and during Akbar's days a new translation of this work was produced among the disciples of the great Sufi Muhammad Ghaus Gwaliori. But Akbar wanted more: the *Mahabharata*, the *Ramayana* and a number of other important Sanskrit works were rendered into Persian. Badauni, one of the translators, hated this assignment thoroughly. Could there be anything more foolish than the nightmare-like stories of the *Mahabharata*?

Yet other translators participated in the task so that the translation was completed in 1587, and three years later the Persian version of the *Ramayana* was finished. We deal here not with direct translation in the modern sense of the word; Badauni, Faizi, and other intellectuals were brought up in the Arabo-Persian tradition and it is difficult to imagine that these men should have known enough Sanskrit to undertake the task of rendering these enormous works into Persian. They worked with Hindus who were conversant with Persian and/or early Hindi and translated the texts word by word while the Muslim translators then polished the text. The same method was employed three generations later when Prince Dara Shikoh translated the *Upanishads* into Persian. One aspect of the great Indian epics was highly important for Mughal culture: the illustrations of the *Mahabharata*, *Harivamsa* and other epics. Many painters who lived at Akbar's court were Hindus whose style was increasingly refined under the influence of Persian artists, and many of their miniature paintings and illustrations of the great epics are of breathtaking beauty. The Hindus Govardhan and Basawan were among

Akbar's most appreciated artists, and paintings that show ascetics, dust-covered yogi or meetings of Mughal princes with a yogi are among the finest and most spiritual works of the Akbar and Jahangir periods.

The mystical aspects of Hinduism proved quite attractive to some Muslims, in particular to Akbar and to a certain extent his son Jahangir and his great-grandson Dara Shikoh. Both book illustrations and single miniatures show scenes of meetings between the ruler and a yogi. We read that Ganga Rishi came to Akbar during his stay in Kashmir, and Jahangir was fascinated by the yogi Gosain Jadrup in Ujjain in 1617 as he tells in his *Tuzuk* (I 355 ff.). The exact influence of the Natha Siddhas and the entire Bhakti movement on mystical Islam is not yet completely elucidated, but the feeling that (as Jahangir writes) 'the science of Vedanta is the science of Sufism' fascinated some Mughal rulers.

Certain Hindu rites and customs which on the whole seemed appalling to the normal Muslim, such as *suttee* (self-immolation of a widow on her husband's funeral pyre) played a role in Mughal home politics: Akbar once voiced his admiration for Hindu widows who were willing to perform *suttee* after their husbands' death; yet, in 1583 he ordered that no wife should be forced to follow her husband on the funeral pyre. But it was during his reign (and would probably not have been possible under another Muslim king) that a Persian epic poem about a woman committing *suttee* was composed in India. This is Nawi's '*Soz u gudaz*', which was dedicated to Prince Danyal and was lavishly illustrated by contemporary artists. One should not forget that a considerable number of Hindu writers enjoyed Akbar's patronage, and Sanskrit learning was encouraged by the court. Even the powerful Hindu minister of finance, Todar Mal, composed an encyclopaedia of Sanskrit knowledge with the help of some Pundits, and more than one poet was honoured by Akbar with the title *Mahakavirai*, which corresponds approximately to *Malikush-Shuara*, the poet laureate. Scholarly works, especially treatises about astrology, were appreciated by the Mughals up to the reign of Shahjahan. Other Hindus using Hindi for their poetical works, such as the great Tulsidas, a friend of Akbar's leading commanders, the Khankhanan and Man Singh, appear several times among those honoured by the rulers.

Under Jahangir the situation changed slightly. As much as he enjoyed talking to Gosain Jadrup and as much as in his time the *Yoga Vahishta* was rendered into Persian, yet, when it came to hard reality he could be quite intolerant. In his *Tuzuk* he tells how he broke an idol with a boar's head (that is, an incarnation of Vishnu as a boar) and speaks of the 'worthless religion of the Hindus'. Nevertheless, to destroy temples was only permissible in wartime; new temples, however, should not be built.

Under Shahjahan, no proselytising activities of the Hindus were allowed. Yet the interest in Hinduism continued to be strong. Hindu poets lived at court and were highly esteemed by the ruler—we need only to remember Chandarbhan Brahman, Dara Shikoh's secretary whose detailed descriptions of the activities and peculiarities of Shahjahan's court are found in his *Chahar chaman*, 'Four Meadows', which contains also a fine description of Lahore.

The prince-royal Dara Shikoh, mystically-minded as he was, tried once more to bridge the gap between the two religio-social systems in his hoped-for future kingdom, thus extending Akbar's plans, though without his ancestor's immense strength. Dara Shikoh's conversation with Baba Lal Das, which took place in Kashmir in 1653, shows this lively interest in Hinduism. That holds even more true for his translation, or better, rendering, of fifty *Upanishads* into Persian, which he undertook with the help of some Pundits. This was published in 1657 under the title *Sirr-i Akbar*, 'the greatest secret'. It was this Persian translation which was later rendered into Latin by the French orientalist, Anquetil Duperron, under the title of '*Oupnekhat, id est secretum tegendum*'. The translation appeared in 1803 and kindled the interest of European (and in particular German) philosophers in the mystical heritage of ancient India, thus creating a romantic image of India that still looms large in the minds of some people.

It is not surprising that Dara Shikoh was an admirer of the mystical philosophy of the great Andalusian (Spanish) theosophist Ibn Arabi (1165-1240) and a friend of one of his greatest Indo-Muslim interpreters, Muhibbullah Allahabadi, for the idea of 'Unity of Being' as proposed by the Muslim thinker seemed to be related to, nay, even identical with the *Advaita* of the *Upanishads*. This mystical attitude would enable people to experience the *Majma al-bahrain*, the 'Mingling of the Two Oceans' (as Dara Shikoh called one of his books, using a Quranic expression). The similarities of expressions and imagery

THE ASCETIC AND THE QUEEN.
Late Mughal, Lucknow or Bikaner; second quarter of the 18th century.
Courtesy of the Goenka Collection.

in mystical trends of Islam and Hinduism could easily lead to a blurring of the boundaries both in high literature and in mystical folk tradition.

We can add that Hindus would (and still will) participate in the *melas*, the fairs, of Muslim saints, for 'while the mosque separates, the shrine unites'. Dara Shikoh's younger brother Aurangzeb however considered such movements dangerous for the position and survival of the Muslim kingdom; but he too, though disallowing some practices, employed numerous Hindu military leaders and administrators.*

Hinduism remained vital and creative throughout the Mughal period. The most sober definition of Hinduism in later Mughal times was given by Mazhar Jan-e Janan of Delhi (d. 1781), a leading master of the Naqshbandiyya order, who, in contrast to the usual stance of this order, stated that Hindus are basically monotheists, but after the Prophet's appearance their religion should be regarded as abrogated.

Christians

Christians had been living in the southern part of India from very early times, and after the Portuguese captured Goa in 1510, contacts between them and the Muslims were soon established. Akbar had his first encounter with the Portuguese in 1573 during the siege of Surat, and in 1578 a Jesuit father from Satgaon appeared in Fatehpur Sikri. The most important contact between Akbar and the Christians took place when the Jesuit fathers, Rudolfo Aquaviva and Montserrate were invited to the capital in 1580. Akbar, keenly interested in learning more about Christianity, often listened to them. The letters sent by Montserrate to Rome give a lively picture of Akbar's attitude. Mughal miniature pictures show the venerable fathers in their black habit among the colourfully attired Mughal nobles and religious leaders.

Montserrate mentions Akbar's interest in and admiration for the Virgin Mary and Jesus—a fact that should not have astounded him for in many places the Quran mentions Isa ibn Maryam (Jesus) and his virgin mother with great reverence, as Jesus is the last of the God-sent prophets before Muhammad (PBUH). The Jesuits took the emperor's interest in the Christian tradition as a sign of his willingness to be baptised. But they were mistaken, even though the emperor—seemingly no longer bound to the rules and customs of Islam—once even celebrated Christmas with them. In 1603 a *farman* permitted the Christians to make converts in the country, and already somewhat earlier churches had been built in Agra (on land gifted by the emperor), Lahore, Cambay, and Thatta. The Jesuit fathers even received a daily allowance from the emperor so that they could live in India without difficulties. It sounds strange too that the little sons of Akbar's youngest son Danyal were baptised in 1611 under Jahangir, only to re-enter the fold of Islam shortly afterwards. But that was done for political reasons, in order to exclude them from a possible succession.

The *Akbarnama* (III 874) also mentions the visit in 1590 of a Greek Orthodox priest from Goa, who was asked by Akbar about a possible translation of Christian books into Persian, but nothing is mentioned about the case later. Although the Jesuits naturally failed in their attempts at converting Akbar, yet their presence inspired many an artist at court. The precious gift of the Polyglot Bible, which had been prepared for Philip II in the years 1569-72 and contained many pictures, was regarded at the court as a true treasure. This Bible and other books with pictures inspired Mughal painters; thus we find not only more or less faithful copies of drawings of the Virgin and Child and even of the crucifixion (despite the Quranic statement in Sura 4:157 'They did not kill him and did not crucify him') but more importantly the Mughal painters became interested in the technique of perspective, of naturalistic flowers and of buildings as they were found in the Christian painterly tradition. The influence extends also to buildings whose mural decorations clearly show traces of Christian influence, in particular in Jahangir's time.

The Jesuit fathers were not the only ones to inform the Mughals about life in the Christian world. Some ambassadors from Europe reached 'Agra and Lahore of Great Moghul' (as Milton says), for instance Sir Thomas Roe, or fortune seekers such as Manucci. Their reports from the court are important sources of knowledge of Mughal life (the fact that some of the European visitors posed—apparently successfully—as physicians allowed them quite a few insights into Mughal life).

---

* Editor's Note: For more information on the increase in employment of Hindus in Aurangzeb's reign, see p. xix n. 1.

The interest of Mughals in Christian literature continued to a certain extent after Akbar. The Portuguese Father Jerome Xavier, who even accompanied the emperor to Kashmir, wrote two works about Christianity, one of which was completed under Jahangir. Later, however, the attitude toward the Christians hardened, for the simple reason that the Portuguese tried to extend their power in Hughli, Bengal. Therefore Shahjahan destroyed the church in Agra. Increasing tensions between Muslims and Christians resulted from the fact that more and more Europeans arrived in India; the age of colonisation began, and this fact, naturally, induced the rulers to counteract the activities of the Portuguese, French, and British who were slowly settling in the country.

The fruitful discussions with priests from Europe which had begun in Akbar's *ibadatkhana* seemed to be finished for two centuries, until during the last decades of the Mughal empire religious debates of Muslim scholars with European missionaries began to occupy Indian intellectuals. But that is another story.

Zoroastrians

In the late seventh and early eighth centuries a number of Zoroastrians (Parsees) left Iran to settle on the west coast of India, mainly in Bombay and Gujarat. Karachi too boasts a small but active Parsee community. They were mainly merchants and apparently came into prominence under Akbar when some of their priests, *mobeds*, participated in the discussions in his *ibadatkhana* (thus in 1578). The emperor was apparently very impressed by their work ethic as well as by the purity of their practices, and his love of light (a Muslim symbol) and fire was possibly strengthened by his appreciation of their fire worship: a fire was kept burning constantly in his palace and his devotions were connected with the light; they took place at sunrise, noon, evening, and midnight (which of course is contrary to the Muslim prayer times, which never coincide with the actual sunrise or sunset). The dualistic Zoroastrian worldview and the emphasis upon the eternal struggle between good and evil interested him as well. We may speculate as to whether or not some elements of the *Din-i Ilahi* were adopted from or at least influenced by Zoroastrian thought.

Peaceful relations between the empire and Parsees continued into the later Mughal time; during the last decades of the Mughal period they began to participate actively in the cultural and educational life of the Subcontinent.

Jews

A group of Jews also found a place in Gujarat, since that part of the Subcontinent was so easy to reach from the Middle East—the sea route between Hadramaut and the west coast plays an important role in South Asian history. Long before Islam spread in the Subcontinent, a number of Jews had settled on the coast, and to this day an interesting Jewish community lives in Bombay. But this small group apparently did not attract the interest of the Mughals.

One strange Jewish character, however, appeared in Shahjahan's days—that is Sarmad, a Persian or Armenian Jew who was interested in religion; after studying Christian and Islamic theology in Iran with Mullah Sadra he converted to Islam. He then reached Karachi as a merchant, fell in love with a Hindu boy and turned into a wandering dervish, walking around stark naked (which is prohibited by the *shariah*). Sarmad became known as the author of excellent quatrains, (*rubaiyat*) and began to live in the tradition of the martyr mystic al-Hallaj (executed in 922). Like this great Baghdadi Sufi, he too was executed, in 1661. Dara Shikoh's friendship with this exotic figure doubtless contributed to the aversion of the orthodox to the prince-royal; but that certainly had nothing to do with his Jewish background. Recently, however, some Jewish writers from Bombay have tried to revive Sarmad's memory and to celebrate his anniversary at his modest tomb near the Great Mosque of Delhi.

Jains

The Jains were a small religious community in Gujarat who continued the ascetic practices of olden times. They were vegetarians, something that attracted Akbar to a certain extent; but otherwise they had little impact on Mughal culture. During Akbar's time some Jain monuments were destroyed, but the emperor asked the governor of Gujarat to protect the temples from further damage; new temples were also erected there during his reign.

In 1583, some Jain monks appeared in Fatehpur Sikri for the first time but did not play a major role in Akbar's religious scheme. Some Muslims disliked them as the sect of *Digambaras* used to walk around only 'clad in air' and were thus in conflict with the *shariah*. However, some Jain scholars who composed major Sanskrit works were honoured by Akbar—one of them even composed 128 Sanskrit verses in praise of the emperor! Another Jain scholar was honoured by Akbar with the title of *Jagat Guru*, the Teacher of the World.

The only major clash between the Mughals and the Jains was a result not of religious but rather of political reasons; during Jahangir's time Rai Singh of Bikaner rebelled because a Jain prophecy had announced that Jahangir would be overthrown. This rebellion led to Rai Singh's punishment and the expulsion of the Jains from the imperial territory.

Sikhs

Many syncretistic movements appeared in India in the course of time, and mystics from both the Hindu and the Muslim tradition felt the necessity of working for a better understanding between their adherents. The poetry of the fifteenth-century mystic Kabir, who is claimed by both Muslims and Hindus, is a fine example of this trend.

Out of such feelings grew a group of seekers under the leadership of *Guru* Nanak: the Sikhs. Akbar gave Amritsar as a grant to *Guru* Ramdas, and ever since this city with its Golden Temple has remained the centre of the Sikh religion.

Sikhism is probably the only religion that developed from a mystical, peaceful faith with a tendency to unify the different religions, into a militant group of devoted warriors who are no longer known as worshipful, mild mystics but rather as energetic, martial men, mainly from the Punjab. The reason for this surprising change lies probably in the fact that Jahangir, shortly after his accession to the throne, had executed *Guru* Arjun (1606)—as so often happens, not for religious but for political reasons. For when Prince Khusrau, Jahangir's firstborn son, rebelled against his father, the Sikh *Guru* Arjun sided with him and blessed him. This, understandably, resulted in Jahangir's revenge.

Guru Arjun's role in Sikh history is central not only because of his execution, which made him the arch-martyr of Sikhism, but even more as the one who is credited with the collection of the *Adi Granth*. The importance ascribed by the Sikh to this sacred book may well be inspired by the Muslim reverence for the Quran. The *Adi Granth* contains mystically coloured poetry by Hindu, Muslim, and Sikh poets. *Guru* Arjun was apparently the first to organize his followers into a closely knit group.

Somewhat later, and again for political reasons, *Guru* Hargovind was imprisoned. This was not a persecution of the Sikh community for religious reasons, although Hargovind's two sons were also killed.

Yet again, under Aurangzeb, politics contributed to a further deterioration of relations. During the struggle for Shahjahan's succession, the Sikh *Guru* Har Rai sided with Dara Shikoh (only to desert him later) and it was his successor *Guru* Teg Bahadur who was executed in 1675 on Aurangzeb's order. This execution resulted in the active rebellion of the Sikhs, and when in 1710—three years after Aurangzeb's death—the tenth *Guru*, Govind Singh, was assassinated, the Sikhs gathered momentum and committed terrible atrocities in the Punjab. From that time onwards the group—consisting of fierce Punjabi warriors—turned into dangerous enemies of the Mughal rulers. The Mughal empire was, in any case, weakened by corruption and an interminable struggle against the Marathas approaching from the south, the British from Bengal, and a number of so-called Muslim friends, be it the Afghans or the Rohilla. Thus the Sikh community finally achieved such political power that the Punjab fell completely into their hands. The British installed Ranjit Singh as ruler of the Punjab, only to incorporate this region also into their own possessions in 1849.

MUSLIM RELIGIOUS MOVEMENTS

The Mahdawiyya

One movement that played a considerable role in the early Mughal period was the Mahdawiyya. Many people have claimed, in the course of Muslim history, to be the promised *Mahdi* who will appear at the end of

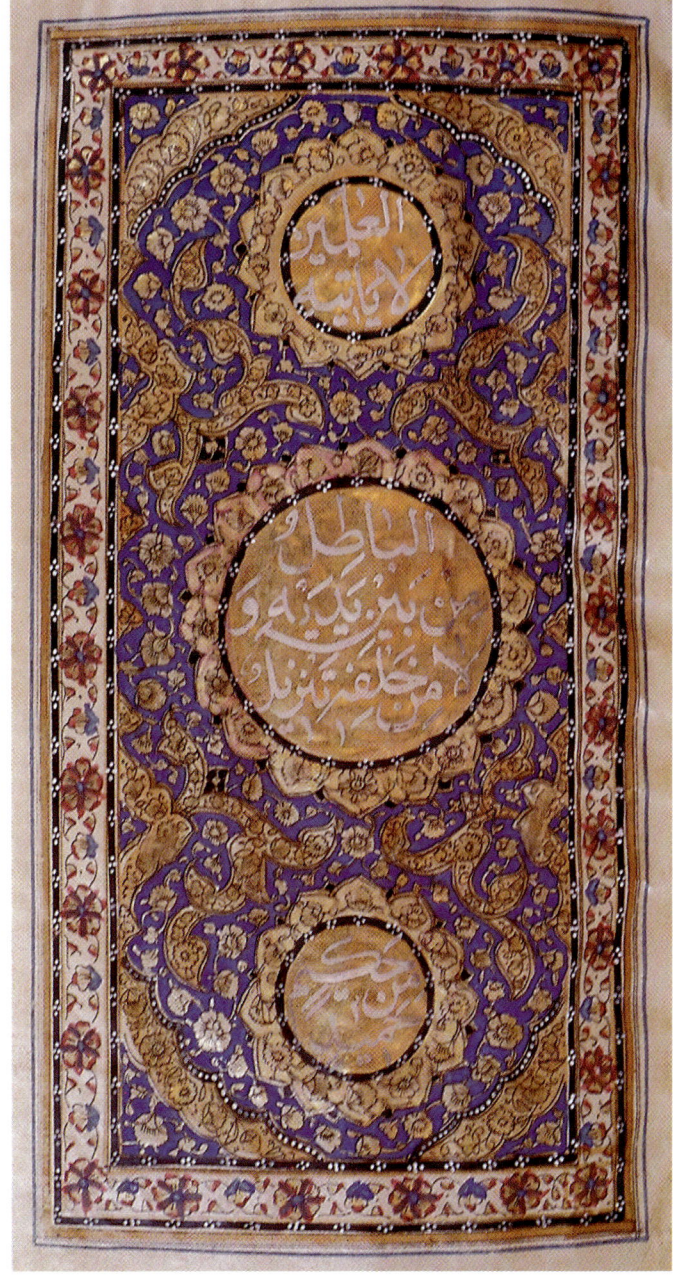

MANUSCRIPT OF THE QURAN.
Naskh script. 18th century. Photo: Mohammed Ali Qadir.
Courtesy of Mohatta Palace Museum, Karachi. Qalam: The Arts of Calligraphy exhibition. NM1972-86.

Meccans, wisely, did not react to this claim, but on his return Kazimi had to face many hardships inflicted by orthodox theologians, especially in Gujarat. He died, a fugitive, in 1505, not far from Herat in present-day Afghanistan.

His tenets were simple. The greatest importance was given to the performance of the *dhikr*, the constant recollection of God. The disciples gathered twice a day for meetings during which the divine name was repeated. Poverty was one of the tenets of the Mahdawis and equal distribution of possessions was expected.

The centre of Mahdawi worship is not the mosque but the *daira*, a simple meeting place. Similarities abound with early, sober Sufism; however, contrary to some Sufi orders the *Mahdi* prohibited music and ecstatic dance. The influence of this movement on serious Muslims went so far that at times anyone who was leading a particularly sober and law-abiding life was regarded as a Mahdawi, hence sometimes persecuted.

The persecutions reached their apex during the Sur interregnum with the connivance of Makhdum ul-Mulk, the *Shaikh ul-Islam*. Shaikh Alai, one of the foremost disciples of the Mahdawi leader Abdullah Niyazi, a Pathan, was cruelly tortured. Shaikh Mubarak, the father of Akbar's friends and his religious guide, actively supported Alai against both the Suris and Makhdum ul-Mulk. Therefore even Shaikh Mubarak was later accused of having been a Mahdawi. Badauni, the pious Muslim, speaks very highly of Alai and Niyazi, admiring their piety and devotion, and even lauds Mubarak's efforts in saving Alai's life. The latter, barely surviving the severe beating that was administerd to him by the Suri authorities, turned back later to orthodox Islam, denying his former association with the Mahdawis.

The persecution and the clashes between the Sunnis and the Mahdawis continued during the latter half of the sixteenth century but the sect survived in small pockets in the Deccan and Sindh despite renewed persecution under Aurangzeb.

The full impact of Mahdawi ideas on literature and politics has still to be studied in detail; it should be mentioned that one of the earliest poets to write in a regional language, namely Malik Muhammad Jayasi, who wrote the epic *Padmawat* in Purabi, was a disciple of Burhanaddin (d. 1562-3), one of the leading Mahdawis of his time. About the same time, the first

time to fill the earth with justice as it is now filled with injustice. One of these preachers was Sayyid Muhammad Kazimi of Jaunpur who during his pilgrimage to Mecca declared himself as the *Mahdi*. The major Sindhi mystic, Qadi Qadan of Sehwan, was, according to some reports, a Mahdawi.

The Raushaniyya

Slightly later than the Mahdawiyya, another religious movement appeared in Subcontinental Islam. This was the Raushaniyya, founded by Bayezid Ansari, called by his followers *pir-i raushan*, 'the luminous master,' and by his adversaries *pir-i tarik*, 'the dark master'. Bayezid came from Waziristan, in the north-west, and at the legendary age of forty he called people to join him in a religious movement that seems to have its root again in Sufism. Bayezid taught the mystical path that began with *tauba*, repentance, and passed through eight steps (as opposed to the generally accepted seven steps of most mystical movements in East and West). The last stage was *sukunat*, 'tranquillity', and the eight may point to the paradisiacal bliss connected with this number, which means 'completion' in many religious traditions.

The origins of Bayezid's ideas have been discussed time and again. He apparently taught his disciples to perform the *chilla*, the forty day seclusion, as do the Sufis. Some scholars regard the movement as born out of Pathan independence ideas. One can also find some similarities with Ismaili thought (were there influences from the Ismaili pockets in Badakhshan via Hunza?).

Whatever the inspiration, Bayezid's great contribution to Muslim culture is that he was the first to compose a religious work, *Khair al-bayan*, in his mother tongue Pushto, which thus became a literary vehicle. Not only did Bayezid's later adversary Akhund Darweza (d. 1631) compose his refutation of Bayezid's teaching, the *Makhzan al-Islam*, in Pushto, but from his time on, Sufis as well as warrior poets in that area used the Pushto language in their works. This movement culminates on the Sufi side in Rahman Baba (d. ca. 1709) and, in general terms, in the poetry of the warrior Khushhal Khan Khattak who, though by no means a late member of the Raushaniyya, voiced his hatred against Aurangzeb in his verse.

The Raushaniyya appeared to Akbar as the most dangerous enemy as they controlled parts of the vulnerable north-western areas of the Subcontinent, and history shows time and again that the security of the country was threatened mostly by invaders from the mountains north and south of the Khyber. We should not forget that Kabul was part of the Mughal empire, and Qandahar a bone of contention between Mughal India and Iran. Hence Akbar sent Man Singh to check the activities of the Pathan tribesmen who had joined Bayezid and his Raushaniyya, endangering the stability of the expanding empire. Although Bayezid was slain in battle in 1575, the danger continued and some of his descendants were killed in Jahangir's time near Attock at the confluence of the Indus and Kabul River. Thus, this important religio-political movement was mercilessly crushed.

The Shia

The dynasties that ruled northern India from the beginning of the second millennium onward were Sunni Turks and Afghans. Small pockets of Shia Muslims were found in the country, and the sources mention the *ibahatiyan*, people who did not follow the official religious line. It may have been members of the Ismaili community whose missionaries had reached the Subcontinent (mainly Gujarat and Sindh) in the twelfth century.

However, neither the Khoja nor the Bohra factions or the Sathpanthis (all parts of the Ismaili movement) seem to have played a particular role during the Mughal period until, in 1839, about twenty years before the end of the Mughal period, the Aga Khan—coming from Iran—settled in Bombay.

As for the Twelver Shia, their role became more conspicuous after Shah Ismail, the first Safavid king, introduced Shia Islam as the official state religion in Iran in 1501, for that made the Shia a political factor. After Humayun's years in Iran, where he allegedly embraced the Shia form of Islam, we witness a steady influx of Shia artists from Iran as the Iranian regime, from the days of Shah Tahmasp's 'sincere repentance' was not very interested in poetry and fine arts. Thus the Shia influence grew in the Subcontinent, and one of the leading figures in early Mughal history, Bairam Khan the Turkoman, was Shia. The fact that the Deccani kingdoms were predominantly ruled by Shia princes gave the defenders of Mughal Sunni supremacy (often called Turanis) an additional reason for caution.

Apparently, Shia scholars did not occupy very high positions during the sixteenth century, and it was a novelty that one of the leading scholars, Nurullah Shushtari, was appointed by Jahangir as chief *qazi* of Lahore. The learned *qazi*, whom even a strict Sunni such as Badauni praises highly, authored a number of important books, among them the *Majalis al-Muminin*, biographies of the major literary figures of Iran and the neighbouring countries; all of them were regarded by the *qazi* as Shias practicing *taqiya*, 'dissimulation', that is, posing as Sunnis to avoid persecution. Shushtari himself was accused of *taqiya* and Jahangir had him flogged to death in 1610 so that he became the 'third martyr' of the Shia.

Despite this cruel act, Jahangir became more lenient toward the Shias after marrying Nur Jahan in 1611. The queen and her family supported Shia tendencies in the court—that was probably one reason for the aversion of the orthodox Sunnis and especially the Naqshbandi Sufis to the regime. From that time onward, the Shia become more prominent, and a certain group of Shia nobility supported Dara Shikoh while Aurangzeb was regarded as a model of a strict Sunni Muslim.

After Nadir Shah's invasion in 1739, members of the Shia nobility were granted the province of Awadh, whose capital was first Faizabad, then Lucknow. The nawabs (from 1819, kings) of Awadh developed a distinct Shia culture, and the province became a haven for Shia literati who no longer found patronage in Delhi after the constant attacks on the once so glorious capital. Delhi, plundered and pillaged more than once from 1739 onward, lost its pivotal cultural importance while in Awadh, both in the field of architecture (the splendid *imambaras*) and literature a highly sophisticated Shia culture developed. Sauda, the satirist who settled late in his life in Awadh, had composed *marsiyas* commemorating the tragedy of Karbala, and the art of *marsiya* became increasingly important in Lucknow. There it was given its ideal form, that is, the form of the *musaddas*, six-line stanzas which enabled poets to tell longwinded stories without boring the audience by the monotony of the traditional mono-rhyme or by the classical *masnavi* form. In the end the *marsiya* was often understood as a symbol for the oppression of Indian Muslims by the British who treated them, as it were, in the same way as Yazid treated the Prophet's (PBUH) grandson Husain.

MYSTICAL POETRY IN THE VERNACULARS

After Dara Shikoh's defeat the Qadiriyya chose to withdraw to a certain extent from public life, but a number of Qadiri Sufis in the Punjab continued teaching and writing. While using Persian for their didactic works they wrote poetry in their local idioms. The development of a literature in the regional languages is a result of Sufi activities during the Mughal period. That is true for Sindh as well as for the Punjab, and to a certain extent for the Pathan areas as well as for the Deccan.

The first poet known to us in this field is Qadi Qadan (d. 1551) of Sehwan in Sindh, Mian Mir's maternal grandfather. He is sometimes thought to be a Mahdawi, but his poetry is no different from any other Sufi writing, except perhaps for the poignant images taken from his environment, the banks of the Indus close to the old Shiva sanctuary of Sehwan, and since the thirteenth century a centre of ecstatic Sufism connected with the name of Lal Shahbaz Qalandar. Qadi Qadan's poetry was known only in a few fragments until some twenty years ago, when a considerable number of *dohas* were discovered in a Hindi manuscript in Haryana (whose authenticity is not beyond doubt). The poet expresses his loving trust in God, who can, for example, be symbolized by a banyan tree that looks like an entire forest and yet is only one tree; and the lover's narrow heart cannot withstand the influx of grace nor contain it but must speak up, just as the canals cannot contain all the water when the Indus is in spate. And if the pilot trusts in God, even a fragile boat can reach its goal and cross the waves better than a strong, tall ship. But Qadi Qadan's most famous *doha* is:

> Leave grammar and syntax to the people
> I study the beloved.

This verse is a kind of keynote for all subsequent mystical poetry in the vernaculars. The piety of learned people is too cerebral for the true lover, and the poets outside the towns never ceased ridiculing the learned jurist who relies on *kanz*, *quduri*, *kafiya*, i.e., the books on hadith, Hanafi law, and Arabic grammar as taught in the *madrasa*. Is it not enough to know the *alif*, the first letter of the Arabic alphabet, which is at the same time a cipher of Allah's unity and unicity and of the slim, graceful stature of the human beloved, as already Hafiz had sung?

The fact that in the mid-sixteenth century religious poetry in the vernaculars appears in the Subcontinent has a parallel in Christian mysticism in the thirteenth century when German or Italian was used instead of the Church's Latin. In the Subcontinent, again, the *bhaktas* used no longer the sacred Sanskrit but sang of their love for the deity in Punjabi, Rajasthani and other languages. The problem as to what extent *bhakti* mysticism and popular Sufism have influenced each other still awaits solution. For not only did the Sufis in Sindh, the Punjab and the Deccan utilize their native idioms from the early Mughal period onward, they also took over the typically Indian concept of the *virahini*, the woman longing for her absent husband or lover, while in the Hindu tradition the emphasis on the personal deity may have developed under the influence of Islamic ideas. In any case, in both traditions, many similar strands can be discovered, and this movement culminates in the Mughal period.

It was not only Qadi Qadan in Sindh who sang mystical poetry in his mother tongue; slightly later we meet Madho Lal Husain (d.1593) in Lahore whose modest tomb at the corner of the Shalimar Gardens is the place of the *chiraghan mela*, the 'candles' fair' in late March. Madho Lal used Punjabi for his daring mystical verse; he must have been a fascinating personality, who was visited by Mughal courtiers (the court was at that time in Lahore), and it is possible that the Khankhanan Abdul Rahim, Akbar's generalissimo, may have been in touch with him. For the commander of Akbar's army was a mystically-minded poet who wrote not only Persian and Turki poems but sang numerous Hindi *dohas* in the style of the contemporary Hindu *bhakti* poets, whom he patronized, beside the numerous Persian poets who adorned his court (it should be recalled that Tulsidas was among his friends). During his long stay in Burhanpur the Khankhanan was in close touch with the mystics of this area.

Burhanpur's mystical tradition should be mentioned here in passing; named after the music-loving Chishti saint Burhanuddin Gharib (d. 1337) and situated at the strategically important river Tapti that formed the border between the north and the Deccani kingdoms, Burhanpur became a refuge for a group of Sindhi weavers who left Sindh in the wake of the wars between Humayun and his adversaries in the early 1540s. Among them were some Sufis, and in the course of the sixteenth century a genuine mystical tradition of mainly Qadiri Sufis developed there. Even a lady mystic, Bubu Rasti, is mentioned as an expert on classical Persian mystical poetry. And it was a Sufi master who came to console the Khankhanan after the assassination of his last son. Not to forget that an important work on the Prophet (PBUH) and his veneration, *Tuhfa al-Mursala ila'n-Nabi*, was composed, in 1620, by Muhammad Fazlullah Burhanpuri, and gained wide acceptance in the eastern part of the Muslim world. Furthermore: Burhanpur became a centre of the Sathpanthi branch of the Ismailis who settled there after a split in the community after 1512. It seems that some of their writings were influenced by Qadiri Sufi literature. However, the different aspects of poetry in the vernaculars, where Muslim and Hindu strands are intricately woven together, have still to be carefully disentangled.

To return to the religious poetry in the vernaculars we have to follow the development of Sindhi as it was first used as a literary language in early Mughal times (as for precedents, nothing written has come down to us). We learn from Badauni that Sindhi singers came to Akbar's court. Akbar also had very friendly relations with the former ruler of Sindh, Mirza Jani Beg, after the Khankhanan had conquered the province in 1591. Both the emperor and his 'prisoner' were fond of the same religious music, and the Sindhi ex-ruler was one of the few members of the *Din-i Ilahi*. Sindhi religious poetry appears first on a larger scale in the work of Abdul Karim of Bulri, who used—apparently for the first time—allusions to the Sindhi folktales such as *Sussi Punhun* or *Sohni Mehanval*. This trend becomes clearly visible in the poetry of Abdul Karim's descendant Shah Abdul Latif of Bhit (d. 1752) whose *Risalo* is the sacred book of every Sindhi, whether Muslim or Hindu. The poet takes up the tragic tales of the Indus valley to transform them into symbols of the soul's longing for the Divine Beloved, and the soul, always a brave woman, undergoes trials and tribulations on the difficult path to be finally united with her beloved through death. Or else she resembles the reed flute cut off from the reedbed and complaining of separation, as Rumi had expressed it in his *Masnavi*.

These similarities are not fortuitous. Rumi's *Masnavi* was well known all over the Subcontinent from the fourteenth century onward and there is barely any mystically-inclined poet who does not allude to at least the first eighteen verses of this great poem. Stories from the *Masnavi* are inserted everywhere, and it would be useful to enumerate and study all the commentaries on and translations from the *Masnavi* during Mughal times. Not only were Mughal princesses like Jahanara and her niece Zebunnisa interested in this book—Akbar liked to listen to it, Dara Shikoh collected lengthy excerpts from it, and even Aurangzeb used to shed tears when the *Masnavi* was read to him. The verses of many Persian-writing poets in India during the Mughal period are replete with allusions to, and insertions from, Rumi's book. *Masnavikhwan*, reciters of the poem, were found everywhere from the capital to the villages in Sindh. The most famous commentary on the *Masnavi*, that by Bahr al-ulum of Lucknow (d. 1810), was completed in Madras.

While Shah Abdul Latif was the singer of 'love in suffering', his younger contemporary Sachal Sarmast, who composed his lyrics in Sindhi, Siraiki, Persian and Urdu, is a typical representative of the ecstatic trends in Sufism, expressing a borderless pantheism. 'Everything is one', and there is no difference between the martyr mystic Hallaj and his judge, nor between Pharaoh and Moses—'everything is He'. Such songs can excite the listeners into near ecstasy even in our day.

But it is understandable that the officials disliked this kind of mystical frenzy, all the more as the political situation in the Indus valley and the Punjab had changed. In 1739, the Persian ruler Nadir Shah asked the Sindhi ruler for an enormous indemnity before proceeding to Delhi. The wise Hindu minister brought him a little bag which, as he claimed, contained the most precious things Sindh possessed, that is, the dust of saints and sayyids (descendants of the Prophet)… Shortly before this happened some Mughal officers had allegedly discovered attempts at overthrowing Mughal rule; it was a Sufi who had been accused by colleagues who were jealous of his attracting numerous poor villagers. This Shah Inayat of Jhok, who had studied in Burhanpur, seemed to preach a kind of religious communism and was then executed for rebellion against the Mughals in 1718.

While the Sindhi poets sang of Divine Love or the Unity of Being, the Naqshbandiya, having established themselves in the Delhi kingdom, reached the provinces and counteracted the ecstatic movement that had inspired so many simple, loving souls. It is to the credit of the Naqshbandis that they attempted to introduce a better understanding of the Quran and the religious tradition. We owe to them some fragmentary translations of the Quran into Sindhi as well as some simple and straightforward introductions to dogmatic and ritualistic questions in Sindhi, through which the language slowly became capable of expressing all themes and topics.

We mentioned in passing, the role of Bayezid Ansari's first religious work in his mother tongue, Pushto, which belongs to the same period as the writings of Qadi Qadan in Sindh and Madho Lal Husain in the Punjab. A long line of Punjabi Sufi poets, mainly connected with the Qadiriyya order, followed. Among them, the master of Jhang in the southern Punjab, Sultan Bahu, must be singled out. Although he wrote theoretical treatises in Persian, he is mainly known for his *Siharfi*, a 'Golden Alphabet', in which each verse begins with one letter of the alphabet, and each line ends with the exclamation *Hu*—'He'. In the first line the poet compares God to a jasmine tree planted by the master into his heart and watered with the water of the profession of faith until it fills his whole being with fragrance. The use of the 'profession of the faith' as *dhikr* formula shows that the author belonged to the Qadiriyya. Some decades later in the northern part of the Punjab, Bullhe Shah of Qasur (d. 1758) sang in the same ecstatic strain as did Sachal, expressing the Unity of Being in his verse. The loving soul represented by the girl Hir is transformed into Ranjha, her beloved, after repeating his name with every breath, or else, the poet, taking up an image typical of the cotton growing areas, sees that 'white are all the cotton flakes' and that the differentiation appears only after the cotton is spun, woven, or coloured: everything is God, the differences are external illusions. Here, again, cross fertilization with the Hindu tradition is visible and it is typical that Hindu expressions found in Bullhe Shah's verse are always glossed over by modern Pakistani translators.

The situation in the Deccan before the Mughal conquest of 1686 and 1687 was similar in form and content, and in the tendency of the Sufis to use their native idiom (Dakhani Urdu) and images taken from the daily life of simple people—especially of women, such as 'spinning songs' or songs for the grinding of flour for the *chapattis* (bread), so that the women could easily follow the descriptions of the religious, the mystical way. Richard Eaton has lucidly shown this development in his book *Sufis of Bijapur*.

RELIGIOUS CUSTOMS

It seems that many of the customs practised today in the Subcontinent were known in Mughal times as well. A typical example that seems to be restricted to the Subcontinent is the introduction of a child to the Quran at the age of 4 years, 4 months and 4 days, which makes the boy *bismillah ka dulha* 'the bridegroom of the *bismillah*.' The child—boy or girl—is given a tablet inscribed with the word *bismillah*, which he or she has to lick off. Both Akbar and Jahangir practised this custom.

The two major religious feasts, Id ul-fitr (celebrating the end of Ramadan) and Id ul-adha (commemorating the sacrifice of Abraham), were of course celebrated. The Id ul-adha, however, caused much pain to the Hindus (as some Muslims would sacrifice cows) and to the strictly vegetarian Jains. Thus, the great feast could become a cause for riots.

A non-Quranic feast was the *shab-i barat*, the night of the full moon in the eighth lunar month, Shaban, when according to common belief the fates are fixed for the next twelve months—it was probably an old New Year's rite. In the Persianate areas it is mentioned at least from ca. 1100 onward. This night is celebrated in prayer and, even more, with fireworks and—as on every special occasion—sweets are made and distributed.

It seems that the *shab-i barat* was more intensely celebrated than the Prophet's (PBUH) birthday. For formerly 12 Rabi al-Awwal (the third lunar month) was celebrated to commemorate the Prophet's death, *barah wafat*, and this is still the case among certain tribes, especially in the Pathan areas. Later, the celebration of this day as the Prophet's (unknown) birthday became widespread, and it was celebrated not only with prayers but with songs in honour of the Prophet (PBUH). The poets, in particular the folk poets writing in the vernaculars, liked to enumerate the miracles ascribed to the Prophet; but even high-ranking theologians like Shah Waliullah composed grand Arabic odes celebrating Muhammad's (PBUH) greatness. And even though Badauni claims that Akbar did not want to hear the Prophet's name mentioned, yet his favourite court poet Faizi composed glorious Persian hymns about the Prophet (PBUH). A special aspect of this hymn form are the simple Sindhi *maulud*, poems about the Prophet, who appears as the beloved bridegroom of the soul. In other songs the bards express their longing for Medina, where his last resting place is located.

The Shia population observed the Muharram rites. These became more elaborate with the establishment of Shia principalities in the former realms of the empire, as in Lucknow and, on a different level, in the Deccan. The Muharram processions, in which participants beat themselves and lament in heartrending tunes, often aroused the anger of orthodox Sunnis, and led to riots between the two factions; that is why Aurangzeb prohibited them. It is worthy of mention that in some parts of the Subcontinent such processions, in which even firewalking was (and still is) practised, could turn into a kind of carnival with strange figures in masks playing an important role, as we can see in eighteenth century miniature paintings from Hyderabad.

The development of dirges, *marsiya*, especially in Lucknow, was mentioned before, as was the importance of the *imambaras*, large and often luxurious buildings where the implements for the Muharram processions (flag, standards, drums, etc.) are preserved during the year. In Muharram, men and women used to, and still do, attend *majlis*. These gatherings during the first ten days of Muharram in private houses kept, and still keep, the ladies busy; they would appear there without makeup and jewellery to listen to the sad stories of Imam Husain's (the martyred grandson of the Prophet) suffering and the recitation of poetry.

Everyone, beginning with the ruler, visited sacred places, such as the shrines of Sufis (Ajmer, Pakpattan, Multan, Rudauli Sharif, Delhi, and others). Shrines were often repaired or built anew. The religious predilections of a prince or an official can be recognized from his interest in certain shrines. The Mughal ladies participated in these activities as well.

The pilgrimage to Mecca was a duty for everyone, but could not be undertaken too frequently as the dangers were very great; the Portuguese had captured Goa and parts of the western coast of India, which made the journey through that region perilous. Some leading Mughal officials such as the Khankhanan Abdur Rahim built special boats to facilitate the pilgrimage. The second route to Mecca was also not without tribulation as it led through parts of Iran where the Shia persuasion was ruling, considered heretical by some staunch Sunnis who therefore avoided journeys through these areas. One should not forget that a pilgrimage to Mecca could also be ordered as a kind of punishment, or in order to get rid of an official who had lost the emperor's favour. On the other hand, the royal ladies—Akbar's aunt and his wife Salima, and numerous noble women—thoroughly enjoyed their lengthy stay in Mecca, despite a dramatic shipwreck on their return trip.

Footprints of the Prophet (PBUH) were venerated in various places and so was the hair of the Prophet. In mosques in different parts of the Subcontinent one finds such a hair which is encased in fine glass and wrapped in layers and layers of perfumed silk. It is somewhat surprising that the chronicles rarely mention one of the most important activities of the Mughals, that is, the building of mosques. A Prophetic tradition used in India from early times claims 'Someone who builds a mosque, even though it be only as small as a qata-bird's nest—God will give him a house in Paradise.'

The majestic mosques built by the Mughals are among the finest examples of religious architecture, as are some of the mausoleums of the sixteenth to eighteenth centuries. The great mosques in Agra, Delhi and finally in Lahore are good examples of the religious strength of the Mughal rulers. Provincial religious architecture is often also of great beauty—suffice it to mention the wonderful mosque in Thatta, Sindh, with its fine blue tilework, or the enormous mosque on the steep rock of Asirgarh—both built by Shahjahan in gratitude for the fact that he found shelter once in Thatta, and once in Asirgarh.

Sometimes the Mughal rulers participated in the festivities of other religious groups, as in the Christmas celebrations of the Jesuits, or in Hindu festivities. Hindu customs such as celebrating Holi were quite generally enjoyed, as becomes evident from their representation in painting.

The Mughals believed firmly in astrology, and miniature paintings depicting the birth of a prince show astrologers sitting in front of the gate, figuring out the future of the child. Even Aurangzeb, after dismissing his Hindu astrologers, employed Muslim astrologers. And poets, such as Ghalib, at the very end of the Mughal period, gives his own horoscope in the first part of a religious Persian poem in honour of Hazrat Ali (RA). Not only that, horoscopes were cast for each and every important action: when to ascend the throne, when to enter a city and much more. Humayun was the ruler who was most dependent upon horoscopes and omens, whether derived from names or from animals, from interpreting birds' flight or, in good old Mongol fashion, looking at a sheep's shoulderblade. He had arranged his entire life according to strict rules depending upon stars, numbers, and names so that each hour was connected with certain occupations or with a specific group of people who were then, and only then, allowed to wait upon him. The influence of the Sufi master Shah Phul is quite clearly visible.

The Mughals also believed in the magic circle: did not Babur walk three times around the bed of the ailing Humayun to take over his illness and substitute his own life for that of his son? The search for omens was also practised by opening the *Divan* of Hafiz. A copy of this book (now in Patna-Bankipore) contains remarks of Humayun and other Mughals about the meaning of this or that verse of Hafiz and its role in their lives. And it is not surprising that Abul Fazl, with his tendency to see Akbar as the Perfect Man, ascribes miracles to him such as producing rain or saving, by the power of his very name, a man from a tiger's attack!

GLOSSARY

Ahl al-Kitab	those who own a God-sent book, i.e., Christians, Jews and Sabians, to whom the Zoroastrians (and Hindus in India) were later added. They have full religious freedom under Muslim rule. The men are exempted from military service. However, since their lives, property and places of worship are protected, the able-bodied men have to pay an exemption tax, *jizyah*, in lieu of military service.
Bhakti	popular mystical current in medieval Hinduism in which the love relation between man and God is emphasized.
Brahmin	a Hindu of the highest caste traditionally assigned to the priesthood.
Chishtiyya	one of the main Sufi orders.
Farman	an order issued by a ruler.
Fatwa	formal legal opinion, pronounced by a lawyer trained in *shariah* law.
Hadith	any authenticated report of what the Prophet Muhammad (PBUH) said or did.
Hijra	emigration of the Prophet Muhammad (PBUH) from Mecca to Medina in AD 622; marks the beginning of the Muslim calendar.
Ijtihad	'striving', the right to go back to the roots of jurisprudence in order to interpret the law, and not to be confined to the solutions codified by one of the legal schools.
Imam	in general, the leader in prayer and/or in other activities; in particular for Shias, a spiritual guide.
Jizyah	(from *jaza*, 'as a compensation') exemption tax paid by the able-bodied men of the *ahl al-kitab* who are in turn protected by the Muslims, and the men exempted from military service.
Madrasa	a school for secular and religious studies; historically, associated with a mosque.
Muharram	first lunar month of the Islamic year. On the 10th of Muharram AD 680 the Prophet's (PBUH) grandson Husain was martyred in the battle of Karbala, an event mourned by all Muslims, especially the Shia.
Mujtahid	someone who exerts the right of *ijtihad*.
Naqshbandiyya	one of the main Sufi orders.
Qazi	a judge who administers Islamic law.
Qadiriyya	one of the Sufi orders.
Sabiri	a sub-order of the Chishtiyya.
Shariah	the Muslim code of law, based on divine revelation, which regulates all aspects of Muslim life.
Shia	see 'Sunni'. From 'Shi-an-Ali' (Friends of Ali). The Muslim sect that asserts the precedence and ascendance of Ali [the son-in-law and cousin of the Prophet (PBUH)] over the first three of the Rightly Guided Khalifas (Abu Bakr, Omar, Usman); and believes that the leadership (*Imamat*) of Islam was bestowed on Ali and his descendants.
Sufism/Sufi	Sufism has been variously described as Islamic esotericism, gnosis and spirituality. Sufis practice all the tenets of the faith, but their special focus is on internalizing the message and spirit of Islam, which emphasizes the primacy of mercy over wrath. The goal of the Sufis is to achieve nearness to God, by assuming the attributes of God as their own, the foremost being love. Sufis seek to emulate the Prophet whom they regard as the embodiment of perfect character. Since Islam is particularly open to diversity of expression, there are many Sufi paths (*tariqas*) to the same goal. The seeker (*salik*) progresses through the stages of extinction of the ego (*fana*), and gnosis (*irfan*), to ultimate union (*wisal*).
Suhrawardiyya	one of the Sufi orders.
Sunni	one who follows the tradition (*sunna*) of the Prophet (PBUH). The Shia also follow the main creed of Islam and the *sunna*, with slight variations of interpretation of the *sunna*.
Tariqa	'way', used especially to refer to the mystical paths of the Sufis; by extension, an order of those who follow a Sufi path.
Urs	'wedding', celebration of a saint's death anniversary when his soul was united with God.
Waqf	an endowment, usually in the form of lands, for the upkeep of a mosque, *madrasa*, or some other religious enterprise.

4
LITERATURE
Wheeler M. Thackston

The history of literature in the Mughal empire is basically the history of Persian. With the exception of the later period, when Indian vernacular languages entered the literary sphere and aside from a very limited number of exceptional oddities here and there, all official, high, and courtly literature was produced in the normal language among educated people in Mughal India—Persian. Since Persian is no longer a living language in the Subcontinent, and it did not originate there either, it may be helpful to trace its development in brief.

Persian was introduced into the South Asian Subcontinent as an administrative vehicle at the end of the tenth century by the invading Ghaznavids, Oghuz Turks who established an empire in the Punjab that outlasted their home empire in Ghazna (south of Kabul) by almost a century and a half. Although by no means the first contact between the Subcontinent and Muslim civilization, the Ghaznavid incursion is responsible for the lasting Islamization of northern India and the pervasive Persianate civilization it embraced. Throughout the rapidly changing dynasties that succeeded, the Persian language and its cultural baggage remained stable, spreading downward into society as Islamization—either religiously or culturally—filtered down from the ruling classes and upward with the activity of Persian-educated Sufi missionaries. What is now called the 'Mughal Empire'[1] was founded in the Subcontinent in 1526 by Babur, who was descended from the Turkish conqueror Amir Timur (known in the West as Tamerlane) and was originally from the Ferghana Valley in what is now Uzbekistan and Tajikistan. Like every educated Central Asian Turk at the time, Babur was bilingual in his native Chaghatai Turkish and in Persian, so when he came to the Subcontinent, the language neither of the bureaucracy nor of the ruling class or 'polite society' had to be changed in the slightest, for culturally speaking Babur and his men, Central Asian Turks though they were, were completely acculturated to the same Persianate civilization that had long since been domesticated in the Subcontinent. Turkish-speaking rulers were also nothing new to the Subcontinent: all dynasties ruling in Delhi from around 1200 were either Turks or Afghans, and all used Persian as the language of administration and culture. In fact, over the century of Mughal rule before Jahangir, the Persianization of India had only increased. When Humayun returned to the throne in 1555 after his fifteen-year exile in Safavid Iran, he brought with him many Iranians, and this influx further reinforced the already entrenched position of Persian. To this can be added the immigration of a large number of talented Iranians fleeing Safavid Iran for either religious or economic reasons in the early sixteenth century. On the religious side, the Safavids had made Twelver Shiism the state—and sole tolerated—religion within their realm. Those who chose not to convert from Sunnism had to emigrate to Sunni lands, either westward to the Ottoman empire, whither many of the religious classes went, or eastward to the Subcontinent. Economically, the creation of the highly centralized Safavid empire had deprived Iran of a number of local gubernatorial courts and petty kingdoms, which historically had given employment to a large number of poets, bureaucrats, and administrators, among others. These out-of-work educated elite also left Iran, generally for the Subcontinent, where opportunities for employment were more promising. An excellent example of such Iranian emigrants is Ghiyas Beg, the future Itimaduddaula, who left Iran and, after harrowing experiences en route, arrived in India with his wife, his son Abul Hasan, who became Asif Khan, and his daughter Mihrunnisa, who eventually married Jahangir and became the famous Nur Jahan.

Poets also came to the Subcontinent in record numbers. Although the Safavids were not hostile to literature *per se* and patronized some poets, the reduction in the number of courts left little opportunity for employment in the field of poetry, and poets began to flock to the Subcontinent, mostly to the Deccani kingdoms but also to the Mughal realm in the north, where they could find patronage with kings and nobles. It is telling that, of the four persons who held the title of *Malik-ush-Shuara*, 'king of poets' or poet laureate, under the Mughals, only one was a native-born Subcontinental. The first was Ghazali of Mashhad, appointed to the post by Akbar. At Ghazali's death in 1572, the title was conferred upon Faizi, the son of Shaikh Mubarak of Nagaur. Under Jahangir the title went to an Iranian *émigré*, Talib of Amul, and in Shahjahan's reign it was held by Kalim of Kashan, who was the last to bear the title before it was abolished as frivolous by Aurangzeb.

This said, we have to begin our survey of Mughal literature with an important work that is not in Persian.

The autobiography of the founder of the empire, Babur (1483-1530), was written in Babur's native and family language, Chaghatai Turkish, the language of the Ulus Chaghatai, which included what is now Uzbekistan, Tajikistan, Turkmenistan, Kyrghyzstan, parts of Afghanistan, and much of Kazakhstan. Babur's memoirs are of great importance on several fronts: it is the first true autobiography in any Muslim language, and it is the longest piece of expository prose in the Chaghatai language.

Babur had been raised in the hills of the Ferghana Valley and spent many years (1504-26) in and around Kabul, and he comments as follows on the things he missed most:

> Hindustan is a place of little charm. There is no beauty in its people, no graceful social intercourse, no poetic talent or understanding, no etiquette, no nobility, or manliness. The arts and crafts have no harmony or symmetry. There are no good horses, meat, grapes, melons, or other fruit. There is no ice, cold water, good food, or bread in the markets. There are no baths and no madrasas. There are no candles, torches, or candlesticks.[2]

Babur was accustomed to the mountainous terrain of the kingdom of Kabul, and the flatness of the Gangetic plain was not to his liking. A great builder of gardens and orchards, Babur once set out to find a site for a garden:

> I always thought one of the chief faults of Hindustan was that there was no running water. Everywhere that was habitable it should be possible to construct waterwheels, create running water, and make planned, geometric spaces. A few days after coming to Agra I crossed the Jumna with this plan in mind and scouted around for places to build gardens, but everywhere I looked was so unpleasant and desolate that I crossed back in great disgust. Because the place was so ugly and disagreeable I abandoned my dream of making a *charbagh*.
>
> Although there was no really suitable place near Agra, there was nothing to do but work with the space we had. The foundation was the large well from which the water for the bathhouse came. Next, the patch of ground with tamarind trees and octagonal pond became the great pool and courtyard. Then came the pool in front of the stone building and the hall After that came the private garden and its outbuildings, and after that the bathhouse. Thus, in unpleasant and inharmonious India, marvellously regular and geometric gardens were introduced. In every corner were beautiful plots, and in every plot were regularly laid out arrangements of roses and narcissus.[3]

Babur had not planned to remain in India. He had proposed to consolidate his Subcontinental gains, turn it over to his son Humayun, and then retire back to his beloved Kabul. Fate had other plans for him, however. When Humayun fell ill at his fief at Sambhal,

> the malady gradually increased and his Majesty Giti-sitani Firdus-makani [Babur], growing disturbed at the alarming news, ordered, in his affection for him, that he be brought to Delhi and thence by water to Agra, in order that he might be treated by skilful physicians under the Emperor's own eyes. A large number of learned doctors who were always in attendance at the royal Court, were directed to employ their talents in effecting a cure. In a short space of time, he was conveyed by boat. Though physicians used their skill and exhibited Messiah-like science, he did not get better. As the sickness was prolonged, the Emperor one day was seated with the wise men of the Age by the Jumna and considering about remedies. Mir Abu Baqa who was one of the most distinguished saints of the Age, represented that it had been received from the ancient sages, that in a case like this, when

---

1. It is worth repeating here that the 'Mughals' did not refer to themselves as Mughals at all. It is a misnomer picked up in the sixteenth century by Europeans, mainly the Portuguese, from a local usage, probably derogatory, and perpetuated thereafter. From the common European appellation the word has even re-entered Indian languages as *mughlai* and *mughli* (as in Mowgli, the name of the young hero of Kipling's *Jungle Book*). 'Mughal' comes from the same word that gives our 'Mongol,' and in Babur's time it referred not to actual Mongols from Mongolia but to the highly Mongolianized Turks of Moghulistan. It is true that Babur's mother was the daughter of the khan of Moghulistan, but Babur, who had nothing good to say about the Moghuls in his employ, would have been dismayed had he known that his dynasty would be known by this name. It is, of course, far too late now even to contemplate changing our common name for the dynasty, but the reader should be aware that the 'Mughals' referred to themselves as Timurids, and in the rare instance in which they applied anything like an official name to their dynasty, they called themselves the *Silsila-i Gurkaniyya* 'the Gurkanid Dynasty,' a reference to Amir Timur's title of *Gurkan*, from the Mongolian *guragan* 'son-in-law,' a title dating back to before the time of Genghis Khan and accorded all who married princesses of Genghisid blood, as did Amir Timur and Babur's father, Umar Shaikh Mirza.
2. Babur, *Baburnama*, 350.
3. Babur, *Baburnama*, 359f.

physicians were at a loss, the remedy was to give in alms the most valuable thing one had and to seek cure from God. His Majesty Giti-sitani said, 'I am the most valuable thing that Humayun possesses; than me he has no better thing; I shall make myself a sacrifice for him. May God the Creator accept it.[4]

And he died shortly thereafter in Agra in 1530. His body was conveyed to Kabul, where he was laid to rest in the open in a garden, as he had requested.

Babur not only wrote prose but also composed a *Divan* (a collection of verse) in Turkish and has some Persian poems to his credit too. One senses that, unlike most of the poets dealt with in this survey, his poetry is expressive of experience and true feelings. Occasionally we even know the instance at which a poem was composed. The following selection is from the *Baburnama* and dates from the winter of 1506-7:

> Our guide was a Pashai named Sultan. Whether he was too old or faint-hearted, or whether because of the depth of the snow, in any case he had lost the road and could not guide us. Since it was at Qasim Beg's insistence that we had come by this road, and it reflected upon his honor, he and his sons trampled down the snow, found the road again, and went on ahead. One day the snow was so deep and the road so obscured that no matter what we did we could not go on. There was nothing for us to do but turn back and camp in a place with firewood. I appointed seventy or eighty warriors to retrace our steps to find and bring to guide us any Hazaras who were wintering in the valley. We did not move from this camp for three or four days until those who had gone out returned. When they did return, they did not bring with them anyone who could show us the way. Trusting in God, we sent Sultan Pashai ahead and set out back down the very road where we had gotten lost. During those few days we endured much hardship and misery, more than I had experienced in my whole life. At that time I composed this line:

چرخ نینگ مین کورماگان جور و جفاسی قالدی مو
خستہ کو نگلوم چیکماگان درد و بلاسی قالدی مو

> Is there any cruelty or misery the spheres can inflict I have not suffered? / Is there any pain or torment my wounded heart has not suffered?[5]

The following poem from Babur's *Divan*, presumably written to be sent to someone, perhaps a family member still in Kabul, was composed in India:

غربت تہ اول آی ہجری مینی پیر قیلیب تور
ہجران بیلہ غربت منگا تاثیر قیلیب تور
مقدور باریچہ قیلورام سعی وصالینگ
تا تینگری بیلمان کہ نی تقدیر قیلیب تور
تقدیر دور اول یان و بویان سالغوچی، یوقسہ
کیم گا ہوس سنبل و نظیر قیلیب تور
بو ہند پیری حاصلی دین کوپ کونگول آلدیم
نی سود کہ بو پیر مینی دلگیر قیلیب تور
سیندین بو قدر قالدی پیراق اولمادی بابر
معذور توت ای یارکہ تقصیر قیلیب تور

> In exile, separation from that moon has made me old.
>   Separation and exile have taken their toll on me. 1
> I am trying as hard as I can to be with you,
>   But I know not what destiny God has decreed. 2
> Were it not for destiny on one side and obligation on the other,
>   Who would have any desire for Sambhal and the like? 3
> I have taken much heart from the land and produce of India,
>   But to what avail? for this place disgusts me. 4
> Fate has put him distant from you, but Babur has not died—
>   Forgive him, my beloved, for he has made a mistake. 5

One of the best poets of Chaghatai Turkish in India was Bairam Khan, the regent during Akbar's minority. He composed poetry in both Turkish and Persian. His son Abdul Rahim Khankhanan (1556-1627) was an accomplished poet in Persian, Turkish, Arabic, and Hindi. He produced and presented to Akbar in 1589 the Persian translation of the *Baburnama*, the only version of the memoirs known for many centuries and the basis for the early translations into English and other western languages until the rediscovery of the Turkish text in 1900. Abdul Rahim was a great patron of literature and had a number of poets in his entourage. His life, times, and accomplishments are described in Abdul Baqi Nihawandi's *Maasir-i Rahimi* (1616).

It is difficult to say for certain how long Turkish remained a true living language in the royal family. Humayun was certainly fluent in Turkish, as is shown by the letters Babur wrote to him in that language. Akbar must also have been conversant in it; his regent Bairam Khan was certainly a master of it, and Bairam Khan's son Abdul Rahim was also well versed in it; he is the last major figure to have written in that language. Jahangir claimed that he also knew some Turkish, his ancestral language, but the way he says it makes one think that his Turkish was limited—'Although I grew up in Hindustan, I am not ignorant of how to speak or write Turkish.'[6] From Jahangir's time on, the languages of the imperial harem must have been Persian and some form of Indian vernacular, and the Turkish that had formerly been the 'family language' of the Timurids died away. It was around the same time that the emperors themselves began to speak the vernacular in addition to Persian. Jahangir certainly must have learned to speak some local form of the common language of north India from his mother or other Rajput women in the harem, although he never says so. It is difficult to imagine how else he might have communicated so well and so often with the hermit Gosain Jadrup, for example, but one can read his memoirs from cover to cover and never guess, aside from a few Hindi words he gives for things peculiar to the Subcontinent and for which Persian has no words, that he knew how to speak it. There is not, to my knowledge, any reference to Shahjahan's familiarity with Turkish, and it was probably all but gone by that time.

Babur was not the only member of the imperial family to write his memoirs. Inspired by his great-grandfather, Jahangir also kept a meticulous record of his daily doings, the *Jahangirnama*. Of course, Jahangir did not have the adventurous experiences that Babur had, and the rough-and-tumble of Babur's life was far removed from Jahangir's pampered, luxurious existence, which was always circumscribed by the court even during his fairly extensive travels. Yet Jahangir, like Babur, was a keen observer of nature, and his memoirs are of interest for the insight they offer into Jahangir's emotional states and his day-to-day life:

> In Ahmadabad I had two markhor goats along with me. Since there was no female in the establishment to mate with them, I wondered what sort of offspring would be produced if they were mated to the Barbary goats that are brought from Arabia, particularly from the port of Dofar. In short, they were mated to seven Barbary females, and six months later in Fatehpur they all produced young, four females and three males. They were extremely good-looking, well formed, and nicely colored. Among the colors, the ones that more resembled the markhor males, like the dun-colored ones with black stripes down the back and the ones that were dark red, looked better than the others and the good breeding was more obvious in them.
>
> What can be written of their playfulness, the funny things they do, and their leaping and bounding about? They do things that make one want to watch them in spite of oneself. What is well known among the people—that it is impossible to imitate the leaping and gamboling of a kid goat—has certainly been proven true. If occasionally someone can successfully imitate a kid goat's tricks, there is no doubt that one must acknowledge one's inability to imitate their strange antics, various leaps and bounds, and comical movements. One kid a month old—actually only twenty days old—leapt onto the ground from such a high place that if it had been anything other than a goat, not one of its limbs would have remained unscathed. I enjoyed them so much I ordered them always to be kept nearby, and each of them was given a suitable name.
>
> I enjoy them immensely and take great care in the breeding of markhors and thoroughbred goats. I want their offspring to multiply and become popular. When their offspring are mated to each other, it is thought that they will be even more valuable. One of the peculiar characteristics of these is that, whereas when a goat kid is born it does not immediately take the mother's teats in its mouth and suck milk but bleats and cries, these by contrast do not cry at all but act extremely independent: Their meat may also be quite delicious.[7]

Also like his great-grandfather, Jahangir was immensely fond of gardens and was always on the look-out for a promising site:

> [The Vernag Spring in Kashmir] is the source of the Bahat River. It is situated at the foot of a mountain, but there are so many trees, so much greenery, and so many plants that the earth cannot be seen. When I was a prince I ordered a building worthy of the site constructed at this spring. It has recently been completed. It has an octagonal pool forty-two cubits across and four ells deep. The water looks dark green because of the reflection of the greenery that grows on the mountain, and there are many fish in the pool. All around the pool are arched walkways, and there is a garden in front of the building. From the edge of the pool to the garden gate runs a canal 4 ells wide, 180 ells long, and 2 ells deep. On both sides of the canal are avenues paved with stone. The water is so pure

---

4. Abul-Fazl, *Akbarnama* 1:275.
5. Babur, *Baburnama*, 240f.
6. Jahangir, *Jahangirnama*, 77.
7. Jahangir, *Jahangirnama*, 302f.

The Magnificent Mughals

PAGE OF CALLIGRAPHY
By Imdad al-Husayni (d. 1615), one of the geatest Irani Masters of calligraphy. Rare work in Chaghatai Turkish and Persian, dated 1609-1610. *Nastaliq* script. From the Mughal album of the National Library of Romania.

and clear that, although it is four ells deep, if a chickpea fell to the bottom it could be seen.

What can be written of the purity of the canal or of the greenery and the plants that sprout below the spring? Bitter herbs, aromatic herbs, various dark green and pale green herbs all grow together. One bush that was seen was as multicoloured as a peacock's tail and shimmering like wavy water with isolated flowers blooming here and there. In all of Kashmir there is no scenic spot so beautiful or charming as this one. It is obvious that Kashmir above the river is beyond any comparison with what is below the river. I should really have stayed in this area for a few days and enjoyed myself fully, but since the hour for marching was near and it had begun to snow in the passes and there was no time to stop, I turned my reins back toward the city. It was ordered that plane trees should be planted on both sides of the canal.

On Saturday the fourth [17 September] camp was made at the Lukabawan spring. This spring is also a nice place even if at present it is not equal to the others. If it were repaired it would be a beautiful place. I ordered a building worthy of the site constructed and the pool in front of the spring repaired. Along the way we passed by a spring called Anantnag. It is well known that the fish of this spring are blind. I stopped a moment at the spring and cast a net in. Twelve fish were caught in the net. Three of them were blind, and the other nine had eyes. Apparently the water of this spring has the effect of making the fish blind. In any case, it is not a little strange.[8]

Jahangir continued Babur's family tradition of being addicted to drink. Although Babur managed to give it up at age forty, Jahangir did not have the fortitude to stop drinking, but he did not mind sharing intimate details of his habit with his readers:

I myself did not drink until the age of eighteen, except during my infancy, when two or three times my mother and nurses asked my exalted father for liquor to treat infantile complaints and gave me a tola of it mixed with rose water and water as cough medicine. Then, when my exalted father's entourage was camped to deal with the Yusufzai Afghans in the Attock fortress on the banks of the Nilab River, one day I mounted to go hunting. Since I overdid it and got exhausted, a wonderful gunner named Ustad Shah-Quli, the chief of my uncle Mirza Muhammad-Hakim's gunners, said to me, 'If you drink a beaker of wine, it will relieve the exhaustion'. Since I was young and my nature was inclined to do these things, I ordered Mahmud the water-carrier to go to Hakim Ali's house and bring some alcoholic syrup. The physician sent a phial and a half of yellow-coloured, sweet-tasting wine in a small bottle. I drank it and liked the feeling I got.

After that I started drinking wine, increasing it day by day until I no longer got a kick out of grape wine and started drinking liquor. Little by little, over nine years, it increased to twenty phials of double-distilled spirits, fourteen during the day and rest at night. By weight that much is six Hindustani seers, which is equivalent to one and a half Iranian maunds. During those days my only food was the equivalent of one meal with bread and radishes. In this state no one had the power to stop me. Things got so bad that in my hangovers my hands shook and trembled so badly I couldn't drink myself but had to have others help me. Finally I summoned Hakim Humam, Hakim Abu'l-Fath's brother and one of my exalted father's confidants, and informed him of my condition. In perfect sincerity and compassion he said, with no beating around the bush, 'Highness, the way you're drinking, in another six months—God forbid—things will be so bad it will be beyond remedy.' Since his words were spoken in benevolence, and life is precious, it made a great impression on me.

From that date I began to decrease the amount and started taking philonium, increasing it by the amount I decreased the wine. Then I ordered the spirits mixed with grape wine, two parts wine to one part spirits, and I kept decreasing the amount I drank every day. Over a period of seven years I got it down to six phials, the weight of a phial being seventeen and three-quarters mithcals. I have now been drinking like this for fifteen years without increase or decrease. I only drink at night, but not on Thursday, the day of my accession, or on Friday eve, a blessed night of the week. Out of these two considerations I drink at the end of the day because I don't like to let the night go by in negligence without rendering thanks to the True Benefactor. On Thursdays and Sundays I don't eat meat—Thursday because it is the day of my accession, and Sunday, my exalted father's birthday, because he venerated it greatly.

After a while I substituted opium for the philonium. Now that I am forty-six years and four months old by solar reckoning or forty-seven years and nine months by lunar reckoning, I have eight surkhs of opium after the elapse of five gharis of the day and six surkhs after the first watch of the night.[9]

---

8. Jahangir, *Jahangirnama*, 346.
9. Jahangir, *Jahangirnama*, 184f.

PERSIAN POETRY

The highest literary art form throughout the Mughal period was Persian poetry, and the poetic tradition in Persian had been accumulating since the tenth century. Here we will deal with the three most prominent forms of Persian poetry, the *qasida* (ode), the *ghazal* (lyric), and the *masnavi* (narrative). *Qasidas* and *ghazals* share a form: they both consist of successive lines, each of which is divided into two metrically equal half-lines divided by a metrical caesura; the first line shows the rhyme at the end of both half-lines; thereafter, only the end of the line shows the rhyme. Graphically represented, both the *qasida* and the *ghazal* have the following shape:

```
————a | ————a
————x | ————a
————x | ————a
```

The Qasida. *Qasidas* are typically quite long (anywhere from fifty to two hundred lines or more); *ghazals* are necessarily quite short (five to twelve lines). Meter is strict in Persian, and once a meter is established in the first half-line, it must be maintained without deviation until the end of the poem.

In *qasidas* the tradition of the highly artificial, courtly production designed to dazzle the hearer with the poet's erudition and mastery of the language was continued. *Qasidas* designed for the main occasions for court celebration, Nauroz, the end of Ramadan, the imperial weighing ceremony etc., abound. Congratulatory *qasidas* composed for special occasions such as victory in battle, birth of a prince, and accession to the throne are to be found throughout the period, but one example will suffice here.

A good specimen of a *qasida* written for a court occasion is the following one by Kalim,[10] Shahjahan's poet laureate. It illustrates the motifs and images brought into play for the encomiastic *qasida*, the spring ode, the festival congratulatory, and the purpose-poem such as for an imperial edifice or some article of regal paraphernalia. Written in 1635 for a gala festival for Nauroz and Id ul-fitr, which happened to coincide that year, at which the famous Peacock Throne was first unveiled, this *qasida* typifies the use of Indian-style conceits in the *qasida* form and the contrapuntal technique of interlacing main themes with subtle repetitions of minor strains. Here there are four main themes: the end of Ramadan, the advent of spring, the magnanimity of Shahjahan (encomium), and a description of the Peacock Throne, all of which are carefully introduced in turn and held together by a delicate weaving of nature—and element—allusions and by transitional lines in which one theme is concluded and the next major topic is introduced. The technique of parallel construction and balancing of contrast pairs, so characteristic of the *ghazal*, is lacking in the *qasida* in general; instead, the rhetorical devices of *muraat-i nazir* (maintaining images of similar properties) and *husn-i talil* (fanciful reasoning) are relied upon almost exclusively. Here similar pairs are juxtaposed one against the other to express similar qualities by means of similarity albeit in a different context, rather than by stressing similarity through dissimilarity in a like context, as in the *ghazal*.

In the first two lines the coincidence of the Id ul-fitr and Nauroz is introduced along with the figure of the *saqi* (cupbearer), which leads to a minor incursion of wine-poetry:

فشانده اند چه گلهای عیش بر سر سال   خجسته مقدم نوروز و غرّهٔ شوال
ضرورتست بلی این دو عید را دو هلال   بزم عیش دو جام است در کف ساقی

Happy advent of Nauroz and new moon of Shawwal:
  Petals of delight have been strewn over the heads of the month and the year. 1
In the banquet of delight the *saqi* holds two cups:
  Two crescents are necessary for these two feasts. 2

As the end of Ramadan signals an end to abstinence, and the festival of Nauroz heralds the advent of spring, the season for indulgence in pleasure and drinking, the cupbearer's two goblets hold two 'crescents' of wine, which the poet fancifully likens to two crescent moons, although only the moon of Shawwal shows in the sky. From the very beginning, lines are linked one to another by the repetition of a key word: lines 1 and 2 are thus held together by the word *aysh* 'pleasure', the antithesis of which is typified by the 'dry ascetic' of line 3. The pleasure theme is picked up again in line 8.

Now the 'wetness' of the two goblets of wine is contrasted with the 'dryness' of the ascetic during his fast:

> The ascetic's dryness has increased with fasting.
>   To cure his aridity two cups brimful are needed. 3
> Should I compensate for thirty days of thirst?
>   I have opened both hands in supplication to the cupbearer. 4

With line 3, the first major theme proper begins, i.e., the end of Ramadan, during which month abstinence from wine has increased the ascetic's natural aridity, and for which abstinence the poet now holds out both hands to the cupbearer in supplication to make up for his thirty-day thirst/fast.

> The twice-fired wine of lightheartedness is so sharp that we may infuse the water of fatigue. 5
> The slit of my red bud has opened, and fasting is past.
>   What better could you wish of a barren one? 6
> On account of fasting, the child of desire was at school.
>   The feast came, and the children were dismissed from school. 7

The 'fatigue' induced by enforced fasting and abstinence can now be poured into the heady wine, which is said to be strong enough to dispel the effects of fatigue (line 5). At last the poet's parched lips ('red bud') are opened, and his desires, pent up during Ramadan like children in school, are free to be indulged.

> The plenitude of pleasure is manifest from the outcome of labour.
>   From this spring the goodness of the year is obvious. 8
> From this good beginning a good end is in sight:
>   Even the philosopher has ceased to worry about end results. 9
> Pleasure has become so perfectly mellow that the night of union is no longer blamed for being short. 10
> Pleasure goes out on his father's back to greet the traveller
>   Who comes toward the realm of existence. 11
> Because of the wax of restoration, in our time nothing is broken
> But the geomancer's die. 12

The theme of pleasure is again taken up in line 8, in which the second main theme, spring, is also introduced as herald of a good year, for the combination of perfect pleasure and perfect spring cannot but bode a good end

---

10. Kalim, *Divan*, 12-14.

(line 9). Next (line 10), the shortening of the night (characteristic of spring) is introduced, but this 'fault' is counterbalanced by the mellowness of pleasure. In line 11 a characteristically Indian-style cerebralism portrays this newly-born Pleasure as a child riding on his father's back, rushing forward to greet the long-awaited traveller who approaches the 'realm of existence', i.e., spring, which is slowly coming into being from the realm of non-existence whence it had been banished by autumn and the approach of winter.

Line 12 then introduces the spirit of perfection that comes with spring, for it is in spring that the times are not felt to be 'out of joint': all the 'disjointedness' of winter has been 'set right' by the 'wax of restoration', an allusion to the wax then used to set broken bones. Only the geomancer's die is left crushed, no longer able to forecast dire events.

> No two days of ours are alike, as conditions have begun to wax like the crescent moon. 13
> Time has blocked the road of depression from all directions,
>   As they carry water from the sea in a sieve. 14
> Spring has brought water on the face of earth's labour.
>   The jeweller cannot distinguish crystal from clay. 15

With the advent of spring, Time itself is daily waxing as mirrored by the crescent moon that grows larger night by night as the length of daylight increases. In line 14 the poet introduces the abstract figure of Time, who is said to have 'stopped up' the way of depression (*tanazzul*, which contrasts with 'advancement', *taraqqi*, in line 13), as people might stop up a sieve in order to carry water from the sea.

With line 15 the spring-theme proper begins. The earth in spring so glistens with moisture that it resembles crystal, and even a jeweller is unable to distinguish between true crystal and the crystalline clay of the earth.

> The world seeks pretexts for becoming verdant:
>   Since it finds moisture in the mouth, the toothpick turns green. 16
> See the zenith of growth: out of the moisture of perspiration the seed of the mole has sprouted like the verdure of the downy cheek. 17
> The appearance of the dew-dropped verdure is like water in a fountain:

> From the moment it raises its head above the meadow there is a shoot. 18
>
> Such purity of earth there is that the fish in water lift their fins above the surface out of longing for the land at this time. 19

The next characteristic of spring introduced is the appearance of tiny shoots of greenery. Indeed, the 'whole world' is only seeking pretexts for becoming green: even a toothpick will sprout buds when it comes in contact with moisture in the mouth (line 16). Maintaining the classical images (mouth, downy cheek, mole), Kalim compares the tender verdure with the down on the cheek and sees the mole as a seed watered by beads of perspiration. So fast do the shoots of greenery sprout from the earth (line 18) that one would think them jets of water shot up by a fountain. Again in line 19 the silvery slivers of greenery are likened to fish that raise their fins above the level of the water out of longing for the land (= space, which belongs idiomatically with 'time').

> Without a moving breeze the silver-scattering blossoms are so generous that
> They bestow before being asked. 20
> At the hand of the dyer of new spring, in only one vat the rosebud's cloak is turned green and his shirt pink. 21
> In the defile of the branch's veins blossoms and leaves struggle with each other to get out first. 22

In line 20 the silvery blossoms of fruit trees that fall early in spring are imagined to be so generous that they scatter silver coins without being asked and without even a breeze to blow them off. Continuing the theme of colour introduced in line 16, the poet marvels at spring as a dyer and how it can colour the rose's leaves, which he calls its cloak, green and its shirt, the bud itself, pink all in one vat (line 21). The rose bushes also sprout and bloom so quickly that Kalim remarks that the leaves and blossoms must be vying with one another to get out first (line 22).

Having thus 'set the stage' in the blossom of spring, the poet now engages in a 'fugue' of five lines (23-27) he weaves together with strands of the four elements and their properties and by juxtaposing opposing qualities which resolve themselves in line 27 with the harp of the world striking the note of the golden mean. Lines 23 and 24 are held together by the repetition of *hawa* 'air', the properties of which, cold and dry, and shared with iron, are mentioned in line 23:

> The clouds' air has so softened iron that it has become like stirrup-leather toned by heavy feet. 23
> By mingling with the air has fire become so moist that charcoal has washed its innate blackness from its face. 24
> The earth has such limpidity that the seeds beneath the dirt have swollen of their own accord
> Like fever blisters. 25
> During this spring, were an angel to write down a sin,
> The moisture of the air would wash it away from the Book of Deeds. 26
> Time has so plucked the harp of moderation that the singer's drum has ceased its mildness and irascibility. 27

The property of hardness innate in iron is opposed to the softening action of the air, just as the innate colour (black) of charcoal has been opposed by the colourlessness of air (line 24). The second element, fire (hot and dry), is opposed to the moistness of the atmosphere, thus introducing the third element, water (cold and wet), which is again taken up with 'limpidity' and water itself in line 25. As the 'earthiness' of iron and charcoal links lines 24 and 25, the heat of fire is implicit in 'fever blister', which also contains water (line 25). The last element, earth (hot and wet), is twice mentioned in line 25, but it is the watery theme that is carried on to line 26 in a delightful conceit: the air is so moist that the ink would be washed away from the register of deeds if a recording angel were to write down a sin, thus nullifying the possibility of anything but goodness coming from such temperateness. The whole gist of the preceding four lines is captured in line 27, where the world is said to have struck the chord of the golden mean and to be in such harmony with itself that even the singer's drum has rested from the extremes of its art, 'mildness and irascibility', i.e., slow and fast beats (literary 'water and fire').

> If anyone were to take an augury from an unwritten ledger,
> Joy would extend a commentary upon it to a thousand verses. 28

This line continues the theme of writing and related images from line 26 and also provides a closing to the spring section, whereas lines 29 and 30 form a localizing transition into the third main theme, the coming of Shahjahan from Akbarabad (Agra) to Delhi, and his generosity and magnanimity are praised from line 35 through line 39:

> I am the destruction of the people of Akbarabad's happiness,
>   Who have derived their heart's desire from the three festivals this year. 29
> In the eyes of the people of Delhi is a new festival:
>   The dust of the train of Shahjahan is a world of majesty. 30
> The Milky Way has come to the second Sahibqiran:
>   O heavens! take pride in the dust of his armies. 31
> Spring sold its honour to the tutty-vendor of the north wind
>   To buy the dust of his road. 32
> The dust of his charger's hoof, in the eye in which it set,
>   Settled like tutty in the ranks of horseshoes. 33
> The king's approach is like the Fountain of Life with grace.
>   Gently the ship of hope touched the shore. 34
> The clouds, jealous of his generosity, are so despondent of existence that
>   They hurl themselves against the mountain peaks. 35
> His palm is so opened that were a mute to drink water from his hand,
>   His tied tongue would open. 36
> In the banquet of generosity he sits at the head of kings,
>   For supplication does not precede his bestowal. 37
> One who has not a sou to hand, because of his generosity,
>   Can trample of wealth. 38
> At the time of liberality, like a torrent, all haste;
>   At the time of punishment, like the razor-edge of the mountains, all neglect. 39

Next are mentioned the emperor's awesomeness, his might, his innate qualities, his justice, and omniscience:

> From fear of his prohibition, his likeness, were it to enter a house of mirrors,
>   Would not be able to go away without permission. 40
> During his reign the lion has so washed any sign of his prey's blood from his hand that
>   The red (*al*) has disappeared from his claw (*changal*). 41
> His innate excellences have no need of praise.
>   How could the sanctuary doves be adorned with anklets? 42
> During his reign the world has become so filled with justice
>   That brokers can find no place in the market. 43
> Fate does not hide its secrets from him,
>   Like a patient who does not fail to describe his symptoms to a doctor. 44

From line 45 to line 60, the last theme, the Peacock Throne, is maintained. Like the throne itself, this section is a study in precious gems, with conceits constructed on the theme of the play of light refracted through these jewels and the dazzling brilliance produced thereby:

> As the Lord of the World is the Shadow of God,
>   So also is his throne an image of the Throne on high. 45
> On such a festival Nauroz itself gains honour when the king is seated on the Throne of Sovereignty. 44a
> I am about to scatter pearls of description of the bejewelled throne.
>   May God grant me Khizr's life and length of speech. 46
> A thousand Ceylons of carnelians and a hundred Badakhshans of rubies glitter on it to display elegance. 47
> The rays of its rubies and emeralds fall on diamonds like lamplight playing on a water-cascade. 48
> Its ancient emeralds are fresher than young verdure.
>   Who says the coincidence of opposites is impossible? 49
> The gold on the throne might become molten from the fire of the rubies,
>   Or droplets might scatter from the pearl waterfall. 50
> Before its design the Garden of Iram's spring would be as ashamed of showing itself
>   As a peacock whose feathers had been shed. 51
> Lamps can be lit from the fire of its carnelians such that
>   No harm comes from wine or from rain. 52
> Even one who has not seen it can describe it.
>   The lightning of the jewels burns from afar the feathers of the bird of sight. 53
> If the luster of its jewels be recalled,
> The tempers of the ignorant are destroyed out of perplexity. 54
> From contemplating its design, the brocade of imagination is woven of a thousand colours in the workshop of poetry. 55
> The galaxy of gems that has reached the foot of this throne—
>   Were it to pass over Caesar's head, he would succumb to the pox. 56
> Were the keeper of the throne to cover it with his shawl,
>   It would become a *gulband* [a type of silk brocade] from the resplendence of the jewels. 57
> In shape like a mountain, yet full of bubbles like the sea—
>   Bubbles of different colours, of various shapes. 58
> No jeweller can ever determine its worth.
>   How can an ounce-scale weigh a mountain? 59
> It has no price, yet whatever else you want it is:
>   Splendor, grandeur, dignity, pomp, beauty, and elegance. 60

The *qasida* ends with a petition for the emperor:

> Forever, so long as the Chosroës of the planets is seated in sovereignty on the gilded throne of the spheres, 61
> May you on the imperial throne be as constant as the poles!
> May the star of your augustness never see change! 62

Qasidas were recited at court, as is recorded by court histories, and sometimes astounding rewards were bestowed upon the poets for their efforts.

The Ghazal.* The main artistic form of the age was the *ghazal*, a short verse form (five to twelve lines) that necessarily deals somehow, no matter how tenuously, with love. By the time our survey of Mughal literature begins in the sixteenth century, the *ghazal* had already undergone centuries of development and conventionalization, and the stereotypical conventionality of the *ghazal* is perhaps its most distinguishing feature. The 'landscape' of the *ghazal* was fixed. The characters who could appear in a *ghazal* were limited. And, most importantly, the language deemed suitable for a *ghazal* was severely restricted.

The dominant style in the *ghazal* during the sixteenth and seventeenth centuries (the 'High-Period') has been labelled the 'Indian-style' (*sabk-i hindi*). There is nothing wrong with this label so long as we realize that there is nothing particularly Indian about the 'Indian-style'. Poetry composed in Iran and Central Asia at the same time exhibits the same characteristics, and many, perhaps even most, of the practitioners of the 'Indian-style' were actually Iranian, even though they may have produced most of their poetic output in the Subcontinent. The style has been labelled as 'Indian' because in Iran a reaction set in during the eighteenth century against hypercerebralization and euphuism and a conscious effort was made to 'return' to an older, more classical style, hence the movement known as the *bazgasht-i adabi*, the 'literary return'. Since the Subcontinent did not take part in this movement and continued writing in the High-Period style, it has been called 'Indian-style'. The more accurate description is 'High-Period' style.

The High-Period style, unfortunately, has been described mainly in negative terms:

> Many westerners seem to identify it with a vague 'baroquism'... and with a linguistic heaviness and complication, bad taste, cerebralism, ridiculously exaggerated comparisons, etc.—things which, basically, say almost nothing that is stylistically precise.[11]

It has fared little better at the hands of Iranian critics, although most have felt themselves constrained to admit that there is much of beauty in the same exaggerated hyperbole they criticize. An Iranian historian of Persian stylistics, Bahar, produced the following list of characteristics of the Indian-style:[12] (1) little attention paid to eloquence of diction; (2) unusual and exotic words not used; (3) archaic expressions never employed; (4) more attention given to new conceits than to anything else; (5) psychic states and internal excitement were not expressed by means of words but through conceit and metaphor; (6) lofty ideals and high thoughts expressive of noble life and extraordinary character are not found; (7) the majority is *ghazal* in form, and the contents convey feelings of debilitation, humility, and vileness; (8) vocabulary drawn from the bazaar and low level of diction as compared with previous eras; (9) many new expressions that had not existed before; (10) the greatest fault is that the personality of the poet cannot be known through his poetry; the poet does not invent conceits to suit his 'message', rather he first finds the conceit and then invents a 'message' to fit the conceit; (11) monotonous.

As regards pure stylistics, few, if any, of these characteristics distinguish the High-Period style from the classical style that preceded it, especially in the realm of exaggerated metaphor and the artificial conceit, to which Persian poetry, as a tradition, tended practically from its nascence. Bahar's observation that a poet's 'personality' cannot be known through his poetry certainly applies to all Persian poetry, for the conceit and traditional diction almost always masked the poet's individuality. Bahar is correct in observing that archaisms and recherché vocabulary are lacking in Indian-style poetry, for the trend to adornment with conceit rather than with minute care to eloquence was also a natural outgrowth of the previous (classical) style and represented a shift in mode of thought rather than being a break with tradition and formation of a completely new style.

---

* Editor's Note: Also see *Ghazal* in the Urdu chapter, pp. 118-131.

To accomplish their goals the poets of the Indian-style relied mainly on three devices, the creation of a novel metaphor, the sustaining of this metaphor by hyperbole, and the 'presentation of some poetical (fanciful) sentiment which is not true to experience, but which the poet invents, substantiating it by an equally poetic (fanciful) reasoning.'[13] On the purely lexical level, there was produced

> a tendency, which may be in a certain sense a logical consequence of the greater freedom of choice for the objects of comparison brought about by the preceding process [i.e., the rupture of the law of formal harmony], to use purely abstract conceits, verbs often in the infinitive, …abstracts in—*í* or nouns of the form taf'íl, or semipersonified ideas and metaphorical plays on the objects.[14]

A historian of Urdu literature, Muhammad Sadiq, holds that the very names by which the adherents characterized their style (*khayal-afarini* 'creating a mental image', *mazmun-bandi* 'making a conceit', and *nazuk-khayali* 'making a subtle image') indicate that their 'poetry was conceived in the intellect, and its function was not to represent or interpret life.'[15]

The rupture of the law of formal harmony in poetry resulted in poetry dominated by the literary device. In fact, the older subordination of the device to form as a mere embellishment does break down, leaving the embellishment as the apparent reason for the structure itself. This trend is coincidentally visible in the ideals of Mughal architectural ornamentation:

> So effectively do these modes of decoration applied in such profusion, dominate the architectural composition, that it becomes obvious one of the essential principles of the building art has been ignored, for instead of the ornamentation being subordinated to the structure, it controls it. Everywhere the architect has been impelled so to devise his construction that it may provide spaces or receptacles for coloured embellishment.[16]

So too does High-Period style poetry appear superficial. Bahar's characteristic number ten says essentially the same thing: the poet, having thought of a good conceit, then invents an experience to bear out the content of the conceit. On this score the style was not without severe critics in its own heyday, when it was hostilely referred to as the 'new style' (*tarz-i taza*) and 'newspeak' (*tazagui*). Mulla Shaida is said to have detested the style: 'He was a sworn enemy to the new style and considered the new-stylists more useless than last year's calendar.'[17] Others complained of the excessive imagic complexity, yet the poets themselves apparently considered this quality essential to their mode of expression. When Inayat Khan criticized the complexity of Ghani of Kashmir's poetry, the poet is reported to have said, 'Until now I had always relied on Inayat Khan's ability to comprehend poetry, but today that reliance is gone forever.'[18] On the necessity for metaphor in poetry Talib of Amul comments:

زسادہ گوئی افسردہ نادم طالب
من وسخن بہمان طرزِ استعارۂ خویش[19]

I regret, Talib, having written in the 'worn-out' simple style: I had better write in my own metaphorical style.

سخن کہ نیست در و استعارہ نیست ملاحت
نمک ندارد شعری کہ استعارہ ندارد[20]

Verse that has no metaphor in it has no sweetness. Poetry that does not have metaphor is insipid.

The High-Period style poetry was aristocratic, born of minds highly educated, cultivated, and elitist in character. *Ghazals* were typically recited in the intimate setting of an evening assembly (*majlis*) hosted by a noble and attended, by invitation, by poets and literati. Poetry in such an environment demanded of its immediate audience not only a familiarity with the vast corpus of the tradition of Persian poetry and the literary arts but also a knowledge of the totality of the sciences of the universe. If the conceits and expression current were not 'true to life', it is because the poets were not attempting

---

11. Bausani, *Storia delle letterature del Pakistan*, 54f. My translation.
12. Bahar, 'Saib u shiva-i u,' 264f.
13. Shibli-Nu'mani as quoted by M. Sadiq, *A History of Urdu Literature*, 28.
14. Bausani, 'Contributo a una definizione dello 'stile indiano', 176f. Translation mine.
15. M. Sadiq, *A History of Urdu Literature*, 29.
16. Percy Brown, *Indian Architecture*, 115.
17. Abdul-Hamid Lahauri, *Badshahnama* 2:396.
18. Ikram al-Haqq, *Shi'r al-'ajam fi'l-Hind*, 93.
19. Talib Amuli, *Kulliyyat*, 635, line 13,557.
20. Talib Amuli, *Kulliyyat*, 447, line 10,046.

to express or interpret life on an ordinary plane; rather they were trying to illustrate a mode of thought that viewed this world and its life as essentially unreal, a mere reflection of the Real Universe that lies beyond the boundaries of sense perception where the earthly laws of phenomenology are not applicable. By necessity, therefore, familiar images, limited as they are to the observable and tangible universe defined by this world, do not 'work'. Images were pushed to unfamiliar lengths precisely because what the poets tried to visualize in their poetry was unfamiliar, yet they were forced at the same time to utilize familiar images and expressions from the body of tradition, not wishing (perhaps unable) to break totally with the narrow strictures that defined poetry as poetry.

Poetry had been extensively used as a didactic vehicle for Islamic mysticism by the great exponents of mysticism like Sanai, Attar, Rumi, Iraqi, and Jami, yet didacticism is not at all apparent in the High-Period style, which is nonetheless pervaded with mystical notions and concepts. This style may in fact be seen as the fruition of the labours of the theorists and practitioners of Sufism in its codified form of post-Timurid eastern Islam. It was an attempt on the part of the poet to express by means of word pictures the Sufism then current—not true asceticism or mysticism (though individually many may well have been true mystics in every sense of the word) but rather Sufism as a way of life consisting mainly of ethical and also, to an extent, philosophical doctrines propagated through the Sufi orders. The language of poetic Sufism continued, as it had always done, to afford poets an opportunity to express sentiments that could never have been said openly or written in prose since, if objections were made, almost anything couched in poetry could be explained away as poetic license and metaphor.

As Sufism progressed through the ages and was incorporated as an institution, it had of necessity divested itself of much of its individual character and taken on the attributes of a much larger vehicle, wider in scope, to meet the needs of all those who sought an interiorization of the precepts of Islam. From a movement primarily concerned with union with the ultimate Reality in the here-and-now, Sufism gradually widened and spread and became a mass movement associated with trade guilds, chivalric orders, and finally the educational establishment. The basic teaching of Sufism shifted to a set of ethical values largely geared to teach individuals to incorporate other-worldly concerns into their daily lives.

By the time of the establishment of the Mughal empire, the fabric of Muslim society was so shot through with the threads of Sufism, or, as it may be conveniently termed to distinguish it from classical Sufism, 'sufistic thought', that all aspects of society had come to rely to some extent on the institution of Sufism. It was an age when kings and emperors paid court to the masters of the Orders, and princes of the blood were handed over to Sufi masters for their education. The *ghazal* had also been so suffused with Sufism from the fourteenth century on that it was, practically speaking, impossible to compose a lyric poem that did not reverberate with overtones of mysticism. The common stock of images forever played upon in the *ghazal*— 'night of union', 'cupbearer', 'drunken Turk', 'intoxicated eyes', etc.—were all bequeathed by the mystics and retained something of their mystical signification.

Unfortunately, *ghazals* do not make the transition into western languages well because of the very conventional quality that makes them what they are. When so much depends upon the language itself, and no western language has the stock of conventional images that Persian has built up, translations can convey only the most superficial or, at best, a one-dimensional level of a *ghazal*.

Two outstanding poets of the Akbar period were Faizi and Urfi. Abul Faiz (1547-1595), who used two pen names, Faizi and Fayyazi, was Akbar's poet laureate. A prolific author, in addition to his many fine *ghazals* and *qasidas*, he composed *masnavis* on the Indian story of Nala and Damayanti (*Nal u Daman*) from the *Mahabharata* and tales from the *Bhagavad Gita*. He wrote a treatise on Vedantic philosophy, *Shariq-ul-marifat*, translated Bhaskaracharya's *Lilawati* on arithmetic and geometry and Somadeva's *Kathasaritasagara*, and wrote a commentary on the Quran in Arabic, *Sawati-ul-ilham*, that contains no dotted letters, a feat of extraordinary erudition in consideration of the fact that fourteen of the twenty-eight letters of the alphabet would be unavailable. Like many other poets, he planned a set of five long poems in imitation of Nizami's *Khamsa*, but only the first, *Markazul-adwar*, and the third, *Nal u Daman*, were completed. In lines in

Faizi's *ghazals* the tendency to the *mazmun*, a play on a literary topos, can be seen. For instance, in the first line of the *ghazal* that follows it is taken for granted that the celestial sphere turns 'crookedly' because as it turns it produces untoward events that mar every individual's happiness. Taking this as the given, Faizi tells the celestial sphere to keep on with its crooked turning; he begs only that it turn a little slower because it is the night of union, when the poet is enjoying his beloved:

فلک، زین کجروی‌ها یت نمیگویم که برگردی
شبِ وصلست، خواهم اندکی آهسته‌تر گردی

زمهتاب رُخش ویرانهٔ من روشنست امشب
اگر وقتِ طلوعت آید، ای خورشید، برگردی

پس از عمریست امشب کوکبِ اقبالِ من طالع
ترا، ای شب، نمیخواهم بوقتِ خود سحر گردی

عجب نبود که جز روزِ قیامت پرده نگشائی
که ای صبحِ سعادت از شبِ من باخبر گردی

تو ای اختر شناس امشب توانی گفت گردون را
که بهر خاطرم برعکسِ شبهای دگر گردی

مها امشب بجانان دردِ دل دارم، میا بیرون
که میترسم خدنگِ آهِ فیضی را سپر گردی

Celestial sphere, I do not say that you should cease your crookedness. It is the night of union: I just want you to turn a little slower. 1

From the moonlight of his face my ruined hut is filled with light tonight. If the time of your rising comes, O sun, turn back! 2

After a lifetime, the star of my good fortune is rising tonight. O night, I don't want you to turn into dawn in your own time. 3

It is no wonder you won't lift your veil except on the day of resurrection, for, O morning of felicity, you will know of my night. 4

Astrologer, tonight you can tell the celestial sphere, for my sake, to turn in the reverse of other nights. 5

O moon, tonight I am unburdening my heart to my beloved. Do not come out, for I fear you will be a shield against the arrow of Faizi's sighs. 6

Jamaluddin Muhammad Urfi (1556-1591) was born in Shiraz, but early in life he went to Fatehpur Sikri, where he was patronized by Faizi and then by the court physician Hakim Abul Fath Gilani, who introduced him to the grand literary patron of the age, the Khankhanan Abdul Rahim. After gaining appreciable fame, he was enlisted in Akbar's retinue. The following pessimistic lines are taken from a long *qasida* in praise of the Imam Ali ibn Abi-Talib:

جهان بگشتم و در دل بسی شهر و دیار
نیافتم که فروشند بخت در بازار

کفن بیاور و تابوت و جامهٔ نیلی کن
که روزگار طبیبست و عافیت بیمار

زمانه مردِ مصافست و من ز ساده دلی
کنم بجوشنِ تدبیر وهم دفع مضار

زمنجنیقِ فلک سنگِ فتنه میبارد
من ابلهانه گریزم در آبگینه حصار

چنین که ناله ز دل جوشد و نفس نزنم
عجب مدار گر آتش بر آورم چو چنار

اگر کرشمهٔ وصلم کُشد و گر غمِ هجر
نه آفرین ز لبم بشنوند و نه زنهار

دلم ز درد گر انما یه چون جگر ز فغان
دماغم از گله خالی چو خاطرم ز غبار

گلِ حیاتِ من از بسکه هست پژمرده
اجل نمیز ندازد تنگ بر سر دستار

ز دوستانِ منافق چنان رمیده دلم
که پیش روی ز الماس میکنم دیوار

برونِ صورتِ دیبای پالشم کس نیست
کز آستین نم اشکم بچیند از رخسار

کدام فتنه بشب سر نهاده بر بالین
که صبحدم نشد از خواب روبمن بیدار

I have toured the world, but, alas, in no city or region have I found that luck was sold in the market. 1

Bring shroud and coffin, and dye your clothes indigo, for fate is a doctor, and health is his patient. 2

Time is a champion in battle, and I foolishly imagine that I can ward off loss with a breastplate of strategy. 3

From the catapult of the celestial sphere rain down stones of trouble: I stupidly flee into a crystalline fortress. 4

So much do cries boil up out of my heart, and yet I do not say a word—do not be surprised if I burst out in flame like a plane tree. 5

Whether flirtatious promises of union kill me or the grief of separation, neither will 'bravo' be heard from my lips nor 'beware'. 6

My heart is as heavy with pain as my liver is with cries; my mind is as empty of complaint as my mind is of worry. 7

The rose of my life is so withered that death will not stick it in to its turban. 8

My heart has so shied away from hypocritical 'friends' that I put a wall of diamond before my face. 9

Other than the pictures in the brocade of my pillow, there is no one who will wipe my tears from my cheeks with his sleeve. 10

What trouble has ever laid its head on the pillow by night that did not wake up in the morning with its face toward me? 11

Jahangir's poet laureate was Talib Amuli. He came to India from Iran and got himself attached to a provincial governor, Mirza Ghazi Beg Tarkhan in Qandahar, and he was in his retinue until Mirza's death in 1611. Next he became a protégé of Abdullah Khan, the governor of Gujarat. Through the good offices of Itimaduddaula, Nur Jahan's father, he became known in court circles, and in 1618 he was appointed poet laureate:

> On this date Taliba received the title of Maliku'sh-shu'ara [king of poets] and was clad in a robe of honour. He is originally from Amul. He was with Itimaduddaula for a while, but since the level of his poetry surpassed that of all others, he was enrolled as a court poet. These few lines are by him:
>
> Spring is much in your debt for having plundered the meadow, for the rose stays fresher in your hand than on the stem.
> I have so closed my mouth to speaking that you would say my mouth was a wound on my face that had healed.
> Love, from first to last, is nothing but singing and dancing. It is a wine that is enjoyable both new and aged.
> If I were a mirror instead of being a substance, how could I reveal you to yourself without a veil?
> I have two lips, one devoted to wine and the other apologizing for drunkenness.[21]

The following *ghazal* is a good example of his extremely large corpus:[22]

بتن بویا کند گلهای تصویرِ خالی را
بپا در جنبش آرد خفتگانِ قالی را
من و اندیشهٔ بوس و کنارِ او محالست این
مگر بینم بخواب این آرزوهای خیالی را
ترا باید ز خویش آموختن علمِ وفاداری
چه حاجت با معلم صاحبانِ درکِ عالی را
هنوز اندک شعوری دارم ای ساقی زمن مگذر
بچشمِ مستِ خود تکلیف کن این جامِ خالی را
حجابم غنچه سان در پردهٔ ناموسِ غم دارد
دریغا کاش مچیدم گلِ بی انفعالی را
گهی ابر تر و گاهی ترشّحِ گونهٔ باران
بیا در چشمِ من بنگر هوای بر شکالی را
فلک عاجز پسند افتاد، من هم در مماشاتش
تتبّع میکنم با شیرِ طبعی ها شکالی را
فرنگی شاهدانت ساقی بزرگمندهان ای دل
صنم میگوی و میکش بادهای پرتگالی را
زمرّدگانِ غزالانِ خامه ها سر کرده ای طالب
رقم زن بر بیاضِ دیده این اشعارِ عالی را

With his body he makes the roses in the design of a pillow fragrant. With his foot he makes the sleepers of a carpet (the fallen pile) come into motion. 1

Me and my thoughts of his kisses and embraces—it is impossible unless I see these fantastic wishes in a dream. 2

You will have to learn the science of faithfulness from yourself. What use do those possessing outstanding comprehension have of a teacher? 3

I still have a bit of feeling left, *saqi*. Don't pass me by. With your intoxicated eyes offer me this empty goblet. 4

My being veiled like a rosebud behind a curtain of honour gives me grief. Alas! Would that I had plucked the rose of immodesty. 5

Sometimes a damp cloud, and sometimes flowing like rain. Come, see in my eyes the monsoon weather. 6

The celestial sphere likes weaklings; I too follow in its footsteps. I follow the jackal with those whose natures are like lions. 7

European beauties are cupbearers at your banquet. Beware, O heart. Keep speaking of idols and quaffing Portuguese wine.8

From the eyelashes of gazelles you have made pens, Talib. Draw these wonderful lines of poetry across the whiteness of the eye. 9

This was also an age of witticism in poetry. Many a correspondence turned on an apt line or two of poetry, and many a place was secured by a witty response. When Jahangir offered Talib the post of keeper of the imperial seal, he refused in a long occasional poem in which these two lines occur, in which he puns on *mihr* 'affection' and *muhr* 'seal', which are written identically in Persian:23

ز شاعر ثنا سنجی آید، نه خدمت
که بلبل نوازن بود، نی شکاری
چو مهرِ تو دارم، چه حاجت به مُهرم
مرا مهر داری، به از مُهر داری

Singing praise is a poet's job, not service: a nightingale is a singer of tunes, not a bird of prey.
Since I have your affection, what need have I of a seal? For me to keep your affection is better than to keep your seal.

This was one area where secluded ladies could participate in life as actively as men, and many of the women of the Mughal house were accomplished poets, and through their screens they carried on repartees with the outside through the medium of poetry. We may mention particularly Shahjahan's daughter Jahanara Begum and Darashikoh's wife, Nadira Banu Begum, both of whom were known for their poetry, which varies between witty and delicately lyrical.

---

21. Jahangir, *Jahangirnama*, 319f.
22. Talib Amuli, *Kulliyyat*, 226.
23. Talib Amuli, *Kulliyyat*, 155, lines 4426, 4438.
24. Kalim, *Divan*, 414f.
25. Here the poet plays on the word *rifat* ('exaltedness'), which shares its initial letter, r, with the word for 'rank' (*rutba*).
26. Kalim, *Divan*, 294.
27. Kalim, *Divan*, 154.

During Shahjahan's reign the poet laureate was Abu Talib Kalim of Kashan (d. 1651). In many respects Kalim's career is typical of *émigré* poets, but he was more successful than most. Born around 1582, he came to the Subcontinent from Iran and is first heard of as a member of the retinue of Shahnawaz Khan Shirazi, the minister of Ibrahim Adil Shah of Bijapur in the Deccan. In 1619 he returned to Iran, which was several years after his patron's death in 1611. Then, in 1621, he was back in India under the patronage of Muhammad Amin Shahrastani Mir Jumla, who then held the position of *arz-mukarrir*, reviser of petitions, at the Mughal court. Kalim received his first reward from court, and his official recognition from the emperor, as the result of a quatrain he composed for the completion of a courtyard before the Hall of Public Audience in August 1628:

این تازه بنا که عرش همسایهٔ اوست
رفعت حرفی ز رتبهٔ پایهٔ اوست
باغیست که هر ستون سبزش سرویست
کآسایش خاص و عام در سایهٔ اوست 24

This new building, of which God's throne is a neighbour— 'Exaltedness' is only one letter of the rank of its pedestal.25
It is a garden, every green pillar of which is a cypress,
For the repose of elite and common alike is in its shadow.

It must have been around that time that he was given the title of poet laureate, for his occasional poems and chronograms for court events proliferate after that time. By 1645 he had retired to Kashmir with a court stipend. Kalim's poetry is filled with superb examples of constructed conceits:

با من آمیزشِ او الفتِ موج است و کنار
روز و شب با من و پیوسته گریزان از من 26

His affection for me is like that of the wave and the shore: day and night with me yet continually fleeing from me.

دل گمان دارد که پوشیده است رازِ عشق را
شمع را فانوس پندارد که پنهان کرده است 27

The heart thinks it has cloaked the secret of love: the lantern imagines it has hidden the candle.

PAGE OF CALLIGRAPHY
By Abdul-Rashid Daylami (d. ca. 1670), a famous Irani calligrapher who moved to the Mughal Empire during Shahjahan's reign. Persian. *Nastaliq* script. From the Mughal album of the National Library of Romania.

He is considered one of the chief exponents of the High-Period style, and he managed to introduce 'new words' (i.e., words not sanctioned by classical usage) into his poetry in a novel fashion, like the use of 'spectacles' in the following in conjunction with the classical *barikbini* (acuteness of sight, but literally 'thin-seeing', to accord with the slender waists that follow):

پیری رسید و موسم طبع جوان گذشت
ضعفِ تن از تحملِ رطلِ گران گذشت
باریک‌بینیت چو ز پهلوی عینکست
باید ز فکرِ دلبرِ لاغرمیان گذشت ²⁸

Old age has arrived, and the season of youthful nature has passed. The body is too weak to hold a heavy measure of wine.
Since your ability to see acutely comes from spectacles, you must give up thinking about slender-waisted charmers.

In Kashmir, he and a host of poets congregated at the assemblies of Zafar Khan (d. 1670), the governor of Kashmir and patron of literature, who also wrote poetry under the pen name of Ahsan.

Another master of the High-Period style (Indian-style) was Mirza Muhammad Ali Saib (1601-1678), who was from Isfahan. He came to India during Shahjahan's reign in 1628 and remained until 1657, when he returned to Iran to become Shah Abbas's poet laureate. His forte was the apophthegmatic *bayt*, or eminently quotable line, another hallmark of the style. As shown by the anthologies of the period, the outstanding individual line was appreciated far more than was the *ghazal* as a whole in which the line may have occurred, and every 'good' *ghazal* has at least one outstanding line designed to be a 'hit' at an assembly. The ingenuity and cerebral juggling of Sufistic and pseudo-philosophical themes reached their climax with Saib, whose poetry exerted great influence on the poets of the Subcontinent and the Ottoman empire for another century and a half:

این ناکسان که فخر به اجداد میکنند
چون سگ به استخوان دل خود شاد میکنند

These nobodies who take pride in their ancestors are like dogs making themselves happy with bones.

خروشِ سیلِ حوادث بلند میگوید
که خواب امن در این خاکدان نمی باشد

The shout of the torrent of events cries out, 'There is no sleep of security in this dust heap.'

با کمالِ احتیاج از خلق استغنا خوشست
بادهانِ تشنه مردن بر لبِ دریا خوشست
فکرِ شنبه تلخ دارد جمعهٔ اطفال را
عشرتِ امروز بی اندیشهٔ فردا خوشست
هر چه رفت از عمر یادِ آن بنیکی میکنند
چهرهٔ امروز از آیینهٔ فردا خوشست ²⁹

Despite all one's need, to be able to do without people is nice: To die thirsty-lipped on the edge of the sea is nice.
The thought of Saturday embitters the children's Friday: today's pleasure without thought of tomorrow is nice.
All that has gone of life is remembered with fondness: the face of today is nice in the mirror of tomorrow.

گفتگوی کفر و دین آخر بیکجا میکشد
خواب یک خوابست اما مختلف تعبیرها ³⁰

All this talk of infidelity and religion finally leads to one place: the dream is the same dream, only the interpretations differ.³¹

رفتن از عالم پر شور به از آمدنست
غنچه دلتنگ بباغ آمد و خندان برخاست

To leave this troubled world is better than coming into it: the rosebud comes into the garden with straitened heart and departs smiling.³²

---

28. Kalim, *Divan*, 123.
29. Saib, *Kulliyyat*, 262.
30. Saib, *Kulliyyat*, 75.
31. Browne, *Literary History* 4:271.
32. Translation cannot capture the pun on *khandan*, which literally means 'smiling, laughing' but of a flower also means 'blossoming,' which is, of course, how a rose leaves the garden. *Diltang* 'of straitened heart' was commonly used to describe a rosebud, which is tightly closed.

The ultimate in the High-Period style was reached by Bedil (1644-1721), who was universally recognized as the absolute master of the intricate conceit, and his poetry is still popular among Persian-speaking and-reading peoples in the Subcontinent and Afghanistan, though it is all but unknown in Iran. Typical of Bedil's poetry is the following, in which his pessimism is obvious: the only thing existence has to offer is trouble, and we would all have been better off resting where we were in our 'corner of nonexistence'. The perplexity engendered in the human heart by existence does not possess the power to boil up much in complaint; we are only a small whimper, but it echoes through the world:

مطلبی گر بود از هستی همین آزاد بود
ورنه در کنجِ عدم آسودگی بسیار بود
حیرتِ دل این قدر ها جوشِ نالیدن نداشت
ماحهان یک ناله ایم اما جهان کهسار بود ³³

> If there was anything to existence it was this very trouble; otherwise there would have been much repose in the corner of nonexistence.
> The heart's perplexity did not involve so much ferment of outcry: we are this one scream, but the world was mountainous.

Bedil's poetry also contains many lines with apophthegms like the following, which, while ultimately true, would not have been considered properly poetic in the slightest in the classical period:

مگذر از موقع شناسی ورنه در عرضِ نیاز
بیش از آروغ است نفرت آهِ بیهنگام را ³⁴

> Do not neglect to find the right moment; otherwise, in exhibiting your misery an ill-timed sigh is more disgusting than a belch.

Persian *ghazals* continued to be written well into the nineteenth century. The last Mughal ruler, Bahadur Shah Zafar (r. 1837-58), wrote *ghazals* in Persian, as did many of the nineteenth-century educated elite. But once Urdu became a respectable vehicle for poetry, Persian gradually receded into the category of a learned language and lost its immediacy.

The Masnavi. If the conventionality of the *ghazal* exerted an effective ban on incorporating the actual environment into poetry, this was not true of the *masnavi*. In form, the *masnavi* is an unlimited series of rhyming couplets held together by a common meter:

```
— — — —a | — — — —a
— — — —b | — — — —b
— — — —c | — — — —c
```

Masnavis have been written on every conceivable topic, and practically all poets tried their hand at the genre. It had always been the vehicle for narrative in Persian, and it was free of the conventional constraints that defined the *ghazal*. There are *masnavis* written about palaces, pavilions, and bathhouses—many of them actually inscribed on the edifices in question—and chronogrammatic *masnavis* for every conceivable event, births, marriages, deaths, journeys, battles, and victories. In one specialized type of *masnavi* called *shahr-ashob* the poet makes an imaginary tour through a city, detailing the devastating effects the arrival of a beauty in town has had on members of the various classes, trades, and crafts, punning for each with its own technical vocabulary. With this unfettered form, poets of the Subcontinent were at liberty to versify native Indian stories and legends. We have already mentioned Faizi's versification of the story of Nala and Damayanti. The Punjabi legend of Hir and Ranjha and the Sindhi tale of Sussi and Punhun also found their way into Persian *masnavis*. In 1730 the poet Afarin produced a version of Hir and Ranjha. One version of Sussi and Punhun, *Zeba u nigar*, was completed by Muhammad Rizai in 1643; another, *Sassi Pannun*, was composed by Jaswant Rai Munshi in 1727. During Akbar's reign Nawi wrote *Soz u gudaz*, the story of a Hindu woman who commits *suttee*. Based on a Hindi tale of Ratan Sen and Padmawat composed by Malik Muhammad Jayasi in 1540, is a Persian version by Bazmi (d. 1662) that was dedicated to Jahangir. Around 1601, Idraki Beglari wrote his Persian *Chanesarnama*, the Sindhi story of Lila Chanesar, in the style of Jami's *Yusuf u Zulaykha*.

HISTORY WRITING

Historical literature during the Mughal period is characterized by extremely florid, artful prose, and court-sponsored histories are even more so. This trend in Persian historiography was neither new nor developed by the Mughals but had been part and parcel of Persian prose writing long before the Mughals had anything to do with the Subcontinent. Prose embellished with internal rhymes and *tarsi*, a rhetorical device that uses Arabic words of identical patterns but different root letters to provide a jingly, quasi-rhyming character to prose, had been a hallmark of high historical prose from early Timurid times, when Sharafuddin Ali Yazdi's history of Timur, the *Zafarnama*, a prime example of the type, was considered the quintessence of artful prose. An example of *tarsi* taken from Muhammad Salih Kambo's history of Shahjahan's reign, *Amal-i salih*,[35] is as follows:

Chon asálat-i ummahát ʿumdatarin-i asbáb-i karámat u jalálat-i awlád
va najábat-i wálidát sharíftarín báʿis-i sharáfat u nabáhat-i abná-yi saʿádatnihád ast…

Here Muhammad Salih has said exactly the same thing twice ('since the blue blood of mothers is the surest means to assure the nobility of children'), but each time he has used completely different words, all synonyms, and each parallel pair contains the same sequence of vowels either completely (<u>karámat u jalálat</u> and <u>sharáfat u nabáhat</u>) or to a large degree (<u>asálat-i ummahát</u> and <u>najábat-i wálidát</u>); and even when the sequence of vowels is not the same, the parallel phrases rhyme (<u>awlád</u> and <u>abná-yi saʿádatnihád</u>). This is fairly easy to do using the Arabic vocabulary of Persian, but it is not easy to sustain through a long prose work. It is the sort of rhetorical trick the great master of Persian prose Saadi used to such good effect—and in great moderation—in his *Gulistan*. Once the style invaded history-writing, it became ever more complicated and tortuous, and rhyming devices protrude at every turn: the emperor is no longer simply *shahanshah* (king of kings) or *shah-i ru-yi zamin* (the king of the face of the earth), but he becomes *hazrat-i khilafat-martabat* (the presence as exalted in rank as the caliphate), which provides a triple rhyme in *-at*. When the tendency to periphrasis and metaphorical expression was given free reign, it resulted in passages like the following, which become all but mandatory to introduce any new rubric:

> Since constantly hidden in the recesses of the effulgent mind of the presence at which the caliphate takes refuge (= the emperor) was [a desire to] witness the manifestation of the loveliness and beauty of the exciting, sweet-zephyred charmer which is peerless Kashmir in the initial period of the season of spring, and a yearning to behold blossoms and flowers and observe tulips and hyacinths in the vigor of the age of youthfulness continually increased the degrees of desire, during this period, when the benevolent [imperial] mind was inclined on all sides to collectedness and no anxiety remained in any direction or on any account, therefore on the fifth of Shawwal in the Hijra year 1028 the banners of grandeur and majesty were raised in that direction.[36]

All court-sponsored Mughal histories indulge in this type of writing to some degree. Even histories that cannot be categorized as court literature, that is works produced outside the sphere of courtly literature and not sponsored directly or indirectly by the sovereign or court, are never free of what is now thought to be 'prolixity', which was considered a mandatory mark of erudition and good prose style. What we might consider good, straightforward prose would have been thought totally inappropriate for the history of such lofty, noble individuals. Of the myriad of histories written during the Mughal period, only a few can be mentioned here. The major histories of the individual reigns are as follows:

For Babur's reign there are Babur's own memoirs. His time is also chronicled in the *Habibus-siyar* by Ghiyasuddin Khwandamir (ca. 1475-1535), who was in India with Babur and Humayun from 1528 until his death.

Humayun's reign (1530-40, 1555-56) was chronicled by Mihtar Jawhar Aftabachi in his *Tazkiratul-waqiyat*, by Bayazid Bayat in his *Tarikh-i-Humayun* (covering the years 1542 through 1591), and by Humayun's own sister Gulbadan Begum in her *Humayunnama*. Khwandamir also wrote a *Humayunnama* in which are given the rules and ordinances established by Humayun.

---
33. Bedil, *Kulliyyat* 1/2:642.
34. Bedil, *Kulliyyat* 1:72.
35. Muhammad-Salih Kambo, *Amal-i salih* 1:46.
36. Muhammad-Salih Kambo, *Amal-i salih* 1:129f.

Akbar's reign (1556-1605) is well documented in the voluminous *Akbarnama* by the poet Faizi's younger brother, Abul Fazl (ca. 1551-1602), one of Akbar's intimates. The third book, the *Ain-i-Akbari*, contains a detailed historical, geographical, and institutional description of the empire. An indispensable tool for the study of the period, the *Akbarnama* remains a model of historiography. It has been translated into English, but no translation can capture the elegance or the difficulty of Abul Fazl's Persian prose. A master of Persian style, Abul Fazl also produced *Iyar-i danish*, yet another reworking of the Bidpai fables, which has a long history of translation, from Sanskrit into Middle Persian and then into Arabic by Ibn al-Muqaffa, and thence into New Persian by Nasrullah as *Kalila u Dimna-i Bahramshahi*, which in turn was rewritten as *Anvar-i Suhayli* by Mulla Husayn Waiz Kashifi in the late fifteenth century.

An unofficial, and often disapproving, history of Akbar's reign is contained in Abdul Qadir Badauni's *Muntakhabut-tawarikh*. It may be of interest here to compare the tenor of Badauni's history with that of Abul Fazl's. The author of the *Akbarnama* gives the following passage on the proceedings in Akbar's famous *Ibadatkhana*, in which account the rhetorical flourishes mentioned above are more than obvious, even in translation:

> At this time when the capital (Fatehpur Sikri) was illuminated by his glorious advent, H. M. ordered that a house of worship ('Ibádatkhána) should be built in order to the adornment of the spiritual kingdom, and that it should have four verandahs. Though the Divine bounty always has an open door and searches for the fit person, and the inquirer, yet as the lord of the universe, from his general benevolence, conducts his measures according to the rules of the superficial, he chose the eve of Friday, which bears on its face the colouring of the announcement of auspiciousness, for the out-pouring. A general proclamation was issued that, on that night of illumination, all orders and sects of mankind—those who searched after spiritual and physical truth, and those of the common public who sought for an awakening, and the inquirers of every sect—should assemble in the precincts of the holy edifice, and bring forward their spiritual experiences, and their degrees of knowledge of the truth in various and contradictory forms in the bridal chamber of manifestation.
>
> Wisdom and deeds would be tested, and the essence of manhood would be exhibited. Those who were founded on truth entered the hall of acceptance, while those who were only veneered with gold went hastily to the pit of base metal. There was a feast of theology and worship. The vogue of creature-worship was reduced. The dust-stained ones of the pit of contempt became adorners of dominion, and the smooth-tongued, empty-headed rhetoricians lost their rank. To the delightful precincts of that mansion founded upon Truth, thousands upon thousands of inquirers from the seven climes came with heartfelt respect and waited for the advent of the Shahinshah. The world's lord would, with open brow, a cheerful countenance, a capacious heart and an understanding soul, pour the limpid waters of graciousness on those thirsty-lipped ones of expectation's desert, and act as a refiner. He put them into currency, sect by sect, and tested them company by company. He got hold of every one of the miserable and dust-stained ones, and made them successful in their desires—to say nothing of the be-cloaked and the be-turbaned. From that general assemblage H. M. selected by his far-reaching eye a chosen band from each class, and established a feast of truth. Occasionally he, in order to instruct the courtiers, sent perspicuous servants who could discriminate among men, and these reflective and keen-sighted men brought every description of person to perform the kornish. Then that cambist and tester of worth examined them anew and invited some of them. There were always four noble sections in that spiritual and temporal assemblage. In the eastern chamber of worship ('Ibádatkada) were the great leaders and high officers who were conspicuous, in the courts of society, for enlightenment. In the southern compartment the keen-sighted investigators, both those who gathered the light of day (i.e., the Illuminati) and those who chose the repose of the night-halls of contemplation, sate in the school of instruction. In the western compartment those of lofty lineage practised auspicious arts. In the northern compartment were the Sufis of clear heart who were absorbed in beatific visions. A few of felicitous and wise comprehensiveness—which they had attained to by the bliss of H. M.'s holy instructions—lighted the torch of knowledge in all four compartments. Lofty points and subtle words passed from the holy lips, and physical and Divine truths trickled from that soothsayer of the court of variety, so that the leaders of the arena of manifestation, and the swift coursers on the mountains of contemplation burned with shame. It is of this condition that Zahir sings:
>
> In the glorious assemblage of his thoughts / Shame befalls the rose and the rosarium.
>
> A set of wisdom-hiving, judicious men were in readiness to propound questions and to record views. The difficulties of the various classes of men were fittingly resolved. The mirrors of the inquirers of the Age were polished. The whole of that

night was kept alive by discussions which approved themselves to one and all. The degrees of reason and the stages of vision were tested, and all the heights and depths of intelligence were traversed, and the lamp of perception was brightened. By the blessedness of the holy examination, the real was separated from the fictitious, and the uncurrency of those who were only coated with wisdom was brought to light… The various forms of ability came from the darkness of concealment to the hall of manifestation. Rather they came from the abyss of non-existence and were resplendent on the height of existence. If I were to record in detail the illustrious events of these glorious assemblages, and describe the attainments in learning of this school of truth, a separate volume would be required.[37]

Badauni's more sober account of the *Ibadatkhana* is as follows:

In the year 983 A.H. (1575 A.D.), the buildings of the Ibádat-Khánah, or 'Hall of Worship', were completed. The cause of their erection was as follows. In the course of the last few years the emperor had gained many great and remarkable victories, and his dominion had grown in extent from day to day, so that not an enemy was left in the world. He had taken a liking for the society of ascetics and the disciples of the celebrated Mu'iniyyah, and spent much time in discussing the Word of God and the sayings of the Prophet, likewise devoting his attention to problems of Sufism, science, philosophy, law, and similar matters. He passed whole nights in meditation upon God and upon the modes of addressing Him, and reverence for the great Giver filled his heart. In order to show his gratitude for his blessings, he would sit many a morning alone in prayer and mortification upon the stone bench of an old cell in a lonely spot near the palace. Thus engaged in meditation, he gathered the bliss of the early hours of dawn.

Having completed the construction of the 'Hall of Worship', he made a large chamber in each of its four divisions and also finished the construction of the tank called *anúptaláo*. After prayers on Fridays he would go from the monastery of the Shaikh-al-Islam and hold a meeting in this new building. Shaikhs, learned and pious men, and a few of his own companions and attendants were the only people who were invited, and discussions were carried on upon all kinds of instructive and useful topics. Every Sabbath evening he invited Sayyids, shaikhs, theologians, and nobles, but ill feeling arose in the company about the order of precedence, so that his Majesty commanded that the nobles should sit on the east side, the Sayyids on the west, the theologians on the south, and the shaikhs on the north. His Majesty would go to these various parties from time to time and converse with them to ascertain their thoughts. Quantities of perfume were used and large sums of money were distributed as reward of merit and ability among the worthy people who obtained an entry through the favour of the emperor's attendants. Many fine books which had belonged to Itmad Khan Gujarati and had been acquired in the conquest of Gujarat were placed in the royal library, but were subsequently brought out and distributed by the emperor among learned and pious men. One night the vein of the neck of the chief theologian of the age swelled up in anger and a great outcry and tumult arose. This annoyed his Majesty, and he said to the humble writer of these lines: 'In future, report any one of the assembly whom you find speaking improperly, and I will have him turned out.' Thereupon I said quietly to Asif Khan: 'According to this, a good many would be expelled.' His Majesty asked what I had said, and when I told him, he was much amused, and repeated my saying to those who were near him.[38]

He continues after a short digression:

His Majesty used frequently to go to the 'Hall of Worship' and converse with the theologians and shaikhs, especially on Sabbath evenings, and would sometimes pass the whole night there. The discussions always turned upon the principles and divergencies of religion, and the disputants used to exercise the sword of their tongues upon each other with such sharpness and animosity that the various sects at length took to calling each other infidels and renegades. Innovators and schismatics artfully started their doubts and sophistries, making right appear to be wrong and wrong to be right, and thus his Majesty, who had an excellent understanding and sought after the truth, but was surrounded by low irreligious persons to whom he gave his confidence, was plunged into scepticism. Doubt accumulated upon doubt and the object of his search was lost. The ramparts of the law and of the true faith were broken down, and in the course of five or six years not a single trace of Islam was left in him.

There were many reasons for this, but I shall mention only a few. Learned men of various kinds and from every country, as well as adherents of many different religions and creeds, assembled at his court and were admitted to converse with him. Night and day people did nothing but inquire and investigate. Profound points of science, the subtleties of revelation, the curiosities of history, and the wonders of nature were the continual themes of discussion. His Majesty collected the opinions of every one, especially of those who were not Mohammedans, retaining whatever he approved and rejecting

---
37. Abu'l-Fazl, *Akbarnama* 3:157-60.
38. Elliot, *History of India* 5:277-80.

everything which was against his disposition and ran counter to his wishes. From his earliest childhood to his manhood, and from his manhood to old age, his Majesty passed through the most diverse phases and through all sorts of religious practices and sectarian beliefs, and collected everything which people can find in books, with a talent of selection peculiar to him and a spirit of inquiry opposed to every Islamitic principle.

Thus a faith, based on some elementary principles, traced itself on the mirror of his heart, and as the result of all the influences which were brought to bear upon him, there grew (as gradually as the outline on a stone) the conviction in his heart that there were sensible men in all religions, and abstemious thinkers and men endowed with miraculous powers among all nations. If some true knowledge was thus to be found everywhere, why should truth be confined to one religion or to a creed like Islam, which was comparatively new and scarcely a thousand years old? Why should one sect assert what another denies, and why should one claim a preference without having superiority conferred on itself?

Moreover, Hindu ascetics and Brahmans managed to get frequent private interviews with his Majesty. As they surpass all other learned men in their treatises on morals and on physical and religious sciences, and since they attain a high degree of knowledge of the future and of spiritual power and human perfection, they brought proofs based on reason and testimony for the truth of their own religion and the falsity of other faiths, and inculcated their doctrines so firmly, and skilfully represented things as quite self-evident which require consideration, that no man, by expressing his doubts, could now raise a doubt in his Majesty, even though the mountains should crumble to dust or the heavens be torn asunder.

Hence his Majesty cast aside the Islamic revelations regarding the resurrection, the Day of Judgment, and the details connected with it, together with all ordinances based on the tradition of our Prophet. He listened to every insult which the courtiers heaped on our pure and glorious faith, which can so easily be followed; and eagerly seizing such opportunities, his words and gestures showed his satisfaction at the treatment which his original religion received at the hands of these apostates.[39]

And he continues in this vein, listing separately the gross offenses of every non-Muslim group and the heinous influences they exerted upon the emperor.

In line with Akbar's catholic interests, it was under him that translations from Indian literature flourished. The *Mahabharata* was translated at Akbar's order in 1582 by a collaborative effort involving the above-mentioned Abdul Qadir Badauni, Ibn Abdul Latif Husayni Naqib Khan, Muhammad Sultan Thanesari, and Mulla Sheri.

An abridged paraphrase of the *Mahabharata* was also made at Akbar's order by Tahir Muhammad Sabzawari, who also made a prose translation of the *Bhagwatapurana*. *Rajatarangini*, a twelfth-century history of Kashmir in verse by Kalhana, was translated at Akbar's order by Mulla Shah Muhammad Shahabadi in 1590 and rewritten by Badauni in 1591. Badauni also translated *Singhasanadvatrinshatika* (thirty-two tales of the throne) as *Nama-i khirad-afza* in 1574 and then revised it twenty years later. Always a very popular work, it was retranslated into Persian as *Singhasan battisi* any number of times, at least once during each reign until Aurangzeb's time (there is one by Chaturbhuja in Akbar's time, one by Baharmal Khattri in 1610, one by *Mahakavirai* (poet laureate) Sundardas in 1631, and one by Bisabrai also done during Shahjahan's reign). Badauni also made a translation of Valmiki's *Ramayana*, but he disapproved heartily of all these endeavours. Of the completion of the *Ramayana* he wrote:

> I seek refuge with God from that black book, which is as desolate as the record of my life. Reproduction of infidelity is not infidelity, and I utter a word in refutation of infidelity, for I fear that this book, all of which was written with loathing but in obedience to command, will cause deprecations to be rained down upon me.[40]

Shahjahan's eldest son, Dara Shikoh, was also deeply influenced by Sufism and mysticism, topics he treats in his *Majma al-bahrain*. As its title, which means 'Confluence of the Two Seas', indicates, it is an attempt to bridge the gap between Hinduism and Islam through mysticism. Translations from the *Upanishads* (*Sirr-i akbar*) were made by Dara Shikoh in 1657, and he commissioned Habibullah to translate the *Yogavasishtha* in 1655 (*Jog Bashist*). A translation of the *Bhagavad Gita* (under the title *Ab-i zindagi*) is also attributed to Dara Shikoh, as are translations from the *Mahabharata*.

For Jahangir's reign (1605-27), there are only Jahangir's own memoirs, selections from which have been given above, and the *Iqbalnama* by Jahangir's

---

39. Elliot, *History of India* 281-84.
40. Bada'uni, *Muntakhabu't-tawarikh* 1:366.

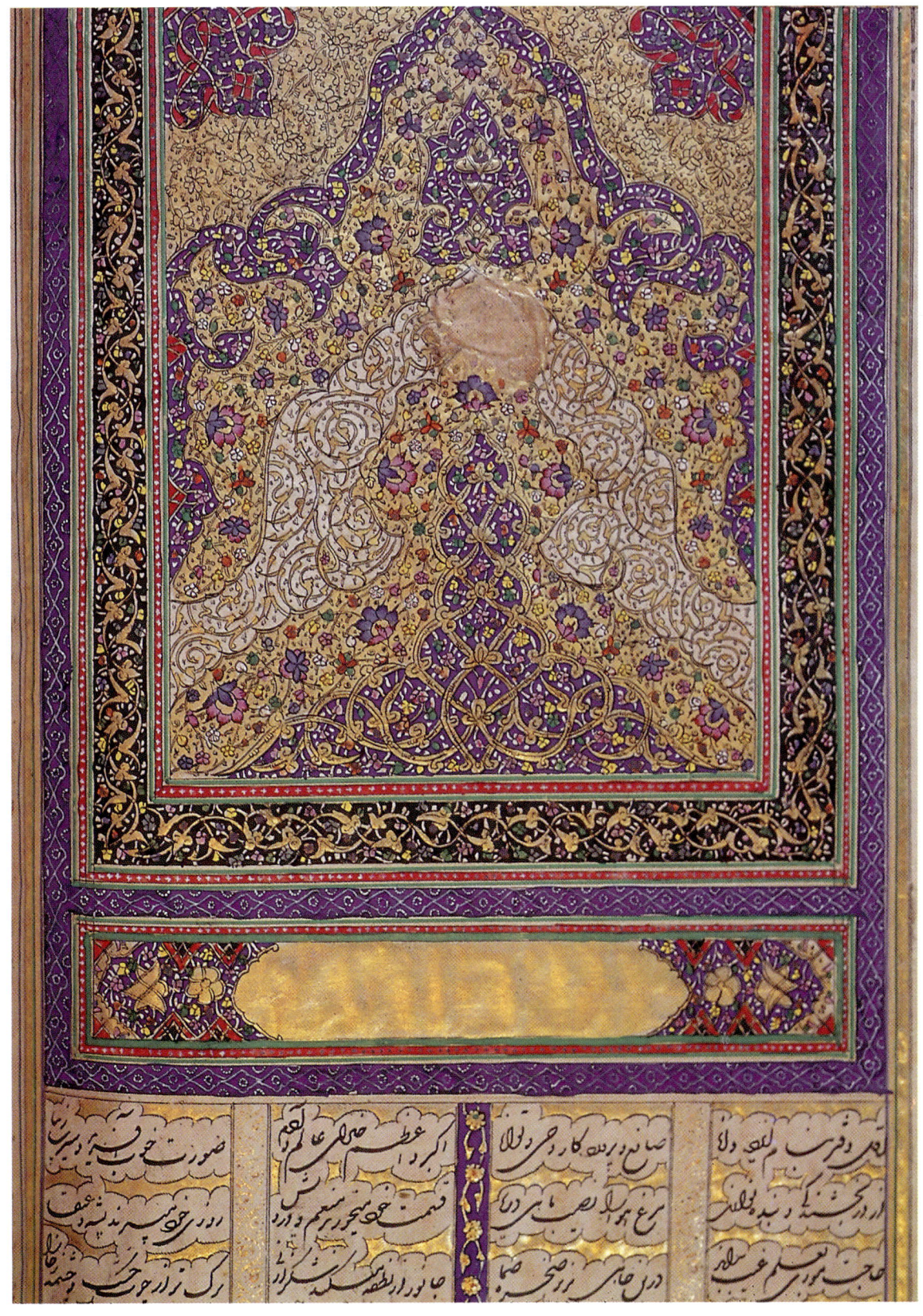

PAGE OF AN ILLUSTRATED MANUSCRIPT OF KULLIYAT-E-SAADI.
Shafia script with gold leaf, 1838. Photo: Mohammed Ali Qadir. Courtesy of Mohatta Palace Museum, Karachi.
Qalam: The Arts of Calligraphy Exhibition. NM 1958-226/3

private secretary, Mutamad Khan, whose work is based largely on the memoirs.

Shahjahan's reign (1628-58) was exceptionally well recorded by the historians Muhammad Salih Kambo in his *Amal-i-Salih*, Abdul Hamid Lahawri in his *Padshahnama*, Inayat Khan in his *Shahjahannama*, Sadiq Khan in his *Shahjahannama*, and Chandarbhan Brahman in his *Char chaman*, to mention but a few. There are also unfinished versified histories by two first-rate poets, Muhammad Jan Qudsi, *Zafarnama-i Shahjahani*, and Abu Talib Kalim, *Shahjahannama*, but they are of interest now only as specimens of literature, not as history.

Aurangzeb's reign (1658-1707) is chronicled in Muhammad Kazim's *Alamgirnama* and Mustaid Khan's *Maasir-i-Alamgiri*.

Three general histories deserve mention for their coverage and importance, particularly for the latest period treated by each: Mulla Ahmad Tattawi's *Tarikh-i alfi*, a commemoration of the first millennium of the Muslim world, was commissioned by Akbar in 1585. After Mulla Ahmad's death in 1588 it was continued by Jafar Beg Asif Khan and completed in 1589. Abdul Qadir Badauni's *Muntakhabut-tawarikh* covers the period from 997 to 1595, and it is useful for Akbar's reign 'as correcting, by its prevalent tone of censure and disparagement, the fulsome eulogium of the *Akbarnama*. Despite this systematic depreciation, it has been observed that Abdul-Kadir's narrative conveys a more favourable impression of the character of Akbar than the rhetorical flourishes of the Court journalist.'[41] Khwafi Khan's *Muntakhabul-lubab* covers the history of India from the Muslim conquest to 1731. Although Khwafi Khan's history is late, it is particularly valuable for the reigns of Shahjahan and Aurangzeb because it incorporates material written by eyewitnesses.

After Aurangzeb, prose and verse histories proliferate, but most are of limited interest. Ghulam Husayn Khan Tabatabai's (1727-ca. 1815) *Siyarul-mutaakhkhirin* should be mentioned, however. It covers the history of India from Aurangzeb's death to 1781 and is particularly valuable for the history of Bengal. Another work of great importance is Shahnawaz Khan Aurangabadi's *Maasirul-umara*, a biographical dictionary of nobles from the reign of Akbar down to the author's time (mid-eighteenth century). As enlarged by Shahnawaz Khan's son, Abdul Hai, who completed the revision in 1780, it is now an indispensable reference work.

BIOGRAPHY

Accounts of the lives of holy men and saints, as one might expect, flourished mightily in the Mughal empire. Only a small number of the many works devoted to holy men in general, saints of particular orders, or individuals can even be mentioned.[42] Jamali Dihlawi's (d. 1536) *Siyarul-arifin* is devoted to the lives of fourteen Chishti saints. Abdul Haqq Dihlawi's (d. 1642) *Akhbarul-akhyar* consists of short biographies of two hundred and fifty-five Sufi saints of India. Dara Shikoh's *Safinatul-awliya* (1640) contains notices of holy men, and his *Sakinatul-awliya* (1642) is an account of his spiritual mentor, Mian Mir, and his disciples. Dara Shikoh's sister Jahanara Begum wrote a biography of the great saint of Ajmer, Muinuddin Chishti, entitled *Munisul-arwah*, in 1640, and in 1641 she wrote her *Sahibiyya*, an account of Molla Shah, who died in Lahore in 1661. Shah Waliullah's *Anfasul-arifin* is on the lives, sayings, and miracles of the author's kinsmen. Ghulam Ali Azad Bilgrami's (1704-1786) *Rawzatul-awliya* treats the lives of ten saints buried at Khuldabad. Ghulam Sarwar Lahauri's *Khazinatul-asfiya* (1863) treats the great holy men of the Qadiris, Chishtis, Naqshbandis, Suhrawardis, and miscellaneous orders, saintly women, and deranged holy men.

TAZKIRA WRITING

The writing of *tazkiras*, biographical dictionaries of poets (or saints) with selected specimens of their poems, may not have been invented in India, but far more works of this genre have been produced there than elsewhere. To mention but a few,[43] Taqi Awhadi's (1565-1630) *Arafatul-ashiqin* contains mentions of over 3000 Persian poets. Amin Razi's *Haft iqlim* (1594) deals with 1500 poets, saints, and scholars arranged according to their country of origin. Mirza Muhammad Afzal Sarkhwash's (1640-1714) *Kalimatush-shuara* has short notices of two hundred poets who flourished during the reigns of Jahangir, Shahjahan, and Aurangzeb. The *Safina-i Khwashgu* (1724) by Bindraban Das Khwashgu is arranged chronologically and contains notices of 'ancient' poets, 'medieval' poets, and 'moderns' and contemporaries. Finally, Ali Quli Khan Walih Daghistani's *Riyazush-shuara* (1747-48) is arranged alphabetically and has notices of 2500 poets.

LEXICOGRAPHY

Jamaluddin Husayn Inju's (d. 1626) dictionary of Persian, *Farhang-i Jahangiri*, was begun by order of Akbar and upon completion in 1623 was presented to Jahangir, who notes the fact in his memoirs: 'He presented for my inspection the dictionary he had composed. He really took a lot of trouble with it and persevered in citing examples for all the words from the poetry of the ancients. There is no other such book in this field.'[44] A revised version, the *Farhang-i Rashidi* was made in 1654 by Abdul Rashid Tattawi. During the very late period, 'poetizing' versifiers demanded more and more rhyming words, necessitating ever more dictionaries and specialized glossaries of obscure and obsolete words and constructions. Scholars were happy to oblige, of course. What has been called 'one of the grandest dictionaries ever written by one man' is Rai Tekchand Bahar's (d. 1775) *Bahar-i ajam*, a voluminous dictionary of words and idioms used by Persian poets supported by copious examples.

---

41. Elliot, *History of India* 5:477.
42. See Storey, *Persian Literature* 1:967-1066.
43. For an exhaustive list, see Storey, *Persian Literature* 1:781-923.
44. Jahangir, *Jahangirnama*, 394.
45. See, for example, Stuart Cary Welch et al., *The Emperor's Album: Images of Mughal India* (New York: The Metropolitan Museum of Art, 1987), which reproduces an album made for Jahangir and Shahjahan. Virtually all the calligraphies are either signed by or attributed to Mir Ali, who flourished in the first half of the sixteenth century in Herat and Bukhara.
46. For reproduced examples of text pages, see Milo Beach et al., *King of the World: The Padshahnama* (Azimuth Editions & Sackler Gallery, 1997), 16.

* Editor's Note: Also see section on 'Mystical poetry in the vernaculars' in Annemarie Schimmel's chapter on 'Religion' in this volume.

CALLIGRAPHY

Throughout the Mughal period the normal style for calligraphic specimens and fine book production, at which the Mughal workshops certainly excelled, was the refined and elegant *nastaliq* character (a very debased form of which is the normal hand seen in Urdu signage these days). This style was raised to an art form in Timurid Herat at the beginning of the fifteenth century, and the Mughals were avid collectors of specimens of the classic masters of *nastaliq*, as only a glance at any of the many albums of calligraphy and painting made for them will attest.[45] Noted practitioners of calligraphy in Mughal India include Abdul Rashid Tattawi, Mir Muhammad Salih Kashfi (d. 1651) and his brother Mir Muhammad Mumin Arshi, sons of the calligrapher Mir Abdullah Tirmizi Wasifi (who received the title *Mushkin-Qalam* 'musky pen' from Akbar), and Muhammad Amin Mashhadi, who copied the text of the Windsor Castle *Padshahnama*.[46] Calligraphy in the 'classic' six pens also abounded in India, as one may readily see on practically any of the architectural monuments from the period. The calligraphy of the Taj Mahal is by Abdul Haq Amanat Khan. One innovation made during the Mughal period was the use of the *nastaliq* script as architectural ornamentation, and one may justifiably marvel at the poetry in *nastaliq* inlaid in black marble in Shahjahan's buildings in the Delhi Fort.

REGIONAL LITERATURE*

Literature in the regional languages of the northern Subcontinent scarcely figures during the high period of the Mughals. Most of the work done to reduce the regional languages of the Subcontinent to written form was done during the reign of the later Mughals, but there were a few early attempts, generally poetry of a Sufi and devotional nature.

For Pushto there was the famous poet Khushhal Khan Khattak (1613-1689), a contemporary of Shahjahan, and his Pushto poetry is still much appreciated.

For Sindhi, an early attempt was made in 1611 by Samayasunderji to write in Sindhi in a work called *Mrigavati charitra*. The poets Raju Darwesh (d. 1569), Abdul Karim Bulri (d. 1622), and Usman Ihsani (fl.

1640) all wrote on mystical themes. Sindhi literature flourished around the time of Shah Abdul Latif of Bhit (d. 1752), whose *Shah jo Risalo* is considered the great masterpiece of Sindhi literature. Of local interest to Sindh, though not in Sindhi, are the works of Ali Sher Qani Tattawi. His *Tuhfatul-kiram* (1766) deals in large part with the history of Sindh, and his *Maqalatush-shuara*, completed in 1760, consists of biographies of Persian poets of Sindhi origin. He also wrote an account of the saints buried on Makli Hill near Thatta, the *Maklinama*.[47]

Literary Punjabi began with the first *guru* of the Sikhs, *Guru* Nanak (1469-1538), and subsequent Sikh literature is written in Punjabi in an indigenous script based on Devanagari called Gurmakhi. The Punjabi poets Madho Lal Husain (1539-1593) and Sultan Bahu (d. 1691) both expressed popular, devotional Sufism in their native language. Another Sufi poet of the Punjab who used the rural folk idiom to express mystical experiences is Bullhe Shah (d. ca. 1758). The ever-popular Punjabi tale of Hir and Ranjha has been versified many times. One was mentioned in the section on *masnavis* above. Prose versions were produced in 1744 by Mansaram Munshi in Persian and in 1764 by Waris Shah in Punjabi.

Unlike any of the other regional languages, Bengali had a highly developed tradition of literature. Bengali flourished in the autonomous Hindu states of the eastern marches, where the local rajas patronized Bengali literature. In Rozanga, Dawlat Qazi (1600-1638) wrote a narrative poem, *Sati Moina*, representing the stages of union, separation, and reunion. Alaul (1607-1680), also a poet at the court of Rozanga, produced a Bengali version of Malik Muhammad Jayasi's *Padmawat* and a poem based on the *Arabian Nights* story of Saifulmulk and Badiuljamal.

Scarcely a vernacular tongue, Sanskrit also needs to be mentioned. Of course, the Mughal period falls long after the traditional end of Sanskrit literature, but works continued to be written by learned pundits. Samayasunderji presented a Sanskrit work, *Ashtalakshi*, to Akbar and received the title *Upadhyaya* in 1592. Jagannath Pandit was awarded the title of poet laureate, *Mahakavirai*, by Shahjahan and was a close friend of Asif Khan's and Dara Shikoh's. His *Jagadabharana* is a eulogy to Shahjahan and Dara Shikoh, and his *Asafvilasa* is a poem in praise of Asif Khan. His masterpiece is the unfinished exposition of literary criticism, *Rasagangadhar*. Also by him is a popular devotional poem, *Gangalahari*, also called *Piyushlahari*.

The bulk of what is now considered classical Hindi poetry was composed during the Mughal period, but till the seventeenth century the world of Hindi poetry was remote from the Mughal literary sphere, which was overwhelmingly Persianate.* Hindi poets were fostered at the Mughal court, and several were awarded the title *Mahakavirai* (great lord poet). In 1608 Jahangir writes of a Hindi poet who had written in praise of him:

> On the twenty-fourth [31 March], Raja Suraj Singh, my son Khurram's [later Shahjahan] uncle, came to pay homage. He brought Shyam, a cousin of the damn Rana's [Amar Singh of Mewar]. He is quite honourable and knows how to ride an elephant well. Raja Suraj Singh had brought along a poet who composed in Hindi. He presented a poem in praise of me that said, 'If the sun had a son, it would always be day and never night because after sunset the son would take the sun's place and keep the world bright. Thanks be to God that He granted your father such a son so that after his death the people should not have to wear mourning, which is like the night. The sun itself is jealous and says, "Would that I too had a son to take my place and not allow night to come to the world." By your brightness and brilliance, despite such a catastrophe, the world is so illuminated that it is as though night had neither name nor trace.' Rarely have I heard such subtle conceits from the poets of India. As a reward for this eulogy I gave him an elephant. The Rajputs call a poet *charan*. One of the poets of the age versified these sentiments [in Persian] as follows:
>
> If the world illuminator had a son, there would be no night and it would always be day / Because when he hid his golden crown, the son would show his diadem. / Render thanks that after such a father such a son has taken his place / That with the passing of that king no one made his clothes black in mourning.[48]

The tradition of conferring the title of *Mahakavirai* continued into Aurangzeb's reign. Two of his sons, Moazzam and Azam, were known for their patronage of Hindi literature.

---

*   **Editor's Note:** See chapter on Urdu Literature.

---

47. For works written in Persian on local and dynastic history for various regions in the Subcontinent, see Storey, *Persian Literature* 1:651-780.
48. Jahangir, *Jahangirnama*, 93.

BIBLIOGRAPHY

Abdul-Hamid Lahauri. *Badshahnama*. Edited by Kabir al-Din Ahmad and Abd al-Rahim. 2 vols. Calcutta: *Bibliotheca Indica*, 1867-78.

Abu'l-Fazl. *Akbarnama*. Translated by Henry Beveridge, 3 vols. *Bibliotheca Indica*, 138, 1897-1921; reprinted, Delhi: Rare Books, 1972-73.

Babur, Zahiruddin Muhammad. *The Baburnama: Memoirs of Babur, Prince and Emperor*. Translated by Wheeler M. Thackston. New York: Oxford University Press, 1996.

Badauni, 'Abdul-Qadir. *Muntakhabu't-tawárikh*. Volume 1. Edited by W. N. Lees, Kabir al-Din Ahmad, and Ahmad Ali. Calcutta: *Bibliotheca Indica*, 1864.

Bahar, Muhammad-Taqi. 'Saib u shiva-i u.' *Yaghma* 23, no. 5 (Murdad 1349).

Bausani, Alessandro. 'Contributo a una definizione dello "stile indiano" della poesia persiana'. *Annali dell' Istituto Univ. Orientale* 7 (1958): 167-78.

Bausani, Alessandro. *Storia delle letterature del Pakistan*. Milan: Nuova Accademia Editrice, 1958.

Bedil. *Kulliyyat*. 4 vols. Kabul: Pohni Matba'a, 1341-44.

Brown, Percy. *Indian Architecture: The Islamic Period*. Bombay: Taraporevala, n.d.

Browne, Edward Granville. *A Literary History of Persia*. 4 vols. Cambridge: At the University Press, 1956.

Elliot, Sir Henry Miers. *The History of India, As Told by Its Own Historians: Muhammadan Period*. Edited by John Dowson, 8 vols. London: The Grolier Society, 1907.

Ikrám, Shaikh Muhammad. *Rod-i Kawsar: Islámí Hind awr Pákistán-kí mazhabí awr rúhání táríkh*. Lahore: Feroz Sons, 1958.

Ikram al-Haqq, Shaikh. *Shi'r al-'ajam fi'l-Hind az avakhir-i 'ahd-i Shahjahan ta asas-i Pakistan*. Multan: al-Ikram, 1961.

Jahangir, Nuruddin Muhammad. *The Jahangirnama: Memoirs of Jahangir, Emperor of India*. Translated by Wheeler M. Thackston. New York: Oxford University Press, 1999.

Kalim Kashani, Abu-Talib. *Divan*. Edited by H. Partaw-Bayza'i. Tehran: Khayyam, 1336.

Marek, Jan. 'Persian Literature in India'. In Jan Rypka, ed., *History of Iranian Literature*. Dordrecht: D. Reidel, 1968. Pp. 713-34.

Marshall, D. N. *Mughals in India: A Bibliographical Survey of Manuscripts*. London and New York: Mansell Publishing Limited, 1967.

Sadiq, Muhammad. *A History of Urdu Literature*. London: Oxford University Press, 1964.

Saib Tabrizi. *Kulliyyat*. Edited by Amiri Firuzkuhi. Tehran: Khayyam, 1333.

Schimmel, Annemarie. 'Classical Urdu Literature from the Beginning to Iqbal'. *A History of Indian Literature*, vol. 8, ed. by Jan Gonda. Wiesbaden: Otto Harrassowitz, 1975.

Schimmel, Annemarie. 'Islamic Literatures of India'. *A History of Indian Literature*, vol. 7, ed. by Jan Gonda. Wiesbaden: Otto Harrassowitz, 1973.

Schimmel, Annemarie. *Pain and Grace: A Study of Two Mystical Writers of Eighteenth-Century Muslim India*. Leiden: E. J. Brill, 1976.

Storey, C. A. *Persian Literature: A Bio-Bibliographical Survey*. Vol. 1. London: Royal Asiatic Society of Great Britain and Ireland, 1970-72.

Talib Amuli, Maliku'sh-shu'ara. *Kulliyyat-i ash'ar*. Edited by Tahiri Shihab. Tehran: Kitabkhana-i Sana'i, 1346.

The Magnificent Mughals

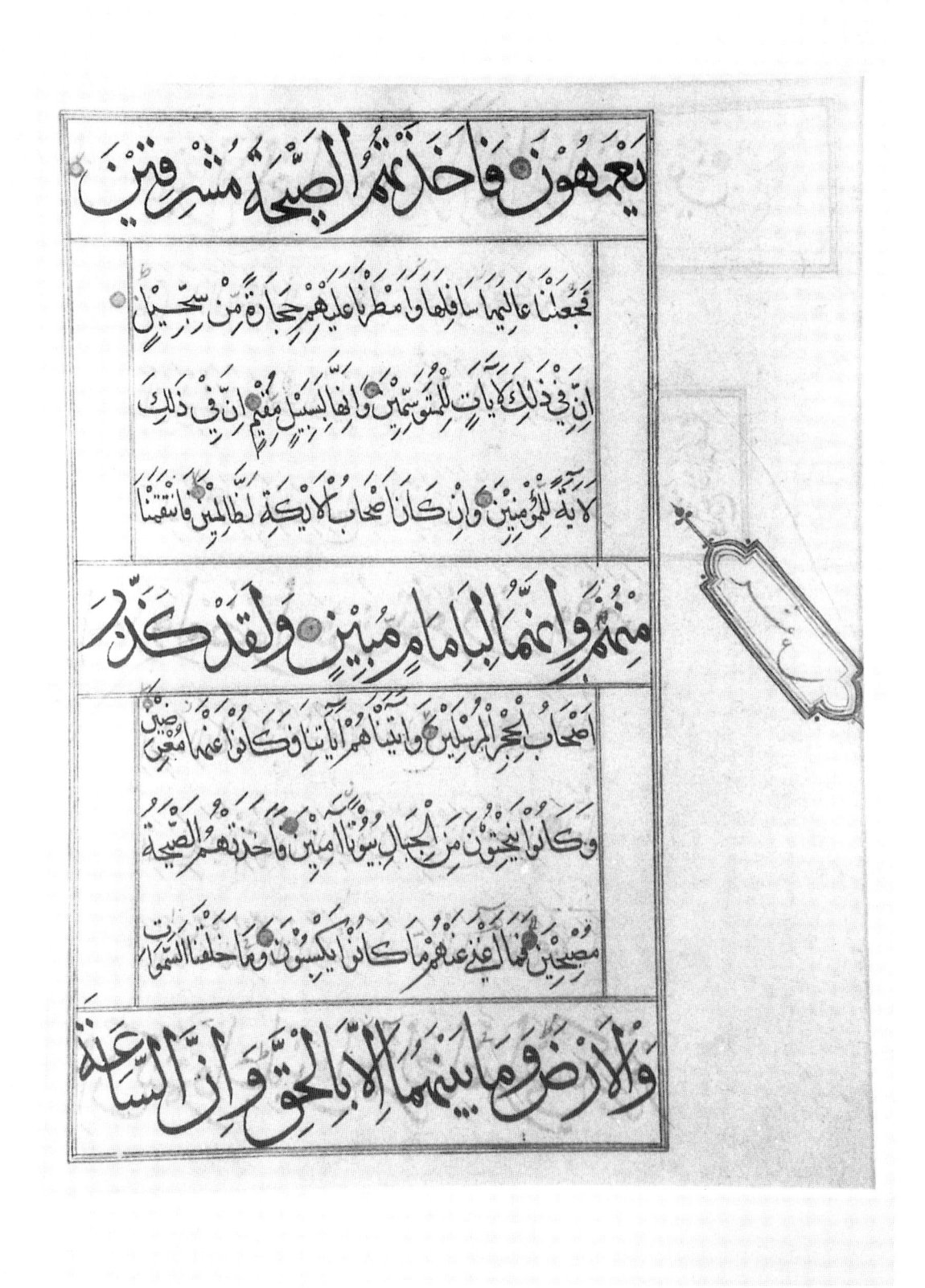

PAGE OF A QURAN.
Inscribed by Abdullah al-Khadim. 1616.
Photo: Homayra Ziad

5

URDU LITERATURE

Shamsur Rahman Faruqi

A GARDEN PARTY. Poetry, music, wine, a cloudy sky, the sound of flowing water: it seems to be a perfect occasion. Mughal, ca.1600. Courtesy of the Goenka Collection.

EARLY HISTORY

The story of early Urdu consists of a few small events and some large gaps. It also presents the historian with many puzzles whose existence, far less their solutions, had remained unsuspected until quite recently. Although the language must have existed by the early eleventh century, it was not known by the name 'Urdu' until the late eighteenth century. Continuous literary activity in the language is not traceable before the fifteenth century. The birth of the language most probably took place in the area around Delhi, which means chunks of territories now in modern Rajasthan, Haryana, and the western part of Uttar Pradesh. Regular literary production in the language began, however, not in Delhi, but in far away Gujarat. From Gujarat it spread to the true South and had many centuries of powerful growth in Gujarat and the Deccan.

No influence of Delhi can be seen on the Urdu literature of Gujarat and Deccan. The main reason is that Delhi did not then have any Urdu literature of its own, to influence or be influenced by others. Delhi had long remained a haven for Persian and continued to be so until at least the first half of the eighteenth century. Urdu literature in the meantime continued to flourish elsewhere, and the language over the centuries acquired a number of names: Hindvi/Hindi, Dihlavi, Gujri, Dakani/Dakhani/Dakhini. 'Hindustani' also seems to have been used, but not very frequently. Rare instances of the name being pronounced 'Hindui' (from *hindu* = Indian) are also known. 'Rekhta' as another name for this language became common in Delhi, along with 'Hindi', in the eighteenth century. The language name 'Urdu' appeared quite late in that century, but over the next hundred years it outbid all other names for the language and is its only name today.

The first known literary writing in Urdu was the product of Mas'ud Sa'd Salman's erudite and prolific mind. Salman (1046-1121), who lived in Lahore and was widely regarded as the greatest Persian poet of the age, is reported to have put together a *divan* (formal collection of poems) in 'Hindvi'—Urdu's most popular early name. Nothing of this collection survives, and the earliest indication even of its existence comes a century after Salman, in Muhammad Aufi's *Lubab-ul Albab*, a biographical dictionary of poets compiled in Sindh around 1220. Three quarters of a century later, Khusrau (1253-1325) wrote a seminal *Dibacha* (Preface) to one of his *divans* which he called *Ghurrat-ul Kamal* (1294). In this Preface, Khusrau mentioned Salman's Hindvi *divan*, and said that he (Khusrau) had also produced, for the delectation of his friends, 'a few quires of verse in Hindvi'. Unfortunately, almost nothing of Khusrau's Hindvi verse survives.

Thus there was nothing by way of Urdu literature in the two centuries between Salman and Khusrau, and another century had to pass after Khusrau before literary activity in Urdu can be discerned. Owing to the vast geographical spread of the language, and the flux of both time and its speech community, Urdu quickly developed a number of registers: Gujri; 'hard', or Sanskrit *tatsam*-and-Telegu influenced Dakani; 'soft', or Sanskrit *tadbhav*-and-Braj influenced Aurangabadi Dakani/Hindi; Dihlavi; Murshidabadi; and so on. Yet inspite of the great longevity, range and sophistication of the literature in Dakani, neither it nor any other register could acquire pan-Indian authority and normativity.

By the end of the seventeenth century, Urdu, or Hindi/Hindvi/Dakani as it was then called, had became the koine for the Subcontinent. India's greatest modern historian Tara Chand says that over the centuries (before English supervened), 'Hindustani', that is 'Hindi' with an overlay of Persian (=what is now called Urdu) was the lingua franca for all polite speakers throughout the Subcontinent. The Dihlavi register of Urdu had by that time already burst its local linguistic boundaries and had become established far into the South, in and around Aurangabad, as the Aurangabadi register of Hindi/Dakani. Now in the eighteenth century this powerful koine, as practiced in Delhi, became the measure and the lodestar against which all other registers were tested.

Ahad Ali Khan Yakta in his *Dastur-ul Fasahat* (composed in 1798, with emendations carried out until 1815), and Inshallah Khan Insha and Muhammad Hasan Qatil in their *Darya-e Latafat* (composed 1807) affirm the supremacy and normativity of Delhi's Urdu. Although none of the three came from the South, they did come from different backgrounds and places, and none of them was truly from Delhi either. In the South, Muhammad Baqar Agah (1745-1806) of Vellore, the greatest writer of that time in the 'hard' Dakani mode, also wrote in 'Rekhta', confirming thus not only his virtuosity but also the availability of 'Rekhta' as a literary medium that far into the South.

The acceptance of the Dihlavi register of Urdu as the pristine, authentic tongue was due in no small measure to one poet: Vali. Variously called Vali Gujrati/Vali Dakani/Vali Aurangabadi, he was born around 1665/7, and died in 1707/8. Already a substantial poet in Aurangabadi Hindi/Dakani, Vali's language was mutually comprehensible with the Delhi Hindi/Rekhta when he came to Delhi in 1700. There was very little Hindi/Rekhta poetry in Delhi at that time. Whatever there was, was in the *rekhta* genre. Rekhta was originally a kind of macaronic verse where a Hindi template was used for grafting Persian vocables onto it, or there was a Persian template with Hindi/Hindvi vocables grafted onto it.

That Vali's example must have shaken the polite society of Delhi out of its Persian-induced hubris is not to be doubted. The Persianate Delhi must have been somewhat shocked to realize that Aurangabadi Hindi/Dakani/Rekhta, in the hands of a true poet, was as flexible a medium of literary production as Persian. Whatever doubts remained, must have been blown away twenty years later when Vali's *Divan* arrived in Delhi. Shah Hatim (1699-1783), himself a major bilingual poet in Persian and Hindi/Rekhta was an eye witness to the frisson, the thrill, the new fire of inspiration that swept through Delhi at that time. As Hatim told Mus'hafi (1750-1824) later, poetry in Vali's style became in no time the only game in town.

The success story of Dihlavi Urdu must have caused divers kinds of discomfort to several sorts of historians. If Delhi and its Empire in the eighteenth century presented an unrelieved scene of decay, corruption and disintegration, how did a new and sophisticated linguistic-literary mode spring out of such chaos? And how could poor, battered, effete Delhi have had the authority to enforce that mode throughout the vast stretches of the Subcontinent? Urdu/Hindi/Rekhta was never the court language anywhere in the North. So even that *deus ex machina* couldn't be implored to provide the solution. Such questions were therefore not asked, and 'mainline' historians preferred not to make any observation on the literary-cultural vitality, power and resilience of Delhi in the eighteenth century.

Urdu was not even the court language at Lucknow, and in fact none of the regional courts that sprang up in the eighteenth century used Urdu as the court language, or a language in which official business could be transacted. Tipu Sultan perhaps did permit the Dakani mode of Hindi along with Kannada, but his reign ended in tragic defeat, and his example was not followed anywhere. Persian persisted well into the twentieth century as the official language at the court of Nizamul Mulk at Hyderabad.

Of course, all courts, whether regional, or at Delhi, began to employ Hindi/Rekhta poets from the eighteenth century. This was by way of patronage, and providing sustenance to a favoured subject, and had nothing to do with treating Hindi/Rekhta as a language of the court. Yet the very fact that the Mughal emperor Muhammad Shah (r. 1719-1748) was a connoisseur of Hindi/Rekhta poetry, and that Shah Alam II (r. 1759-1806) conducted informal conversations in Hindi/Rekhta, and was himself a Hindi/Rekhta poet and author of some distinction, lent immense prestige to Hindi/Rekhta throughout the Subcontinent.

As for those who like to put down—by way of praise or blame—all Urdu as a pale imitator of Persian, their dilemma was equally horrible. Delhi liked to see itself as home to Persian, and Khan-e Arzu, the greatest linguist and lexicographer of the eighteenth century, declared in his major work *Musmir* (Fruit-bearing Tree, ca. 1754) that the language of Delhi was Persian, the same as that of the great Iranian poets of the past, and Delhi's Persian was in fact better than that of other extant Iranian cities for Delhi's Persian register was normative for the entire country.

There is considerable force in Khan-e Arzu's assertion, because the elite of Delhi, and many commoners and unlettered people too, were then perfectly fluent in spoken, even literary Persian. Khwaja Nasir Andalib (1696/7-1758/9) was a major Sufi of Delhi. Khan-e Arzu describes him as 'not having acquired knowledge of the outer sciences, *tahsil-e ilm-e zahir na karda*.' The saint also occasionally describes himself as 'unlettered' (*ummi*). Apparently he knew just enough to write, and nothing more. Yet he composed huge Sufiistic texts in highly literary and learned Persian; the texts were taken down to his dictation mostly by his even more famous son Khwaja Mir Dard (1720-1785). Occasionally, when no amanuensis was at hand, he himself did the writing.

Given this background, our Persianate historians held that Urdu poetry in Delhi, if not everywhere else, was bound to be just an appendage of Persian. Yet Delhi, great House of Persian for at least seven centuries, had no tradition of Urdu (= Hindi/Dihlavi /Rekhta) poetry. Persian alone could not provide the creative fillip that was needed to effect the switch from Persian to Hindi/Rekhta. The great flowering of Urdu /Hindi/Rekhta in Delhi came to be only when the Dakani creative strain impinged upon the admittedly puissant creative forces that were already in Delhi, like sun-dried earth, waiting to be quickened by the warm, welcome, but alien rain.

That Delhi Urdu did as much for literature as all Gujri and Dakani put together again attests to the vast creative urge for Urdu that had lain dormant in Delhi, its ear to the ground, keen to descry, however dimly, the coming of the catalyst which would open up the ground for ever. Urdu in Delhi at that time was, as Rumi said in another context, like:

Deep into the bush—
Tigers
Waiting for the command;
Come!

* This section was originally published as 'Conventions of Love, Love of Conventions: Urdu Love Poetry in the Eighteenth Century', in *The Annual of Urdu Studies*, No. 14 (1999); ed. Muhammad Umar Memon.

✦ Author's Note: Original texts of the Urdu and Persian *shers* quoted by me can be seen in the Appendix. All translations from Urdu and Persian are by me. Following the convention of English literature, I have translated the poems depicting the beloved as female, though that may not be necessarily the case in the actual text. In the actual text, the beloved's gender would often be indeterminate; in many cases, the beloved's grammatical gender would be male, but the beloved himself/herself could well be read as female. In some cases the gender is specifically male. Where the gender, and not only grammar, is clearly male, I have allowed for it in the translation, trying to make the gender aspect as unobtrusive as the demands of translation authenticity would permit. Always provided that in very many cases the poem could sustain a Sufistic interpretation, the beloved's gender notwithstanding. This section deals only with the *ghazal*, but many of the ideas suggested here can be applied to non-*ghazal* love poetry of the period in question.

I must thank Nasir Ahmad Khan of the Jawaharlal Nehru University whose persistent reminders made me collect my ideas on this subject and attempt this paper.

'Official' historians find nothing but negative images in the Delhi of the eighteenth century because such a view is on all fours with the colonialist discourse, and, let me add, even the Marxist discourse. For did not Marx view the British rule in India as a potent instrument of History which catapulted India into the pre-Industrial society? The actual reality was rather more complex. Certainly the eighteenth century did not view itself as living at the edge of an Apocalypse or Armageddon. It saw itself as a continuation of the ages of Babur and Akbar through Aurangzeb. Wars of succession, temporary failure of the Centre to hold together, or the emergence of new alignments, were nothing new to the Indo-Muslim political culture.

Culturally and spiritually, the eighteenth century was more vibrant than its predecessor. In the field of Urdu and Persian literature, it was the inheritor and perfector of the 'Indian style' of literary expression which had over the centuries been fashioned alike by Hindu, Indian Muslim, Iranian, Tajik, Uzbek and Pathan and by a variegated host of poets like Kabir and Malik Muhammad Jayasi who did not write in Urdu or Persian. But for Delhi and the eighteenth century, Urdu literature would have remained locked away in distant places, like the obscure contents of the treasure chests of provincial families.

URDU LOVE POETRY IN THE EIGHTEENTH CENTURY*✦

Next to our own, the eighteenth century is the most exciting, vibrant, and productive century in more than five hundred years of literary production in Urdu. Perhaps the most remarkable thing that happened in Urdu literature during that time—traditionally represented by British historiography-influenced writers as a period of decay and disintegration—was the consolidation and discovery of a poetics, of a whole new way of charting out a course for literary creativity in a language that, in Delhi at least, was still a little tottery on its legs in the field of literary production. Delhi, even in the middle of the eighteenth century, boasted of Persian as the *zaban-e urdu-e mua'lla-e shahjahanabad* (the language of the exalted city of Shajahanabad). It described Sanskrit as *hindi-e kitabi* (learned *hindi* = Indian), and the city's common, spoken language, was known as plain *hindi*. Very little literature in *hindi* was produced in Delhi during the period 1600-1700—and hardly any during the four preceding centuries—and the literary form of *hindi* in which the literature was produced was called *rekhta* (mixed, poured, cement-and-mortar, etc.) The term Urdu as a language name came into use much later.* Rekhta/Hindi remained the universal name for the language until the end of the eighteenth century.

Rekhta may have begun independently, as a pidgin. It is more likely that it began as a kind of macaronic verse in Hindi, and gradually assumed a life of its own, so much so that the pidgin element was eliminated, giving room to a literary Hindi, such as was already being written in the Deccan, particularly Aurangabad, under the name of Dakani and/or Hindi. However, Delhi, with its cosmopolitan cultural environment, long continued to look upon Rekhta with a faint air of disapproval, as something different from, and inferior to Persian. There is a famous verse by Qa'im Chandpuri (1724-94):

(1) Qa'im, it was I who gave
To Rekhta the manner
Of the *ghazal*. For otherwise
It was just a feeble thing,
In the language of the Deccan.

This tendency for the word *ghazal* to be taken to mean only Persian *ghazal*, continued until quite late in Delhi. Thus we have Ghulam Hamdani Mus'hafi (1750-1824), writing around 1820:

(2) Mus'hafi, I compose Rekhta
Better than the *ghazal*. So why
Should now one be
A devotee
Of Khusrau and Sa'di?

Delhi's Rekhta/Hindi acquired a literary status and a sophistication that was soon to surpass, or equal, the best achievements of the past three centuries in Gujarat and the Deccan. This happened mainly due to Vali (1665/7-1707/8), an Aurangabadi by birth, who came to Delhi in 1700. At that time, he was a substantial poet in his own right, regarding only the Persian poets—Iranian or Indo-Persian—as worthy of his mettle. There is a story about Vali being advised at that time by Shah Gulshan in Delhi to appropriate the rich store of themes and images in Persian and thus introduce a new depth and space in his Hindi/Dakani. There are reasons to disbelieve this story. There is, however, little doubt that Vali's full *Divan* arrived in Delhi in 1720. According to Mus'hafi, Shah Hatim (1699-1783), who was an eyewitness to this event, told him that Vali's poetry took Delhi by storm, and became instantly popular with young and old, rich and poor.

It is this *Divan* which provided a jumpstart to Rekhta/Hindi poetry in Delhi, not only by providing an active model, but also by introducing new theoretical lines of thinking about the nature of poetry, and about how to make poems. In short, Vali seems to have provided both the model, and the theory that went with it.

There is an interesting *sher* (verse), again by Mus'hafi, in his third *Divan*, compiled in 1794. He says:

(3) Oh Mus'hafi, I have,
In this *urdu* of the *Rekhta*
Introduced a thousand new things
Of my own making.

There is a certain piquancy in the phrase '*urdu* of the *Rekhta*.' (Does it mean Urdu language as derived from the Rekhta, or does '*urdu*' mean 'royal court, camp, camp-market'? 'Royal court' seems the more likely meaning.) Yet what is most notable here is the bold assertion of invention, the poet's confidence and assurance in his own role as a 'maker,' and not just 'imitator' of things in poetry. Judging from the fact that this proudly soaring self-belief is of a poet who wasn't even born in Delhi, and was not a witness to the momentous arrival, more than sixty years ago, of a new wave of poetry in Delhi, it is easy to see that Rekhta/Hindi poetry in the North came of age within a very short time, and the tree of invention in Rekhta continued to give off new shoots for a long time to come.

The major discovery in the theory—we first hear about it in the Deccan, in *'Ali Nama* (1672), a long poem by Nusrati Bijapuri—was in the concept of *ma'ni*. Nusrati speaks of *mazmun*, and *ma'ni*, as two separate entities. Classical Arab-Persian literary theory spoke

---
* **Editor's Note:** For further elaboration, see pp. 136-137.

only of *ma'ni*—a word now universally translated as meaning—in the sense of the 'content' of a poem, the assumption being that a poem meant what it 'contained.' Nusrati, however, uses *mazmun* in the sense of theme, content, the thing/object/idea, which the poem is about. The term *ma'ni* he uses to connote the 'meaning,' that is, the inner, deeper, or wider signification of the poem. Vali too uses the two terms in the senses described above. After him, all Rekhta/Hindi poets in Delhi constantly make use of the distinction for making points about the nature of poetry.

Since the 'theme/meaning' distinction doesn't occur in Arabic or Persian, it is strongly probable that Nusrati, a man of great learning, picked it up directly from the Sanskrit, or from Telegu and Kannada, languages which he would have known, and whose poetics is almost entirely derived from Sanskrit. Or he may have come across this idea in the Persian poets of the 'Indian style' (*sabk-e hindi*) who themselves may have developed it through their direct and indirect contact with Sanskrit language and literature from mid-sixteenth century on. These contacts, by the way, remained very strong in the eighteenth century all over the Subcontinent, and their effects permeated Rekhta/Hindi poetry as well.

Many advantages accrued to Rekhta/Hindi from this discovery about the dual nature of meaning. For our purposes, the most important seems to have been the change in the ontological status of the lover and the beloved. Now, the lover in the poem need not have been the poet himself, nor did the beloved necessarily have to be 'real' or a 'real-life' person. In the Deccan, Dakani/Hindi poets often spoke in the female voice—poets like Hashimi Bijapuri (1635-1697/8) consistently adopted the female persona in the *ghazal*. Others moved freely from one persona to the other.

The recognition of the poem being splittable into 'What is it about?' and 'What does it mean?' meant that the poet could assume any persona—now it was not, for instance, Vali the person, who was speaking in the poem, but there was a voice, and Vali the poet was only the articulator of that voice. Again, if the poem could mean something else, or more, or different, from what it was about, the person or object or thing about whom, or as a result of transactions with whom, the poem came into existence, need not be fixed in any particular gender, for that would tend to limit the 'meaning' aspect of the poem.

Ghalib (1797-1869) made the point nicely, more than two centuries later. Qadr Bilgrami, a pupil of his, sent him a *ghazal* for correction. The *matla'* (opening verse) can be translated as follows:

(4) You brought me into the world
     And gave me the poison
     Of mortality. What a pity!
     You cheated, leaving me alone
     In this maze.

Ghalib wrote back,

> Tell me, who is it you are addressing here? Except for Fate and Destiny none else, no boy, no woman, can be imagined to be the addressee.... So I changed the person of the verb to plural...now the utterance is directed equally to the worldly beloveds, and Fate and Destiny.

The contribution of Vali in the development of the new ontology is that in his case, the beloved is occasionally female, often it/he is male, and in many cases indeterminate. The significance of this is that the notion—articulate or inarticulate—of the protagonist or the speaker in the poem assumes a critical importance. The protagonist-lover could now be just a notion, an ideal lover, whose gender was not so important as the ideas that could be expressed and realized in the poem by whatever metaphorical construct lent itself conveniently at the moment. Just as the woman/man lover was not actually a woman or a man, so the woman/man/boy beloved was not actually a woman, man, or boy.

Since the convention of having the 'idea' of a lover or beloved instead of an actual lover/beloved freed the poet-protagonist-lover from the demands of 'reality,' or 'realism,' love poetry in Urdu from the last quarter of the seventeenth century onwards consists mostly—if not entirely—of 'poems about love,' and not 'love poems' in the Western sense of the term. This is true of almost all of Indian style Persian poetry too—for obvious reasons—and even a lot of other Persian poetry of earlier times. But the distinction between poet—the person, who actually wrote the poem—and protagonist—the person, or the voice, which articulated the poem—was nowhere so seriously adduced and practiced as in the Indian style Persian poetry, and Urdu love poetry of the eighteenth century.

The *ghazal* is often described by West-oriented Urdu critics as a 'lyric,' and the main quality of the *ghazal* as 'lyricism.' Modern Urdu critics even invented a new term, *taghazzul* (*ghazal*-ness), to describe this quality. It comes as a surprise, if not an incredible and unpleasant shock, to modern students to be told that the term *taghazzul* does not occur in any work or document extant to us from before 1857, the time when a great discontinuity began in our literary culture through colonialist interventions.

There are serious flaws in the proposition that a *ghazal* is a lyric, and that a rose by any other name, etc. While there is no one, hegemonic, seamless image of the lyric in Western poetics, the lyric is generally understood there to be a poem in which the poet expresses 'personal' emotions and 'experiences,' and does not, in the nature of things, assume an external audience for his poem. Both these assumptions are false for the *ghazal*. We just saw how new developments in Urdu poetics split the poet-poem-as-one notion, in which a main line 'lyric' poem would seem to be anchored. As for the audience, since the *ghazal* was intended to be recited at *musha'iras* and public gatherings, and was in any case largely disseminated by word of mouth, the whole proposition of the *ghazal* as a 'personal-private-no-audience-assumed' text becomes ridiculous.

The fact that the *ghazal* is a poem in which oral performance plays a great part has other important consequences. One consequence is that a *ghazal* may perhaps be expressive of 'emotions,' in the ordinary sense of the term. But these are not necessarily the poet's 'personal' emotions 'recollected in tranquility' (Wordsworth), or 'the spontaneous expression of the powerful feelings of the heart' (Wordsworth), or the 'lava of the imagination whose eruption prevents an earthquake' (Byron). It was the 'verbal contraption' in the poem, to use Auden's phrase, which became the chief object of the poetic exercise. Poems needed to make sense of the experience, or the idea, of love, and in terms that made sense to the audience as a whole, and not a specific individual, beloved, or friend.

Byron was nearer the mark when at another place he said that the poet was 'the most artificial' of the artists. But the ideas about the nature of poetry—*all* poetry—that won the day in Urdu, through the efforts of the great modernizers of the late nineteenth century, were those of the 'lava of the imagination' type, and echoed writers like Wordsworth and Hazlitt, who insisted that a certain lack of 'art' and an overflow of 'passion' were the hallmarks of poetry. Hazlitt, one might recall, said that there was a natural and inalienable connection between passion and music, and music and poetry. Then he went on to say, 'Mad people sang.' Small wonder that phrases like *shirin divanagi* (delectable madness) became the stock in trade of our modern critics when they spoke of the kind of *ghazal* they admired.

The distinction between *mazmun* (theme, motif) and *ma'ni* led to the recognition of the fact that there was a universe of discourse particular to the *ghazal*. Certain kinds of *mazmuns* were admissible in this universe of discourse; others were not. Thus while *mazmuns* were infinite in theory, each *mazmun* had to have affinity with other *mazmuns* before it could be considered a proper subject for poetry. Hence one major convention—common, by the way, to Sanskrit, Indian style Persian poetry, and Indian style Turkish poetry—was that *mazmuns*, even words and images, already used, should be reused, though in a new way or with a new slant. 'Personal' or 'personalized' narration was by no means barred, but was not to be encouraged, and preferred only when it made sense in general terms.

One of the recurrent themes in the eighteenth-century Urdu *ghazal* is the poet's self-denigration as a 'writer of elegies,' and not of poems proper. Here are some examples:

(5) Nothing falls from the lips of Qudrat
But lamentation. He's no poet
But an elegist for his own heart.
(Qudratu 'l-Lah Qudrat, 1713-91)

(6) It's a whole age
Since Mazhar has been pouring
His lamentations into meter,
And yet in the beloved's mind,
He doesn't speak like a poet.
(Mirza Mazhar Jan-e Janan, 1699-1781)

The above verse is in Persian; Mazhar was a major Sufi and an important Persian and Urdu poet in Delhi, and is described as having influenced a great number of Urdu poets, especially in the first half of the century.

(7) Don't describe me as a poet, Oh Mir,
   I collected numerous griefs and sorrows
   And made up a *Divan*.
   (Mir, 1722-1810, in the first *Divan*, compiled around 1754)

(8) I just don't know
   If my *Divan* is a book,
   Or an elegy, or
   Anything at all.
   (Mus'hafi, in *Divan* I, ca. 1785)

(9) I am not really a poet, Oh Mus'hafi,
   I am an elegy-reciter;
   I recite the *soz*, and make
   The lovers weep.
   (Mus'hafi, *Divan* III, ca. 1794)

In fact, we can see this convention in action even in the nineteenth century. Here is Saiyad Muhammad Khan Rind (1797-1857):

(10) Those of a loverly temperament
    Often weep while reading them;
    Indeed, the poems of Rind
    Are not poems, but elegies.

Poetry thus was basically a quest for themes, and love was just another theme, not an event in the poet's real life; only that in the *ghazal*, love was the most important theme. And the core function of love was to soften the heart, to make it receptive to more pain, which ultimately made the human heart a site for the Divine Light to be reflected upon and into it. Pain, and things that caused pain, had a positive value. The lover's place was to suffer; the beloved's function was to inflict suffering. This was a Sufistic formulation, but was regularly taken by the *ghazal* poet to be true for the *ghazal* universe. Shaikh Ahmad Sirhindi, a leading Sufi of the early seventeenth century, wrote that the lover should desire that which is desired by the beloved. Since the lover suffered pain and grief, it is obvious that that was what the beloved desired for the lover. To ask for, or long for, comfort was therefore 'unloverly'.

All this was *mazmun* for Urdu love poetry in the eighteenth century. The poet suffered pain also in search of *mazmuns*. Or he wept for a *mazmun* that was lost, or couldn't be realized, or which was experienced for a moment, and then lost. One is reminded of Shelley's characterizing the creative process as being

> conscious of evanescent visitations of thought and feeling sometimes associated with a place or person, sometimes regarding our mind alone, and always arising unforeseen and departing unbidden....

So the poet toiled to get the lost visitations back, or mourned at their departure. Mir said:

(11) You have neither grief in your soul
    For the *mazmun*,
    Nor is your heart soft with pain.
    So even if your face was pale like
        parchment,
    What of it?
    (*Divan* IV, ca. 1794)

The lover-protagonist and the beloved-object both live in a world of extremes: supreme beauty, supreme cruelty, supreme devotion—all things are at their best, or worst, in this world. The beloved-object is not a passive recipient of the lover-protagonist's tribute of love, or a helpless non-entity unable to alleviate the lover's pain or ameliorate his condition. The beloved's 'cruelty' may be real, or act as a metaphor for his/her indifference or physical distance from the lover. But the indifference of the beloved is an active stance, it makes a point. The lover-protagonist would prefer death at the hands of the beloved to his/her indifference. Or if one does find oneself to be lucky enough to be killed by the beloved, there are degrees of merit and distinction in death, too. The lover-protagonist is the only true lover: all the rest are false, and given to *havas* (lust), rather than *shauq* (desire), or *'ishq* (love). There is a famous Arabic saying: *al-'ishqu narun yuhriqu ma siva al-matlub* ('ishq is a fire that burns down everything but the object of desire). The rival, the Other (*ghair*) doesn't burn with that fire; even if the beloved kills him, he earns no distinction:

(12) There's the difference of earth and sky
    Between the death of the *ghair*
    And my giving up the ghost:
    Doubtless, she killed us both, but me
    She killed with torture.
    (Mir, *Divan* V, ca. 1789-1803)

Also, even if there are other true lovers—though not really possible, such a state can at least be imagined—the lover-protagonist of the *ghazal* deserves special treatment:

(13) She ought to have maintained
My distinction at the moment
Of killing. What a pity, she
Trampled me into dust, roiling me
With others.
(Mir, *Divan* II, ca. 1775-8)

(14) She was heard telling someone
The other day: I'll kill someone.
Well, there's no one who so deserves
To die, but me.
(Muhammad Rafi' Sauda, 1706?-1781)

It should be obvious that in such a scheme of things, 'success in love' is not a valid, or powerful, category of thought. No doubt, eighteenth-century Urdu *ghazal* contains some extremely erotic poetry, and these poets are more conscious of the body and its pleasures, and the transactions that give rise to or lead to such pleasures, than their nineteenth-century successors. Yet success in terms of this universe is unsuccess—the greatest success is therefore death. This poetry is thus quite naturally more occupied with dying than most love poetry that one is likely to encounter in other cultures. It reverberates throughout with the terror, and the ecstasy, of dying. Death, in spite of all its uncertainty and unfamiliarity, is an achievement, a respite, a transition:

(15) I hacked through life in every way,
Dying, and having to live again
Is doomsday.
(Shah Mubarak Abru, 1683/5-1733)

(16) From being to non-being
The road is just a few breaths
It's not much of a journey—
Passing from this world.
(Sauda)

It thus follows that so long as Death does not come to him, the lover-protagonist seeks, or gets, suffering and ill luck, disapproval of the 'worldly,' loss of honour and station. Madness and banishment, or imprisonment or general 'ill fame,' are the functions of true love: the stronger the madness, the farther the wandering, the blacker the ill fame, the truer and deeper the love. All this is often expressed with the subtlest of word plays, in the most vigorously metaphorical language, and occasionally, with extremely vivid but generally non-carnal realizations of the beloved's body. Since the beloved-object is the ideal in physical beauty too, his/her body can be evoked freely, but because the idea of the beloved is not anchored into any particular person or gender, the narration, though bold, is rarely physical in the modern sense of the word.

Evocation, rather than description is the rule in the *ghazal*. This is also true of all other characteristics, circumstances, transactions, of the lover and beloved. The only items somewhat firmly anchored in quotidian, recognizable reality are the 'other.' 'Others'—friends, advisors, preachers, censors, the devout, and the priestly—that is, all those who are in principle not in favour of the lover throwing his life away, or destroying his faith by following the course of love rather than that of the world, and of God, as seen by the worldly and priestly. The lover rarely listens to them, and generally holds them in contempt, regarding them as benighted, materialistic, and mundane, having no understanding of the inner life. The phrase *'ahl-e zahir'* (the people of the obvious and apparent) sums it all up. The world of the *ghazal* is one world where the Outsider is the Hero, where non-conformism is the creed, and where prosperity is poverty.

In spite of its idealistic and unworldly air, the poetry of the *ghazal* wears an air of delight, of enjoyment, in making up poems through words, in making the language strain its limits, and yet remain *ravan* (flowing, felicitous, smooth in reading aloud, easy to remember: all these things are denoted by the term *ravani*). All poets, in even conventionally 'sad' narration, employ word play to the best of their power. A certain restraint in physicality, and a certain exuberance in execution, mark much of the best Urdu love poetry from the eighteenth century:

(17) In Time's garden, Oh how well
My fortune sleeps. I am verdant
And prosperous like the green grass;
But it's a sward that's crushed

To sleep by the feet that walk
Upon it.
(Khwaja Mir Dard, 1720-85)

The verse turns on a play on *'sar sabz'* (verdant, thriving), *sabza* (greenery), and *khufta/khvabida* (sleeping) whose subtlety can't really be conveyed in any translation or explication. Most modern Urdu readers, brought up on false notions of 'naturalness' of expression, are taught to feel disappointed and let down to see a 'serious' poet like Dard indulging in the 'frivolity' of word play. Yet the poets knew better. They knew that word play infuses new life into old themes, expands the horizon of meaning, and often makes for an ambiguity of tone which enriches the total feel of the poem. Here is an almost exact contemporary, using the same image, to a different effect:

(18) Like the grass
That grows on the roadside,
I was trampled off
By the multitude
In a single sortie.
(Qa'im Chandpuri, 1724-94)

It is a powerful verse, but lacks the additional energy of meaning that Mir gives to the same theme by word play:

(19) I was grass newly sprung
On the roadside. I raised
My head to be crushed down
By feet.
(Mir, *Divan* I, c. 1754)

The word play revolves around *'nau rasta'* (newly liberated, newly sprouted, newly sprung), *'sar uthana'* (to raise one's head, to rise in rebellion), and *'pamal hona'* (to be trampled under foot). It is obvious that Qa'im's verse lacks these dimensions which are afforded to the poem by word play.

As we can see, 'sadness' of theme or 'authenticity' of emotion is not the point here. The poet and the audience both know that it is in the nature of certain themes to be sad, and they are not interested in how 'sad' is 'sad.' Their primary concern is to renew, and refashion, and thus demonstrate and realize the potential of the language. Intertextuality, imagination, audience expectation, all play their part. Obviously, eighteenth-century poets did not have twentieth-century readers in mind.

Let's now examine how 'erotic' is erotic in this kind of poetry. Word play is important here, too. But other devices like all kinds of sensuous imagery, metaphor, and a sense for dialogue and drama also come into play. An epistemological convention almost always respected here more than most is that things are expressible by their essence, or epitome. There is an essential 'itselfness' in each thing, and it is this, rather than specific points, which needs to be indicated by the poet. Ghalib (1797-1869), though not of the period we are discussing, put it best:

(20) The rose, the poppy, the eglantine
Are all of a different colour.
In every style, every colour
One needs to affirm the spring.

Thus the rose is the essence of all roses, and since the beloved is the essence of all beloveds, so *'gul'* (rose) is often employed to mean 'beloved.' The central image of the rose generates an almost infinite complexity of metaphors, but the human body beats it all:

(21) How can the rose
Have the clearness, the finish
Of your body? And then,
There is the bride-like fragrance
Of good fortune,
Poured into it to the full.
(Shaikh Jur'at, 1748-1809)

This is based on Shah Hatim, and reading Hatim's verse, one can see how great a difference the suggestive memory has made in the case of Jur'at:

(22) You whose body is like a rose,
How exciting are the waves
Of fragrance from your perspiration,
Roses are now perfumers, and
The breeze is ever so pleased.
(Shah Hatim)

Doubtless, Hatim is more earthy in talking of the perspiration as a heady perfume, and his globalization of the perspiration-as-fragrance is piquant, but the verse feels bookish when put beside that of Jur'at.

> (23) Morning, she rolled her sleeves
> Up to the elbows—
> The nakedness of her body, entire,
> Was drawn into the hands.
> (Mus'hafi, *Divan* III, ca. 1794)

> (24) How closely it clings
> To her gold-like body,
> There's someone whose
> Sulfur-colored dress burns
> My heart with much envy.
> (Mir, *Divan* I, ca. 1754)

Mir and Mus'hafi both use the image of the clinging dress over and over again, and always to great effect:

> (25) If you would always wear
> Dresses of this design
> I for one would never say,
> 'Please put off your dress.'
> (Mus'hafi, *Divan* III, ca. 1794)

> (26) My heart is torn to pieces
> Envying her clinging dress
> How tightly the dress
> Hugs the body.
> (Mir, *Divan* VI, ca. 1809/10)

Consider the date: Mir was nearly eighty-eight when he put together this last, sixth *Divan*. Also consider the word play: the heart that tears, and the dress that clings. It should be clear that the verse wouldn't have had much to do with Mir's 'real life' at that time. It is the play of imagination on a favourite theme, the life of the mind, and the poet boldly writing and rewriting on the palimpsest that enables such vivid and 'naughty' poems to be made.

The question that most bothers Western readers (and, unfortunately, now a number of native readers too) is that of the beloved's gender. The fact that in many *ghazal shers* the lover and beloved can be construed as male, or the beloved can be construed to be a boy, was seen by the modernizing Urdu critics of the late twentieth century as an embarrassment, if not an indictment of the whole *ghazal* culture. It never seems to have bothered anyone else before. Many reasons are offered by the modern critics for this 'lapse of taste' committed by eighteenth-century Urdu poets: an almost universal vogue of various kinds of same-sex love—from homoeroticism to open pederasty; segregation of women in the society; influence of Iran; 'corrupt' practices prevalent in religious and Sufi institutions; general decline of 'moral' values, encouraging every kind of dissolute life; and so on.

No one, of course, seems to have asked the 'accused' if they had any explanation or defence. All of us were in the greatest hurry to apply the moral standards of Victorian-Colonial India to a culture that was nowhere near being colonized at that time. In fact, during a great part of the eighteenth century, the boot was on the other leg: it was the English who were trying to adopt what they thought was the Indian lifestyle. Throughout the eighteenth, and through much of the nineteenth century, Indians looked down upon the English as essentially uncivilized. A white complexion was not yet a thing of universal praise and desire.

> (27) One who, in preference
> To those of a dark-complexion,
> Hankers after the white ones—
> Regard him as heart-dead.
> (Shah Mubarak Abru, 1683/5-1733)

> (28) Let me go hunt the Dark-
> Colored Beauty. Why die
> At the hands of the light-weight
> White ones?
> (Muhammad Shakir Naji, 1690?-1744)

The point that I want to make here is that by late nineteenth-century standards, fairness of complexion was the greatest of merits in a person, but poets of the eighteenth century should not be blamed for holding a different opinion. Similarly, questions about the beloved's gender didn't bother the poets of that time because they weren't practicing 'realism' or writing autobiographical poems. The beloved was, first and foremost, an idea, and that idea could be represented in one of many ways. The beloved's anthropomorphic character was often left vague, especially by poets inclined toward Sufism. The general literary feeling was, anyway, in favour of ambiguity and richness of interpretive potential.

Once the beloved was no longer anchored in any given entity, it became possible to play with all kinds of possibilities. Man, woman, boy, God himself, all, or none of them but a general sense of 'belovedness' became possible. The 'you' of the *ghazal* assumed a life of its own. There is no question that some of the poems are clearly homoerotic or even pederastic. Also, there is no question that in many such poems it is very hard to determine the tone—ironic, self-mocking, or just conventional or maybe all of these rolled into one. Similarly, the *shers* in which the gender or the identity of the beloved is so vague as to encompass both 'profane' and 'sacred' love would perhaps outnumber all other kinds of *shers* put together in the eighteenth-century *ghazal*.

What is really important here is not the question of who or why, and how bad or good a light it reflects on the poets. Literature is a system on its own right; it needs to be understood and judged, first and foremost, on its own terms. Is the system coherent? Do all its parts make sense separately or collectively? These questions are more valuable than those of 'moral soundness' or 'political correctness' in regard to the literary output of a culture.

The matter of real importance, thus, is to understand the poetics which enabled poems to be written where the poet could be heterosexual, Sufistic, homoerotic, or pederastic at the same time, and where the beloved could have characteristics of both man and woman in the same poem, often in the same *sher*. This is how it came about.

The liberation of the beloved from the constraints of gender identity enabled the poet to use all possibilities as it suited him. For example, let the beloved be a boy. Now the convention is that the beloved is always assumed to be youthful in age and appearance. Since intensification is a common device in this poetry, the age of the beloved became gradually so reduced that he could be imagined, without any sense of incongruity, as little more than a baby. Little children everywhere love to ride a short staff, or the cane-reed, pretending to be expert horsemen. In Urdu, the word for such children is *nai savar* (cane-reed rider). Now this is Mir:

(29) Well, love is a terrible thing indeed
 Even Mir, much given to lamenting
 Ran on and on, like a petty servant
 Yesterday, alongside the cane-reed riders.
 (*Divan* IV, ca. 1794)

There is a bit of word play here, but it is not a great *sher*. Still the great thing about it is that Mir carries off the image of a grown up person running hot like a footman behind a reed-riding child. Even in English translation the poem doesn't sound risible. In Urdu it sounds entirely appropriate. Here is a *sher* by Mus'hafi:

(30) Wearing my heart on my sleeve,
 I was always there, around him
 Even in the days when he played
 Marbles with the urchins of the street.
 (*Divan* I, ca. 1785)

Mus'hafi's *sher* does not have the *ravani* that Mir's has, but the point, I think, is clearly made by the two examples: the poet-protagonist-lover is not a paedophile. It is the convention—the *ecriture*, to use a fashionable word—that's doing the writing here. And by the same token, if the beloved is assumed to be a grown up man, he is conventionally seen as a boy or adolescent on whose face the down has not appeared, or is just appearing. All these are again full of possibilities for *mazmun*-making. It is quite common, for instance, to say that the appearance of the down on the face has made the beloved more beautiful, hence more cruel, less truthful, and more prone to break promises. The word most often used for 'down' in such cases is *khat*, which also means writing, and therefore, *a written agreement* or *letter*. Mir Tahir Vahid, a noted Iranian poet of the Indian style, makes the point beautifully:

(31) How can Vahid claim his heart
 Back from you now?
 The day he gave it to you,
 There was no *khat* between us.
 (Mir Tahir Vahid, d. 1708)

In the following verse, Naji (1690?-1744) implies that the bearded face of the beloved is more devastating than a clean one. Unfortunately, my translation loses a delightful word play:

(32) For how long the practice
 Of tyranny, dearest?

> Cut your hair short,
> Shave off your beard.

Taking advantage of the fact that the beloved's hair is occasionally described as the rays of the sun, and the sun's rays are supposed to kiss the dew drops on the rose, Naji says:

(33) If you desire union with
The sun, keep your eyes wet
With tears, like the dew.

The two eighteenth-century poets who are most given to *mazmuns* of boy-love, homosexuality, homo-eroticism, and so forth are Shaikh Mubarak Abru (1683/5-1733) and Muhammad Shakir Naji (1690?-1744). It is not clear that their interest in these themes was based on an actual propensity, and if so, how far this propensity entered their real life. Abru never married, and if the following verse from him is taken as a true statement of personal preference, he looked down upon heterosexuality as improper and 'unloverly':

(34) One who passes by a boy
And loves women
Is no lover. He is
A man of lust.

We know that there were many women in Mus'hafi's life, yet he claims—again, if the poem is accepted as true personal evidence—a certain proclivity for bisexuality:

(35) Though the catamite gives pleasure
Of a sort, I didn't find
The true pleasure of love
But in Women.
(*Divan* IV, ca. 1796)

In any case, such verses, whether true testaments or false, would not have shocked their audiences in the eighteenth century. South Asian society has never looked upon homosexuality with the horror and anxiety that have characterized Western responses to it since the early modern period. K.J. Dover tells us that among the Greeks, homosexual transactions were intercrural, and anal penetration was not permitted, at least in theory. If some of the eighteenth century accounts are to be believed, while there were any number of professional boy-beloveds in Delhi at that time, even touching and kissing were considered improper and were to be discouraged strongly.

The story is told, for instance, of the poet Aftab Ra'e Rusva's love for a boy. Rusva came from a well-to-do family, and was gainfully employed when he fell in love with a boy. He gave up his job, began to wander naked in the streets of Delhi, mad and uncaring. Once he found his beloved holding court, surrounded by friends and admirers. Apparently there had been no physical contact between Rusva and the boy up until then. Finding him in open company, Rusva was overwhelmed by passion, and boldly kissed his beloved. This lapse of decorum so enraged the boy that he fatally stabbed Rusva who refused medical aid and all other succour. He recited the following verse (apparently his own) as he died:

(36) Though my master may not
Sew up the wound in my heart,
What of it if I die,
Let my master live.

Abru has left us a long poem in the *masnavi* form, addressed to a young male who wants to set up as a beloved. Detailed instructions about toilette, make up, hairstyle, deportment, and speech are given. He is also advised to retire as soon as his beauty starts declining, though not immediately after the down appears, or even the whiskers grow stiff, necessitating their removal: for the down also is 'the secret of beauty and goodness.' It is God's 'artistry on the face.' Coquettish behaviour is okay, but things should never be allowed to become physical:

(37) Be sure that among your lovers
There's none that is vulgar,
Lustful, unchaste, filthy hearted

(38) You already have beauty, now
Look for sophistication,
A bad living person is
No beloved at all.

Choudhri Muhammad Naim has an excellent analysis of the poem, and the issues involved in it (see Bibliography). The interested reader is referred to it. My limited concern here is to show that however much

PAGE OF AN ILLUSTRATED MANUSCRIPT OF GULISTAN-E-BUSTAN OF SAADI.
Nastaliq script. 19th century. Photo: Mohammed Ali Qadir. Courtesy of Mohatta Palace Museum, Karachi.
Qalam: The Arts of Calligraphy Exhibition. NM 1958-394.

rooted in the social mores of the eighteenth century, boy-love and man-love, as depicted in this poetry are, for us, not 'social' but literary issues. These themes, and their treatment in the extant form, became possible due to literary reasons. And in any case, since poetry then was not expected to reflect social reality (as if there could be one seamless, omni-where social reality which poetry could catch hold of), but deal with *mazmuns*, the issues of the beloved's gender, age, profession, and social status never arose, and we would be doing serious injustice to this poetry if we raise such issues now.

Mir described *ada bandi* as one of the qualities of his poetry he was particularly proud of. This term, vague in itself, is hard to translate. It means something like 'depiction and narration of the beloved's coquetry, dress and manners, speech and body language.' Mir, no doubt, excels here, as he does in many things. But he does much more. The depths and intensities of experience, coupled with the fullest possible vocalization of the mysterious power of love, that Mir is able to achieve are not seen elsewhere in this century, or in any century for that matter. In Mir's poetry, the dimensions of both loss and gain are infinite, and yet the poems are strictly earthly, not abstract or cerebral. A great deal of Urdu love poetry can be interpreted as Sufistic, but Mir retains the everyday, human dimension even while suggesting things best seen on a cosmic scale.

The thing that immediately strikes the reader's mind about the eighteenth century—as compared to the nineteenth—is the human relationship aspect, the *ada bandi*, the rare meetings and closeness, the all too frequent partings, and the distressing distances between lover and beloved, that the eighteenth-century poetry highlights for us. Mir was thus quite correct in giving *ada bandi* such importance in his scheme of things.

It is largely because of *ada bandi* that the beloved in the eighteenth-century *ghazal* is not the passive, hiding-behind-the-*purdah*, slightly tubercular, recoiling from the slightest physical contact, shrinking-violet type of girl much touted by modern critics as the optimal beloved in the *ghazal*. This image gained currency through modern 'classicist' poets like Hasrat Mohani (1875-1951), and attempts continue to be made to fit all *ghazals* to this image, but even a brief look at the *ghazal* of this period will demonstrate the falseness of this image. Here is Hatim:

> (39) Our bodies and souls were one
> There were no cracks
> But both our hearts longed
> Just for a word or two.

> (40) I still remember that heart enticing
> Hint of yours, making up
> A little *pan* from a filbert
> Leaf, and flinging it toward me.

> (41) At that time, right then
> My heart was in your firm grasp
> When you let your hand
> Touch with mine.
> (Shah Hatim, composed 1736-37)

> (42) Scooting over a little bit, bit by bit
> You came to sit right next to me
> What skittishness, effrontery,
> Self-assurance!
> (Shah Hatim, composed 1743)

The beloved here is a conscious participant, and since gender is not specific in any of the four *shers* I quoted above, the lover-protagonist here need not necessarily be male, just because the poet is male. In fact, in the general scheme of things, even though the lover/beloved became essentially genderless, the lover-protagonist inherited some of the qualities from the original, female protagonist in the *ghazal*. That is, many qualities which are generally identified in South Asian society with women—steadfastness against the (male) beloved's fickleness, being patient and self-surren-

dering—came more and more to be the mark of the lover-protagonist in the eighteenth-century *ghazal*. I have discussed the 'female' aspects of the lover-protagonist's personality elsewhere (see Bibliography). One might recall here that Muhammad Hasan Askari, Urdu's most distinguished modern critic, identified Mir's greatest strength and poetic quality as his ability to fully and unconditionally surrender his lover's self to the beloved.

We will now look briefly at one point relating to the epistemology of metaphor, and close this necessarily brief discussion of a wide and difficult subject. Non-native readers, and now even most of the native ones, are shocked and even revolted by the image of the beloved and the lover as presented in the *ghazal*. The beloved seems mindlessly given to bloodshed, kills countless people at one stroke, lets rivers of blood flow in the streets, cuts the lover up into pieces, is deliberately and sadistically cruel, and so forth. The lover is apparently the most wretched of persons, partly or wholly mad, revelling in being denigrated, often grovelling in the dust or mud in the beloved's street, and so on. These things are true, except that they are seen in the *ghazal* universe as positive, not negative, characteristics, and the reason for their being where they are is again literary, not the social or mental backwardness of our poets.

Metaphors are also to be understood in their 'literal' sense, before they can start making sense as metaphor. Abdul-Qahir Jurjani held that in some cases, rejection or deferment of the literal sense would lead to losing all the sense contained in metaphor. Schleirmacher made a very similar point seven centuries later, when he said, 'Words used in the figurative sense retain their proper and specific meaning, and achieve their effect only through an association of ideas on which the writer depends.'

One implication of the 'literalness' of metaphor was on the epistemological level: metaphors do not represent facts; they are facts. Thus a metaphor could be treated as a fact, and another metaphor drawn from it. From that metaphor again, another one could be derived, and so on. Instead of the frightening 'infinite regress' of meaning that one finds in Derrida, here was an exhilaratingly infinite progress of metaphor, and each metaphor was a fact in its own right. Consider the following:

The lover obviously loves the beloved more than he

loves his own self. This leads to the metaphor/idiom: *kisi par marn*a = to die for someone. Or there is the metaphor/idiom: *kisi par jan dena* = to give up one's life for someone. This leads to the proposition: The beloved can cause death. This is followed by the proposition: The beloved can kill. This is followed by: The beloved is a killer. Now a new line of metaphorical reasoning takes over: The beloved kills—with a look. Her eyes therefore are daggers, or swords, or a weapon of killing. Now swords etc., need to be sharpened; so kohl applied to the eyes is a sharpener. But why should only the eye be the sword/dagger etc.? The beloved's coquetry can also kill. So another set of metaphors comes into existence. Then since the beloved has a number of lovers, and all lovers by definition get killed, so the beloved can kill a whole host of people in one glance = blow. Then killing with a dagger or similar weapon causes blood to flow. Hence the beloved's street is a place where one smells blood, like Cassandra, anticipatively, or actually. If a number of people get killed at the same time, rivers of blood flow in the city, and the beloved can be seen riding his/her/its charger in triumph.

Then, the beloved does not necessarily kill; she may inflict a wound or two and stop at that. The lover can now react in any number of ways, given the 'fact' that the wounds are real wounds. For example: The lover writhes in pain, ecstatically, hoping to 'enjoy' the moment for as long as possible; the lover may complain to the effect that the beloved was casual, and not in earnest; or worse still, she was deliberately casual and intentionally delivered only a glancing blow, so as to deprive (because she is perceived as perverse by definition) the lover of the pleasure and honour of dying. The lover may plead for the killing blow, or feel angry and disappointed at being reprieved.

A casual blow, or refusal on the beloved's part to kill the lover, may also involve a value-judgment: the lover is poor material, not fit to kill. This may again be due to one of many reasons: the lover is qualitatively inferior; he is not a good enough lover, or distinguished enough as a person to deserve killing at the hands of the beloved. Or, it may be that the lover has grown 'pale, and spectre thin,' has wasted away, and is therefore not worth the trouble of killing. Or maybe the beloved or her sword—yes, even the sword, because the shine and sharpness of a sword is described as its *ab* = water—may perspire out of shame at having to kill such a wretch who is more than half-dead.

And if there are wounds, then there are doctors, surgeons, expert or inexpert sewers up of the open wound. The lover should, by definition, refuse any kind of aid, medical or spiritual. This gives rise to another set of metaphors. Or the lover's wound may have been sutured, but the sly lover knows his job. He has fingernails to pick at the stitches or reopen the wound.

The wounds may be self-inflicted in a fit of frenzy, for instance, but not with a view to suicide. Or the wounds may have been inflicted by the street Arabs, who harass and torture the mad lover and pelt him with stones. The lover actually desires this, because loss of dignity, honour, and station, being insulted by the meanest, and treated with contumely even by street urchins, ensures the death, or at least the suppression, of his own self, and thus makes him more suitable for 'dying' in the beloved. Negating his own being, he affirms the being of the beloved, who alone is sufficient as life and as life-giver. So the lover actually desires and welcomes the rocks thrown at him by naughty children. In a *sher* of Mir's, the protagonist-lover heaps rocks and stones in his street so as to make it easy for the street Arabs to throw them at him. A seventeenth-century Persian poet of the Indian style put it most piquantly, summing up a whole culture of love, madness, and self-effacement, in this couplet:

> (43) The madman goes his way,
> And the children go theirs;
> Say, friends, does this city of yours
> Have no rocks or stones?
> (Saiyad Husain Khalis, d. 1710)

All this, and much more, could become possible for the simple reason that in the poetics of Indian style Persian poetry, and all classical Urdu poetry, the metaphor of dying is treated as a fact from which another metaphor can be generated, and the resultant metaphor, in turn, treated as fact generates other metaphors. What sounds bizarre or distasteful to minds untrained in this poetics, falls quite naturally into place as proper and desirable—in fact unique in all poetry since early modern times— once it is seen as a rhetorical system which permits metaphors to be made both paradigmatically and syntagmatically.

Western poetics has generally treated metaphor as a paradigmatic device, which is true as far as it goes. But the picture changes drastically once metaphor and fact are treated as interchangeable, as in the Urdu and Indian-Persian poetics. Now metaphors can be generated syntagmatically as well. Thus: if *p* is the same as *q*, then the characteristics of *q* also apply to *p*. The lover is a captive (of the beloved or of love.) Birds also are made captive, so the lover is a bird. A captive bird is kept in a cage, so the lover is in a cage. In order to be made captive, the bird has to be captured; the person who captures a bird is a hunter=*saiyad*. So the protagonist-lover-bird was made captive by a hunter. But the bird-protagonist is the lover, too. And the person who captured the lover is the beloved, who thus equals *saiyad*, and so on.

Syntagmatic thinking makes for an infinity of metaphors, because the metaphors generated by it do not depend on similitude between two apparently dissimilar objects (which, Aristotle said, was the soul of metaphor), but on association. Western philosophers have long held that there are no rules for metaphor making. This is quite true, so long as metaphors are seen hinging upon similitude. Once that barrier is broken, a simple rule emerges: metaphors can be made by the power of association, so long as each metaphor is taken as the fact itself, and the substitute for that fact. A delightful example of this procedure is that the eyes of the beloved are often described in this poetry as *bimar*=ailing, indisposed. Apparently there could be nothing more dissimilar to the beloved's eyes than ailment or indisposition. Syntagmatism makes this possible, thus: *ankh uthna/uthana* is for the eyes to be raised. Those who are ailing cannot rise. The eyes cannot rise, so they are indisposed. Thus, the more indisposed or ailing the beloved's eyes, the better it is, for it affirms both her status and chastity as beloved.

Going back to the status of the beloved as the rightful taker of lives, it is natural that there are no suicides in the eighteenth-century *ghazal*, or any classical *ghazal* for that matter. There are countless deaths and woundings, burials and half-burials, but no one ever kills himself. For that would deprive the lover of the merit of being killed by the beloved, and worse still, by killing himself, the lover would presume to occupy the space that can be occupied only by the beloved. There is scarcely any talk of suicide in this world, and Mir, who has a few delightful verses on this theme, makes it do more work than its nature (and the nature of the *ghazal* universe) would seem to imply. The following is from *Divan* II, put together around 1775-78:

(44) Don't leave sword or ax
Anywhere near Mir;
Lest he waste himself.

The idea here is not so much to emphasize the act of Mir's killing himself, as his character: Mir is no wilting lily, or an adolescent in the throes of calf love. The other point is that by killing himself, he would be wasting himself; he is too valuable to be wasted. The ambiguity of the verb used to indicate the act of suicide permits two meanings. The other *sher*.

(45) I said to her: I am
Out of patience, entirely:
What should I do,
Kill myself? She said,
'Oh yes, man must
Do something.'
(*Shikar Nama* II, c. 1790)

The ironical dimensions of this verse can only find a match in the miraculous economy of the diction. The two-line *sher* in the original, though in a meter of normal length, that is a meter that requires four feet to a line and not three, contains eighteen words, of which fully eight have only one syllable. Of the rest nine are disyllabic; there is only one trisyllabic word. Those who read Urdu would know that Urdu favours disyllabic and trisyllabic words. Words of four syllables, too, are quite common. A verse having a heavy preponderance of unisyllabic and disyllabic words, and packing so much meaning in it, is a rarity, even in Mir.

The final impression that a major eighteenth-century poet's *ghazal* leaves on us is not that its protagonist (and some tend to identify protagonist with poet) is a person much given to wine and love, but who is essentially a helpless slave to social power or sexual desire, battered and defeated. Instead, we are left with the feeling that we have been in close touch with a vigorous, complex intellect, a mind capable of self-mockery and introspection, a body and spirit that have suffered and enjoyed, and are still prepared to suffer and enjoy, a soul that is no stranger to the mystic dimensions of existence, an outsider and nonconformist who cannot be patronized. An invitation to pity is nowhere to be found in his vocabulary.

INSTITUTIONS OF *MUSHA'IRA* AND *USTAD/SHAGIRD*

With eighteenth century Delhi must also lie the credit for introducing, or in fact creating, two new institutions in Urdu literature: the *musha'ira*, and the master (*ustad*) who gave formal or informal instruction in the art of poetry and prose to aspiring or practicing writers (*shagirds*).

The *musha'ira*, as a formal gathering of poets at a well-to-do person's, or at another poet's place, does not seem to occur anywhere in the main Muslim lands in medieval or pre-modern times. Yet it must have existed in the Subcontinent from around the sixteenth century. Such gatherings must have had an audience, of both poets and non-poets, from quite early on, if not from the very beginning. The presence of a poet among the audience would imply that he wasn't regarded as senior enough to recite his poetry at such an assembly. One of the reasons for the *musha'ira* to have originated in the Subcontinent may be the fact that from the sixteenth century, there was a greater influx of Persian poets into the Mughal empire than ever before. Persian poets not only from Iran, but also from the Persianate Central Asia migrated, or travelled to India for extended sojourns. Akbar actively promoted Persian at court and in government, and this must have given an extra fillip to Persian poets from abroad to come to India in search of employment or patronage. These poets, finding many of their profession in the same city, or even at the same court away from home, would have tended to gravitate toward each other for comparing notes, for conversation, and recitation of their new compositions.

The word *musha'ira* is apparently not a proper Arabic derivative from the root *shin*, *'ain*, *ra*. The word is also not found in any authoritative Persian dictionary before the early nineteenth century. *Shamsul Lughat* (composed 1804-5, printed 1891), and *Ghiasul Lughat* (composed 1826, numerous printings in the nineteenth century) seem to be the earliest to enter it. While according to the former, the word has an agnostic sense in the context of public recitation of poetry; the latter glosses it as 'reciting poetry to one another'. The fact that none of the authoritative Persian dictionaries of the eighteenth and earlier centuries recognize it, would suggest that poets of repute did not use this word in their works, regarding it probably as spurious, or a neologism. Thus the institution itself could not be very ancient. It was very much in place, however, by the early eighteenth century.

When Hindi/Rekhta poetry became popular in Delhi, assemblies of poets of that language too began to take place frequently. However, with characteristic snobbishness, the word used for the assemblies was *murakhita*, an Indianistic (and grammatically illegal) derivative from the Persian '*rekhta*'. The 'high' word *musha'ira* was thus reserved for the 'high' poetry of Persian.

The *murakhita*, however, soon overtook the Persian-language assemblies in popularity, if not exactly in prestige and the word '*musha'ira*' began also to be used for Hindi/Rekhta assemblies. The earliest use of *musha'ira* denoting an assembly of Hindi/Rekhta poets is in the first *divan* of Muhammad Taqi Mir (1722-1810), compiled before 1752. We have accounts, or reports, of *musha'iras/ murakhitas* by poets like Sa'adat Yar Khan Rangin (1758-1834/5), Mus'hafi (1750-1824), and by poets and biographists like Qudratullah Qasim (d. 1811). The *musha'ira* soon became a lively place, amenable to agnostic confrontations and rivalries, and attracting poets of different ages and attainments. It was not uncommon for a poet to be challenged in open assembly to scan a line, or give 'authoritative proof' of the correctness of a word or phrase used by him. Qudratullah Qasim, in his *tazkira* (biographical dictionary) *Majmu'a-e Naghz* (final draft composed around 1806/7) gives us the story of Azim Dihlavi (d. 1806/7), a not very accomplished poet, but given to much self-regard, being challenged by Inshallah Khan Insha (1756/7-1817) when the former unwittingly mixed two metres in one poem. Tempers ran high, and remained so for a long time. In his biographical dictionary *Nikatush Shu'ara*, composed in 1752, Mir tells us about the *musha'iras* at the residence of Khwaja Nasir Andalib, and how the venerated Khwaja later delegated to Mir himself the duty of organizing as well as presiding over the *musha'iras*.

There is little doubt that the *musha'ira* helped improve the standard of composition in Hindi/Rekhta.

From the point of view of the sociology of literary production in a given milieu, an even more important consequence of the spread of the *musha'ira* as a creative, competitive arena was, in Delhi and elsewhere, a phenomenal increase in the number of poets, and the love and praxis of poetry trickling down to the so called lower classes. Qasim's *Majmu'a-e Naghz* lists 693 poets. Khub Chand Zaka's (d. 1846) *'Ayarush Shu'ara* (final draft finished around 1812/3, begun 1798/9) has 949 poets. 'Azamuddaula Sarvar's (d. 1835) *'Umda-e Muntakhaba* (begun 1801, final draft may have been prepared much later) gives us information about 996 poets. Not all the poets listed by these authors are from Delhi. But there is very little Hindi/Rekhta literature in Northern India (including all of Punjab) and Eastern India (including Assam and all of Bengal) before the eighteenth century. The proliferation of Hindi/Rekhta poets in all the territories of the North and East at that time must have owed a great deal to the example of Delhi. Abul Hasan Amrullah Ilahabadi wrote his *tazkira* called *Masarrat Afza* in 1779-80; one of his stated purposes was to write about poets of the East not mentioned in the *tazkiras* produced a few years earlier in Delhi.

Among the professions of poets reported by Qasim are: Husain Bakhsh Bakhshi, clothier; Madhu Singh Shigufta, ironsmith; Khwaja Hinga, gold lace maker and braider; Mir Sadiq Ali, elephant keeper; Shambhu Nath Aziz, money lender; Mir Latif Ali Latif, gemstones broker; Mughal Ali Mughal, braider and merchant; Badruddin Maftun, cloth merchant; Yakrang, goldsmith; Pandit Ganga Das Taskin, brahmin; Muhammad Hashim Sha'iq, tailor; Muhammad Arif, darner; Inayatullah aka Kallu, barber; Ghulam Nasir, lancer and dresser of boils and wounds; Mirza Raja Shankar Nath Haya, nobleman; Maqsud, water carrier; Shiv Singh Bejan, geomancer. There is even a sweeper, called Qarin. Let it be noted that some of the above poets are Hindu. Hindus, who had been concentrating on Persian up until the middle of the century, seem to have lost their heart to the elegance of Hindi/Rekhta by the time its *musha'iras* became popular in Delhi. As the century progresses, we encounter more and more Hindu names among Hindi/Rekhta poets. Soon they are joined by Christians, mostly Europeans, but also second generation Indian Christians.

Women also make their appearance quite early on the literary scene. Contrary to common belief, not all of them came from the 'nautch girl' class, though that class did have its representatives. The best and, justly, the most celebrated woman poet of the century was indeed a dancing girl called Mah Laqa Ba'i Chanda (1768-1820) in the South. A woman of great elan and social prestige in Hyderabad, she had poets writing *qasidas* (odes) in her praise. In Delhi, there was Gunna Begum (d. 1773). Married to Ghaziuddin Khan, Prime Minister to Shah Alam II, she was a poet of substantial elegance, and a person of great beauty, ready wit, and a patron of poets. Then there was Yasman, housemaid to Inshallah Khan Insha. Some of her verses rival those of much better known poets.

Women poets attracted the attention of *tazkira* writers by virtue of their considerable numbers, and the quality of their poetry. *Baharistan-e Naz*, the first *tazkira* devoted to women poets alone, was published in 1864-5 by Fasihuddin Ranj. It contained accounts of 174 poets, some of whom wrote in Persian. Durga Parshad Nadir published his *Chaman-e Andaz* in 1877; its first edition contained 144 women poets, while in the second (1884), the number went up to 196. In his *Shamim-e Sukhan* (1872-3), Safa Badayuni took care to separate the 'professional' women from those who observed *purdah* and were *sharif* by birth and circumstance.

We have seen how Persian was the main, and almost the first language of all the elite and many of the middle classes in Delhi up until the first half of the eighteenth century. However, when Hindi/Rekhta began to tug at the hearts and minds of the poets of Delhi, they turned to it with a zest and verve never seen before or after in the history of Urdu letters. Yet, however much the poetry in Hindi/Rekhta may owe to Persian, it was a different language, and those who wanted to compose in it had no real perspective to determine what was excellent and acceptable as poetry in Hindi/Rekhta. They needed someone to put them through their paces, to give them a surer footing in what essentially was an alien idiom for them. This felt need gave rise to the institution of *'ustad'* (master) to whom a 'pupil' (*shagird*) poet would submit his verse, and also prose, for 'correction', and to whom he would defer in matters of idiom, usage, and other finer aspects of the art of composition.

The origin of this system seems to have been unique

to Delhi, and to Hindi/Rekhta. Doubtless, we hear of an occasional Persian poet being a pupil of a major writer like Mirza Abdul Qadir Bedil (1644-1720) or Sirajuddin Ali Khan-e Arzu (1689-1756) in Delhi. Vali himself was a pupil of a Sufi and a Persian poet Shah Gulshan (1662/3?-1727), and Vali is also reported to have had a couple of pupils of his own. But the nature of the relationship is not clear in these cases. Vali certainly was not a pupil of Shah Gulshan's in Rekhta/Hindi poetry. He may have learnt some other discipline from him. Similarly, we know about Vali's pupils from indirect sources alone, and he may have acquired them on his return from Delhi. As far as Persian is concerned, it seems that Bedil and Arzu were consulted, but informally, except where Arzu's expertise as linguist and master of literary as well as colloquial Persian were made use of by other poets. Arzu was certainly the *ustad* of some of the earliest Hindi/Rekhta poets in eighteenth century Delhi.

In Urdu, the *ustad-shagird* institution very soon became a commonplace of the literary environment. Protocols, unwritten but fairly strong, were in place by about the middle of the eighteenth century. For example, the *ustad* need not have been much older than the *shagird*, but must have been someone with a big reputation. One did not change *ustads* casually. Those who changed *ustads* without a proper reason, or due to their temperament not being suitable to the *ustad*, were not admired. Often the new *ustad* would refuse to accept the pupil, unless the matter had been run by the previous *ustad* and his consent obtained. Payment to the *ustad* for services rendered was not obligatory, but expected. Women also had access to the *ustad*. Mah Laqa Ba'i Chanda's *ustad* was Sher Muhammad Khan Iman (d. 1806/7). Hayatunnisa Haya, a daughter of emperor Shah Alam II, was the *shagird* of Shah Nasir (1760/61?-1838).

The *ustad* never solicited *shagirds*, and had full right not to accept a given person as *shagird*, either due to the lack of ability in the prospective *shagird*, or lack of inclination on the part of the *ustad*. Mir tells us in his autobiography of Raja Jugal Kishor, a rich patron of poets who desired to appoint Mir his *ustad*. Not finding the Raja's poems 'worthy of correction', Mir turned him away, having 'scrawled a line across most of' the Raja's verses. Mir was practically destitute at that time, and would not have been more than thirty-five years of age.

His refusal to accept the Raja as *shagird* must have meant hardship and maybe loss of future patronage from others as well. The fact that Mir had no hesitation to turn down the Raja reflects light on the value he placed on the *ustad's* calling and also on the station of the poet: not everybody could become a poet, poetry was not a class privilege. It was a matter of talent. A nobleman's or an affluent person's appointing a poet his *ustad* was also a way of bestowing patronage. There have been suggestions that sometimes the *ustad* composed virtually all the poetry that went under the rich or powerful *shagird's* name. But no one has ever proved this. Instances, however, of the *ustad* giving away to, or 'bestowing on' a *shagird* a whole verse or *ghazal* are not unknown.

The *ustad-shagird* institution thrived and became widespread in a short time because it answered a need, was an easy means of showing favour to poets, and finally, because it suited the nature of the oral society. The *ustad* passed on, by word of mouth or by example, the nuances of the art of writing to his *shagird*. No recourse to the written word was needed, because the *ustad's* authority subsumed, and perhaps even surpassed, the authority of the book. The 'new' poetics that developed and flourished in Hindi/Rekhta over a century and a half between 1700 and 1850 remained unrecorded, for the *ustad's* oral transmission of all subtleties of theory and practice was available when needed. This also suited the genius of the society which was very largely oral, and which respected immediate authority and oral instruction as an important part of cultured existence. This is also reflected in the fact that in due course, one's excellence as a poet became partly a function of whose *shagird* he or his *ustad* was, and to a certain extent, the *ustad's* excellence and status too were judged in terms of the number of *shagirds* he had. Similarly, while the *ustad* might authorize a *shagird* to recite his poems in *musha'iras* without 'showing' them first to the *ustad*, many poets still preferred, if feasible, to have the *ustad* look over their poems before they recited them in the *musha'ira* or put them into their collection. No poet would, unless he was a 'rebel', take *shagirds* of his own unless the *ustad* permitted him.

All this is reminiscent of the practice in musical *gharanas* (houses), and Sufi orders. The air was entirely secular, and Muslims would cheerfully take a Hindu as *ustad*. The example of Rai Sarb Sukh Divana (1727?-

1788/9) among whose *shagirds* were the redoubtable Ja'far Ali Hasrat, and Haidar Ali Hairaan, is perhaps the best known, though not as well known today as one would like it to be.

The 'new light' of the post-1857 age extinguished the light on many traditions, including the *ustad-shagird* tradition. One of the many charges brought against it was that the *ustad* stifled the originality of the *shagird*. This argument, though misconceived, was never really answered by the *ustads* who had remained in business even after the call for 'natural poetry' and 'poetry based on true emotions' apparently seemed all set to abolish the old order of excellence in poetry. The answer to the charge was not far to seek, and the fact that it was never made indicates the intellectual disarray and loss of self-confidence which became the lot of our cultural consciousness after the defeat of the 1857 movement.

I.A. Richards taught in China during 1930-31 and thus had an opportunity to learn at first hand the fundamentals of Chinese literary culture. He was delightfully surprised to find that the Western concept of 'originality' had no counterpart in China where remaking an old thing in a new way was considered the mark of true originality. Bertrand Russell had made a similar discovery when he went to China a few years earlier. Similarly, 'realism' was never an issue with the Chinese. While the Westerners asked about a work of art, 'Is it true?', the Chinese simply asked, 'Is it human?' Long before Pankofsky, the Chinese had realized that 'art' is just a set of rules that tell us how 'reality' should be represented. There is no such thing as a reality 'out there' which can be captured by the artist without any frills or strings. In a painting one doesn't represent reality so much as to organize pictorial surfaces in given ways.

Those of us who are familiar with the Sanskrit or Arabic literary culture will immediately recognize that in regard to 'originality' and 'realism' in literature, our own position is very similar to the Chinese. A necessary concomitant to the idea of originality is that of plagiarism. The great Arab literary theorist Al Jurjani (d. 1078) practically denied the existence of plagiarism, saying that literary themes are the common property of all. The Sanskrit as well as the Arab literary traditions insisted on 'meaning' and not 'truth' as the object of art. The Arabs had the same word, *ma'ni*, to denote 'meaning' and 'literary theme'.

Of course, poets do influence each other, in big ways or small. But since 'originality' was not a value in our literary tradition, it was never at risk at the hands of the *ustad* when he dealt with his *shagird*. In fact, sometimes the *ustad* would write in the manner of the *shagird*, if he found that the *shagird's* manner was more in keeping with the demand of the times. The classic case is that of Mus'hafi (1750-1824) who during the evening of his life readily adopted the manner of his *shagird* Atash (1777-1847) who was very good at *khiyal bandi*, a mode that had then become fashionable due to Shah Nasir and Nasikh.

The *ustads'* inability to meet the charges of the modern age diminished the prestige and also the geographical spread of their institution. The *ustad-shagird* nexus was, however, so strongly suited to the genius of Urdu literary culture that it never ceased to exist. It exists even today, though the excellence of the *ustad*, as well as the authority that the institution wielded in the culture are things of the past.

Delhi did some bad things too, and some bad things were interpreted as good, and were added to Delhi's crown by later historians. In 1755-6, Shah Hatim wrote a Preface for his *Divan Zada*, a selection of his poetry that he compiled, implying that whatever else he wrote in the past should not be regarded as authentic. He strongly advocated the primacy of the accepted colloquial idiom over the 'bookish' idiom. This was quite proper, but in that Preface, he also suggested that he had given up the use of some words, which were not on the tongues of elegant speakers of Delhi. The words that he singled out were mostly of Sanskrit *tatsam* type, but had entered Rekhta/Hindi perhaps through Braj. He also frowned upon what he called '*Bhakha*'. His last suggestion was that poets should use Arabic and Persian words according to their 'original' pronunciation.

It is not quite clear what motivated Hatim to say all this. Perhaps he was desirous of distancing himself from Vali whose attitude to language was practical and non-bookish. Be that as it may, in his *Divan Zada* itself, which according to Hatim was the epitome of his work purged of all 'objectionable' usages, Hatim used freely and frequently the very words and constructions that he had held blameable in his Preface. Unfortunately, later historians and grammarians of poetry chose to ignore Hatim's emphasis on the superiority of educated, everyday speech over pedantic, overburdened speech.

IN PRAISE OF SLIMNESS.
Folio from an unidentified, illustrated poetical work, showing a poet reciting a poem on the theme of 'slimness' to his well-endowed patron. Mughal, last decade of the 16th century. Courtesy of the Goenka Collection.

They placed great value on the negative aspects of Hatim's formulations which were hailed as 'reformist'. Hatim was, on the basis of his negative and restrictive pronouncements, honoured as having made the first attempt at 'purifying' the language.

All this was bad history and even worse linguistic theory, but it gained enormous and very quick currency. Other 'reformers' of the language duly appeared or were invented, especially in the first half of the nineteenth century. This resulted in loss of flexibility in the language and established the false power ratio of the grammarian laying down the law for the poet, though the natural equation works the other way around. The situation became even more dire because the *ustad-shagird* system permitted the poet to assume the grammarian's role as well. For all its brilliant elegance, the language of Urdu poetry in the nineteenth century doesn't always reflect the ground level linguistic reality.

THE FICTION ABOUT THE NATURE AND ORIGIN OF URDU†

The belief that Urdu originated in Muslim army camps and cantonment bazaars helped generate and sustain two myths: Urdu was the language of the Muslims, and being originally the language of camp and cantonment, it stood in natural need of being refined and gentrified, and this process was initiated by the master poets of Delhi in the second half of the eighteenth century.

Small wonder, then, that the name 'Urdu,' which didn't come into use for the language before the 1780s, is invariably invoked by our historians to 'prove' that since 'Urdu' means 'army, army camp, or the market of a camp,' the Urdu language was born as a result of 'foreign' Muslims and local 'Hindus' interacting with each other for petty trade and commerce. None stopped to consider that the only foreign armies in India during and from the 1780s were British (and some French). There were no Arabic- or Persian- or Turkish-speaking armies in India in the 1780s, and the language of Urdu had by then been in existence for several centuries.[1] Thus the name 'Urdu' which first came into use apparently in the 1780s could not have been given to the language because of the putative army connection.

The word 'Urdu' as a language name does not appear in old Persian dictionaries though they were all compiled in India and very often do enter or mention some words as 'Hindi.' Let's take a look at some of the specifically Urdu-English dictionaries. They were mostly compiled in the nineteenth century, and almost always by the British. Duncan Forbes (1866) defines 'Urdu' as follows:

> An army, a camp; a market, *urdu, i mu'alla*, the royal camp or army (generally means the city of *Dihli* or *Shahjahanabad*; and *urdu i mu'alla ki zaban*, the court language). This term is very commonly applied to the Hindustani language as spoken by the Musalman population of India proper.[2]

And this is Fallon (1873):

> Originally, a camp,
> 1. An army; a bazar attached to the camp [...]
> 2. The Hindustani language as spoken by the Mohamedans of India, and by the Hindus who have learnt of them or have intercourse with them [...] Urdu-i mualla 1. The court language. 2. The Delhi idiom.[3]

Here is Platts, who came after the above two:

> Army; camp; market of a camp; s.f. (= *urdu zaban*), The Hindustani language as spoken by the Muhammadans of India, and by Hindus who have intercourse with them [...]:— *urdu-i-mu'alla*, The royal camp or army (generally means the city of Delhi or Shahjahanabad); the court language (= *urdu-i-mu'alla ki zaban*); the Hindustani language as spoken in Delhi.[4]

I don't need to point out the political underpinnings which have, perhaps unconsciously, let colonialistic biases creep into these definitions. Those will become clear when I quote John Gilchrist who wrote when colonialistic thought was just being crystallized in the British mind. Suffice it to say at present that even these comparatively late arrivals on the Urdu linguistic scene were not able to suggest that the language name had anything directly to do with the army, Muslim or any other. They have, of course, suppressed the major fact that the language was also, and more commonly, and even at the time of their writing, known as Hindi, or Rekhta.

The earliest traceable use of 'Urdu' as language name is in a *sher* of Mus'hafi (1750-1824), in his first *divan*, compiled around 1782-85. It must have contained poems from earlier dates too, but not much earlier, because his actual first *divan* was stolen in Delhi. He said in a later *divan*, 'My *divan* was stolen in Delhi too.'[5] The *sher*, suggesting that 'Urdu' is a language name, is as follows:

> Mus'hafi has, most surely, claim
> of superiority in Rekhta,
> That is to say, he has
> Expert knowledge of the
> language of Urdu[6]

---

† This is an extract from S.R. Faruqi, 'Unprivileged Power: The Strange Case of Persian (and Urdu) in Nineteenth-Century India', published in *The Annual of Urdu Studies*, No. 13 (1998), ed. Muhammad Umar Memon.

Since Urdu has no definite article, the word 'Urdu' in the *sher* could theoretically refer to Delhi, but we will assume that 'Urdu' is used here as a language name. Yet another *sher* of Mus'hafi's had been cited in *Nuru'l-Lughat*[7] under the entry 'Urdu' as a language name. It has also been cited by Mahmud Sherani.[8]

> May God preserve them, I have
> heard the speech of Mir and Mirza,
> How can I truthfully claim, oh Mus'hafi
> that my language is Urdu?

I have been unable to trace this *sher* in eight *divans* of Mus'hafi, and neither *Nuru 'l-Lughat* nor Sherani cites the source. However, if the *sher* is by Mus'hafi, it should push back the date of the first use of 'Urdu' as a language name by a few years, for the reference to Mirza (Sauda) suggests that Sauda may have been alive at the time. Sauda died in 1781. It must be said, though, that the phrase *'Khuda rakkhe'* ('may God preserve') could well refer to the language, and thus need not necessarily be of a date prior to 1781. Even if the *sher* dates from before 1781, it won't push back the history of the word 'Urdu' by very many years.

Khan-e Arzu composed his Urdu dictionary *Navadiru 'l-Alfaz* around 1747. In this work, he doesn't use the word 'Urdu' in such a way as to indicate that it is a language name. He speaks of 'people of [the] Urdu,' 'popular speech of [the] Urdu,' 'language of [the] Urdu,' and so on. It is not before Gilchrist (1796) that we have a linguist's—or even a poet's, for that matter—unambiguous reference to 'Urdu' as language name. Gilchrist clearly defined 'Urdu' to mean 'the polished language of the court.' In 1796, he wrote his *Grammar of the Hindoostanee Language*. In this book, we find Gilchrist saying that poets have composed 'their several works in that mixed Dialect, also called Oordoo [...] or the polished language of the Court.'[9]

By the 1800s, however, British colonial imperatives were creating another source for Urdu's origin. Seizing upon the etymology of the word 'Urdu', and taking advantage of the fact that it also meant 'camp, or market of a camp' (though never 'army'), they proposed that Urdu was born in Army camp markets. The earliest printed source for this fiction seems to be Mir Amman's *Bagh-o-Bahar*, produced at the College of Fort William in 1803. Mir Amman said:

> Finally, Amir Taimur (with whose House the rule still remains, though only in name) conquered India. Due to his coming, and staying here, the bazaar of the army entered the city. And that's why the market place of the city came to be called 'Urdu.' [...] When King Akbar ascended the throne, people of all communities, hearing of the appreciation and free glow of generosity as practiced by that peerless House, came from the lands of the four sides and gathered in his presence. But each had his distinctive talk and speech. By virtue of their coming together for give and take, trade and commerce, question and answer, a [new] language of the camp-market came to be established.[10]

This theory of the 'lowly' origins of Urdu, perpetrated by the British for their own purposes, was disseminated through educational establishments for many generations, and thus fiction became accepted as fact.

---

1. Urdu's earliest and most popular name was 'Hindi' or 'Hindvi'. Khusrau uses both. Much before Khusrau (1253-1325), Ma'sud Sa'd Salman (1046-1121) is reported to have compiled a divan in Hindvi. See Jamil Jalbi, *Tarikh-e Adab-e-Urdu*, (4 vols. Delhi: Educational Publishing House, 1977-84), vol. 1, p. 23.
2. Duncan Forbes, *A Dictionary, Part I, Hindustani and English, Part II, English and Hindustani* (facsimile ed., Lucknow: UP Academy, 1987 [1866]), p. 28.
3. S.W. Fallon, *A New Hindustani-English Dictionary* (facsimile ed., Lucknow: UP Academy, 1986 [1866]), p. 69.
4. John T. Platts, *A Dictionary of Urdu, Classical Hindi, and English* (Oxford, 1974 [1884]), p. 40.
5. Nuru 'l-Hasan Naqvi, ed., *Divan-e-Mushafi* (5 vols. Lahore: Majlis-e-Taraqqi-e Adab, 1968-83), vol. 3, p. 26.
6. Ibid., vol. 1, p. 67.
7. Naiyar Kakorvi, *Nuru 'l-Lughat*, vol. 1 (facsimile ed. Lahore, 1988), p. 265.
8. Mazhar Mahmud Sherani, ed., *Maqalat-e-Hafiz Mahmud Sherani* (7 vols. Lahore: Majlis-e-Taraqqi-e Adab, 1966-76), vol. 1, p. 41.
9. Second edition published apparently by the author at Chronicle Press, Calcutta, 1796, p. 261.
10. Rashid Hasan Khan, ed., *Bagh-o-Bahar*, by Mir Amman Dihlavi (Delhi: Anjuman Taraqqi Urdu, 1992), pp. 7-8 (main text).

BIBLIOGRAPHY

Abrams, M.H. *The Mirror and the Lamp: Romantic Theory and the Tradition*. London: Oxford University Press, 1977.

Abru, Shaikh Mubarak. *Divan-e Abru*. Ed. Muhammad Hasan. New Delhi: Bureau for the Promotion of Urdu, 1990.

Abu'l-Hasan Amru'l-Lah Ilahabadi. *Tazkira-e Masarrat Afza [1780-1]*. Abridged and translated by 'Ata Kakvi. Patna: Azimushshan Book Depot, 1968.

'Askari, Muhammad Hasan. *Majmu'a-e Muhammad Hasan 'Askari*. Lahore: Sang-e Meel Publications, 1994.

'Askari, Muhammad Hasan. *Takhliqi 'Amal aur Uslub*. Ed. Muhammad Suhel 'Umar. Karachi: Nafis Academy, 1989.

Arzu, Sirajuddin Ali Khan. *Majmuan Nafais*. Ed. Abid Riza Bedar. Patna, n.d.

Arzu, Sirajuddin Ali Khan. *Musmir*. Ed. Raihana Khatun. Karachi 1989.

Cowl, R.P., Ed. *The Theory of Poetry in England*. London: Macmillan, 1914.

Danto, Arthur C. Review of Erwin Pankofsky: 'Perspective as Symbolic Form', in the London Review of Books, dated 9 April 1992.

Faruqi, Shamsur Rahman. 'Expression of the Indo-Muslim Mind in the Urdu *Ghazal*.' *Studies in Urdu Ghazal and Prose Fiction*. Ed. Muhammad Umar Memon. Madison: University of Wisconsin, Madison, 1979. (A slightly enlarged version of this article appears in Faruqi, *The Secret Mirror: Essays on Urdu Poetry*. Delhi: Progressive Book Service, 1981).

Faruqi, Shamsur Rahman. *Early Urdu Literary History and Culture*. New Delhi: Oxford University Press, 2001.

Faruqi, Shamsur Rahman. *She'r-e Shor Angez*. Vol. III. New Delhi: Bureau for the Promotion of Urdu, 1993. (All four volumes were reprinted in 1998.)

Ghalib, Mirza Asadu'l-Lah Khan. *Ghalib ke Khutut*. Vol. IV. Ed. Khaliq Anjum. New Delhi: Ghalib Institute, 1993.

Ghiasuddin Rampuri, Mulla. *Ghiasul Lughat* [1826]. Kanpur, 1893.

Hasrat Mohani, Maulana, Ed. *Intikhab-e Sukhan*. Vol. I. Lucknow: UP Urdu Academy, reprint of the original 1929 [?] edition. (The selection from Hatim is particularly valuable.)

Hatim, Shah Zahuru 'd-Din. *Intikhab-e Hatim*. Ed. 'Abdu 'l-Haq. New Delhi: Delhi Urdu Academy, 1991.

Hatim, Shah. *Divan Zada*. Ed. Ghulam Husain Zulfiqar. Lahore, 1975

Insha, Inshallah Khan, and Qatil, Mirza Muhammad Hasan. *Darya-e Latafat*. Murshidabad, Publisher: Aftab Alam Taab, 1850.

Jan-e Janan, Mirza Mazhar. *Divan*, with *Kharita-e Javahir*. Kanpur: Matba'-e Mustafa'i, 1855. (The Saiyad Husain Khalis and Mir Tahir Vahid *shers* are taken from *Kharita-e Javahir*, an anthology of Persian poetry put together by Mirza Mazhar Jan-e Janan.)

Jur'at, Shaikh Yahya Man (Qalandar Baksh). *Kulliyat-e Jur'at*. Ed. Nuru'l-Hasan Naqvi. Aligarh: Litho Colour Printers, 1971.

Khusrau, Amir Yaminuddin. *Dibacha-e Ghurratul Kamal*. Ed. Vazirul Hasan Abidi. Lahore: National Book Foundation 1975.

Mir, Muhammad Taqi. *Kulliyat-e Mir*. Vol. I. Ed. Zill-e 'Abbas 'Abbasi. Delhi: 'Ilmi Majlis, 1968.

Mir, Muhammad Taqi. *Nikatu'sh-Shu'ara'*. 1752. Ed. Muhammad Ilahi. Delhi: Idara-e Tasnif, 1972.

Mir, Muhammad Taqi. *Zikr-e Mir* Translated as *Zikr-i Mir, the autobiography of the Eighteenth Century Mughal Poet: Mir Muhammad Taqi Mir* by C.M. Naim. New Delhi, 1999.

Muhammad Aufi. *Lubab-ul Albab*. Ed. Edward Browne and Mirza Muhammad Qazvini. Teheran, 1343 (1964).

Muhammad Husain Azad. *Ab-e Hayat: Shaping the Canon of Urdu Poetry* [1880]. Translated and edited by Frances W. Pritchett with Shamsur Rahman Faruqi. OUP, New Delhi, 2001

Mus'hafi, Shaikh Ghulam Hamadani. *Divan-e Mushafi*. [The Eighth Divan.] Ed. 'Abid Raza Bedar. Patna: Khuda Baksh Oriental Library, 1995.

Mus'hafi, Shaikh Ghulam Hamadani. *Kulliyat*, Divans VI and VII. Ed. Hafeez 'Abbasi. Delhi: Majlis-e Isha'at-e Adab, 1975.

Mus'hafi, Shaikh Ghulam Hamadani. *Kulliyat-e Mushafi*. 5 vols. Ed. Nuru'l-Hasan Naqvi. Lahore: Majlis-e Taraqqi-e Adab, 1968-83. Vol. I.

Mus'hafi, Shaikh Ghulam Hamadani. *Tazkira-e Hindi*. Ed. Maulvi 'Abdu'l-Haq. Aurangabad: Anjuman Tarraqi-e Urdu, 1933.

Naim, C.M. 'The Theme of Homosexual (Pederastic) Love in Pre-Modern Urdu Poetry.' *Studies in Urdu Ghazal and Prose Fiction*. Ed. Muhammad Umar Memon. Madison: University of Wisconsin, Madison, 1979.

Naji, Muhammad Shakir. *Divan-e Shakir Naji*. Ed. Fazlu'l-Haq. Delhi: Majlis-e Subh-e Adab, 1968.

Nusrati Bijapuri. *'Ali Nama*. 1672. Ed. 'Abdu'l-Majid Siddiqi. Hyderabad: Salar Jung Dakani Publishing Company, 1959.

Pritchett, Frances W. *Nets of Awareness: Urdu Poetry and its Critics*. Berkeley, California, 1994.

Qaim Chandpuri, and Shaikh Qiyamu 'd-Din. *Kulliyat-e Qa'im*. Vol. I. Ed. Iqtida Hasan. Lahore: Masjlis-e Taraqqi-e Adab, 1965.

Qasim, Qudratullah. *Majmua-e Naghz*. Ed. Hafiz Mahmud Sherani. New Delhi, 1973.

Richards, I.A. *Coleridge on Imagination*. London: Routledge & Kegan Paul, 1962

Safa Badayuni. *Shamim-e Sukhan, Hissa-e Avval*. Lucknow, 1891.

Shamsul Lughat [1804-5]. Two volumes. Mumbai, 1891.

Shelley, P.B. 'A Defence of Poetry.' 1821. *English Critical Essays*. Ed. Edmund D. Jones. London: Oxford University Press, 1919.

Tara Chand. *The Problem of Hindustani*. Allahabad: Indian Periodicals Ltd., 1944.

Vali. *Kulliyat*. Ed. Nurul Hasan Hashmi. Lahore, 1996.

Wordsworth, William. 'Poetry and Poetic Diction'. *English Critical Essays*. Ed. Edmund D. Jones. London: Oxford University Press, 1919.

Yakta, Ahad Ali Khan. *Dastur-ul Fasahat*. Ed. Imtiaz Ali Khan Arshi. Rampur: Raza Library, 1943.

Yusuf Taqi, Ed. *Murshidabad ke Char Klasiki Shu'ara*. Calcutta: published by the author, 1989.

APPENDIX

A Note on Transliteration

Vowels: *a*   *ā*   *ē*   *e*   *i*   *ī*   *o*   *ō*   *u*   *ū*   *ai*   *au*

Consonants:

bē	b	*dāl*	d	*ṣuād*	ṣ	*gāf*	g
pē	p	*ḍāl*	ḍ	*ẓuād*	ẓ	*lām*	l
tē	t	*żāl*	ż	*ṭō'ē*	ṭ	*mīm*	m
ṭē	ṭ	*rē*	r	*ẓō'ē*	ẓ	*nūn*	n/ṅ
s̱ē	s̱	*ṛē*	ṛ	*'ain*	'	*vā'ō*	v
jīm	j	*zē*	z	*ghain*	gh	*hē*	h
čē	č	*žē*	ž	*fē*	f	*dōčash-mī hē*	h
ḥē	ḥ	*sīn*	s	*qāf*	q	*yē*	y
khē	kh	*shīn*	sh	*k̲āf*	k	*hamza*	'

1. Word-final *h* is indicated only when it is pronounced, for example, in *nigah*, but not in *qaṣīda*

2. *Iẕāfat* is indicated by adding *-e* to the first member of such compounds, for example, *nigah-e čashm-e surma-sā*.

3. The Arabic definite article is transliterated *al-* or *'l-*, for example, *'ilm al-ḥadīs̱* or *'ilmu 'l-ḥais̱*. Note, however, the transliteration of such common words as *bilk̲ul* and *allāh*.

4. The *v* of conjunction is written *-o-*.

Persian and Urdu originals of the verses quoted in the text:

1. *Qā'im maiṅ ghazal ṭaur kiyā rēkhta varna*
   Ik bāt lačar sī ba-zabān-e dak̲anī tʰī

2. *Muṣḥafī rēkhta kahtā hūṅ maiṅ behtar ze ghazal*
   Mu'taqid kyūṅ ke kō'ī Sa'dī-o-Khusrau kā hō

3. *Yeh rēkhta ka jo urdu hai Muṣḥafī is mēṅ*
   Na'i ṅikaali haiṅ baateṅ hazaar ham ne tō

4. *Lā ke dunyā mēṅ hamēṅ zehr-e fanā dētē hō*
   Hā'e kis bʰūl-bʰulaiyāṅ mēṅ daghā dētē hō

5. *Lab qudrat sē juz faryād kucʰ rēzish nahīṅ kartā*
   Ye kucʰ shā'ir nahīṅ hai apnē dil kā mars̱iya-khvaṅ hai

6. *Nāla mauzūṅ mī-kunad 'umrīst amma pīsh-e yār*
   Nīst Maẓhar dar shumār-e shā'irāṅ gōyā hanōz

7. *Ham k̲ō shā'ir na kahō Mīr ke ṣāḥab ham nē*
   Dard-o-gham kitnē kiyē jama' tō dīvān kiyā

8. *Ma'lūm nahīṅ ke apnā dīvāṅ*
   Hai mars̱iya yā kitāb kyā hai

9. *Kuchʰ maiṅ shā'ir nahīṅ ae Muṣḥafī hūṅ marsiya-khvaṅ*
   Sōz paṛh paṛh ke muḥibbōṅ kō rulā jātā hūṅ

10. *'Āshiq-mizāj rōtē haiṅ paṛh paṛh kē bēshtar*
    Ash'ār rind kē na hū'ē marsiyē hū'ē

11. *Gham-e maẓmūṅ na khāṭir meṅ na dil meṅ dard kyā ḥāṣil*
    Hūvā kāghaẕ namaṭ gō raṅg tērā zard kyā ḥāṣil

12. *Ghair kē mērē mar jānē meṅ tafāvut arz-o-samā kā hai*
    Mārā un nē dōnōṅ kō lēkin mujʰ kō kar kē sitam mārā

13. *Rakʰnā tʰa vqt-e qatl mirā amtiyāz hā'ē*
    Sō khāk meṅ milayā mujʰē sab meṅ sāṅ kar

14. *Kahtā tʰa kal kasū sē karūṅgā kisī kō qatl*
    Itnā tō kushtanī nahīṅ kō'i magar ke ham

15. *Zindagānī tō har ṭaraḥ kāṭī*
    Mar ke pʰir jēvnā qayāmat hai

16. *Hastī sē 'adam tak nafas-e čand kī hai rāh*
    Dunyā sē guzarnā safar ēsā hai kahāṅ kā

17. *Ham gulshan-e daurāṅ meṅ aē khuftagī-e ṭāli'*
    Sar-sabz tō haiṅ lēkin jūṅ sabza-e khvābīda

18. *Us sabzē kī ṭaraḥ sē ke hō rahguzār par*
    Rauṅdan meṅ ēk khalq kī yaṅ ham malē ga'ē

19. *Sabza naurasta rahguzār kā hūṅ*
    Sar utʰāyā ke hō gayā pāmāl

20. *Hai raṅg-e lāla-o-nasrīṅ judā judā*
    Har raṅg meṅ bahār kā iṡbāt čāhiyē

21. *Kahāṅ hai gul meṅ ṣafā'ī tirē badan kī sī*
    Bʰarī suhāg kī tis par ye bū dulhan kī sī

22. *'Ajab lapaṭ hai pasīnē kī gul-badan tērē*
    Ke gul hai 'iṭr-farōsh aur hū'i ṣabā maḥẓūẓ

23. *Āstiṅ usnē jō kuhnī tak čaṛhā'ī vaqt-e ṣubḥ*
    Ā rahī sārē badan kī bē-ḥijābī hātʰ meṅ

24. *Uskē sōnē sē badan sē kis qadar časpāṅ hai hā'ē*
    Jāma kibrītī kasū kā jī jalātā hai buhat

25. *Ham tō kabʰī kaheṅ na ke kapṛē utāriyē*
    Pahnā kareṅ gar āp isī vaz' kā libās

26. *Jī pʰaṭ gayā hai rashk sē časpāṅ libās kē*
    Kyā taṅg jāma lipṭā hai uskē badan kē sātʰ

27. *Qadrdāṅ ḥusn kē kahtē haiṅ usē dil-murda*
    Sāṅvrē čʰōṛ kē jo čāh karē gōrōṅ kī

28. *Namkīṅ ḥusn kā shikār karūṅ*
    Kyūṅ marūṅ halkē-pʰulkē gōrōṅ sē

29. *Čāhat burī balā hai kal Mīr-e nāla-kash bʰī*
    Hamrāh nai-savārāṅ dōṛē pʰirē nafar sē

30. *Ham dil ba-kaf nihāda tabʰī uskē gird tʰē*
    Vo jin dinoṅ ke kʰēlē tʰā laṛkōṅ meṅ gōliyāṅ

31. *Imrōz bā tū da'va-e dil čūṅ kunad Vaḥīd*
    Rōzē ke dāda būd khaṭē darmiyāṅ na būd

32. *Ẓulm kī mashq kab talak pyārē*
    Mū qalam kar kē khaṭ kō ṣāf karō

33. *Khurshīd-e khaṭ-e rukh sē tū čāhē ke hō'ē vaṣl*
    Shabnam kī niman čashm kō anjʰvāṅ satī nam rakʰ

34. *Jō lōṅdā čʰōṛ kar randī kō čāhē*
    Vo kō'ī 'āshiq nahīṅ hai bulhavas hai

35. *Har čand ke amradōṅ meṅ hai ik rāh kā mazā*
    Ghair az nisā valē na milā čāh kā mazā

36. *Gō zakhm-e dil mirē kō na sīvē mirā miyāṅ*
    Maiṅ mar gayā tō kyā huā jīvē mirā miyāṅ

37. *Par khabar rakʰnā kō'ī khanda na hō*
    Bulhavas nāpāk dil ganda na hō

38. *Ḥusn hai hī mīrzā'ī kar talāsh*
    Vo nahīṅ ma'shūq jō hō badma'āsh

39. *Sab jān-o-tan milā thā na thā kuch khalal magar*
    Dōnōṅ kē dil us ān tarastē thē bāt kō

40. *Vo ramz-e dil-farēb tirī ab talak hai yād*
    Bīrā banā kē phēṅknā bērī kē pāt kō

41. *Us vqt dil mirā tirē panjē kē bīč thā*
    Jis vaqt tunē hāth lagāyā thā hāth kō

42. *Ṭuk ik sarak sarak kar ā bēṭhnā baghal mēṅ*
    Kyā ačpalā'iyāṅ haiṅ aur kyā dhiṭā'iyāṅ haiṅ

43. *Dīvāna ba rāhē ravad-o-ṭifl ba rāhē*
    Yārāṅ magar īṅ shahr-e shumā saṅg na dārad

44. *Tēgh-o-tabar rakhā na karō pās Mīr kē*
    Aēsā na hō ke āpko ẓā'' vē kar rahēṅ

45. *Maiṅ nē kahā taṅg hūṅ mār marūṅ kyā karūṅ*
    Vo bhī lagā kahnē hāṅ kuch tō kiyā čāhiyē

6

IMPERIAL MUGHAL PAINTING
Joseph M. Dye III

Fig. 1: Akbar, Jahangir, and Shahjahan with their Ministers.
By Bichitr from the Minto Album, 1630. Reproduced by kind permission of the Trustees of the Chester Beatty Library, Dublin (7A.19).

The single most important event in the history of later Indian painting was the arrival of the Mughals in 1526.* For several hundred years, the emperors of this dynamic Muslim dynasty (Fig. 1) patronized an atelier of artists and artisans that produced illustrated manuscripts and individual paintings depicting poetic, historical, and religious subjects as well as portraits and nature studies. The vast imperial library at Agra contained 24,000 volumes. These books and pictures were highly valued by the Mughals: they were regarded as tangible evidence of wealth, refinement, and power; they were frequently used as ceremonial gifts; and they were taken as spoils of war.[1]

Imperial Mughal painters, calligraphers, paper makers, leather workers (for book covers), gilders, illuminators, and apprentices were both Muslims and Hindus; they came to the atelier from different parts of South Asia as well as from Persia and Central Asia (Fig. 2). Their work was organized by studio masters or administrators who assigned projects to artists and supervised their efforts. Some painters specialized in depicting specific subjects or themes (portraits, court scenes, etc.). Since they belonged to the imperial studios, these artists had access to the finest papers, pigments, brushes, and other materials, all of which they used with great and increasingly refined skill.

The painting techniques employed by members of the imperial Mughal studio were demanding. Once the subject of a picture was determined, its composition was drawn on a sheet of burnished paper in black or ochre; and then covered with a thin priming layer of white paint. Different coloured pigments prepared from mineral and vegetable sources were applied with animal-hair brushes. After each layer of paint was laid down, the back of the paper was rubbed with a stone to smooth the pigments and impart an attractive sheen to the surface. This burnishing was followed by additional refinements: outlines were carefully reinforced; minute details were added; pictorial elements were modelled to give them volume and depth; and gold and silver were applied in appropriate areas. Upon completion, the painting or manuscript was presented to the ruler-patron for his approval (Fig. 3).[2]

Imperial Mughal painters worked in a distinctive style that began in the sixteenth century as an eclectic, somewhat awkward idiom. At first, the different components of Mughal painting were fairly easy to distinguish: its expressive line and decorative polish were taken from Persia; its compositional energy and bright colours came from India; and its illusionistic devices were selectively borrowed from Europe. By the late sixteenth century, however, these diverse components were skillfully blended into a coherent and highly refined whole that was neither Persian, nor Indian, nor European, but distinctively Mughal.

The evolution of the imperial Mughal style was profoundly influenced by the personality, preferences, and needs of each Mughal ruler. It is, of course, not likely that the emperor administered the day-to-day activities of his studio (although it is well-known that the artists were closely and regularly supervised by the emperors), but in the final analysis, the painters worked to please him and to gain his favours. The emperor's tastes inevitably shaped the aesthetic vision that guided the imperial Mughal studio as a whole: it is no accident, for example, that dynamic and innovative paintings were produced for the charismatic young Akbar; or that under the ever-curious and scientific-minded Jahangir, Mughal pictures became increasingly refined and naturalistic.

While the emperor's preferences were important, they were not the only factors that influenced the work of the imperial atelier. Of great importance, too, were the talents, interests, and personalities of the studio's artists and their supervisors.[3] Atelier masters exercised considerable power over individual projects and each painter developed his own version of the studio's general style. Artistic individuality was, for the most part, recognized, encouraged, and highly valued in the imperial atelier.

---

* Editor's Note: For more on Mughal Painting, see Foreword.

1. The contents of this chapter owe a great deal to the works of S.C. Welch, M. Beach, M. Brand, L. Leach, J. Losty, G. Lowry, J. Seyller, and other scholars listed in the bibliography. In particular I am indebted to the efforts of S.C. Welch and M. Beach. No scholar of Mughal painting can capture the essence of a miniature or manuscript illustration like Mr Welch. Dr Beach's conclusions, based upon sensitive and discriminating stylistic analysis and comparisons, are always stimulating.
2. This account of Mughal painting technique is taken from Dye, 1989, p. 88.
3. Several detailed studies of individual Mughal painters have appeared in recent years: Beach 1978, Beach 1981, Dye 1989, Verma 1994, and Das 1998.

Fig. 2: THE MANUSCRIPT ATELIER.
From a copy of the *Akhlaq-i Nasiri* ca. 1590-95. Collection Prince and Princess Sadruddin Aga Khan (Ms 39, f. 196a).

The development of the imperial Mughal style in the sixteenth and seventeenth centuries is traced in the following pages. Mughal painting is one of the most exhaustively investigated areas in the entire history of South Asian art; the views presented here represent a consensus of current academic opinion. Despite heroic scholarly efforts, many questions remain: the origins of the Mughal style, for example, are still debated as are the relative contributions of patrons, artists, and studio masters to the school's evolution. While the history of Mughal painting in the sixteenth and seventeenth centuries is fairly well known, the fate of the style after Aurangzeb remains to be explained, an extraordinary task that lies well beyond the scope of this study.

BABUR (r. 1526-30)

The history of Mughal painting probably begins with Babur, the dynasty's founder, but there is no evidence to prove that it did. Like all his family, Babur was a multi-talented individual; he was a poet, scholar, and book collector. He wrote a lively autobiography that not only chronicles his eventful life, but also preserves his acutely observant reactions to the Subcontinent—its varied people, its ancient cultures, and its exotic flora and fauna. Given Babur's natural curiosity and visual sensitivity, it is quite likely that he had artists illustrate his books; but not one of these works has survived.[4]

When he died in 1530, Babur left his descendants with a fledgling empire, a distinguished Muslim lineage, and highly refined sensibilities rooted in the Persianate court culture of his Timurid ancestors. Most of all, the inquisitive Babur passed on to his descendants a zest for life and a fascination with the unique qualities of the physical world: these attitudes would be of fundamental importance to the development of Mughal painting.[5]

HUMAYUN (r. 1530-40; 1555-56)

Babur's son Humayun ascended the throne immediately after his father's death, but his efforts to hold the empire were challenged by several of his brothers (especially Kamran) and by Bahadur Shah, the ruler of Gujarat. In 1540, Humayun was forced out of India by Sher Shah, a brilliant Afghan adventurer. The emperor retreated to Lahore; then to Sindh; then to Rajasthan; and back to Sindh. Finally, in 1544, he sought refuge with Shah Tahmasp, the Safavid ruler of Iran (r. 1524-1576).

Humayun waited for some time at the Safavid court before Shah Tahmasp decided to provide the money and troops that he needed to regain the throne. After conquering Qandahar and Kabul he succeeded in capturing his brother Kamran, and went on to defeat the sons and relatives of Sher Shah. In 1555 he entered Delhi and restored the Mughal dynasty.

Humayun was a gentle, superstitious man deeply interested in books and paintings and had set up an atelier before his exile. According to the Mughal historian Abul Fazl, Humayun was so fond of manuscripts that he took his favourite volumes with him on military campaigns; an artist, it is said, accompanied him during his long exile.[6] It is not surprising, then, that while waiting at the Safavid court Humayun hired several artists who had formerly worked for Shah Tahmasp: two painters, Mir Sayyid Ali and Abdus Samad, joined Humayun at Kabul in 1550; they were soon followed by Mir Musavvir and Dost Muhammad. These talented men brought the latest Persian techniques and styles to the Mughal court.

Portrait of a Young Scholar painted about 1550 and inscribed to Mir Sayyid Ali demonstrates the type of work that was done by these Safavid masters (Fig. 4). It shows a handsome scribe kneeling on a carpet in a grassy sward. He pensively contemplates a book resting on a stand, presumably an example of his work. Sheets of paper, an inkpot, and a pen case are scattered around him. The grass is strewn with flowers. A golden sky and lavender hills fill the background.

Like other mid-sixteenth century Safavid court paintings, this picture is a paradise of jewel-like flowers, gilded skies, and pastel hills. Mir Sayyid Ali is intensely interested in surface ornament (fabrics, bookstand, etc.) and minute details as well as in beautiful and independently expressive lines. Even the attenuated, weightless figure of the scribe, which occupies a shallow spatial stage, is treated almost like another meticulously delineated pattern.[7]

Aside from the employment of these Safavid court painters, not much is known about the size, organization, and administration of Humayun's studio. Extant paintings, however, suggest that the imperial atelier was more complex and innovative than one might think. It was Humayun's artists, according to M. Beach, who created the earliest known Mughal portraits as well as the first representations of contemporary events and studies of flora and fauna (Humayun shared his father's interest in natural history).[8] Some scholars think that Humayun hired painters not only from Shah Tahmasp's court, but also from other Timurid centres, most notably Bukhara. His studio did not seem to develop a single homogeneous style, though virtually all extant paintings attributed to it are done in a Persian or Persianate manner.

The state of Humayun's atelier at the time of his death is to some extent indicated by *Prince Akbar Hunting a Nilgae*, a painting from an album, ten pages of which are now at the Fitzwilliam Museum, Cambridge (Fig. 5). This picture, dated about 1555 (when Akbar

---

4. Although no illustrated books made expressly for Babar survive, there are volumes that bear his seal, for example a *Shahnama* of ca. 1440 illustrated in Herat and now in the Royal Asiatic Society, London.
5. Beach 1978, p. 15.
6. See Brand and Lowry 1985, p. 89.
7. See Brand and Lowry 1985, pp. 24-25.
8. See Beach 1987, pp. 7-49, for a reevaluation of Humayun's patronage.

Fig. 3: ABU'L HASAN PRESENTING A PAINTING TO JAHANGIR. Attributed to Abu'l Hasan ca. 1605. Bibliotheque Nationale de France, Paris (Estampes, Od49/4, no. 40).

was thirteen) depicts an event later recorded in the *Akbarnama*:

> On this day and while on the march His Majesty the Shahinshah struck a *nilagao* [an antelope]…with his sword and took it as a prey so that the huntsmen were surprised, while the acute obtained a sign of his capturing the booty of sublime intention and were made glad.[9]

This painting portrays an actual event, but owes much to standardized representations of the royal hunt from Persia. It shows Akbar on horseback pursuing a *nilgae*; behind him a falconer kneels near a river; the walls and turrets of a fortress rise in the distance. Though awkward, this composition clearly demonstrates that an interest in naturalistic effects had already begun to blossom in Humayun's studio: the landscape is more spatious and plausible than the flat, Persian-inspired setting of *Portrait of a Young Scholar* (Fig. 4); and it is inhabited by pictorial elements that are treated not as ornamental details, but as lively, full-bodied entities, each with its own integrity. The energetic figure of Akbar, the scampering animals, and the freely rendered tree on the lower left are filled with an exuberance that anticipates developments to come.

Humayun died in early 1556 after he slipped on his library steps attempting to respond to a *muezzin's* call to prayer. His life, often viewed as a tragedy, was not without its triumphs: Humayun did return to his empire; he did regain his lost throne. Most importantly for us, Humayun also established a firm foundation for the future development of Mughal painting.

AKBAR (r. 1556-1605)

Born in 1542 in the deserts of Sindh while Humayun was fleeing India, Akbar (Fig. 6) was barely a teenager when he ascended the Mughal throne in 1556; but in a few short years he proved his mettle by stamping out rebellion and expanding his empire in northern and central India. Athletic, generous, and brave, Akbar was a charismatic leader as well as a gifted administrator and a brilliant strategist. Like his grandfather, he was intensely curious about everything, especially the religions of his subjects, most of whom were Hindus, Jains, or Zoroastrians. Christianity, introduced by Portuguese Jesuits from Goa, also fascinated him.

Akbar quickly decided that the imperial atelier must be expanded. To accomplish this he turned to Humayun's Persian painters—Mir Sayyid Ali and Abdus Samad. These two masters hired local artists trained in various styles: some worked in simplified and/or Indianized versions of Persian schools favoured by India's pre-Mughal Sultans; others painted in various indigenous South Asian styles used to illustrate texts in Indic languages; and still others worked in the Jain styles of Gujarat and Rajasthan.

Fig. 4: PORTRAIT OF A YOUNG SCHOLAR.
By Mir Sayyid Ali. 1549-1556. Los Angeles County Museum of Art, Bequest of Edwin Binney III (M.90.141.1). Photograph ©2001 Museum Associates/LACMA.

---

9. Quoted in Brand and Lowry 1985, p. 27; see Brand and Lowry 1985, p. 25, and Beach 1987, pp. 18-21 for a discussion of this painting.

Fig. 5: PRINCE AKBAR HUNTING A NILGAE.
Ca. 1555-1560. Fitzwilliam Museum, Cambridge (PD 72.1948).

Fig. 6: AKBAR PRESIDING OVER DISCUSSIONS IN THE IBADATKHANA (House of Worship).
By Nar Singh from a copy of the *Akbarnama* ca. 1604. Reproduced by kind permission of the Trustees of the Chester Beatty Library, Dublin (Ms. 3,f. 263v).

Since Akbar, like Babur, welcomed energetic activity and artistic experimentation, it is not surprising that these newly employed artists (and perhaps others left over from Humayun's reign) set out to forge a dynamic new style under the guidance of Mir Sayyid Ali and Abdus Samad. Their initial efforts are preserved in the Cleveland Museum's *Tutinama* (Tales of a Parrot), an anthology of stories told by a parrot to its mistress on each of twelve successive nights.[10]

The style of this manuscript's illustrations is, as one might expect, rather inconsistent and depends upon the specific artistic background of each painter. Some of Akbar's artists found it difficult to work out of their old, pre-Mughal modes and into the studio's new style. The painter of folio 99v (*The Merchant's Daughter Encounters a Wolf and Bandits*), for example, originally worked in the so-called Chaurapanchasika style, an indigenous Indian mode featuring flat compositions, vigorous lines, bold colours, formulaic figural types, and expressive gestures. It is hardly surprising, then, that the landscape, trees and female figures in his *Tutinama* folio (Fig. 7) look like those in such Chaurapanchasika style paintings as *Krishna Stealing Butter* (Fig. 8). This artist's only concessions to the newly emerging Mughal style are the softly modelled tree trunks and tufts of grass.

For other painters working on the *Tutinama*, however, the transition to the new style was much easier. The artist responsible for folio 32r (*The Parrot Mother Cautions Her Young*) is completely committed to the bold, naturalistic interests of Akbar's studio (Fig. 9) adumbrated in such late Humayun period pictures as *Prince Akbar Hunting a Nilgae* (Fig. 5). His landscape is open, airy, and evocative. The quickly brushed trees, which recall those in the lower left corner of *Prince Akbar Hunting a Nilgae*, are carefully observed and beautifully rendered.

The early Akbari style in a far more unified, but not fully resolved state is seen for the first time in a magnificent set of paintings made a few years after the *Tutinama* was completed. They illustrate the *Hamzanama* (Story of Amir Hamza), a legendary tale that recounts the exploits of Hamza, the Prophet Muhammed's (PBUH) uncle. This chaotic story, full of love, magic, and high adventure appealed to the energetic Akbar who, like many young men, enjoyed the legendary and the poetic.

Work on the *Hamzanama*, Akbar's first truly major manuscript project, commenced in 1562 and was completed by 1577. It originally consisted of fourteen volumes, each with 100 illustrations done on large sheets of cloth (about 27 by 20 inches). This undertaking was so vast that more painters trained in different regional traditions had to be hired. The work of the studio was supervised by Mir Sayyid Ali, and later by Abdus Samad, who seems to have watched over the project very carefully.

Paintings from the *Hamzanama*, like Akbar's empire, blend various Persian and indigenous South Asian idioms with much greater consistency and refinement than they had been in the *Tutinama*. *Aemr Disguised as the Surgeon Mizzmuhil Arrives before the Fort at Antalya* (Fig. 10), for example, includes individual motifs and intricately patterned surfaces ultimately derived from Persian painting, but the bright colours, agitated composition, emphatic gestures, and overall intensity are decidedly Indian. The painting's limited but relatively spacious stage, as well as the use of shading to give weight and volume attest to the growing interest of Mughal artists in naturalistic effects.[11]

So demanding was the *Hamzanama* that little else was painted between ca. 1562-77. When this mammoth project was completed, the imperial studio was left with a more coherent style and with an army of highly experienced artists eager for new challenges. Akbar responded by ordering many important manuscripts, but these commissions differed from those of his youth. As he matured, Akbar abandoned his taste for fantastic adventure stories in favour of more sober subjects that were 'rational' and 'verifiable'. Most of Akbar's later projects were, therefore, focused upon dynastic histories and portraits as well as texts related to the traditions of Islam and Hinduism.[12]

The illustrated historical manuscripts made by the imperial atelier shortly after the *Hamzanama* included: the *Timurnama* (ca. 1584) or 'Story of Timur', a history of Timur and his descendants down to Akbar; the first *Baburnama* or 'Story of Babur' (ca. 1589) which recounts the events of his grandfather's reign; and the first *Akbarnama* or 'Story of Akbar' (ca. 1590 or earlier)

---

10. See Chandra 1976 for a complete discussion of this manuscript.
11. See Beach 1981, p. 65.
12. See Beach 1981, pp. 18-22.

Fig. 7

Fig. 9

which documents the emperor's own career. These lavish books celebrating Akbar and his glorious ancestors were deliberately intended to present the Mughals as the legitimate heirs of the Timurids and the just rulers of India. Each manuscript contained an average of 150 full-page paintings, most of them highly descriptive scenes of battles, hunts, and sieges. No Persian ruler before Shah Tahmasp, J. Losty notes, had the resources to include more than thirty or forty large paintings in a single manuscript.[13]

Akbar's studio could produce so many illustrated books because it was organized rather like a modern factory. Paintings and illustrations were usually a joint effort: a master sketched the composition, a second (often inferior) artist applied the colours; and sometimes a third who specialized in portraits painted the faces. The quantity of pictures and manuscripts made by this assembly-line process was staggering, but the aesthetic quality was often uneven and, at times, pedestrian.[14]

During the 1580s, the imperial studio also produced several manuscripts dealing with the traditions of Islam and Hinduism. In 1581-82, Akbar commissioned the text and production of the *Tarikh-i Alfi* (History of a Thousand), a 'factual' account of the history of Islam's first millennium. This illustrated manuscript was completed in ca. 1592-93. He also ordered Persian translations of important Hindu texts: the two great epics, the *Mahabharata* or *Razmnama* as it is called in Persian (ca. 1582-86), and the *Ramayana* (1584-89), as well as the *Harivamsa* or genealogy of Vishnu (ca. 1585).

Krishna and Balarama Arriving in Vrindavan (Fig. 11), an illustrated page from the *Harivamsa* of ca. 1585, demonstrates just how far the imperial Mughal style had evolved since the *Hamzanama*. The *Harivamsa* painting shows the arrival of the two young Hindu gods in a landscape of spatial pockets, each one of which reveals a 'secret world'. These vignettes are tightly structured by a series of compositional triangles that, organized around the central vertical axis, move back and into the painting: the first and largest is established by the figural group in the foreground; the second, by the mauve rocks and green trees in the middle ground; and the third by the distant mountains at the top centre in the background. The spatial depth created by this progression in and back is amplified by other illusionistic devices: for example, many of the pictorial elements in the fore—and middle—ground (especially the trees) are larger than those in the background; and virtually every one of these elements is modelled to give it volume and weight.

In contrast, the spatial stage of the *Hamzanama* page (Fig. 10) seems much shallower and its contents less refined. Although its composition is also structured by triangular movements around the central vertical axis, the *Hamzanama* painting's middle ground is obscured and flattened by the rocks rising in front of it. Rather than diminishing in size, the pictorial elements in the background (especially the faces of the figures) are about as large as those in the foreground. Since narrative clarity is all-important to the *Hamzanama* artist, his rough-hewn figures are far more emphatic than the relatively restrained inhabitants of the *Harivamsa* page.

The growing interests in naturalism and illusionistic effects evident in the *Harivamsa* and other imperial Mughal manuscripts of the 1580s were, in large part, inspired by contacts with European prints, drawings, and paintings.[15] In 1580, Akbar invited Jesuits from Goa to the Mughal court where they participated in theological discussions and debates. This mission brought a copy of the eight-volume *Royal Polyglot Bible* printed at Antwerp (1568-1573) by Christoph Plantin and illustrated with engravings (Fig. 12).[16]

Members of the imperial atelier avidly studied these illustrations and many other northern European prints, paintings, and drawings presented as gifts to Akbar and his court. Some Mughal artists made fairly close (but not necessarily identical) copies of them (Figs. 13, 14): for example, the painter Kesu Das' version (ca. 1590) of an engraving after the Nuremberg artist Georg Pencz's *Joseph Relating His Dreams* (ca. 1544).[17] Other artists, created clever pastiches made up of exotic European

---

13. Losty 1982, p. 79.
14. Beach 1981, pp. 9-11.
15. Evidence suggests that Western pictorial sources influenced Mughal artists from at least the beginning of Akbar's reign, if not earlier.
16. For a discussion of this topic, see Brand and Lowry 1985, pp. 96-105.
17. See Brand and Lowry 1985, p. 100.

Fig. 7: THE MERCHANT'S DAUGHTER ENCOUNTERS A WOLF AND BANDITS. *Tuti-Nama (Tales of a Parrot),* (f. 99v), ca. 1560 © The Cleveland Museum of Art, 2000, Gift of Mrs A Dean Perry, 1962.279.

Fig. 8: KRISHNA, THE BUTTER THIEF. From a copy of the *Bhagavata Purana* ca. 1540. Virginia Museum of Fine Arts, Richmond (64.36.1).

Fig. 9: THE PARROT MOTHER CAUTIONS HER YOUNG. *Tuti-Nama (Tales of a Parrot),* (f. 32r), ca. 1560. © The Cleveland Museum of Art, 2000, Gift of Mrs A Dean Perry, 1962.279.

Fig. 8

Fig. 10: Aemr, Disguised as the Surgeon Mizzmuhil, Arrives Before the Fort at Antalya.
From a copy of the *Hamzanama* ca. 1562-77. Courtesy of the Freer Gallery of Art, Smithsonian Institution, Washington, D.C.

Fig. 11: KRISHNA AND BALARAMA ARRIVING IN VRINDAVAN.
From a copy of the *Harivamsa* ca. 1585. Virginia Museum of Fine Arts, Richmond (68.8.50).

The Magnificent Mughals

Fig. 15: THREE ANGELS.

Fig. 12: POLYGLOT BIBLE.

Fig. 12: 1568-72 Vol. I, Page H. Houghton Library, Harvard University, Cambridge (f Bible A.569)

Fig. 13: George Pencz, German, 1544 Engraving. Courtesy, Museum of Fine Arts, Boston. Reproduced with permission. ©2000 Museum of Fine Arts, Boston. All Rights Reserved. Harvey D. Parker Collection (P2355)

Fig. 14: Attributed to Kesu Das. From the *Muraqqa-i Gulshan* ca. 1590. The Saint Louis Art Museum, (403.52).

Fig. 15: Ca. 1585. Reproduced by kind permission of the Trustees of the Chester Beatty Library, Dublin (Ms. 62, no. 2).

Fig. 13: JOSEPH RELATING HIS DREAMS.

Fig. 14: JOSEPH TELLING HIS DREAM TO HIS FATHER.

elements taken from various sources and placed in Mughal or Mughalized settings: *Three Angels* (ca. 1585), for example, features celestials copied from a European print and set in a Euro-Mughal landscape (Fig. 15).[18]

Throughout the late Akbari period, Mughal artists were especially interested in the illusionistic creations of Western pictorial conventions and techniques: the concepts of spatial planes, single point perspective, and spatial recession; the use of pictorial elements that diminish in size according to distance; and shading to give figures a sense of volume and weight. Mughal artists remained true to their basic Persianate idiom, but they did borrow many Western techniques to help clothe their work in increasingly more naturalistic garb.

By the late 1580s-1590s, the imperial Mughal style was a coherent, fully realized whole. The youthful energy and narrative directness of early Akbari painting gave way to subtle elegance and heightened naturalistic effects. The best imperial Mughal pictures of the late sixteenth century are highly controlled works of art that make brilliant use of delicate line, quiet colour, deep spatial recession, and sensitive modelling. The different components of the Mughal style, so easily distinguished in the *Tutinama* and the *Hamzanama*, are now fully integrated.

Without doubt, the finest imperial Mughal pictures of the late 1580s and the 1590s illustrate several small, personal volumes created for Akbar when he lived in Lahore (1585-98): the *Divan* of Anvari (1588); the *Baharistan* (1595), the *Khamsa* of Nizami (1595), the *Khamsa* of Amir Khusrau Dehlavi (1597-98); and an *Anvar-i Suhayli* (1596-97). These luxurious manuscripts, most of them Persian poetical anthologies, were made from the finest papers and illustrated with expensive pigments. Each illustration was usually the responsibility of one painter, rather than a team of artists.

A painting from the *Baharistan* (ca. 1595) epitomizes the breathtaking quality of these precious little books from Lahore (Fig. 16).[19] This lush illustration shows the moment when a wise sage encountered an all too stylish dervish sewing his robe: 'That robe is your God' the sage declared. This scene is presented in a deep and elaborately detailed stage consisting of three well-defined spatial planes: a foreground filled with rustic details; a middle ground occupied by the two holy men and a large Mughal building; and an enigmatic background consisting of a pavilion, two men, and a leafless tree.

Compositional movements and charming details lure one into this picturesque work, especially the curious rooms and chambers of its architectural setting, placed as they are at different angles to suggest depth. The gnarled tree in the foreground, the dervish's wiggling coat, the stout ceiling rafters, and virtually every other pictorial element are carefully rendered to capture their external appearance with complete exactitude. The artist obviously delights in portraying the psychological tension between the two men: the firm, but calm face of the sage; and the sharp gaze of the dervish.

Little could match the rich, opulent illustrations from such small Lahore manuscripts as the *Baharistan*, but so controlled is the atelier's production in the 1590s that even the large historical manuscripts produced by joint effort—the second *Akbarnama* (ca. 1597-98), the *Chingiznama* (1596), and several *Babarnamas* (ca. 1590, 1593, 1597-98)—adhere to certain minimum standards.

Hulagu Khan Destroys the Fort at Alamut a page from the *Chingiznama* or 'Story of Genghis' (Fig. 17), a history of Genghis Khan and the Mongols, is typical of the imperial atelier's standard joint production in the 1590s. This painting shows Hulagu Khan, the grandson of Genghis Khan, standing atop the gate of the fort at Alamut: his left hand holds a bow; with his right hand he whistles in amazement. Below him, men demolish Alamut's walls and, in the foreground, Hulagu's victorious army rides up to the captured fort on spirited chargers.

According to inscriptions, this painting was designed by Basawan and coloured by Nand Gwaliori. Its composition, filled with amply modelled figures, is organized into three planes (foreground, middle ground, and background) linked together by the files of soldiers who ride across and through the picture. The diagonal movements of these troops give the painting a strong feeling of depth; it is further augmented by progressively reducing the size of figures as one moves back through the composition. The transitions between the three planes are smoothed by systems of colour

---

18. See Leach 1995 (vol. 1), p. 143.
19. For a discussion of this painting, see Welch 1978, pp. 54-55.

Fig. 16: THE FOPPISH DERVISH REBUKED.
From the *Baharistan* ca. 1595. Bodleian Library, University of Oxford (MS.*Elliott* 254, f. 9r).

Imperial Mughal Painting

Fig. 17: HULAGU KHAN DESTROYS THE FORT AT ALAMUT.
Designed by Basawan, coloured by Nand Gwaliori. From the *Chingiznama* 1596. Virginia Museum of Fine Arts, Richmond (68.8.53).

Fig. 18

Fig. 19

Fig. 20

Fig. 18: AKBAR'S EXPEDITION TO THE EASTERN PROVINCES.
From a copy of the *Akbarnama* ca. 1597-98. Present location unknown.

Fig. 19: TWO ROSY PASTORS.
From the Berlin album ca. 1570 Staatsbibliothek zu Berlin-Preussischer Kulturbesitz, Orientabteilung (A 177, f. 17b).

Fig. 20: RAM DAS KACHHWAHA.
Attributed to Manohar ca. 1590-95. Reproduced by kind permission of the Trustees Chester Beatty Library, Dublin (11A.35).

Fig. 21: A SINNER'S PASSIONATE PLEA TO GOD.
From a copy of the *Kulliyat* of Sa'di ca. 1604. Collection Prince and Princess Sadruddin Aga Khan, (Ms. 35, f. 107b).

Fig. 22: AN ALTERCATION IN THE BAZAAR.
From a copy of the *Kulliyat* of Sa'di ca. 1604. Collection Prince and Princess Sadruddin Aga Khan, (Ms. 35, f. 19b).

Fig. 21

Fig. 22

patterning that enable one's eye to move with a measured rhythm through the composition.[20]

Even richer and more complex than the paintings from the *Chingiznama*, were those produced for the 'second' *Akbarnama*, at one time dated to 1604, but recently redated by J. Seyller to ca. 1598. *Akbar's Expedition to the Eastern Provinces* (Fig. 18) is a fine example of illustrations from this superb manuscript: its paintings are closely related in style and quality to those in the small volumes of poetry produced during the 1590s in Lahore. The painting shows Akbar seated on a grand, ram-bowed barge at the centre of the composition issuing orders to his subordinates; surrounding him in the turbulent waters are barges filled with courtiers, attendants, learned men, and elephants.

20. As competently rendered as it is, Basawan's picture is not without precedents. Its subject—the siege of a fortified town—appears in many Akbari period historical manuscripts. Most Mughal siege paintings follow the general format employed here by Basawan, i.e., a walled city in the upper right or left corner attacked or approached by an army in the fore and middle-grounds.

Fig. 23: DARBAR OF JAHANGIR.
By Abu'l Hasan ca. 1615. Courtesy of the Freer Gallery of Art, Smithsonian Institution, Washington, D.C.

Fig. 24: PRINCE KHURRAM WEIGHED AGAINST METALS.
Ca. 1615. The British Museum, London (1948 10 – 9 069).

Fig. 25: Peafowl in a Landscape.
Attributed to Mansur ca. 1620. Courtesy of the Arthur M. Sackler Museum, Harvard University Art Museums, Cambridge, Private Collection.

The captivating detail and visual polish of this painting recall *The Foppish Dervish Rebuked* from the *Baharistan* (Fig. 16). Like the architectural setting in the *Baharistan* painting, Akbar's boats are set at various angles within the composition's clearly defined spatial planes to suggest depth. Visual details, energetic action, and complex spatial construction mark this painting as a product of Akbar's studios during the 1590s. The palette is rich but controlled, and each pictorial element is carefully modelled to give it a sense of volume and weight.[21]

The naturalistic concerns encountered in the second *Akbarnama,* and of course in other late sixteenth century Mughal manuscripts, imply a genuine belief in the validity and value of the phenomenal world, an attitude initially fostered by Babur and one that contrasts sharply with the traditional Indian emphasis on ideal types and visual unities. The Mughal's commitment to such ideas is especially evident in the nature studies made during Akbar's reign, for example *Two Rosy Pastors in a Landscape* of ca. 1570 (Fig. 19). Though probably based upon earlier prototypes rather than direct observation, these two birds are, nonetheless, rendered with meticulous attention to naturalistic detail: the volume and the poses of the birds are especially striking.[22]

Akbar's interest in realistic portrayal extended not only to animals and birds, but also to people. Portraits were created in India long before the Mughals, but they were always idealized representations of individuals, not exact likenesses. The Mughals were the first to introduce visually accurate portraiture to India. According to Abul Fazl, Akbar commissioned true likenesses of important nobles, courtiers, and other personalities, many of which were mounted in large albums.[23] A typical example, the portrait of Ram Das Kachhwaha (Fig. 20) shows the subject standing against a plain green ground, wearing a transparent *chakdhar jama* over purple pajamas tied with a gold sash. Ram Das served as a deputy of the important minister Todar Mal during Akbar's reign; he was later promoted by Jahangir. A tough survivor, Ram Das is shown here as a solid, dignified man, who managed to hang on through two emperors and, no doubt, endless court intrigue.[24]

Mughal manuscript illustration and miniature painting during Akbar's reign had been dynamic, innovative, and experimental, very much like the emperor himself. By the late 1580s-1590s, the Akbari style emerged in its fully evolved, classic state. It was characterized by dynamic compositions often filled with hosts of energetic figures engaged in some kind of activity. The studio's interest in naturalistic effects, encouraged by Akbar and facilitated by contact with European pictorial sources, was profound: constructing a deep, complex pictorial space seems to have been a major preoccupation of Akbari artists, but modelling to create a sense of volume as well as visually accurate characterizations were also of great interest. The imperial Mughal style is, at this point, a long way from its awkward, sometimes clumsy, infancy as recorded a few decades earlier in the *Tutinama*.

During the last six or seven years of Akbar's life the imperial atelier focused on texts that had deep personal meaning for the emperor.[25] These books, like those from Lahore, were mostly small volumes of poetry, illustrated with a few superb miniatures, each executed by a single artist. Some of these illustrations are rather conservative. *A Sinner's Passionate Plea to God* of ca. 1604 (Fig. 21) from the *Kulliyat* of Saadi (the Works of Saadi, renowned

Fig. 26: A CHAMELEON. By Mansur ca. 1610-15. Her Majesty Queen Elizabeth II, The Royal Collection ©2000, (RL. 1208).

---

21. See Goswamy and Fischer 1987, pp. 84-85; Beach 1992, pp. 64-67.
22. See Beach 1987, p. 27.
23. Beach 1987, pp. 128-131.
24. For a discussion of this painting, see Leach 1995, pp. 140-141.
25. Beach 1987, pp. 128-134.

Muslim poet and philosopher), for example, recalls the lush complexity and intriguing visual detail of the classic 1590s style.[26]

Other pages from the same manuscript, however, anticipate trends that would fully surface under Akbar's son Jahangir. *An Altercation in the Bazaar* (Fig. 22) also from the *Kulliyat*, for example, abandons the opulent detail of *A Sinner's Passionate Plea to God* in favour of a less cluttered and even more exquisitely realized picture.[27] The thoughtful composition is made up of a few pictorial elements, many with richly modulated monochromatic surfaces and restrained designs. Facial expressions, gestures, glances, and figural placement are used to define the relationships between the picture's two major combatants as well as the varied reactions of the surrounding crowd. The artist's emphasis upon psychological interaction and elegantly articulated visual details hint at things to come.

JAHANGIR (r. 1605-1627)

The imperial Mughal studios, which had been somewhat of a factory for much of Akbar's reign, were destined to be something quite different under Jahangir (Fig. 23). Born in 1569 and known until his coronation as Salim, Jahangir spent his childhood in the shadow of his dynamic father. He had little of Akbar's charisma; and there was a kind of indolence about him born of opulent court life and sustained by too much opium and wine. He was, as one might expect, torn between admiration and rejection of his father.

In July 1600, Salim tried to seize the Agra fort while Akbar was in the Deccan. This rebellion was unsuccessful and Salim fled to Allahabad, where he assumed the title of *shah* (king) and established his own court. Akbar eventually forgave Salim, but their relationship was never quite the same. The rebellious prince remained in Allahabad until shortly before his father's death in 1605.

Salim's court at Allahabad was a dissolute and dramatic establishment. The quixotic prince was given to sudden acts of cruelty and of kindness fuelled, in part, by his excessive consumption of opium and wine. Nonetheless, Salim's flamboyant Allahabad years were crucial to his development as a patron and connoisseur of painting. Long before his rebellion, the prince had exhibited a special love for painting; in his early twenties, for example, he actively supported painters such as the *émigré* Persian Aqa Riza and his young son Abul Hasan.

Given his fondness for painting, it is not surprising that Salim established an atelier soon after he arrived in Allahabad. The artists of this studio worked in two distinctive modes: the first was a simplified and more focused version of the Akbari court style; the second was a precise, flat, and highly decorative style, inspired by Safavid Persian paintings, especially those of Aqa Riza. Though he sponsored work in both modes, the prince was especially fond of the refinements of the second.[28]

Salim took the name Jahangir or 'the World Seizer' when he ascended the throne; but the world over which he ruled was much different than the one that his father inherited in 1556. By 1605, the Mughals were not a royal house in the making, but a secure, established dynasty with an increasingly ritualized court. Jahangir was neither a brilliant military leader nor a great empire builder, but he was an intelligent and highly sensitive man deeply interested in the world around him. During his reign, Jahangir would prove to be one of the Mughal dynasty's most engaged and astute patrons of art. He wrote in his memoirs, the *Tuzuk-i Jahangiri*:

> As regards myself, my liking for painting and my practice in judging it have arrived at such a point that when any work is brought before me, either of deceased artists or those of the present-day, without the names being told me, I say on the spur of the moment that it is the work of such and such a man. And if there be a picture containing many portraits, and each face be the work of a different master, I can discover which face is the work of each of them. If any other person has put in the eye and eyebrow of a face, I can perceive whose work the original face is, and who has painted the eye and eyebrows.[29]

Unlike Akbar, who often commissioned large manuscripts illustrated by armies of artists, Jahangir favoured small, elegant books with fewer and finer illustrations, each one the work of a single artist. Poetic

---

26. See Goswamy and Fischer 1987, pp. 158-59. The *Kulliyat* of Saadi discussed in the text is a transitional work placed late in Akbar's reign or early in Jahangir's reign depending upon the scholar and/or date of publication.
27. See Goswamy and Fischer 1987, pp. 131-132.
28. See Beach 1992, pp. 68-78.
29. Quoted in Beach 1978, p. 23.

Fig. 27: Inayat Khan Dying.
Ca. 1618. Courtesy, Museum of Fine Arts, Boston (14.679). Reproduced with permission. ©2000 Museum of Fine Arts, Boston. All Rights Reserved

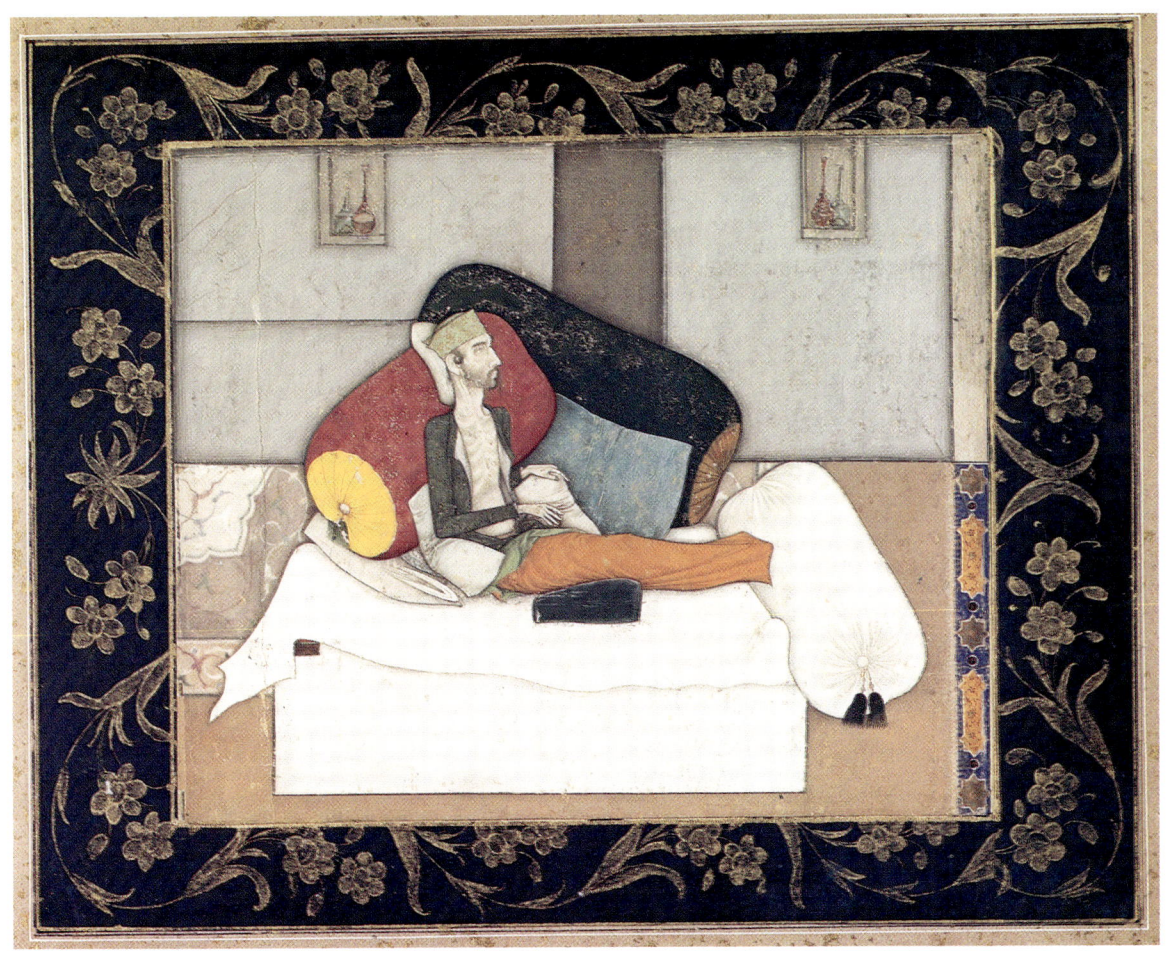

Fig. 28: Inayat Khan Dying.
Ca. 1618. Bodleian Library, University of Oxford (MS.*Ouseley add.* 171b f. 4 r).

Fig. 29: JAHANGIR EMBRACING SHAH ABBAS.
By Abu'l Hasan, from the Leningrad Album ca. 1618. Courtesy of the Freer Gallery of Art, Smithsonian Institution, Washington, D.C. (45.9).

Fig. 30: Shahjahan Honouring Prince Aurangzeb at Agra Before His Wedding.
By Payag, from the *Padshahnama* ca. 1640. The Royal Collection ©2000, Her Majesty Queen Elizabeth II (f. 214B).

and historical texts were prepared for Jahangir, but he preferred individual paintings depicting what by now were standard Mughal themes: the pleasures and pastimes of court life; portraits; studies of birds, animals, and flowers; scenes derived from European pictorial sources; and studies of holy men. These independent pictures, framed by exquisitely painted borders, were usually bound into sumptuous albums or *muraqqas* that also contained Deccani, Persian, or Turkish miniatures and examples of calligraphy as well as European prints and Mughal copies of them.[30]

When Jahangir became emperor, he dismissed many of his father's less talented artists, preferring instead to nurture a small group of highly gifted painters. Jahangir encouraged his artists to develop their own particular talents: for example, Abul Hasan concentrated upon court scenes and official portraits; Mansur did natural history subjects, Daulat created portraits, and so forth. No doubt, artistic individuality was stimulated by a studio environment that was less rigidly organized than it had been under Akbar.

Over the course of the next twenty-two years, Jahangir's painters focused upon realizing their own distinct version of the imperial Mughal style. In so doing, they refined the energetic naturalism of the Akbari period into a calmer, even more intensely realistic style capable of revealing not only the outer appearance of physical reality, but also its unique inner spirit. The ability of Jahangiri painters to penetrate deep into the heart of reality was made possible by their extraordinary technical skills. They were especially interested in modelling in light and shade to give weight and volume to their figures; and they laboured long and hard to record the unique qualities of human character and psychological inter-relationships.[31]

Many features of the new Jahangiri style, a combination of highly analytical realism and exceptional technical virtuosity, had already begun to surface late in Akbar's reign. By 1615, the heightened realism of Jahangir's studios was in full bloom. It can even be seen in such formal court paintings as *The Emperor Weighs Prince Khurram* (ca. 1615), a picture which was probably intended for a *Jahangirnama* ('History of Jahangir') and is now in the British Museum (Fig. 24). This painting depicts an event in 1607 that Jahangir describes in his memoirs:

On Friday...I came to the quarters of Khurram which had been made in the Urta Garden. In truth, the building is a delightful and well-proportioned one. Whereas it was the rule of my father to have himself weighed twice every year, (once) according to the solar and (once according to the) lunar year, and to have the princes weighed according to the solar year, and

Fig. 31: SHAHJAHAN EXAMINING THE ROYAL SEAL. (Below) by Abul Hasan ca. 1628; PORTRAIT OF JAHANGIR. (Above) by Balchand. Collection Prince and Princess Sadruddin Aga Khan (M. 140).

moreover in this year, which was the commencement of my son Khurram's sixteenth lunar year, the astrologers and astronomers represented that a most important epoch according to his horoscope would occur, as the prince's health had not been good. I gave an order that they should weigh him according to the prescribed rule, against gold, silver, and other metals, which should be divided among faqirs and the needy.[32]

The event is shown in a complex, but rationally organized space. Rather than the multitudes of scampering, energetic figures that one might encounter in an Akbari painting, one sees only a few stately participants. Jahangir stands under a red canopy in the middle ground, steadying the weighing pan in which Prince Khurram (later Shahjahan) sits; the emperor is assisted by the Khankhanan who stands at the right. Behind him at the right appears a row of four courtiers (left to right)—Itimaduddaula, Asif Khan, Mahabat Khan, and Khan Jahan Lodi. Behind the emperor at the left, two attendants hold a weighing pan filled with sacks of treasure; a third stoops to place elegantly wrapped bundles on the carpeted floor. Khurram's gifts to Jahangir (trays of silks, daggers, jewellery, and gold vessels) cover the foreground; they are catalogued by a royal steward (lower right) and watched by a guard (lower left). The interior of a pavilion as well as a terrace and garden view fill the background.

The extraordinary technical skill and a deep commitment to realistic representation so typical of Jahangir's studio are evident in this painting. The fabric patterns, the rugs, *blanc-de-chine* porcelain in the niches of the pavilion's interior are rendered with great precision. Regardless of these arresting details, however, one's eye moves immediately to the two main figures—Jahangir and Khurram—who occupy the central vertical axis of the composition. Jahangir's eyes and carefully modelled face are filled with affection as he beholds Khurram, shown as a poised, if not haughty young prince. The powerful exchange of their gazes and the interrelationship that they reveal dominate all other elements in this dense, visually demanding painting.

The imperial studio's commitments to intensely

---

30. Dye 1989, p. 89.
31. Beach 1978, pp. 23-27.
32. Quoted in Welch 1978, p. 75.
33. See Welch 1985, p. 217.

Fig. 32: SHAHJAHAN, MASTER OF THE GLOBE.
By Hashim, from the Kevorkian album 1629.
Courtesy of the Freer Gallery of Art, Washington, D.C. (39-49a).

analytical realism and great technical virtuosity are even more fully exhibited by the many studies of flowers, animals, and birds made during Jahangir's reign. The extraordinary accuracy of these paintings reflects the skill of Jahangir's painters as well as the emperor's own keen scientific interest in the diverse forms of nature. In *Peafowl* (Fig. 25) attributed to Mansur, a cock quickly devours a wiggly worm just as his peahen turns to look at him. As S.C. Welch notes: 'The peacock's forward rush and the peahen's split-second turn are recorded with lightening speed.'[33] Probably sketched in part from life, these naturalistically conceived birds are balanced against a sketchy and stylized Mughal landscape.

Jahangir delighted in the odd or eccentric forms of nature that his artists frequently painted. One such work, *A Chameleon* of ca. 1610-15 attributed to Mansur,

Fig. 33: SHAHJAHAN HUNTING.
From the *Padshahnama* ca. 1645. The Royal Collection ©2000, Her Majesty Queen Elizabeth II (f. 165A).

demonstrates how his studio used drawing and painting to capture the appearance of even the ugliest creatures in the phenomenal world, the reality of which were fully accepted (Fig. 26).[34] Sinister and predatory, the prehensile lizard is shown here gripping a tree branch. He is about to devour a dainty butterfly. In this picture, which is really a drawing heightened with colour, the artist uses delicately naturalistic line, wash, and colour with an exactitude that is almost unbearable in its perfection.

Perhaps the epitome of Jahangiri realism is a drawing that records the last moments of Inayat Khan (Fig. 27), as well as a painting based upon it (Fig. 28). Jahangir describes in his memoirs the circumstances under which this pictorial record was made:

> On this day news came of the death of 'Inayat Khan. He was one of my intimate attendants. As he was addicted to opium, and when he had the chance, to drinking as well, by degrees he became maddened with wine. As he was weakly built, he took more than he could digest, and was attacked by the disease of diarrhoea and in this weak state he two or three times fainted. By my order Hakim Rukna applied remedies, but whatever methods were resorted to gave no profit… At last, he became dropsical, and exceedingly low and weak. Some days before this, he had petitioned that he might go to Agra. I ordered him to come into my presence and obtain leave. They put him into a palanquin and brought him. He appeared so low and weak that I was astonished. 'He was skin drawn over bones' (verse) or rather his bones, too, had dissolved. Though painters have striven much in drawing an emaciated fact, yet I have never seen anything like this, or even approaching to it. Good God, can a son of man come to such a shape and fashion?' As it was a very extraordinary case, I directed painters to take his portrait.[35]

Inayat Khan, emaciated and pale, is shown sitting upright on a palanquin, his disease ravaged body supported by bolsters and pillows. His eyes are glazed, but he remains at attention, wearing a hat and jacket as a gesture of respect for his ruler and for court etiquette. This stark image of death's nobility and its indignities is frank and unsentimental. It is exactly what the eye sees and what the painter records.

Pictures like *Inayat Khan Dying* move far beyond the naturalism of the full-blown Akbari style. In fact, Jahangiri paintings can often be so probing that they make the contents of Akbari pictures, no matter how realistically rendered, seem generic. *Inayat Khan Dying* is, perhaps, one of the most moving Mughal paintings ever created. This deeply contemplative study of human frailty could not have been done during Akbar's heady reign, nor would such a touching subject be found in the grand albums of Shahjahan.

In the later years of his reign, Jahangir's addiction to opium and wine worsened, and he became increasingly isolated by the ceremonial life of the court. It is not surprising, then, that the emperor eventually began to patronize allegorical paintings with a political and adulatory slant.[36] A fine example of these pictures, Abul Hasan's *Jahangir Embracing Shah Abbas* (Fig. 29), demonstrates how such works can harness the intense naturalism of the Jahangiri style to the demands of political ideology, rather than the truth.

This picture shows the mighty Mughal ruler standing on a globe and affectionately embracing a submissive Shah Abbas of Iran; both rulers are surrounded by a halo composed of the sun and the moon. As grand as it is, this composition has very little to do with historic fact; in reality, Jahangir and Shah Abbas were deeply at odds over the fate of Qandahar, a Mughal territory and fortress in Afghanistan that the Persians, after a futile attempt in 1606, managed to seize in 1622. At the time this picture was painted (ca. 1618), Shah Abbas was hardly submissive and Jahangir was by no means the master of their antagonistic relationship.[37] Despite its grandiose imagery, this painting suggests that Jahangir was somewhat discomforted by their military rivalry.

Allegorical portraits like this one, which support dynastic claims and promote the inviolability of the emperor, were often based upon Western models: for example, *Jahangir Embracing Shah Abbas* is modelled on European portraits showing a monarch standing on a globe against a dramatically lighted sky.[38] Before 1615, Jahangir's painters usually presented the emperor in a narrative context; but after that time he is often shown as a majestic figure isolated with symbols of wealth and power. These changes, which deliberately glorify

---

34. See Welch 1985, p. 217.
35. Quoted in Welch 1978, p. 81.
36. Leach 1995 (vol. 1), p. 35.
37. For a discussion of this painting, see Beach 1981, pp. 169-170.
38. See Beach 1981.

Jahangir, reflect the increasingly sacral character of the Mughal emperor. Such a conscious use of painting for political ends would come to dominate the imperial atelier under the next emperor, Shahjahan.

SHAHJAHAN (r. 1628-1658)

Shahjahan, who succeeded his father Jahangir, was a strong, extremely capable leader who presided over a glittering court trapped in elaborate ceremony and infatuated with conspicuous display (Fig. 30). Most Mughal emperors were concerned with their imperial image, but none more so than Shahjahan: he seems to have been almost obsessed with the substance and external expression of Mughal power. Shahjahan wanted to be known by all as the just and glorious ruler of a mighty empire which, with divine blessings, had entered into a golden age of peace and prosperity.[39] Everything associated with this rather formal man seems to have conformed to a guiding vision of the Mughal empire as a heaven on earth.

Shahjahan's passion for Mughal grandeur especially revealed itself in the spectacular building projects that he initiated, like his new capital Shahjahanabad in Delhi and his wife's tomb, the Taj Mahal in Agra. It is indeed appropriate, as John F. Richards notes, that one of Shahjahan's first commissions was the fabled Peacock Throne: it took seven years and millions of rupees worth of precious stones to create this opulent marvel.[40]

Shahjahan inherited not only a well-established and immensely wealthy realm, but also Jahangir's carefully nurtured atelier of talented artists capable of deep psychological insight and consummate technical virtuosity. The emperor wisely decided to keep most of his father's painters, thereby guaranteeing the continuity of the highly naturalistic Jahangiri style and its established subject matter categories. Shahjahan, like Jahangir, preferred individual paintings done by a single artist and mounted in albums.

Although Shahjahan's painters continued many features of Jahangiri painting, they soon transformed it into something quite different. Under Shahjahan, the realistic techniques of Jahangir's artists were not used to define the inner character and outward appearance of a subject, but to idealize and glorify it. Shahjahan's artists wanted to show the Mughal world, not as it was, but as the emperor wanted it to be—a

Fig. 34: RAM SINGH OF AMBER. From the Late Shahjahan Album ca. 1650. Virginia Museum of Fine Arts, Richmond (68.8.64).

harmoniously ordered, sublimely beautiful heaven on earth. Shahjahan's artists employed the accurate techniques of Jahangiri naturalism to invest their idealized pictorial worlds with a kind of pseudo-reality; and they did so with an unearthly and, at times, almost eerie perfection.[41]

Nowhere are the new aesthetic values better seen than in the many official portraits of Shahjahan created under his patronage. One such likeness, a portrait by Abul Hasan done in the first year of the emperor's reign, reveals how the imperial atelier used the precise techniques of Jahangiri realism to glorify the royal house (Fig. 31). This state portrait is hard, polished, and flawlessly rendered. It shows a haloed, rather stiff Shahjahan holding symbolic attributes as though he were a Hindu god: an accession seal marking the first year of his rule appears in his left hand; his right hand touches the hilt of a sword, an emblem of imperial power. His smooth pink *jama* serves as a plane upon which superbly rendered jewellery is displayed.[42]

This icy likeness differs considerably from a smaller portrait of Jahangir mounted above it on the same album page (Fig. 31). Painted by Balchand towards the close of the old emperor's life, this perceptive likeness records with great sensitivity what the artist saw and felt. Jahangir is nimbused and bejewelled, but he is lovingly shown for exactly what he was at that very moment: a vulnerable old man increasingly addicted to drugs and wine and tormented by family tragedies.

The cool formality of Abul Hasan's portrait characterizes almost every likeness of Shahjahan made during his reign, regardless of the artist. No matter what he is shown doing, Shahjahan always appears as an aloof man with a halo around his head. He bears fixed symbolic attributes that proclaim his superior wisdom, taste, and power (sword, dagger, turban ornament, flywhisk, amulets, etc.). Transient feelings and human vulnerability are never revealed in his face; his eyes always stare firmly into the distance.

Allegorical portraits of Shahjahan are even balder

Fig. 35: TULIPS AND AN IRIS.
Attributed to the Master of the Borders ca. 1650.
Collection of Prince and Princess Sadruddin Aga Khan, (M. 127).

statements of imperial power than state portraits. *Shahjahan, Master of the Globe* of ca. 1629 (Fig. 32) is obviously based upon such paintings as *Jahangir Embracing Shah Abbas* (Fig. 29), but it differs from them in telling ways. Symbolic portraits made for Jahangir often had a decidedly human dimension: they revealed the emperor's hopes and sometimes, his fears; and they frequently referred to specific historical events.

In comparison to such Jahangiri prototypes, *Shahjahan, Master of the Globe* is a superficial icon created for one purpose—to impress us with the majesty of the Mughal dynasty in general and of Shahjahan in particular. The emperor, holding a sword and amulet, is

---

39. The following discussion of Shahjahani painting is based upon the author's 1989 study; see Dye 1989, pp. 88-127.
40. Richards 1993, p. 123
41. Dye 1989, p. 89.
42. Dye 1989, pp. 90-91; Goswamy and Fischer 1987, pp. 96-97.

Fig. 36: Aurangzeb and his Third Son, Sultan Azam, with Courtiers.
By Hashim ca. 1658. Courtesy of the Arthur M. Sackler Museum, Harvard University Art Museums, Cambridge, Private Collection.

shown atop a globe inscribed with a panegyric and painted with standard allegorical figures: the scales, symbolizing justice; the lion lying with the lamb, representing the peace that follows from the emperor's just rule; and delicately drawn holy men who attest to his 'humility' and wisdom. Three putti descending from the clouds bear an imperial sword and diadem as well as a royal parasol inscribed with the emperor's genealogy. The meaning of this portrait is more than clear: Shahjahan's just and legitimate rule, sponsored by the powers of heaven, has brought about a harmoniously ordered world; a place where the lion can lie with the lamb.[43]

Given Shahjahan's passion for such grand imagery, it is not surprising that depictions of his life and court were also transformed into visions of cosmic splendour. Many of these paintings are found in an illustrated copy of the *Padshahnama* ('History of the Emperor') now in the Royal Library, Windsor Castle; the text of this official history of Shahjahan's reign was composed by

Abdul Hamid Lahawri. A number of the manuscript's paintings belong stylistically to the 1630s, but the initial portion of Lahawri's text, which documents the first decade of Shahjahan's rule, was not completed until 1641; and the history of the second decade was finished in 1648. Most probably, the *Padshahnama* paintings of the 1630s were made before Lahawri composed his text: they may have been originally intended for another project or were simply taken from a stock of paintings kept on hand for use when necessary.[44]

The Windsor *Padshahnama* pictures record the principal activities of Shahjahan's highly ritualized public life: military campaigns; formal audiences of the emperor with his subjects; imperial hunts; visits to Muslim shrines; and royal celebrations. The aesthetic quality of these paintings varies depending upon the artist engaged, but those done by the studio's most prominent masters (Abid, Murad, Govardhan, Payag, Bichitr, etc.) are highly accomplished, self-confident works of art.

Payag's *Shahjahan Honouring Prince Aurangzeb at Agra before his Wedding*, painted about 1640, is a typical work (Fig. 30). Though by no means Payag's most brilliant effort, this picture is a competent example of a standard Shahjahani *durbar* or royal audience scene.[45] It shows the emperor seated in the *jharoka*, a balcony at the back of the royal audience hall (*Diwan-i Khass*) where he conducted affairs of state before an assembly of noblemen, grandees, and others. Remote and haloed, Shahjahan is presented in a typically iconic manner, attended by Prince Dara Shikoh and Prince Murad Baksh who stand in the upper left. Aurangzeb, garbed in a yellow *jama* and green jacket hails his father from below, his right hand raised to his forehead. Nobles, servants, and spectators stand in rapt adoration, like hierarchies of angels around the throne of God.

Although Payag probably presents a factual record of this event, his painting has the perfection of a dream. Like other Shahjahani artists, he skillfully manipulates composition, space, figural groups, and visual details to heighten the scene's opulence and grandeur. The emperor, seated on high, is placed directly on the central vertical axis. His exalted position is reinforced by the balanced arrangement of richly clad courtiers standing beside and below him. It is further augmented by diagonal compositional movements that progress up and back through the picture and culminate in the central vertical axis.

The rows of courtiers attending the emperor wear gorgeously coloured robes shimmering with gold, silver, pearls, and precious stones. Many of these men can be precisely identified, but the almost identical size and weight of each figure as well as the dense crowding transform them into a host of supplicants as tightly packed and interchangeable as the minor celestials of a Buddhist or Hindu relief.[46]

Iconic depictions of Shahjahan's *durbars* dominate the *Padshanama*, but the manuscript also includes fine paintings of less static subjects. *Shahjahan Hunting* (Fig. 33), for instance, is an example of Shahjahani painting at its very best.[47] The emperor, crouching on a small carpet at the right, raises his matchlock to shoot an antelope coming to drink water just before sunrise. He is accompanied by Prince Dara Shikoh, who stands to his immediate left, and assisted by Jafar Khan, who holds a fresh rifle. The courtiers Salabat Khan and Asalat Khan stand in front of Dara Shikoh. Two huntsmen also appear: one squats, balancing the emperor's matchlock on his shoulder; the other one, who keeps the game in shooting range, stands at the front.

The royal party is surrounded by a panoramic landscape of low ochre hills punctuated with trees and filled with animals and farmers that diminish in size as the landscape recedes into the distance. So effortless and naturalistic is this sweeping vista that one almost forgets that the idealizing tendencies of Shahjahani painting are still present: the emperor is shown here with his head surrounded by a radiant halo; his richly dressed noblemen look and behave as though they are attending an imperial *durbar* rather than a hunt; and the peaceful landscape, is bathed in a golden glow, suggesting the prosperity and tranquility brought about under Shahjahan's rule.[48] In many respects, this painting is almost as much an assertion of imperial glory as *Shahjahan, Master of the Globe* (Fig. 32), but it is done in a far more subtle way.

---

43. Dye 1989, p. 91-92.
44. Beach and Koch 1997, pp. 15-19.
45. Beach and Koch 1997, pp. 206-207.
46. Dye 1989, p. 93.
47. Beach and Koch 1998, pp. 192-194.
48. Beach and Koch 1997, p. 192.

The desire to present the world as a harmoniously ordered, sublimely beautiful paradise inhabited by perfected images of real people, or in many cases, simply ideal figural types, permeates Shahjahani painting. These preferences were especially evident in the portraits of noblemen and retainers that fill Shahjahan's many *muraqqas*, such as the full-length likeness of Ram Singh of Amber from the *Late Shahjahan Album* ca. 1650 (Fig. 34).[49] In this portrait, as in many others, the primary aim is to suggest that the sitter is of sufficient importance to be included in the emperor's album. Thus, while Ram Singh's face is probably more or less accurately rendered, it is really his costly garments and their patterns that are of the greatest interest to the artist. Standing on a grassy field beneath a prettily coloured sky, the Rajput prince wears a colourful turban of gold-and-red patterned fabric, a white gauze *jama* tied with a floral sash, and pajamas made of opulent gold cloth covered with rows of flowers. Ram Singh's reputation as a military leader is indicated by the array of weapons that he bears (push dagger, sword, and shield).

The portrait's surrounding borders, like others from this album, are filled with figures related to the main subject—in this case, four of his military subordinates who bear arms; a musician playing a stringed instrument; and two custodians who examine trays of their chief's jewellery. The presence of this retinue tells us that Ram Singh is a powerful warrior, a wealthy ruler, and a cultivated man. It is not so much the Rajput chieftain's character that is assessed here, as much as it is his power, status, and social role. This portrait does not analyze Ram Singh; it simply glorifies him.

The love of Shahjahani painters for idealized physical reality as well as for lush colour and opulent effects even extends to depictions of birds, animals, and flowers—subjects far from the realms of imperial power and glory. Jahangiri studies of tulips or narcissus record the appearance of each flower with almost scientific accuracy; Shahjahani flower paintings, in contrast, are usually rendered with a sense of dramatic exaggeration. The flowers in *Tulips and an Iris* (Fig. 35) painted in the mid-seventeenth century are so stylized that, as S.C. Welch has noted, they seem to have human characteristics: a royal tulip, a demure iris, and a slightly embarrassed *tulipa montana*.[50] More richly coloured than they would be in real life, these flowers grow in heaven, not on earth.

AURANGZEB (r. 1658-1707)

Shahjahan's reign ended with his imprisonment and the war of succession between Crown Prince Dara Shikoh and his three younger brothers—Shah Shuja, Aurangzeb, and Murad Baksh. The ultimate victor was Shahjahan's third son, Aurangzeb. Aurangzeb was a man of austere outlook who neither drank alcohol nor took opium. He was well versed in jurisprudence and frequently took advice from members of the *ulema* or *shaikhs* from the orthodox Naqshbandi order.

The quantity, quality, and range of Mughal painting declined during Aurangzeb's reign. The imperial atelier could only flourish under enlightened and engaged patronage. Unfortunately, Aurangzeb was not interested, largely because painting did not fit into his vision for the future. Aurangzeb hoped to transform the Mughal empire into a staunchly orthodox Muslim state. As John F. Richards notes, a new moralistic and legalistic tone began to undermine the eclectic, inclusive Mughal court culture so brilliantly nurtured by Akbar and Jahangir.[51] Rather than supporting painting, Aurangzeb patronized books on religious law and the repair and maintenance of mosques.

In some respects, too, the imperial Mughal style had started to ossify of its own accord by 1658. What began in an extraordinary burst of creativity under Humayun and Akbar, had now slowly hardened into an officially accepted style with increasingly rigid representational and thematic conventions. Later Mughal artists found it easier to follow established studio formulae, rather than to invent new ones. Towards the end of Shahjahan's reign, the grand painters began to die off: those that replaced them were fewer in number and, in many cases, lesser talents.

The decline of the Mughal studio, however, does not mean that imperial Mughal painting ceased to exist under Aurangzeb. Portraits, more politically useful than illustrations to 'effete' poetic texts or romantic literature, continued to be produced, especially in the early years of Aurangzeb's reign. *The Durbar of the Emperor Aurangzeb* of ca. 1658 (Fig. 36), for example, maintains the idealizing tendencies of Shahjahani painting.[52] A haloed Aurangzeb is shown, like his father, seated on a canopied throne at the centre of the composition surrounded by courtiers, relatives, and servants. He holds a predatory falcon in his hand. The Shahjahani concern with immaculately rendered garments, patterns, and other visual details remain, but in comparison to *durbar* scenes from the *Padshahnama*, this painting with its undefined background and inconsistent modelling seems somewhat simplified and flat.

IMPERIAL PAINTING AFTER AURANGZEB

The fate of the imperial style after Aurangzeb's death in 1707 is a story that remains to be told. The political decline of the Mughal empire during the eighteenth century meant that imperial patronage was neither as plentiful nor as demanding as it had once been. Certainly, the most enlightened imperial Mughal patron of this period was the emperor Muhammad Shah (r. 1719-48). Pictures painted by artists of his studio, such as Chitarman, Muhammad Afzal, and Govardhan (not the Jahangir and Shahjahan period painter), were not as ambitious as those of the sixteenth and seventeenth centuries, but they are often beautiful.* The worlds shown in Muhammad Shahi works are gentle, dream-like places, inhabited by dignified men and beautiful ladies enjoying a variety of courtly pleasures. Portraits of the emperor, hunting scenes, and depictions of festive occasions on terraces and in pavilions were especially favoured.

The sack of Delhi in 1739 by Nadir Shah of Persia changed the course of imperial Mughal painting. Many Mughal artists, fleeing the capital, migrated to the courts of powerful Mughal noblemen in the provinces who pledged allegiance to Delhi, but maintained strong, independent territories. The Muslim rulers of such places as Awadh and Bengal supported flourishing ateliers of painting at various times during the eighteenth and early nineteenth centuries. The artists who worked in these studios evolved distinctive variants of the imperial Mughal style, some of them influenced by European naturalism.

Not all Mughal painters abandoned Delhi after Nadir Shah's raid. Some of those artists who stayed on continued to work for the increasingly weak Mughal emperors; others churned out opulent paintings for the commercial market; and still others copied seventeenth century Mughal paintings or 'refurbished' old albums and manuscripts.[53]

IMPACT OF THE IMPERIAL MUGHAL STYLE

Throughout its long history and even at its weakest moments, the imperial Mughal style exerted enormous influence over the development of Indian painting. The technical refinements and pictorial conventions of Mughal artists were widely admired, not only for their beauty, but also because they were closely associated with the Subcontinent's paramount political power. It is not surprising that a desire to emulate the imperial Mughal style appears as early as Akbar's reign, when the nobility, the wealthy and other rulers patronized works in a simpler, more indigenized version of the imperial mode. These sub-imperial patrons enjoyed the standard subjects of Mughal painting, but they were also fond of Hindu stories and literature.[54]

So prestigious was imperial Mughal painting that it even impressed the Rajputs, staunchly Hindu rulers of Rajasthan, Central India, and the Punjab Hills. Akbar initiated what was to become a long and fruitful association between Mughals and Rajputs. After they were brought under Mughal hegemony, many Rajput kings began to serve in the imperial armies and to attend events at the Mughal court. These rulers soon began to emulate their Mughal overlords by patronizing painters and manuscript illustrators. By the seventeenth century (if not earlier), painting studios were established in many Rajput states, each one of which combined indigenous and Mughal elements in its own distinctive way.[55]

---

* **Editor's Note:** See Figs. A and B (pp. 180-1). These works, discovered in 2000 in the National Library of Romania, are from the middle of the eighteenth century. This is the first-ever reproduction of Fig. B. Also see p. 71 for another later Mughal painting.

49. Glynn 1996, pp. 67-93.
50. Welch 1985, p. 245.
51. Richards 1993, pp. 171-174
52. Welch 1998, pp. 112-113.
53. Artists would 'refurbish' from the imperial libraries by remounting their paintings in sumptuous new borders, or by removing these illustrations and replacing them with copies (see Losty 1982, pp. 111-112).
54. Two of the most important sub-imperial patrons were Abdul Rahim Khankhanan, leader of the Mughal armies under Akbar and Jahangir (1561-1626/27); and Mirza Aziz Koka Muhammad Khan (ca. 1542-1624), Akbar's foster brother.
55. In many cases, Rajput artists learned Mughal pictorial conventions by copying Mughal paintings; in others, however, it seem likely that they learned them from Mughal artists who for one reason or another left imperial employ.

BIBLIOGRAPHY

Beach, Milo C. 'The Context of Rajput Painting.' *Ars Orientalis* 10 (1978): 11-17.

Beach, Milo C. *The Imperial Image: Paintings from the Mughal Court*. Washington, D.C.: Freer Gallery of Art, 1981.

Beach, Milo C. *Early Mughal Painting*. Cambridge Mass., and London: Harvard University Press, 1987.

Beach, Milo C. 'Mughal and Rajput Painting'. Pt. 1, Vol. 3 of *The New Cambridge History of India*. Cambridge: Cambridge University Press, 1992.

Beach, Milo C., and Ebba Koch with new translations by Wheeler Thackston, *King of the World: The Padshahnama, An Imperial Mughal Manuscript from the Royal Library, Windsor Castle*. London and Washington, D.C.: Azimuth Editions and Smithsonian Institution, 1997.

Brand, Michael, and Glenn D. Lowry. *Akbar's India: Art From the Mughal City of Victory*. New York: The Asia Society Galleries, 1985.

Chandra, Pramod. *The Tuti-Nama of The Cleveland Museum of Art. Commentarium*. Graz: Akademische Druk u. Versagsanstalt, 1976.

Das, Ashok Kumar, ed., *Mughal Masters: Further Studies*. Bombay: Marg Publications, 1998.

Dye, Joseph M. III. 'Artists for the Emperor.' In *Romance of the Taj Mahal*, P. Pal et al. Los Angeles and London: Los Angeles County Museum of Art with Thames and Hudson, 1989.

Glynn, Catherine. 'Evidence of Royal Painting for the Amber Court'. *Artibus Asiae* 56, nos. 1/2 (1996): 67-93.

Goswamy, B.N. and Eberhard Fischer. *Wonders of a Golden Age: Painting at the Court of the Great Mughals*. Zurich: Museum Rietberg, 1987.

Leach, Linda York. *Mughal and Other Indian Paintings from the Chester Beatty Library*. 2 vols. London: Scorpion and Cavendish, 1995.

Losty, Jeremiah P. *The Art of the Book in India*. London: The British Library, 1982.

Pal, Pratapaditya. *Master Artists of the Imperial Mughal Court*. Bombay: Marg Publications, 1991.

Richards, John. 'The Mughal Empire'. Pt.1, Vol. 5 of *The New Cambridge History of India*. Cambridge: Cambridge University Press, 1993.

Verma, Som Prakash. *Mughal Painters and Their Work; A Biographical Survey and Comprehensive Catalogue*. Delhi: Oxford University Press, 1994.

Welch, S.C. *Imperial Mughal Painting*. New York: George Braziller, 1978.

Welch, S.C. *India: Art and Culture, 1300-1900*. New York: The Metropolitan Museum of Art and Holt, Rinehart, and Winston, 1985.

SECONDARY SOURCES

Beach, Milo C. *The Grand Mogul: Imperial Painting in India 1600-1660*. Williamstown, MA, 1978.

Gascoigne, Bamber. *The Great Moghuls*, 1971. Reprint, Delhi, Bombay, Calcutta, Madras: Dass Media in association with Jonathan Cape, Ltd. 1985.

Koch, Ebba. *Shah Jahan and Orpheus: The Pietre Dure Decoration and the Programme of the Throne in the Hall of Public Audiences at the Red Fort of Delhi*. Graz: 1988.

Seyller, John. 'Model and Copy: The Illustrations of Three Razmnama Manuscripts'. *Archives of Asian Art* 38 (1985): 37-66.

Seyller, John. 'Scribal Notes on Mughal Manuscript Illustrations'. *Artibus Asiae* 48, nos. 3/4 (1987): 247-77.

Seyller, John. 'Codicological Aspects of the Victoria and Albert Museum Akbarnama and their Historical Implications'. *Art Journal* 49, no. 4 (Winter 1990): 379-87.

Skelton, Robert. *The Indian Heritage: Court Life and Arts under Mughal Rule*. London: The Victoria and Albert Museum, 1982.

Welch, S.C. *Gods, Thrones, and Peacocks*. New York: The Asia Society, 1965.

Welch, S.C., Annemarie Schimmel, Marie L. Swietochowski, Wheeler M. Thackston. *The Emperors' Album: Images of Mughal India*. New York, N.Y.: The Metropolitan Museum of Art, 1987.

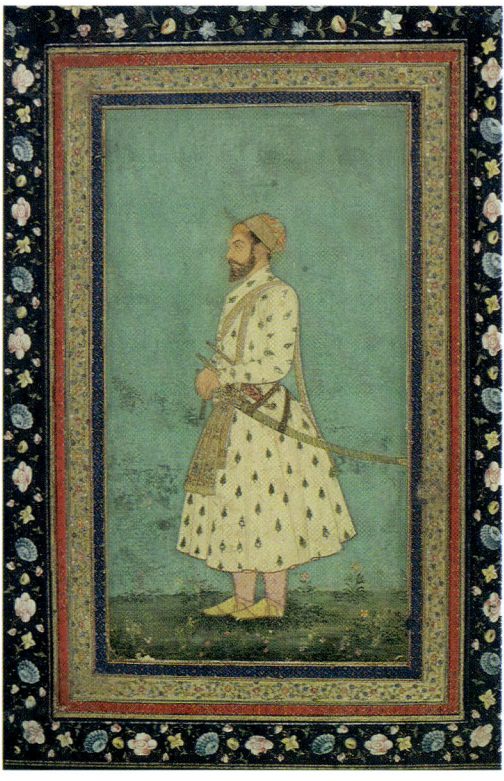

Fig A: A NOBLEMAN. Late Mughal, ca. middle of the 18th century. From the collection of the National Library of Romania.

Fig B: A Lady.
By Faqirullah, late Mughal, ca. middle of the 18th century. From the collection of the National Library of Romania.

The Magnificent Mughals

Major Architectural Sites and Cultural Centres in the Mughal Empire

7
ARCHITECTURE
Catherine B. Asher

ARCHITECTURAL PRECURSORS: THE TIMURID AND INDO-MUSLIM TRADITIONS

Zahiruddin Muhammad Babur, the first Mughal ruler of the Subcontinent, assumed the throne in 1526. His assumption of power in India was not without precedent, for he claimed legitimacy based on the actions of his ancestor, Timur, headquartered in Samarkand (today in Uzbekistan) who had captured Delhi in 1398. In fact, the house we know today as the Mughals is actually a continuation of the Timurid line. The Mughal dynasty treasured its Timurid roots, and thus it is no surprise that Timurid traditions informed the development of Mughal visual culture.

Just as Babur's Timurid heritage remained important to him and subsequent Mughal rulers, so too the magnificent architectural heritage of Samarkand, Herat, and other Timurid cities played a major role in the development of the Mughal architectural tradition.[1] During the fourteenth and fifteenth centuries, first Timur and then his successors created structures known for their truly impressive scale, an example of which is Timur's own Aq Serai Palace in Shahr-i Sabz which looms high above ground and is visible from a distance of at least seven kilometres (Fig. 1). The figure included here indicates the enormous scale of the building in relation to the people in the photograph. Scale would play an important role in imperial Mughal architecture. So too did the Timurid preoccupation with symmetry, a feature that was to become the hallmark of much Mughal construction. Understanding complex geometrical proportions, Timurid architects were able to create innovative spaces that were vertical in nature using elaborate transverse arches to create spectacular interiors. Once the Mughals mastered these Timurid technologies they too began to create structures with elaborate interior plans, elevations and arches embellished with net pendentives[2] in emulation of Timurid works. Brightly glazed tiles enriched the exterior surfaces of Timurid buildings. Under the Mughals, juxtaposed inlaid stones would more likely be the source of colour on a facade, but tiles were used as well. Gardens were another important Timurid tradition that the Mughals continued to follow, but we are unclear about the precise appearance and form of earlier Timurid gardens. Babur and his immediate successor, Humayun, were personally acquainted with much Timurid architecture and gardens. In his memoirs Babur describes the Timurid buildings of Samarkand and Herat in the most glowing terms.[3] Emulating Timurid buildings was a major, though often unattainable, goal of the early Mughals who had actually seen these structures; even after the mid-sixteenth century when no Mughal ruler ever again visited the Timurid homeland the memory of a Timurid past remained important, particularly to Shahjahan, the fifth Mughal ruler.

When the Mughals established their rule in India, they were hardly the first Muslim presence in the Subcontinent. As early as the eighth century, Muslims had settled near what today is Karachi and since that time there had been a continuous Muslim presence in the Indus Valley. However, the architectural trends of

Fig. 1: Timur's Aq Serai Palace, Shahr-i Sabz, Uzbekistan

the Indus Valley appear to have had little influence on the subsequent development of Mughal architecture. In 1192 the Ghorid dynasty, who were ethnic Turks ruling in Afghanistan, first established themselves in Delhi. Subsequently, Muslim authority spread throughout west, north, and east India. It is the architectural developments that transpired between 1192 and the advent of Babur that left their mark on much of Mughal architecture. What is important to remember here is that many features of Mughal architecture commonly associated with Hindu and Jain structures came long before the Mughal period and were used in structures built by the various Muslim dynasties of India.[4] Such structural features include trabeated (post and lintel) construction where flat or corbelled[5] roofs are used rather than domes or vaults. Curved brackets and deep eaves[6] were also associated with pre-Mughal architecture. Non-imperial Mughal mosques often adhered to a single aisled multi-bayed[7] plan that was established under the previous dynasty, the Lodis. Mughal imperial mosques followed Timurid models, that feature a large central bay flanked on either side by rows of multiple bays. This plan-type was similar to those used by some Indian Sultanates. Motifs used in Mughal architecture, such as the bell and chain, the chandrasala[8] and the torana,[9] are often assumed to be derived directly from the Hindu architecture. However, all of these and more had long been used in India's pre-Mughal Muslim architecture, especially that of Gujarat and Bengal, the source of much Mughal inspiration. Thus even in this brief introduction we can see that Mughal architecture is heir to the rich traditions of both Central and South Asia.

BABUR (1526-30)

Babur was essentially a prince without land. Born in Ferghana—a territory today divided between Uzbekistan and Kyrghyzstan—he lost his father, and ultimately his lands, at a young age. Briefly he held Samarkand, that queen of Timurid cities, but by the turn of the sixteenth century he had to settle for only Kabul, today the capital of Afghanistan. About this time he realized that, for a variety of reasons, hegemony over the Timurid homeland was not possible.[10] He then turned his attentions to India, the land that his ancestor, the great Timur, had acquired in 1398, although his acquisition had long since been forgotten on the Indian front. In 1526, after several forays into the Indian plains, Babur with a motley crew of men possessing firearms not yet acquired in India at that time, was able to defeat the last independent Sultan of Delhi, Ibrahim Lodi, at Panipat, about eighty kilometres north of Delhi. Immediately upon entering Delhi Babur retraced the footsteps of Timur, visiting each site, including the *dargahs* (tombs) of the Sufi saints, at which his predecessor had paid homage some 125 years earlier. This re-enactment was geared at underscoring his legitimate claim to India.[11]

Babur was one of many who aspired to hold the throne of Delhi at this time. His charismatic personality and the effective deployment of gunpowder, enabled him to overcome much more powerful opponents. Once his rule was established, Babur, like all new monarchs,

---

1. See Lisa Golombek and Donald Wilber, *The Timurid Architecture of Iran and Turan*, 2 vols. (Princeton, 1988) for the best coverage of Timurid material. Ebba Koch, *Mughal Architecture: An Outline of its History and Development (1526-1858)* (Munich, 1991) and Catherine B. Asher, *Architecture of Mughal India* (Cambridge, 1992) are the two best sources for Mughal architecture and the most accessible sources for plans, illustrations, and detailed bibliographic sources. To eliminate numerous citations in this essay, I will rarely make direct reference to these two works; they, however, include most of the material discussed here.
2. Pendentive: a concave triangular surface that allows a square structure to support a dome. Net pendentive: stucco decoration in vaulting or pendentives.
3. Zahiruddin Muhammad Babur, *The Baburnama: Memoirs of Babur, Prince and Emperor*, tr. Wheeler M. Thackston (Washington D.C. and New York, 1995), pp. 82-90, 237-39.
4. For a detailed discussion see Asher, *Architecture of Mughal India*, pp. 1-18.
5. Corbel: a projection of stone, timber, etc. jutting out from a wall to support a weight.
6. Eave: an overhang to prevent excessive sunlight from entering a chamber.
7. Bay: individual chambers formed by pillars that are often covered by single domes.
8. Chandrasala: an elaborate niche-like structure topped by an ogee arch and is found as a decorative device on Sur and Akbar's architecture.
9. Torana: serpentine-like lintels often formed as a gate, again found on Akbar's architecture.
10. Catherine B. Asher, 'Babur and the Timurid Char-Bagh: Use and Meaning,' *Environmental Design* 1-2 (1991), p. 46.
11. Ebba Koch, 'The Delhi of the Mughals Prior to Shahjahanabad as Reflected in the Patterns of Imperial Visits,' in Ahsan Jan Qaisar and Som Prakash Verma, eds., *Art and Culture: Felicitation Volume in Honour of Professor S. Nurul Hasan* (Jaipur, 1993), p. 4.

needed to assert his authority. To accomplish this he chose not only traditional hegemonic manners, but visual affirmation of his role as king. He did this in two ways: one was via the construction of mosques and the other by the creation and planting of gardens. Babur is traditionally associated with building three mosques in the Subcontinent, a form of patronage in which he never engaged in the Timurid homelands—there his patronage was always much more secular, largely in the form of pleasure gardens.[12] However, having proclaimed himself emperor he needed to legitimize himself and Mughal rule. He thus cast himself as a faithful Muslim ruler over idolatrous non-Muslim subjects, for indeed the majority population of the Subcontinent was and continues to be non-Muslim. The patronage of two of these three mosques was probably not directly Babur's, so here we will focus only on the one, the Kabuli Bagh mosque, known by inscription to have been built by Babur between 1527-28 (Fig. 2). Located at Panipat where he defeated Ibrahim Lodi, the mosque was clearly geared toward proclaiming political aspirations over religious ones, for the latter were minor to Babur. Underscoring this is the fact that the plan of the Kabuli Bagh mosque emulated the imperial Timurid mosque types as much as was possible in India—a land at this point lacking Timurid trained architects and engineers. In contrast to the single aisled multi-bayed contemporary north Indian imperial mosque, the Kabuli Bagh mosque was much closer in plan to the four-*iwan* (vaulted entrance) royal ones in Timurid Iran. Moreover, details on the mosque's pendentives suggest an attempt to use artistically, although not structurally, the design concepts employed in the vaulting and net pendentives of Timurid architecture. Built at the site of Babur's victory, the Kabuli Bagh mosque, while ostensibly a religious structure, was undoubtedly meant to serve as a political statement of new Mughal hegemony.

If Babur's patronage of the Kabuli Bagh mosque was essentially driven by the normative expectations of a Muslim ruler in newly acquired territory, his patronage of gardens was from the heart. While Babur himself created many Timurid-inspired gardens and urged his highest ranking followers to do the same, in fact, we know more about these gardens from his memoirs than from any extant garden. Only one in Dholpur about fifty kilometres due south of Agra, his capital at the time, survives in any original sense. Carved from the living rock, the garden consists of a series of terraces linked by water channels and pools, one in the form of an open lotus (Fig. 3). Since the site today sits under a village, it is difficult to grasp its overall appearance, although

Fig. 2: Babur's mosque, known as the Kabuli Bagh Mosque, Panipat

Fig. 3: Lotus Pool, Dholpur

Elizabeth Moynihan has drawn its plan.¹³ Such gardens were called *char bagh*, meaning four-part gardens. However, it is not clear if what *char bagh* came to mean in Mughal India was the same as what it meant to the Timurids. In India, at least by the late sixteenth century, a *char bagh* was a terraced garden each of whose tiers were divided, by straight bisecting water channels, into four symmetrical quadrants. Whatever the actual appearance, Babur's writings and those of his contemporaries make clear that his gardens had political significance, for Babur considered himself a master gardener who was able to subdue what he terms, 'unpleasant and inharmonious India.'¹⁴ For Babur the ability to organize, control, and beautify the dusty plains of India was a metaphor for his ability to rule.

Babur was in India only for four years. Nevertheless he inspired others to build, especially gardens, which he prized most highly, and religious structures. One mosque in Ayodhya (Faizabad District, Uttar Pradesh), known as the Babri Masjid, and commonly believed to be Babur's, was in fact built by one of Babur's nobles, Mir Baqi Beg, in 1528-29 (Fig. 4). It was an ordinary structure built in the single aisled multi-bayed plan of the Lodi dynasty. However, since its destruction on 6 December 1992 by right wing Hindu groups who believe it rested on the birth place of the god Rama, an incarnation of Vishnu, its fame has spread. There is no reason to believe, however, that the association of this mosque with the birthplace of Rama existed before the nineteenth century.¹⁵ Thus for historical purposes the Babri Masjid should be understood as a manifestation of a regional architectural style that reflected older styles and values, not those current at the imperial centre.

Fig. 4: Babri Masjid, view from west, Ayodhya

HUMAYUN (1530-40; 1555-56) AND THE SUR INTERREGNUM (1540-55)

Babur died in 1530 bequeathing the throne to his oldest son, Humayun. This second Mughal emperor was a man with many aspirations—one scheme involved the construction of fantastic wooden palaces, some of which were intended to float on water. His dealings with political realities were less inspirational. Between 1530 and 1540 he was pursued by his major adversary, an upstart of Afghan descent named Sher Shah Sur, who eventually chased him out of India and into Central Asian territory controlled by Shah Tahmasp of the Safavid dynasty. During this period, however, Humayun was able to build a mosque in Agra (today known as the Kachpura mosque) that closely adheres in style and plan to his father's Kabuli Bagh mosque, thus suggesting that ideologically it echoes Babur's concept of state. Humayun is also known for his construction of an entire new citadel within Delhi that he called Din Panah, Refuge of Religion (today called Delhi's Purana Qila). In spite of effusive poetic Mughal texts eulogizing the fort, most of it was probably completed by Sher Shah Sur, who ruled Delhi from 1540-45. During the years that Humayun spent in Iran, making important contacts that allowed for the subsequent flourishing of Mughal culture, his arch enemy Sher Shah was able to consolidate power.

Sher Shah and his successors held first east and then all of north India from 1538-55. Although the Sur interregnum was brief, Sher Shah was able to introduce major administrative reforms that were adopted by Akbar, the next Mughal ruler. For our purposes his

12. Howard Crane, 'The Patronage of Zahir al-din Babur and the Origins of Mughal Architecture,' *Bulletin of the Asia Institute* 1, 1987, p. 101.
13. Elizabeth B. Moynihan, 'The Lotus Garden Palace of Zahir al-din Muhammad Babur,' *Muqarnas* 5, 1988, pp. 135-52.
14. Babur, p. 359.
15. The literature on this mosque is vast, although most deals with politics and not the structure itself. See, for example, Sarvepalli Gopal, ed., *Anatomy of a Confrontation: The Babri Masjid-Ramjanmabhumi Issue* (New Delhi and New York, 1991).

architectural and public works projects are significant, especially when their largely utilitarian nature is contrasted with Humayun's frivolous architectural patronage.[16] Renowned for his justice, Sher Shah built and repaired major highways connecting the Subcontinent from modern Peshawar to modern Dhaka (the present Grand Trunk Road), providing trees for shade, caravanserais, wells and mosques for the welfare of travellers and constructed strategically located forts for the security of the state. The two most famous of these forts, both originally named Shergarh, are today known as Rohtas (one in Punjab, Pakistan; the other in Rohtas District, Bihar). While most of his forts were mud-constructed, these two are massive stone fortifications. In providing public works including fortifications, Sher Shah was following the obligations of a good Muslim ruler established in well known texts on kingship since at least the twelfth century. Future Mughal rulers too would provide similar structures for the welfare of their subjects.

Sher Shah also built tombs for his long deceased low-ranking father and grandfather in Narnaul (Mehendiragarh District, Haryana) and Sasaram (Rohtas District, Bihar). His grandfather's mausoleum was a beautifully constructed square-plan building, the sort usually erected for high-ranking nobles, but the Narnaul tomb was more splendid than any previous one. It was octagonal—the type often associated with royal tombs—but larger than others of this sort. In doing this, Sher Shah was attempting to create a fictitious genealogy to indicate that he had the requisite high-birth and breeding demanded of Muslim rulers. For himself, Sher Shah built an enormous octagonal mausoleum, also in Sasaram, situated in an artificial lake (Fig. 5). The largest tomb at that time ever built in India, its setting is a visual allusion to the abundant waters of paradise described in the Quran, a reference carved on the tomb's interior. Thus Sher Shah's tomb suggests this ruler had qualities of both piety and high-birth. The scale of all three tombs doubtless played some role in the Mughal decision to construct monumental imperial mausolea, so as not to be outdone by their enemy.

By 1555, with the Safavid Shah Tahmasp's help Humayun was able to regain the Delhi throne. He brought with him several painters from the Iranian court and while it seems no architects accompanied him, it is clear that the buildings he experienced in Iran appealed to him. In the year between his return and death in 1556, Humayun provided a two-storeyed octagonal pavilion built in the Timurid-Safavid manner, inside his Din Panah (the Purana Qila) known today as the Sher Mandal (Fig. 6). While the red sandstone facing was to become a Mughal hallmark, its central interior chamber linked by axial passages to the outer

Fig. 5: Sher Shah's Tomb, Sasaram

Fig. 6: Humayun's Sher Mandal, Delhi

ambulatory (a passageway circling an interior room or space) derives from similar pavilions in Iran.[17] The net pendentives in the vaulting, as at the Kabuli Bagh mosque, are an attempt to emulate Timurid Iranian forms. When Humayun fell from this pavilion in 1556 and died, his young thirteen-year-old son, Akbar, inherited a shaky state at best.

AKBAR (1556-1605)

Many consider Akbar the greatest of all the Mughal emperors, for he not only expanded but also consolidated his empire making it the strongest, largest and richest Muslim state of its time and the wealthiest state in the world. Akbar did this through marriage, battle, and treaty, but most importantly through administrative reform. He understood that the support of the Hindu majority as well as Indian Muslims was imperative to maintaining strong control, and thus over time he both reduced the power of Iranian and Central Asian Muslims and extended the canopy of justice to all Mughal subjects. This was an official policy of Universal Toleration known as *Sulh-i Kul*.

For about the first thirty years of his reign, Akbar showed a profound reverence for saints, especially those associated with the Chishtiyya, a Sufi order, and this is reflected in certain aspects of his architectural patronage. However, by the 1580s Akbar turned away from saint veneration. A little later, about 1589, Abkar's close companion, Abul Fazl, commenced the *Akbarnama*, a history of his reign, in which Akbar takes on the status

Fig. 7: Humayun's Tomb, Delhi

of a Sufi saint. He is presented not as a mere mortal, but as an emanation of divine light who had a special relationship with God.[18] This concept of Mughal kingship is perpetuated in one degree or another until the end of the dynasty in 1858. It was also manifested in Akbar's relationship with his nobility which was likened to that between a Muslim spiritual guide (*pir*) and his disciples (*murid*). This close relation between king and noble, known as the *Din-i Ilahi*, is often misconstrued as Akbar's creation of a new religion. In fact, it was simply Akbar's attempt to consolidate his role as the benevolent and wise head of state; and as a father to his people, an age-old Indian concept of kingship. All of these concepts are fundamental to not only understanding Akbar's architecture, but also much of the Mughal architectural patronage in general.

During the initial years of Akbar's reign he remained under the control of a few powerful persons, including a wet nurse and a guardian, and it was these influential members of the court who embellished the area around the Din Panah, where Akbar resided until about 1565, with mosques and tombs. Akbar's first monumental architectural project, a tomb for his father, Humayun (Fig. 7), was also situated in this same area and across from the tomb of Delhi's most famous saint, Nizamuddin Auliya, another Sufi who belonged to the Chishti order.[19] Completed in 1571, the tomb was designed by a father-son team from Bukhara who were trained in both landscape as well as traditional

---

16. See Catherine B. Asher, 'Legacy and Legitimacy: Sher Shah's Patronage of Imperial Mausolea,' in Katherine P. Ewing, ed., *Shari'at and Ambiguity in South Asian Islam* (Berkeley, 1988), pp. 79-97 for a detailed discussion.
17. Attilio Petruccioli, *Fatehpur Sikri: Citta del Sole e delle Acque* (Rome, 1988), fig. 234.
18. Abul Fazl, *Akbarnama*, 3 vols., transl. H. Beveridge (reprint ed., Delhi, 1972-73), I:37. Hereafter cited as *Akbarnama*. Also see J.F. Richards, 'The Formulation of Imperial Authority Under Akbar and Jahangir,' in J.F. Richards, ed. *Authority and Kingship in South Asia* (Madison, 1978), pp. 260-66.
19. Glenn Lowry, 'Humayun's Tomb: Form, Function and Meaning in Early Mughal Architecture,' *Muqarnas* 4, 1987, pp. 133-48.

architecture. Ghiyasuddin, the lead architect, placed the enormous mausoleum in the middle of a walled *char bagh*; waterways divide the garden into four symmetrical units which are further sub-divided by narrower waterways. This setting, probably intended to evoke paradise on earth, became the standard for imperial Mughal tomb architecture.

The monumental mausoleum sits on an elevated square plinth 99 metres per side. Faced with red sandstone (quarried nearby between Mathura and Dholpur) that is trimmed with white marble, the facade is embellished in the local Indian tradition. In elevation and plan, however, it derives from Timurid traditions. From the exterior the tomb is square with chamfered corners[20] (called a Baghdadi octagon); the interior consists of a central chamber surrounded by eight smaller ones, known as a *hasht behisht* plan. If translated literally from the Persian this means an eight-paradise plan and derives from Timurid type plans. Humayun's tomb is the most Timurid-like structure of Akbar's reign and was probably intended to recall the dynasty's roots.

A second structure, which commenced about the time that Humayun's tomb was completed, also reflects the dynastic ties. This is the Akbari mosque (Fig. 8) located at the most important Chishti Sufi shrine in all South Asia, the *dargah* of Muinuddin Chishti in Ajmer. Although we do not have absolute proof that it was provided by Akbar, he issued orders in 1570 that mosques should be constructed around this important shrine and this one is probably his own contribution. Its plan, even more than the earlier Panipat and Kachpura mosques, evokes the architectural traditions of the Mughal's Timurid origins. Now the multi-bayed prayer chamber with its enormous central entrance arch is not free standing as were the earlier Mughal examples, but as in the Timurid tradition there are enclosed galleries on the east, north and south sides. This mosque was probably intended as an official statement encompassing the spectrum of current Mughal political and religious ideology.

Fig. 8: Akbari mosque at the Dargah of Muinuddin Chishti in Ajmer

To provide security for the empire Akbar, like Sher Shah, needed to build forts. But while Sher Shah's had been mostly mud-constructed, Akbar in 1565 began to build a series of strong stone-constructed fortified palaces across his domain from Attock to Allahabad. The first was his fort at Agra built to replace an older mud structure. Its red sandstone walls are impressively spectacular, enough to evoke fear in the mind of any potential rebel. According to Abul Fazl, Akbar's confidant, the fort once had 500 buildings in the 'fine styles of Bengal and Gujarat,'[21] but today only a few survive, for most were dismantled when the fifth Mughal emperor, Shahjahan, remodelled the forts. The most notable of these is the so-called Jahangiri Mahal, part of the women's quarters (Fig. 9). Its exterior, like Humayun's tomb, is red sandstone traced

Fig. 9: Jahangiri Mahal, Agra

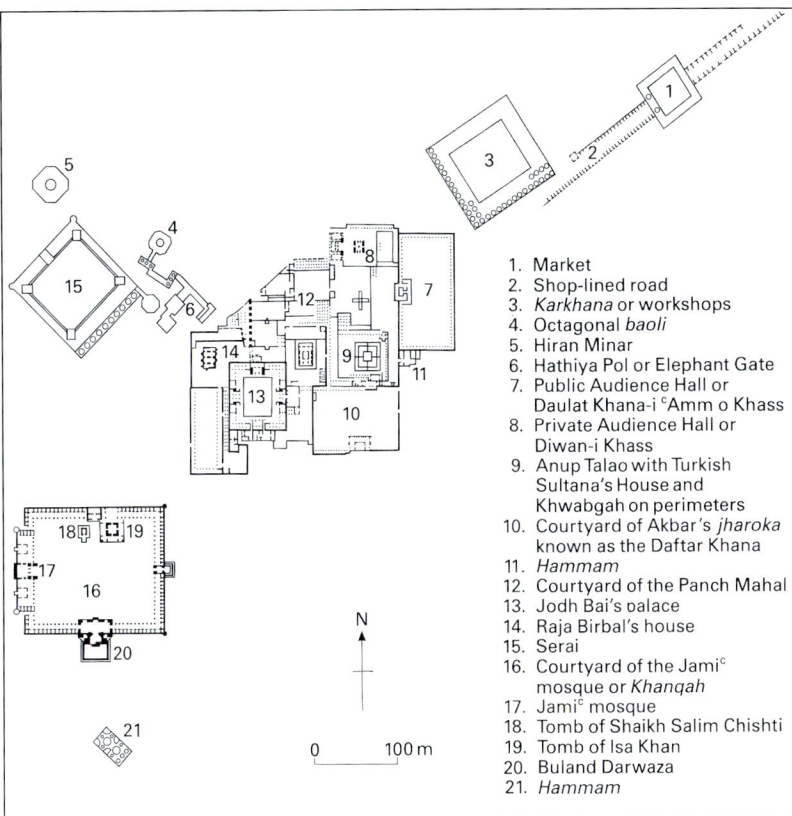

Fig. 10: Plan of Fatehpur Sikri, after Attilio Petruccioli

Key:
1. Market
2. Shop-lined road
3. *Karkhana* or workshops
4. Octagonal *baoli*
5. Hiran Minar
6. Hathiya Pol or Elephant Gate
7. Public Audience Hall or Daulat Khana-i ʿAmm o Khass
8. Private Audience Hall or Diwan-i Khass
9. Anup Talao with Turkish Sultana's House and Khwabgah on perimeters
10. Courtyard of Akbar's *jharoka* known as the Daftar Khana
11. *Hammam*
12. Courtyard of the Panch Mahal
13. Jodh Bai's palace
14. Raja Birbal's house
15. Serai
16. Courtyard of the Jamiʿ mosque or *Khanqah*
17. Jamiʿ mosque
18. Tomb of Shaikh Salim Chishti
19. Tomb of Isa Khan
20. Buland Darwaza
21. *Hammam*

Fig. 11: Buland Darwaza, Fatehpur Sikri

with white marble. Here the carving is intricate, similar to that found inside. The interior combines both South and Central Asian elements; for example, the open central courtyards recall those of the ca. 1500 Gwalior palace, while some of the pillared interiors are stone translations of pillar types used in Timurid buildings. Other courtyards feature elaborately carved brackets recalling those of western India. The plan and decor of this pavilion highlight the particularly rich fusion of South Asian and Timurid traditions which were brought together in Akbar's fortified palace in Agra, which Abul Fazl called 'the centre of Hindustan.'[22]

In addition to the fortified palaces, Akbar constructed an entire city and palace 35 kilometres west of Agra at Sikri, the abode of the saint, Salim Chishti. Akbar began the complex in 1571 to honour Salim Chishti, who had predicted the birth of his son and heir. While ostensibly built to celebrate Akbar's successful acquisition of Gujarat in western India, it more immediately underscored Akbar's links with the Chishti order. The city was not used after 1585 due to pressing political concerns in the northwest which necessitated shifting the capital to Lahore. Walled but not fortified, it was named Fatehabad (City of Victory) but became popularly known as Fatehpur Sikri (Fig. 10). One focal point of the palace was the *khanqah* (residential compound for spiritual study) built for Salim Chishti. It is entered on the south through an enormous arched gateway known as the Buland Darwaza (Fig. 11), which at 54 metres surpasses in height Timur's own Aq Serai palace. In the *khanqah*'s inner open courtyard is an enormous congregational (*jami*) mosque, the largest in Akbar's India, whose facade and interior reflect a combination of Timurid and South Asian elements. However, the focus of the courtyard is the white marble tomb of Salim Chishti himself (Fig. 12). He died in 1572, but his tomb was not completed until 1580-81, when ironically Akbar had begun to break with saint

---

20. Chamfered corners: right angles that have been cut to form a third surface or angle.
21. Abul Fazl, *Ain-i Akbari*, 3 vols. Vol. I, tr. H. Blochmann, Vols. II and III tr. H.S. Jarrett (reprint eds. Delhi and New Delhi, 1965-78), II:191.
22. *Akbarnama*, II:372.

The Magnificent Mughals

Fig. 12: Tomb of Shaikh Salim Chishti, Fatehpur Sikri

veneration. The use of white marble should be noted, for at this time white marble was reserved for saints' shrines alone. For instance, some twenty years earlier the shrine of the Chishti saint, Nizamuddin Auliya, in Delhi had been renewed in white marble. Moreover, in paintings intended for inclusion in Akbar's official history, the *Akbarnama*, he is often depicted wearing the white simple garb of a saint, not the elaborate robes usually worn by royalty.[23] This suggests an intentional visual link between king and saint.

The exquisitely designed tomb of Salim Chishti derives in plan and overall appearance from earlier ones in Gujarat, for example, the premier fifteenth century shrine of Shaikh Ahmad Khattu (at Sarkhej) which, like the setting for the tomb of Salim Chishti, was part of the palace of the Gujarat Sultans. The interior square chamber containing Salim Chishti's cenotaph, like similar tombs in Gujarat, is provided with an enclosed passage to allow for circumambulation of the grave, a common practice at saints' shrines. The delicate pierced stone screens of the outer walls are also found on the tomb at Sarkhej; the magnificently carved brackets too are a common feature of the architecture of western India. Not only had Akbar recently conquered Gujarat, but the noble who provided the tomb's flooring and screens at his own expense had also served in Gujarat.[24]

The palace portion of the Fatehpur Sikri complex can be entered through a number of ways, but the main entrance is the Hathiya Pol or Elephant Gate which was probably intended as a grand ceremonial gate for Akbar himself. Once inside, the palace consists of numerous pillared pavilions,[25] most composed of red sandstone, much of which is ornately carved. The post and lintel nature of the structures is a long-standing Indian feature, but the carved motifs are derived from both Indian and Timurid forms. These structures are grouped in clusters and as a whole are related to the

Fig. 13: Akbar's Throne, Diwan-i Amm, Fatehpur Sikri

khanqah in axial and geometric terms.[26] The exact purpose of many of these remains unclear, although a large quadrangular courtyard to the east of the Elephant Gate served as the Public Audience Hall (Diwan-i Amm) with Akbar's pillared throne in the west wall (Fig. 13). Thus when Akbar's subjects faced him they were looking in the direction of the *qibla*, that is, the direction of Muslim prayer,[27] indicating that at this time Akbar's concept of Mughal imperial ideology was already evolving.

The area to the west of the Public Audience Hall appears to have some ceremonial and administrative purpose. At the southernmost end was Akbar's window through which he presented himself to his subjects,[28] thus playing out his role as a father to his people. Moving north on a direct line is Akbar's bedroom known as the Khwabgah or Abode of Dreams and the Anup Talao, a square pool in the centre of which was a pavilion; today only the base remains. Its use as a place for discussion is noted in contemporary texts. Then proceeding to the northern most structure on this same axis one finds the Diwan-i Khass or Private Audience Hall (Fig. 14). From the exterior this square-plan trabeated structure looks similar to others at Fatehpur Sikri, but its interior is unique. In the centre of the room is an elaborately carved pillar that extends about halfway up the room's total height (Fig. 15). Its capital consists of S-shaped brackets, fuller at the top than at the bottom, similar to those found on Sultanate architecture, especially that of Gujarat. These brackets support a circular platform which is connected to each corner by walkways. This platform is believed to have served as Akbar's throne where he projected himself as the pillar of the Mughal state.

Further west of this administrative and ceremonial area appears to have been the *zenana* or women's quarters. Composed of a series of trabeated pavilions it seems that most of these were once linked with covered

Fig. 14: Diwan-i Khass, Fatehpur Sikri

Fig. 15: Interior Pillar, Diwan-i Khass, Fatehpur Sikri

23. Geeti Sen, *Paintings from the Akbar Nama* (Varanasi, 1984), pp. 42, 134-5.
24. Ebba Koch, 'Influence of Mughal Architecture,' in George Michell, ed., *Ahmadabad* (Bombay, 1988), pp. 169-70.
25. Pavilion: a free-standing structure, often associated with pleasure.
26. Attilio Petruccioli, 'The Geometry of Power,' in Michael Brand and Glenn D. Lowry, eds., *Fatehpur Sikri* (Bombay, 1987), p. 57.
27. Glenn D. Lowry, 'Urban Structures and Functions,' in Michael Brand and Glenn D. Lowry, eds., *Fatehpur Sikri* (Bombay, 1987), p. 33.
28. Koch, *Mughal Architecture*, p. 58.

The Magnificent Mughals

Fig. 16: Panch Mahal, Fatehpur Sikri

Fig. 18: Jal Mahal, Narnaul

Fig. 19: Govind Deva Temple, interior, Vrindavan

Fig. 17: Bridge over the Gumpti River, Jaunpur

passages to Akbar's own quarters. Among these are the so-called Panch Mahal, or five storeyed palace, which in spite of its open nature today, probably was faced with pierced stone screens (Fig. 16). Given its height, women of the imperial family could watch the court proceedings but not be seen themselves. It is important to understand that just because women were not visible to outsiders, they did not lack tremendous influence. In many ways the royal ladies were potent forces behind many imperial decisions.[29]

Beyond these portions of the palace were other important areas whose function is known, but the actual structures are no longer extant. These include areas for gambling and drinking, an experimental school set up to discover the natural language of all humans, and a chapel for the Jesuit priests who were often invited to court. Some of the buildings that do survive are *hammams* (baths), pavilions, deep stepped wells (*baolis*) and small mosques as well as the city walls.

Fatehpur Sikri is considerably more Indian in appearance than Humayun's tomb or even the Agra Fort's Jahangiri Mahal. It was during the time that he was building at Fatehpur Sikri that Akbar was concerned with winning the favour of both his Indian Muslim and Hindu subjects while reducing the power of the dominant Iranian and Central Asian nobility.[30] These politically motivated moves appear to be reflected in the architectural style chosen for the site.

While at least through the mid-seventeenth century the Mughal emperors continued to be the leading patrons of architecture, the nobility were active builders as well. In part, construction was encouraged by the enormous wealth of the Mughal state; moreover, once a noble died his entire estate reverted to the state, thus encouraging expenditure during his lifetime. By the reign of Jahangir, the next Mughal emperor, we have proof that building activity on the part of the nobility often led to an increase in rank and salary, but this was probably true under Akbar as well. The building types constructed by nobles during Akbar's reign were extensive including, of course, mosques and tombs, but also additions to forts, gardens, and caravanserais. One such noble was Muhammad Munim Khan who in 1567 was appointed governor of one of Akbar's eastern territories, Jaunpur. This city, until it was ruined by the Lodi dynasty, had been considered the Shiraz of India. He extensively refurbished Jaunpur and rebuilt an older massive fort. Additions to the older fort included a public viewing window (*jharoka-i darshan*), a palace, a bath (*hammam*), and an entrance gate. But his most valuable contribution was a massive bridge over the Gumpti river (Fig. 17).[31] A marvel of technological achievement the bridge rests on massive pylons and is surmounted with covered kiosks (*chattris*) to provide shade for travellers. It gained both Mughal and British praise when in the eighteenth century it sustained no damage even after having been covered completely by the raging waters of a violent flood.

Shah Quli Khan, another of Akbar's faithful nobles, was an equally prolific patron of architecture in western India, although the nature of his patronage was somewhat different from that of Munim Khan. Very wealthy and highly regarded, in 1571-72 he provided the needed enclosures at another Chishti shrine at Ajmer, the *dargah* of Sayyid Husain Khing Sawar on Taragarh hill overlooking the premier Sufi *dargah* of Muinuddin Chishti. Sayyid Husain was a fourteenth century saint whose shrine received little notice until Akbar issued his general orders to build in Ajmer. Shah Quli spent the last thirty years of his life in the western city of Narnaul, and there constructed his own tomb (1574-75) clearly inspired by pavilions of the Sher Mandal type. On the Narnaul estate he built a pleasure pavilion known today as the Jal Mahal (Fig. 18). Situated in the middle of a pool of water, much like Sher Shah's tomb, the square-plan building's facade is pierced by arched openings and surmounted by *chattris*. The interior is a version of the *hasht behisht* plan used by this time for both pleasure pavilions and tombs.

The patronage of individual nobles like Munim Khan and Shah Quli Khan was generally limited to a single region since very few of the nobility had truly pan-South Asian connections. A notable exception was the Hindu Raja Man Singh who was also a prince with long-established ancestral lands (*watan jagir*). He

---

29. D. Fairchild Ruggles, 'Vision and Power: An Introduction', in D. Fairchild Ruggles, ed., *Women, Patronage and Self-Representation in Muslim Societies* (Albany, NY, 2000), pp. 1-15.
30. Iqtidar Alam Khan, 'The Nobility Under Akbar and the Development of his Religious Policy,' *Journal of the Royal Asiatic Society* 1-2, 1968, pp. 31-32.
31. Catherine B. Asher, 'Sub-Imperial Palaces: Power and Authority in Mughal India,' *Ars Orientalis* XXXIII, 1993, pp. 283-84.

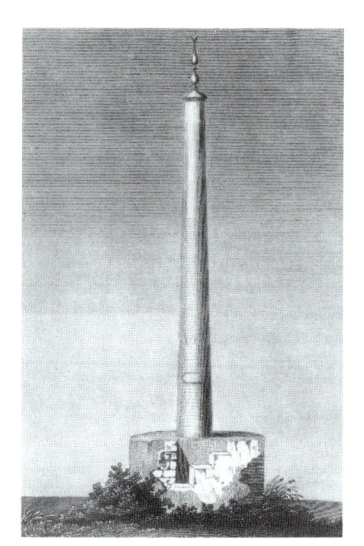

Fig. 20

Fig. 21

Fig. 20: Jami Mosque, Rajmahal
Fig. 21: Allahabad pillar, third century BCE inscribed with Shah Salim's intentions to ascend the throne. Drawing by James Hoare, from Asiatic Researches VII (1803), Plate XIII
Fig. 22: Akbar's Tomb, Sikandra
Fig. 23: Akbar's Tomb, open top floor, Sikandra

Fig. 23

Fig. 22

belonged to the Kachhwaha family which had been the first house of Rajasthan to give their daughters in marriage to the Mughals. Akbar called Man Singh *'farzand'*, (son, in Persian) and he became the highest ranking noble in the Mughal empire. His architectural patronage was awesome, including Hindu temples, mosques, Muslim shrines, gardens, palaces, and pleasure pavilions built throughout much of north India. One question that arises is whether Raja Man Singh's architectural patronage was representing Man Singh as independent Raja or Man Singh as Mughal agent. The answers are complex, and reveal the elastic yet patrimonial nature of Mughal kingship.

First among Raja Man Singh's projects was a garden at Wah, today in Pakistan.[32] Highly praised by Mughal emperors, Wah appears at first glance as an ideal Mughal garden. However, its setting and appearance, when studied alongside texts on ideal dwellings for

Hindu gods, suggest that Wah may have had a dual meaning—one understandable to all those attuned to Persianate culture but another directed solely at a Hindu elite who would recognize the setting as ideal for the gods. The Raja's best known structure is the Govind Deva temple that he provided in 1590 in Vrindavan (Mathura District, Uttar Pradesh), an area which at that time was becoming a major pilgrimage site associated with the deity Krishna, an incarnation of the Hindu god, Vishnu. The temple, the largest one built in north India since the thirteenth century, is constructed entirely of red sandstone.[33] Its exterior follows the traditional trabeated mode of building temples, but its interior is a spectacular display of vaulting, especially the central vault which is an enormous version in red sandstone of the Timurid vault type (Fig. 19).[34] The result is a sense of height and openness hitherto unprecedented in temple architecture. The question is: why did Man Singh decide to build such a temple? There is reason to believe that after winning a military victory, he vowed to build this temple; moreover, inscriptional evidence suggests that the temple was constructed, in part, to commemorate his recently deceased father. All the same, the choice for this particular location needs to be examined, for it is the only structure he provided which was neither on his own ancestral lands nor on land where he served in his capacity as a Mughal officer. The fact that Akbar had invested in Vrindavan's temples as early as 1565 doubtless played a major role in his own decision to build at the site, suggesting that the Govind Deva temple was designed to reflect both the Kachhwahas' personal and official image.[35]

Man Singh's patronage in territories where he acted as a Mughal governor reflects a similar duality. A case in point is a mosque he provided around 1600 in Rajmahal (Sahibganj District, Bihar), then the capital of Bengal, which emulated the great mosque at Fatehpur Sikri (Fig. 20). This resemblance might not seem so apparent today, but nineteenth century drawings indicate that originally it had inlay much like that found at Fatehpur Sikri. While he commissioned a mosque to represent official Mughal presence, he named the new capital Rajanagar, the City of the Raja, reflecting his personal role in its creation, but popularly it was and still is known as Rajmahal. Man Singh built an enormous palace in Rohtas, at that time the capital of Bihar, to serve as a Mughal administrative centre. It was loosely modelled on prototypes at the imperial centres. There on a stone plaque are two inscriptions: one in Persian, the Mughal court language, indicates that Man Singh built the palace as Akbar's servant; the other, in Sanskrit, has no mention of Akbar, but instead praises Man Singh as 'king of kings' suggesting he was the supreme monarch. These examples underscore the dual nature of the relationship between the Mughal ruler and the Raja. Under the Mughal state system serving the emperor *included* defending one's own religion, honour, and even patrimony if necessary. Evoking a title which symbolized Rajput ideals or aspirations did not conflict with the Raja's role as Mughal governor, for both were part of the integral success of the functioning Mughal empire.[36]

JAHANGIR (1605-1627)

Prince Salim, named after the Chishti saint who had predicted his birth, aspired to be emperor, and in 1600 rebelled and established a counter-court in Allahabad. Shortly before Akbar's death in 1605, father and son reconciled. The prince assumed the title, Nuruddin Muhammad Jahangir Badshah Ghazi. Upon his accession he began writing his memoirs, stating that he took the title Jahangir, World Seizer, since controlling the world was the concern of kings; the title Nuruddin, Light of the Faith, was appropriate since his accession to the throne, 'coincided with the rising and shining on the earth of that great Light, the Sun.'[37]

Jahangir made essentially no real changes to Mughal

---

32. Catherine B. Asher, 'Gardens of the Nobility: Raja Man Singh and the Bagh-i Wah,' in Mahmood Hussain, Abdul Rehman and James L. Wescoat Jr., eds., *The Mughal Garden: Interpretation, Conservation and Implications* (Lahore, 1996), pp. 61-72.
33. For a recent and detailed discussion of this temple, see the articles in Margaret Case, ed., *Govindadeva: A Dialogue in Stone* (New Delhi, 1996). This site is also spelled Brindavan.
34. Koch, *Mughal Architecture*, p. 69.
35. Tarapada Muhkerjee and Irfan Habib, 'Akbar and the Temples of Mathura and its Environs,' *Proceedings of the Indian History Congress, 48th Session* (Panajim, Goa, 1988), p. 235.
36. See Catherine B. Asher, 'Sub-Imperial Patronage: The Architecture of Raja Man Singh,' in Barbara S. Miller, ed., *The Powers of Art: Patronage in Indian Culture* (New Delhi, 1992), pp. 183-201, for a detailed discussion.
37. Muhammad Nur al-Din Jahangir, *Tuzuk-i Jahangiri*, 2 vols. tr. A. Rogers (reprinted, Delhi, 1968), 1:2-3. Hereafter this is called *Tuzuk*.

The Magnificent Mughals

Fig. 24: Akbar's Tomb, south entrance gate, Sikandra

Fig. 26: Hunting Tower, Shaikhupura

Fig. 25: Garden pool, Vernag, Kashmir

state polity as it had evolved under Akbar. Content with the empire he inherited from his father, military campaigns were few; Prince Khurram, the future Shahjahan, was active in battles, not the emperor himself. Jahangir was spiritually inclined, reviving Mughal ties with the Sufi Chishti order abandoned by Akbar some twenty-five years earlier.

During the period that Prince Salim established his counter-court at Allahabad fort, and assumed the name Shah Salim, he sponsored a painting atelier and indulged a penchant for inscribing objects proclaiming his intention to succeed Akbar. Among these were a black stone throne inscribed with verses praising Shah Salim, and a pillar dating to the third century BC, where even more explicit verses indicate his determination to assume the Mughal throne (Fig. 21).[38] On this pillar, interspersed with edicts issued by the famous Maurya ruler, Ashoka, in an inscription dated to several months before his official coronation, his entire lineage is traced back to Timur, naming the rebel prince, not Shah Salim, but Jahangir. The Names of God are interwoven with those of his ancestors, thus underscoring the Mughal concept of divinely chosen kings. By placing such an inscription on an ancient Indian pillar, Jahangir, like the father he was so desperate to replace, linked Mughal rule to both South Asian and Timurid tradition.

In spite of his estrangement from Akbar, upon his death Jahangir arranged for a monumental tomb, set in the middle of a *char bagh*, to be constructed at Behishtabad (the Abode of Paradise) in Sikandra, a suburb of Agra (Fig. 22). Not at all pleased with its appearance when he first saw the tomb in 1608, he ordered it to be rebuilt; inscriptions on the southern gate of the complex indicate that it was completed by 1614. The tomb itself is a multi-tiered structure that sits on a high plinth similar in design to the one at Humayun's tomb. The arched openings in the plinth housed readers of the Quran. The plinth is stucco covered while the first three pillared tiers are red sandstone, but the top floor, left open to the air, is white marble (Fig. 23). The tiered appearance of the tomb set in a *char bagh* is probably inspired by the promised mansions of Paradise which according to the Quran will be 'one above the other' and 'beneath them flow rivers of delight'.[39] The use of white marble, a material previously associated only with saints' tombs, suggests a blurring of the distinction between kings and saints, and thus projects the Mughal concept of sanctified sovereignty.[40] The explanation for why the uppermost storey was left open to the air is found in an inscription on the tomb's southern gate, the final verse of which reads, 'May his [Akbar's] soul shine like the rays of the sun and the moon in the light of God.'[41] This magnificent gate is crowned with four towering white marble minarets, one at each corner, thus initiating a new Mughal tradition of associating imperial mausolea with minarets (Fig. 24). The entrance is beautifully inlaid with coloured stones and white marble. Its

Fig. 27: Cheshma-i Nur (Fountain of Light), Ajmer

inscription indicates that visual devices on Mughal tombs are references to paradise, by stating, 'These are the gardens of Eden, enter them and live forever.'[42]

Jahangir's patronage of Akbar's tomb is well known, but it is usually assumed that in general he had little interest in architecture. However, his memoirs are full of accounts of both the structures he built as well as those of his nobility. When he was pleased with the appearance of a new mansion or garden, he frequently rewarded the person with money and an advance in rank. Among his own buildings were palaces, gardens, and hunting pavilions in various locales. In Kashmir he ordered that natural streams, waterfalls, and springs be turned into gardens, for example at Vernag where walls were erected around a spring and eventually a larger garden was built around it (Fig. 25). The architect Haider was responsible for part of this project. Shortly after he assumed the throne his favourite antelope died at Shaikhupura, not far from Lahore. It was given a suitable burial at the site and then a watch tower for hunting (Fig. 26) and a tank with a pavilion were added. The tower closely resembles Akbari prototypes, but the pavilion centred in the tank was restored in Shahjahan's reign. Among Jahangir's most beloved country palaces was the Cheshma-i Nur, Fountain of Light, completed in 1615 in the hills around Ajmer. There pillared pavilions face each other on either side of a running stream that tumbles below just next to a vaulted chamber (Fig. 27), providing cooling breezes for its occupants. Although remote from the city, Jahangir visited Cheshma-i Nur over thirty-eight times during the few years that he lived in Ajmer.

---

38. Catherine B. Asher, 'Appropriating the Past: Jahangir's Pillars,' *Islamic Culture* LXXXI 4,1997, pp. 1-16.
39. Quran, 39: 20.
40. For a more detailed discussion see Asher, 'Sub Imperial Palaces,' p. 283.
41. Edmund W. Smith, 'Akbar's Tomb, Sikandarah,' Archaeological Survey of India, *New Imperial Series*, XXV (Allahabad, 1909), p. 35.
42. Smith, pp. 31-35.

Jahangir built palace pavilions in Akbar's Agra and Lahore forts, as well as in an older fort at Mandu and one in Delhi known as Salimgarh. At least two architects, Jahan Muhammad Dost and Mamur Khan, were involved in several of these projects, thereby providing a uniformity of appearance in all of Jahangir's palaces. Of Jahangir's few palace pavilions that survive is one inside the Lahore fort known today as the Kala Burj, Black Tower, probably because of its external appearance of unadorned, and now black, stucco. Recent conservation work on its interior, however, indicates that angels and birds were painted on its walls and vaulted ceiling (Fig. 28), similar in theme to those depicted on tiles on the fort's exterior walls. These figures were intended to represent the heavenly retinue of King Solomon, considered an ideal ruler, and to whom Jahangir is likened in his only inscription on this fort.[43]

Increasingly women were responsible for embellishing Mughal cities, following Timurid (like the prolific patronage of the fifteenth century queen Gawharshad) and Muslim precedent. Such construction is a genuine reflection of the wealth and influence of the court's highest ranking women and served as a statement of dynastic loyalty.[44] Many mosques and public works were provided by women as acts of charity. Near the Lahore fort is the Mosque of Maryam Zamani (also known as the Begum Shahi mosque) completed in 1611-12, which was commissioned by the queen mother. The mosque's most notable feature is a spectacular dome with a central medallion from which radiate stellate (star-like) and net forms in stucco exquisitely painted in blues, golds, and reds. Variations of this dome type are found in somewhat later tombs as well, for example, those in Khusrau Bagh in Allahabad built in the 1620s by one of Jahangir's daughters, and at the tomb of Itimaduddaula in Agra provided by the queen, Nur Jahan.[45]

During Jahangir's reign by far the most important female patron and indeed perhaps the most powerful and influential person in the Mughal empire was his wife Nur Jahan. In 1611 the emperor married the then widow, bestowing on her the title Nur Jahan, Light of the World, in 1616. She soon assumed an unprecedented role in court and political affairs, becoming Finance Minister when her father, the previous minister, died. As much as she was appreciated by the emperor, others disliked her intensely, creating factions among the nobility. After Jahangir's death in 1627, she lost her influence and lived quietly until her death in 1645 in Lahore.

Nur Jahan amassed enormous wealth, in part by building caravanserais on lucrative trade routes, giving her control on tariffs levied on important goods. One of her serais known as Serai Nur Mahal is still extant in a town also known as Serai Nur Mahal in Punjab (Jalandhar District). Begun in 1618 it contained 124 rooms for travellers, a mosque, and a three-storeyed royal apartment. Its fine entrance is embellished with carved animal and mythic figures similar to those on her husband's Lahore fort walls (Fig. 29). In building this serai Nur Jahan was following a well established tradition in the Subcontinent and the larger Muslim world. In India, similar structures, usually much less elaborate, were built across major trade routes about the distance of a single day's journey. They provided safe lodging for the traveller and his goods, thus stimulating trade and thereby, the economy.

Nur Jahan also created a number of gardens, including the refurbishment of one of Babur's in Agra, called the Bagh-i Nur Afshan, today popularly known as the Ram Bagh. But her most important architectural contribution is the tomb she built in Agra for her parents which is dated between 1626-28 (Fig. 30). Although the tomb was constructed for both her parents, it is known after her father, Itimaduddaula. Set in a *char bagh*, the tomb has two storeys and engaged corner turrets crowned by *chattris*. The ground floor interior consists of nine chambers, a *hasht behisht* plan, but unlike the arrangement at Humayun's tomb the central chamber is surrounded by two rooms on each side. The second floor is a single chambered room whose exterior resembles the canopied structures over the graves of saints,[46] thus blurring the distinction between saints and the royal queen's parents. The walls of this chamber are largely exquisitely carved marble screens through which light floods the room (Fig. 31), a metaphor for God's presence

---

43. Ebba Koch, 'Jahangir and the Angels: Recently Discovered Wall Paintings under European Influence in the Fort of Lahore,' in J. Deppert, ed., *India and the West* (New Delhi, 1983), pp. 182-86.
44. Ruggles, pp. 4-9.
45. Koch, 'Jahangir and the Angels,' p. 176.
46. Koch, *Mughal Architecture*, p. 74.

Fig. 28

Fig. 29

Fig. 31

Fig. 28: Kala Burj (Black Tower), interior with painted vaulting, Lahore Fort
Fig. 29: Serai Nur Mahal, Punjab. Photo: Subash Parihar
Fig. 30: Tomb of Itimaduddaula, Agra
Fig. 31: Tomb of ltimaduddaula, detail of interior, Agra

Fig. 30

and a reference to the imperial Mughals who were obsessed with light imagery. The exterior too is white marble, delicately inlaid with semi-precious stones in the shapes of vessels, especially wine vessels, fruit, flowers, and cypress trees. These visual devices probably allude to Quranic passages and Persian poetry describing paradise.

Other important female patrons of architecture included the queen mother, Maryam Zamani and Sultan Nisar Begum, sister of the ill-fated Khusrau, the eldest son of Jahangir, whose death allowed Shahjahan to succeed Jahangir. Sultan Nisar Begum, built herself a tomb (1624-25) in a *char bagh* in Allahabad, already the site of the tomb of her mother, Jahangir's first wife, Shah Begum (Fig. 32). Shah Begum's multi storeyed edifice was probably the model for Akbar's mausoleum. It is likely that Sultan Nisar Begum provided the tomb for Prince Khusrau as well. The square-plan tombs commissioned by her follow much older architectural types, in that they appear from the exterior as two-storeyed structures but the interior is a single chamber. As cited earlier, each interior features spectacular vaulting.

Monumental tombs were the most widely constructed edifice type and are found throughout Muslim India. Among the many notable mausolea is the tomb of Shah Daulat at Maner (Bhojpur District, Bihar). Built in local sandstone between 1613 and 1619, the two-storeyed square plan tomb has a single central chamber surrounded by an ambulatory, recalling in some ways the tomb of Salim Chishti at Fatehpur Sikri (Fig. 33). Their overall appearances are quite different, however, for this tomb is considerably larger and the buff coloured stone facade is magnificently carved with fine designs.

Jahangir considered it the responsibility of his nobility to provide religious and secular buildings to 'encourage population' and stability throughout the empire; this was one of the twelve orders he issued upon his accession.[47] Thus shrines, bridges, wells, serais, mosques, and other structures were provided across Mughal territory, often by officers wishing to gain favour with the emperor. One notable example is the fine red sandstone mosque in Agra attributed to Mutamid Khan, a noble for whom Jahangir had considerable regard.[48] Although undated, the mosque's facade is divided into a series of grids carved with intricate geometric patterns and slender necked vessels similar to other structures of this period (Fig. 34), like the Serai Nur Mahal and some garden entrances in Agra (the Kanch Mahal, for instance) which are also rendered in red sandstone.

Hindu princes provided palaces and temples in Jahangir's India. Often that construction took place on ancestral lands, but Vrindavan continued to receive imperial land grants[49] and new temples there were built in the typical red

Fig. 32: Shah Begum's Tomb, Allahabad

Fig. 33: Tomb of Shah Daulat, Maner

sandstone so closely associated with imperial Mughal architecture. The Jugal Kishore temple appears to date from this period; above its entrance is a large carving of an elaborate *chandrasala*, similar to those found earlier at Fatehpur Sikri. Jahangir, who visited Vrindavan, admired its temples built in the pan-South Asian Mughal aesthetic.[50]

One Hindu raja, Bir Singh Deo, was but a minor figure, who rose considerably in status by assassinating Abul Fazl, Akbar's adviser and confidant, in 1602 at the future Jahangir's request. From then on he advanced steadily in rank, receiving the title Maharaja (great prince) in 1623.[51] This increased wealth made it possible for Bir Singh to build two palaces, one in Orchha (Jhansi District, Uttar Pradesh) and another in Datia (Datia District, Madhya Pradesh), about 30 kilometres apart (Fig. 35). Both appear to be modelled on Rajput palaces constructed in Rajasthan, and elsewhere, such as Raja Man Singh's palace at Rohtas (Bihar). They consist of large multistoreyed square structures with high exterior walls and chattris. Bir Singh also built a sizeable temple, now partially ruined, at Orchha whose interior vaulting and dome may have been inspired by Man Singh's earlier temple at Vrindavan. Clearly, Bir Singh also wished to participate in highly visual temple construction, for at Mathura, only 10 kilometres from Vrindavan, he built an enormous red sandstone temple dedicated to Keshava Deva, a form of the Hindu god, Krishna. Mathura was another important site associated with the now extremely popular Krishna cult. Although the temple was dismantled in the seventeenth century under Aurangzeb in a political protest, a French traveller noted that it was visible for 16 kilometres, indicating its tremendous scale.[52]

Fig. 34: Mutamid Khan's Mosque, Agra

Fig. 35: Bir Singh Deo's Palace, Datia

SHAHJAHAN (r. 1628-58; d. 1666)

During his thirty-year reign, Shahjahan, the fifth Mughal emperor, was the Subcontinent's most prolific patron of architecture. Under him the empire achieved unprecedented stability and wealth and,

---

47. *Tuzuk*, I: 7-8.
48. *Tuzuk*, II: 246.
49. Tarapada Mukherjee and Irfan Habib, 'The Mughal Administration and the Temples of Vrindavan during the Reigns of Jahangir and Shahjahan,' *Proceedings of the Indian History Congress, 49th Session* (Dharwad, 1989), pp. 287-89.
50. *Tuzuk*, II: 103-04.
51. *Tuzuk*, I: 24-25; II: 253
52. Jean-Baptiste Tavernier, *Travels in India*, 2 vols., tr. V. Ball, ed. William Crooke, 2nd ed. (London, 1925), II:186-89.

Fig. 36: Jahangir's Tomb, Lahore

simultaneously, courtly culture and its setting—architecture—became increasingly formalized and symmetrical. The favourite son of Jahangir, the future Shahjahan was treated as the heir apparent, until about 1622 when he fell from Nur Jahan's avour. For a short while the future Shahjahan rebelled establishing a counter-court in eastern India, but several years before Jahangir's death acknowledged imperial authority. When Jahangir died in 1627, Shahjahan had powerful supporters at court who assisted in eliminating rivals, and he acceded to the throne in early 1628, assuming titles which specifically linked him to his Timurid predecessors. While memoirs and histories of the previous Mughal rulers provide considerable insight into their colourful personalities, we have little knowledge of Shahjahan's personal thoughts. Voluminous official histories present him as an ideal aloof ruler who upheld orthodox Islam. It is true that mosque construction increased under Shahjahan but there was no change in the percentage of Hindus serving his military/administrative bureaucracy; some temple construction was banned and a few temples even dismantled. But contradictions abound: like his father and grandfather he continued to maintain the temples of Vrindavan, and supported as his heir apparent, Dara Shikoh, his mystically inclined son who wrote highly unorthodox religious treatises claiming Hindu and Muslim thought were essentially one.[53] Perhaps the best insight into the image Shahjahan wished to project is found in his portraits. Regardless of age, Shahjahan, always shown in profile, is perfect in physique and physiognomy. His face unlined and surrounded by a halo, he is depicted as the pious and just king of the world, a play on the very meaning of his title, Shahjahan. In some portraits he is even crowned by angels from heaven, while the lion and lamb, symbols of just rule, reside at his feet.[54]

Shahjahan had so many architectural commissions carried out concurrently that it is difficult to discuss the material chronologically. As a prince, he had already established himself as a patron of some note by building, for example, a palace for himself known as Moti Bagh, in Ahmedabad when he was governor of Gujarat, and dwellings in Udaipur, the ancestral lands of the recalcitrant Rana of Mewar whom he had successfully subjugated. At the time of his accession three large projects were initiated: a mosque and palace pavilions at Ajmer; public audience halls at the Agra and Lahore forts; and his father's tomb at Lahore. Within three years, his favourite wife, Mumtaz Mahal, died and then the construction of a monumental tomb, the Taj Mahal, in Agra was added to those projects. Simultaneously, other pavilions were added to the Lahore and Agra forts and gardens were built. Once much of this was completed by the late 1630s, Shahjahan decided to construct an entire new city and fortified palace in Delhi, known as Shahjahanabad, the Abode of Shahjahan. Other architectural projects were pursued as well.

Of the two tombs that Shahjahan began early in his reign, the Taj Mahal appeared to occupy much of his attention, while fewer contemporary references are found to Jahangir's tomb in Lahore (Fig. 36). Set in a huge *char bagh*, Jahangir's tomb today consists of a large sandstone platform with arched openings that are marked at each corner by a towering minaret; marble inlay forms decorative elements. Originally screens

---

53. See Bikrama Jit Hasrat, *Dara Shikuh: Life and Works* (New Delhi, 1982).
54. For example, see Ebba Koch, *Shah Jahan and Orpheus* (Graz, 1988), pls. 54-55.

Fig. 37: Taj Mahal, Agra

Fig. 38: Mosque at Dargah of Muinuddin Chishti, Ajmer

Fig. 39: Diwan-i Amm (Public Audience Hall), Agra Fort

made from carved marble surrounded a cenotaph that at Jahangir's wish was left exposed to the air. Under this spot is an interior sepulchral chamber which is magnificently painted; it contains a marble sarcophagus that, like those at the Taj Mahal, is exquisitely inlaid with rare stones. Construction commenced in 1628 and, according to contemporary sources, took ten years to complete.

While the construction of Mumtaz Mahal's tomb was of considerable interest to the grief stricken ruler, this enormous white marble structure set at the end of a *char bagh*, in fact, had little impact on future South Asian architecture (Fig. 37). Much has been written on the Taj Mahal, including controversial scholarly material arguing that the tomb and its garden setting are depictions of Islamic cosmological concepts.[55] More likely the Taj Mahal is simply a continuation of the paradisiacal theme set forth in the earlier Mughal imperial mausolea. Briefly stated, the mausoleum portion of the Taj Mahal complex is derived from Humayun's tomb constructed nearly one hundred years earlier, a reflection of Shahjahan's interest in his Timurid past. Minarets are added to its plinth, a feature also seen at Jahangir's tomb. The Taj Mahal though, is much more than simply a mausoleum; an entire village was part of the complex, as were mosques, a forecourt and other structures including a second garden across the river. The complex was initiated in 1632, six months after Mumtaz Mahal died; much of it was finished by 1636 and it was virtually complete in 1643.

The Taj Mahal is a structure whose significance is greater today than it was at the time of its construction. True, it was admired by the Mughal family, members of the nobility, and European travellers throughout the Mughal period and beyond, but it essentially marks the end of the tradition of building large scale tombs for the royal family. But today its image, more than any other in the world, symbolizes perfection. Over the last twenty years advertisements featuring the Taj Mahal have been associated with fine china, expensive cars, aged whisky, top end cameras, premier quality life insurance, luxury hotels and more.[56] The Government of India features this tomb in glossy advertisements inviting tourists to experience paradise on earth.

The association of Shahjahan's white marble mausoleum with excellence is harmless—perhaps the proud emperor would have been delighted with this universal acclamation of his architectural output. But other modern interpretations are pernicious. Land for the Taj Mahal was purchased from Jai Singh, the Hindu Raja of Amber, a descendant of Raja Man Singh who was discussed in connection with Akbar.[57] This fact has been distorted by authors such as P.N. Oak, a member of the Institute for Rewriting Indian History, who have presented not just the Taj Mahal but also a number of other structures built by Muslims in the Subcontinent, as products of Hindu patronage.[58] Oak's ideas, while patently insupportable, have been popularized through various media, among them books, e-mail list servs and web sites on the Taj Mahal which claim, for example, that it was constructed as a temple.[59] Such claims manipulated by members of the Hindu right wing, whether in the Subcontinent itself or in the diaspora, use artistic creation to discredit Muslims and the very basis for a secular democracy in modern India.

Although no other structure created by Shahjahan has generated so much attention as the Taj Mahal, at least in today's world, his other extant gardens, mosques, and

Fig. 40: Royal Quarters, Agra Fort

Fig. 41: Naulakha, Shahi Burj, Lahore Fort

palaces are universally acknowledged as magnificent. While Akbar constructed two mosques early in his reign and Jahangir none, Shahjahan built mosques throughout his entire reign. Among these are a mosque he provided at the *dargah* of Muinuddin Chishti in Ajmer in response to an earlier vow; the mosque was completed in 1637-38 (Fig. 38). Shahjahan considered this of all his projects in Ajmer to be the most important. Built, like the nearby saint's tomb, completely of white marble, the double-aisled mosque has a flat exterior roof. The mosque's location, due west of the tomb, allowed the emperor to be positioned between saint and the mosque's *qibla* during prayer. Shahjahan's eldest daughter Jahanara, who served as first lady once her mother, Mumtaz Mahal, died, was a devotee of Muinuddin Chishti. She wrote his biography and just at the tomb's east entrance provided a pillared marble porch known as the Begumi Dalan. Thus the tomb of the Subcontinent's most important saint was sandwiched, so to speak, by white marble structures provided by the leading members of the imperial family; the imprimatur of Mughal hold over the shrine is heralded visually.

White marble was associated with saints' shrines and increasingly with Mughal royal tombs; under

---

55. See Wayne E. Begley. 'The Myth of the Taj Mahal and a New Theory of Its Symbolic Meaning,' *The Art Bulletin*, 61, 1979, pp. 7-37. Later this author and Z.A. Desai produced, *Taj Mahal: The Illumined Tomb: An Anthology of Seventeenth-Century Mughal and European Documentary Sources* (Cambridge, MA, 1989); here there is no reference to his original theory.
56. See Pratapaditya Pal, Janice Leoshko et al., *Romance of the Taj Mahal* (Los Angeles and London, 1989), pp. 9-12 for some of these.
57. Begley and Desai, pp. 163-67.
58. P.N. Oak, *Taj Mahal is a Hindu Palace* (New Delhi, 1968) and his, *The Taj Mahal is a Temple Palace* (New Delhi, 1974). Other examples include P.N. Oak, *Delhi's Red Fort is Hindu Lal Kot* (Bombay, 1976).
59. Khan, Zulfikar. 'The Taj Mahal—A Hindu Temple-Palace.' <http://www.flex.com/~jai/satyamevajayate/tejo.html> (17 June 1999). **This is a particularly insidious site which cites Oak's work frequently. The author's highly inflammatory discussion of Islam and Muslims in general makes it unlikely that Zulfikar Khan is his or her real name; rather, this Muslim name seems to have been adopted to give the site a sense of legitimacy that is otherwise lacking.**

Fig. 42

Fig. 42: Water Pavilion, Shaikhupura
Fig. 43: Shalimar Garden, Lahore
Fig. 44: Plan of Jami Mosque, Agra. American Institute of Indian Studies, Center for Art and Archaeology

Fig. 43

Shahjahan it was also used for those palace pavilions which were reserved for imperial use. In both the Lahore and Agra forts most of the Akbari and Jahangiri structures were cleared to make way for Shahjahan's own designs. It appears that the ones in Lahore fort were completed before those at Agra, but the bulk of the work at each was completed by the end of the 1630s. At both forts the Public Audience Halls were rebuilt. Pillared halls were placed before a white marble imperial throne at both Lahore and Agra (Fig. 39). Similar in layout to some imperial contemporary mosques, these halls were important places of court ceremonial and served multiple purposes including as mosques. They were intended to replicate the great audience hall of Persepolis believed to have been founded by Solomon, who was considered the ultimate symbol of justice.[60]

A second remodelled area in the Agra and Lahore forts was the royal quarters. Maintaining Mughal tradition, Shahjahan placed the imperial quarters on the edge of the fort that overlooked water. These white marble structures often embedded with hard precious stones, consisting of private quarters, public viewing windows, Private Audience Halls among others, were the finest in each palace. They tended to be elevated above walled courtyard gardens; in the Agra fort, the quadrangle was composed of Shahjahan's bed chamber, the residence of his daughter Jahanara, and the pavilion from which he presented himself to the public (Fig. 40).[61] Of particular note here is the Public Viewing Window, a low triple arched pavilion surmounted with a curved gilt roof in which the emperor appeared before his subjects. His official chronicler noted that when Shahjahan was under the roof, it appeared as if there were two suns, the emperor and the reflection of light from the shining roof.[62] Similar pavilions are part of Shahjahan's additions to the Lahore fort. In a quadrangle known as the Shahi Burj are a mirrored marble hall, and a pavilion known today as the Naulakha while others are clustered around a courtyard in whose centre is a pool (Fig. 41). The Naulakha was originally covered with a curved roof similar to that on the Agra fort's viewing window suggesting it may have served as the imperial window.

Other architectural enterprises included the building of hunting pavilions in country estates, such as the one in Bari (Dholpur District, Rajasthan) and Hashtsal, just outside modern Delhi. In 1634, Shahjahan remodelled Jahangir's water pavilion at the Shaikhupura hunting pavilion (Fig. 42). An elegant three storeyed octagonal structure, it is set in the middle of a tank and a causeway connects it to land. Pleasure came not only from hunting; Shahjahan also enjoyed gardens, especially those in the hills of Kashmir. There in 1634 on the edge of Dal Lake in Srinagar he further embellished the world famous Shalimar garden that he had started as a prince. Consistent with gardens of this sort, the entire space is divided laterally by a broad stream that runs from the mountains behind through a series of terraces to the lake below. A pillared pavilion in a local dark stone was built over the rushing stream.

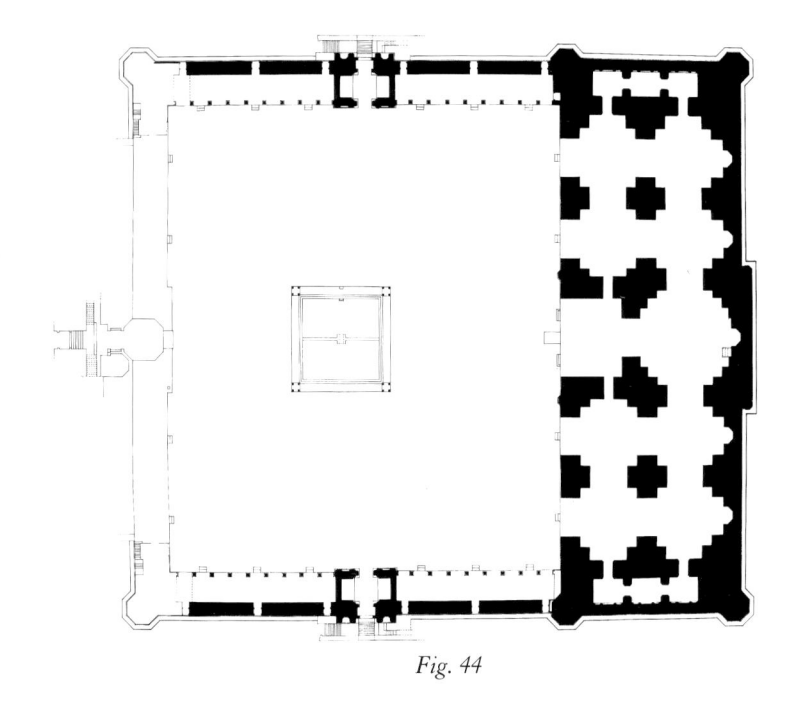

Fig. 44

Shalimar was divided into two parts, one for private imperial use (Faiz Bakhsh) and the other for imperial audiences (Farah Bakhsh). Others, including his daughter Jahanara and high ranking nobles, also adorned the Kashmir hills with terraced *char baghs* often around natural springs and waterfalls. (These gardens brought in considerable revenue through the sale of flowers and fruit). There are reputed to have been 777 Mughal gardens in Kashmir. Kashmir was the home of another well-known saint, Molla Shah Badakhshi. Both Jahanara and her brother Dara Shikoh were his disciples and provided for him a mosque and school, the Pari Mahal, in Srinagar.

The Kashmir Shalimar garden served as the prototype for one constructed on the plains of Lahore in 1641. A remarkable engineering feat largely masterminded by Ali Mardan Khan brought water to Lahore from a considerable distance thus enabling the construction of the Lahore Shalimar garden. Here a third terrace was placed in the middle of the original two found in the Kashmir garden. Its marble throne served as a royal seat surrounded by cooling waters (Fig. 43).

Although building activity was concentrated on Shahjahanabad during the 1640s there were some notable exceptions. One was Shahjahan's construction of a large white marble mosque inside Agra fort that was completed in 1653; its plan and that of imperial

---

60. Ebba Koch, 'Diwan-i 'Amm and Chihil Sutun: The Audience Halls of Shah Jahan,' *Muqarnas* 11, 1995, pp. 148-53.
61. Koch, *Mughal Architecture*, p. 106.
62. Lahauri in Nur Bakhsh, 'The Agra Fort and its Buildings,' *Annual Report of the Archaeolgical Survey of India, 1903-04* (Calcutta, 1906), p. 180.

Fig. 45: Wazir Khan's Mosque, Lahore

Public Audience Halls are remarkably similar,[63] again suggesting the Mughal ruler's sanctified status. Another was Jahanara's provision of a Jami mosque for Agra city built between 1643 and 1648. This mosque, faced with red sandstone and white marble, served as a model for Shahjahan's great Jami mosque of Delhi. The plan of the Agra mosque (Fig. 44) is based on the splendid one in Lahore ordered by Wazir Khan, governor of Punjab, in 1634-35 (Fig. 45). The Wazir Khan mosque, however, is faced with glazed tiles, typical of much architecture in Lahore and is brilliantly painted inside recalling the Jahangir-period mosque of Shah Begum. Wazir Khan was one of Lahore's most active patrons; he also built a garden estate complete with residence and a large public bath.

In the 1640s Shahjahan focused his attention on the construction of an entire planned city and palace, Shahjahanabad, north of Humayun's and Akbar's Din Panah in Delhi. After deciding that Agra and Lahore were inadequate for the observation of appropriate ceremony and the processions required by the court, work commenced on the new city and its palace in 1639. Designs for both were executed by Ustad Ahmad Khan and Hamid Khan while the first project supervisor was Ghairat Khan followed by Makramat Khan. The dedication took place in 1648. Ebba Koch, the only scholar permitted to measure the entire palace, today known as the Red Fort, has determined that the whole plan was based on a mathematically proportioned grid which allowed Shahjahan to build a palace on the principles of bilateral symmetry (Fig. 46).[64] After the Revolt of 1857, unfortunately most of the original walls that divided the various parts of the fort into garden courtyards and much more, were destroyed by the British. Thus the experience of visiting it today is a far cry from its original conception.

The main gate, centrally located on the fort's west, fed immediately onto a long covered bazaar, which in turn led directly to the Naqqar Khana, an entrance to the palace's Public Audience Hall. The pillared Public

Audience Hall (Diwan-i Amm) is similar in form and function to those at Lahore and Agra, but here Shahjahan's marble throne, embedded in the central bay of the east wall, is considerably more elaborate (Fig. 47). It is designed as a high platform surmounted by a curved roof supported on bulbous baluster columns, drawn from European illustrations of holy and royal settings. These architectural features at this time were exclusive to Shahjahan.[65] Visually they emphasised this emperor's special majesty. So, too, the inlaid, largely Italian panels of birds, animals, and even one of the Greek figure Orpheus taming wild animals embedded in the back walls of the throne were used to depict an Islamic understanding of Solomon's throne—the seat of the ideal just ruler—a notion we have seen earlier in both Jahangir's and Shahjahan's conceptualization in the Lahore fort.

Due east of the Public Audience Halls are the royal chambers that overlook the Jumna river. Arranged on a north-south axis, a canal bisects each room, including among others the royal quarters for Shahjahan and his daughter, Jahanara, the Private Audience Hall and a bath. Most of these chambers feature bulbous baluster columns; an example can be seen in the Shah Burj which was used exclusively by Shahjahan and his offspring. The white marble of these chambers is often

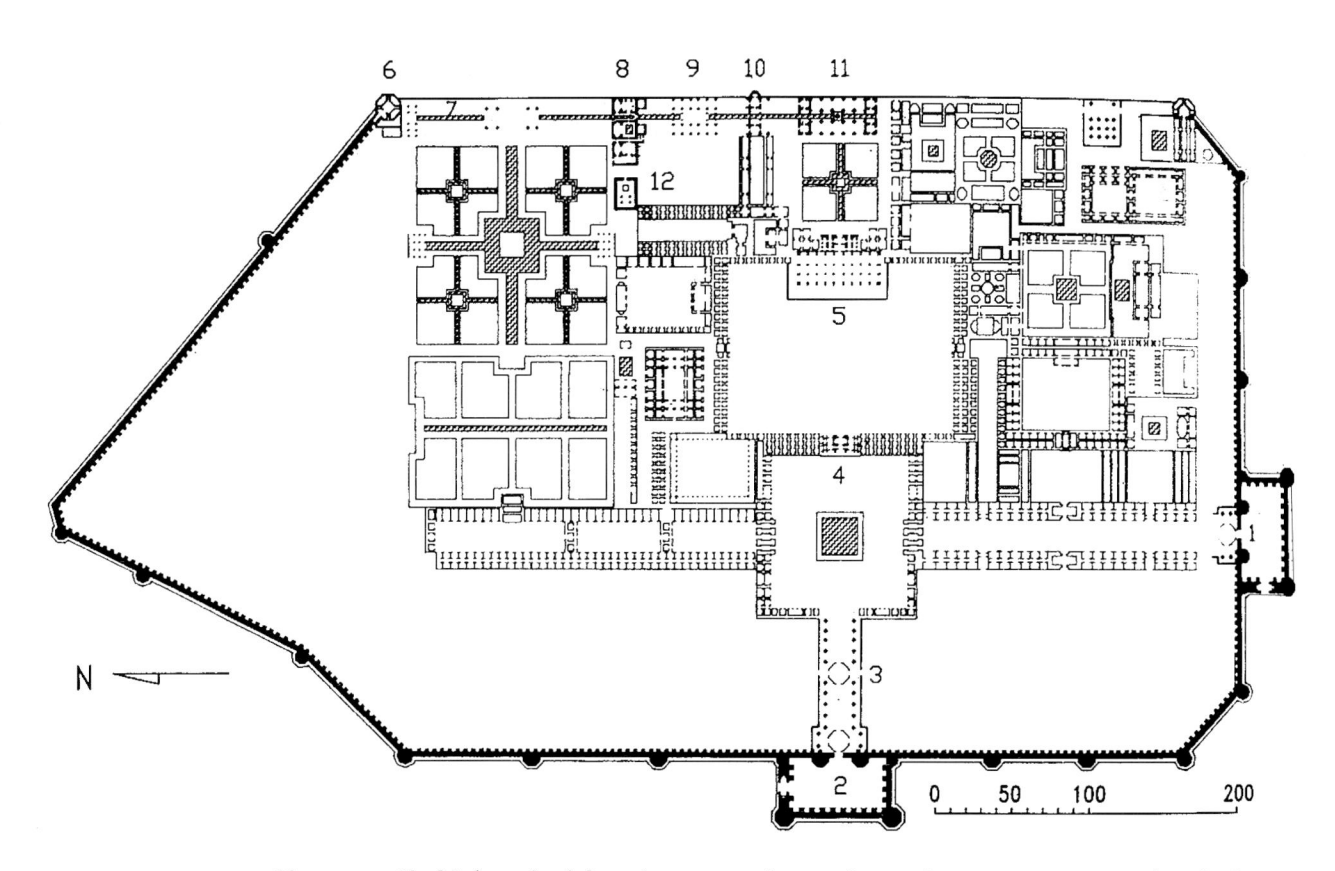

Plate 118. Shahjahanabad fort, known today as the Red Fort, Delhi. 1. Akbarabad (Delhi) gate; 2. Lahore gate; 3. Covered bazaar; 4. Naqqar Khana (Drum Room); 5. Daulat Khana-i Khass o ᶜAmm (Public Audience Hall); 6. Shah Burj; 7. Nahr-i Behisht (Canal of Paradise); 8. *Hammam* (bath); 9. Daulat Khana-i Khass (Private Audience Hall); 10. Khwabgah; 11. Imtiyaz Mahal (Hall of Distinction); 12. Moti (Pearl) mosque

---

63. Koch, 'Diwan-i 'Amm,' p. 155.
64. Koch, *Mughal Architecture*, pp. 109-110.
65. Koch, *Shah Jahan and Orpheus*, pp. 12-16, 23-28, 31-33.

Fig. 46: Plan of Shahjahan's Palace, Shahjahanabad (Delhi). After O. Reuther

Fig. 47: Marble Throne, Public Audience Hall, Shahjahanabad (Delhi)

inlaid with rare stones; beautiful examples are in the bath, the Private Audience Hall, and Jahanara's quarters. In this portion of the palace, Shahjahan's continued fascination with paradisiacal imagery as well as visual themes of just rule is manifest. On a panel leading into Shahjahan's sleeping quarters is a high relief carving in marble covered with gold gilt of the scales of justice, a reference to the emperor's perception of his own rule (Fig. 48). Close to this carving is a lengthy inscription which praises Shahjahan and likens his creation to the mansions of paradise. In the nearby Private Audience Hall are verses from the fourteenth century Indian Muslim poet, Amir Khusrau, painted on the walls that proclaim the structure a paradise on earth.

The fortified palace included much more—quarters for ladies, servants, kitchens, and even workshops for required goods existed. All this served only the palace. It was the city that served the needs of nobility, ordinary persons, and servants. Shahjahan defined the city by first constructing mud walls around it and then in 1653 replacing them with red sandstone walls. Stephen Blake estimates about 400,000 people lived in the approximately 6500 acres that comprised the city.[66] Shahjahan commissioned two mosques, one an Idgah (place for Id prayers) just outside the city in 1655, and an enormous Jami mosque close to the fortified palace (Fig. 49). Initiated in 1650 and completed in 1656, it was at that time the largest mosque in Mughal territory. Called the World Showing Mosque (Masjid-i Jahannuma), it stands at the city's highest point. Shahjahan himself claimed it was modelled on Akbar's great mosque at Fatehpur Sikri;[67] similarities include the impressive entrance gates approached by high stairs, the interior court and facade. Shahjahan's mosque bears inscriptions on its facade that are written in a manner that suggests they are Quranic verses, since all the vowels are marked as in the Arabic of Quranic texts. In fact, they are in Persian and are not religious in content; rather they are encomiums praising Shahjahan and his just rule.[68]

Shahjahan provided two bazaars including the most important one that linked the palace's main west gate with the city's west gate, organized rigidly in a straight line. Today known as Chandni Chowk, this area was a tree lined esplanade through whose centre ran a canal, probably inspired by reports of Isfahan which had been built about forty years earlier in Safavid Iran. Here and elsewhere in the city the leading ladies of the court played a significant role in its embellishment. Two of Shahjahan's wives, Fatehpuri Begum and Sirhindi

Fig. 48: Relief, Shahjahan's Sleeping Quarters, Shahjahanabad (Delhi)

Fig. 49: Jami Mosque, Shahjahanabad (Delhi)

Begum erected mosques and serais, while Jahanara, built the most important serai of the entire city in the centre of Chandni Chowk. Jahanara has been mentioned as an active patron of major works throughout Shahjahan's rule. As discussed earlier, her generosity as well as that of other important women patrons, was not an innovation; such beneficence, essentially an investment in charity and dynasty, is an extension of the female patronage also found under the Mughal's ancestors, the Timurids.[69] In fact, public buildings were commissioned as an act of charity by women throughout the Muslim world.

Mosques were provided in unprecedented numbers during the reign of Shahjahan. Some, like the Jami mosque in Thatta (Pakistan) (Fig. 50) were ordered by Shahjahan (and built between 1644 and 1647), but it is improbable that the emperor was as personally involved in this project as he was, for instance, in his Delhi Jami mosque. Constructed in local brick and decorated with blue and yellow tile work, the interior's richness suggests that the mosque benefited from funding from the imperial coffers. One unusual and creative feature is found on the three *mihrabs* (prayer niches) which feature pierced stone screens that allow for the entrance of light, a reference to the Quranic verse which likens God's presence to a lamp in a niche. Mosques were also built by the nobility, such as Wazir Khan's famous one in

---

66. Stephen P. Blake, *Shahjahanabad: The Sovereign City in Mughal India 1639-1739* (Cambridge, 1991), p. 67.
67. Ebba Koch, 'The Architectural Forms,' in Michael Brand and Glenn D. Lowry, eds., *Fatehpur Sikri* (Bombay, 1987), p. 122.
68. *List of Muhammadan and Hindu Monuments: Delhi Province*, 4 vols. (Calcutta, 1916-22), I: 143-44. Hereafter cited as *List*.
69. Ruggles, p. 5.

Fig. 50: Jami Mosque, interior, Thatta, Pakistan

Fig. 51: Jagdish Temple, Udaipur

Lahore, discussed earlier. Now nearly every major Mughal city features a Shahjahan period mosque. This is true of smaller towns as well; for example, there are several in the eastern India mercantile city of Patna. This increase in mosque construction may be seen as a reflection of the upsurge of orthodox Islam within all sections of South Asia's Muslim population.

While orthodox Islam was definitely in the ascendence, official Mughal policy *vis-à-vis* the Hindu and Jain traditions is less clear cut. It is true that Shahjahan ordered the destruction of Bir Singh's temple at Orchha in 1635, but that was because his successor had rebelled against Mughal authority.[70] At the same time the grants extended to the Hindu temples at Vrindavan were maintained throughout his life,[71] suggesting that actions which could be construed as anti-Hindu were in fact politically, not religiously, motivated. All the powerful Hindu rajas of north India built both magnificent palaces and temples during this period, probably as a response to Shahjahan's own patronage. Perhaps the most interesting of the religious structures is the Jagdish temple in Udaipur (Fig. 51) erected by the Mewar king in 1652, just two years after construction commenced on Shahjahan's Delhi Jami mosque. Mewar had been subjugated by Shahjahan when he was still a prince; under his regime, the two houses had an uneasy alliance. For example, one of the terms to which Mewar had to agree was that no fortification could occur without prior Mughal permission, so when the Mewar house rebuilt their great fort, Chittorgarh, Shahjahan had it torn down.[72] As Jennifer Joffee has argued, the Jagdish temple was clearly the Mewar ruler's response to both Mughal authority and to Shahjahan's great mosque as is apparent in their scale, the parallel meaning of their names, and the position of their patrons. Joffee indicates that the Mewar house was suggesting that in spite of its vassal status, its prowess was as great as that of the Mughals.[73]

Although numerous palaces were commisioned by Hindu princes, they are little studied.[74] While the Mewar kings built fine palaces in Udaipur it is often difficult to distinguish any precise phases since they were continuously added to over time. In general, like Man Singh's Amber palace, they are situated on high terrain overlooking water and are massive walled structures with numerous compartments inside their multi-levels. An example is the City Palace in Udaipur which was built between the sixteenth and twentieth centuries, but much of it is a seventeenth century creation. Easier to understand are Jai Singh's additions to Man Singh's palace in Amber. This is because once Jaipur replaced Amber as the new capital in the early eighteenth century, relatively little important construction took place in the former capital of Amber. The position of the Amber Kachhwahas was very different from that of the Mewaris of Udaipur, for the descendants of Man Singh continued to serve as high ranking officers of the Mughals. It thus comes as no surprise that Jai Singh's new palaces at Amber are very close in appearance and layout to those of Shahjahan's Agra fort. This is especially apparent at the Jai Mandir, also known as the Shish Mahal, in Amber (Fig. 52). The pavilion's curved roof is clearly derived from the Agra fort pavilion at which Shahjahan presented himself to the public.

---

70. Muhammad Salih Kanbo, *'Amal-i Salih*, 3 vols. (Lahore, 1967), II: 102-03.
71. Mukherjee and Habib, 'The Mughal Administration and the Temples of Vrindavan during the Reigns of Jahangir and Shahjahan,' 287-99.
72. Kanbo, III: 147.
73. Jennifer Joffee, 'The Art of Politics, the Politics of Art: The Jagdish Temple in Udaipur,' presented at the American Council of Southern Asian Art Symposium, Charleston, South Carolina, November 1998. This is at the heart of her dissertation which is currently in progress.
74. G.H.R. Tillotson, *The Rajput Palaces: The Development of an Architectural Style, 1450-1750* (New Haven, 1987), is a notable exception.

Fig. 52: Jai Mandir (also known as the Shish Mahal), Amber

AURANGZEB (1658-1707)

In 1657 Shahjahan became extremely ill and it was believed he would die, triggering a war of succession among the imperial princes. Aurangzeb, Shahjahan's third son, emerged victorious crowning himself in 1658. Although Shahjahan recovered, he was imprisoned by Aurangzeb in Agra fort until his death in 1666. Aurangzeb is generally considered the last notable Mughal ruler, but his long-term warfare in the Deccan as well as increased factionalism in the court ultimately weakened the Mughal state. During his fifty-year reign Aurangzeb maintained much of Akbar's concept of state, but due to his personal orthodoxy showed less tolerance than did his predecessors for non-Muslims. Many histories of this sixth Mughal ruler, especially the five volume one by J.N. Sarkar, go to great lengths to present Aurangzeb as a bigot who, without reason, destroyed numerous temples.[75] It is true that Aurangzeb did ruin temples, but a careful reading of the primary sources indicate that his reasons were political and not religious. Moreover many of the temples involved, such as the Govind Deva temple in Vrindavan, had been built by Mughal nobles; in the case of this particular temple, Mughal grants had funded its construction and maintenance. Thus in Aurangzeb's eyes it was Mughal property. So when Ram Singh, the then Kachhwaha ruler, sheltered the emperor's arch enemy, Shivaji, the destruction of the temple, the seat of the raja's most important deity, was the result of the emperor's revenge.[76]

In his personal life Aurangzeb was a devout Sunni Muslim who read the Quran in his spare time and even penned copies of this sacred text. Thus it is no surprise that among the structures he commissioned, including serais, baths, gardens, tombs and fortified walls, mosques were his primary concern. He repaired mosques of the earlier rulers, including pre-Mughal ones, and built many inside captured forts during his twenty plus year campaign in the Deccan. Best known are the three he erected during the initial years of his reign: one in his father's Shahjahanabad fort, one in Lahore, and another in Mathura on the site of the former Keshava Deva temple after it was destroyed in 1669-70 to avenge rebel forces (Fig. 53).[77] The mosque in Mathura resembles the type of imperial congregational mosque built by Shahjahan and ladies of the royal family, but is austere in its ornament. More ornate are the two he built within the Delhi and Lahore forts. The exquisite white marble Moti (Pearl) mosque, completed in 1662-63 inside Delhi's fortified palace, was intended as the emperor's private mosque (Fig. 54). It

Fig. 53: Aurangzeb's Mosque, Mathura

Fig. 54: Moti Mosque, Delhi

Fig. 55: Badshahi Mosque, Lahore

Fig. 56: Tomb of Rabia Durrani (also known as Dilras Banu), Aurangabad

75. For example, Jadunath Sarkar, *History of Aurangzeb*, 5 vols. (Calcutta: 1925-30), III: 285.
76. S.N. Sinha, *Subah of Allahabad under the Great Mughals* (New Delhi, 1974), pp. 65-68, and Asher, *Architecture of Mughal India*, pp. 253-55.
77. Tavernier, *Travels in India*, II:186-189, and Saqi Must'ad Khan, *Maasir-i 'Alamgiri*, tr. Jadu Nath Sarkar (Calcutta, 1947), pp. 57-61, for the Keshava Deva temple and its destruction.

Fig. 57: Grave of Jahan Ara, Dargah of Nizamuddin Auliya, Delhi

Fig. 58: Jami Mosque, Mathura

closely follows in style a small mosque that Shahjahan had built inside Agra fort, but the ornamentation is richly organic. While Koch sees this as a reflection of Aurangzeb's lack of personal interest in his architectural commissions, it could be argued that forms once appropriate for palace architecture, such as the ornament on Shahjahan's Delhi throne, were now utilized on palace mosques which for Aurangzeb would be worthy of the finest embellishment.[78] Equally elaborately decorated, especially in the interior, is his Badshahi (Imperial) mosque in Lahore completed in 1673-74 under the supervision of a foster brother, Fidai Khan Koka (Fig. 55). Closely patterned on the Shahjahanabad Jami mosque, this red sandstone and marble mosque is enormous; its courtyard can hold 60,000 people. Located just outside the walls of Lahore fort, Badshahi mosque was intended for both the city's Id and Friday congregational prayers.

When Aurangzeb's wife, Rabia Durrani, died in 1657 the emperor ordered his eldest son to build her tomb (completed in 1660-61) in the city of Aurangabad in the Deccan (Fig. 56). A smaller version of the Taj Mahal, the tomb reflects the new aesthetic that developed very early in Aurangzeb's reign. In lieu of the perfect balance of proportions featured in Shahjahan's architecture now there is an emphasis on verticality. This tomb is generally discussed in disparaging terms, but this new spatial arrangement as well as its highly naturalistic fine floral ornament, much of it rendered in stucco, render it innovative, not just a poor copy of the Taj Mahal.

Rabia Durrani's tomb truly ends the long-established imperial tradition of monumental mausolea set in a *char bagh*. Now members of the Mughal imperial family were buried in the courtyards of mosques or shrines with simple cenotaphs that were surrounded by marble screens. The grave of Jahanara, who died in 1681, is situated in the *dargah* of Nizamuddin Auliya in Delhi (Fig. 57). In addition to the simple grave and enclosure screens is a beautifully inscribed marble slab

---

78. Koch, *Mughal Architecture*, p. 130.

proclaiming her pious devotion to Chishti saints. Aurangzeb, too, was buried in a similar grave at a Chishti shrine at Khuldabad in the Deccan.

Considering the length of his reign, Aurangzeb built relatively little, but patronage on the part of the nobility escalated. Like Aurangzeb, these people commissioned all building types, but mosques appear to have predominated. Most large north Indian cities tend to feature Aurangzeb period mosques, like Mathura's Jami mosque, completed in 1660-61 (Fig. 58). This building shows the same tendency towards verticality as the tomb of Rabia Durrani finished in the same year, but located in the Deccan. It is interesting to note that even though Aurangzeb was considerably less committed to architecture than was Shahjahan, during his reign, just as in earlier Mughal periods, a uniform aesthetic quickly spread throughout the empire. Yet another mosque, this one in the town of Merta (Nagaur District, Rajasthan) reflects some of these same tendencies (Fig. 59). Built by the son of a local religious official in 1665, the emphasis on verticality is achieved by two towering minarets that flank the front corners of the facade. Since the mosque is already situated on a very high plinth, these slender

Fig. 60: Madrasa of Ghaziuddin, Delhi

minarets are visible for a considerable distance. Made of local reddish stone, the facade is similar to Shahjahan's Delhi mosque; especially noteworthy is the central dome which is decorated with bands of red and white like those on the Delhi mosque. Following imperial practice, mosques now tended to feature very tall minarets, for example the Jami mosque in Gwalior (1664-65) and the Jami mosque on the Varanasi river front, although its minarets no longer survive. It can be assumed that these highly visible minarets, especially in these two cities, one the seat of a Hindu raja and the other, one of the Subcontinent's most sacred pilgrimage sites for Hindus, were intended as bold statements proclaiming the heightened status of orthodox Islam in the Mughal state. Along with this revitalization of Islam came the popularity of the *madrasa*, a school for secular and religious instruction, as an independent building type. Of course *madrasas* had existed in the Subcontinent as an institution, but in Mughal India (as well as during some other periods) the *madrasa* was rarely realized as an independent building. Some were built in Shahjahan's time; Saif Khan, related to Mumtaz Mahal, commissioned one in Patna between 1629 and 1634. Today it is ruined beyond recognition. More seem to have been built in Aurangzeb's reign, such as the Hadayat Bakhsh *madrasa* in Ahmedabad (1690-1700). The *madrasa* of Ghaziuddin, known in the nineteenth century as Delhi College and now as the Anglo-Arabic School, was built sometime between 1683-1709 in Delhi (Fig. 60). The patron came from Bukhara in 1683, and

Fig. 59: Jami Mosque, Merta

the *madrasa's* general layout reflects contemporary trends in Bukhara where *madrasas* were built in large numbers. It is a quadrangular building, entered on the east by a fine gate with projecting extended windows surmounted by curved roofs. In Shahjahan's time this feature was reserved for imperial use, but as early as 1660-61, as is seen on the curved roof surmounting freestanding pavilions at the Mathura Jami mosque, became common on much Mughal architecture.

The imperial Mughals having forsaken large scale tombs for humble ones intended to reflect their own piety, clearly influenced the pious wealthy to follow suit. Ghaziuddin's own tomb set inside his Delhi *madrasa* compound, is an example of this sort. In Ajmer, too, the tomb of Abdullah's wife (dated 1702) is similar in appearance, but in the same complex the tomb of her husband (father of the Sayyid brothers who held the reigns of power during the rule of a later Mughal ruler) is a structural one. Others continued to build in the monumental tradition; the tomb of Sardar Khan in Ahmedabad is illustrative of this.

Fig. 62: Zafar Mahal, Dargah of Bakhtiyar Kaki, Delhi

THE LATER MUGHALS (1707-1858)

The Mughal dynasty lasted 150 years after Aurangzeb's death, but as the strength and wealth of the imperial Mughals waned, so too the size of the empire decreased until finally it was reduced to the city of Delhi. Tormenting the Mughal dynasty were issues of political intrigue, financial problems, invasions and simply ill-prepared rulers. As the Mughal empire diminished new powers emerged in its stead: in the east, north and Deccan, Shia Muslim houses came to the fore, while elsewhere Rajput Hindus were able to assert their authority as never before. Marathas, also Hindu and one of Aurangzeb's biggest headaches, became powerful forces in the west, while Hindu Jats were able to carve out kingdoms in western India and areas around Delhi. Sikh rulers asserted themselves in the Punjab, the hilly areas of northwestern India, and in Lahore. To add to this potpourri of new players were also the British who slowly but surely built their own empire which replaced Mughal authority in 1858. Architectural production is rarely considered during these last 150 years; when buildings are discussed they are generally deemed to be decadent, as if political decline is reflected in architectural terms. Even when the architecture of many of these splinter states is discussed (although it rarely is), it too is seen as being a Mughal derivative with little redeeming qualities. In fact a good deal of innovation is seen in buildings produced under the later Mughals and particularly in those built by the many new emerging Indian powers.

Significant Mughal contributions to architecture were essentially limited to the walled city of Delhi and its suburbs during this last century and a half of Mughal rule. Here we see a change from patronage dominated by the imperial family to that dominated by wealthy nobles and even an increasingly wealthy merchant class. The imperial family largely restricted their beneficence to *dargahs*, including the placement of their own tombs inside those compounds. Muhammad Shah (1719-1748) was buried at the *dargah* of Nizamuddin Auliya, next to Jahanara's earlier tomb; it is similar in appearance although it lacks an inscribed marble headstone (Fig. 61). For political reasons Mughal access to Ajmer was difficult, hence patronage at yet another Delhi shrine, the *dargah* of the fourteenth century Chishti saint, Qutbuddin Bakhtiyar Kaki, increased. Babur while reenacting Timur's tour of the city had visited the *dargah*, but since then there had been little imperial interest in the shrine. From Aurangzeb's time the shrine became more significant; under Shah Alam (1707-19) and subsequent rulers this *dargah's* importance escalated. Shah Alam commissioned a mosque and built his tomb here following the pattern initiated with Jahanara's tomb. By placing their own white marble tombs at these shrines, the later Mughals were still asserting their elevated status; but now they emphasized their own piety in a much more public manner than the earlier Mughals.

The last Mughal emperor, Bahadur Shah II (1837-58) constructed his own palace known as the Zafar Mahal at the shrine of Bakhtiyar Kaki (Fig. 62) in Delhi. All that survives is its entrance gate dated 1847-48; its red sandstone facade faced with white marble recalls the palace architecture of the earlier Mughals. Its appearance, more than the pure white structures provided by rulers such as Shahjahan, indicates unambiguous imperial presence at the shrine. Moreover, it was here that the drums were sounded to announce that the king was in residence—in this case, at the *dargah*. Thus this last Mughal ruler, himself a Sufi and a great poet, merged the two meanings of *dargah* which are palace and shrine, blurring further than ever before the line between saints and royalty.

Although the construction of large scale tombs was relatively rare during this period, two notable ones exist. Both the tomb of Safdar Jang, the Mughal governor of Awadh, and the tomb that Shah Alam II built for his mother and daughter are located south of the walled city where there was plenty of space for gardens and large structures. Shah Alam ordered a red sandstone building, known today as Lal Bangala, for his female

Fig. 61: Grave of Muhammad Shah, Dargah of Nizamuddin Auliya, Delhi

family members. The single domed structure has an internal *hasht behisht* arrangement. Safdar Jang (d. 1754) is buried in an enormous edifice, provided by his son, that resembles Humayun's mausoleum in both plan, appearance and setting.

During the eighteenth and nineteenth centuries dozens of mosques were built in Delhi and its surroundings. These relatively small mosques were paid for by a variety of people from prime ministers to milkmaids,[79] suggesting that wealth, not only rank, empowered people to build. Most of these mosques, such as the one provided in 1721-22 by an immensely powerful noble, Roshanuddaula, in Chandni Chowk, are surrounded by shops on the increasingly crowded thoroughfares. This mosque, like most then being built in Delhi, was faced with stucco on the exterior and interior, but a notable example of a red sandstone and white marble mosque is the Fakhr al-Masajid (Pride of the Mosques). In the tradition of the female elite embellishing the city, it was built in 1728-29 by a noblewoman, Fakhr-i Jahan, in honour of her recently deceased husband who had served Aurangzeb. Nearly all these mosques are single aisled, with three entrances from the east and are surmounted by three domes. Fakhr-i Jahan's mosque's appearance, more than any other contemporary structure in Delhi, links the building and thus the patron with the earlier Mughal

---

79. List I: 114-15. See my 'Mapping Hindu-Muslim Identities Through the Architecture of Shahjahanabad and Jaipur,' *Beyond Turk and Hindu: Rethinking Religious Identities in Islamicate South Asia*, in David Gilmartin and Bruce Lawrence, eds., (Gainsville, FL, 2000), pp. 121-148, for a more detailed discussion.

glory. Only a century later Ghalib, the famous poet, would pen verses proclaiming Shahjahan's reign as a golden age.[80]

During this period the wealth and power of the merchant class, many of them Hindus and Jains, increased. Architecturally this is manifest in the numerous temples that began to be built in the walled city of Delhi: some originally date to the eighteenth century, but the bulk were constructed in the nineteenth century. Most of the Hindu ones are dedicated to the deity Shiva, and are usually small circular temples whose single domes are supported by pillars; they are often located inside walled courtyards and, hence, are not readily visible from outside. The Jain temples are larger, although they have often been increased in size since 1858. Their interiors are generally sumptuously covered with gold gilt and fine painting.[81]

In 1803 the British gained control of Delhi. The Mughal emperor, however, was retained on the throne, in recognition of his great symbolic authority. Although the British resided mostly north of the walled city and established estates with colonial style bungalows, a few churches were built within the walled city. The most significant is St. James's church located just near the city's Kashmir gate. Provided by the colourful Colonel James Skinner (d. 1841), whose father was European and mother Indian, this domed Greek-plan church was consecrated in 1836. The interior, however, is similar in plan to octagonal tombs of the pre-Mughal period, also in Delhi. Skinner played a major role in the consolidation of north Indian territory for the British in the first half of the nineteenth century.

East of Delhi two former imperial governors established independent states. The more powerful of the two was the Nawab of Awadh whose headquarters were in Lucknow. The other was the Nawab of Murshidabad in Bengal. These rulers, however, were reluctant to completely break with the Mughals. They continued to send tribute, for Mughal custom and culture stood for an established and highly regarded social order. In both Lucknow and Murshidabad numerous palaces, gardens, tombs, and mosques were constructed. In addition, new building types developed as a direct result of their devotion to the Shia sect. The history of the *imambara*, *medina*, *husainia* and *karbala* (all structures associated with the ritual commemoration of Husain's martyrdom) in north India is still obscure. But starting from the eighteenth century such structures were built in large numbers at these Shia courts. Of particular note was the truly gigantic *imambara* commissioned in 1784 by Nawab Asifuddaula in Lucknow. This enormous complex consisting of the *imambara* hall itself, a huge mosque, several courtyards, a stepwell and a massive gate, known as the Rumi Darwaza (Fig. 63) was built to provide work for subjects suffering from a serious famine. Encouraging even the

Fig. 63

Fig. 64

Fig. 63: Rumi Darwaza, central bay, Lucknow
Fig. 64: Hazarduari Palace of Nawab Humayun Jah, Murshidabad

Fig. 65: Govind Deva Temple, Jaipur.

high-born to join in, the ruler himself laboured on the project as an act of piety. The gate, whose central elevation was surrounded by a finial from which water spouted, was highly creative and considerably more flamboyant than the more orderly Mughal architecture on which it is loosely modelled.

Muslim religious architecture in north India during this period is largely based on Mughal prototypes and bears, like Mughal architecture itself, little if any imprint of any European architecture. This is not the case with secular architecture constructed in the very same locales which is often influenced by European styles. Such palaces were erected in both Murshidabad and Lucknow, the most extreme example being the Hazarduari (1000 doors) Palace, built between 1829-37 by Nawab Humayun Jah in Murshidabad (Fig. 64). The palace was designed by a European, Duncan McLeod, and modelled on European country estates. Whether or not the Nawab had any say in the plans is unclear, for by now a British agent of the East India Company essentially ruled the area. He certainly never lived in the palace, but used it for administrative purposes and for entertaining the British who, as the style of the enormous neo-classical building suggests, were the real masters.[82]

To the West of Delhi, Rajput houses formerly loyal to the Mughals sought independence as well. An excellent case in point are the Kachhwaha Rajputs of Amber who by the early-eighteenth century had distanced themselves from Mughal authority. In 1727 Jai Singh (1688-1743), the Kachhwaha raja, built a new city, Jaipur, on the flat plain beneath Amber fort which was, like all older Rajput citadels, sited on hilly terrain. Based on ancient Sanskrit texts that discuss ideal cities, Jaipur was completely planned. Wide streets intersect the city in a grid like manner making it much more orderly than Shahjahanabad which was only partially planned. The two main streets lead to two important temples situated outside the city's walls and atop high hills. Although small, these temples can be seen from a considerable distance. This is not true, however, of the city's most important temple, the Govind Deva temple (Fig. 65), which is situated in the Raja's palace grounds. Like contemporary temples of Delhi, it is essentially invisible from the exterior. Only the raja, looking down on it from the multi-storeyed palace pavilion which

---

80. Ralph Russell and Khurshidul Islam, eds., *Life and Letters, vol. I of Ghalib, 1797-1869* (London, 1969), 73, and Pavan K. Varma, *Ghalib— the Man, the Times* (New Delhi, 1989), p. 35.
81. List I: 36, 125, 127, 130, 132, 137-8, 140-1, 151. Also see this author's, 'Hidden Gold: Jain Temples of Delhi and Jaipur and Their Urban Context,' in Olle Qvarnstrom, ed., *Essays in Honour of Padmanabh Jaini* (Lund: University of Sweden), forthcoming and 'North India's Urban Landscape: The Place of the Jain Temple,' *Islamic Culture*, LXXIII, 3 (1999), pp. 109-50.
82. Catherine B. Asher, 'Architecture of the Later Mughals and Mughal Successor States,' in Christopher London, ed., *Architecture in Victorian and Edwardian India* (Bombay, 1994), pp. 91-92.

The Magnificent Mughals

Fig. 66: Hawa Mahal, Jaipur

Fig. 67: Life Insurance Building by Charles Correa, Delhi

contained his living quarters, could see the temple and its *char bagh* setting from afar. This temple houses the same image that was originally in the Govind Deva temple in Vrindavan, but had been shifted when Aurangzeb issued orders to damage it. Patterned on Shahjahan's Public Audience Halls in the Delhi, Agra and Lahore forts, this structure introduced a new temple design that later became typical throughout much of north India. Here the deity is situated in the position of a Mughal ruler's throne. Thus the notion of the temple conceived as a palace comes into play. Many such temples were built throughout Jaipur during the eighteenth and nineteenth centuries; all of them from the exterior appear as simple dwellings or shops, perhaps underscoring the secular nature of Jai Singh's city.[83]

Jai Singh's palace is a vast complex consisting of numerous pavilions as are Mughal palaces. However the Mughal emphasis on symmetry is avoided. Instead there is an emphasis on height, as in the raja's dwelling, the Chandra Mahal; or in the Hawa Mahal, an addition to the palace almost surely used as a viewing platform for women, provided by a Kachhwaha successor in 1799 (Fig. 66).[84] Its facade, overlooking the main street where processions were held, resembles a honeycomb with six storeys of projecting windows. Each floor duplicates the other utilizing traditional Indian building concepts, while the eighteenth century characteristics of height, lightness, and grace are maintained.

Elsewhere, palaces and forts were constructed in areas once held by the Mughals, for example, by the Jat Hindu rulers of Deeg and Bharatpur. While the general shape of individual chambers and vaulted roofs derive from Shahjahan's architecture, as in the Keshav Bhavan at Deeg, an interest in highly articulated designs and even mechanical devices that emulate rain and thunder give these buildings a playfulness not found in Mughal architecture. Rain and thunder evoke the relief from intense heat brought by the monsoon and are often used as a metaphor for the yearning of lovers, a theme of much Hindu poetry and painting.

AFTERMATH

The Mughal dynasty ended in 1858 when the British tried the last Mughal emperor Bahadur Shah for 'treason' in connection with the Revolt of 1857. He was then exiled to Rangoon.[85] At his death in 1862 his supporters, who saw him as a martyr and Sufi, wished to build a mausoleum for him in the tradition of the Taj Mahal.[86] That proposal was flatly rejected by the British as they had no wish to valorize him or the dynasty. The British were only too aware of the power of Mughal architecture and earlier had fully acknowledged the importance of the Mughal architectural tradition in two ways. One was the construction of the Prince of Wales' Royal Pavilion in Brighton in the early eighteenth century, whose rather fantastic domed and arched exterior is an amazing interpretation of Mughal mosque architecture. The second was the creation by the British of an entirely new architectural style, known as the Indo-Saracenic.[87] Such buildings were a pastiche of elements from past Indian architectural traditions, especially Mughal ones. An example is the Mayo College in Ajmer (1875-85), built to educate the Indian princes in a 'proper' British manner. Arches, domes, and *chattris* are found on a structure whose features, while Indian, had been manipulated and placed on it in a unique manner expressing, ultimately, British authority. Indo-Saracenic buildings were constructed well into the twentieth century and the British even introduced a Mughalized style which they felt was appropriate for mosque architecture in British-controlled Malaya.[88]

Today though, the most significant reference to a Mughal architectural past is seen in the Life Insurance Building (1975-86) designed by the Indian architect, Charles Correa (Fig. 67). Situated at the edge of Connaught Circus (the British-provided neo-classical shopping centre), the facade of this multi-storeyed high

---

83. Joan L. Erdman, 'Jaipur: City Planning in eighteenth Century India,' in Anna Libera Dallapiccola et al., ed., *Shastric Traditions in Indian Art*, 2 vols. (Stuttgart, 1989), I: 233.
84. Deborah S. Hutton, ' "Purdah Palace" and Political Space: A Reinterpretation of the Hawa Mahal,' unpublished paper.
85. Percival Spear, *Twilight of the Mughuls: Studies in Late Mughul Delhi*, Cambridge, 1951, p. 226.
86. Madhi Husain, *Bahadur Shah II and the War of 1857 in Delhi with Its Unforgettable Scenes*, Delhi, 1958, pp. 429-34.
87. Thomas R. Metcalf, *An Imperial Vision: Indian Architecture and Britain's Raj*, Berkeley, 1989, pp. 55-104.
88. Thomas R. Metcalf. 'Past and Present: Towards an Aesthetics of Colonialism,' in G.H.R. Tillotson, ed., *Paradigms of Indian Architecture: Space and Time in Representation and Design*, Richmond, Surrey, 1998, pp. 20-24.

rise building is a combination of red sandstone and a glass curtain window. The building itself is a statement of modernity whose glass facade reflects the nearby colonial arcade, while the towering structure with its red sandstone facing is, in the words of Correa himself, a reference to the Mughal past, most especially the high entrance gates at Fatehpur Sikri and Shahjahan's Delhi mosque.[89] Here is an instance where the Mughal past becomes part of South Asia's present on a building whose interior activities are intended to serve the Subcontinent's future.

BIBLIOGRAPHY

Abul-Fazl. *Ain-i Akbari*. 3 vols. Vol. I, tr. H. Blochmann, Vols. II and III tr. H.S. Jarrett, reprint eds. Delhi and New Delhi, 1965-78.

Abul-Fazl. *Akbar Nama*. 3 vols., tr. H. Beveridge, reprint ed., Delhi, 1972-73.

Ambashtya, B.P., ed. *Contributions on Akbar and the Parsees*. Patna, 1976.

Asher, Catherine B. 'Appropriating the Past: Jahangir's Pillars,' *Islamic Culture* LXXXI, 4, 1997, pp. 1-16.

Asher, Catherine B. 'Architecture of the Later Mughals and Mughal Successor States,' in Christopher London, ed., *Architecture in Victorian and Edwardian India*. Bombay, 1994, pp. 85-98.

Asher, Catherine B. *Architecture of Mughal India*. Cambridge, 1992.

Asher, Catherine B. 'Babur and the Timurid Char-Bagh: Use and Meaning,' *Environmental Design* I-2, 1991, pp. 46-55.

Asher, Catherine B. 'Gardens of the Nobility: Raja Man Singh and the Bagh-i Wah,' in Mahmood Hussain, Abdul Rehman and James L. Wescoat Jr., eds., *The Mughal Garden: Interpretation, Conservation and Implications*. Lahore, 1996, pp. 61-72.

Asher, Catherine B. 'Hidden Gold: Jain Temples of Delhi and Jaipur and Their Urban Context,' in Olle Qvarnstrom, ed., *Essays in Honor of Padmanabh Jaini*. Lund: University of Sweden, forthcoming.

Asher, Catherine B. 'Legacy and Legitimacy: Sher Shah's Patronage of Imperial Mausolea,' in Katherine P. Ewing, ed., *Shari'at and Ambiguity in South Asian Islam*. Berkeley, 1988, pp. 79-97.

Asher, Catherine B. 'Mapping Hindu-Muslim Identities Through the Architecture of Shahjahanabad and Jaipur,' in David Gilmartin and Bruce Lawrence, eds., *Beyond Turk and Hindu: Rethinking Religious Identities in Islamicate South Asia*. Gainsville, FL, 2000.

Asher, Catherine B. 'North India's Urban Landscape: The Place of the Jain Temple,' *Islamic Culture*, LXXIII, 3, 1999, pp. 109-50.

Asher, Catherine B. 'Sub-Imperial Palaces: Power and Authority in Mughal India,' *Ars Orientalis* XXXIII, 1993, pp. 281-302.

Asher, Catherine B. 'Sub-Imperial Patronage: The Architecture of Raja Man Singh,' in Barbara S. Miller, ed., *The Powers of Art: Patronage in Indian Culture*. New Delhi, 1992, pp. 183-201.

Babur, Zahir al-Din Muhammad. *The Baburnama: Memoirs of Babur, Prince and Emperor*, tr. Wheeler M. Thackston. Washington D.C. and New York, 1995.

Begley, Wayne E. 'The Myth of the Taj Mahal and a New Theory of Its Symbolic Meaning,' *The Art Bulletin* 61, 1979, pp. 7-37.

Begley, Wayne E. and Z.A. Desai. *Taj Mahal: The Illumined Tomb An Anthology of Seventeenth-Century Mughal and European Documentary Sources*. Cambridge, MA, 1989.

---

89. Vinod Gupta. 'Changing Trends in Office Building Design.' *Architecture and Design* 9, 6, 1992, pp. 30-37.

Blake, Stephen P. *Shahjahanabad: The Sovereign City in Mughal India 1639-1739*. Cambridge, 1991.

Brand, Michael and Glenn D. Lowry, *Akbar's India: Art From the Mughal City of Victory*. New York, 1985.

Case, Margaret, ed. *Govindadeva: A Dialogue in Stone*. New Delhi, 1996.

Crane, Howard. 'The Patronage of Zahir al-Din Babur and the Origins of Mughal Architecture,' *Bulletin of the Asia Institute* 1, 1987, pp. 95-110.

Erdman, Joan L. 'Jaipur: City Planning in 18th Century India,' in Anna Libera Dallapiccola et al., ed., *Shastric Traditions in Indian Art*, 2 vols. Stuttgart, 1989, 1:219-33.

Golombek, Lisa and Donald Wilber, *The Timurid Architecture of Iran and Turan*, 2 vols. Princeton, 1988.

Gopal, Sarvepalli, ed., *Anatomy of a Confrontation: The Babri Masjid-Ramjanmabhumi Issue*. New Delhi and New York, 1991.

Goswamy, B.N. and J.S. Grewal, *The Mughals and the Jogis of Jakhbar: Some Madad-i Ma'ash and Other Documents*. Simla, 1967.

Gupta, Vinod. 'Changing Trends in Office Building Design', *Architecture and Design* 9, 6, 1992, pp. 30-37.

Hasrat, Bikrama Jit. *Dara Shikuh: Life and Works*. New Delhi, 1982.

Husain, Madhi. *Bahadur Shah II and the War of 1857 in Delhi with Its Unforgettable Scenes*. Delhi, 1958.

Hutton, Deborah S. " 'Purdah Palace' and Political Space: A Reinterpretation of the Hawa Mahal," unpublished paper.

Jahangir, Muhammad Nur al-Din. *Tuzuk-i Jahangiri*, 2 vols., tr. A Rogers, reprinted. Delhi, 1968.

Joffee, Jennifer. 'The Art of Politics, the Politics of Art: The Jagdi Temple in Udaipur,' presented at the American Council of Southern Asian Art, Symposium VIII, Charleston, South Carolina, November 1, 1998.

Kanbo, Muhammad Salih. *'Amal-i Salih*, 3 vols. Lahore, 1967.

Khan, Iqtidar Alam. 'The Nobility Under Akbar and the Development of his Religious Policy', *Journal of the Royal Asiatic Society* 1968 (1-2), pp. 29-36.

Khan, Saqi Must'ad. *Maasir-i Alamgiri*, tr. Jadu Nath Sarkar. Calcutta, 1947.

Khan, Zulfikar. "The Taj Mahal—a Hindu Temple-Palace." <http://www.flex.com/~jai/satyamevajayate/tejo.html> (17 June 1999).

Koch, Ebba. 'The Architectural Forms,' in Michael Brand and Glenn D. Lowry, eds., *Fatehpur Sikri*. Bombay, 1987, pp. 121-48.

Koch, Ebba. 'The Delhi of the Mughals Prior to Shahjahanabad as Reflected in the Patterns of Imperial Visits,' in Ahsan Jan Qaisar and Som Prakash Verma, eds., *Art and Culture: Felicitation Volume in Honour of Professor S. Nurul Hasan*. Jaipur, 1993, pp. 1-20.

Koch, Ebba. 'Diwan-i 'Amm and Chihil Sutun: The Audience Halls of Shah Jahan,' *Muqarnas* 11, 1995, pp. 143-65.

Koch, Ebba. 'Influence of Mughal Architecture,' in George Michell, ed., *Ahmadabad*. Bombay, 1988, pp. 168-85.

Koch, Ebba. 'Jahangir and the Angels: Recently Discovered Wall Paintings under European Influence in the Fort of Lahore,' in J. Deppert, ed., *India and the West*. New Delhi, 1983, pp. 173-95.

Koch, Ebba. *Mughal Architecture: An Outline of its History, and Development (1526-1858)*. Munich, 1991.

Koch, Ebba. *Shah Jahan and Orpheus*. Graz, 1988.

List of Muhammadan and Hindu Monuments: Delhi Province, 4 vols. Calcutta, 1916-22.

Lowry, Glenn D. 'Humayun's Tomb: Form, Function and Meaning in Early Mughal Architecture,' *Muqarnas* 4, 1987, pp. 133-48

Lowry, Glenn D. 'Urban Structures and Functions,' in Michael Brand and Glenn D. Lowry, eds., *Fatehpur Sikri*. Bombay, 1987, pp. 25-48.

Metcalf, Thomas R. *An Imperial Vision: Indian Architecture and Britain's Raj*. Berkeley, 1989.

Metcalf, Thomas R. 'Past and Present: Towards an Aesthetics of Colonialism,' in G.H.R. Tillotson, ed., *Paradigms of Indian Architecture: Space and Time in Representation and Design*. Richmond, Surrey, 1998, pp. 12-25.

Moynihan, Elizabeth B. 'The Lotus Garden Palace of Zahir al-Din Muhammad Babur,' *Muqarnas* 5, 1988, pp. 135-52.

Mukherjee, Tarapada and Irfan Habib. 'Akbar and the Temples Mathura and its Environs,' *Proceedings of the Indian History Congress, 48th Session*. Panajim, Goa, 1988, pp. 234-50.

Mukherjee, Tarapada and Irfan Habib. 'The Mughal Administration and the Temples of Vrindavan during the Reigns of Jahangir and Shahjahan,' *Proceedings of the Indian History Congress, 49th Session*. Dharwad, 1989, pp. 287-99.

Nur Bakhsh. 'The Agra Fort and its Buildings,' Annual Report of the Archaeological Survey of India, 1903-04. Calcutta, 1906, pp. 164-93.

Oak, P.N. *Delhi's Red Fort is Hindu Lal Kot*. Bombay, 1976.

Oak, P.N. *Taj Mahal is a Hindu Palace*. New Delhi, 1968.

Oak, P.N. *The Taj Mahal is a Temple Palace*. New Delhi, 1974.

Pal, Pratapaditya and Janice Leoshko et al., *Romance of the Taj Mahal*. Los Angeles and London, 1989.

Petruccioli, Attilio. *Fatehpur Sikri: Citta del Sole e delle Acque*. Rome, 1988.

Petruccioli, Attilio. 'The Geometry of Power,' in Michael Brand and Glenn D. Lowry, eds., *Fatehpur Sikri*. Bombay, 1987.

Petruccioli, Attilio. *Fatehpur Sikri*. Bombay, 1987, pp. 49-64.

Prasad, Pushpa. 'Akbar and the Jains,' in Irfan Habib, ed. *Akbar and His India*. Delhi, 1997, pp. 97-108.

Richards, J.F. 'The Formulation of Imperial Authority Under Akbar and Jahangir,' in J.F. Richards, ed., *Authority and Kingship in South Asia*. Madison, 1978, pp. 252-85.

Ruggles, D. Fairchild. 'Vision and Power: An Introduction', in D. Fairchild Ruggles, ed., *Women, Patronage and Self-Representation in Islamic Societies*. Albany, NY, 2000.

Russell, Ralph and Khurshidul Islam, eds., *Life and Letters, vol. I of Ghalib, 1797-1869*. London, 1969.

Sarkar, Jadunath. *History of Aurangzeb*, 5 vols. Calcutta, 1925-30.

Sen, Geeti. *Paintings from the Akbar Nama*. Varanasi, 1984.

Sinha, S.N. *Subah of Allahabad under the Great Mughals*. New Delhi, 1974.

Smith, Edmund W. 'Akbar's Tomb, Sikandarah,' Archaeological Survey of India, *New Imperial Series*, XXV. Allahabad, 1909.

Spear, Percival. *Twilight of the Mughuls: Studies in Late Mughul Delhi*. Cambridge, 1951.

Tavernier, Jean-Baptiste. *Travels in India*, 2 vols., tr. V. Ball, ed. William Crooke, 2nd. ed. London, 1925.

Tillotson, G.H.R. *The Rajput Palaces: The Development of an Architectural Style, 1450-1750*. New Haven, 1987.

Varma, Pavan K. *Ghalib—the Man, the Times*. New Delhi, 1989.

Top: Jami Mosque (Shahjahani), gallery, Thatta
Photo: Fahd Beg
Left: Tomb of Mirza Isa Khan Tarkhan, Mughal Governor of Sindh, ca. 1630. Makli, Thatta, Pakistan
Photo: Homayra Ziad

8
MUSIC AND DANCE
Bonnie C. Wade

The history of music in the Mughal period is the story of a very gradual synthesis of South Asian with Central and West Asian musical traditions on the one hand, and the gradual indigenization of Mughal court music and dance on the other. Hazarding an extreme generalization, it can be said that there were three particularly significant causal factors in that synthesis: (1) socio-politically, inclusive rather than exclusive *modus operandi* on the part of the Mughal rulers, including intermarriage; (2) the shared religious experience of similar devotional currents in Hindu (*bhakti*) and Muslim (Sufi) life of the time; and (3) a mutual cultural appreciation of dance traditions including the music. This chapter shall discuss music during the period of Mughal rule in the Subcontinent (1526-1858) both at the imperial court and later in regional centres, following the story in chronological order, from Babur (r. 1526-30), the founder of the Mughal dynasty, through Bahadur Shah II (r. 1837-58), the last occupant of the throne.

The process of synthesis of the Hindu South Asian and Muslim Central and West Asian (Persia and the Arab lands) cultures had long been underway in the northern and central regions of the Subcontinent, initiated by Muslim rule starting from the eleventh century. It is well known to music historians that a synthesis of West Asian music with South Asian had been in progress for a considerable time when the *Sangita Ratnakara*, a thirteenth-century Sanskrit treatise confirmed it in theoretical writing. In the fourteenth century, the storyteller, Nakhshabi, suggested as much in the story of the thirteenth night in his *Tutinama*.

> O Nakhshabi, playing the *tar* with skill is a rare art. Listening to doleful music makes the tears flow like streams. Who can make a melody out of the sound of the wind? To play the *tar* and sing, one must originate new themes. A person should know...out of how many Indian melodies one Persian melody can be formulated, or how many Indian melodies are contained in one Persian melody. He must know which of these [Indian] melodies is masculine and which is feminine... If in the process of composition, the masculine of a melody is combined with the feminine of another, neither will the listener derive any pleasure from hearing it, nor will the musician have any desire to play or to sing it. He should know who the originators and the masters of this science were.[1]

Instruments of various origins were not only played in discrete ensembles in one locus—in a court context, for instance—but were also performed together in ensembles, if pictorial evidence can be believed. In a painting dated to 1534 of the Sultanate ruler Muhammad Tughluq (r. 1325-51), for instance, two dancer-with-ensemble groups are depicted (Fig. 1). The instruments are a mixture of South and West Asian: in one group a woman musician is playing the South Asian plucked stick-zither (*rudra vina*), the other is blowing a West Asian vertical flute (*na'i*); in the second ensemble, a player of the South Asian barrel-shaped drum (*pakhavaj*) and singers—one of whom holds the South Asian hand-cymbals used for dance (*tala*)—perform while others play on the West Asian frame drum (*da'ira*) and long-necked plucked lute.

The process of synthesis in the sphere of dance was much slower than in music. In Fig. 1, the dancers hold a South Asian stance: bent knees, and one leg lifted toward the other at about the level of the knee. Dance historian Kapila Vatsyayan confirms that Sultanate paintings from the twelfth to the sixteenth centuries, and particularly from the fourteenth to the sixteenth centuries, show no evidence that other dance styles had fused with South Asian.[2] The first evidence occurs in Mughal paintings.

The heralding ensemble (*naubat*, or *naqqara khana*), an extremely important West Asian symbol of power for rulers, was another product of earlier cultural integration; both the instruments and the fact that it symbolized kingship were already well in place before the Mughals arrived. That the immediate Muslim predecessors of the Mughals in India practiced the periodic daily sounding of an imperial musical ensemble is well-documented.[3] In Fig. 2, the *naubat* ensemble is lined up to the right.

BABUR

The cultural situation was already complex when Babur came to Hindustan. From Babur's memoirs (the *Babur Nama*), we learn that he was a musically-involved person, and we also obtain a sense of the important role that music continued to have in the lives of the imperial family. As Babur moved—from Andijan, his Central Asian home, to Kabul, and finally

Fig. 1: A Nautch Party at the Court of Mohammed Tughluk.
From a Sultanate manuscript, 1534, by Shapur of Khurasan. After *Imaging Sound*, University of Chicago Press, 1998, by Bonnie C. Wade, Fig. 60. The top ensemble consists of a singer at the top who holds the South Asian *tala* cymbal and possibly a second singer down to her right. Below the singer is a player of the South Asian *pakhavaj* drum. The long-necked plucked lute and tambourine-type instrument (*da'ira*) are West Asian. The dancers' style is South Asian.

to Delhi—he commented in great detail on people, customs, events, nature, and much else. Babur was a music critic with acumen, which permitted him to observe that there were distinct regional as well as individual musical styles: 'Hafiz Haji sang well, as Heri people sing, quietly, delicately, and in tune. With Jahangir Mirza was a Samarkandi singer Mir Jan whose singing was always loud, harsh, and out-of-tune'.[4] Visiting his Timurid elder relative's court in Herat, among the most cultured in the early sixteenth century Persian sphere, he made a detailed accounting of the Sultan's personnel including musicians, again revealing his own musical acuity:

> Of musicians, no-one played the dulcimer so well as Khwaja Abdul-lah Marwarid. Qul-i-Muhammad the *oud* player also played the *ghichak* beautifully and added three strings to it. For many and good preludes (*peshrau*) he had not his equal amongst composers or performers, but this is only true of his preludes. Shaikhi the flutist (*nayi*) was another; it is said he played also the *oud* and *ghichak*, and that he had played the flute from his twelfth or thirteenth year. He once produced a wonderful air on the flute, at one of Badiuz-zaman Mirza's assemblies; Qul-i-Muhammad could not reproduce it on the

---

1. Simsar 1978, p. 98.
2. Vatsyayan 1982, p. 89.
3. *Tabakat-i Nasiri*, pp. 619-21 for example.
4. *Babur Nama*, p. 303.

ghichak, so declared this a worthless in strument; Shaikhi Nayi at once took the *ghichak* from Qul-i-Muhammad's hands and played the air on it, well and in perfect tune.[5]

From such entries we gain as much detail about music as any specifically Mughal source provides, with the single exception of a remarkable compendium, the *Ain-i Akbari*, written two generations later. The instruments Babur mentions are three varieties of plucked lute (*oud*, *rabab*, and *tambur*), a vertical flute (*nayi*), two bowed lutes (*ghichak* and *qubuz*), the heralding/signalling trumpets and drums, the 'Jews'-harp', and a board zither (*qanun*). (See Fig. 3 for some of them.) Of these, the *tambur* (a long-necked lute), the heralding instruments, and the *qanun* remained viable instruments in Hindustani music throughout the entire Mughal period.

We also learn from Babur that musicians were versatile: the flutist played both a plucked and bowed stringed instrument; the *oud* player also played *ghichak*. In addition, he tells us that composers were sometimes different persons from performers (unlike in much improvised music where the two roles are taken by one individual);[6] this impression is confirmed at other points in the memoirs. Indeed, Babur himself may have composed, according to the entry for 7 January 1520:

> Mulla Yarak played an air he had composed in five-time and in the five-line measure (*makhammas*), while I chose to eat a confection (*ma'jun*). He had composed an excellent air. I had not occupied myself with such things for sometime; a wish to compose came over me now, so I composed an air in four-time.[7]

It is clear from the *Babur Nama* that musicians toured from place to place to earn a living within the Persian cultural sphere. It is therefore not surprising to learn that a number of them migrated to South Asia in a steady stream for at least the next fifty years.

Several contexts for music-making were noted through Babur's memoirs—drinking parties, river rafting and boating parties, 'assemblies' hosted by noblemen and princes (*mirza*). The extremely observant and curious Babur even noted details of a ritual that involved instruments—the old Mongol ritual of the proclaiming of the standards when 'hautbois and drums were sounded…'.[8] Celebrations of numerous types called for music and dance—a feast held on the birth of a prince, an important military or political triumph, a marriage festivity. Most of the celebrations were arranged by women in the family, so they as well as the men were important patrons of musicians and dancers in Mughal life. Dancing was enjoyed by Babur's peers themselves:

> After the Evening Prayer we left the Tarab-Khana for a new house in Muzaffar Mirza's winter-quarters. There Yusuf-i-ali danced in the drunken time, and being, as he was, a master in music, danced well. The party waxed very warm there.[9]

That Yusuf-i-ali was not a professional musician is clear in other passages in the *Babur Nama*;[10] he was a commander of military forces, in the service eventually of Babur's son Humayun also.

The presence of female dancers seems to have been taken for granted; they certainly did not cause much evaluative comment. Miniature paintings from the time of Babur's grandson, Akbar, that illustrate books on Timurid and Mongol history place the dancers at important celebratory occasions as just part of the event; perhaps oral tradition informed the painters that such occasions would have necessitated their presence. An energetic male style of dancing with one or two swords can also be found in depictions of the time of Babur, Humayun, and of Akbar who was responsible for the production of the paintings (Fig. 4).

HUMAYUN AND AKBAR

For the period of Humayun (r. 1530-40, 1555-56) there is little direct evidence concerning music. Fortunately, his sister Gulbadan Begum's recollections of the time (the *Humayun Nama*), contain some references to musical entertainment. She seems not to have been as involved in music as Babur, because she provides no real detail about the music and dance she patronized. For instance, on the occasion of a celebration to mark the completion of Humayun's first year on the throne, she remarks: 'Young men and pretty girls and elegant women and musicians and sweet-voiced reciters were ordered to sit'[11] and 'young people sat in the room and players made music'.[12] This suggests that both instrumentalists and reciters (of poetry, perhaps, or singers) performed in the same context and that they entertained young people.

Gulbadan Begum also recalled the time in November 1545 when, after five years of exile in Persia, Humayun finally controlled his rebellious half-brother, Kamran, and was reunited with his sisters and mother: 'Again and again we joyfully made the prostration of thanks. There were many festive gatherings, and people sat from evening to dawn, and players and singers made continuous music'.[13] 'Grand entertainments' were held on the occasion of the delayed circumcision of Humayun's heir, the child Akbar; a miniature painting produced for Akbar illustrates both the male and female types of dance entertainment (Fig. 4). Manipulating castanets, the women dancers must have accentuated the rhythm of their movements, as did the player of *da'ira* (frame drum); melody was added by the flutist and it is probable that the drummer sang as well. The male sword dancer was always accompanied in paintings on a pair of bowl-shaped *naqqara* beaten with sticks and with the double-reed *shahna'i*. In Fig. 4, *shahna'i* are blown by two musicians behind the drummers; the addition of a long horn (the instrument is not painted distinctly; its stem is held in the hands of the player but then fades into the balustrade) suggests that this male ensemble also constitutes the heralding ensemble that signified the presence of the ruler.

In the cultural sphere, Humayun can be credited most for having brought to the Subcontinent artists from the Persian court who would guide local and other painters in the development of the Mughal style of miniature painting. Then, under the watchful eye of his successor, Akbar (r. 1556-1605), hundreds of artists in the imperial atelier produced illustrated manuscripts—perhaps as many as forty-six—many of them in multiple copies for presentation as gifts. These illustrations, a remarkable number of which abound with 'sound', together with an assortment of contemporary writings provide an invaluable source about music at the court of Akbar.

Akbar's agenda was one of synthesis: the creation of a distinctly Mughal polity and culture from the fusion of what he and his predecessors had brought with them to South Asia and what he found there. His reign was sufficiently long, so that despite continuous military ventures to expand the territory under his control, a highly creative intellectual and cultural milieu was fostered. In a very real sense, Akbar garnered to a centre (himself and his extensive imperial household) all those elements he needed to establish that distinct culture: good administrative ideas of the Afghani challenger to his father, Sher Shah; loyalty of the strong leaders of competitive Indian groups such as the Rajputs, and to cement those loyalties, Rajput wives who brought with them fully staffed mini-households that contributed to a quintessentially multi-cultural imperial household; musicians from diverse areas of the Persianate world, and others such as the great singer, Tansen, who had adorned rival Indian courts; painters of many styles; and abundant wealth to finance his efforts, from an effective taxation system which drew upon improving economic conditions; among others.

To document his administrative establishment, Akbar commissioned from his official historian, Abul Fazl, the *Ain-i Akbari*—a priceless compendium rich in information for all who study the Akbari period. For instance, along with other ensigns of royalty are meticulously listed the instruments in the imperial heralding ensemble, the *naubat* (or *naqqara khana*); it was both a military band for signalling and a concert band which performed each morning from the tallest gateway to awaken the Mughal sovereign and all within hearing of the imperial household.[14] In Fig. 2 the grand ensemble is there to represent Akbar, at whose behest the occasion was being held.

Like his grandfather, Akbar was a musically-involved person, and he filled his imperial sphere with numerous musicians from various locales in the Timurid/Persianate spheres as well as South Asians. The *Ain-i Akbari* lists thirty-two of the imperial musicians, and passages in his official court chronicle, the *Akbar Nama*, add more information. Instrumentalists came from Transoxiana and Khurasan in Central Asia, cities in Persia such as Mashhad and Herat, and from Kashmir. Singers mentioned were associated with

---

5. Ibid., p. 291.
6. Ibid., pp. 291-2.
7. Ibid., p. 422.
8. Ibid., pp. 154-55; see Wade 1998, p. 47.
9. Ibid., p. 303.
10. Ibid., p. 675, 687.
11. *Humayun Nama*, p. 118.
12. Ibid., p. 126.
13. Ibid., p. 178.
14. *Ain-i Akbari* I, p. 53.

Fig. 2: Royal Musicians Perform at a Marriage.
Akbarnama, 1590 or earlier. Courtesy of the Board of Trustees of the Victoria and Albert Museum, IS.2-1896 f.8/117. The heralding ensemble (*naubat* or *naqqara khana*) on the right announces the presence of the Emperor. Three Indian women in the centre sing and play the drum (*dhol*) and cymbals (*tala*), while Central Asian female musicians accompany dancers on tambourine (*da'ira*).

the South Asian city of Gwalior, among whom was Tansen, the most famous singer of the age. Undoubtedly, also important for the development of music at the court was Baz Bahadur, the ruler of Malwa, whose political downfall brought a talented singer, instrumentalist, and lover of music to the court in the person of the ruler himself (along with some of his female musicians who had been captured earlier).[15]

Akbar participated in the Sufi religious experience and was deeply moved by the devotional genre of *qawwali* (see Glossary for definitions); his official chronicle attests to this by describing his having attained a state of ecstasy:

> At this time, Bakhshu Qawwal recited before him two heart-ravishing stanzas in a pleasing manner. That Syllabus of the roll of recognition (of God) displayed a countenance flashing with Divine lights. Those whose vision did not extend beyond the plain outward appearance received spiritual delight (from the singing)...When H.M. returned from that wonderful condition he gave thanksgiving to God, and filled the hopeskirt of the songster with rich coin.[16]

Badauni also recorded Akbar's visit to the shrine of Khwaja Muinuddin Chishti, the founder of the Chishti order in India, at Ajmer:

> And daily according to his custom held in that sacred shrine by night intercourse with holy, learned, and sincere men, and *seances* for dancing and sufism took place. And the musicians and singers, each one of whom was a paragon without rival, striking their nails into the veins of the heart used to rend the soul with their mournful cries. And *dirhams* and *dinars* were showered down like raindrops.[17]

These insights into Mughal participation in Sufi practice, in particular, hearing a specifically named singer of *qawwali*, are important for situating the importance of Sufism in the Mughal period.

Most of the instruments in early Mughal sources, that is, in the paintings—whether depicting history or contemporary times—or mentioned in writing of the Akbari period are not South Asian instruments. Among the most important was the *tambur* (Fig. 3, bottom row, third from the left). In Babur's time an instrument called *tambur* was used in ensembles and, indeed, in Akbari-period paintings it is depicted with flute and drum. The paintings show a long-necked plucked lute with a shallow wooden bowl, and an ovoid face that tapers to meet a thin, straight neck, along the end of which the pegs are inserted laterally. Strikingly, although four players of *tambur* (one from Herat, one from Mashhad, and two others with Muslim names but whose origin is not given) are included in the list of important imperial musicians in the *Ain-i Akbari*, in Akbari paintings this instrument is placed in scenes depicting locations outside the Subcontinent, or is being held up entreatingly by a marginalized player who stands in a crowd outside a wall, seeking admission to the enclosed favoured internal space. The *tambur* was clearly an instrument on which melody was produced; in some paintings the neck is ringed by frets marking the placement of pitches. The *qanun*, another instrument mentioned in Babur's memoirs, is seldom depicted in Akbari-period paintings, but it was definitely part of the court instrumentarium (Fig. 3, top row, second from the right). Abul Fazl compares it to a similar instrument with an Indian name, the *svarmandal*. This board-zither survives to the present day, utilized to provide a drone background by Punjabi singers of classical music. The *oud*-type of plucked lute that is mentioned by Babur never seems to have found favour in the Mughal sphere. The *ghichak*, a spiked lute that was popular in the Persian cultural sphere particularly for relatively casual male gatherings, is seldom depicted in Akbari-period paintings and when it is, seems to suggest locales outside the Subcontinent (Fig. 3, top row, far left).[18]

A West Asian instrument mentioned by Babur and clearly important in Akbar's sphere as well was the *na'i*, a vertical flute (Fig. 3, bottom row, far left). The *na'i* is a relatively long, thin flute with a cylindrical bore; held in a downward and slightly angled position, it produces a low and sweet tone. A flute-type instrument was likely to play a prominent role in cultural synthesis because it was an instrument of choice in ensembles that accompanied dance across the West, Central and South Asian regions. However, the type of flute used historically in South Asian ensembles was not like the *na'i*: sculpture shows it to have been a side-blown horizontal flute.[19]

---

15. Wade 1998, p. 90.
16. *Akbar Nama* III, p. 378.
17. *Muntakhabu-t-Tawarikh* II, p. 188.
18. Wade 1998, p. 69.
19. Kramrisch 1965, figs. 117 and 118, for example.

Already in the Sultanate period, paintings have the vertical flute rather than the horizontal flute in the hands of musicians accompanying Indian-style dance (Fig. 1), and it is this type which is depicted consistently in Mughal illustrations. Thus, the *na'i* provides historical evidence of cultural synthesis and here the point about the shared appreciation of dance traditions by West, Central, and South Asian audiences also comes into play.

Gender may also have played a role in the process of synthesis. There is some pictorial evidence that women played the vertically-held *na'i* in Persian culture,[20] as there is sculptural evidence that women played the horizontal flute to accompany dance in South Asia. It may be likely that during the *bhakti* movement, which began in the Sultanate period, the Indian horizontal flute became a thoroughly gendered male instrument, strongly associated with religious devotion through music. It is the instrument of Lord Krishna, the capricious cowherd deity who dances and plays his way into the heart of every female. For South Asian women to have played it in the period of the flourishing *bhakti* religious movement may not have seemed appropriate, with the result that Indian female dance accompanists replaced it with the West Asian *na'i*.

In Akbar's court the Turki women dancers of Central/West Asia shared performance time and space with South Asian dancers. Accompanying the Turki dancers was likely to be a player of *na'i* as well as of the frame drum, *da'ira* (Figs. 1-4). Thus, that instrument (*na'i*) was shared as the accompaniment of different dance styles. Dancers would have been able to observe each others' styles in Akbar's extended imperial household and to hear the accompanying music.

Accompanying the South Asian dancers along with *na'i* was the barrel-shaped drum, the *pakhavaj*, that has been in use in the Subcontinent since ancient times (Fig. 2). In Mughal paintings and from the description of the instrument by Abul Fazl it is clear that characteristics of the modern *pakhavaj* were already in place: wooden wedges were inserted near one end under the lashing between the two heads, to permit careful tuning of the drumhead. The paintings consistently show the use of tuning paste as well.

With so much Persianate culture in his court that could be taken for granted, Akbar took pains to learn about and to have recorded (or translated) information about Indic culture. As a result, in the *Ain-i Akbari*, there is a long section on '*Sangita*', 'the art of singing, accompanied by music and dancing',[21] which speaks of the nature of musical sound and musical pitches, intervals, and modes (*ragas*), some performance genres, and elements of improvisation as well as instruments and 'classes' of singers. It is possible to correlate information on musicians and instruments in the miniature paintings with information given in this important source.[22]

One performance genre that Abul Fazl mentions in the *Ain-i Akbari* as performed by Indian musicians who were clearly present in the imperial household is *dhrupad*. In historical accounts of Hindustani music, the development of *dhrupad* has been associated mostly with Gwalior, a kingdom ruled from 1486 to 1516 by an important patron of music, Man Singh Tomar. With wonderful singers in his employ, *dhrupad* emerged as a court genre. Composed in the oldest and best-known *ragas* of the existing classical form, *prabhanda*, but also in more locally known *ragas*, *dhrupad* was an immediately accessible genre; and unlike earlier South Asian classical vocal music, the texts of which were in Sanskrit, the texts of *dhrupads* were in the vernacular Hindi language. Finally, eschewing the classical poetic meters of earlier song, *dhrupad* texts were unconstricted by prosodical length of words or syllables. Of the *dhrupad*, Abul Fazl reported:

> The *Dhrupad* (Dhruva-pada) consists of four rhythmical lines without any definite prosodial length of words or syllables. It treats of the fascinations of love and its wondrous effects upon the heart. In the Dekhan these songs are expressed in their language by the term Chind, and consist of three or four lines, and are chiefly laudatory.[23]

We learn in the *Ain-i Akbari* that performance of the genre by other than the classically-trained musicians continued in the court context at least through Akbar's reign.[24] Developed further into the most prominent vocal genre at the Mughal court by the great singer Tansen, however, *dhrupad* marked the beginning of a new era in Hindustani classical music (see Glossary).

As ruler of the Subcontinent, Akbar asserted his possession of explicitly Indic culture in several ways, including music. (We can know this more from a large number of paintings than from written sources.) In miniature illustrations of formal Akbari court sessions, for example, we see singers with a player of the Indian *rudra vina* (stick zither-type of stringed instrument shown in Fig. 3) embellishing the *durbar* (court), rather than the Persianate ensemble of bowed or plucked lute with frame drum. It probably did not escape Akbar's acute sensitivity that the *vina* was an instrument explicitly associated with numerous Hindu deities and that it was the instrument of the *bhakti* musicians. The *dhrupad* genre which the vocalists were likely to have been singing in the court sessions was one as closely associated with praise of a deity as praise of a king. To be shown seated on his throne with those particular musicians facing him, may very well have suited Akbar's idea of portraying himself as a divinely-inspired monarch. Viewers of the paintings saw a refined assertion of the Mughal ruler's agenda of cultural synthesis.

From paintings one can literally see the prestige of the *rudra vina* increase as it developed into a more substantial instrument in morphological terms, more complex in terms of number of strings and frets, and more ornately adorned (Fig. 4, bottom row, second from left). Naubat Khan, a high-ranking *binkar* in Akbar's court (and in Jahangir's), may have been the individual musician responsible for those physical changes and in playing technique as it was developed toward a solo instrument;[25] this corpulent son-in-law of the great singer, Tansen, is the subject of portraits by Akbari painters and others later in the Mughal period.

Akbar used music in another way as well. Miyan Tansen, who, by oral tradition, is considered the most illustrious singer-musician of the time, graced the court of Akbar from 1562 until his death in 1586. It is clear from the *Akbar Nama* that Tansen had no choice but to leave a Rajput patron, Ramchand, with whom he was happy, to join the Mughal establishment;[26] Akbar insisted, using this occasion to assert his power as the emperor. It is said that Akbar gifted Tansen two hundred thousand rupees on his first performance at court.

In addition to Akbar's avid interest in music, his political power play in depriving Ramchand of his treasured musician, and his patronage of the best contemporary artists, there was probably another element that made Tansen attractive to the Mughal sovereign: there seem to have been multiple cultural strands in Tansen's life—both Hindu and Muslim. For Akbar, whose cultural agenda was to foster synthesis to the maximum extent, such a musician would have been invaluable. The great Hindu saint-singer Sur Das is said to have been a friend of Tansen[27] and Swami Haridas is widely thought to have been his teacher. Other accounts also associate him with Muhammad Ghaus Gwaliori, one of the great Sufi saints of India who was particularly welcoming of Hindus.[28] Muhammad Ghaus may have been the spiritual guide of Tansen. One piece of documentary evidence puts Tansen into an explicitly Sufi context: as told by Jahangir, he was called to sing by the dying Shaikh Salim Chishti, the Sufi saint who had foretold the birth of Akbar's three sons.[29] Sources disagree about whether or not Tansen actually converted to Islam. Two of his five children had Hindu names, although that in itself is not very significant, and the three others may themselves have converted to Islam. In any case, Tansen had a Muslim funeral, as described in the *Akbar Nama*,[30] and was buried in Gwalior, under a *neem* tree in the southwest corner of the mausoleum of Muhammad Ghaus.[31]

Very little is actually known about Tansen's singing style, but his musical legacy as a composer of *dhrupad* and as a singer are legendary. He is credited with the creation of new *ragas* such as *Darbari Kanada*, *Miyan ki Malhar* and *Miyan ki Todi* ('Miyan ki' indicating Tansen's form of a traditional *raga*). That Tansen sang to the accompaniment of the Indian drum, the *pakhavaj*, was asserted by Faqirullah, Mughal governor of Kashmir in the seventeenth century and translator of the book *Raga Darpana*, and it is certainly reasonable to assume that he must have done so. However, there is no *pakhavaj* in the Akbari-period illustrations that show the court ensembles of singers with their *rudra vina* accompanists. At least in the contexts depicted in paintings, marking of the rhythm would not have been

---

20. Wade 1998, p. 89.
21. *Ain-i Akbari* III, pp. 260-73.
22. See Wade 1998, pp. 77-9.
23. *Ain-i Akbari* III, p. 266.
24. Ibid., p. 271.
25. Wade 1998, p. 118-21.
26. *Akbar Nama* II, pp. 279-80.
27. Schimmel 1983, p. 36.
28. Ibid., p. 29.
29. *Tuzuk-i Jahangiri* II, pp. 70-71.
30. *Akbar Nama* III, p. 816.
31. For a full discussion of Tansen, see Wade 1998.

done on a drum, but in the traditional manner of a singer clapping out the metric cycle, or by rhythmic plucking on the *rudra vina*.

The imperial household was inhabited by wealthy women and men whose constant, enthusiastic involvement in the arrangement of festivities made them significant patrons of music and dance. It was a very cosmopolitan, multi-ethnic atmosphere, conducive to cultural synthesis. In artistic terms, Akbar patronized West, Central, and South Asian artists and stimulated Persian-style painting by both Hindus and Muslims, creating the now-familiar style of Mughal miniature painting. In architecture, too, the synthesis of West Asian and South Asian traditions which had begun earlier became more refined under Akbar with the introduction of Timurid and Safavid elements. In addition, regional South Asian styles had been proven to work with non-Indian structures in ways that were extremely satisfactory, aesthetically as well as practically.[32]

Strikingly, while Akbar's patronage of musicians from multiple cultures was undoubtedly fostering synthesis in that sphere as well, the only sure evidence of it in visual sources relates to instruments—presence or absence of one instrument or another, instrument construction, playing position or technique, and other hints. Another indication is the clothing of women musicians. If pictorial content is accurate, the process of synthesis seems to have been slower in music than in art or architecture, relatively speaking. That should not be surprising, as it seems to be axiomatic that music changes more slowly than most other spheres of culture. The reasons for this were probably many. For instance, the South Asian musicians named in the *Ain-i Akbari* list of imperial musicians, had been trained in the traditional Indian system in Gwalior, a system that cultivates ideals of musical discipleship and adherence to tradition. These (along with the several other groups of Indian musicians mentioned by Abul Fazl with specializations other than 'art music') would have been the artists involved in synthesis in the 'art music' sphere. Tansen's presence in Akbar's court may have been especially valuable precisely because he, more than these other musicians, would be likely to encourage musical change.

JAHANGIR AND SHAHJAHAN

The soundscape of the imperial court continued under Jahangir and Shahjahan. Processions and receptions and royal audiences were heralded by ever-larger *naubat* ensembles, with 'the loud beating of the royal drums [making] the glad sounds of rejoicing through the universe'.[33] Some musical changes were occurring—the drums in the *naubat* for one. The magnificent ensembles of the Akbari period, shown in miniature paintings, feature multiple sizes of the bowl-shaped *naqqara* drums, gradually ranging from smaller to larger in a diagonal line (Fig. 2). In the grand *naubat* ensembles pictured both in Jahangiri- and Shahjahani-period paintings, however, relatively smaller drums make an appearance and a tall single drum will contrast with much smaller pairs of drums (Fig. 5). Instead of the straight-down pounding drumming technique of Akbari drummers, the two drums of Jahangiri-period pairs are tilted toward each other, with players shown hitting them with various techniques—crossing hands to strike a drum with the opposite stick, for example. There is a strong possibility that dance-drumming was influencing the ensemble tradition (compare the male drummers in Fig. 4 with those in Fig. 2). In addition, by Shahjahan's time, three major changes occur with respect to the trumpets and horns in the ensemble. The *karna* trumpet with swan's-neck-curved tube disappears from most depictions of the group and the straight-necked version of the *karna* becomes larger and heavier, with a huge bell. Further, the South Asian C-shaped horn appears to be included in the ensemble more frequently.

Beyond the imperial court, the Mughal model of grand marriage processions was taken up. In Fig. 6 a procession in Bilaspur or Mandi (painted ca. 1680) passes through a bazaar. The heralding ensemble features the entire instrumentarium, old and new: the Indian cylindrical drum as well as the *naqqara*, the C-shaped horn (*sing*), and the swan-shaped and straight *karna* as well as *shahna'i*.

---

32. See Asher 1992, pp. 41-67.
33. *Shah Jahan Nama*, p. 408.

Fig. 3: TWELVE MUSICIANS PLAYING INDIAN AND PERSIAN INSTRUMENTS.
Saqi Namah of Zuhuri, Deccan, 1685. By permission of the British Library, OR.338, f.54B. Instruments on the top from left to right: *ghichak*, *rabab*, *qanun*, *sarangi*; in the middle from left to right: *da'ira*, *chang*, *dhol*, panpipe; on the bottom from left to right: *nayi/na'i*, *rudra vina*, *tambur*, *jaltarang*.

Fig. 4: Emperor Humayun at the Celebration of his son Akbar's Circumcision.
Akbarnama, 1596-97 or 1604. By permission of the British Library, OR12988 f. 114A. Female musicians entertain in the private family quarters; dancers dressed in Turki clothing and holding castanets are accompanied by women players of the tambourine (*da'ira*) and vertical flute (*na'i*). In front of the walls a sword dancer is accompanied by dance drums of the *naqqara* type, two double-reed *shah'nais* (one hidden) and a trumpet (*qarna*) that is not completely drawn.

Fig. 5 includes a prominent plucked lute of the Mughal period that resulted from synthesis: a long-necked lute of West Asian origin that came to be used for *dhrupad*-type music (and therefore was referred to as the *dhrupad rabab*). Featuring a ram's horn-shaped protuberance where the long neck is attached to the bowl of the lute, and a distinctive mechanism for attaching the strings, the *dhrupad rabab* does not appear to have been part of the instrumentarium fostered by Akbar. It is in a few paintings, but always contextualizable as South Asian—appearing in a *Mahabharata* illustration, for instance. It may be that this version of the West Asian long-necked plucked lute had been adopted into South Asian culture at some earlier point and was fully in use but in particular sites. In an act of imperial patronage, Jahangir brought it into Mughal court music; being the child of a Rajput mother, he might have known musicians who played this type of *rabab* in his mother's mini-household within the imperial fortress.

To Jahangir's patronage as well can be attributed the fostering in Mughal court music of the South Asian practice of devoting an instrument to keeping a drone pitch. This is perhaps the most significant instance of indigenization of the performance practice of music in the Mughal sphere. Evidence, that devoting an instrument to keeping a reference pitch had been well underway in regional South Asian music in the sixteenth century, can be found in numerous paintings of the genre called *ragamala*. The *ragamala* paintings are so stylized and iconographical (relative to Mughal miniatures) as to warrant only very careful use of them for historical information. However, the consistency with which one-gourd stick zithers (*vinas*) are shown being played over the shoulder with one hand plucking, leaves little doubt that the instruments are being used for something other than producing melody. Rather, the *ragamalas* suggest that keeping a constant drone in *raga*-associated music was common in musical practice in those regions. One can conjecture that Jahangir was familiar with that practice, too, from his mother's household musicians.

It was not a South Asian instrument, however, but the West Asian *tambur* that came to be the drone-keeping instrument in Hindustani classical music (Figs. 3 and 5). From the Jahangiri period on, many works produced in the imperial atelier depict the delicate lutes with long, narrow necks held over the shoulder by musicians in such a position that they could only be played to produce a drone.[34] While male musicians are playing them in the earliest depictions, they quickly appear in illustrations of women musicians as well.

Women dancers and singers were a continuing presence in court life in both the reign of Jahangir and his successor, Shahjahan. An Italian observer of the court of Shahjahan commented on them on the occasion of birthdays and the New Year celebrations at the palace, when the noble ladies of the court were obliged to pay their compliments to the queens and princesses and to offer costly gifts:

> The dancing-women and singing-women receive on these occasions handsome presents from the princesses and other great ladies. They either sing to compliment them on their birthday, or invoke on them all kinds of prosperity when congratulating them at the New Year. The ladies respond then to all the praises, which the singing-women never failed to shower on them, by full trays of gold and silver coin which they throw to them.[35]

While there were certainly women musicians and dancers in Akbari-period paintings, the presence of such large groups of them in the paintings of the *Padshahnama*, the chronicle of Shahjahan's reign, is truly striking. A joyously improvisatory dance is being performed on the occasion of the weighing of Shahjahan on his forty-second lunar birthday (Fig. 5).

In Inayat Khan's condensed version of the chronicle of Shahjahan's reign, there are suggestions that the sovereign took a serious interest in music. That he himself sang may be indicated in the doleful account of the monarch's reaction to the death of his beloved wife Mumtaz Mahal on 17 June 1631:

> For a whole week after this distressing occurrence, His Majesty from excess of grief did not appear in public nor transact any affairs of state... After this calamity, he refrained from the practice of listening to music, singing, and wearing fine linen.[36]

---

34. See Wade 1996.
35. Manucci 1907, II, pp. 322-3.
36. *Shah Jahan Nama*, p. 70.

Otherwise, enjoyment of music was part of the daily routine which Shahjahan followed strictly whether he was in camp or at the capital.[37]

The grand numbers of performing forces in the celebratory paintings of Shahjahan (such as Fig. 5) impart the sense of security of the ruler amidst extreme wealth and elevated status. He was an impressive administrator who consolidated the empire, provided stability and a splendour which exuded the aura that imperial greatness had reached its zenith.

Information on music in regions away from the court is gained primarily from sources that chronicle relationships of the Mughal sovereigns to local cultures. Through illustrations of a manuscript of a *Masnavi* by Zafar Khan, who served as governor of Kashmir under Shahjahan, we glimpse the gracious life led by a Mughal officer in the valley of Kashmir. In 'A Review of Troops' (Fig. 7) three different dance styles are shown. The character with bare torso is doing a folk style called *ghumb*. The stylishly dressed man holds a pose familiar from paintings of dance at court. The long sleeves on one of the two remaining dancers identify him as a dervish.

Dance historian Kapila Vatsyayan sees the trance dance of Sufi dervishes as important in the development of dance in South Asia:

> One aspect of the collective singing of the Sufi devotees was the 'trance dances' of the *dervishes*. Trance dances were performed not in the courts. The Sufi singers and dancers were followers of Nizamuddin Chishti and were known for their dancing in a trance called *Sahebe Hala*. They travelled far and wide and were accompanied by the *Qawaals*. The story of the spread of Sufism is well known, but it is often not recognised that this particular type of singing and dancing also contributed to the making of a distinct North Indian dance style which is identified today as Kathak.[38]

We also learn about music outside the imperial sphere through the political relations of the Mughals as in the case of Baz Bahadur of Malwa, whose fame as a patron of musicians and dancers was well known at the Mughal court. When Akbar took Malwa by force his singers and dancers were taken as booty. Their appearance before Akbar provides us a precious 'photo' of a dance style that appears to be at least related to *Kathak* (Fig. 8).

AURANGZEB THROUGH MUHAMMAD SHAH

It is well known that the youthful Aurangzeb patronized and partook of music and dance just as his predecessors had; it was part of the refined fabric of life at court. Indeed, after the death of his brother Dara Shikoh, Aurangzeb demanded Dara Shikoh's women singers from Shahjahan 'as there is no skilled songstress with me whose music may soothe my ear'.[39] It is equally well known that shortly after succeeding to the throne, Aurangzeb (r. 1658-1707) experienced a change of heart; in 1659 he issued a series of edicts, including appointment of a censor, which were more or less heeded. His proscription of music, historical painting, alcohol, and the drug *bhang* came in a second wave of restrictions in 1668; initially transgressors were severely punished, and the female dancers who had enjoyed great liberty during his father's time were ordered either to marry or leave the court. Indeed, if Manucci's number of five hundred dancers in the court sphere is even anywhere near correct, that group had become excessive. Perhaps balance in the performing ranks really did need to be restored.

As regards music history, Aurangzeb's notoriety has persisted through an oft-told story of his treatment of musicians:

> Aurangzeb took steps against the excessive number of musicians. In Hindustan both Moguls and Hindus are very fond of listening to songs and instrumental music. He therefore ordered [an] official to stop music. If in any house or elsewhere he heard the sound of singing and instruments, he should forthwith hasten there and arrest as many as he could, breaking the instruments. Thus was caused a great destruction of musical instruments. Finding themselves in this difficulty, their large earnings likely to cease, without there being any other mode of seeking a livelihood, the musicians took counsel together and tried to appease the king in the following way: About one thousand of them assembled on a Friday when Aurangzeb was going to the mosque. They came out with over twenty highly-ornamented biers, as is the custom of the country, crying aloud with great grief and many signs of feeling, as if they were escorting to the grave some

---

37. Saksena 1962, pp. 238-43.
38. Vatsyayan 1982, p. 89.
39. Sarkar 1972, III, p. 147.

Music and Dance

Fig. 5: THE WEIGHING OF SHAH JAHAN ON HIS 42ND LUNAR BIRTHDAY.
Painted by Bhola. *Padshah Nama*, ca. 1635. The Royal Collection © 2000 Her Majesty Queen Elizabeth II.
Holmes Binding 149, p. 140, f. 70b. The *naubat/naqqara khana* musicians play from the balcony, while below dancers are accompanied by singing, *dhrupad rabab, rudra vina, dhol, tambur*, castanet and possibly other instruments.

Fig. 6: A Marriage Procession in a Bazaar.
Mandi, Punjab Hills. Mid-17th century. Collection Howard Hodgkin. Reproduced by permission of Howard Hodgkin.

distinguished defunct. From afar Aurangzeb saw this multitude and heard their great weeping and lamentation, and, wondering, sent to know the cause of so much sorrow. The musicians redoubled their outcry and their tears, fancying the king would take compassion upon them. Lamenting, they replied with sobs that the king's orders had killed Music, therefore they were bearing her to the grave. Report was made to the king, who quite calmly remarked that they should pray for the soul of Music, and see that she was thoroughly well buried. In spite of this, the nobles did not cease to listen to songs in secret. This strictness was enforced in the principal cities.[40]

Certain types of music-making continued, however: the official heralding ensemble remained in place, and in the women's quarters music-making could continue. If the gossipy Italian sojourner is to be believed, Aurangzeb's prohibition of music did not extend to the quarters of the queens or his daughters. He even conferred special names on the female superintendents of the women musicians and dancers; Manucci listed thirty-three superintendents with a translation of the titles: 'Surosh Bai' was 'The lady with the good voice' for instance; 'Chanchal Bai' was 'The Bold'; 'Dhyan Bai' was 'The Well-informed'; 'Kesar Bai' was 'Saffron'.[41]

All of the above names are Hindu, and ordinarily these overseers of the music are Hindus by race, who have been carried off in infancy from various villages or the houses of different rebel Hindu princes. In spite of their Hindu names, they are, however, Mahomedans. Each has under her orders about ten apprentices; and along with these apprentices they attend the queens, the princesses, and the concubines. Each one has her special rank according to her standing. The queens and the other ladies pass their time in their rooms, each with her own set of musicians. None of these musicians are allowed to sing elsewhere than in the rooms of the person to whom they are attached, except at some great festival. Then they are all assembled and ordered to sing together some piece or other in praise of, or to the honour of, the festival.[42]

Beyond the imperial household music had to go underground; not buried deeper as Aurangzeb is alleged to have suggested, but kept discreetly out of royal hearing. Although some musicians left for centres such as Alwar in Rajasthan, a large number of musicians remained in Delhi.[43] In the capital, patronage shifted more to princes and members of the nobility and thus musicians catered to a broader audience.

Musical intellectual activity continued, as two of the major Persian-language works on music, *Rag Darpana* and *Tuhfat-al-Hind*, were written during Aurangzeb's reign; both are crucial sources for Hindustani music history. In the reign of Shahjahan Amir Faqirullah had joined imperial service; under Aurangzeb he fought several wars, and was honoured with the title of Saif Khan, as well as the governorship of different states—Kashmir, Allahabad, Multan—from time to time. Faqirullah was a patron of musicians himself, and was highly knowledgeable about music. In 1665 while in Kashmir, he started work on the *Rag Darpana*, a translation of the treatise, *Man Kautuhal*, that had been written during the period of Raja Man Singh Tomar of Gwalior (r. 1486-1516), 'an old manuscript that Faqirullah found'.[44] *Tuhfat-al-Hind* was written either for Aurangzeb himself, or more likely, for his third son, Mohammad Azam, who was a great connoisseur of literature, poetry and music. There is a difference of opinion about its author, who is given as Mirza Jaan, Mirza Khan and Mirza Mohammad in three different manuscripts.[45] One of five parts of the book concerns music. When it was written, the system of *ragas* and *raginis* that are depicted in *ragamala* paintings in a number of regional styles was very much in vogue. While *Tuhfat-al-Hind* refers to previous writing (the *Raga Darpana* of Amir Faqirullah, for instance) the explanation of theory is more comprehensive and clearer and, unusually, it features a detailed chapter on *talas* (musical meters).[46]

In addition, an important Sanskrit text on music was written in 1665: the *Sangitaparijata* of Ahobala. Whereas paintings in the first two decades of the 1600s show the *tambur* being used as a drone instrument with the frets still on it in case melodic playing was desired, the *Sangitaparijata* confirms the full indigenization of the *tambur*, describing both a fretted version for melody and an unfretted version of the instrument for drone-keeping.[47] This text was translated into Persian (called the *Parijatak*) by one Pandit Dinanath in 1724, and Maharaja Sawai Pratap Singh of Jaipur used it as the textual model for his *Sangit Sar* of 1790.

In view of the changes that had already occurred in the reigns of Jahangir and Shahjahan, it seems likely that musicians were ready for further evolution and that the constraining cultural hegemony of the Mughal court

---

40. Manucci 1907, II, p. 5-6.
41. Ibid., p. 313.
42. Ibid., pp. 313-14.
43. B.R. Sharma, 1980, p. 106.
44. Ahmad 1984, pp. 19-21.
45. Ibid., p. 34.
46. Ibid., pp. 34-5, 54-5.
47. Miner 1997, p. 31.

Fig. 6: A MARRIAGE PROCESSION IN A BAZAAR. (DETAIL)
Mandi, Punjab Hills. Mid-17th century. Collection Howard Hodgkin.

Fig. 7: A Review of Troops.
From the *Mathnavi* of Zafar Khan, 1663. F.12r. Courtesy of the Royal Asiatic Society, London.

needed to be disrupted to some extent. Rather than revile Aurangzeb for that, it might be more appropriate to credit him for making possible the acceleration of further significant developments.

For the remainder of the eighteenth century most of the sources available for Hindustani music history are still those of the Mughal court in Delhi, but the stories they tell reveal a gradual popularization of music and dance in relative terms. That is to say, music and dance which must have been going on beyond the imperial household in the early eighteenth century are gradually encompassed by the Mughal court as well. As is frequently the case in historical accounts of change, popularization is interpreted in negative terms; in the case of Hindustani music, the metaphor for negative change was 'the dancing girl'. The vitality that multiple dance styles had imparted to Mughal court culture from the time of Babur onwards took on a different cast in socio-political terms, in the light of eighteenth century events. In 1707, Aurangzeb was succeeded by his already-elderly oldest son, Muazzam, who took the title of Bahadur Shah (r. 1707-12). 'A fairly successful sovereign',[48] Bahadur Shah I is assumed by Hindustani musicologist Brhaspati to have renewed patronage of music in his imperial household, as *dhrupad* compositions containing his name can be found.[49] Furthermore, it was in his court that Na'mat Khan, who would become the most famous of eighteenth century musicians, began his training from the court artists, Tatari Qawwal, Lala Bangali Natva, and Devdat Kabishar—a singer of *qawwali*, an actor, and a poet.[50]

On the death of Bahadur Shah I in 1712, all his four sons vied for control of the empire. They were puppets of leaders of increasingly powerful regional entities such as Zulfiqar Khan Bahadur, head of the Persian and Shia faction at the court, and Asif Jah, his Sunni rival whose family was originally from Bukhara and who now, as Nizam, established an independent dynasty in Hyderabad. In addition, another influential Muslim

---

48. Irvine 1922, I, p. 137.
49. Brhaspati 1974, p. 78.
50. Miner 1997, p. 79.
51. In the period of Akbar, Baz Bahadur was such a person; see the *Akbar Nama*, II: p. 212 and in the nineteenth century another such person was Wajid Ali Shah of Awadh who is discussed later.
52. Miner 1997, p. 80.

Fig. 7: A Review of Troops. (Detail).

family, the Sayyids of Baraha in Uttar Pradesh, claimed the right to command the vanguard of the imperial army. In 1712 that family was headed by two brothers, Husain Ali, deputy-governor of Patna, and Abdullah, governor of Allahabad. In this competitive climate, three of Bahadur Shah's sons were quickly dispatched and the fourth, Jahandar Shah, briefly came to the throne under the auspices of Zulfiqar Khan.

Jahandar Shah (r. 1712-13)—an entirely ineffectual sovereign—stands among those kings of the Subcontinent who are reviled in history for having devoted themselves too much to 'music and dance'.[51] With accounts of Jahandar we see the metaphor of the dancing girl for the popularization of music and dance at the Mughal court played out in literal terms. Jahandar seems to have been controlled not only by Zulfiqar as *Vazir* and his father as *Vakil-i mutlaq*, but also by musicians and dancers. In particular, a favourite concubine by the name of Lal Kunwar held power over the Mughal sovereign; she was a singer and dancer whose relationship with Jahandar began before he assumed the throne. Contemporary sources say that Lal Kunwar was the daughter of one Khasusiat Khan (she has a Hindu name although he is Muslim; Muslim singers/dancers sometimes adopted Hindu names, a practice that continues till today), a descendant of Tansen, and that the famous player of *rudra vina*, Na'mat Khan, was one of her several brothers.[52] Under the sway of Lal Kunwar, Jahandar enriched them all

Fig. 8: Celebrated (Captive) Dancers (from Mandu) Perform before Akbar.
Painted by Dharmdas, composed by Kesu Kalan. *Akbarnama*, 1590 or earlier. Courtesy of the Board of Trustees of the Victoria and Albert Museum, IS.2-1896 f.16/117.

with gifts and imperial privileges: the brothers were granted the *naubat* (heralding) ensemble and drums of authority, and Lal Kunwar was allowed to display the imperial umbrella and to march in public with drums beating as if she were the emperor in person.[53] Lal Kunwar and her family supposedly contributed greatly to corruption at the court. By early 1713, in a swift coup, Jahandar and his powerbrokers were swept aside by the Sayyid brothers and replaced by Farrukhsiyar, Bahadur Shah's grandson.

Farrukhsiyar (r. 1713-19) was cruel and vicious, but also dissolute, pleasure-loving, and popular with the people. We gain some insight into his character and that period of Mughal life from William Irvine's account of Farrukhsiyar's marriage celebration.[54] Women musicians and dancers were ever-present:

> [On 17 December, 1715] the whole of the Diwan-i-Amm and the courtyard, both sides of the road within the palace, and the plain towards the Jamuna were illuminated by lamps placed on bamboo screens. About nine o'clock in the evening, Farrukhsiyar came out by the Dihli Gate of the palace, seated on a moveable throne and wearing, according to usage, the clothes sent to him by the bride's father...The Emperor was preceded by platforms, on which stood women singing and dancing as they were carried along. Fireworks were let off.[55]

Farrukhsiyar proved difficult to control and between 1713 and 1719 Delhi was distracted by political squabbles. In a style reminiscent of earlier Mughal court chronicles, Irvine describes the challenge of a rival prince, Husain Ali Khan in February of 1719:

> Husain Ali Khan at the head of his army, estimated to include 30,000 horsemen, marched to Wazirabad, one of the imperial hunting preserves about four miles north of the city on the Jamuna bank. As they passed, his troops plundered the shops and trod down, in the most merciless manner, the standing crops in the fields outside the city. By this time he had often been heard to say, that as he no longer considered himself to be in the imperial service, why should he respect the rules of etiquette...Disregarding the rules forbidding the playing of the naubat within one mile of the capital, he marched in with sovereign state, kettle-drums beating and clarions sounding... Farrukhsiyar, owing to the presence of the rival Prince, was in such a state of trepidation that, as one writer says, 'his liver melted through fear'.[56]

Interestingly, for such a pleasure-loving emperor, beyond such vague descriptions as these citations from Irvine, no musical references have been found relating to this period.[57]

Farrukhsiyar was ultimately assassinated and for a few months the Sayyid brothers raised a series of puppet sovereigns to the throne in very quick succession, including two more grandsons of Bahadur Shah I. However, the third grandson of Bahadur Shah I, Raushan Akhtar—who took the title of Muhammad Shah—had the capacity for survival, as well as intelligence, shrewdness, and deception. Though he was only eighteen when he came to the throne, he had observed the seven years of Sayyid politics and correctly assessed the hatred that seven years of their unrestrained power had bred. The new emperor made the astute decision to ally with Asif Jah, whose base in Hyderabad in the Deccan made him less likely to constantly interfere in Delhi and who could eliminate the Sayyid brothers, thus leaving Muhammad Shah free to rule for more than a quarter century (1720-1748).

While there were no huge surpluses to support grand imperial schemes, under the new emperor the ritual and protocol at the Mughal court remained the same: formal apearances in the *Diwan-i Amm*, many festivities, traditional ceremonies. Known as Muhammad Shah *Rangila* (Pleasure Lover), he supported poets—both Persian and Urdu-language—painters, and musicians. He is credited with fostering more popular forms of music and dance—most specifically *khyal*, a developing vocal genre.

The impression one gains from contemporary sources about music at court is contradictory. The debates about musical quality and newer versus older musical and dance forms indicates an abundance of musical activity at court. The author of an important contemporary commentary, *Muraqqa-e Dehli*, mentions musicians who perform at the court as being old-fashioned:

---

53. Irvine 1922, pp. 193-4.
54. This can be compared with marriage celebrations in the period of Shahjahan, in Wade 1998.
55. Irvine 1922, I, pp. 304-305.
56. Ibid., p. 373-74.
57. Miner 1997, p. 81.

[Bole Khan] is in the service of the *Badshah* [Mohammad Shah *Rangila*] and holds a position of repute and confidence amongst the imperial supervisors. He has an antiquated style of singing.[58]

Then there is a description of a female singer who was sometimes patronized by the sovereign:

A well known personality of Dehli, [Chamani] has access to the *Badshah*. Confident of her talent, she competes with great musicians and is honoured…She enhances the eloquence of her conversations with the use of appropriate idioms, and she is an excellent company to be with. Having crossed the threshold of youth her maturity attracts only those who are fond of singing. The *Badshah* also enjoys her company occasionally.

Her singing is intoxicating and rekindles the dormant desires. In the singing of *tarana* her tongue moves sharper than the scissors. Her mastery is acknowledged by her contemporaries. She is a worthy woman, skillful and learned and kind to those who know her.[59]

The tone in this quote is quite different from that taken by a historian of *dhrupad*, Srivastava, who commented about Muhammad Shah in a manner that reflects his bad repute in modern South Asian musicology:

Besides *dhrupada* he was also fond of the newer styles of singing. Therefore only few *dhrupada* singer were in his court. The main reason for this seems to be that by this time the newer styles of music like *khyala*…*tappa*, etc. had become more popular than the dhrupada style and Muhammad Shah was more fond of these newer styles which were more erotic than the *dhrupada*.[60]

Most importantly, though, Muhammad Shah is credited with fostering the ubiquitous Na'mat Khan whose early appearance in the Mughal court of Jahandar Shah is remembered more for scandal than for music. Dargah Quli Khan, author of the *Muraqqa-e Dehli*, convinces us that Na'mat Khan's career had taken a turn for the better:

His existence in *Hindustan* is a blessed gift. He is renowned for his compositions…and is on par with the *nayaks* of bygone days. He innovated a variety of beautiful *khayyals*. The works of [Ne'mat Khan] are in different languages and he is considered the master of all contemporary musicians of Dehli. During the reign of Shah Muhammad Mui'zud-din [Ne'mat Khan] was a highly honoured and respected [person]. He takes part in the ceremony of the *urs* of the saints and himself performs the celebrations of the 11th day [the death anniversary]. There is a musical gathering at his residence on the 11th day of every month when a large section of the populace [including the nobles of high rank and elites] of *Dehli* gather…The *mehfil* lasts till the break of dawn, when it is culminated with *raag bibhas* [a *raga* calm and sung at dawn].

His expertise in the art of playing the *bin* has no parallel in this world.[61]

Despite imperial revival under Muhammad Shah, he and the empire were dealt an economic and cultural blow with the sacking of Delhi in 1739 by Persia's Nadir Shah, stripping more psychological and imperial authority away from the emperor and leaving increasingly potent leaders in various sections of the Subcontinent. Muhammad Shah was certainly unprepared for the Persian invasion and not predisposed to fight, but he nonetheless marched to meet the enemy. The ubiquitous Mughal camp-fortress was set up at Karnal—in Nadir Shah's path—with great quantities of gear and the usual camp followers, but despite the huge military force (ca. 300,000 soldiers, 2000 elephants, and plenty of guns), the emperor was forced into the most humiliating defeat by a Mughal ruler since Humayun, nearly 200 years earlier. After a brief, uneasy truce, the citizens of Delhi began a campaign of guerrilla warfare against the Persian forces and Nadir Shah used the incidents as an excuse to sack the city, substituting in memory the scorched earth policy of Timur's three-and-a-half centuries earlier. Indeed, the term *nadirshahi* has been used since in Delhi as synonymous with a disaster of the greatest magnitude. Two months of systematic plunder, rape, murder, arson, and other atrocities committed in the city and surrounding countryside yielded the great accumulated treasures of the empire—art, manuscripts, monies, jewels, the royal stables, arms, and the like—and the necessity for the emperor to surrender the territories of Sindh, Kabul, and the districts west of the Indus, not to mention most of the glory of the empire. Sated, Nadir Shah returned to Persia, leaving the dynasty stripped of military might, major resources, and political influence.

Muhammad Shah reigned for nine more years in a devastated city and empire which took that decade of

Fig. 9: DANCING VILLAGERS.
Painted by Pandit Seu ca. 1730. Los Angeles County Museum of Art. From the Alice and Nasli Heeramaneck Collection. Museum Associates Purchase. M.77.19.24.

struggling to recoup. Nonetheless, he continued to support the arts. While the results of Nadir Shah's venture on the Subcontinent severely reduced Muhammad Shah's appetite for play and also his ability to patronize musicians and dancers, Dargah Quli Khan gives the impression that cultural life in the Delhi court continued unabated. But from this point on, the history of music in North India becomes a history of dispersion from the central court, to urban life in Delhi and to other territories in the Mughal empire.

---

58. *Muraqqa-e Dehli* 1989, p. 91. Henceforth *Muraqqa*.
59. Ibid., p. 107.
60. Srivastava 1977, p. 38.
61. *Muraqqa*, pp. 75-6.
62. Ibid., p. 8.

MID-EIGHTEENTH CENTURY

An important musical activity in Delhi in which both Hindus and Muslims participated were regular events at the shrines of historic Muslim saints and contemporary ascetics. Prominent at those events were *qawwals*, singers of ecstatic devotional texts whose musical style was very significant for Hindustani classical music. From Dargah Quli Khan's descriptions of the events, we can gain a sense of their prominence. Concerning an annual *Urs* (death anniversary of a saint):

> The *Urs* [of *Qutb-ul-Aqtab*] is held on the sixteenth of the month of *Rabi'ul-Awwal*. A large number of people perform pilgrimage and then enjoy themselves in the surroundings for two days. The *qawwals*, sometimes sitting or standing recite continuously around the blessed Grave.[62]

There were also regular weekly events and the citizens could anticipate the calendar to plan their outings. On Tuesdays:

> His [Shah Ghulam Muhammad] Khanqah is adjacent to the stables of Dara Shikoh. On every Tuesday the gatherings of *sama* are celebrated here and the *qawwals* of the city and those desirous of taking part gather and derieve (*sic*.) great pleasure out of it.[63]
>
> The grandeur of his asceticism [Shah Ghulam Muhammad Dawal Pura] and the magnificence of his conversations stupefies even the greatest of men... A group comprising *derveishes*, *faqirs*, and dependants live day and night in the vicinity of his felicitious residence and obtain the agreeable share from the offered victuals...The largest portions of the gifts are bestowed on the *qawwals* who reside in these felicitious surroundings. They live like his shadow, insperable (*sic*.) and maintain an atmosphere of ecstacy with their singing.[64]

On Wednesdays:

> The blessed abode of his Holiness [*Hazrat* Nizam-ud-Din Aulia] is situated at a distance of half *croh* from Old *Dehli*...Every Wednesday the nobles and plebians dress themselves [and gather here] for pilgrimage and the *qawwals* perform the ceremony of salutation with full traditions and regard.[65]

On Sundays:

> The illuminated mausoleum of this exalted being [*Hazrat* Nasir-ud-Din Chiragh Dehli] is at a distance of 3 *croh* from Old *Dehli*...Pilgrimage at his *mazar* is performed on Sunday. To obtain the felicity of *ziyarat* large crowds gather on this day, particularly, on the last Sunday of the month of *Diwali*...Both Hindus and Muslims perform the same rituals of pilgrimage. Caravans of pilgrims arrive from dawn till sunset and setting up their tents in the shadow of the walls [they] amuse themselves. The place is a spectacle of musical assemblies of good cheer and from every corner sounds of *moor chang* and *pakhawaj* emanate. His *Urs* is performed with full regulations.[66]

Week-long festivities were also held. The pleasant and easy mingling of Muslim and Hindu life can be seen in a description given by Dargah Quli Khan:

> Festivity and hustle bustle can be found in Qadam Sharif of the Holy Prophet in the month of Basant. [The festival of Basant was celebrated among Muslims since the time of Hazrat Nizamud-din Aulia.]...In the courtyard and surroundings of this place of felicity, everyone tries to surpass the other in making merry and wait impatiently for the *qawwals*, dancers, and pilgrims. The *qawwals* and singers pay their tributes by reciting their compositions in a delightful manner and [the pilgrims] present colourful bouquets and pray for the pious soul of the Prophet. With perfect humbleness the singers lead with slow, deliberate steps...On the other side of the pious place the old *qawwals* pay homage by rubbing their foreheads of the threshold with dedication. Singers and dancers exhibit their art which for them is their kind or worship. Devout pilgrims send their greetings to the Prophet. From sunrise to the time of *Namaz-e-'Asr* the singers pay their tributes turn by turn with deep regard...
>
> Similarly, on the second day the singers and musicians visit [the *Dargah* of] Hazrat Qutbul-Aqtab [Hazrat Bukhtiyar Kaki] and offer salutations... On the third day a large number of people can be seen moving towards the mausoleum of Hazrat Sultanul-Mashaikh [Hazrat Nizamud-din-Aulia] which being close to the city makes everyone inclined to visit it. A *majlis* of *sama* is organized here, and each sufi tries to out do the other in attaining the state of ecstasy...
>
> On the 4th day, the singers and the musicians who have faith in *Hazrat* Shah Rasul Numa, gather at his grave, in the heart of the city. ...On the 5th day the *mehfil* takes place at the threshold of *Hazrat* Shah Turkman. Amongst those who gather there are *sufis* and beautiful women who are a source of envy for even the stars and the paradise. All the singers and *qawwals* who reside in the neighborhood come and sing in turn and receive many thanks from the listeners.
>
> According to their schedule on the sixth day they go to the residences of the *Badshah* and the nobles with the desire of receiving some worldly goods. On the night of the 7th [day] of this month, all the dancers [of the city] get together and go to the grave of *Azizi*, in *Ahadipura*, and wash it with wine, and take it in turn to dance. They feel their dancing and singing will provide peace and pleasure to his soul. Gradually the *qawwals* also gather and the *mehfil* becomes very gay, and men and beautiful women also join in...Thus, the pleasure seekers and the visitors join in the revellry of these six days and derive a year worth of pleasure. What Good Luck they have.[67]

Although Fig. 9 (ca. 1730) was not drawn in Delhi, it is in the style of Mughal painting from Muhammad Shah's reign and gives a flavour of the ecstatic dancing of the dervishes.

Fig. 10: NEW YEAR'S TRIBUTE.
Lucknow ca. 1760-64. Reproduced by kind permission of the Trustees of the Chester Beatty Library, Dublin.
T.306 (c) of CBL. Ms. In. 69.5.

Musical gatherings (*mehfils*) were also held at the homes of nobles in Delhi. One learns that at these sophisticated soirees both instrumental and vocal music were performed. Humour and skilled repartee employing proverbs and idioms, perhaps in multiple languages, were cultivated:

[Latif Khan] is the son of a nobleman and all his energies are devoted to organising *mehfils* of music. He himself is so well versed in *raag* that even N'emat Khan visits him at his house and applauds his style of singing. His recitation is so popular and amusing that even those in high offices find it difficult to gain admission to his *mehfils*. He is par excellence in singing and colourful speech…Everyone enjoys wine in his company. Beautiful *huqqas*, wine goblets and flagons along with eatables are put forth individually for everyone. The singers and musicians give an account of their talents alternately. Along with singing a lot of jokes are recited and repartee takes place.[68]

As regards instrumental music, the quintessential South Asian drum, the *pakhavaj*, seen in the hands of female and male dance accompanists in Mughal miniature paintings from the time of Akbar (Fig. 8), is in full use in mid-eighteenth century urban Delhi. So,

63. Ibid., p. 36.
64. Ibid., p. 27.
65. Ibid., p. 9.
66. Ibid., p. 11.
67. Ibid., p. 42-4.
68. Ibid., p. 40.

Fig. 11: MAHARANA AR SINGH PERFORMING PUJA IN BADI MAHAL.
Rajput, Rajasthan at Udaipur. 1764. Courtesy of the Freer Gallery of Art, Smithsonian Institution, Washington D.C. f.1987.7.

too, is the *dholak* and the stringed instrument, the *rabab*.

Since *dhrupad* is mentioned only once in the *Muraqqa-e Dehli*, we might assume that that august vocal genre of the Mughal court had fallen into eclipse in the capital, being considered old fashioned; on the other hand, it is possible that the author of the commentary was just not interested in *dhrupad* and therefore did not mention more singers of it. Indeed, Na'mat Khan was cited in another contemporary source as a *dhrupad* performer.[69] Furthermore, Na'mat Khan's nephew, Firoz Khan (Adarang) was known for excellence as a composer of *dhrupad* as well as the more popular *tarana* and *khyal*.[70] Whether or not *dhrupad* was a popular vocal genre, it continued to serve as the repository of Mughal courtly prestige and of musical knowledge and was/is therefore the genre relative to which the histories of all others have been elucidated. While Delhi and Rajasthan had long been centres of *dhrupad* singing, musicologist Srivastava states that in the period of Muhammad Shah, *dhrupad* singers settled in several locations, some in the proximity of Delhi (Mathura, Vrindavana, and Haryana), others to the east or west of Delhi: Rampur, Jaipur, Indore, Vishnupur, Darbhanga, Varanasi, and Lucknow, for instance.[71]

What *dhrupad* actually sounded like, or indeed what *qawwali* actually consisted of, can only be assumed from occasional references. Dargah Quli Khan commented on a *drupadiya*: '[He] is a master in the singing of Dhruvapad. His style of *alap* is like the slow advance of spring'.[72] A centuries-old fact that *qawwali* induced ecstasy is reiterated in a passage in the *Muraqqa-e Dehli*:

> [Jatta] is a prominent [*qawwal*] in the *mehfils* of the *sufis* and ascetics and they derieve (sic.) pleasure from his presence. He recites Quranic texts in a meloncholic voice which expound on the unity of being and causes the sufis to suffer [from unrequited love] in the state of ecstasy…The sounds of his instruments and song enrapture the heart for ecstacy is an inseperable (sic.) element of his singing.[73]

A wide vocal range was apparently desirable in the singing of *qawwali*:

> [M'uin-ud-Din *qawwal*] is one of the contemporary and eminent master *qawwals* and has outshone the others in the art of *qawwali*…He has command over the different pitches of his voice and often experiments with the extremes [high and low pitches] which [the audience] find appealing.[74]

Allyn Miner concludes from various sources: 'We get the idea of a fast-moving, energetic and ornamented music, not unlike the *qavvali* known today'.[75]

With this description of *qawwali*, one wonders if *qawwaliyas* are depicted in Fig. 10, a painting from Lucknow, ca. 1760-64, showing a bearded nawab in a scene of greeting at New Year.[76] Among the entertainers to the right at a lower level are a number of musicians; notably, there are singers whose hand gestures are quite different from each other, indicating perhaps singers of different styles. The relatively sedate, traditional Mughal-painting style of hand position for singers can be seen on the far right, in the second last row of men: Two *tambur* players and three singers can be identified, with the hands uplifted but close to the body. Perhaps they are *dhrupad* singers—or in any case, *kalavants*. In contrast, next to the balustrade stand two musicians with right arm lifted high; one holds a smaller *tambur*; perhaps a third musician with arm lifted but not so high belongs with them. The exuberant gesture might indicate a more flamboyant vocal genre—*qawwali* perhaps. In front of those singers stands a player of cylindrical *dhol*, and *tala*, but it is not possible to be sure that the group constitutes an ensemble.

Mid-eighteenth century Delhi also witnessed the emergence of *khyal* as a major vocal genre. While the early history of *khyal* is uncertain, it is clear that something called *khyal* existed before the great *binkar* Na'mat Khan 'innovated a variety of beautiful *khayyals*'.[77] It may have existed in some form, associated for instance with *qawwali* through the great musician Amir Khusrau of the fourteenth century and the Sufism of Nizamuddin Auliya.[78] In Delhi, that city of free musical associations, musicians of all sorts heard each other's performances, and continuing influences from one genre to another can be taken for granted:

---

69. Miner 1997, p. 86.
70. Ibid., p. 88.
71. Srivastava 1977, p. 38.
72. *Muraqqa*, p. 82.
73. Ibid., p. 101.
74. Ibid., p. 84.
75. Miner 1997, p. 83.
76. Leach 1995, pp. 687-9.
77. *Muraqqa*, p. 75.
78. See for example, Dhond 1980; Meer 1980.

[Mir Abdullah] is one of the mourners of Hazrat Abu-Abdullah-Al-Hussain. He recites elegies composed by Hazeen and Nadim in such a meloncholic way that the laments and wails of the mourners reach a high pitch. His style of tender rehearsal [of the initial verse] is worthy of mention and has a soul-wrecking impact...The great musicians are unanimous in their opinion that a superior elegist with a rhythmic voice such as his [Mir Abdullah] has never been heard before...Many people, including the *kalawants* and *qawwals* gather at his residence to imbibe the art of recitation of elegies.[79]

It is possible that *khyal*, a song style with a long-standing connection to *qawwali* and probably not strictly based on *ragas*, was classicized through an addition of *dhrupad* elements by Na'mat Khan. The fact that the name '*khyal*' was retained is evidence that in the original mixture of the earlier *khyal* and the *dhrupad* genres, the balance tilted toward the former.[80] Using the name Sadarang, Na'mat Khan composed new songs that, said Dargah Quli Khan 'these days in *Dehli* are in vogue'.[81] Whether he performed *khyal* himself or taught it to courtesans or to other singers is not clearly documented. Na'mat Khan was a musician whose sister had been a courtesan and whose professional sphere traversed both the Mughal court of Muhammad Shah and diverse performance contexts of urban Delhi; like the great singer Tansen before him in the court of Akbar, Na'mat appears to have been a figure whose breadth of cultural associations and musical achievements permitted him great influence.[82] Vim van der Meer proposes that the new classicized form of *khyal* permitted courtesans to sing the *ragas* that were previously restricted to *dhrupad* singers.[83] In any case, the new form of *khyal* flourished, and developed with the artistry of singers in other cities, as discussed below.

In most mid-eighteenth century commentaries that mention music and/or dance, the ubiquitous female dancer(s) and their accompanists are likely to be included. Their dancing must have been an entertainment rage, to have attracted such consistent attention. Dance entertainment in the private court context was certainly not a new phenomenon as we have seen, but what drew the attention now was performance in non-court *mehfils* (still a private context) and also public performance. The impression one frequently gains in the descriptions is of lascivious sensuality; there had historically been a connection between the role of courtesan and dancer, but now there was a sort of deliciously suggestive negativity attached to the word 'nautch'. In fact, there was a wide range of skills and roles among women who earned their living as dancers in the private and public contexts. Fig. 11 of 1764 from Udaipur in Rajasthan demonstrates this point. The Rajput Maharana Ar Singh performs *puja* (prayer) in his palace in the middle of the picture, while closer to the viewer a dance ensemble performs, with all figures in dignified formal posture. Significantly, the instruments used to accompany the dancer are the same selection that later accompany the *Kathak* dance style.

What is important about such a painting for the history of music during the Mughal period is the instrumentarium of the ensemble. Rather than the single hand-played barrel-shaped *pakhavaj*, the cylindrically shaped *dhol*, or the stick-played bowl-shaped pair of *naqqara* that are depicted in dance ensembles in Mughal paintings through the mid-seventeenth century (Figs. 3, 5, 7, 8, 9, and 10), the drums used to accompany female dancers in paintings of the mid-eighteenth century are a hand-played pair suspended in playing position in a wide sash tied around the player's waist. The first pictorial evidence of paired hand-played drums is found in paintings done at the Punjabi hill court of Jasrota (ca.1745), by the Mughal artist Nainsukh who had lately arrived from the court of Delhi;[84] in some paintings the drummer is male, in others female but in either case the drummer accompanies dance. In one painting the drum pair is cylindrical, but in others the shape is hidden. Slightly later, hand-played hemispherical pairs are found in paintings from Rajasthani courts and Faizabad. Thus, the use of hand-played paired drums seems to have been widespread beyond the Mughal court sphere. With them probably lies the origin (albeit still murky) of the most important drum used in Hindustani music today—the *tabla* (*tabl*: Arabic for drumming. *Tabla* is the Arabic name of the goblet drum popular in the Muslim world), a pair of tuneable hand-played drums.[85] An important link of paired drums to 'classical music' is provided by Fig. 12, a rare *ragamala* produced in Murshidabad in Bengal, ca. 1760 as a section of a tent wall.[86]

Widespread use of this hand-played pair of drums as well as the drums of long-standing popularity—the *pakhavaj*, *dhol*[*ak*], and *naqqara*—in the eighteenth century is an important factor in the history of drumming. On the basis of reconstructions of the genealogy of interrelated families of *tabla* players whose members had played other drums as well, music scholar Rebecca Stewart suggests that a shared history of performance practice stretched back to eighteenth century Delhi. Through analysis of drumming patterns, she elucidates the techniques, indeed the 'musical style' of the *pakhavaj*, *dholak*, and *naqqara* historically and she concludes: 'The closeness of the relationship between the tabla and the naqqara, dholak and pakhavaj, at the level of the stroke and bol pattern, is indisputable'.[87] Sharing may very well have taken place primarily in the sphere of dance accompaniment, particularly the most representative form of North Indian dance—*Kathak*. This link and the further development of *tabla* drumming will be discussed below.

Also of note in the painting of the dance ensemble in Udaipur (Fig. 9) are the players of the bowed lute, the *sarangi*, another instrument which drew increasing attention through the eighteenth century. European travellers occasionally mentioned the *sarangi* as part of a musical ensemble. John Burnell, travelling through Bengal in 1712, for instance, enumerated a bowed lute, bowl-shaped drums, played with singing; he also heard double-reed instruments played 'in concert':

79. *Muraqqa*, p. 68.
80. Miner 1997, pp. 84-6.
81. *Muraqqa*, p. 113.
82. See Wade 1998.
83. Meer 1980, pp. 57-8.
84. Stewart 1974, p. 7.
85. Stewart concluded: Whether the hybridized instrument which we recognize today as 'the' *tabla* can also be traced back to [eighteenth century Delhi] is another matter. Judging from both pictorial and literary descriptions, this instrument...underwent several minor and not so minor alterations during the 100 years between 1750 and 1850. The instrument we see today is probably no more than 75 to 100 years old at the most (Stewart 1974, p. 7).
86. Leach 1995, II, p. 93.
87. Stewart 1974, p. 69.
88. Burnell 1967, p. 130.
89. See Wade 1998, pp. 189-92.
90. English translation by Allyn Miner from Khwaja Hassan Nizami, *Purani Dihli ke Halat*. Delhi: 1949, p. 69 (Urdu translation from Persian of the *Muraqqa-e-Dehli*). Cited in Bor, 1986/87, p. 66.
91. Bor 1986/87, pp. 66-67.
92. Bor 1986/7, p. 77, Fig. 74. All nineteenth century writers, including F.J. Fetis (1869) and V.C. Mahillon (1880, 1893) seem to agree that the *sarangi* was a relatively small, box-shaped instrument with eleven or thirteen sympathetic strings. By that time, a larger type had emerged in Delhi.
93. Bor 1986/87, pp. 80-81.
94. Ibid., p. 70.

Cojey Surratt [Khwaja Israil Sarhad], a merchant...resident in Calcutta, paid us a visit...and brought with him his musick consisting of a Georgian violin, two small kettledrums and the like number of hautboys with which he entertained us. The instruments were costly and of curious workmanship. To the violin the drums were added in concert, assisted with the voice of the musicians....[88]

Bowed-lute type instruments of several sorts are depicted in Mughal paintings.[89] However, Joep Bor suggests that it was only in the second half of the seventeenth century that the *sarangi* became acknowledged as a stringed instrument used in Hindustani classical music. Dargah Quli Khan places it squarely within the sphere of *raga* music: '[Ghulam Mohammad] is a master of melody and has specialized in playing sad and serious ragas with deep feeling. Not a single musician can play sarangi like him, so profound is his training'.[90] Even in the eighteenth century, however, most musicologists ignored it, probably because it originated as a humble instrument of the common man.[91]

Sarangis with a waisted, box-shaped resonator became gradually more prominent during the latter part of the eighteenth century.[92] Bor concludes that the 'modern' classical *sarangi* probably developed in or around Delhi, approximately 145 years ago.[93] Further, he suggests that rural male *sarangi* players who had settled in the cities in the second half of the eighteenth century soon discovered that it was virtually impossible to compete with *rabab* and *tambur* players, let alone with the aristocratic *binkars*:

They must have realized that, in order to make a reasonable living, the only solution was to associate with courtesans. As singing and echoing their own songs on the sarangi had for centuries been the main occupation of these bards, it was not difficult for them to accompany the songs of female vocalists. These women must have welcomed the wistful sound of the sarangi, which blended so well with their voices, and gave them support and inspiration.

Through their association with famous courtesans, sarangi players were able to participate in musical sittings and enter the courts. In this way, they began to be known in the world of classical music, and the move from rural to urban society was complete. Sarangi players, however, did not have the status of vocalists nor instrumentalists; they did not belong to the category of solo performers and were relegated to a subordinate position.[94]

Fig. 12: TODI RAGINI. Also called *'SECTION OF A QANAT (TENT WALL)'*
17th-18th century, unidentified artist. Bengal, Murshidabad, ca. 1760. Cincinnati Art Museum, The William T. and Louise Taft Semple Collection, 1962.461.

Significantly, the *sitar* as well, in fully developed form is first named in writing in *Muraqqa-e Dehli* of 1739;[95] its association with mid-eighteenth century Delhi is thereby established. (Here I summarize the conclusions by Allyn Miner in her carefully-documented study of the history of this important instrument of Hindustani music.) One theory about the origin of the *sitar* (a composite Persian word meaning three strings) is that it was developed from the melody *tamburs* of Mughal court musicians; Miner thinks not, based on Darqah Quli Khan's clear separation of the two in his accounts of instrumental performance and on the lack of association of the two in oral tradition.[96] The thin-necked lutes in eighteenth century paintings are *tamburs*, with lateral tuning pegs, a tapering neck and a thin bridge; there is no mid-eighteenth century visual representation known for the *sitar*. The earliest known surviving thin-necked lute with lateral pegs but non-tapering neck, a flat-surface bridge and a gourd body is an instrument of about 1790 that is preserved in the Maharaja Sawai Man Singh II Museum in Jaipur. What is labelled the *sitar* first appears in European and Company style art only in the late-eighteenth, early nineteenth century.[97]

The *sitar* may be related to the Kashmiri *setar*, an instrument directly traceable to the Persian *setar* that had found its way into courts and also regional use in North India. The *setar* was associated particularly with *sufiana kalam* (Sufi poetry) in Kashmir, thought to date to at least the fifteenth century, which blended Persian and South Asian influences.[98]

A musician at the court of Muhammad Shah by the name of Khusrau Khan is said to have visited or resided for some time in Kashmir and brought the idea for *sitar* back to Delhi. Once more, significant musical innovation of the mid-eighteenth century is linked to the Mughal court and also to an innovative musical family: Khusrau Khan was Na'mat Khan's brother and was later known as Amir Khusrau (not to be confused with the celebrated fourteenth century Sufi poet and musician, Amir Khusrau). Given the corroboration of oral accounts and contemporary written records, it seems fairly conclusive that Khusrau Khan and also Firoz Khan (Na'mat Khan's nephew) were responsible for the introduction of the *sitar* in Delhi.[99]

The development both of *sitar* and vocal genres is attributed to Firoz Khan (Adarang) who was a talented composer and versatile musician:

> A nephew of Ne'mat Khan [Ada Rang who innovated various new notations to be played on the *sitar*] is skilled in playing the *sitar* and composes new notations. He also plays notations on the *sitar* usually played on other instruments. In the world [of music] he is incomparable. The author [of this book] has attended his musical gatherings many times and regards him with respect. Endowed as he is with this unique talent, his

mehfils are popular, and carry on all night. Inspite of the instability [caused by the invasion of Nadir Shah] the spirit of revellry is extant [and continues] til pre-dawn darkness.[100]

THE RISE OF REGIONAL CULTURAL CENTRES

Muhammad Shah was succeeded by his son Ahmad Shah, whose reign was neither easy nor long (1748-54). The real direction of the empire was in the able hands of Safdar Jang of the Awadh ruling line, but when he died in 1753 the realities of the power structure in the Subcontinent were swiftly and substantially exposed.[101] The main regional challenger was the capable grandson of Asif Jah, Ghaziuddin Imadulmulk, who rightly saw Delhi as a better centre than Hyderabad from which to exercise power. Upon Safdar Jang's death, Ghaziuddin immediately seized Ahmad Shah, had him blinded and deposed, and placed the elderly, inept grandson of Jahandar Shah on the throne. Ruling as Alamgir II (r. 1754-59) he eventually incurred Ghaziuddin's displeasure and was put to death.

Along with the growing influence of the princely states there loomed a potent new player on the Subcontinent's stage, the Afghan chieftain Abdali, who had carved out an extensive kingdom comprising present-day Afghanistan, most of eastern Iran, Sindh, Kashmir, and the Punjab. During the reign of Alamgir II in 1757, Abdali repeated the sack of Delhi and, in 1761, with Alamgir II's successor, Shah Alam II (r. 1760-1806), comfortably ensconced in Allahabad, annihilated the Maratha confederacy, one of the greatest threats to the empire's survival. With the Marathas eliminated and Abdali preoccupied with his northern possessions, the role of potential protector of the empire again fell to the *nawab-vazirs* of Awadh, Persians from Khurasan, who were a focal point for Shi'ism on the Subcontinent and welcoming to intellectuals and artists. The empire would see only two more rulers after Shah Alam II—Akbar Shah (r. 1806-1837) and Bahadur Shah II (r. 1837-58) who was forced into exile in Burma by the British.

After the death of Alamgir II in 1759 the history of music has to be told from the perspective of regional centres as well as from that of the Mughal capital. So unsettled was life in mid-eighteenth century Delhi that what began as a gradual exodus of musicians turned into a veritable flood.

The region of Awadh with its capital at Faizabad became a cultural magnet, a phenomenon made possible by the close supporting ties with Muhammad Shah of the first two Nawabs (Saadat Khan, r.1722-39, and Safdar Jang, r.1739-53) but 'enacted' by the third Nawab, Shujauddaula (r. 1753-75).

> Fyzabad had risen to a height of unparalleled prosperity under Shuja ud-Daula and almost rivalled Delhi in magnificence; it was full of merchants from Persia, China and Europe, and money flowed like water…[102]

In 1775, after a decade of steady inroads by the increasingly confident British, the territories of Jaunpur and Ghazipur, including Varanasi, were ceded to the British East India Company and the next Nawab, Asifuddaula (d. 1793), moved the capital of Awadh from Faizabad to Lucknow. To the new capital flocked numerous musicians from Delhi and the stage was set for a vigorous artistic quasi-renaissance in the last quarter of the eighteenth century. Details of musical life under both Nawabs Shujauddaula and Asifuddaula are known from a single important source: a detailed list by Muhammad Karam Imam that provides for documentary historians the sort of information provided for mid-eighteenth century Delhi by Dargah Quli Khan (although the format of the two works was very different).

Connections between Delhi and Lucknow are clear, and the traditional musical forms were maintained. There was a revival of *dhrupad* among the singers from

---

95. Miner 1997, p. 32.
96. Ibid., p. 33.
97. Ibid., p. 32.
98. See Pacholczyk 1978; During & Dick 1984, p. 354.
99. Miner 1997, p. 24.
100. *Muraqqa*, p. 76.
101. The founder of the Awadh ruling line, Saadat Khan Burhan ul-Mulk, had been appointed *subahdar* of Awadh by emperor Muhammad Shah in 1722 and had run the province as an independent ruler, a *nawab-vazir*. Having failed to stop Nadir Shah at the side of Muhammad Shah, he committed suicide and was succeeded by his nephew Safdar Jang.
102. Neville 1928, p. 223.

the line of the legendary Tansen (and also among musicians in Rajasthani courts). This sustained the performance of the form through the next century. The instrumentalists who came to Lucknow included descendants of *binkar* Sammokhan Singh (Tansen's son-in-law) and players of *dhrupad rabab*, most notably the brothers Chajju Khan and Jivan Khan. Miner points out that no *sitar* player is mentioned for this period in Lucknow, either by Karam Imam or in oral histories.[103]

Two factors for musical change were noted by Karam Imam. One factor was the loosening of hegemonic musical constraints by *dhrupad*-style instrumentalists. Pyar Khan, for instance, who was the teacher of Nawab Wajid Ali Shah (r. 1847-1856), is credited by Imam with the invention of the *sursingar*, a metal-stringed hybrid instrument. After Pyar Khan died (ca. 1857), the instrument was cultivated further in Lucknow and Calcutta by the next generation of musicians.[104] In addition, the *dhrupad* repertoire was extended by an instrumentalist to include not only the venerable court repertoire but regional music as well: *Dhrupad rabab* player Jivan Khan 'played both Marg and Desi *ragas*'.[105] The second factor for musical change was the cultivation of the vocal style, *khyal*. Ghulam Rasul and Jani, two musicians mentioned by Dargah Quli Khan as singers of *qawwali*, are noted by Imam as singers of *khyal*—the first of a string of noted *khyal* singers of Lucknow.

Another region became prominent as well: Rohilkhand, due east of Delhi. One important exodus from Delhi to Rohilkhand serves as a quintessential example of the continuing influence of Mughal court culture. Rohilkhand was an area to which a number of Afghans had migrated and whose leader, Ali Muhammad, had been given the title of 'Nawab' by Muhammad Shah. Experiencing Mughal court culture, Ali Muhammad determined to adopt the appreciation of the arts that were appropriate to his new status and forthwith offered patronage to some of Delhi's musicians. Sometime before 1760, the great sitarist Firoz Khan moved to Rohilkhand. Initially under the patronage of one of Ali Muhammad's sons, Sadullah Khan, he later moved to Ali Muhammad's court. In Rohilkhand there was a flourishing but non-professional cultivation of performance on Afghani-style *rabab*. The arrival of Firoz Khan and other Delhi musicians brought *rababiyas* their first extended contact with Hindustani mainstream court music. Musical ferment continued in the area; the city of Rampur, founded in 1775 by another of Ali Muhammad's sons, Faizullah Khan, quickly became a cultural centre.

The processes of indigenization and musical synthesis were later to result in the development of the *sarod*, most likely from the Afghani-style *rabab*. The first musician associated with an instrument called *sarod* was Ghulam Ali Khan, a *rababiya* who lived in the first half of the nineteenth century, for a while in Lucknow and finally in Gwalior, another new cultural centre, discussed below. Grandson of a *rababiya* from Afghanistan, he learned Hindustani music at the various courts where he lived. It is likely that Ghulam Ali instituted some changes to the *rabab* and/or called it by the new name.[106] The development of the modern instrument with its steel strings and metal fingerboard occurred, however, after the end of the Mughal empire.

Musical remnants of the *rababiyas* are represented in the *sarod* playing of their descendants such as Radhika Mohan. Suited specifically to a medium speed, Firozkhani *gats* have stroke patterns set in varied and interesting rhythms, their melody lines cover the entire gamut of the *raga* and their melodic movement is characterized by large intervallic jumps.[107] Firozkhani *gats* have an association with the *sitar* as well, as they are mentioned in several of the nineteenth century *sitar* handbooks, where they must be considered the earliest of all recorded *gat* forms.[108]

While the great sitarist Firoz Khan moved to Rohilkhand, Masit Khan, an important musician who was probably his son, remained in Delhi. He contributed significantly to maintaining Delhi's high culture during the reign of Shah Alam (r. 1759-1806). To Masit Khan is attributed the introduction of the *gat-toda* genre of *sitar* music. The *gat* is a composition in *tala* with fixed strokes and melody; '*gat*' being a term used in drumming and dance, its use for *sitar* music probably shows the *sitar*'s early role as an accompanying instrument for dance. *Toda* are melodic lines that embellish on and are interspersed with the *gat* melody; the chain-type of ornamentation follows the pattern of *dhrupad* exposition, i.e., gradual increase into wider ranges of tonal space and rhythm but employing techniques used on the *bin*. Analysis of surviving Masitkhani *gats* and also organological information about the *sitar* of his period causes Allyn Miner to suggest that the instrument had metal frets, and a capacity for a degree of pulling; therefore Masit Khan could imitate techniques involving deflection of the main string and particular *bin* patterns of right hand strokes. When performance practice on *sitar* began to encompass an aspect of *dhrupad* structure (the pattern of exposition) and also techniques used by players of the venerable *bin*, a systematic classicizing process was initiated that permitted a rise in status for the *sitar*—the very same classicizing process which Na'mat Khan had enacted with *khyal*.

Later writers have emphasized the elements of *dhrupad* in describing the style of Masit Khan and the generations which followed him in Delhi, i.e., the Delhi style. Miner, however, concludes that 'written *gats* and performance tradition show that it was very much a genre of its own, one having the qualities of experimentation and eclecticism that characterized *sitar* music throughout its history'.[109] She found no evidence of the presence of drone strings on any eighteenth century *sitar* or the capacity for sustained tone.[110] Masitkhani *gats*, imitative of *dhrupad*, were to be played at a slow speed, but 'slow' was considerably faster than the 'slow' speed practiced today. Being imitative of *dhrupad* might have meant that the *gat* melodies were created according to *raga* rules and were meant for solo music.[111]

Although Shah Alam II ruled over a waning empire, he involved himself with the culture around him as his predecessors had. He is said to have had good knowledge of music, and in 1797 had a collection of Persian, Hindi, and Punjabi songs made under the title of *Nadirat-e-Shahi*. All but a few of the 606 songs have *raga* and *tala* specified at the beginning; included are a wide range of genres—*ghazals*, marriage songs, *kavitt*, *horis*, and *taranas*, among others. From the large number of *taranas* in *Nadirat-e-Shahi*, it is clear that that vocal genre had become an important form of court music; *tarana* consisted of Urdu couplets along with Persian *rubaiyat*, and emphasized rhythmic syllabic play. A study of the songs suggests that various Muslim and Hindu festivals were celebrated with equal enthusiasm—the *urs* of Khwaja Muinuddin Chishti and Sheikh Abdul Qadir on the one hand and Holi, Diwali, and Basant on the other hand.[112]

Insight into melodic theory of the late eighteenth century has been gleaned by musicologist Najma Ahmad from *Usulun-Naghmat-e-Asifi*, a comprehensive Persian-language work on music. The two main ideas—and the original contributions of this source—are a new viewpoint on the systems of classification of *ragas* and *raginis*, and the treatment of Bilawal scale as the Shuddha scale. While the author did not elaborate those points in detail, Ahmad points out that the approach followed is more or less similar to the present-day *'that'* system for classifying *ragas*;[113] this should have considerable significance for the modern scholars of music.

In Delhi, Masit Khan's son, Bahadur Khan (d. ca. 1841), and nephew, Dulha Khan, continued the family tradition, playing both *bin* and *sitar*. Dulha Khan was known as a great performer—a singer of *dhrupad* as well as an instrumentalist—but Bahadur Khan's memory lives on in *gat-toda* compositions. His *gats* contain *mid* and *zamzama*, among the earliest of the named *sitar* techniques. Developments by them and their disciples (including a female artiste, Biba Jan Sahiba) came to be called the Delhi *baj* of *sitar* playing.[114]

It was probably in the last quarter of the eighteenth century that the *sitar* was taken to Jaipur in Rajasthan: the *Sangit Sar*, written by Maharajah Sawai Pratap Singh describes a *sitar* that had probably arrived recently from Delhi.[115] Up to that point, miniature paintings in Rajasthani and Pahari hill styles show *bins* and *tamburs*, but no *sitars*. In the nineteenth century, however, Jaipur and other cities of Rajasthan would be the centre of the activities of Masit Khan's followers who would form the important Jaipur Senia line of *sitar* players, independent of the Delhi *baj*.

In Varanasi to the east and Rajasthan to the west of Delhi, high levels of patronage through the eighteenth and entire nineteenth centuries continued under Hindu

---

103. Miner 1997, p. 97.
104. Ibid., p. 119.
105. Miner interprets this to mean both *dhrupad* and non-*dhrupad* music; 1997, p. 237, n. 101.
106. Miner 1997, p. 67.
107. Ibid., p. 91; citing Radhika Mohan Maitra.
108. Miner 1997, p. 95.
109. Ibid., p. 104.
110. Ibid., pp. 38, 94.
111. Ibid., pp. 93-94.
112. Ahmad 1984; pp. 74-8, 128-9.
113. Ibid., p. 72.
114. Miner 1997, pp. 103-104.
115. See Miner 1997, p. 36, for a translation of the passage.

rulers also. Not surprisingly, *bin* playing continued to flourish. After the demise of the Mughal empire (1858), the courts of Alwar and Jaipur would be famous for the important *binkar* line of Rajab Ali Khan and the later Senia *sitar* players (see below). In Varanasi, *binkars* Jivan Shah and his brother Pyar Khan were particularly noted. Situated near Lucknow in that eastern (*purab*) area, musical developments in predominantly Hindu Varanasi were intertwined with those of the Muslim cultural centre of Lucknow.

Early nineteenth century Lucknow saw some musicians leaving the city, while others stayed through a period of relative political instability following Asifuddaula's death in 1798. The British signalled their approval of the ending of Awadh's support for the Mughal emperor, by gifting the title of 'king' to Ghaziuddin Haidar (r. 1814-27) and by tightening their grip over his state. The *sitar* seems to have made its way there as accompaniment to dance[116] which was a central part of court entertainment.

There is little of importance to note about music in the court of Awadh in the early nineteenth century but the second surge of cultural activity, one with important effects on music throughout Hindustan, took place in the nine-year reign in Awadh of Wajid Ali Shah (r.1847-1856), in the twilight of the Mughal period. It was a time of extravagant refinement in all the arts—clothing, etiquette, architecture, music, dance, and poetry. While in Delhi the last Mughal ruler Bahadur Shah II (r.1837-58) was patronizing Ghalib, the brilliant poet of Urdu, Urdu poetry flourished in Awadh as well. Wajid Ali Shah was an exceptionally talented and cultured individual, an able administrator, and a popular ruler (the proof of his popularity came when all Awadh rose against the British in 1857). He was, however, rendered ineffective due to the constant interference by the British who disrupted the administration to create a pretext to annex Awadh. Wajid Ali turned his creative energies to culture and the arts. Apart from his patronage of, and contributions to, poetry, dance, and music he is also credited with introducing modern drama and opera into the Subcontinent. As a young man Wajid Ali had been surrounded by courtesan musicians and dancers; Ghulam Raza was one of the teachers of the courtesans, a musician of the socially low *dhari* group. Ghulam Raza, with several members of his family established themselves in favour once Wajid Ali became the ruler; they were given titles, meddled in political affairs, and engaged in corruptive activities to the point that they were ultimately exiled. This contributed to the ammunition that the British could use against Wajid Ali and in 1856, having arbitrarily annexed Awadh, he was given no choice but to relinquish his throne; he left to live in Calcutta. In the meantime, culture and the arts at the court in Awadh had been glorious.

In Awadh, Ghulam Raza Khan created a new style of showy fast-speed *gats* for performance on sitar; Imam suggests that he introduced another influence into *sitar* music, namely fast *gats* composed on the basis of *thumri*, a vocal style associated with dance which had not yet come into its own as a significant Hindustani genre. Razakhani *gats* became indistinguishable from other *gats* in the *sitar* style that developed throughout the eastern region—the Purab *baj*.

As has so frequently been the case in Hindustani music, it was a talented individual who injected personal creative artistry and skill into the course of history: Purab *baj* was spurred by the respected musician Ghulam Muhammad who transferred to the *sitar* techniques and style of the *bin* he had learned from Umrao Khan, the leading *binkar* of the day. In this case, conservatism was the force behind musical change; the *binkars*, steeped as they were in *dhrupad* and invested as they were in their high cultural status, would not teach disciples beyond the family to play the *bin*. Ghulam Muhammad was apparently a more flexible type of musician. He is also credited with having developed a new *sitar* which later came to be called *surbahar*. This instrument, according to Tagore,[117] may have introduced the addition of drone strings (*cikari*) to *sitar*. Another influence on the developing Purab *baj* came from Rampur, with musicians who played the music of Firoz Khan and the Afghani *rabab*, an instrument especially suited to rhythmic work.

The Purab *baj* came to be characterized by a mixture of musical elements from various musical styles: *bin*-inspired *alap* and *jhala*, and also middle or fast-speed *gats* with a variety in *mizrab* (plectrum) patterns, syncopated and complex rhythmic movements and quick melodic movement over the range of the *raga*. This 'eastern style' contrasted with the Delhi instrumental style with its faster speed, constant variety and focus on non-*dhrupad* styles and *ragas*.

Vocal genres mentioned for mid-eighteenth century Delhi are cited by Imam as cultivated in early nineteenth century Lucknow as well: *tarana* as well as *dhrupad* and *khyal*. *Tappa*, which Ahmad did not find discussed in any of the seventeenth or eighteenth century texts that she examined (aside from a short description in *Raga Darpana*), is among the genres mentioned by Imam.[118] *Khyal* appears to have become mainstream music, accepted even by musical families steeped in the *dhrupad* tradition.

Central to Lucknow court culture was *Kathak* dance, which began to develop there into the form familiar to North Indians and Pakistanis today—a dance style marked by virtuosity and complicated rhythmic patterns. The Lucknow style of *Kathak* no doubt developed from a variety of dance styles. Abdul Halim Sharar, for instance, attributes it to a fusion between the styles of the courtesans who flocked to the court of Shujauddaula in Faizabad and the Hindu Kathaks (professional storytellers) of Ayodhya and Benares.[119] As mentioned earlier, dance historian Kapila Vatsyayan believes *Kathak* was influenced by the dance of the dervishes. Furthermore, she adds:

> Exponents [called bhand] in this dance style who lived in the courts of Mohammed Shah Rangila dispersed into various remote regions and established themselves into little sects of dancers, [seeking] the patronage of the royal courts at Lucknow, Rampur, Jaipur, Raigarh, Gwalior and Datia... Pandit Thakur Prasad of Lucknow is the great name with whom the entire development of the Lucknow school of Kathak is associated. [He] served both at the court of Nawab Wajid Ali Shah and the Nawab before him...The patronage of Wajid Ali Shah laid the foundations of this lyrical and delicate school of Kathak at Lucknow.[120]

The connection of *Kathak* with drumming is profound, wherein particular sounds that emerge from the feet and the ankle bells are related to sounds of strokes on *pakhavaj* and *tabla* (and the mnemonic syllables called *bols* by which they are spoken):

> The dancer starts with the simpler rhythmic pattern of the *tabla*, moves to the *pakhawaj*, to the soft jingling sound of the bells themselves and finally to...where the Sahitya [text] comes to play a part in the rhythmic compositions...It is this great subtlety and variety of the *bols*...which makes a Kathak performer stop in the middle of the performance very often to recite loudly the entire rhythm sequences of the *nrtta* composition and to follow it up with the performance of the feet.[121]

With the waning of the Mughal empire and centralized cultural hegemony, the number of smaller courts which emulated Mughal patterns of artistic patronage increased. This had two quite different effects. On the one hand, localized developments were generously fostered. On the other hand, with so many courts being too small for rulers to retain a large number of musicians, the custom developed of a concert circuit. That permitted much greater flexibility in terms of what musicians heard from one place to another. While local specializations had flourished throughout the Mughal empire, the new concert circuit increased the possibility that practitioners of one musical style would take up traits of another. This effectively put into place a mechanism for both local specialization and a pan-Hindustani style that was not imposed by politico-cultural hegemony. *Sitar* music is a case in point:

> When, after the time of Bahadur and Dulha Khan, the descendants of Masit Khan moved from Delhi, a new phase in sitar music began with...Rahimsen [in Rajasthan]. Around this time, the title 'sen,' and the designation 'senia,' came to be considered a mark of the family line descending from Tansen, and Masit Khan and his son Bahadur Khan began to be called Masitsen and Bahadursen by some followers. The so-called Senia sitar line was subsequently traced to them. It is more expressive of the developmental phases of sitar music, however, to separate [them] from the sitar players in Rajasthan beginning with Rahimsen.[122]

Rahimsen is said to have been a descendant of Tansen through a son's line and was the first among those descendants to play the *sitar*; Rahimsen's father was a *dhrupadiya*. Employed at a small court, Jhajjar, located very close to Delhi, tradition must have weighed

---

116. Miner 1997, p. 110.
117. Tagore 1976, pp. 34-5.
118. Ahmad 1984, p. 142.
119. Sharar 1975, p. 142.
120. Vatsyayan, 1956, pp. 76-7. The patronage of the Jaipur courts produced a more austere and slightly less lyrical school of *Kathak*.
121. Vatsyayan 1956, p. 81.
122. Miner 1997, pp. 104-5, drawing on Sastri 1916.

heavily on Rahimsen, but having taken up a new instrument on the death of his father, he was willing to cast his musical net even further. He turned to *khyal*, the vocal genre that was fast becoming a respectable form of music, taking from it '*fikre*, passages played in imitation of a section called *fikrebandi* in a *khyal* performance'.[123] (*Fikra* in *sitar* music came to have a range of meanings.) Drawing of course on his family's musical tradition as well, Rahimsen and his prodigy son Amrtsen (b. 1814) developed a style of *sitar* music that was characterized by attention to *raga*, with *gats* that encapsulated the essence and rules of the *raga* in which they are composed. Unlike Masitkhani style, in imitation of the *bin*, Rahimsen and Amrtsen played an *alap* before the *gat* and *toda*, albeit perhaps somewhat simpler and faster-moving *raga* development than the extremely slow modern *alap*.[124] Amrtsen's rhythmic work surpassed even the skill of *pakhavaj* players with whom he performed.

Drawing on Sastri, Allyn Miner asserts an earlier and greater influence of *khyal* on Senia *sitar* music than has been widely acknowledged. The influence came through that very concert circuit, when Amrtsen performed with the brothers Hassu and Haddu Khan, two of the most important *khyal* singers of the nineteenth century, who were court musicians at Gwalior. 'There is little doubt that Haddu-Hassu Khan's best-known innovations, varieties of fast speed *tans*, had an impact on Senia *sitar* music, despite the prevalent modern view that fast *tan* playing [i.e., *khyal* influence] was instituted in the early 20th century...by *sitar* players Imdad Khan and Inayat Khan'.[125]

The vocal genre *khyal* offers perhaps the best example of the development of local stylistic specializations, though in a pan-Hindustani context.[126] Principally as a patron of *khyal* singers, Daulat Rao Sindhia (r.1794-1827) rejuvenated the centuries-old reputation of Gwalior as a centre of vocal music, attracting most importantly the *khyal* singer Bade Muhammad Khan from Lucknow. Building on his style, the younger musicians Hassu and Haddu Khan with positions under Jayaji Rao Sindhia (r. 1843-1866) cultivated what became known as the Gwalior *gharana* of *khyal* singing that is significant even to the present day. Another style of *khyal* would develop in the Patiala (Punjab) court in the second half of the nineteenth century, after Tanras Khan, one of the greatest singers, sought refuge there from the Delhi court of the last Mughal sovereign, Bahadur Shah II, in 1857 (the year of the revolt against the British).[127] *Khyal* singing also burgeoned in other locations, but well beyond the end of the Mughal period.

By the middle of the nineteenth century, the *tabla* had become one of the three dominant classical drums of North India. Local styles were fostered. In Lucknow, the *tabla* (along with the *sarangi*) was associated primarily with the dance genre, *Kathak*. While no absolutely consistent parallel between dance *bol*/step and drum *bol*/stroke exists, an interrelationship between the two in the 'eastern style' of *tabla* playing is clear.

> Historically, such a complex relationship exists between the bols of a nucleus as danced, as recited (padhant) and as played by the pakhavaj or tabla, that it is almost a moot question to ask which came first ... The relationship of the kathak tradition and the Purab baj tabla is best covered in the area of the larger elaborative pattern, for it is here that structural parallels...are exposed.[128]

Three major schools of *tabla* playing diverged: the Delhi school, and two Purab *baj* schools—Lucknow and Varanasi. Two major regional offshoots exist: the Farukhabad, related closely to the Lucknowi, and the Ajrara (sometimes referred to as the Meerut), related in origin to the Delhi and later to the Farukhabad; both are dependent upon their parent schools for most of their techniques. Until the popularity of Punjabi performers Allah Rakha and his son Zakir Hussain in the second half of the twentieth century, the later, regionally-defined Punjab school remained almost completely separate from the other three. By the end of the nineteenth century the *tabla* had become the standard accompanying instrument for several types of vocal music and for *sitar*.

Significantly, in the conceptual differences behind the playing of the two drums, *pakhavaj* and *tabla*, the deep and lasting influence of West Asian music that began so long ago in South Asia may be revealed. Here we may see musical synthesis at the deepest, i.e., conceptual, level—in this case, in the organization of time. From the analysis of drumming patterns, Stewart arrives at the following conclusion:

> ...Two distinct metric traditions exists (*sic*) in North India today, the second of which has almost completely replaced the first.
>
> The first is primarily confined to the pakhavaj. It applies to tals which a) are linked with the quantitative, verse-derived

structures still popular in South India such as 2+1, 2+1+1, 2+1+2 and their extensions; b) display internal structures which are not delineated through an heirarchy of accents and c) are not conceived in terms of nuclear or skeletal drum patterns the express function of which is to outline their structure.

The second is primarily confined to the dholak, naqqara and tabla. It applies to tals which a) are linked with qualitatively expressed poetic, dance and instrumental structures (found also in the neighbouring Muslim countries) such as 3+3, 3+4, and 4+4; b) display internal structures which are delineated through a heirarchy of primarily pitch and stress accentuation and c) are conceived in terms of skeletal drum patterns the express function of which is to outline the structure of the tal.[129]

Significant, too, is Stewart's occasional reference to the *daf*, the hand-played frame drum known widely as tambourine; for instance: '…for certain sections of the dance, nuclei are borrowed intact from such drums as the naqqara, tasa and daf, precisely because of their excellent euphonic qualities'.[130] Thus, a historical link to 'structures found also in neighbouring Islamic countries' might very well have come also through the *da'ira/daf* that is the ubiquitous drum for accompaniment of non-Indian dance styles in Mughal miniature paintings (Figs. 2 and 4).

To conclude, I return to a point made at the beginning of the chapter, that a mutual cultural appreciation of dance traditions, including the music, was a particularly significant causal factor in the gradual synthesis of South Asian with West and Central Asian musical traditions. This synthesis was skillfully guided and nurtured by the Mughals—a dynasty exemplary in the refinement of its taste. In paintings from the pre-Mughal Sultanate period, through the Mughal dynasty, the *pakhavaj*, *naqqara*, and *da'ira/daf* are consistently shown in the accompaniment of dance (Fig. 1). Dance provided a performative nexus as the musical systems and ensembles gradually merged in the music of the Mughal court. Energized both by disparate practices such as the use of a drone-producing instrument and an additional concept of meter, and by instruments such as long-necked lutes in different shapes and sizes, the shared experiences of South Asians which extended even beyond the Mughal court and later, beyond the Mughal period, provided the world with one of the marvels of our age—Hindustani classical music.

GLOSSARY OF MUSICAL TERMS

Alap	Improvised melodic structure to introduce a melodic mode (*raga*)
Baj	Instrumental playing style
Bin	Plucked stick-zither with fixed frets; developed from the *rudra vina*
Binkar	Player of the *rudra vina* (now called *bin*)
Bol	'Word' or 'syllable'; in music and dance, also mnemonic syllables for dance steps and drum strokes
Cikari	Drone string
Da'ira/daf	West Asian frame drum (tambourine)
Dhol	Cylindrical or barrel-shaped drum, played by hand and stick or two hands
Dholak	Hand-played barrel-shaped drum
Dhrupad	Type of classical vocal music; also played on *rudra vina/bin*
Dhrupadiya	Singer of *dhrupad*
Dhrupad rabab	West/South Asian long-necked plucked lute used for *dhrupad*-type music
Fikra	Melodic passages consisting of short, quick, ever changing series of pitches
Gat	Instrumental composition
Gat-toda	Type of composition for plucked stringed instruments
Gharana	Musically affiliated group with a distinctive traditional style of singing or playing (literally: household)

---

123. Sastri 1916.
124. Miner 1997, p. 107.
125. Ibid., p. 108.
126. Wade 1984.
127. Ibid., Chapter 8.
128. Stewart 1974, pp. 71-2.
129. Ibid., pp. 100-101.
130. Ibid., p. 72.

Ghazal	Type of song with Urdu text and meter
Ghichak	West Asian bowed spike-lute
Hindustani classical music	('Hindustan': Persian for India) refers primarily to the music of the central and northern regions of the Subcontinent, in which the absorption of Arab, Persian and Central Asian music was the greatest.
Jhala	Playing style on melodic instruments in which constant repetition of pitches creates driving fast rhythm
Kalavant	Historical South Asian term for master musician
Karna	West Asian trumpet, with straight or swan's-neck curved tube
Kathak	Pakistani/North Indian classical dance style
Kavitt	Eighteenth century song-type
Khyal/khayyal	Song style that became a highly improvisational type of classical vocal music
Lute	Stringed instrument on which the strings run over both a resonating chamber and a neck; played by bowing or plucking
Mid/Meend	Term for gliding from one melodic pitch to another
Mizrab	Plectrum used for plucking a stringed instrument
Na'i/Nayi	West Asian end-blown, vertical flute
Naqqara	West Asian bowl-shaped drum, usually stick-played
Naubat/Naqqara khana	West Asian military band and imperial heralding ensemble of wind and percussion instruments
Nayak	Historical category of South Asian musician who was both skilled performer and music theorist
Oud	West Asian short-necked plucked-lute
Pakhavaj	Hand-played barrel-shaped drum with one end wider than the other; used to accompany *dhrupad* and *rudra vina/bin*
Prabhanda	Ancient type of South Indian music with multiple sections
Qanun	West Asian plucked board-zither (dulcimer)
Qawwali	Music genre of South Asian Muslims in which devotional texts are sung to ecstatic music
Qawwal/qawwaliya	Singer of *qawwali*
Qubuz	West Asian bowed lute
Rabab	West Asian long-necked plucked lute without frets
Rababiya	Player of *rabab*
Raga	Melodic mode
Ragamala	North Indian type of painting that depicts the extra-musical associations of melodic modes
Ragini	Term for melodic mode in the *raga-ragini* classification system for modes
Rudra vina	Mughal period plucked stick-zither
Sarangi	Waisted, box-resonated bowed lute
Sarod	Modern short-necked plucked lute
Setar	West Asian long-necked plucked lute
Shahna'i	West Asian double-reed wind instrument
Sing	C-shaped horn
Sitar	Modern long-necked plucked lute with frets
Sufiana kalam	Sufi (mystical) poetry
Surbahar	Large, deep-sounding *sitar*-like plucked lute
Sursingar	Modified form of the *dhrupad rabab*
Svarmandal	South Asian plucked board-zither; similar to *qanun*
Tabla	A pair of hand-played tunable drums; used to accompany *khyal* and some other vocal genres, *sitar* and other instruments
Tala	Small hand cymbals used for dance
Tala	Musical meter
Tambur	West Asian long-necked plucked lute with frets
Tan	A virtuosic fast melodic passage
Tappa	Vocal music derived from rough Punjabi camel drivers' song, refined into a richly ornamented song style
Tar	West Asian long-necked plucked lute
Tarana	Rhythm-oriented type of vocal music featuring vocables, poetry, pitch and drum syllables as text
Thumri	Type of light classical, romantic vocal music originally associated with dance
Zamazama	Trill ornamenting a pitch on a stringed instrument
Zither	Stringed instrument on which the strings run over the full length of the body of the instrument, whether the body is a stick or a box of some shape

BIBLIOGRAPHY

Ahmad, Najma Perveen. *Hindustani Music: A Study of its Development in Seventeenth and Eighteenth Centuries* [sic], New Delhi: Manohar Publications, 1984.

Ain-i Akbari. By Abul Fazl 'Allami ibn Mubarak. 3 vols. Cited from translation by H. Blochmann (vol. 1) and Colonel H.S. Jarrett (vols. 2-3). Calcutta: Royal Asiatic Society of Bengal, 1869-77; 2nd ed.: vol. 1, 1927; vol. 2, 1949; vol. 3, 1948. 3rd ed. with corrections and further annotations to vols. 2 and 3 by Sir Jadunath Sarkar. New Delhi: Oriental Books Reprint Corp., 1977.

Akbar Nama. By Abul Fazl. Cited from translation by Henry Beveridge. 3 vols. Calcutta: *Bibliotheca Indica*, 1873-87. Repr., Delhi: Ess Ess Publications, 1977.

Asher, Catherine B. 'Architecture of Mughal India'. *The New Cambridge History of India* I.4. Cambridge: Cambridge University Press, 1992.

Babur Nama (Memoirs of Babur). Cited from translation by Annette Susannah Beveridge. London: Luzac, 1922. Repr., New Delhi: Oriental Books Reprint Corp., 1979. Also translated by W.M. Thackston, Jr. as *Baburnama*, 3 vols. (Cambridge: HUP, 1993); *The Baburnama* (New York: OUP, 1996).

Bor, Joep. 'The Voice of the Sarangi: An Illustrated History of Bowing in India'. *Quarterly Journal*, Bombay National Centre for the Performing Arts, 15/16: 1-183.

Brhaspati, K.C. *Musalman aur Bharatiya sangit*. Delhi: Rajkamal Prakasan, 1974.

Burnell, John. *Bombay in the Days of Queen Anne* and *Burnell's Narrative of his Adventure in Bengal*, edited by S.T. Sheppard and W. Foster. Nendeln: Lichenstein 2, 1967.

Dhond, M.V. *The Evolution of Khyal*. New Delhi: Sangeet Natak Akademi, 1980.

During, J. and A. Dick. 'Rabab', in *The New Grove Dictionary of Musical Instruments*, edited by Stanley Sadie. London: Macmillan Press, 3: 298-99.

Fetis, F-J. *Histoire générale de la musique: depuis les temps les plus anciens jusqu'a nos jours*. 5 vols. Paris: Librarie de Firmin Didot Fr'eres, Fils et Cie, 1869.

Francklin, W. *History of the Reign of Shah Aulum*. London, 1798.

Hambly, Gavin and Wim Swaan. *Cities of Mughal India. Delhi, Agra, Fatehpur Sikri*. New Delhi: Vikas Publishing House, Ltd., 1977.

Heber, Reginald. *Narrative of a Journey through the Upper Provinces of India, from Calcutta to Bombay, 1824-1825*. 3 vols. 4th edition, London, 1829.

Humayun Nama (The History of Humayun). By Gul-Badan Begam. Cited from translation by Annette S. Beveridge. London: Royal Asiatic Society, 1902. Repr., New Delhi: Oriental Books Reprint Corp., 1983.

Imam, Hakim Mohammad Karam. *Melody Through the Centuries: A Chapter from Ma'danul Moosiqi, 1856*. Sangeet Natak Akademi Bulletin 11-12 (April) 13-26, 33.

Irvine, William. *Later Mughals*, edited and augmented by Jadunath Sarkar. Calcutta: M.C. Sarkar and Sons; London: Luzac, 1922.

Khan, Dargah Quli, Bahadur. *Muraqqa'-e Dehli: The Mughal Capital in Muhammad Shah's Time*. English translation, introduction, and notes by Chander Shekhar and Shama Mitra Chenoy. Delhi: Deputy Publication, 1989.

Kramrisch, Stella. *The Art of India Through the Ages*. New York: Phaidon Press, 1965, 2nd. ed.

Leach, Linda York. *Mughal and Other Indian Paintings from the Chester Beatty Library*. 2 vols. London: Scorpion Cavendish, 1995.

Mahillon, Victor-Charles. *Catalogue descriptif & analytique du Musée Instrumental de Conservatoire Royal de Musique de Bruxelles*. Vol. 1. Gand: Librarie Générale de A.D. Hoste, 1893.

Manucci, Niccalao. *Storia do Mogor (or Mogul India 1653-1708)*. 4 vols. Translated by William Irvine. London: J. Murray, 1907.

Meer, Wim van der. *Hindustani Music in the Twentieth Century*. New Delhi: Allied Publishers, 1980.

Miner, Allyn Jane. *Sitar and Sarod in the eighteenth and nineteenth centuries*. Delhi: Motilal Banarsidas, 1997.

Muntakhabu-t-Tawarikh (The reign of Akbar, from 963 to 1004 AH), by 'Abdul Qadir Ibn-i-Muluk Shah, (known as Al-Bada'uni). 3 vols. Delhi: Renaissance Publishing House, 1986.

Naqvi, Hameeda Khatoon. *History of Mughal Government and Administration*. Delhi: Kanishka Publishing House, 1990.

Neville, H.R. *Fyzabad, A Gazeteer*. Allahabad: Government Press, 1928.

Pacholczyk, Józef. 'Sufyana Kalam, the Classical Music of Kashmir.' *Asian Music*, 1978, 10: 1-16.

Richards, John F. 'The Formulation of Imperial Authority under Akbar and Jahangir,' in *Kingship and Authority in South Asia*, edited by John F. Richards, South Asian Studies, publication 3, Madison: University of Wisconsin, 1978: 252-85.

Rusva, Mirza Muhammad. *Umrao Jan Ada*, translated by K. Singh and M.A. Husaini. Calcutta, 1961.

Saksena, Banarsi Prasad. *History of Shahjahan of Dihli*. Repr., Allahabad: Central Book Depot, 1962.

Sarkar, Jadunath N. *History of Aurangzeb: Mainly Based on Persian Sources*. 5 vols., Reprinted Bombay: Orient Longmans, 1972.

Sastri, S. *Sangit Sudarsan*. Varanasi: Chowkhamba Sanskrit Series Office, 1916.

Schimmel, Annemarie. Introduction to *Anvari's Divan: A Pocket Book for Akbar*. New York: Metropolitan Museum of Art, 1983.

Shah Jahan Nama. Condensed from the *Padshahnama* by Inayat Khan. Cited from translation by A.R. Fuller, 1891 (British Library, ADD30,777); edited and completed by W.E. Begley and Z. A. Desai. Delhi: Oxford University Press, 1990.

Sharar, Abdul Halim. *Lucknow: The Last Phase of an Oriental Culture*. Translated and edited by E.S. Harcourt and Fakhir Hussein. London: Paul Elek, 1975.

Sharma, B.R. 'Contribution of Rajasthan to Indian Music.' In *Indian Music: A Perspective*, edited by G. Kuppuswamy and M. Hariharan. Delhi: Sundeep Prakashan, 1980: 104-21.

Simsar, Muhammed A. (transl.) *The Cleveland Museum of Art's 'Tuti-nama': Tales of a Parrot*. By Ziyauddin Nakhshabi. Cleveland, Ohio: The Cleveland Museum of Arts. Graz, Austria: Akademische Druck u. Verlagsanstalt, 1978.

Smart, Ellen and Daniel S. Walker. *Prince of the princes: Indian Art of the Mughal Era in the Cincinnati Art Museum*. Cincinnati: Cincinnati Art Museum, 1985.

Spear, Percival. *Twilight of the Mughuls: Studies in Late Mughul Delhi*. Cambridge: Cambridge University Press, 1951.

Srivastava, Indurama. *Dhrupada: A Study of its Origin, Historical Development, Structure, and Present State*. Utrecht: Elinkwijk, 1977.

Stewart, Rebecca Marie. *The Tabla in Perspective*. Ph.D. dissertation, University of California, Los Angeles, 1974.

Tabakat-i Nasiri. A General History of the Muhammadan Dynasties of Asia, including Hindustan; from A.H. 194 (810 C.E.) to A.H. 658 (1260 C.E.). Cited from translation by Major H.G. Raverty. New Delhi: Munshiram Manoharlal, 1970.

Tagore, S.M. *Yantra Kosha or a Treasury of the Musical Instruments of Ancient and of Modern India, and of Various Other Countries*. First edition, 1875. Reprint. New York: AMS Press, 1976.

Thielemann, Selina. *The Darbhanga Tradition: Dhrupada in the School of Pandit Vidur Mallik*. Varanasi: Indica Books, 1997.

Tuzuk-i Jahangiri (The Memoirs of Jahangir). Cited from translation by Alexander Rogers and Henry Beveridge. 2 vols. Delhi: Munshiram Manoharlal, 1968.

Vatsyayan, Kapila. 'Kathak'. *The Journal of the Music Academy*, Madras, 1956, 27: 74-88.

Vatsyayan, Kapila. *Dance in Indian Painting*. New Delhi: Abhinav, 1982.

Verma, Som Prakash. *Mughal Painters and Their Work: A Biographical Survey and Comprehensive Catalogue*. Delhi: Oxford University Press, 1994.

Wade, Bonnie C. 'Performing the Drone in Hindustani Classical Music: What Mughal Paintings Show Us to Hear,' in *World of Music*, ed. Bonnie C. Wade, 38 (2), 1996: 41-67.

Wade, Bonnie C. *Imaging Sound. An Ethnomusicological Study of Music, Art, and Culture in Mughal India*. Chicago: University of Chicago Press, 1998.

Wade, Bonnie C. *Khyal. Creativity within North India's Classical Music Tradition*. Cambridge: Cambridge University Press, 1984.

Welch, Stuart Cary. *Imperial Mughal Painting*. New York: Brazillier, 1978.

PORTRAIT OF A VINA PLAYER
This uninscribed work is almost certainly a portrait of the great imperial musician, Naubat Khan. Mughal, Akbar period; last quarter of the 16th century. Courtesy of the Goenka Collection.

9
THE ECONOMY
Irfan Habib

AGRICULTURE AND THE AGRARIAN SECTOR

India (in its pre-1947 frontiers) at the beginning of the seventeenth century was one of the most populous regions of the world. It contained, according to latest estimates, some 145 million inhabitants, which possibly exceeded the size of China's population at that time.[1] But with even this number of inhabitants, the area under cultivation was probably about a half of what it was at the beginning of the twentieth century.[2] This meant for ca.1600 a much larger forest cover, and open waste land for pasturages, and probably a higher level of precipitation.

The forest was, therefore, far more important for the economy than we can now imagine—as a source of timber, firewood, charcoal, lac, wild silks, animal skins, honey, medicinal plants, and elephants (much in demand for military and ceremonial use). Maddison may, therefore, not be far wrong in assigning 10 per cent of the labour force in Mughal India to the tribal sector, as against 5 per cent in ca. 1900.[3]

The availability of virgin land meant that the more intrinsically fertile land would have been brought under cultivation first, although data about crop yields do not suggest that these were very different from what they were in the latter half of the nineteenth century.[4] This is largely because agricultural methods during this period underwent no fundamental alteration. But agricultural production was not static. The large list of crops already cultivated was enlarged by the diffusion in the seventeenth century of tobacco and maize, brought from the New World. In the next century the green chilli also reached Northern India. Sericulture already established in Bengal in the fifteenth century became a very important sector of peasant production in that province in the seventeenth century. The monsoons naturally displayed the same vagaries as at present, and thus the crops had their consequential great ups and downs, leading to periodic gluts or famines and scarcities.[5]

As one may assume, South Asian agriculture in Mughal times was mainly peasant agriculture and, though the land might have been abundant, the average holding owing to the cultivators' limited resources in terms of cattle and plough, was quite small. A remarkably detailed survey of a revenue-grant at Navsari, near Surat in Gujarat, in 1596, discloses that each field with a different crop on average covered barely 0.6 hectare, while the average peasant-holding itself was no more than 2.8 hectare.[6] An official survey of ten villages of Chatsu in eastern Rajasthan in 1666, showed each peasant owning less than three bullocks, on the average.[7]

The peasantry, therefore, presented to the external observer the spectacle of an undifferentiated, impoverished mass. 'Stark want' and 'bitter woe' were the words used by Pelsaert, the Dutch factor at Agra, 1626, to describe the life of the 'common people' in the Mughal empire.[8] Contemporary descriptions of peasants' living conditions—diet, clothing, food—impart substance to this general statement.[9] While famine could always take its toll when it came around, disease and epidemic continually ravaged the countryside. Of twenty-five villagers who appeared before the *qazi* of Mathura between 1653 and 1717 and had their descriptions recorded (in Vrindaban documents), as many as ten bore marks of the dreaded small pox.[10]

Uniformly impoverished as the peasantry looked to the outsider, it had internally its own sub-classes and strata. The Hindu caste system, the regressive nature of the land tax, the fluctuations of prices, and the extensive web of usury, all contributed to such differentiation. But that differentiation existed everywhere is not only attested to by many documents containing records of individual peasant holdings, cattle and tax-payments, but also by official statements distinguishing the 'big men' (*kalantaran*) of the villages from the 'small peasants' (*reza ri`aya*).[11] To give an example from our documentary evidence, a census of plough-oxen in a village of pargana Tijara in Haryana in 1666, showed that out of thirty-eight peasants, twenty-six had only one plough each, but two had three each and two had as many as five.[12]

Those who had more than one plough, for example, a person like Akbar's master dyer Ramdas, who held above 8 hectares as 'self-cultivated holding' in a village near Agra in 1562,[13] must have needed to employ hired labour. Most of such hired labour came not only from pauperized peasants, but also from the so-called 'menial' castes. Prevented from holding land by the caste system, members of these lowly Hindu castes constituted a large rural proletariat, whose very size, if not also the actual repression of upper castes, compelled them to work in the fields for depressed wages. India was probably singular in creating such a class since ancient times through a deliberate piece of 'social engineering'.[14] Agrestic slavery also existed, but was apparently confined to regions like Assam, Mithila (Bihar) and Malabar (Kerala).

The village was the characteristic unit of settlement. The numbers of villages have not grown in the net in most areas since Mughal times, while population has increased many times over. The average village in the seventeenth century must therefore have been far smaller than its successor today. This explains the small number of peasants who are assigned to individual villages in Mughal-period documents. Much has been written on the 'community' that the traditional South Asian village constituted. We are fortunate in possessing a large number of documents in Persian and Braj that the temples of Vrindaban (near Mathura) have preserved, from the sixteenth and seventeenth centuries. These show peasants belonging to different families (and therefore possibly to different castes, and, certainly, often of different faiths, since Muslim names also occur), coming together as *panch* or *muqaddams* and 'in agreement' disposing of or selling away plots of waste land of the village. These *panch* also controlled the village fund, into which proceeds from the sale of waste land were paid, with some shares appropriated by the individual *panch* themselves.[15] Official Mughal documents make it clear that it was these 'big men' who collected the revenue shares (*behrimal*) from each individual peasant (*asami*) to meet the *jama*, or tax-demand upon the village as a whole.[16] The village community was thus by no means democratic, but provided a mechanism for surplus-extraction to the ruling class, while sustaining a kind of sub-exploitation of the poorer peasantry and labourers by the village upper elements.

Yet surplus extraction could succeed only if certain needs of the peasants were also met. Thus there were land-allotments made out of village land for 'artificers and labourers' comprising persons of 'menial' caste like *chamars* or artisans like blacksmiths, carpenters, barbers, etc., all claiming petty shares in harvests as well.[17] These relationships seem to have been with the village as a whole, and not with individual 'patrons' (*jajmans*) as Wiser had suggested.[18] It is probable that the arrangement enabled the village to function partly within a 'natural economy', while the relationship with the market in the case of the bulk of the peasantry was confined merely to the sale of a part of the produce in order to obtain money to pay tax.

Alongside such peasant-held (*ra'iyati*) villages, there were villages controlled by a superior rural class, for whose members the designation *zamindar* was adopted by the Mughal chancery from Akbar's time onwards, though earlier use of the term is also documented. Their rights over peasants could have originated in various ways: they could be descendants of earlier ruling clans (*ranakas*, *rautas*, etc.) depressed by the imperial regime into hereditary intermediaries under various fiscal arrangements; or their ancestors had established

---

1. The estimates for India's population, ca.1601, have been revised upwards: 100 million (Moreland); 125 million (Kingsley Davis); 145 million (S. Moosvi). For the method leading to the last estimate see Shireen Moosvi, *The Economy of the Mughal Empire, c. 1595*, Delhi, 1987, pp. 395-406, where the earlier estimates are also discussed.
2. See Irfan Habib, *Agrarian System of Mughal India (1556-1707)*, Bombay, 1963, pp. 1-22; S. Moosvi, *Economy*, pp. 39-72.
3. Angus Maddison, *Class Structure and Economic Growth: India and Pakistan since the Moguls*, London, 1971, pp. 33, 166-7.
4. S. Moosvi, *Economy*, pp. 73-92.
5. I. Habib, *Agrarian System*, pp. 100-10.
6. See my analysis of the document in *Proceedings of the Indian History Congress*, 54th session, 1993, Mysore, pp. 248-50.
7. See table in S.P. Gupta, *Agrarian System of Eastern Rajasthan*, Delhi, 1986, pp. 256.
8. 'Remonstrantie', transl. W.H. Moreland and P. Geyl, *Jahangir's India*, Cambridge, 1925, p. 60.
9. Cf. I. Habib, *Agrarian System*, pp. 90-99.
10. These documents comprise a large collection, preserved in photographs, gathered by the late Dr Tarapada Mukherji, of the School of Oriental and African Studies, London. Dr Mukherji most generously sent me photocopies of all documents that were in Persian or were bilingual.
11. Cf. I. Habib, *Agrarian System*, pp. 19-21.
12. Cf. Satish Chandra in *Indian Historical Review*, III (1), p. 26.
13. See *Akbar and his India*, ed. I. Habib, Delhi, 1997, p. 283.
14. Cf. I. Habib, *Agrarian System*, pp. 119-22. The social engineering extended to Muslim communities as well: 'kamins' in Western Punjab and 'Hindkis' in Pukhtun areas, corresponded to landless menial castes in other parts of the country.
15. See I. Habib in: *Peasants in Indian History*, ed. V.K. Thakur and A. Aounshuman, Patna, 1996, pp. 354-66, for an analysis of this evidence.
16. I. Habib, *Agrarian System*, pp. 126-7.
17. Ibid., pp. 366-68.
18. On this see H. Fukazawa's important article, 'Rural Servants in the Maharashtrian Village: Demiurgic or Jajmani System', reprinted in the posthumous collection of his essays, *The Medieval Deccan Peasants, Social Systems and States—Sixteenth to Eighteenth Centuries*, Delhi, 1991, pp. 199-244.

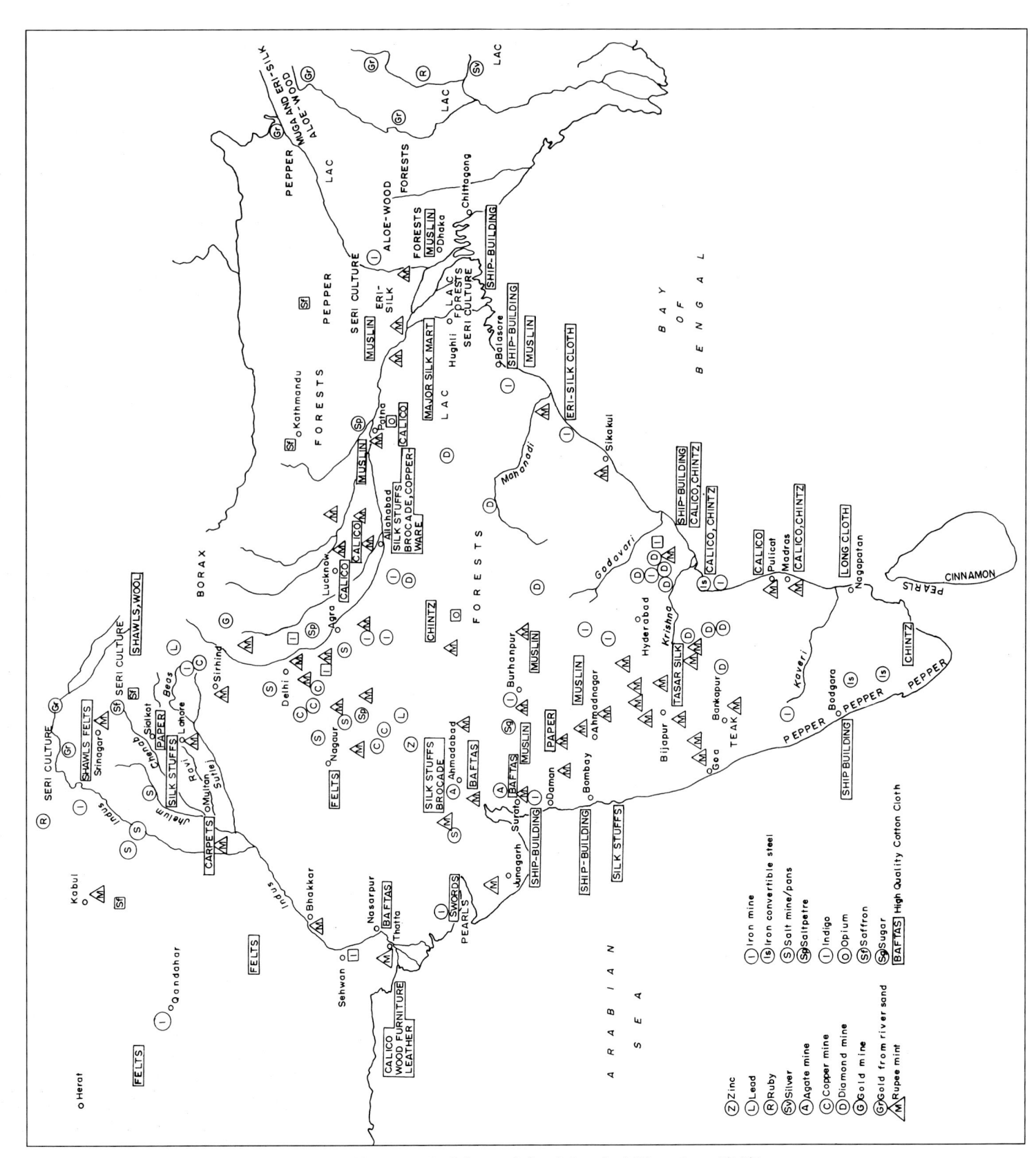

Economic Map of the Mughal Empire, 1707

themselves by force at some earlier time compelling peasants to recognize their claims to certain levies (as was the case with the *girasiyas* in Gujarat and Western Malwa), or they had arranged to settle peasants who thereupon became their particular clients (*chhappar-band*, or, in Rajasthan, *basi*). Of such heterogenous origins, the *zamindars'* status and the exact nature of their rights varied; but the Mughal administration seems to have striven with some success to establish certain common essentials. The right was coupled with the duty to collect taxes from the peasants for which the *zamindar* would receive an allowance (*nankar*). His other entitlements (*haqq*) from the peasants were also sought to be defined; if he did not perform his duty as tax-collector, he could be removed, in which case some compensation for these entitlements (*malikana*) would be paid to him (generally held to be a tenth of the land revenue). Another factor in favour of uniformity was that, as an article of property, the *zamindari* right was universally held to be saleable; and the market should have encouraged certain common expectations from the title. Caste bastions were undoubtedly eroded thereby, and so isolation broken, as land grantees (for example *madad-i ma'ash* holders), rival *zamindars* and money-lenders purchased *zamindaris* from the traditional, established owners.

Towards the end of the nineteenth century the terms *zamindar* and landlord became synonymous. This was in part because with 'the fall of the rupee', the British-Indian land tax had declined in real magnitude (though the colonial regime made up the loss through indirect taxation which fell mainly on the poor), and in part because with the increasing 'commercialization' of agriculture (especially after railway construction), the money rents paid by peasants to *zamindars* could be raised substantially. Thus the old tax-rent equivalence became a thing of the past, the *zamindars* themselves becoming in effect rent-receivers. But in the seventeenth century conditions were quite different. If prices at which *zamindaris* were sold are to be taken as capitalized values of the net annual income that the buyer would expect to receive, it can be shown that such income must have been much smaller than the annual land revenue from the same land.[19]

THE STATE AND THE ECONOMY

The crucial link between the rural economy and the urban superstructure was the land tax. Detailed taxation documents as they have turned up (notably the Rajasthani *arasathas*) generally confirm the high official rates for revenue in terms of produce as given in administrative texts and manuals. While the tax varied as a share of the produce or in terms of money according to crop, it hardly ever in effect fell below one-third of the value of the produce and tended generally to approximate to a half.[20] The tendency of the Mughal administration was to shift from collection in kind to collection in money.[21]

A few words may be added here about the Mughal land-revenue system. There is no reason to believe that the land-tax was heavier than it was under the previous regimes. There was undoubtedly however, much systematization. Akbar perfected the *zabt* system, under which revenue was realized on the basis of measurement, different tax-rates being fixed for different crops in terms of money per *bigha* (unit of area, equal to 0.24 hectare). In the 1650s the system was extended to Mughal Deccan. But forms of 'crop-sharing', implying fixation or collection of tax in kind also continued to be used. The difference from the later British settlements lay in the fact that the British fixed the tax either on the estate or a particular area of land, irrespective of the crop or crops cultivated in it. In other words, more certainty was attained at the expense of flexibility: it is not easy to say which of the two the peasant found harder to bear.

The right to levy the revenue flowed, in the Mughal system, from the emperor. He could grant it away for life, as was done in the case of the so-called *madad-i ma'ash* grants held by theologians, priests, and the like. These grants, however, did not cover an area larger than 5 or 6 per cent of the revenue-paying land in any province.[22] The larger assignments were those known as *jagirs*, held for short periods, against pay claims under

---

19. I. Habib, *Agrarian System*, pp. 157-9, 162.
20. Ibid., pp. 151-4. In 1672-88 in Bahraich, UP, the price of *zamindari* amounted to 2.27 years' revenue only; in 1861, in UP as a whole it amounted to five years' revenue and in 1899-1900 to twenty-eight years' revenue!
21. Cf. ibid., pp. 190-96; S. Moosvi, *Economy*, pp. 95-125. For the evidence of *arasathas*, see S.P. Gupta, *The Agrarian System of Eastern Rajasthan (c. 1650-c. 1750)*, Delhi, 1986, pp. 140-55.
22. I. Habib, *Agrarian System of Mughal India*, pp. 236-40.

the *mansab* system, which in turn required the *jagir* holder (*jagirdar*) to maintain troops (*tabinan*) of prescribed quality and size. Akbar took the key steps in 1574-75, when he gave all his officers various numerical ranks (*mansabs*), with pay fixed by schedules; and began a long-term effort to fix the estimated annual net revenue-yield (*jama*) of each locality.[23] The system as he bequeathed it to his successors continued for over a hundred years without much fundamental change. The *jagirs* too continued to be transferred after short periods, a fact not only confirmed by documents from different localities, but also by repeated comments from contemporaries and European travellers. Bernier, in particular, underlined the dire results of this system for the peasants, since, under it, the assignees were only interested in immediate gain.[24]

The revenues that the Mughal emperor drew from lands reserved for the treasury—the so-called *khalisa sharifa*—and the princes and the nobility from their *jagirs*, amounted to an enormous drain of wealth from the countryside. Part of the revenues so collected remained within the countryside in the form of expenses on local troops (*sih-bandi*), or allowances to local agents or profits left with revenue-farmers. And some amount was set aside for agricultural improvement, through *taccavi* loans or expenditure on irrigation works, orchards, etc. But there is little doubt that the bulk went to the towns to be spent on the imperial and aristocratic households, or passed on, in pay, to the bureaucracy, troops, retainers, and servants. There was undoubtedly a multiplier effect flowing from the employment so created. As Manucci put it, the presence of 8000 Mughal cavalrymen implied the actual presence of some 30,000 persons to include all those who served them.[25] Even if one held each person to represent a family of four members only, we would have here a dependant population of some 120,000 persons. Since the Mughal imperial army was officially estimated in 1647 to contain 200,000 cavalry,[26] we may suppose that three million persons would have been thereby maintained in towns and camps.

The emperor's and the aristocrats' own establishments consisted of large numbers of officials, servants, and slaves; and these, therefore, also constituted an enormous primary service sector, generating further employment for meeting their own consumption needs. The royal and aristocratic demand for luxuries and craft products not only helped maintain large populations of local craftsmen, but also craftsmen working in towns in distant regions, specializing in particular goods. Even when the demand was for imported horses of high breeds (possibly numbering 25,000 annually) from Iran and Central Asia,[27] this too indirectly assisted the Indian craft sector since the animals were paid for mainly through export of Indian products, notably textiles.[28]

TOWNS AND CRAFTS

It is difficult to estimate the size of the urban population that the diffusion of agrarian surplus would have generated. An estimate of up to 15 per cent of the total population living in towns, giving an absolute urban population of, say, about twenty million for the whole Subcontinent may not be unreasonable, especially if we bear in mind the estimates we have for

---

23. Ibid., pp. 313-4.
24. Francois Bernier, *Travels in the Mughal Empire, 1656-1668*, transl. A. Constable, 2nd ed., revised by V.A. Smith, Oxford, 1916, p. 227.
25. Nicolao Manucci, *Storia do Mogor*, transl. W. Irvine, London, 1907-08, II, p. 75n.
26. 'Abdu'l Hamid Lahori, *Padshahnama*, Bib. Ind., Calcutta, 1866-72, II, p. 715.
27. Bernier, op. cit., p. 203.
28. These points are discussed with references in I. Habib, *Essays in Indian History—Towards a Marxist Perception*, Delhi, 1995, pp. 202-13, and in S. Moosvi, *Economy*, pp. 272-95.
29. See T. Raychaudhuri and I. Habib, *Cambridge Economic History of India*, I, Cambridge, 1982, pp. 170-71.
30. Nizamu'ddin Ahmad, *Tabaqat-i Akbari*, ed. B. De and M. Hidayat Hosain, Calcutta, 1913-35, III, pp. 545-6.
31. The returns for Sojhat (1659-60), Jaitaran (1662), and Merta (1663-64), are those of numbers of houses classified by castes of occupants, given in Nainsi, *Marwar ra pargana ri Vigat* [1664] ed. Narayan Singh Bhati, Vol. I, Jodhpur, 1964, pp. 391, 496-7, and Vol. II (Jodhpur, 1969), pp. 83-86. Even after excluding the extraordinary large number of Mahajans (money-lenders, bankers) put at 738, at Sojhat the remaining upper castes had 891 houses in that town as against 616 of the lower castes. In Jaitaran after excluding a similarly high number (720) of Mahajans, the upper-caste houses numbered 585, the rest but 532. In Merta, the Mahajans' houses numbered 2512, out of a total of 5860.
32. For an insightful survey of non-agricultural production in Mughal India see Tapan Raychaudhuri, *Cambridge Economic History of India*, I, pp. 261-307.
33. See miniatures reproduced in A.J. Qaisar, *Building Construction in Mughal India—the Evidence from Painting*, Delhi, 1988, Plates 3, 4, 5, 6, 7, and detail iii.
34. 'Values as an Obstacle to Economic Growth in South Asia', *Journal of Economic History*, xxvii (1967), pp. 588-607.

A GROUP OF TRAVELLERS.
Mughal, last quarter of the 17th Century. Courtesy of the Goenka Collection.

the populations of several towns in the seventeenth century. Agra led here, possibly reaching 800,000 (1666); Delhi had 500,000 (1659-66); Lahore, 400,000-700,000 (1581 and 1615); and towns such as Thatta (1631-5), Ahmadabad (1613), Surat (1700), Patna (1631), Dhaka (c. 1630) and Machchhilipatanam (1672) had estimated populations of around 200,000 each.[29] Akbar's empire in 1592 was indeed said to contain 120 cities and 3200 townships.[30]

It would seem that the nature of expenditure by the ruling classes often tended to promote the direct service sector even more than production through crafts. Though three small towns in Marwar for which we have good statistics, may not necessarily be typical of their class, it is significant that here the upper castes, whose members served as clerks, soldiers, retainers, attendants, etc., constituted a larger number than the lower castes (*pavan jat*), viz. artisans as well as 'menial' persons from amongst whom day-labourers might have come.[31]

Although the service sector accounted for a large part of the population, the towns were still home to very large numbers engaged in manufactures, extractive industries and construction.[32] Women's labour was extensively used; they worked as spinners at home in the textile industry; they worked also as lime-makers and brick and stone carriers at building sites—to which the Mughal miniatures bear witness.[33] Castes were an important factor behind a fixed division of labour, while making available a large reserve of unskilled labour. But how far caste was economically an absolutely restrictive factor is uncertain. Muslims could move into profitable professions where caste monopoly constrained labour supply; and, as M.D. Morris has shown, there was considerable flexibility in the caste system for professional adjustments in the long term.[34] To European observers, it generally appeared that the South

Asian artisan's tools were crude, and that much larger numbers were employed than in Europe for the same tasks.[35] It is possible that the pressure for technological innovation or diffusion was obstructed by the availability of cheap, highly dextrous labour; but other factors, notably ideological (lack of intellectual interest in technological matters, for one), might also have been at work.

Market relationships dominated craft production outside the villages. Many artisans simply produced their wares and put them for sale in their huts or shops or in the open in fairs and bazaars, especially if the costs of materials were low (of which ordinary potters provide an illustration that comes immediately to mind). But even where materials were more expensive, as in the weaving of 'amberty' calicoes, where the further process of washing had also to be paid for by the weavers, we find the weavers selling their products to merchants waiting for them in the markets ('gonges'—*ganj*).[36] Some artisans, such as goldsmiths, who dealt in still more expensive wares, had workshops (*karkhana*) of their own, working with presumably hired labourers.[37]

The merchants' control over artisanal production began with the effort to induce artisans to produce according to their orders, the obligation secured through the giving of advances (*dadani*).[38] In certain cases, merchants also made the advances not in the form of money but in the form of the material to be worked, for instance silk-yarn to weavers in Bengal.[39] From this the next step was for them to establish *karkhanas* of their own. The way two English factors on their first visit to Patna in 1620, set up a 'Cor Conna' employing nearly a hundred workmen to wind silk, suggests that they were only following a locally established practice.[40]

The emperor, princes, and nobles too had their *karkhanas* where numbers of workmen were employed to manufacture luxury goods, weapons, etc., for their use;[41] but these workshops did not produce goods for the market, and, therefore, could only have limited economic significance.

INLAND TRADE

The large amount of non-agricultural production sustained a large volume of internal trade. It is true that agricultural products and other goods of bulk, such as salt, also had to be moved: this was largely done on backs of bullocks by nomadic carriers known as *banjaras*. It is estimated that they possibly conveyed a total volume of 821 million metric ton-miles a year.[42] Craft products were usually carried on bullock carts and camels, or by boats on rivers. Caravans moved over recognized routes, marked by walled inns (caravansarais), and taken over smaller rivers by masonry bridges—a particular feature of Mughal constructional activity.[43] Road tolls were more infrequent and moderate in directly governed imperial

---

35. Pelsaert, *Jahangir's India*, p. 60; Bernier, *Travels*, p. 254. See also I. Habib, 'The Technology and Economy of Mughal India', *Indian Economic and Social History Review* (IESHR), XVII (1980), pp. 1-34, for a survey of production technology.
36. As reported by the English factor from Patna, 1620 (W. Foster, ed., *English Factories in India, 1618-21*, Oxford, 1906, pp. 192-3).
37. Tek Chand 'Bahar', *Bahar-i 'Ajam* (1739-40), litho. Nawal Kishore, 1916, s.v. *khak-bez*.
38. See the evidence in *English Factories in India, 1624-29*, p. 149; *1637-41*, p. 137; *1646-50*, p. 159; *1661-64*, pp. 111-12; and in H. Yule and A.C. Burnell, *Hobson-Jobson*, revised by William Crooke, London, 1902, s.v. 'Dadny'.
39. *English Factories, 1655-60*, p. 296.
40. *English Factories, 1618-21*, pp. 197-8. See also *1655-60*, p. 296.
41. See the description of these workshops in Bernier, *Travels*, pp. 258-9. References in Persian and Rajasthani sources abound.
42. On *banjaras* see I. Habib in James D. Tracy, ed., *The Rise of Merchant Empire*, Cambridge, 1990, pp. 379-79; the estimate of volume carried is on p. 377.
43. For Mughal bridges see Jean Deloche, *The Ancient Bridges of India*, New Delhi, 1984, pp. 12-21, with a very comprehensive list of pre-modern bridges, pp. 22ff.
44. I. Habib, *Agrarian System*, p. 66n.
45. I. Habib, *Essays*, p. 224.
46. Cf. A.K.M. Farooque, *Roads and Communications in Mughal India*, Delhi, 1977, pp. 125-63; I. Habib in *Proceedings of Indian History Congress*, 46th session, Amritsar, 1985, pp. 236-52.
47. Cf. I. Habib in J.F. Richards, ed., *The Imperial Monetary System of Mughal India*, Delhi, 1987, pp. 137-70.
48. Cf. S. Moosvi, *Economy of Mughal Empire*, pp. 372-4.
49. *Khulasatu't Tawarikh*, ed. Zafar Hasan, Delhi, 1918, p. 25; *English Factories in India, 1642-45*, p. 303.
50. Cf. I. Habib, 'The System of Bills of Exchange (*Hundis*) in the Mughal Empire', *Proceedings of the Indian History Congress*, 33rd session, Muzaffarpur, 1971, pp. 290-303.
51. See I. Habib, 'Banking in Mughal India', in *Contributions to Indian Economic History*, I, ed., T. Raychaudhuri, Calcutta, 1960, pp. 13, 15-17.
52. Cf. A. Jan Qaisar, 'The Role of Brokers in Medieval India', *Indian Historical Review*, I(2)(1974), pp. 220-46.
53. Cf. I. Habib, 'Merchant Communities in Precolonial India', *The Rise of Merchant Empires*, ed., J.D. Tracy, Cambridge, 1990, pp. 389-91, for such large firms.

territories than on routes through the territories of local rulers.⁴⁴ The level of security too must have been good as the insurance (*bima*) rates show. Thus in 1655 the insurance cover for cochineal to be transported from Surat to Agra could be purchased for 2.5 per cent of the insured value, while insurance for cash carried from Machchhilipatanam to Surat cost 1 per cent of the amount.⁴⁵

While the government had a system of rapid communications through mounted relays and relay runners, private persons, especially merchants, used professional messengers to convey letters, commercial papers, and news. The bazaar *qasids*, who waited till enough letters were given to them by private persons for a particular place, were naturally irregular, whereas special 'express' messengers were fast but expensive. There is no evidence in the Subcontinent of the institution of a public postal system of the kind that was coming into vogue in Europe in the seventeenth century, where the government opened its own messenger system for use by private parties at set fees.⁴⁶

Commercial transactions in the Mughal empire were undoubtedly aided very greatly by an imperial coinage of a high degree of metallic purity and uniformity. The Mughal tri-metallic currency was based on the silver rupee of 178-180 grains. The Mughals did not allow regional coinages to function, and as the empire absorbed the larger part of the Indian peninsula by 1700, the rupee began to replace even the traditional gold-money of the south based on the *hun* ('pagoda'). The seventeenth century saw a large withdrawal of copper from circulation, and the use of the silver *ana* ('anna', 1/16th of rupee). Since the Mughal mints were open to all who would wish to convert bullion into coin, Mughal rupee output expanded under the impetus of the great influx of American silver mainly through Europe. A long-term moderate rate of inflation seems to have been the result. Such inflation should generally have benefited commerce, since it would add to the merchants' profits as sale prices constantly had an in-built increment over costs.⁴⁷ There is another possibility too: that the influx of treasure into the Subcontinent partly concealed an inflow of merchant or usury capital from the Mediterranean world in order to take advantage of the higher interest rates in India. These rates not only tended to decline over time, but registered a significant fall around the middle of the seventeenth century, broadly synchronizing with a similar fall in Europe.⁴⁸

Merchant capital in South Asia could also have been augmented by the activities of the *sarrafs*, 'money-changers', who accepted deposits and also discounted bills (*hundis*). The convenience of deposit-banking by the *sarrafs* is commented upon by Sujan Rai Bhandari (1695) and its risks ('as in other partes of the world') described in a lively report by an English factor from Agra (1645).⁴⁹

The use of bills (*hundis*) for raising credit and transferring funds was universal in South Asian markets, with *sarrafs* specializing in drawing and discounting them. As a result, in the brisker markets payments in commercial transactions were generally made in bills, a discount (*anth*) being made if cash was asked for.⁵⁰

We have already referred to the institution of insurance (*bima*). This was purely of indigenous origins, and it had certainly no parallel in the Muslim world. The *sarrafs* again were its major practitioners, insuring merchandise as well as *hundis*. By spreading out risks, this device too undoubtedly encouraged commerce.⁵¹

Both credit and commerce were finally aided greatly by the institution of brokerage, present in all parts of India, except the far south.⁵² The Banyas, whose caste provided the bulk of South Asian merchants and bankers, specialized in this profession as well. To them banking and bill-discounting were also forms of brokerage. Brokers especially met the needs of smaller merchants. There were large firms as well, and we hear of the agents or factors (*gumashtas*, *baparis*), who worked for their principals (*sahs*, *sahus*) in shops (*dukans*, *kothis*) in different places.⁵³

FOREIGN TRADE

While domestic merchant capital undoubtedly dominated the inland trade, the case was naturally different with the Mughal empire's foreign trade, where other countries' merchants too would have had a direct stake and an important role.

India's overland foreign trade was mainly through Afghanistan, with Kabul commanding the trade with Central Asia, and Qandahar with Iran. Horses constituted a very large item of overland imports, paid for mainly by textiles and indigo. The export of slaves from India (largely for domestic work in Central Asia), significant till early in the sixteenth century, practically ceased after Akbar's firm prohibitions against slavery in

the early 1560s. Large annual caravans, carrying goods belonging to Iranian, Armenian, and Indian Banya merchants, came from Iran in the seventeenth century. It is possible that when the overland trade increased substantially (marked by high mintage of north-western Mughal mints in those years), a large part of South Asian exports going overland was meant for the Levant and the Mediterranean, from which much of the imported bullion also came. The fluctuations in overland trade thus became keyed to conditions of trade across the Arabian Sea, where European nations persistently interfered with Indian ships plying to the Red Sea and the Persian Gulf.[54] When such disturbances took place, overland trade seems to have revived.

Coming to the sea trade, the belief that the arrival of the Portuguese (after Vasco da Gama's journey around the Cape in 1498) shifted the main channels of the spice trade to the Cape route is long obsolete. After their initial ravages in the first half of the sixteenth century, the Portuguese settled down to operating a tribute-levying mechanism whereby they exploited the shipping and commerce of indigenous merchants. Indian 'junks' of large tonnage, therefore, now maintained a largely peaceful trade with the Red Sea, indirectly contributing to Venetian trade in Asian pepper and Indian textiles.

The arrival of the Dutch and the English soon after 1600 created a new source of disturbance. The Red Sea trade was forcibly disrupted both by the English and the Dutch Companies, until the attractions of the larger trade with the Subcontinent compelled the two Companies to accept accommodation with the Mughal authorities, and tolerate Indian shipping. The Indians from 1630s onwards began to build excellent vessels modelled after Dutch and English ships. With their large shipping, much of it based at Surat in Gujarat, they recovered the bulk of the Red Sea and Gulf trade, though European (and later Armenian) ships also claimed their shares.[55] By and large, the position of the Red Sea as the main channel of South Asian exports to Europe, was maintained until the close of the seventeenth century, when the great Surat merchant Mulla Abdul Ghafur alone had twenty ocean-going ships, of 300 to 800 tons each.[56]

During the seventeenth century the composition of South Asian exports to Europe also changed. Cotton textiles and Bengal silk enlarged their shares in the total value of exports while the shares of pepper and indigo

---

54. For a recent study of the Qandahar trade see Niels Steensgaard, 'The route through Quandahar [sic]: the significance of the overland trade from India to the West in the seventeenth century', in *Merchants, Companies and Trade*, ed. Sushil Chaudhury and Michel Morineau, Cambridge, 1999, pp. 55-73. For the caravan from Iran to India, see also John Chardin, *Travels of Sir John Chardin into Persia and the East Indies*, I, London, 1686, pp. 363-4: the caravan was robbed in 1672; the total amount of loss was believed by Chardin to amount to £700,000.
55. On this 'revolution' in Indian ship-building industry, see I. Habib, 'Technology and Economy of Mughal India', *Indian Economic and Social History Review*, XVII(1), 1980, pp. 14-16.
56. Alexander Hamilton, *A New Account of the East Indies*, 2nd. ed., London, 1739 (New Delhi reprint, 1995), I, pp. 147-8.
57. See the tables for English East India Company's imports (1660-1760) in K.N. Chaudhuri, *The Trading World of Asia and the English East India Company*, Cambridge, 1978, pp. 524-5 (pepper), 533 (Bengal silk), 540-45 (textiles).
58. S. Moosvi, 'Silver Influx, Money Supply, Prices and Revenue Extraction in Mughal India', *Journal of the Economic and Social History of the Orient (JESHO)*, XXX (1987), pp. 47-94; Najaf Haider, 'Precious Metal Flows and Currency Circulation in the Mughal Empire', *JESHO*, XXIX (1996), pp. 298-304.
59. Yet K.N. Chaudhuri (ibid., p. 462) claims: 'The huge influx of bullion was only one indication of the growth in income and employment' in the regions receiving the influx.
60. For the major statement of this thesis see Niels Steensgaard, *The Asian Trade Revolution of the Seventeenth Century—the East India Companies and the Decline of the Caravan Trade*, Chicago, 1974, esp. pp. 22-59 and 114-153.
61. F. Braudel, *The Wheels of Commerce*, London, 1985, pp. 120-25. See also T. Raychaudhuri in *Cambridge Economic History of India*, I, ed. Raychaudhuri and Habib, Cambridge, 1982, pp. 340-42.
62. Cf. Michel Morineau in *Merchants, Companies and Trade*, ed. Sushil Chaudhury and M. Morineau, Cambridge, 1999, pp. 116-44.
63. 'Agrarian System of Mughal India', *Enquiry*, N.S., II, 1965. I gave a more explicit restatement of my position in *Journal of Economic History*, XXIX (1969), reprinted in my *Essays*, pp. 188-232, esp. 231-2.
64. John. F. Richards, *The Mughal Empire*, [*New Cambridge History of India*, I(5)], Cambridge, 1993, pp. xv, 204, 285.
65. Thapar, *The Mauryas Revisited*, Calcutta, 1987; Fussman in *Indian Historical Review*, XIV (1-2) (1987-88), pp. 43-72.
66. *Peasant, State and Society in Medieval South India*, Delhi, 1980.
67. Perlin in *Modern Asian Studies*, XIX(3)(1985), pp. 415-80; Wink, *Land and Sovereignty in India*, Cambridge, 1986.
68. See Bayly, *Rulers, Townsmen and Bazars: North Indian Society in the Age of British Expansion, 1770-1870*, Cambridge, 1983.
69. As in Muzaffar Alam, *The Crisis of Empire in Mughal North India: Awadh and Punjab, 1707-48*, Delhi, 1986, p. 318.
70. Cf. M. Athar Ali, *The Mughal Nobility under Aurangzeb*, 2nd ed., Delhi, 1997, p. xxv.

contracted.[57] In imports, silver maintained its position as the largest item except for a while in the 1660s and 1670s when gold was also imported in significant quantities.[58] It is always difficult to say what effect a large net influx of bullion would have had on economic growth. If it merely increased local prices by adding to the quantities of the circulating medium, or went into hoards, it is difficult to see how a large growth of employment could have resulted from it.[59]

There has been much debate on the role of the European Companies in Indian Ocean commerce. It has been argued that their success was due to their large size and organization enabling them to have both proper intelligence and to exercise control over flow of supplies. As against them, it is stated, the Asian (including Indian) merchants worked in very small units ('pedlars'), constituting a large, badly organized, ill-informed mass, buffeted between gluts and scarcities.[60] Braudel in his scrutiny of the evolution of capitalism, found this hypothesis unsatisfactory, and specifically mentioned the large size of capital and resources of individual South Asian merchants such as Virji Vora and Abdul Ghafur.[61] And peddling was by no means an isolated institution of European commercial life either, so that Europe's superiority over India on this count is not by any means certain.[62] Indeed, the very fact that the Red Sea route remained till the end of the seventeenth century the main traffic lane of Asia's trade to Europe, a lane in which Indian shipping dominated, proves that South Asian merchant capital, pedlar or not, was efficient enough to withstand the European Companies, given an environment of fair competition.

THE EMPIRE AND ITS COLONIAL SUCCESSOR

These conditions were to change with political and military events, notably, the decline of the Mughal empire and the beginning of the colonial conquest with the mid-eighteenth century Carnatic Wars and the Battle of Plassey (1757).

At this point it is worth looking at what these eighteenth-century phenomena meant for the economy of the Mughal empire. When I published my *Agrarian System of Mughal India* in 1963, my assumption that the decline of the Mughal empire adversely affected urban economy and commerce was so much in line with the historiographic tradition of the day that it provoked no criticism. On the other hand, T. Raychaudhuri in a long review, argued that I had been wrong in overstressing the exploitative pressures of the Mughal state and the parasitical nature of the Mughal-Indian town.[63] Though J.F. Richards has recently taken a position closer to that of T. Raychaudhuri,[64] there has been much criticism of these so-called 'Mughal-centric' views from a number of scholars. Since the 1970s there has been a tendency to question the economic depth of the pre-colonial Indian empires: for example, see Romila Thapar and G. Fussman on the Mauryas;[65] Burton Stein on the Cholas;[66] and Frank Perlin, with his emphasis on *watan*, and A. Wink, with his theory of *fitna*, on the Mughals.[67]

These suspicions about the existence of any economically powerful state have matched well with C.A. Bayly's well-known argument about 'local corporate groups' emerging out of the Mughal empire, and then entering into collaboration with the English, so that the early phase of colonial rule would seem to represent both the continuity and fulfilment of Mughal rule.[68] The decline of the Mughal empire thereupon becomes in the eyes of many scholars an economically positive process, and the growing practice of revenue-farming in the late Mughal empire, denounced so vehemently by contemporaries, has now been identified as a veritable index of 'growth'.[69]

The major difficulty of entering into argument with most scholars of this trend is that they reject, at the very beginning, the use of Mughal documentation of any type—official local records, statistics, private papers—and the official and historical literature of the time, regarding all such documentation as normative or formal (this being borne out by a single critical study).[70] Given this primary disavowal of the bulk of historical evidence, it is not surprising that historians proceeding from such disavowals can rest satisfied with their full-scale revision of the earlier views of empires (let alone, the much reviled 'Oriental Despotism' and 'Asiatic Mode of Production' theories).

If one gets back to the hard evidence, as we should, there will be no doubt that the functioning of the Mughal empire had a profound impact on the economy: the transfer of a large part of the surplus to a non-localized ruling class supported a large urban sector and an extensive commercial network. As the empire broke up, mainly through internal pressures and an agrarian crisis (resulting from excessive revenue demand),[71] both towns and trade could not but be affected. Ashin Das Gupta has shown how Surat began to lose its links with its former hinterland and so declined as a port in the early decades of the eighteenth century for the simple reason that 'the Mughal imperial system with all its imperfections had provided cities like Surat with the support necessary to attain prosperity.'[72] It is at the same time true that the decline of the Mughal empire, while it resulted in a certain contraction of commerce and net loss in urban prosperity, did not by any means bring about an economic collapse. The moderate insurance rates quoted for 1795 by Malcolm show that during peaceful times the routes within Northern and Central India were even then fairly safe in the extensive territories of the Maratha Confederacy.[73]

In much of the recent 'revisionist' historiography the impact of colonialism on the post-Mughal economy is either slurred over or even seen as the working out of processes generated within the Subcontinent itself.[74] Just as votaries of the new historiography pay scant attention to the exaction and distribution of agrarian surplus in Mughal times, they concern themselves even less with the Tribute or Drain of Wealth, the well-known process of economic strangulation of the Indian economy by Britain that began with the Plassey plunder of 1757, and assumed a regular form as the East India Company converted a large part of tax-collection into its own capital ('Investment') and its officials transmitted their own enormous private incomes to England. Its consequences for the Indian economy were wholly destructive. As Cornwallis admitted in his minute of 3 February 1790, a general 'langour' was 'thrown upon the cultivation and general commerce of the country'.[75] One cannot just assume on trust Bayly's soothing assurance that what now took place was only 'the redeployment of merchant capital within India, not its destruction'.[76] The Tribute continued to exert its baneful influence all through the nineteenth century and well into the twentieth. When in 1920, Moreland published his well-known study of the Indian economy, c. 1605, he was concerned to establish that Indian production per capita was not lower around 1910 than it was in Akbar's time.[77] Thus despite 150 years of British rule, the best that could be claimed for it was that conditions under it had grown no worse for the people of India than at its beginning. The 1921 Census proved even this to be a delusion. Over the previous five decades the average expectancy of life in India had fallen by over four years to be now barely above twenty years![78] Compared with such performance, the Mughal empire in its heyday might well have shone.

---

71. I have argued the case for an agrarian crisis in the *Agrarian System of Mughal India*, pp. 317-51. For an explicit criticism of this view, see M. Athar Ali, *Mughal Nobility under Aurangzeb*, 2nd ed., pp. xxiv, 89-92; criticism is implicit in S. Moosvi, *Studies in History*, 1(i), New Series, 1985, pp. 45-55.
72. *Indian Merchants and the Decline of Surat*, Wiesbaden, 1979, pp. 8-10, quotation on p. 2.
73. For these see John Malcolm, *Memoir of Central India*, 2nd ed., London, 1824, II, pp. 92-96, 97-98n, 366-9 for insurance rates of 1795, 1800 (and later years) and 1820. The rates for 1800 and later years were higher than for 1795 and 1820 because of political disorders.
74. Thus Harbans Mukhia: 'The view that colonial society in India was the creation of the colonial state is being slowly questioned' (in *Feudalism and Non-European Societies*, ed., T.J. Byres and Harbans Mukhia, London, 1985, p. 248, fn 13).
75. Bayly, who can speak of 'the indigenous roots of the 'colonial' economy', is perhaps able to do so because in his *Rulers, Townsmen and Bazars* he never takes up the question of the size and effects of the drain at all, although he is aware (pp. 65-66) of the 'want of specie' in 1770 and its baneful consequences for the trade. For the eighteenth-century theories generally, see M. Athar Ali in *Indian Historical Review*, XIII (1-2) (1986-87), pp. 102-110.
76. Bayly, op. cit., p. 462.
77. *India at the Death of Akbar*, London, 1920.
78. Kingsley Davis, *The Population of India and Pakistan*, Princeton, 1951, p. 62.

10

COINAGE AND MONETARY SYSTEM
Aman ur Rahman and Waleed Ziad

The history of the Subcontinent, before colonialism, is characterized by continuous invasion, occupation and eventual assimilation of the outsider into the native population. From the sixth century BC onward, each new wave of invaders attempted to introduce its own coinage into the conquered land. The conquerors found, to their surprise, a monetarily developed society with a well-entrenched system of weights and measures. Faced with such conditions most conquerors failed in their attempts to impose new standards. In contrast, Mughal coinage, fusing elements of the Timurid, Persian and South Asian systems, was successfully established throughout the Subcontinent and endured until recent times. The terminology of Mughal coinage is still in use today.

Every aspect of the Mughal's administrative system reflected the unifying, overarching yet flexible nature of their imperial state. The monetary system was no exception. The development of the coinage parallels the spread and consolidation of the empire. The pragmatic Mughals focussed on the existing and accepted norms, adapting and refining them. Based on the reforms of Sher Shah Sur, the tri-metallic monetary system gradually took shape during the reign of Akbar. In a remarkably short time, Mughal denominations became the dominant currency in India. The empire spanned the Subcontinent, encompassing scores of races, tribes, and cultures, yet all were integrated through the common currency. It was accepted universally and the purity of the metal achieved a degree of fineness that probably no other contemporary empire could boast of, maintaining its standard of excellence even in the last days of the empire. To insure propagation and widespread use, the economy was monetised—with taxes payable in specie rather than in produce—and the use of foreign coins was banned.

To the Mughals, coins were not merely a means of exchange, but also a powerful and efficient means of propaganda: a symbol of imperial grandeur carrying the seal of the emperor to every corner of the empire, a testament to the spread of his domain and unchallenged sovereignty. Mughal coins were characterized by superb calligraphy and high quality execution (Figs. 1 and 2); each piece was an exceptional work of art. The innovations and features of the coins from Akbar's reign were numerous, and, served a political purpose remarkably well. By the end of Akbar's reign, mints were widely dispersed throughout the empire but still remained under the direct control of the central government ensuring that the highest standards were

Fig 1.: Akbar, Jahangir, Shahjahan, Aurangzeb. Selection of gold coins, obverse

Fig. 2: Akbar, Jahangir, Shahjahan, Aurangzeb. Selection of gold coins, reverse

Fig. 3: Punch marked long bar

maintained. Each mint employed sophisticated methods of refining metals, and a whole cadre of officials and workers ensured that the royal standards were adhered to. With a dynamic economy, the empire became the major magnet of precious metals in the world. This continuous influx of silver vitalized the numerous coastal and border mints. In addition to improvements in quality, Jahangir's creativity and artistic taste brought about a number of extraordinary monetary innovations. With such a well-established and successful system in place, later Mughals did not deem it necessary to make any significant changes in the monetary policy.

The *Khutba* and the *Sikka* were the two formal declarations of unchallenged authority from the earliest days of Muslim government. The *Khutba* is the sermon delivered at the Friday congregational prayer; at its end blessings were invoked upon the ruling emperor, thus confirming the legitimacy of his rule. The *Sikka* refers to the issuance of coins with the emperor's name imprinted. Striking of coins was a jealously guarded royal prerogative, since, as mentioned earlier, the circulation of money was one of the most effective means of familiarizing the populace with the names and attributes of the emperor, the expanse of his empire and the longevity of his reign. Whenever a Mughal heir was crowned, his first act would be the minting of coins in his own name. As soon as a town or province was occupied, imperial coins would immediately be issued to honour the conquest. Often, they would be minted even after a momentary triumph or raid, serving as a powerful tool of disinformation and propaganda. When a local ruler, pretender, or rebel wished to assert his independence, he would issue his own coins. 'In places where men did not print, these stamped moneys obtruding into every bazaar constituted the most effective manifestoes and proclamations human ingenuity could have devised: readily multiplied, they were individually the easiest and most naturally transported of all official documents.'[1]

PRE-MUGHAL COINAGE

The history of South Asian money takes us back over 2500 years to the pre-Mauryan period, when the *ratti* standard of measures was first developed. One *ratti* was equivalent to the weight of the seed of the native

Fig. 4: Artemidorus (Indo-Greek), obverse
Fig. 5: Artemidorus (Indo-Greek), reverse

Gunja (abrus precatorius) plant, approximately 0.12 gm. By the sixth to fifth centuries BC it had become widely accepted, and during this period the first coins of the Subcontinent were minted. While the weights of the earliest indigenous coinage are the subject of some controversy, it is generally believed that the basic unit was the small, thick *karshapana* (the silver *puranas*), weighing 32 *rattis* or around 3.6 gm, minted in the form of punch marked silver coins (Fig. 3). The method of reckoning by fours, known as the '*gunda*' system, was common in the Subcontinent and all currency sub-divisions even after the British conquest conformed to this law.[2] Western scholars believe that the Persian satraps in northern Pakistan were among the first rulers in the world to issue coins, ca. 600 BC, in the shape of bent, punch marked bars in the *ratti* standard. Eastern experts place the commencement of Indian coinage at

---

Photographs by Aman ur Rahman. All coins are from the collection of Aman ur Rahman.

---

1. E. Thomas, *The Chronicles of the Pathan Kings of Delhi*, pp. 1-2.
2. Nelson Wright, *The Coinage and Metrology of the Sultans of Delhi*, 1936.

Fig. 6: Kushano-Sassanian

Fig. 7: Mahmud Ghaznavi (bi-lingual)

1000 BC, citing mention in ancient Rig Veda texts.³

The Greeks (326 BC) and their successors introduced Athenian (Attic) weight standards in the coins (Figs. 4 and 5) minted for use in India, but they were unsuccessful in replacing the existing *ratti* weight standards. Each subsequent conqueror introduced his native weight standard, fabric, and design on coins minted under his rule, (for example, the Kushano-Sassanians, Fig. 6) only to have it obliterated by his successors.⁴

When Turkish rulers first conquered northern India (eleventh century), they brought with them their native 'minted mass' system, under which coins were struck without strict regard to the weight of the individual pieces and thus for transactions these had to be weighed rather than counted. The average unit weighed around 4.5 gm and was called the *dirhem*. They too, however, quickly grasped the importance of integration with the local practices and adopted the existing standards, (Figs. 7 and 8).

The name of Iltutmish of the Qutbi slave dynasty stands out in the history of the Subcontinent's coinage. One of the first rulers to consolidate government in the Subcontinent, Iltutmish (r.1211-1236) established a strong, centralized administrative structure for the Delhi Sultanate and instituted an exhaustive coinage reform. He combined Muslim and local Indian traditions (Fig. 9) and introduced a four metal system: the 96 *rattis* gold and silver units (*tankas*) of a very Islamic type, which were inscribed with the *kalima*⁵ and cited the Abbasid Khalifa; and the billon,⁶ and copper coins, which were both called *jital* (approximately 32 *rattis*). In accordance with the native 'gunda' system, the parity of gold to silver was kept at 1:8; the fractions likewise followed the 'gunda' system. Often the gold and billon coins emulated the Hindu Shahi design (a horse

Fig. 8: Ghauri

Fig. 9: Iltutmish

and Devanagari characters) on one side, and, on the other, had the emperor's name and titles in Arabic. This coinage system was also maintained under the later dynasties (Figs. 10, 11, and 12).

During the reign of Muhammad Tughluq (1325-1351), the Delhi Sultanate began to break up due to a number of reasons including expensive wars and prolonged famine. The exchequer was severely strained and the first debasement of the *tanka* occurred (Fig. 13). The invasion of Timur in 1398 weakened the Sultanate even further. A centralized monetary order was not possible during the period that followed the invasion since provinces could no longer be centrally controlled. Thereafter, the situation deteriorated to such an extent that the Lodi Sultanate (1451-1526) was no more than a confederacy of petty states under a weak Sultan. Minting of Sultanate coin was restricted to the capital at Delhi and local kingdoms throughout the Subcontinent issued their own forms of currency. As the economy fell into ruin, the gold and silver *tankas* all but disappeared. When Babur assumed the throne of Delhi in 1526, the coin in circulation, the billon *Sikandari*, contained only a few traces of silver (Fig. 14).

BABUR (r.1526-30), HUMAYUN (r.1530-40, 1555-56), AND THE SUR INTERREGNUM (1540-55)

The reigns of Babur and Humayun can be considered a transition period between the fragmented structure of the Sultanate and the consolidated imperial Mughal state. Both issued coins on an *ad hoc* basis, depending on the needs of the military. Babur minted the Timurid *Shahrukhi* or *miscal* standard in the Subcontinent. It was a broad, thin, silver coin, 4/10 the weight of the Sultanate's *tankas*, bearing a distinct Timurid calligraphic style (Fig. 15). On the obverse were the *kalima* and the names of the Rightly Guided Khalifas (the first four Khalifas after Muhammad [PBUH], Abu Bakr, Omar, Usman, and Ali,

Fig. 10: Razia Sultana (daughter of Iltutmish)

Fig. 11: Sultans of Delhi

Fig. 12: Khilji

Fig. 13: Tughluq

---

3. D.C. Sircar, *Early Indian Indigenous Coins*, University of Calcutta, India, 1971.
4. Boperachi and Aman ur Rahman, 'Pre-Kushana Coins in Pakistan', Islamabad, 1995.
5. *Kalima*: the statement of faith in Islam: 'There is no God but Allah and Muhammad is His Messenger'.
6. Billon: an alloy of gold or silver with a predominating admixture of a base metal.

who are regarded as model rulers), and on the reverse were the names and titles of the emperor, the date, and the mint name. The monetary conservatism of Northern India (Hindustan) did not permit this coin to

Fig. 14: Lodi. Example of debased coins

become very popular in the heartland of the empire. Although both Babur and Humayun had these coins minted in major cities such as Agra, Delhi, Lahore, and Jaunpur, such coin types are today found mainly in the region of present-day Pakistan and Afghanistan, indicating that they had been taken back by Mughal soldiers to their native lands where they were accepted currency. Humayun made a feeble attempt to emulate the Sultanate monetary weight standards in Bengal just prior to his eviction from the throne by Sher Shah Sur. A unique double *miscal* (at 8.85 gm it is twice the weight standard of the Timurid *miscal*) in Rahman's collection and several known specimens of a silver *tanka* and rupee of between 10.4 to 11.25 gm issued from the Bengal and other mints are testimony to this attempt. Both Babur and Humayun adopted the Lodi standard for their copper coins. This was because the copper denomination was the main currency of the Indian masses and the Timurids had no coinage in that metal.

The Sur interregnum represents yet another landmark in the evolution of the currency system of the Subcontinent. Sher Shah Sur revived the pre-Tughluq institutions, creating a centralized government with authority over provincial and sub-provincial governments. Land assessment and revenue collection was also centrally administered, which meant that a stable, uniform currency was necessary. The use of debased silver was discontinued. The purity of his silver coins was based on those of his state, Bengal, which was one of the few regions still minting fine silver. Under his monetary reforms, Sher Shah introduced a bi-metallic coinage with a silver coin of a new weight standard of around 11.5 gm called a *rupiya* (rupee) (Fig. 16) and a copper coin of around 20 gm, named the *paisa*. A very limited number of gold coins were issued, but their extreme rarity leads us to believe that they were of an 'experimental' nature. The judicious choice of name for his basic unit, the *rupiya*—derived from *rupehli*, which means silver in Sanskrit—and the inscribing of his own name in Devanagari characters on the coin were clever moves aimed at increasing its acceptability and winning the goodwill of his Hindu subjects. The Sur dynasty established mints throughout the empire. Mints were located in Malwa, Multan, and other urban and military centres, as well as five in Bengal and two in Bihar.

An interesting instance of coinage serving political ends occurred during Humayun's attempts to re-conquer India. In the very first issue after his conquest of the frontier town of Qandahar, Humayun struck a coin on the obverse of which he imprinted the Shia version of the *kalima* in deference to Shah Tahmasp of Persia who was helping him recover his lost empire. After regaining the throne, Humayun reverted to the original legends used by his father. In his new mintings

Fig. 15: Babur. Shahrukhis

he ignored the reforms of his enemies, the Surs, and returned to the *miscal* standard (Fig. 17). However, a short while before his untimely death he also issued a *rupiya* based on the Suri standard weight, some rare specimens of which are in existence.

AKBAR (r.1556-1605)

> [The rupee] was first introduced in the time of Sher Khan. It was perfected during this reign.
> — Abul Fazl, *Ain-i-Akbari* [7]

Fig. 17: Humayun. Shahrukhis and small gold

Fig. 16: Suri. Rupiya

Since Humayun had only issued coins on an *ad hoc* basis, Akbar, at age thirteen, was saddled with an empire without a stable monetary system. Akbar's monetary order was formulated gradually over a period of years. Initially, the government tried to maintain the Timurid standard for the coinage while also minting silver *rupiyas* in the Suri weight standard from Lahore and Agra. *Shahrukhis* were issued from Lahore, Kabul, and Delhi. However, *Shahrukhis* were not generally acceptable to the people, and by the fourth year of Akbar's reign the coinage system of his ancestors was abandoned. The successful Suri coinage was better suited to the needs of Akbar's progressively strong central government and became the basis for his monetary system, which was in place by the early 1560s.

In the early years the bulk of the minting took place in a few urban financial centres and provincial capitals, where the imperial treasuries and sub-treasuries were also located. Although this made the minting centres less accessible to the public, it allowed for economies of scale and easy supervision to ensure that standards of fineness were maintained.

Silver coinage. Akbar realized that coinage, a seemingly inconspicuous tool, could be used in diverse ways to enhance the prestige of the Mughal court. To legitimize his rule it was necessary to re-coin the silver currency in circulation, most of which was Suri. His new *rupiyas* (rupees) of Delhi, Agra, and Lahore were identical to the Suri: round, broad, and weighing about 11.5 gm. However, they followed the epigraphical pattern set by his grandfather and used by his father, with the obverse bearing the *kalima* and names of the Rightly Guided Khalifas. The reverse bore the name and titles of the emperor, 'Jalaluddin Muhammad Akbar Badshah Ghazi', the mint name, and the date. As well as declaring his sovereignty, the coins attested to the aesthetic refinement of the Timurid tradition, which

---
7. Abul Fazl, *Ain* 7 B. Silver Coins.

Fig. 18: Akbar. Selection of silver coins of various shapes and legends

was to become one of the hallmarks of the empire. The excellent calligraphy and high quality execution reveal Safavid influence. Elaborate borders and geometric designs often framed the legend. In size and shape, however, the currency was definitely Indian. Mughal coinage pragmatically combined the best from each source (Fig 18).

Copper coinage. After recovering his empire from the Surs, Humayun had not reintroduced the Lodi copper *tanka*, but had instead used the Suri *paisa*, and that too in very limited issue. Akbar continued using the Suri standard but the *paisa* became known as the *dam*. Five fractional denominations were issued, as well as a double *dam*. The rate of exchange was set at 40 *dams* to the silver *rupiya*. The coin was 7 mm thick, and inscribed with only the mint name and date. The anonymity of the copper coinage was a notable feature—copper was considered a symbol of low prestige and therefore inappropriate to carry the emperor's name. The copper mints, numbering close to twenty by 1577, were located in administrative centres for re-coinage, as well as in peripheral mint towns which were either clearing centres for copper mines or frontier posts where money entered the empire through trade. This allowed the imported metal to circulate as soon as it entered Mughal domains. Demand kept production at a high level, since for most of Akbar's reign the *dam* was the most popular coin for exchange. The *Ain-i Akbari*, in fact, quotes prices in *dams*. Copper was used in land revenue payments and in purchasing commodities in the market. Salaries for labourers, soldiers, and artisans were usually paid in *dams*. It is interesting to note that the word '*dam*' is used in the Subcontinent today to mean 'price'. For smaller payments, the cowrie imported from the Maldives was often used, and in Gujarat the almond served a similar purpose. The rate of exchange was approximately 2500 cowries to the rupee. It is not hard to understand why the word 'cowrie' is still used today when referring to something very inexpensive.

Gold coinage. Due to the fact that the Surs issued very little gold coinage, and Humayun issued only tiny pieces in Badakhshan used solely in Afghanistan, Akbar did not open mints for gold until 1562. Four mints were set up in the capitals of the central provinces. The traditional gold *tanka* of the Delhi Sultanate, weighing 10.9 gm was reintroduced after a hundred year gap and was called *muhr* or *ashrafi*. The need for a proper gold currency reflected the growing prosperity of the empire and the fact that the more affluent classes were amassing enormous wealth. Gold was used mainly for hoarding purposes. While most of the imported silver was coined, gold was more often sold to goldsmiths.

Like his forefathers, Akbar followed the custom of presenting 'money-gifts' to ambassadors for their living expenses. It seems that it was the Central Asian practice or court etiquette to make the gift not in the form of 'beggarly deniers' but in the shape of a heavy ingot of gold or silver or both. Babur tells us in his autobiography that in 935 Hijra he presented various envoys with 'a silver stone's weight of gold and a gold stone's weight of silver'. He explains 'that the gold stone [*tash*] was 500 miscals, that is to say one Kabul seer [about 1 kg], and the silver stone 250 miscals, that is to say half a Kabul seer [500 gms]'.[8] The difference of course was that while Babur's pieces were crude ingots, Akbar's gifts were beautiful discs or medals representing the perfection of the calligrapher's and engraver's art.

The administrative rationalization and integration of the state was initiated and executed by extremely capable finance ministers, particularly during the years at Fatehpur Sikri (1571-85). This encouraged expansion and productivity in the economy. Among the creative policy decisions taken were the introduction of a new, standardized but flexible, revenue assessment system, the demand for land revenue in specie, decentralized tax collection (through the *jagir* system), standardization of measures, cash payment of state salaries, and incentives to agriculture and trade. A responsive monetary order was taking shape simultaneously. The cash needs of the state, the nobility, and the market were met by the enormous and increasing stocks of coin. Monetization progressed rapidly as did the velocity of coin in circulation. Commercial transactions, loans, and cash salaries brought the coin into even the most remote rural areas. Similarly the vast amounts of money spent on public and private building projects, as well as the custom of largess, charity, and conspicuous consumption served to increase the use of coin. Hoard finds show that the rate of monetary transactions was so fast that within a year of minting, a copper coin from the frontier mints could end up in the central provinces.

To provide for the needs of an expanding economy and for large payments and transactions, credit money came into use in the form of bills of exchange called *hundis*. The *hundis* were generally made payable after a certain number of days, depending on where they were issued, and a deduction was paid for the *anth*, or conversion of the *hundi* into coin. The immediate result was that long-distance transactions were facilitated, becoming less expensive.

By 1577, Akbar's realm had grown to such an extent that it was in need of reorganization; this included restructuring the mints. Since Akbar gave utmost priority to the aesthetic excellence of his coinage, the position of imperial mintmaster was created and awarded to Khwaja Abdus Samad, the renowned artist and calligrapher who directed Akbar's atelier. The number of mints was reduced to six: Lahore, Jaunpur, Patna, Gujarat, and Bengal, and the imperial capital at Fatehpur Sikri. This was further evidence of how important standardization and consolidation were to the emperor. Later that year, a royal decree stated that only square coins were to be issued in silver (the shape bringing in a traditional, distinctly Indian touch dating back to the Mauryan empire). Square gold coins were also struck. These currency reforms did not apply to copper coins.

The Ilahi Era. In 1584, Akbar introduced the *Ilahi* era. He issued a *farman* (royal command) that henceforth all time reckoning would be done in the *Ilahi* calendar which dated from 1556, the year of his accession to the throne. Major changes appeared in coin design and epigraphy. *Ilahi* silver coins were issued in both square and round denominations, and the legend was reduced simply to '*Allah-u akbar, jalla jallaluhu*' (God is the greatest, splendid is His glory). The dates were given in *Ilahi* years, which used the solar calendar as opposed to the lunar Hijra calendar used by all Muslim kingdoms. The month of minting was introduced on the coin face using Persian month names. The first issues were dated as *Ilahi* 30. The coins were of a much finer quality than before: calligraphy was outstanding, with characters stamped in bold relief, and the dies were cut neatly to fit the coin blank. Floral patterns were occasionally used,

---

8. Shahpurshah Hodivala, *Historical Studies in Mughal Numismatics*, 1936.

commemorative coins depicted wildlife, and an extremely rare half *muhr* even depicted the figures of Rama and Sita. 'The coins for the first time reflected the court as a patron of culture and symbolized the security of the emperor's ritual position in the political hierarchy.'[9]

Exactly what was the significance of the *Ilahi* coinage? The introduction of the *Ilahi* era can be seen as a practical move by Akbar since a solar calendar was better suited to an agricultural country like India, and coinage was the most effective means of publicizing his new calendar. Dropping the Muslim epigraphy may possibly have been another measure aimed to show impartiality between the many religions in his domain. Nevertheless, it was a break with tradition. It showed that at this point Akbar was very confident of his position. Some numismatists cite the example of the typical *Ilahi* inscription, 'Allah-u Akbar', which they claim attests to Akbar's belief in self-divinity, since the legend can be translated as 'God is the greatest' or 'God is Akbar', Akbar being the Arabic word for 'greatest'. Badauni's testimony refutes this argument. According to him, when Akbar first proposed the idea of introducing 'Allah-u Akbar' on his coinage, some officials commented that it was rather ambiguous and could be misinterpreted. Akbar replied that 'no man who felt his weakness would claim Divinity, and that he [Akbar] merely looked to the sound of the words, and he had never thought that a thing could be carried to such an extreme.'[10] Throughout the Muslim world, emperors often used punning mottos on their coins. It was not considered irreverence, but rather a reflection of the ruler's wit.

Mints. With the strengthening economy, Delhi, Lahore, Patna, and Agra reopened silver mints. Mints also operated in other important locations, such as Atak Benares en route to the North West. Gradually, silver mints were opened in all except two North Indian provinces. The establishment of so many mints, contrary to Akbar's previous policies, would indicate that by this time the economy had expanded to such an extent that economies of scale could be carried out in almost every province. Local administrations had obviously become efficient enough and so closely tied to the central government as to be able to mint coins of the exacting imperial standard.

The widespread access to the mints facilitated the replacement of the copper *dam* with the silver *rupiya* (rupee) as the common circulating denomination. In sale documents, prices started being quoted in rupees as early as 1592. For copper coins, Delhi remained the largest mint. Agra copper coin production tapered off, probably because most of the Agra *Ilahi* series were a new denomination, and the public was known to have very conservative attitudes towards coinage—only familiar denominations would be readily accepted. By 1595, the empire could boast of four mints for gold coins, fourteen issuing silver coins, and forty-two for copper.

During military campaigns, coins bearing the mint name *Urdu* (camp), or *Urdu Zafar Qarin* (camp associated with victory), were issued by the mobile royal camp mint to cater for the salaries of the army and its vast supporting entourage. Whenever a region was conquered, the imperial mint would immediately strike coins bearing the name of the town as a mark of legitimate victory.

Monetary Integration. Establishing Mughal authority over a realm with extremely varied monetary traditions required Akbar to bring all the provinces under a uniform imperial system. Without such a system, monetization of the economy would be impossible. In the past, empires had tried to impose their coinage on conquered territories with limited success, but never had the area been so extensive. The uniformity of Akbar's coins throughout the empire could only be achieved by suppressing the local customs of coinage in each occupied territory. In areas which did not have a well-developed tri-metallic currency, the Mughal mint system was imposed without delay and thus by the 1600s, Mughal coinage had gained ascendance over nearly all other forms of currency in India. Occasionally, though, local currencies maintained some of their indigenous characteristics within the Mughal monetary framework, so that they would be acceptable to the population. Often Akbar's monetary policies in the provinces reflected the level of autonomy allowed in the area. In Malwa, for example, Baz Bahadur, the last independent Sultan, had issued round silver *tankas* and square copper coins, with the *kalima* on the obverse and the ruler's titles on the reverse. Akbar's initial Malwa series struck in Ujjain followed this pattern. Later when he introduced imperial weight standards into the province, they did not immediately become popular, and both standards were used.

Gujarat had developed a complex system of currency under the Sultanate of Gujarat, and the 7.1 gm silver *Mahmudi*, as well as various copper denominations, were used in some other provinces as well. The coinage bore only the title of the sovereign, the mint, and the date. Akbar declared the local currency obsolete, raised the weights to imperial standards (the silver *rupiya* of 11.5 gm), and introduced the *kalima*. The number of mints in Gujarat were increased, and Ahmadabad soon became the greatest mint in the empire. The reason for such drastic measures in Gujarat was probably due to the fact that Akbar realized the importance of this coastal region to Mughal monetary expansion, and wanted it to be immediately incorporated into the imperial system. Another example worth looking at is that of Bengal. For unknown reasons, the Mughal empire did not open a mint in Bengal until 1593, seventeen years after the province was annexed. Although the general Mughal coinage at that time consisted of *Ilahi* rupees, the Bengal mint issued the old square series, bearing the *kalima* and Hijra years. Since Bengal had been a province with a history of revolt, coinage was probably a sensitive medium and it is possible that the unorthodox *Ilahi* coin series could have met with disapproval.

In Kabul, the standard currency was the 4.6 gm silver *Shahrukhi*, mentioned earlier, since Kabul was governed semi-independently until 1585 by Akbar's half-brother Mirza Mohammad Hakim. Shaibanid coins of Iskandar have also been found bearing the countermarks of Akbar. After Mirza's death, Akbar established greater central control over the region, establishing the Kabul mint and issuing *Ilahi* coins. However, only the half-rupee was popularly accepted and minted in large numbers, since it was closer in weight to the *Shahrukhi*.

Aesthetics of the Coinage. 'The coins are now an ornament to the treasury, and liked by the people,' begins Abul Fazl, before introducing the various denominations issued by Akbar.[11] This statement in itself highlights the importance of coinage as a reflection of the power of the Timurids. They were dependable stores of value, always of the purest quality—symbolizing the prosperity of the empire—as well as works of art, indicative of imperial refinement.

As discussed earlier, the superb gold coins were mainly for use among the affluent classes. They were not only a store of value but a symbol of prestige, and merchants and nobles would take pride in owning these elegant pieces. On the other hand, silver coins were the normal medium of exchange, and copper coins were usually associated with the peasantry. The level of workmanship and type of inscriptions on the coins of each of the three metals were chosen likewise.

Abul Fazl describes a number of gold denominations in the *Ain*, from the one *muhr* coin to the grand 100 *muhr Shahinshah*. Akbar gave names to the various coins, such as the *Aftabi*, the *Adlgutkah*, and the *Salimi*. The *Mihrabi*, a long oblong shaped coin, is an attractive example of a new shape introduced by Akbar. The novel shapes were never very successful, again probably due to the monetary conservatism of the Subcontinent. A considerable variety of coins were issued for hoarding purposes: the *Shahinshah*, the *Rahas* (50 *muhrs*), and the *Atmah* (25 *muhrs*) were the largest mentioned.

Among the fascinating features of Akbar's coins were the poetic couplets inscribed on them. Metrical legends in Persian were found as far back as the fourteenth century on the coins of Muhammad Shah of Gujarat. Such legends figured so prominently in glorifying the Mughal image that the poet laureates were given the duty of composing these couplets. In Akbar's earliest recorded rupees of this variety, Sharif Samadi's compositions are used, and the verses of Faizi are found on the 100, 50, and 25 *muhr* gold pieces.

A royal title and the mint name often preceded the couplet. In a pre-*Ilahi* era 100 *muhr* coin described by Abul Fazl, the title was inscribed in the form of a prayer:

> The great Sultan, the distinguished Emperor,
> May God perpetuate his kingdom and his reign!
> Struck at the capital Agrah.[12]

---

9. J.F. Richards, ed. *The Imperial Monetary System of Mughal India*, 1987, p. 37.
10. Shahpurshah Hodivala, *Historical Studies in Mughal Numismatics*, 1976, p. 83.
11. Abul Fazl, *Ain* 10.
12. Abul Fazl, *Ain* 10 A.

The message served, of course, to eulogize the emperor, and also to praise his realm. This was followed by: 'God is bounteous unto whom He pleaseth, without measure.' Often, we find verses from the Quran in addition to the *kalima* and names of the Rightly Guided Khalifas—a declaration of the piety of the sovereign and the importance of Islam. Even quotes on morality were included, in this particular case encouraging charity:

> The best coin which a man expends
> Is a coin which he spends
> On his co-religionists in the path of God.[13]

The emperor was often referred to by the Muslim title, 'Khalifa', so the coin indirectly legitimized his rule and further conquests.

Abul Fazl explained that later in his reign, Akbar ordered the legend on the 100 *muhr* piece to be replaced with two verses by Faizi:

> It is the Sun from which the seven oceans get their pearls,
> The black rocks get their jewels from his lustre,
> The mines get their gold from his fostering glance,
> And their gold is ennobled by Akbar's stamp,[14]

This is followed by '*Allah-u akbar, jalla jalalahu*'.[15] Often sun imagery is included, referring either to the importance of the sun as a manifestation of God's light in Sufi tradition, or to the Zoroastrian elements in the emperor's *Din-i-Ilahi*; or to the 'Lion and Sun' coat-of-arms of Timur. The lower denominations of gold, which were in circulation more than the giant coins, had simpler legends. The *Lal-i-jalali* two *muhr* coin was inscribed '*Allah-u akbar, Ya Muinu*' (O Helper), and others simply read '*Allah-u akbar, jalla jallaluhu*'.

An ancient Eastern tradition which predates Islam is the scattering of largess on ceremonial occasions. It is known that Alauddin Khilji (r. 1296-1316) used to employ military catapults for this purpose. In his memoirs, Babur describes his uncle Sultan Mahmud Mirza, who sent him gold and silver almonds and pistachios for the wedding of his eldest son. Thin gold coins and fractional rupees were introduced by Akbar explicitly for this purpose. These coins were named *darbs* (half rupees) and *charns* (quarter rupees). These became important features of royal ceremonies and public events to promote the image of a benevolent emperor. Badauni speaks of the scattering of 'dishfulls of gold and jewels to the people' at a feast held in honour of Qutbuddin Khan's appointment as tutor to prince Salim.[16] These coins did not necessarily conform to the official weight standards because the object was to produce only as many pieces as would be required at each occasion to make an impressive ceremony.

Purchasing Power of the Currency. To get a basic idea of the purchasing power of money at the time of Akbar, it is useful to consider the prices of some common food items consumed at that period and the wages of a few categories of workers. The following table has been adapted from E. Thomas' seminal book, and 'will give some idea of the extraordinary cheapness of food, though the prices are sufficiently high for the discriminated articles of luxury'.[17] The calculations are based on approximate conversion of the weight standard of the period, the *man*. At that time the *rupiya* was equal to 40 *dams*.

Commodity	
Wheat	3.3 kgs per *dam*
Wheat Flour [according to fineness]	2-2.5 kgs per *dam*
Barley	5 kgs per *dam*
Ground Barley	3.5 kgs per *dam*
Rice [according to quality]	0.4-2 kgs per *dam*
Pulse *Moong*	2.5 kgs per *dam*
Mash	2.5 kgs per *dam*
Nakhud	2.5 kgs per *dam*
Moth	3.3 kgs per *dam*
Juwar [holcus sorgum]	4.0 kgs per *dam*
White sugar	3.2 *dams* per kg
Brown sugar	1.4 *dams* per kg
Ghee [clarified butter]	2.6 *dams* per kg
Sesame oil	2.0 *dams* per kg
Salt	2.5 kgs per *dam*
Sheep [whole]	1.5-6.5 *rupiya*
Mutton	1.6 *dams* per kg
Goat meat	1.4 *dams* per kg

Labour	
Bricklayer	4-7 *dams* per day
Carpenter	2-7 *dams* per day
Semi-skilled	3-3.5 *dams* per day
Unskilled	2 *dams* per day
Matchlockmen [Royal army]	6 *rupiyas* per month
Archers	2.5 *rupiyas* per month

What is remarkable is that the prices of commodities in the market were at the same level as those during the reigns of Feroz Shah Tughlaq (r.1351-1388) and Alauddin Khilji (r.1296-1316) (who had instituted price controls).

THE OUTPUT OF THE IMPERIAL MINTS

To ensure the maintenance of high standards and uniformity of coinage throughout the empire, the widespread mints were placed under the direct control of a department of the central government. 'When the political situation demanded, this department could arrange the transmission of political propaganda to every corner of the empire, through its control of the information and symbols displayed on the face of every coin at hand.'[18] The mint carried out two functions: minting bullion or copper and re-minting 'discounted' coins. Bullion importers had to go directly from the custom houses to the mint upon arrival into the empire, which accounts for the location of major mints in the frontier and port towns.

The system of 'free coinage' prevailed in the empire, in which any individual could bring bullion or old coins to the mint for reminting, with a charge for the cost of minting and seigniorage. A policy of discounting was put into effect, which meant that newly minted coins were valued highest, and older coins, especially those of previous rulers, had discounted values. The discount was never greater than the minting costs, however. The system of discounting, too, was initially developed to establish Mughal prestige, since the majority of coins in circulation in the early part of Akbar's reign were Sur silver *rupiyas*. No discount was charged on copper *dams*.

The wealth of the Mughal realm was *vast*. The amount of silver used in the empire is estimated to be in tens of millions of rupees, which significantly exceeded that of any previous empire in the Subcontinent, and was much greater than that of Safavid Iran or Ottoman Turkey. European kingdoms could not compare even with Turkey. It is noteworthy that so much coin was produced in a country with very low silver and gold production and only a few copper mines. Apart from the annexation of wealthy provinces, the increase of imperial wealth was based on the influx of foreign money. The Mughal state was the major economic power in the world. The money which entered the state remained within its boundaries because the industrial and agricultural products of the Mughal empire were so much in demand that exports far exceeded imports, and the stock of precious metals continued to increase. New World silver entered India at such an extraordinary rate that the price of silver fell in comparison to the other two metals, and this was another reason why silver replaced copper as the common means of exchange.

Foreign coin was not accepted as a means of payment, and had to be changed as soon as it entered the empire. Mints were set up in such a way as to guarantee that all the foreign money which entered the empire was transformed into acceptable Mughal currency and put into circulation as fast as possible. The quality of Mughal coins was so much superior to that of Europe that when Spanish silver, known as the finest in Europe, was traded in for the rupee, the loss was as much as 15 per cent. Much of the foreign silver and gold which was purified and minted in the coastal mints was brought in by the European trading companies, who also played an important role in spreading Mughal coinage throughout the empire and monetizing the economy.

The supply of silver and the output of the respective mints throughout the empire has been researched by Aziza Hasan and Shireen Moosvi. The only evidence which can provide us with close estimates are the English records of the 1630s regarding the output of the Surat mint; and the distribution of coins that exist today of various mints and years. Starting with Akbar, it is possible to trace the trends in the output of the imperial mints.

As discussed earlier, from 1556 to 1575, imperial expansion under Akbar in North India led to the creation of an extensive network of mints, and it is estimated that the number of rupees which were minted annually grew from 900,000 (approx. 11.4 tons) to six million (76 tons) in this period. Furthermore, at this time the mintage and use of copper currency was being replaced by silver, with the raw material being provided

---
13. Abul Fazl, *Ain* 10 A.
14. Abul Fazl, *Ain* 10 A.
15. Abul Fazl, *Ain* 7 A.
16. Hodivala, 1976, p. 180.
17. E. Thomas, pp. 428-30.
18. Richards, *Imperial*, p. 44.

Fig 19: Jahangir. Selection of silver coins of various shapes and legends.

through conquest and trade as well as from internal reserves. By the end of the century, silver mintage increased to over 26 million rupees (329 tons) per annum. This was primarily due to the annexation of the centre of trade, Gujarat (with output of over 166 tons at the turn of the century), making Ahmadabad one of the largest mints in the empire. This stock included imported silver as well as recoined bullion *Mahmudis*. The late sixteenth century was also the period of highest silver bullion export from the Americas to Spain—it is well known that Europe lost over 80 tons a year to the East, much of which ended up in India.

After 1605, the total annual output of rupees fell to thirteen million (164 tons). Gujarat's mint output dropped drastically to an annual 25 tons, probably because the internal stock had already been minted, the American silver export had declined, and the Portuguese trade was hindered by the Dutch and the English, who themselves did not import much silver. The North Western mints, however, stayed at a high level of around 50 tons, due to the growing overland trade through Qandahar. The restricted silver flow and an even smaller import of gold led to the fall in the silver value of gold from a 9:1 ratio in the late sixteenth century to 14:1 by 1628.

However, a little later the Gujarat mints flourished again, minting 33.3 tons of silver, since the sea and land silver imports from the Levant saw a dramatic increase. The Bengal mint overtook the others in production (an estimated 80 tons annual output), and the North West mints continued to thrive until the Qandahar wars of 1646-55 blocked the trade route, bringing production down to 24 tons.

From the 1650s to 1670s, silver imports were reduced, and the English East India Company began to substitute gold for silver. The Gujarat mints remained the most productive, but production in Bengal fell to 14 tons per year. After 1670, currency output increased, and inland mints became more productive than Gujarat, probably because the imported silver brought by the Dutch, English, and Gulf traders went past the coastal areas directly into the central mint towns. The Bengal mint was not too popular since the bullion conversion rates were unfavourable.

ADMINISTRATION OF THE MINT

The mint was created as a prestigious wing of the administration, since national monetization depended upon its effective functioning. The mint officials were regular staff appointed by a *sanad*, or imperial decree, and were paid monthly salaries of cash or revenue assignments, and occasionally, also given commissions.

The main official of the mint was the *darogha*, a high-level administrator who was recommended by the *Diwan-i-Suba* (the provincial governor), and carried the title *Diwan-i-Ala* (chief governor). Abul Fazl stressed that the holder of the position must be 'intelligent and circumspect', as the burden of the mint was on his shoulders, and he must show 'zeal and integrity'.[19] He was responsible for examining the bullion and old coins, and issuing receipts to those who brought in the metals, and for all other financial matters.

It was the *saraff's* responsibility to determine the degree of purity of the coins. By necessity the *saraff* was required to be highly experienced in his trade, since Mughal gold and silver had to be of the highest degree of fineness. In fact, Abul Fazl wrote that the level of purity achieved in Mughal mints was so spectacular that it was often attributed to witchcraft and alchemy. Edward Terry writes: 'The coin is purer silver than any other that I know, being of virgin silver without alloy, so that in the Spanish dollar, the purest money in Europe, there is some loss.'[20] If any fault occurred in the *saraff's* assessments, he had to personally compensate. Other official positions included the *mu'aiyir*, or assayer, the *mushrif*, in charge of daily expenditures, and the *tahwildar*, who kept a daily account of profits. An important post was that of the *amin*, who insured that differences between the *darogha* and the workers would be resolved; he was described by Abul Fazl as a man of 'impartiality and integrity'.

The *muhr-kan* (engraver) held a highly esteemed position, and when the *Ain-i Akbari* was written the office was occupied by Maulana Alf Ahmad, the finest engraver in the empire. He was given a rank of *yuzbashi* (100 *zat*). The engraved dies would usually be made of steel or another hard metal. A number of skilled workers were employed including, among others, the smelter of ore, the platemaker, the coiner, the stamper, and the *niyariya*, who washed and recovered gold from the ashes. Some of the more interesting mint positions included the *nicho-i-wala*. He would purchase old coins from the market, and bring them in to be reminted. In this way, he was indirectly involved in the royal propaganda effort, making sure the names and titles of former kings were replaced by the current ruler's. Apparently, he made quite a profit in this trade. The *khakshoe* was the official mint sweeper. He would take the sweeping to his house and recover the metals. As a reflection of the prosperity of the mints, Abul Fazl described that 'the sweepers carry on a flourishing trade.' In fact, the sweeper had to pay the government 12.5 rupees a month for the privilege of his position!

Metal as bullion or in the form of coins was brought to the *darogha*, and was then examined and weighed by the *mushrif*, *tahwildar*, *qanungo*, *sarraff*, and *amin*, and a receipt was issued listing the weight and quality of metal. The mint developed a very complex process of refining and separating gold and silver. This has been described in detail by Abul Fazl. The *gudazar kham*, the smelter, refined the metal and cast it into ingots. These were cut into coins by the *zarrab*, and the *sikkachi* stamped each piece of metal between two dies.

The main source of income for the mint was the *mahsul darul zarb*. This refers to the mint charges and seigniorage, about 5 to 6 per cent of the metal coined. The rates remained constant through the seventeenth century, except when Aurangzeb lowered the rate to 2.5 per cent for Muslims. They remained at 5 per cent for Hindus, or 2 to 3 per cent if the Hindus were *mahajans* (traders) or *saraffs* (money changers). There was a further small deduction for the payment of mint wages and the cost of materials. Instances have been noted when the mint closed itself down upon news of arrival of large amounts of imported metal, so the mint workers could extort money from the foreign merchants. Since the mints were a monopoly, they were also often accused of undervaluing bullion brought to them. For these reasons, the money changers were often entrusted with old coins and bullion to be minted, since they had special skills in determining the value of

---

19. Abul Fazl, *Ain* 5.
20. D. Pant, *The Commercial Policy of the Moghuls*, 1930, p. 135.

Fig. 20: Jahangir. Zodiac, obverse

metals. *Sarraffs* often kept ready supplies of coins to provide for the needs of clients. We hear of cases where the *sarraffs* and local merchants conspired and offered English merchants lower prices for their imported coins.

JAHANGIR (r.1605-1627)

'It was under Jahangir that the Mughal coinage attained its highest level of excellence.'[21] To any Mughal numismatist, Jahangir's name is synonymous with refinement and intricacy, as his coins were indeed the finest that Muslim India, or maybe even the finest that the Muslim world had ever seen (Fig. 19): his aesthetic sense was outstanding, and he was extremely fond of innovations.

Jahangir abandoned Akbar's *Ilahi* era but preserved the solar computation for the Persian months. The regnal years were reckoned from one vernal equinox to the next, and the coins are dated by the regnal year with or without the Hijra year. The *kalima* did not always appear on his coins, and the ornamentation and calligraphy were highly elaborate and often exquisite.

His first innovation came at the time of his accession (1605), when he issued a *farman* (royal command) that the weight of gold and silver coins be increased by 20 per cent. In the fourth year he decided to increase it further.

The weights were soon after reduced, as Jahangir tells us in his autobiography, the *Tuzuk i-Jahangiri*:

> At the time of my accession, I had increased weights and measures... At this time it was represented to me that in mercantile transactions it would be for the convenience of the people that *muhrs* and rupees should be of the same weight as previously. As in all affairs the contentment and ease of the people are to be looked to, I gave an order that from the present day...they should strike *muhrs* and rupees of the former weight in all the mints of my dominions.[22]

In December 1617, he ordered that gold and silver coins of twice the weight of the Akbari standard be minted at the Cambay mint. He referred to these as '*tankas*' and claims, 'In no reign before this had *tankas* been coined except of copper. The *tanka* of gold and silver were inventions of my own and I called them Jahangiri *tankas*.' These, however, were only issued once. The inspiration for these coins came, according to the *Tuzuk*, while he was looking out at the sea at Cambay and admiring the waves. Another interesting and unique specimen of Jahangir's coinage bears the mint name *Urdu dar rah-i-Dakhan*, or 'the camp on the road to the Dakhan [Deccan]'.

Fig. 21: Jahangir. Zodiac, reverse

In March 1618 Jahangir writes:

> Previously to this, the rule of coinage was that on one face of the metal was stamped my name. And on the reverse the name of the place and the month and year of the reign. At this time it entered my mind that in place of the month they should substitute the figure of the constellation which belonged to that month; for instance, in the month of *Farwardin* the figure of a ram. And in *Ardibihist* the figure of a bull. Similarly, in each month that a coin was struck, the figure of the constellation was to be on one face, as if the sun were emerging from it. The usage is my own, and has never been practiced until now.[23]

The statement is explicit and contains an excellent description of the coins, now popularly known as the zodiac coins (Fig. 20 and 21). These coins were issued in gold and silver at several of Jahangir's mints.

One of the most rare and sought after of the Mughal series are Jahangir's 'portrait *muhrs*'. In fact these were not coins used for currency but rather tokens, continuing Akbar's tradition in which devoted courtiers would be presented with a miniature portrait of the king, symbolizing their discipleship. Jahangir replaced the miniature with a 'medal', later misnamed 'coins' by numismatists, to give to his most loyal courtiers in a kind of initiation ceremony into his circle of intimates. A contemporary historian writes:

> In this year, he gave orders that a piece of gold weighing one *tola* stamped on one side with the image of the Padshah and displaying on the other the figure of a lion surmounted by a sun should be given to the favourite Amirs or most devoted servants and they were to wear it respectfully on the sash of the turban or on the breast-front as a life-preserving amulet.[24]

The portrait medals are of four types; the first one with four variations. The first type displays the emperor's bust in profile on the obverse and the sun-lion emblem on the reverse. In one variant of this he holds a book; in another there is a fruit in the left hand while in a third, a cup of wine is held in the right hand and the book in the left. The fourth variant has differences on the reverse. All these issues belong to the sixth regnal year and have an identical legend in prose. The second type, issued in the seventh year, has the emperor seated cross-legged. The fourth and last type was stamped at Ajmer in the ninth regnal year; the obverse has a portrait of the emperor with the usual halo and a wine-bowl held near the lips; there is just room enough for a Persian couplet. The reverse depicts the sun in a small central square and

Fig. 22: Nurjahan

is inscribed with a Persian verse (Jahangir's coin couplets were composed by the poet laureate Asaf Khan):

> On the face of gold did Fate delineate
> Jahangir the Emperor's portrait.
> The letters of Jahangir and Allah-u Akbar
> Were from Eternity equal in number.

At the time of initiation, according to the *Tuzuk*, some words of advice were given to the 'disciple':

> He must…follow the rule of Universal Peace with regard to religions, he must not kill any living creature with his own hand…Honour the Luminaries which are manifestations of God's light, and recognize the power and existence of the Almighty God at all times and seasons.

Maintaining the etiquette of Central Asia, Jahangir had presentation pieces of large weight made which are erroneously known as the 'gigantic coins'. Throughout his autobiography Jahangir mentions bestowing these gifts. In keeping with his personality he gave fanciful names to the many varieties of these 'gigantic coins'—from the massive 100 *tola*[25] *Nur-Shahis* and 50 *tola Nur-Sultanis*, to the regular 1 *tola Nur-Jahanis*. Silver coins were given names such as *Kaukab-i-Murad* (Star of

---

21. Whitehead, p. xxi.
22. Hodivala, 1976, pp. 135-136.
23. Hodivala, 1936.
24. Hodivala, 1976, p. 152.
25. A *tola* was about 11.5 gms, i.e., the weight of a silver rupee.

Desire), *Kaukab-i-Bakht* (Star of Good Luck) and *Kaukab-i-Iqbal* (Star of Fortune), and the 1 rupee coin was known as the *Jahangiri*. There are several discrepancies in the weights and names of these pieces in Jahangir's own references. 'It is clear that great confusion existed in the mind of the emperor as to the

Fig. 23: Shahjahan

arbitrary and fanciful names he had given to these pieces and that he was himself liable to mix up one with the other.'[26] Jahangir also minted the largest coin in existence, a 1000 *tola* gold. It measues over 21 cm and weighs about 12 kg!

Jahangir formalized the scattering of largess by introducing a special quarter *rupiya* coin and naming it a *nisari* (*nisar* denotes the act of scattering). The size and weight depended on the amount of money which the imperial or other donor was willing to give away as largess at any particular occasion. He also minted a very small silver coin, the *khair qabul*, literally meaning 'may these alms be accepted [by God]'.

The great variety of coins in Jahangir's reign is indicative of the economic and political stability of the empire, which permitted the Mughal emperors to express their whims on the currency of the day—even if only as a token, advertising their greatness.

During Jahangir's rule, the number of mints decreased, from eighty-three under Akbar, to thirty-two: two exclusively for gold, eleven for silver, three for copper, and sixteen for all three. This is partly due to the fact that copper was replaced by silver as the popular medium of exchange, and the decrease in silver mints is probably because a large number of Akbari rupees continued to circulate in his reign.

In 1622, in one of the rare instances in the Subcontinent's history, the name of the Queen-consort, Nur Jahan, appeared on the coins (Fig. 22). It is a well-known fact that Jahangir shared power with his queen, issuing *farmans* in her name. The issuing of this series probably served to strengthen her position and influence over the nobility as well as the lower classes. The coins were uttered at various mints, in gold and silver (rupees and half rupees). The European traveller Tavernier, as was his wont, decided to spice up this event, fabricating a story to explain the coins. According to him, Nur Jahan danced for Jahangir one day as he 'drank briskly', and in his inebriation decreed that she would be sovereign for a day. He supposedly ordered two million gold and silver coins to be issued in her name. There is no factual basis whatsoever to his story.

Fig. 24: Later Mughals: Selection of Silver

SHAHJAHAN (r. 1628-1658)

One of Shahjahan's first acts upon assuming the kingship was to issue a *farman* that all coins bearing the name of Nur Jahan and the zodiac coins were no longer legal and had to be sent back for reminting. He reverted to the classical epigraphical legends of Babur and Humayun by reintroducing the *kalima* on his gold and silver issues—a reflection of his more traditional attitude (Fig. 23). He assumed the title of *Sahib-e-Kiran Sani* (the second lord of the [fortunate] planetary conjunctions, i.e. of the conjunction of Venus and Jupiter. Timur, the founder of the Timurid dynasty, called himself *Sahib-e-Kiran*) which henceforth appears on many of his coins.

Imperial expansion led to an increased number of mints: forty-one in total, with one exclusively gold mint, thirteen silver, five copper, and twenty-two for all three. Shahjahan made an important mint reform by equalizing conditions of coin minting in Surat and Ahmadabad. Previously Ahmadabad had a more favourable exchange rate for foreign currency. Also, Surat had separate days reserved for the reminting of Portuguese or English coins, which meant that often foreign merchants had to wait several days or months to coin their money. Under his rule, the silver *anna* was introduced, equivalent to 1/16 of a rupee. The name *pice* was assigned to the half *dam*.

Shahjahan followed his predecessors in issuing 'gigantic coins' and *nisars*. A remarkable gold 200 *muhr* coin (of 1635) of Shahjahan from the Shahjahanabad mint was found. Only a cast now survives. The 200 *muhr* piece was over fourteen centimeters in diameter, and weighed over two kg.

AURANGZEB (r.1658-1707)

Aurangzeb improved the purity of the metals for his coins, making them 5/8 per cent finer. The weight of the rupee was increased to 11.56 gms and a lighter *dam* of two-third the weight was introduced. The number of mints increased to eighty-five as the empire expanded southward. Because the emperor objected to the name of God being abused if a coin was mishandled, the *kalima* was dropped. After this point, Mughal rupees became monotonous, with the ruler's name and titles on the obverse, and 'in the year of the reign associated with prosperity', the date, and the mint name on the reverse (the coins, however, maintained their fine engraving and

Fig. 25: Akbar Shah Zafar and Bahadur Shah Zafar. Nazrana coin, obverse

Fig. 26: Akbar Shah Zafar and Bahadur Shah Zafar. Nazrana coin, reverse

purity). This formula was maintained by all of Aurangzeb's successors, save one.

Aurangzeb's coin couplets were composed by Mir Abdul Baqi:

> Struck coin in the world as clear as the sun and moon,
> I, King Aurangzeb, conquerer of the world.

---

26. Hodivala, 1936.

The accounts of a number of European travellers commenting on this verse proves that coin couplets were commonly known and recited. Often, the legends were popularly mocked. For instance, it is known that Shah Abbas II of Iran came up with this parody of Aurangzeb's verse:

> Struck coin upon a round of cheese,
> Aurangzeb, brother-slayer, father-seizer.

Aurangzeb continued the practice of minting 'gigantic coins' and *nisars*. To help his subjects meet their religious and social obligations such as *fitra* (alms), dowry etc., he minted a 'legal' *dirhem*: a square or round coin of about 3 gms with the legend, *dirhem shari*, on the obverse.

THE PRETENDERS

As mentioned earlier, the striking of coins was often used as a symbolic act to legitimize the reign of claimants to the throne. As early as Humayun's time, his rebellious brother Kamran issued coins in his own name. In Akbar's *Ilahi* year 44 (1599), Allahabad, under the governorship of Prince Salim (the later Jahangir), issued anonymous silver coins with Persian couplets, different from the regular *Ilahi* variety. This was part of Salim's declaration of independence from his father. At Jahangir's death, his grandson Dawar Bakhsh (son of Khusrau), proclaimed himself emperor and issued coins from Lahore. After the demise of Shahjahan, Shah Shuja in Bengal and Murad Baksh in Gujarat asserted their claims to the throne by striking coins. Other claimants who struck their own coins included Azam Shah and Kam Baksh after the war of succession following Aurangzeb's death. The situation got worse thereafter with coins being issued even by rebellious cousins and uncles, amongst which the following are known: Azim-u-Shan, Niku-Siyar and Bidar Bakht.

THE LATER MUGHALS

Throughout the last century of Mughal rule, every king, however brief his reign, issued coins (Fig. 24). Almost every ruler had prominent poets compose flowery verse for his currency. Shah Alam prohibited the use of verse legends on his coins, but the ban was lifted by his son Jahandar. In the reign of Farrukhsiyar, the poet Zatali, who was condemned to death after the incident, wrote an insulting parody on the emperor's coin couplet:

> Struck coin on wheat and lentils and peas
> The grain gathering emperor Farrukhsiyar.

The gradual diminution of the South Indian mints reflected the decline of the empire, but the high standards of fineness remained— the elaborate Mughal court culture being maintained till the end, despite the loss of all real power. By the reign of Alamgir II, only fifty-one mints remained. Under Shah Alam II, the number of mints rose to eighty-one, only because now the newly emergent successor states and European companies were issuing coins locally, although almost all had the name of the titular Mughal sovereign inprinted on them. Millions of rupees were minted by the British East India Company under the Mughal king's name. By the time of Bahadur Shah II, the last emperor, the only remaining Mughal mint was in the palace at Delhi. The coins struck here were known as *nazranas* (Fig. 25 and 26), and were minted for distribution as imperial gifts to the few ambassadors and grandees who called on him—a generous, noble gesture in the Mughal tradition that he could ill afford.

Like the Mughal revenue and administrative system, the Mughal symbols of power, and other aspects of Mughal rule, the Mughal classification of copper and silver coins was also borrowed *in toto* by the British. Undeniably, the system devised by Akbar and his successors was so efficient that the colonialists, who tried to wipe out all evidence of Mughal glory, had to acknowledge the superiority of the Mughal monetary system, and it remained in use until the middle of the twentieth century.

BIBLIOGRAPHY

Abul Fazl Allami, trans. H. Blockmann. *Ain-i-Akbari*. Lahore, Qausin, 1975.

Ahmad, Qeyamuddin. 'An unpublished report on the functioning and scope of the Banaras Mint, 1801.' *Indian Numismatic Chronicle*. Patna: The Behar Research Society, 1962.

Biddulph, C.H. 'Countermarked Mughal and Sur Coins.' *The Indian Numismatic Chronicle*. Patna: The Behar Research Society, 1963.

Boperachi, Osmand and Rahman, Aman ur, *Pre-Kushana Coins in Pakistan*, Islamabad, 1995.

Gupta, P.L. 'A Survey of Indian Numismatography (Muhammadan Coinage).' *The Indian Numismatic Chronicle*. Varnasi: P.O. Hindu University, 1968.

Haidar, Najaf. 'Precious Metal Flows and Currency Circulation in the Mughal Empire.' *Journal of the Economic and Social History of the Orient*. Leiden: E.J. Brill, 1986.

Hodivala, Shahpurshah. *Historical Studies in Mughal Numismatics*, Numismatic Society of India, 1936.

Hodivala, Shahpurshah. *Historical Studies in Mughal Numismatics*. Bombay: Prince of Wales Museum, 1976.

Jahangir. *Tuzuk-i-Jahangiri*. Frankfurt: Institute for the History of Arabic and Islamic Science at Goethe University, 1997.

Khan, H. *Sher Shah Suri*. Ferozsons, Pakistan, 1987.

Lane-Poole, Stanley. *The Coins of the Mughal Emperors of Hindustan in the British Museum*. London: Longmans and Co., 1892.

Lowick, N. *Coinage and History of the Islamic World*, Variorum, England, 1990.

Moosvi, Shireen. 'The Silver Influx, Money Supply, Prices and Revenue Extraction in Mughal India.' *Journal of the Economic and Social History of the Orient*. Leiden: E.J. Brill, 1987.

Pant, D. *The Commercial Policy of the Moghuls*. Bombay: D.B. Taraporevala Sons & Co., 1930.

Rajgor, D. *Standard Catalogue of Sultanate Coins of India*. Amrapali Publications, India, 1992.

Raychaudhuri, Tapan and Irfan Habib, ed. *The Cambridge Economic History of India*, Volume I: c.1200-c.1750. Cambridge: Cambridge University Press, 1972.

Richards, John F., ed. *The Imperial Monetary System of Mughal India*. Delhi: Oxford University Press, 1987.

Richards, John F. *The Mughal Empire*. Cambridge: Cambridge University Press, 1993.

Singh, M.P. *Town, Market, Mint and Port in the Mughal Empire*. New Delhi: Adam Publishers, 1985.

Singhal, C.R. 'Remarkable Mughal Coins in the State Museum, Lucknow.' *The Indian Numismatic Chronicle*. Varnasi: P.O. Hindu University, 1964

Singhal, C.R. 'Some Notable Coins in the State Museum, Lucknow, Part I.' *The Indian Numismatic Chronicle*. Patna: The Behar Research Society, 1962.

Singhal, C.R. 'Some Notable Mughal Coins.' *The Indian Numismatic Chronicle*. Varnasi: P.O. Hindu University, 1964.

Sircar, D.C. *Early Indian Indigenous Coins*. University of Calcutta India, 1971.

Thomas, E. *The Chronicles of the Pathan Kings of Delhi*. Trubner & Co., London, 1871. Quasain Reprint, Lahore, 1975.

Valentine, W.H. *The Copper Coins of India, Part I: Bengal and the United Provinces*. London: Spink and Son, Ltd., 1914.

Whitehead, R.B. *Catalogue of the Coins in the Punjab Museum, Lahore, Vol. II: Coins of the Mughal Emperors*. Oxford: Clarendon Press, 1914.

Wright, Nelson. *Catalogue of the Coins in the Indian Museum, Calcutta, Volume III: The Mughal Emperors of India*. Varanasi: Indological Book House, 1972.

Wright, Nelson. *The Coinage and Metrology of the Sultans of Delhi*. OUP, London, 1936.

The Great Mughals

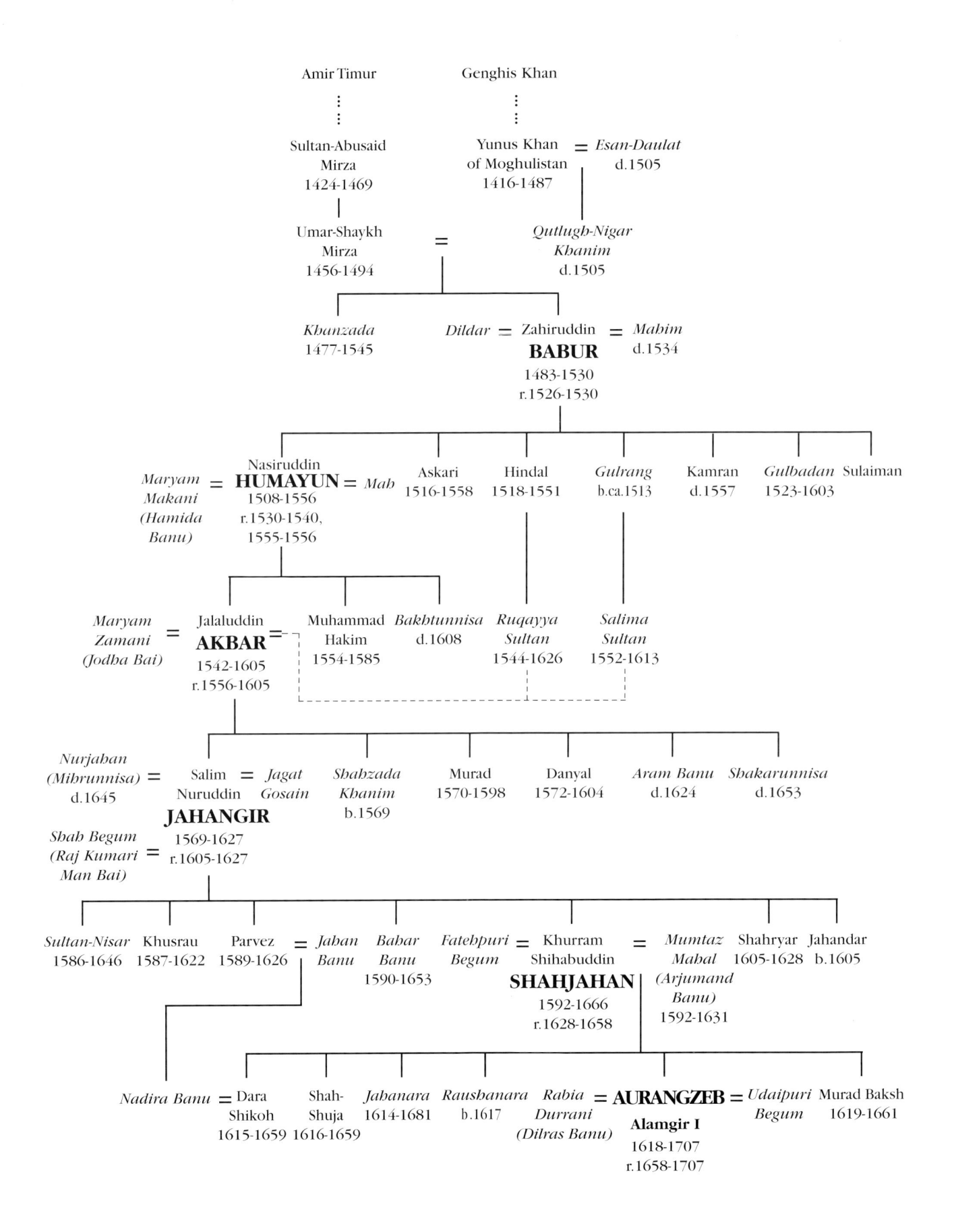

Amir Timur
⋮
Sultan-Abusaid Mirza
1424-1469
│
Umar-Shaykh Mirza
1456-1494

Genghis Khan
⋮
Yunus Khan of Moghulistan = *Esan-Daulat*
1416-1487 — d.1505
│
Qutlugh-Nigar Khanim
d.1505

Khanzada 1477-1545 — *Dildar* = Zahiruddin **BABUR** = *Mahim* d.1534
1483-1530
r.1526-1530

Maryam Makani (Hamida Banu) = Nasiruddin **HUMAYUN** = *Mah* — Askari 1516-1558 — Hindal 1518-1551 — *Gulrang* b.ca.1513 — Kamran d.1557 — *Gulbadan* 1523-1603 — Sulaiman
1508-1556
r.1530-1540, 1555-1556

Maryam Zamani (Jodha Bai) = Jalaluddin **AKBAR** = Muhammad Hakim 1554-1585 — *Bakhtunnisa* d.1608 — *Ruqayya Sultan* 1544-1626 — *Salima Sultan* 1552-1613
1542-1605
r.1556-1605

Nurjahan (Mihrunnisa) = Salim Nuruddin **JAHANGIR** = *Jagat Gosain* — *Shahzada Khanim* b.1569 — Murad 1570-1598 — Danyal 1572-1604 — *Aram Banu* d.1624 — *Shakarunnisa* d.1653
d.1645
Shah Begum (Raj Kumari Man Bai) =
1569-1627
r.1605-1627

Sultan-Nisar 1586-1646 — Khusrau 1587-1622 — Parvez 1589-1626 = *Jahan Banu* — *Bahar Banu* 1590-1653 — *Fatehpuri Begum* = Khurram Shihabuddin **SHAHJAHAN** = *Mumtaz Mahal (Arjumand Banu)* 1592-1631 — Shahryar 1605-1628 — Jahandar b.1605
1592-1666
r.1628-1658

Nadira Banu = Dara Shikoh 1615-1659 — Shah-Shuja 1616-1659 — *Jahanara* 1614-1681 — *Raushanara* b.1617 — *Rabia Durrani (Dilras Banu)* = **AURANGZEB** Alamgir I 1618-1707 r.1658-1707 = *Udaipuri Begum* — Murad Baksh 1619-1661

The Later Mughals

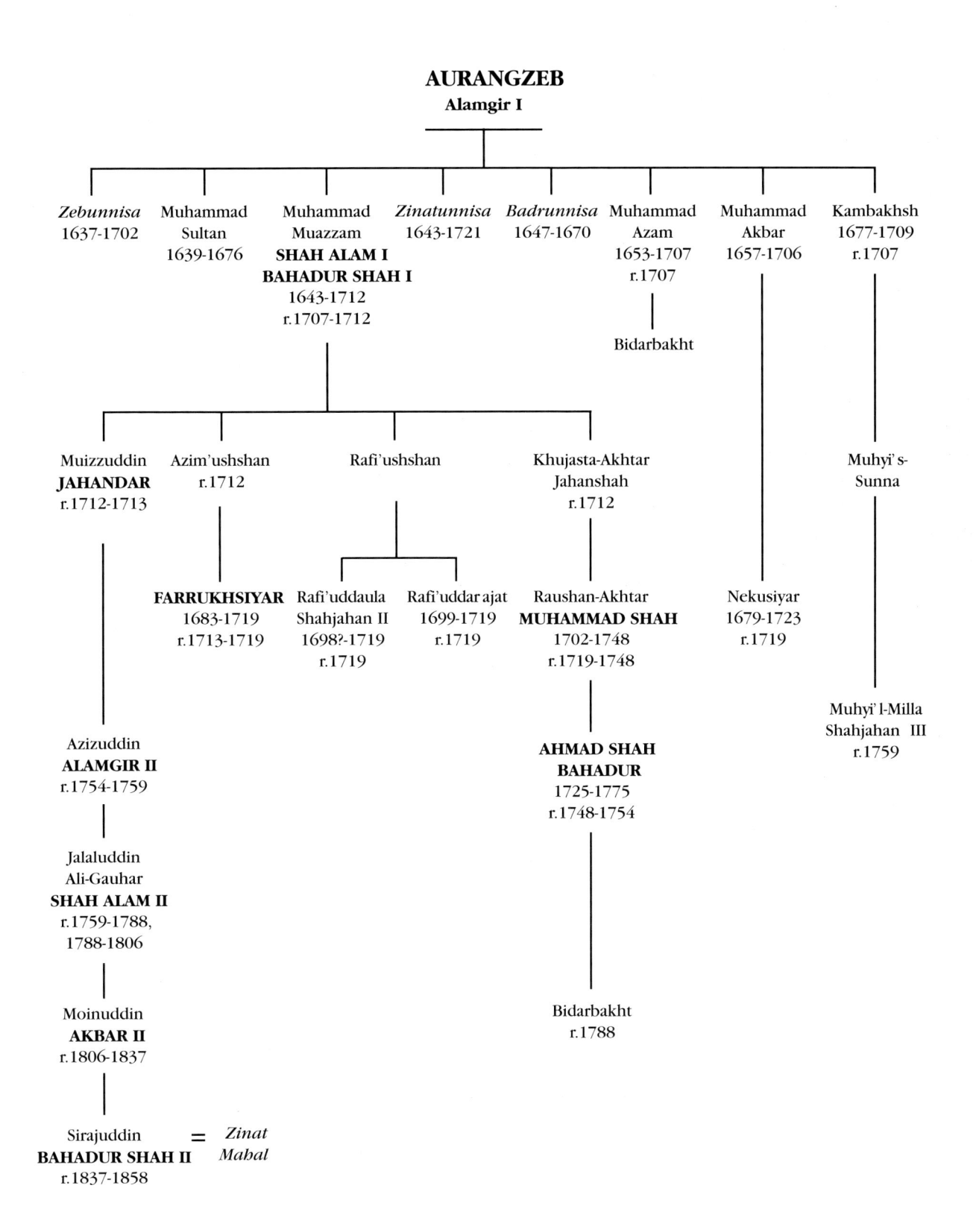

AURANGZEB
Alamgir I

- *Zebunnisa* 1637-1702
- Muhammad Sultan 1639-1676
- Muhammad Muazzam **SHAH ALAM I BAHADUR SHAH I** 1643-1712 r.1707-1712
- *Zinatunnisa* 1643-1721
- *Badrunnisa* 1647-1670
- Muhammad Azam 1653-1707 r.1707
  - Bidarbakht
- Muhammad Akbar 1657-1706
- Kambakhsh 1677-1709 r.1707

Children of Shah Alam I / Bahadur Shah I:
- Muizzuddin **JAHANDAR** r.1712-1713
- Azim'ushshan r.1712
- Rafi'ushshan
- Khujasta-Akhtar Jahanshah r.1712

- **FARRUKHSIYAR** 1683-1719 r.1713-1719 (son of Azim'ushshan)
- Rafi'uddaula Shahjahan II 1698?-1719 r.1719 (son of Rafi'ushshan)
- Rafi'uddarajat 1699-1719 r.1719 (son of Rafi'ushshan)
- Raushan-Akhtar **MUHAMMAD SHAH** 1702-1748 r.1719-1748 (son of Khujasta-Akhtar Jahanshah)

From Muhammad Akbar: Nekusiyar 1679-1723 r.1719

From Kambakhsh: Muhyi's-Sunna
  - Muhyi'l-Milla Shahjahan III r.1759

From Jahandar:
- Azizuddin **ALAMGIR II** r.1754-1759
  - Jalaluddin Ali-Gauhar **SHAH ALAM II** r.1759-1788, 1788-1806
    - Moinuddin **AKBAR II** r.1806-1837
      - Sirajuddin **BAHADUR SHAH II** r.1837-1858 = *Zinat Mahal*

From Muhammad Shah:
- **AHMAD SHAH BAHADUR** 1725-1775 r.1748-1754
  - Bidarbakht r.1788

Charts courtesy of Wheeler M. Thackston

CHRONOLOGY

The following conventional abbreviations are used:

acc.	accedes
b.	born
comp.	composed/compiled
d.	died

1483	Babur b. in Ferghana
1494	Babur acc. to throne of Ferghana
1497	Babur captures Samarkand for the first time
1501	Babur defeated by Shaibani, flees Samarkand
1504	Babur establishes himself at Kabul
1505	Babur's first incursion into India
1508	Humayun b.
1514	Ibrahim Lodi becomes Sultan of Delhi
1518	Babur invades Punjab; Kabir, the celebrated monotheist, d.
1524	Babur takes Lahore
1526	Babur defeats Ibrahim Lodi at Panipat; enters Delhi and founds Mughal/Timurid empire
1527	Babur's campaign against Rana Sanga; defeats Rana of Mewar at Khanua
1528	Babur translates Sufi treatise by Khwaja Ahrar
1530	Babur d.; Humayun acc.
1532	Humayun's campaigns against the Afghans
1535-36	Humayun's campaign against Bahadur Shah of Gujarat
1538	Humayun takes Chunar; Sher Shah takes Gaur
1539	Humayun defeated by Sher Shah at Chausa; *Guru* Nanak (b.1469) d.
1540	Sher Shah overthrows Humayun, establishes Sur empire, institutes reforms
1541	Humayun in exile; marries Hamida Banu
1542	Akbar b. at Umarkot, Sindh
1544	Humayun meets Shah Tahmasp in Iran
1545	Sher Shah killed in accident; Islam Shah acc.; Humayun conquers Qandahar; takes Kabul (lost next year)
1550	Humayun re-occupies Kabul
1554	Islam Shah Sur d.; Humayun invades Punjab
1555	Humayun reoccupies Delhi; brings master artists from Iran
1556	Humayun d. at Delhi; Akbar acc.; Hemu occupies Delhi but is defeated at Panipat
1557	Sikander Shah surrenders

1558	Akbar moves capital to Agra
1560	Akbar dismisses Bairam Khan, assumes full powers
1561	Conquest of Malwa; admission of Rajputs into Mughal nobility begins with the Amber house
1562	First pilgrimage to Ajmer; first marriage to a Hindu princess; Raja Man Singh enters Mughal service; abolition of enslavement in war; Tansen, musician and singer, brought to court
1563	Remission of pilgrim tax for Hindus
1564	Abolition of *jizyah*; construction of Humayun's tomb at Delhi begins
1564-67	Revolts of the Uzbeks and the Mirzas
1568	Akbar visits Sufi saint Salim Chishti in Sikri; occupies Chittor; bridge built over the Gumpti river at Jaunpur
1569	Salim (Jahangir) b.; Ranthambor and Kalingar incorporated into empire
1570	Foundation of Fatehpur Sikri; revision of revenue assessment ordered; Tulsidas comp. *Ramacharitmanas* (Hindi); Baz Bahadur, ex-ruler of Malwa, expert musician, comes to court
1572	Akbar conquers Gujarat, first contact with Portuguese
1573	Capitulation of Surat; introduction of cash salaries
1574	Akbar establishes *mansab* system; resumes *jagirs* on large scale; Abul Fazl and Badauni enter Mughal service; revenue settlement of Gujarat by Raja Todar Mal
1576	Bengal, Bihar and Orissa annexed
1577	Amritsar granted to the Sikhs; reorganization of mints
1579	Religious supremacy claimed for Akbar through theologians' *mahzar*
1580	Akbar sets up systematic *suba* (provincial) administration; faces rebellion in the east; first Jesuit mission arrives on Akbar's invitation; Abdunnabi and Makhdum ul-mulk banished
1581	Mirza Hakim deposed; Akbar's sister appointed Governor of Kabul; Attock Fort built
1582	Akbar liberates his slaves; *Tuhfatu-l Mujahidin* chronicles Malabar people's resistance to the Portuguese
1584	Establishment of *Ilahi* era; change in coinage
1585	Akbar transfers capital to Lahore; occupies Kabul; Bayezid, founder of Raushaniyya sect, d.
1586	Kashmir annexed to Mughal empire; Raja Birbal killed by Yusufzais
1588	Fathullah Shirazi, finance minister, mathematician, astronomer, theologian, technologist, d.
1588-91	Conquest of Sindh
1589	Mahidhara comp. *Mantramahodadhi*; Mukundaram comp. *Chandimangal* (Bengali)
1590	Rebellion in Bengal and Bihar crushed; Man Singh builds Govind Deva temple at Vrindavan with imperial grant; poet Urfi d.
1592	Nizamuddin Ahmad comp. *Tabaqat-i Akbari*, the first history of India
1593	Shaikh Mubarak, liberal theologian, Akbar's advisor d.
1595	Baluchistan and Makran incorporated; Qandahar surrendered to Mughals; Abul Fazl's *Ain-i Akbari* compiled; poet Faizi d.
1596	Berar annexed
1598	Akbar returns from the north and transfers capital back to Agra
1599	Akbar sets out for the Deccan; Mir Masum comp. *History of Sindh*
1600	Akbar conquers Ahmadnagar; Salim rebels; Narayana Bhatta comp. *Manameyo-daya* on philosophy; Ramchandra Patnaik comp. *Haravali* (Oriya); charter of East India Company

1601	Akbar annexes Khandesh, returns to Agra; Salim goes to Allahabad
1602	Abul Fazl (b.1551) murdered
1603	Salim brought to Agra by Salima Sultan Begum for reconciliation, retires to Allahabad
1604	Salim returns to Agra; *Adi Granth Sahib* compiled by Sikh *Guru* Arjun
1605	Akbar d.; Salim Jahangir acc.
1606	Rebellion of Prince Khusrau; Sikh *Guru* Arjun supports Khusrau and is killed
1608	Islam Khan appointed Governor of Bengal, consolidates and enlarges Mughal rule; Inju's lexicon, *Farhang-i Jahangiri*
1610	Shia theologian Qazi Nurullah Shustari killed on Jahangir's orders
1611	Jahangir marries Nur Jahan
1612	Afghan resistance in Bengal broken, leaders treated with clemency; Mughal administration extended over whole province; capital of Bengal shifted to Dhaka
1613	Subjugation of and treaty of peace with Mewar; submission of Jam of Kathiawar and other chiefs
1614	Jahangir resides at shrine of the Sufi saint Muinuddin Chishti at Ajmer
1615	Jahangir's atelier flourishes with master artists like Mansur, Daulat, Abul Hasan, Balchand
1616	Jahangir's first visit to Hindu saint Gosain Jadrup
1617	Surrender of Deccan kingdom of Ahmadnagar
1618	Kingdom of Kangra subdued
1619	Shaikh Ahmad Sirhindi, a leader of Naqshbandi Sufi order, imprisoned by Jahangir
1620	Princess Jahanara and Dara Shikoh become disciples of Sufi saint Mian Mir
1622	Qandahar lost to the Safavids; minister Itimaduddaula d. (buried in superb mausoleum, built by Nur Jahan in Agra); rebellion of Khurram (Shahjahan)
1627	Jahangir d.
1628	Shahjahan crowns himself emperor
1631	Shahjahan's queen Mumtaz Mahal d.
1634	Shalimar Gardens created in Kashmir
1635	Mian Mir, Qadiri saint, d.; Wazir Khan builds famous mosque in Lahore
1636	Ahmadnagar kingdom finally defeated; Shahjahan's compact with Golconda and Bijapur; Shahji Bhonsle submits to Mughals
1637	Aurangzeb marries Rabia Durrani (Dilras Banu Begum)
1638	Qandahar recovered by Mughals; Jahangir's tomb completed in Lahore
1641	Shalimar Gardens created in Lahore through remarkable engineering feat
1642	Mystic and theologian, Abdul Haq Muhaddis, d.
1643	Taj Mahal completed, in eleven years; Vedangaraya comp. *Parasi Prakasha*, glossary of astronomical terms
1645	Nur Jahan d.
1646	Mughal invasion of Northern Afghanistan (fails, 1647)
1647	Encyclopaedia and Atlas of Sadiq Isfahani, comp. at Jaunpur; Shivaji becomes independent
1648	New capital city, Shahjahanabad, (including the Red Fort) completed at Delhi by Shahjahan
1649	Qandahar finally lost; Rupram comp. *Dharmamangal* (Bengali)
1653	Mobad comp. *Dabistan*, unique account of religions

1654	Dara Shikoh comp. *Majma al-bahrain* on identity of Sufic and Vedantic concepts
1656	Mughals take territory from Golconda
1657	Territories cession imposed on Bijapur; Dara Shikoh's translation of the *Upanishads*; Satnami sect founded; Shahjahan falls ill, leading to Wars of Succession
1658	Shahjahan deposed and imprisoned by Aurangzeb; beginning of Aurangzeb's reign
1659	Aurangzeb acc.; Dara Shikoh defeated, d.
1660	First Mughal campaign against Shivaji
1662	Mughal invasion of Assam; Bihari Lal comp. *Sat'sai* (Hindi)
1664	Shivaji sacks Surat; Nainsi comp. *Vigat*; detailed statistical survey of Marwar
1665	Work begins on *Raga Darpana* and *Tuhfat-al-Hind*, two major Persian works on music; *Sangitaparija*, important Sanskrit text on music, comp. in the same period
1666	Mughals take Chittagong from European pirates; Aurangzeb's *farman* to Rasikdas on land revenue administration; *Guru* Gobind Singh acc.; Shahjahan dies; Shivaji given rank of 5000 *zat* after suing for peace; Shivaji violates treaty and escapes to Rajgarh
1667	Yusufzai rebellion in Peshawar
1668	Aurangzeb's *farman* to Muhammad Hashim on land; Aurangzeb recognizes Shivaji as Raja
1670	Shivaji's second sack of Surat; Khushhal Khan Khattak, Pushto poet, flourishes; Yashovijayaji comp. *Jaina tarka-bhasha*
1672	Satnami rebellion; Afridi rising in Northern Frontier
1674	Shivaji crowned; Akho comp. *Akhegita* (Gujarati)
1679	Aurangzeb imposes *jizyah*; annexes Marwar
1680	Shivaji d.; succ. by Shambhaji
1685	Jat uprising under Rajaram begins
1686	Bijapur annexed by Aurangzeb; English in Bengal sack Hughli and begin war; Aurangzeb prohibits all trade with English
1687	Golconda annexed; Mughals occupy Hyderabad
1688	Rajaram, Jat rebel leader, killed; Anglo-Mughal war begins (to end 1689 in English discomfiture)
1689	Shambhaji captured and executed; Rajaram, younger son of Shivaji, acc.
1693	War between Mughals and Portuguese leads to Mughal victory; Viceroy of Goa makes peace
1696	Aurangzeb prohibits Shia Muharram rites
1698	Mughals capture Jinji, key Maratha fort in South India held by Rajaram, son of Shivaji
1700	Rajaram, son of Shivaji, dies; Marathas make peace with Mughals
1702	Theologian and jurist, Shah Waliullah b. (d.1762)
1706	Marathas invade Gujarat and sack Baroda
1707	Aurangzeb d., War of Succession follows; Prince Muazzam defeats Prince Azam and becomes Shah Alam Bahadur Shah I
1708	Sikh *Guru* Gobind Singh d.
1709	Shambhaji's son, Sahu establishes himself as Maratha ruler; Sikh rebellion under Banda begins
1712	Bahadur Shah d.; Jahandar Shah acc.
1713	Farrukhsiyar acc.; abolishes *jizyah*
1716	Banda captured and executed

1717	Farrukhsiyar issues *farman* granting East India Company right to trade in Bengal free of duties on annual payment of three thousand rupees
1719	Farrukhsiyar murdered by Sayyid brothers; Mughal emperor Muhammad Shah acc.; new styles of music, for example, *khyal*, fostered at court; Dargah Quli Khan comp. *Muraqqa-e Dehli*
1720	*Divan* (collection of verse) of Vali, early Urdu poet, arrives at Delhi, initiating development of Hindi/Rekhta/ Urdu
1734	Sawai Jai Singh comp. celebrated astronomical tables, *Zich-i Muhammad-shahi*
1737	Marathas establish supremacy over Malwa and Gujarat; Peshwa Baji Rao I marches to Delhi
1739	Nadir Shah defeats Mughals in battle of Karnal, sacks Delhi; *Hujjat Allah al-Baligha* comp. by Shah Waliullah
1740s	Khusrau Khan and Firoz Khan modify Persian/Kashmiri *setar* and introduce *sitar* to Delhi
1748	Muhammad Shah d.; Ahmad Shah Bahadur acc.; Nizamul Mulk Asaf Jah, autonomous viceroy of the Deccan, d.
1749	Tek Chand Bahar comp. *Bahar-i Ajam*, comprehensive Persian dictionary
1754	Alamgir II acc.
1756	Sirajuddaula, Nawab of Bengal, captures Kolkata
1757	Clive's governorship of Bengal begins
1757	Battle of Plassey
1759	Shah Alam II acc.
1760s	Masit Khan introduces *gat toda* genre of *sitar* music
1761	Afghan king Ahmad Shah Abdali defeats Maratha army in the Third Battle of Panipat
1765	*Farman* of Shah Alam granting Diwani of Bengal, Bihar, and Orissa to the East India Company
1767	First Anglo-Mysore War
1770s	Mir Dard as court poet
1772	Shah Alam II enters Delhi as emperor under protection of Marathas
1774	First Anglo-Maratha War
1775	Jaunpur, Ghazipur ceded to East India Company by Nawab Shujauddaula of Awadh
1788	Shah Alam II reinstated on Delhi throne by Marathas; Na'mat Khan, greatest eighteenth century musician, trains at Mughal court
1793	Permanent Settlement introduced in Bengal by Cornwallis
1797	Shah Alam II commissions collection of Persian, Hindi, and Punjabi music, *Nadirat-e-Shahi*; *Usulun-Nashmat-e-Asifi*, comprehensive work on music comp.
1799	Fourth Anglo-Mysore War
1800-1810	Ghulam Mohammad develops new musical instrument, the *surbahar*
1806	Shah Alam d.; Akbar II acc.
1837	Bahadur Shah II acc.
1849	British seize Punjab
1850	Mirza Ghalib employed by Bahadur Shah II
1856	British seize Awadh
1857	Revolt / First War of Independence
1858	British depose Bahadur Shah II (exiled to Rangoon); sack Red Fort, slaughter imperial family and nobility, plunder and destroy Delhi

CONTRIBUTORS

CATHERINE B. ASHER is Associate Professor, Department of Art History, University of Minnesota. Author of many publications including *The Architecture of Mughal India* and *Islamic Monuments of Eastern India and Bangladesh*.

MILO C. BEACH was Director, Freer Gallery of Art and Sackler Gallery, Smithsonian Institution, Washington D.C. His many publications include *The Imperial Image – Paintings for the Mughal Court* and *King of the World: An Imperial Manuscript from the Royal Library, Windsor Castle*.

JOSEPH M. DYE III is Chairman of the Curatorial Department and E. Rhodes and Leona B. Carpenter Curator of South Asian and Islamic Arts, Virginia Museum of Fine Arts, Richmond. Author of *Shah Jahan and the Vision of Paradise*; *Ways to Shiva: Life and Ritual in Hindu India*.

SHAMSUR RAHMAN FARUQI is Adjunct Professor at the South Asia Center, University of Pennsylvania; was K.A. Ghaffar Khan Professor at Jamia Millia University, New Delhi. Among his many publications are *Early Urdu Literary History and Culture* and *Sher-e Shor Angez*.

ELLISON B. FINDLY is Professor and Head, Department of Religion and Area Studies, Trinity College, Hartford. Author of *Nur Jahan: Empress of India*, *Ananda: Companion of the Buddha* and many other works.

IRFAN HABIB is Professor and Head (Retd.), Department of History, Aligarh Muslim University; Chairman, Indian Council of Historical Research. Has written numerous scholarly papers and books including *The Agrarian System of Mughal India* and *Historical Atlas of Mughal India*.

AMAN UR RAHMAN is a numismatist and a petroleum consultant. Co-author of *Pre-Kushana Coins from Pakistan*.

JOHN F. RICHARDS is Professor, Department of History, Duke University. His numerous publications include *The Mughal Empire* and *Kingship and Authority in South Asia*.

ANNEMARIE SCHIMMEL is Professor (Retd.) of Indo-Muslim Culture, Harvard University; Professor Emeritus, Islamic Studies, University of Bonn. Her many well known books include *Islam in the Indian Subcontinent* and *Mystical Dimensions of Islam*.

WHEELER M. THACKSTON is Professor of Persian and other Near Eastern Languages, Harvard University. Has written *A Millenium of Classical Persian Poetry*, among other works. His translated books include *Jahangirnama: Memoirs of Jahangir* and *Baburnama: Memoirs of Babur*.

BONNIE C. WADE is Professor and Chairperson, Department of Music, University of California, Berkeley. She is the author of *Music in India: The Classical Traditions*, *Performing Arts in India: Essays on Music, Dance and Drama* and other publications.

WALEED ZIAD is a numismatist and a student at Yale University.

The Magnificent Mughals

JAMI MOSQUE (SHAHJAHANI), THATTA
1. *Courtyard*
Photo: Momin Zafar
2. *Central entrance arch (tile and stone work)*
Photo: Homayra Ziad
3. *Detail of tile and stone work at base of central entrance arch*
Photo: Momin Zafar
4. *Brick and tile work of gallery*
Photo: Momin Zafar

INDEX

A

Abdali, Ahmad Shah, 259
Abdul Haq (Muhaddis), 66
Abdul Karim of Bulri, 78, 109
Abdunnabi, 61, 62,
Abdus Samad, artist, xi, 147, 148, 151; as imperial mintmaster, 289
Abid, artist, 179
Abru, Shaikh Mubarak, 122, 126
Abul Fazl, 7, 29, 62, 104-5, 203, 287, 291, 295
Abul Hasan, artist, 166, 170, 173, 175
Adil Shahi dynasty, 9
Administration, 10-15; centralization of, 10, 14; communications, 277; efficiency of local administrations, 290; imperial music establishment, 233-36 passim; monetary system, 282, 287-91; of harem, 40-4; of imperial art studios, see Studios; of mints, 293-6; of religious organizations, 61; of *zamindari* system, 15, 273; provision of public works, see Public works; rationalization and fiscal reforms, 289; Sher Shah's reforms, 286; taxation, see Land Revenue System
Afghans, 66, 76, 259, 260; rulers, 4-5, 14, 61
Aga Khan, 76
Agra Fort, 190-1, 200, 205, 208-9
Agra, 56, 61, 65, 187; church, 72; mint, 286, 287; population, 275
Agrarian sector, 19, 270-1, 273, 289, 293; productivity of, 16
Ahl al-kitab, 61; definition, 82
Ahmad Shah, 259
Ahmadabad, 291, 294, 299
Ahmadnagar, 5, 9
Ahom state, 8,
Ain-i-Akbari, 104; on coinage, 287, 288, 291, 295; on music, 233-8 *passim*
Ajmer, 5, 62, 63, 190, 199; mosque, 207
Akbar Nama, 7, 27, 72, 104, 189, 233, 237; Akbar's birth, 28
Akbar Shah (Akbar II), 259
Akbar, Jalaluddin Muhammad (Fig.1, p. 144), *also see* Dynastic ideology; 5, 27, 31-2, 39, 148; and Islam, 61, 63, 80, 290; and Sufism, 65-6, 189, 191, 235; discipleship of nobles, see *Din-i Ilahi*; Ilahi era, 289-90; military victories, 5, 7, 8; monetary reforms, 287-91; music, 233-8; political strategies, 7, 76, 233 (*also see* Political policies); prohibition against slavery, 278; Rajput policy, 7, 69; religious policies, 61-3; Tomb, 199
Akbar, Prince, 18, 37
Al-Biruni, 69
Ali Mardan Khan, 209
Ali Muhammad, Nawab, of Rohilkhand, 260
Amber, 206, 215, 223
Amirs, 12, 14, 16,
Andalib, Khwaja Muhammad Nasir, 66, 116, 131
Aqa Riza, artist, 166
Arabic, 96, 118-9, 134, 285
Architecture: Hindu, Jain influence, 185; Indo-Muslim influence, 185, 192-3, 204; Mughal concepts, 189, 195; Timurid heritage, 184
Arjumand Banu Begum. *See* Mumtaz Mahal
Arjun, Sikh *Guru*, 63, 74
Army, 12; *also see* Military Campaigns
Artists, 69, 76, 147, 148, 166, 170, 177, 179, 180, 256
Arzu, Khan-e, 116, 133, 137
Asif Jah, Nizam, 247, 249, 259
Asif Khan, 35, 36, 44,
Asifuddaula, Nawab, 222, 259
Askari, Prince, 31
Asmat Begum, 35, 36
Aurangabad, 9, 115-6, 118, 218
Aurangzeb (Fig. 36, p. 176), 37, 39, 110, 178, 216; and Mahdawis, 75; and Rajputs, 18; and Shias, 64, 80; and Sikhs, 74; military campaigns, 9-10; music, 242, 244; painting, xiii, 178; political policies, 18, 216; promotion of Hindus, xixn. 1, 72; Rabia Durrani, 39, 218; religious policies, 64, 216; Tomb, 64, 219
Awadh, 19, 64, 77, 179, 222, 259; culture, 262

B

Baba Lal Das, 69
Babri Masjid (Mosque), 187
Babur Nama, 27, 28, 47, 85; on music, 230-2;
Babur, Zahiruddin Muhammad (Fig. 3, p. 34), 28, 31, 40, 48, 61, 81, 184-7, 292; and Sufism, 65; coinage, 285-6, 289; gardens, 85, 184, 186-7; military victories, 4; music, 230-2; poetry, 86; Tomb, 64, 86
Badakhshan, 5, 33, 76, 288
Badauni, 62, 63, 66, 69, 75, 77, 80, 104, 105-6, 290, 292
Badshahi Mosque, Lahore, 218
Bahadur Shah II (Zafar), 64, 102, 221, 225, 259, 262, 300
Bahar, Rai Tekchand, 109
Bairam Khan, 5, 27, 32, 76, 86
Bakhtiyar Kaki, Qutubuddin, 64, 220-1
Bakhtunnisa, 33
Balchand, artist, xvii, 175
Balkh, 8
Baltistan, 8,
Bangladesh, xi, xixn. 3
Basant, 252, 261
Basawan, artist, 69-70, 157
Bayezid Ansari, 76
Baz Bahadur, Sultan of Malwa, 235, 242, 290
Bedil, 102, 133
Begum Sahib. *See* Jahanara Begum
Bengal, 5, 9, 17, 19, 43, 73, 108, 179, 257, 276, 278, 305, 306; architecture of, 185; coinage, 291; East, 18; mint, 286, 289, 294; Murshidabad, 222, 223; population of Dhaka, 275; sericulture, 270
Bengali language, 110, 306
Berar, 5,

311

Index

Bernier, 29, 36, 39
Bhakti, also see Hindu mysticism; 70, 78, 236, 237
Bichitr, artist, 177
Bihar, 4, 5, 65
Bijapur, 9, 18
Biography Writing, 108
Bir Singh Deo, Raja, 203
Brahmins, 14, 61, 63, 70, 110, 245, 273
British, xiv, 64, 66, 68, 73, 74, 77, 195, 210, 222, 223, 225, 259; attitude to Mughals, xi, xxi, 10, 117, 225; Awadh, 262; coinage, 283, 300; cultural interventions by, 117, 120, 124, 134; economic effects of rule, 280; fiction about origins of Urdu, 136-7; land tax, 273
Bullhe Shah, 79, 110
Burhanpur, 78, 79
Buxar, battle of, 19

C

Calligraphy, 15, 32, 65, 109, 170, 199, 212; on coinage: 282, 288, 289, 296, Abdus Samad as mintmaster, 289; *nastaliq* on buildings, 109
Caste system, xix, 3, 270-3 *passim*, 275
Central Asian, nobles, 8, 189, 195
Chaghatai Turkish, *also see* Turkish language; 84-5, 86
Chandarbhan Brahman, 70, 108
Chandni Chowk, 212-3
Chaudhuris, 14-15
Chaurapanchasika style (art), 151
China, 3, 16, 19
Chishti order, 64-5, 66, 108, 189, 190, 191, 220; and music, 68, 77, 235, 255
Chitarman, artist, 179
Chitor, 5,
Christians, 62, 64, 72, 132; and Akbar, 63; churches, and land grant for, 63, 72
Chunar, 5,
Coinage: *also see* Mints, Calligraphy; 15; Akbar's reforms, 287-91; as work of art, 288-91 *passim*, 291-2; copper, see *Dam*; gifts to ambassadors, 289, 300; gold, see *Muhrs*; Ilahi era, 289-90, 291; Jahangir's innovations: zodiac coins, portrait *muhrs*, 297, gigantic coins, 297-8; Nur Jahan's coin issue, 298; poetry on coins, 291-2, 297, 299, 300; purity of silver/gold, 295; serving political ends, 282, 283, 286, 287, 290-2 *passim*; silver, see *Rupiya*, Silver coins; superiority to European coinage, 293
Colonialism, 300; cultural effects of, xxi, 120, 124, 134; economic effects of, 280
Commerce and Credit: banking, bill discounting, insurance, 17, 277, 289
Crops, 16, 17, 270
Cuisine, Mughal, 47, 55
Cultural synthesis, xii-xiv, xix, xxin. 9; in architecture, 185, 191; in art, 145, 148, 151, 153, 157, 181; in coinage, 282, 288; Hindu/Muslim celebrations, 72, 251-3, 261; in literature, 96, 102, 116, 119, 120, 132-3; and Mughal women, 40, 47, 48, 55; in music, 230: some elements of synthesis, 233, 238; in religion, 70-1, 78

D

Dakani/Dakhani (early names of Urdu), 79, 115-7
Dam, 15, 288, 290, 293, 299
Dance, also see *Kathak*; 230, 249, 262, 265; and Sufis, 242; appreciation of, 232, 236, 241; popularization, 247, 256
Danyal, Prince, 63, 65, 69, 70, 72,
Dara Shikoh, 36, 64, 177, 178; and Sufism, 68, 70, 106; translation of *Upanishads* etc, 70, 106
Dard, Khwaja Mir, 66, 68, 117, 123,
Dargah (shrine/tomb), also see *Qawwali*; xx-xxi, 185, 190, 191-2, 195, 202, 207, 218-9, 220-1, Akbar at, 235; Hindu, Muslim participation at, 72, 251-2
Dargah Quli Khan, 250-7, 258
Daulat, artist, 170
Daulatabad, 9,
Deccan (peninsular India), 3, 9, 18, 68, 273; development of Urdu, 115-8; language, 78, 79; Shia rulers, 76, 80
Delhi College (*Madrasa* of Ghaziuddin), 219-20
Delhi, 4, 5, 61, 65, 66, 77; development of Urdu, 115-8; mint, 286, 287; population, 275; vitality in 18th century: 116, music, 249-56 *passim*, 260
Dhrupad, 236, 255, 260
Dildar, 32, 40
Dilras Banu Begum. *See* Rabia Durrani
Din-i Ilahi (discipleship of nobles), 62-3, 73, 189, 292, 297
Diwali, 261
Dost Muhammad, artist, 147
Durbar (imperial court), 11, 177, 179, 237
Dynastic ideology, 7, 10, 189, 192-3, 198-9, 207, 221, 237

E

East India Companies, *also see* English East India Company; 17, 52, 300; disruption of Mughal trade, 278-9; silver/gold import, 293-4
Economy, *also see* Trade, Commerce; 15-18, 200, 273-4, 282; expansion, 290; impact of Mughal empire, 17, 19, 279-80, 289; output of mints, 293-4; prices, 292; productivity increase, 16-17, 289; silver/gold influx, 17, 277, 283, 293; tax collection, 16
Education, 10, 32, 45, 61, 64, 68, 95-6, 116, 132, 145, 195, 209, 219
English East India Company, 19, 29, 35, 40, 52, 223, 259, 276, 277; disruption of Mughal trade, 278; economic exploitation by, 280; minting, 300; silver/gold import, 293-4
Esan Daulat Begim, 31
Eunuchs, 31, 41, 43, 45
Europeans, 10, 15, 17, 29, 70, 72-3, 206, 223, 257, 258, 278; adoption of Indian lifestyle, 124; gossip, 36, 37n. 96, 39, 47, 298; relations with local women, 40; as Urdu/Hindi poets, 132; wealth of kingdoms relative to Mughal empire, 15-16, 293
Exports. *See* Trade

F

Faizabad, 77, 259
Faizi, 62, 69, 80, 291, 292; his works, 96-7
Family, 31, 40, 48, 232; marriage regulations, 39; senior women of, 40; ties with mothers, daughters, wives, 27, 28
Faqirullah, Amir, 237, 245
Faqirullah, artist, 181
Farrukhsiyar, 19, 64, 249, 300
Fatehpur Sikri, 32, 62, 65; Buland Darwaza, 191; description, 191-5; mint, 289
Faujdars, 10-12, 17

Ferghana, 31, 185
Feroz Shah Tughluq, 61, 293
Firoz Khan (Adarang), 255; developed *sitar*, 258, 260

G

Gardens, 56, 85, 87, 89, 184, 186-7, 195, 199, 209
Garha-Katanga (Gondwana), 5
Genghis Khan, 4, 85n. 1
Ghairat Khan, architect, 210
Ghalib, Mirza Asadullah, 81, 119, 123, 222, 262
Ghazal (Persian), also see *Ghazal* (Urdu); 94-102; High-Period style (Indian-style/*sabk-i hindi*), 94-6, 101, 102, 119; Sufism, 95-6
Ghazal (Urdu), definition, 120; eroticism, gender identity, 123-7; literary theory, 118-9; metaphors, 128-30; Sufism, 121, 124; themes, 120-1
Ghaziuddin, Imadulmulk, 259
Ghiyasuddin, architect, 190
Goa, 28, 72,
Golconda, 9, 17, 18
Gosain Jadrup, 63, 70, 87
Govardhan, artist (17th century), 69-70, 177
Govardhan, artist (18th century), 179
Govind Deva Temple, 197
Govind Singh, Sikh *Guru*, 74
Gujarat, 5, 17, 64, 73, 75; and development of Urdu, 115; architectural influence of, 185, 192-3; 278; coinage, 291; mint, 289
Gulbadan, 31, 32, 40, 47, 103, 232-3
Gwalior, 5, 65, 66, 191; and music, 235-8 *passim*, 264
Gwaliori, Muhammad Ghous, 65, 69, 237

H

Haider, architect, 199
Hamid Khan, architect, 210
Hamida Banu. *See* Maryam Makani
Har Rai, Sikh *Guru*, 74
Hargovind, Sikh *Guru*, 74
Hasrat Mohani, 128
Hatim, Shah Zahuruddin, 116, 123, 128, 134-5
Hindal, Prince, 31, 32, 40, 65
Hindi, 70, 78, 86, 110; and Urdu, 115-6, 118, 131-3
Hindu mysticism and relation with Sufism, 69-70, 72, 74, 78, 79, 106, 230
Hindus, *also see* Caste, Holi; 44, 48, 55, 62, 69, 117, 185, 222; accommodation with Muslims, 4; Akbar, 7, 69, 196; artists, 69, 153, 157, 175, 177, 179, 256; as *ahl al-kitab*, 61; at Muslim shrines, 72, 251-2, 261; Aurangzeb, xixn. 1, 72; conversions, 4, 65; daughters, 27; nobility, xixn. 1, 11; perceptions about Muslims, 69; right-wing groups, 187, 206; seclusion of women, 40; Shahjahan, 204; *suttee*, 29, 70; under Mughal rule, 7, 197; Urdu poets, 132; vitality of Hinduism, 72; writers, 70, 117, 132; *zamindars*, 14
Hindustan, 5, 191, 286; definition, xixn. 3; description in *Baburnama*, 85, 187
Hindustani Classical Music, *also see* Glossary, 265-6; importance for imperial family, 230; important texts in Aurangzeb's reign, 245; major development under: Akbar, 233, 235-7, Jahangir, 241, Shahjahan, 241-2, Muhammad Shah, 249-51, 256, 258, Shah Alam II, 260, 261 (also see *dhrupad*, *tabla*, *sarangi*, *sitar*, *surbahar*, *khyal*, *sarod*, *sursingar*); popularization of, 247; significance of *qawwali*, 251-2, 255, 260; Wajid Ali Shah, 262
Hindustani, 115, 136-7
History Writing, 103-8
Holi, 47, 81, 261
Hujwiri, 64
Humayun, Nasiruddin (Fig. 1, p. 26), 4-5, 28, 31, 32, 40, 48, 61, 146, 187; and astrology, 81; and Shia, 5, 76, 286; and Sufism, 65; books and art, 147; coinage of, 285-7; in Iran, 76, 84, 188; Tomb, 56, 189-90
Humayun-nama, 32, 57, 103; on music, 232-3
Hyderabad (Deccan), 116, 247, 249, 259

I

Ibadatkhana (house of worship), 62, 73, 104-5
Ibn Arabi, 61, 62, 66, 70
Id ul-adha, 80
Id ul-fitr, 80, 90
Iltutmish, 61, reforms, 284
Imambaras, 80, 222
Imports. *See* Trade
Inayat Khan, 173
India (undivided). *See* South Asia
Industry and Crafts, 274-6, 289, 293
Insha, Inshallah Khan, 115
Iran, *also see* Safavid; 76, 84, 230, 282, 289
Islam Shah, 5
Islam, *also see* Sufis, Sufism, Quran, and Glossary of Religion chapter, 82; and beauty, xx-xxi, xxin. 12; and status of mothers, 27; in India, 61, 64-5, 96; marriage to widows, 35; marriage, 39; spread by Sufis, 64-5; veneration of Jesus and Mary, 28, 29n. 8, 72
Ismailis, 76, 78
Itimaduddaula (Ghiyas Beg), 35, 40, 44, 84, 171; Tomb, 200, 202

J

Jagannath Pandit (poet laureate of Shahjahan), 110
Jagat Gosain, 33
Jagdish temple, 214
Jagir system, 16, 19, 273-4, 289
Jagirdar, 16-17, 274
Jahan Muhammad Dost, architect, 200
Jahanara Begum, 36, 47, 99; and Sufism, 37, 65, 68, 79, 108; grave, 218-9; public works, 56, 207, 213
Jahandar Shah, 247
Jahangir, Salim Nuruddin (Fig. 23, p. 162), 8, 27, 28, 32-3, 35, 40, 48, 197-8, 202; and Shias, 77; and Sikhs, 74; and Sufism, 65, 68, 198; coinage, 296-298; gardens, 56, 87, 199; music, 241; painting, 166; rebel court at Allahabad, 166, 198; religious policies, 63, 66; Tomb, 205-6
Jahangirnama. See *Tuzuk-i Jahangiri*
Jai Singh, Raja, 206, 215, 223, 225
Jains, 62, 73-4, 148, 185, 222
Jaipur, 215, 223, 225, 258, 261, 262
Jami Mosque, Delhi, 73, 212
Jaunpur, 5, 195; mint, 286, 289
Jayasi, Malik Muhammand, 75, 102, 110, 117
Jesuits, 32, 81; and Akbar, xii, 63, 72-3, 195; Christian art brought by, 28, 72
Jesus Christ, 39, 65; veneration in Islam, 28, 29n. 8, 72

Index

Jeweled arts, xxin. 9
Jews, 73
Jizyah, 7, 18, 61, 62, 64; definition, 82
Jodha Bai. *See* Maryam Zamani
Jugal Kishore Temple, 203

K

Kabir, 74, 117
Kabul, 4, 5, 8, 33, 64, 76, 85, 277; coinage, 291
Kabuli Bagh mosque, 186
Kalim, Abu Talib, 90-4, 99, 101, 108
Kalima, 284-7 *passim*, 290-2 *passim*, 296, 299
Kambo, Muhammad Salih, 103, 108
Kamran, Prince, 5, 146, 300
Kannada, 9, 116, 119
Kanua, battle of, 4
Karachi, 73, 184
Karam Imam, Muhammad, 259
Kashmir, 5, 48, 55, 70, 73, 87, 99, 101, 199, 209; Srinagar, 56, 209; 242, 258
Kathak dance, 256, 257, 263, 264
Kayasths, 13
Kesu Das, 153
Khadija, 28, 35
Khandesh, 5
Khankhanan, Abdul Rahim, 70, 78, 80, 171; his poetry and patronage, 86, 97, 179n. 54
Khanqah, xx, 191-3, 209
Khanzada Begim, 31
Khilji, Alauddin, 61, 292, 293
Khurram. *See* Shahjahan
Khushhal Khan Khattak, 76
Khusrau Khan (18th century musician, developed *sitar*), 258
Khusrau, Amir (14th century Sufi/poet/musician), 115, 157, 212, 255, 258
Khusrau, Prince, 33, 51, 74
Khyal: and association with *qawwali*, 255-6, 260; influence on *sitar*, 264; styles, 264

L

Lahawri, Abdul Hamid, 108, 177
Lahore Fort, 205, 208-9; Kala Burj, 200
Lahore, 5, 41, 43, 61, 63, 68, 70, 78, 115, 161, 210, 218; Akbar transfers capital to, 65, 191; centre of Persianate culture, 64; mint, 286, 287, 289; population, 275
Lal Shahbaz Qalandar, 77
Land revenue system, 14-17, 273-4, 288, 289; reforms of Sher Shah, 286
Law and order, 10-11, 17, 203, 277
Legacy of Mughals, xi, xx, 19, 36, 47, 55, 57, 85, 109-10, 117, 131, 145, 165, 179, 184, 206, 225-6, 230, 265, 277, 282, 288, 300
Lexicography, 109, 116
Lodi dynasty, 185, 285, 286
Lodi, Ibrahim Khan, 4, 186; mother of, 29
Lucknow, 77, 80, 116, 222, 259, 260, 262, 263

M

Maclagan, 28, 39
Madho Lal Husain, 78, 110
Madras, 10, 17, 79
Madrasa (school), 32, 82, 61, 195, 209, 219-20
Mahabat Khan, 52, 171
Mahabharata, 69, 96, 106, 152
Mahakavirai (poet laureate of Sanskrit/Hindi), 70, 106, 110
Maham Anaga, 32
Mahdawiyya, 74-5
Mahim Begim, 28, 31, 32, 40
Mahmud Ghaznavi, 61, 84,
Mahzar, 62
Makhdum ul-Mulk, 61, 62, 75
Makramat Khan, architect, 210
Malik Ambar, 9
Malikush-shuara (poet laureate of Persian), 70, 84, 291
Malwa, 5, 290
Mamur Khan, architect, 200
Man Singh, Raja, 63, 69, 70, 76, 215; architectural patronage, 196-7
Mansabdars, 12-13, 16, 19, 274
Mansur, artist, 170, 171
Manufactures. *See* Industry
Marathas, 9, 18, 29, 68, 220, 259, 280; under Peshwas, 19
Marsiya, 77
Marwar, 18, 275
Marx, 117
Maryam Makani (Hamida Banu), 27, 28, 32, 56
Maryam Zamani (Jodha Bai), 28, 32, 45, 202; and international trade, 33, 52
Masit Khan, musician, 260-1
Masnavi: as poetic form, 90, 102; Rumi's *Masnavi*, *see* Rumi
Mauryas, 3
Mazhar Jan-e Janan, 68, 72, 120
Merchant capital, 9, 17, 277-9
Meritocracy under Mughals. *See* State system
Mewar, 18, 214-5
Mian Mir, 63, 68, 108
Mihrunnisa. *See* Nur Jahan
Military campaigns, 4, 5, 7-10
Mints, 17, 282; administration of the mints, 295-6; expansion, 290; function and output, 293-4; in Jahangir's reign, 298; in Shahjahan's reign, 299; restructuring and appointment of Abdus Samad, 289; under later Mughals, 300
Mir Amman, 137
Mir Masum Nami, 65
Mir Musavvir, artist, 147
Mir Sayyid Ali, artist, 147, 148, 151
Mir, Mir Muhammad Taqi, 121-4 *passim*, 125, 127, 130, 131, 133
Mirza Jani Beg, ruler of Sindh, 63, 78
Mogul, xi, 85n. 1,
Molla Shah Badakhshi, 37, 68, 108, 209
Monetary system, *also see* Mints; 287-91
Moti Mosque (in Red Fort), 216, 218
Mughal, origin of designation, 85n. 1
Mughal Studies: neglect/ misrepresentation of 18th and 19th centuries: xiii, xiv, xviii, 116-7, in art, 146, 179, in architecture, 220; on economy, 279

Muhammad (PBUH), Prophet, 27n. 3, 62, 72, 78; and status of mothers, 27; footprint of, 63, 81; odes to, 80; relationship with wife Khadija, 28, 35
Muhammad Afzal, artist, 179
Muhammad Azam, Prince, 110, 245
Muhammad bin Qasim, 61
Muhammad Hakim, Mirza, 8, 33, 291
Muhammad Muazzam (Bahadur Shah I), 110, 247
Muhammad Munim Khan, 195
Muhammad Shah, 19, 116, 179; patronage of music, 249-50; Tomb, 220
Muharram, 80, 82
Muhrs, *also see* Coinage; 17, 288-9; excellence of Jahangir's, 296; giant, names of, 291; gigantic, names of, 297-8; largest coin in existence, 298; poetic couplets on, 291-2, 297; rare, 290; Shahjahan's gigantic *muhrs*, 299; zodiac, portrait, 297
Muinuddin Chishti, Khwaja, 32, 62, 64, 108, 190, 235, 261; mosque, 207
Multan, 5, 64, 80
Mumtaz Mahal (Arjumand Banu Begum), 36, 44, 47, 205-6, 241
Murad Baksh, Prince, 178, 300
Murad, Prince, 63, 178
Muraqqas, 170, 178
Mus'hafi, Ghulam Hamdani, 118, 121, 124-5 *passim*, 131, 134, 136-7
Musaddas, 77
Musha'ira, 120, 131-3
Music. *See* Hindustani Classical Music

N

Na'i, 235-6
Na'mat Khan, musician, 247, 250, 255, 258, 261
Nadir Shah, 64, 66, 77, 79, 179, 250
Nadira Banu, 39, 99
Naim, C.M., 126
Nainsukh, artist, 256
Naji, Muhammad Shakir, 126
Nanak, Sikh *Guru*, 74
Nand Gwaliori, artist, 157
Naqshbandi order, 18, 61, 65, 77, 79, 178; attitude to music, 66
Naubat Khan, musician, 237,
Nauroz, 35, 45, 47, 90
Nizam Shahi dynasty, 9
Nizamuddin Auliya, 65, 68, 189, 192, 218, 255
Nobility (service elite), *also see Mansabdars*, *Jagirdars*; 11-13, 16; and personal ties with emperor, 13-14 (also see *Din-i Ilahi*); increase in power of, 19; patronage of: architecture/public works, 195-7, 199, 202, 205, 210, 219, 220, art, 179, literature, 84, 86, 95, 97, 98, 99, 101, 116, 131, music, 232, 245, 250, 253
Nur Jahan, Nur Mahal (Mihrunnisa), 32, 33, 43-4, 48; and English, 52-3; and Shia, 77; charity, 35; daughter Ladli, 35; influence and power, 35, 36, 51-2; minting of coins, 298; public works and gardens, 56, 200; trade, 35, 52
Nurullah Shushtari, 77
Nusrati Bijapuri, 118, 119

O

Oak, P.N., distortion of history, 206, 207n. 58, 207n. 59
Orissa, 5,
Ottoman empire, 3, 4, 19, 84, 101; Piri Reis, 65; wealth relative to Mughal empire, 15, 293

P

Padshahnama, 29, 176-7, 179, 241
Painting, *also see* Artists; art for political purposes, 152, 173, 176, 178; brought by Jesuits, 28, 72, and English, 53; contact with European styles, xii, 53, 72, 153, 157; critique of art historians' interpretations, xii, xiii, xiv; development of Mughal style, introduction of portraiture, 165; influence of Mughal style, xiv, 179, 256, 261; under later Mughals, xiii, 179; women's patronage, 55
Paisa, 288, Sher Shah's nomenclature, 286
Pakhavaj, 236, 253
Panipat, first battle of, 4, 186
Pargana, 10, 14-16
Pathans, 76, 77, 80, 117
Payag, artist, 177
Peacock Throne, 90, 93, 174
Peasantry, xix, 15-17, 270-1, 273
Persia. *See* Iran, Safavid
Persian language, 13-14, 67, 69, 70, 77-80 *passim*, 84, 115; common usage of, 116
Persian Poetry, also see *Ghazal* (Persian and Urdu); 90-102; and Sufism, 95-6; influence of Sanskrit, 119; poets, 131; Sindhi legends in, 102
Persianate high culture, 13, 64, 84, 95, 146
Plassey, battle of, 68, 279; plunder after, 280
Poetry, also see *Ghazal* (Persian, Urdu), Urdu; 90
Political policies, xiii, 14, 15, 63, 72, 73, 74, 76, 185-6; art for political purposes, *see* Painting; coinage serving political ends, *see* Coinage; music for political purposes, 237; women's influence on, 27, 49-51
Population, 3, 270; of cities, 275
Portuguese, *also see* Jesuits; 4, 9, 72-3; harassment of Indian shipping, 33, 52, 80, 278; trade, 17
Prophet, the. *See* Muhammad
Protocol, imperial, 13; in harem, 27, 31, 40-1
Public works, 188, 195, 197, 200, 202, 209, 212-3, 214, 216, 274; bridges, 276; Gumpti river bridge, 195
Pundit Dinanath, 245, 273
Punjab, 5, 68, 74, 77, 79
Punjabi language, 77, 78, 79, 235, 261
Purabi, 75
Purchasing power of currency, 292
Purdah, 40, 57, 132
Pushto, 76, 109

Q

Qadi Qadan, 76, 77
Qadiri order, 37, 63, 68, 77-9 *passim*
Qandahar, 8, 35, 76, 173, 277, 286, 294
Qasida, 90-4

Index

Qawwali, xx-xxi; at shrines, 235, 251-2; 247; significance for classical music, 251-2, 255-6, 260
Quran, *also see* Islam; 18, 67, 68, 69, 74, 79, 80, 188, 199, 213; marriage, 39; spirit of Islam, xx-xxi, xxin. 12; veneration of Jesus and Mary, 65, 72; verses on coins, 292
Qutb Shahi dynasty, 9
Qutluqh Nigar Khanim, 31

R

Rabia Durrani (Dilras Banu Begum), 39, 218
Rahman Baba, 76
Rajputs, 4, 43, 165, 178; and Akbar, 7, 69, 233; and Aurangzeb, 18; architecture, 196-7, 202-3; art, xiv, 165, 178, 179; music, 255, 256, 261-2; nobility, 11; under Mughal rule, 197; women, 29
Ram Das Kachhwa, Raja, 165
Ram Singh, Raja of Amber, 178
Ramadan, 47, 63, 80, 90-1
Ramdas, Sikh *Guru*, 63
Rampur, 260, 262
Rana Sanga, Raja of Mewar, 4
Ranjit Singh, Sikh ruler of Punjab, 74
Ranthambor, 5
Ratti standard, 283
Raushanara Begum, 37
Raushaniyya, 69, 76
Red Fort (Palace of Shahjahanabad), Delhi: destruction of, 210; use of calligraphy on, 109
Regional cultures and languages, xiv, 75, 76-80, 109, 179; music, 242, 255, 259-65
Rekhta, *also see* Urdu; definition, 116, 118
Respect for other traditions, xiii, xix, xx, 28, 40, 47, 65, 69, 70, 151, 197, 230, 261, 290-1
Revolt of 1857, 64, 120, 262; destruction of Red Fort, 210; intellectual disarray after, 134
Rightly Guided Khalifas, definition, 285, 287, 292
Roe, Thomas, 35, 40, 53, 55
Rohilkhand, 260
Rohtas Fort, Bihar, India, 188
Rohtas Fort, Punjab, Pakistan, 188
Rohtas Palace, 197
Rudra vina, 237
Rulership, Mughal model of, 10, 61, 63, 188, 196-7, 200, 292, 296
Rumi, Maulana Jalaluddin, xx, 64, 65, 96, 117; and imperial family, 79; his great book, *Masnavi*, 61, 68, 78-9
Rupiya/Rupee, 15, 277, 287-8, 293; nomenclature of Sher Shah, 286; widespread use of, 290
Ruqayya Sultan Begum, 32, 56
Rusva, Aftab Ra'e, 126

S

Saadat Khan, Nawab, 259
Sachal Sarmast, 79
Sadr as-sudur, 61, 63
Safavid, empire of Iran, 5, 8, 76, 84, 147, 288; wealth relative to Mughal empire, 293
Safdar Jang, Nawab, 259; Tomb, 221
Saib, Mirza Muhammad Ali, 101
Salim Chishti, Shaikh, 33, 62, 65, 191; and Tansen, 237; shrine, 191-2
Salim. *See* Jahangir
Salima Sultan Begum, 27, 32
Salman, Mas'ud Saad, 115
Samarkand, 31, 184, 185
Sanskrit, 78, 117, 286; influence on Persian/Urdu, 119; similarities with Arabic/Persian traditions, 120, 134; text on music synthesis, 230, 245; translations from, 69, 70, 96, 104, 106; works in, 70, 74, 110
Sarangi, 257
Sarmad, 73
Sarod, 260
Sauda, Mirza, 77, 122, 137
Sawai Pratab Singh, Maharajah of Jaipur, 245, 261
Sayyid brothers, 19, 247, 249
Sayyid Muhammad Kazmi, 75
Service Sector, 275
Shah Abbas, ruler of Safavid Iran, 173
Shah Abdul Latif Bhitai, 78, 79, 109
Shah Alam II, 66, 68, 116, 259, 260, 261, 300; daughter of, 133; Tomb, 221
Shah Begum (Raj Kumari Man Bai), 33, 202
Shah Ismail, first Safavid ruler of Iran, 76
Shah Quli Khan, 195
Shah Shuja, Prince, 35, 178, 178
Shah Tahmasp, ruler of Safavid Iran, 5, 76, 146, 286
Shah Waliullah, 61, 66, 80
Shahjahan, Khurram Shihabuddin (Fig. 30, p. 169), 18, 51-2, 110, 203-4; and Mumtaz Mahal, 36, 205-6, 241; coinage reform, 299; justice, 63, 174; military campaigns 8-9, 16; music, 241-2; religious policies, 63
Shahjahanabad, 16, 205; description, 210-12
Shahji Bhonsla, 9
Shahrukhi, 285, 287, 291
Shaibani Khan, 31
Shaikh Mubarak, 62, 75
Shaikh ul-Islam, 61
Shalimar Gardens, Kashmir, 209
Shalimar Gardens, Lahore, 78, 209
Shambhaji Bhonsla, 10, 18
Sher Afgan, 35
Sher Shah Sur (Sher Khan, Sher Shah) 5, 61, 146, 233; architecture and public works, 187-8; monetary/fiscal reforms, 286, 287
Shia, 63, 64, 68, 76-7, 80, 84, 220, 222, 259; and Humayun, 5, 76, 286
Shipping/Ship building, 9, 278-9
Shivaji Bhonsla, 9-10, 29, 216
Shujauddaula, Nawab, 259
Sikander Shah Sur, 5,
Sikhs, 66, 68, 74, 220; grant of Amritsar, 63, 74; literature, 110
Sikri, 33, 62, 63
Silver coins, also see *Rupiya*; Aurangzeb's *dirhem*, 300; Jahangir's *nisar, khair qabul*, 298; Jahangir's zodiac, 297; Shahjahan's *anna, nisars*, 299
Sindh, 5, 61, 64, 65, 68, 78, 79, 110, 115, 146,
Sindhi language, 76, 78-9, 109
Sirhind, 5, 66,
Sirhindi, Ahmad, 66, 121,
Sitar, also see Khusrau Khan, Firoz Khan; 258, 260-4 *passim*,
South Asia: definition, xixn. 3; diversity of, 3; unification under Mughals, xix, 5, 14-5, 19, 189, 273, 277, 289
State system, *also see* Rulership; xviii, 8, 189, 196-7, 216, 230, 233, 273, 282,

290-1; meritocracy, xix, xixn. 1, 7, 11-12, 15, 69, 72, 84, 97, 133, 196
Studios, imperial art: organization of, 145, 147, 148, 152, 166, 170
Subcontinent. *See* South Asia
Sufis: and beauty, xx-xxi, xxin. 12; and dance, 242; and music, 65, 66, 235, 258 (also see *Qawwali*); and regional languages, 75-80; and spread of Islam, 64-5, 84; buildings, see *dargahs/khanqahs*; definition, 82; influence on Mughals, xx-xxi, 62-66, 68, 96, 189, 198, 207, 218; Persian/Urdu poetry, 95-6, 121, 124; practice of universalism, xx, 65, 72, 78-9, 251-2; saintly women, 68, 78, 108; saints, 15, 64-5, 108, 185
Sufism, *also see* Sufis; xx-xxi; as a way of life, 96; definition, 82; diffusion in society, 75-80, 96
Sulaiman, Prince, 5
Sulh-i Kul, policy of, 63, 189
Sultan Bahu, 79, 110
Sultanate of Delhi, 3, 148, 230, 284, 285
Surat, 17, 72, 278, 280; mint, 293, 299; population, 275
Surbahar, developed by Ghulam Muhammad, 262
Sursingar, invented by Pyar Khan, 260
Suttee, 29, 70
Suwar, 12

T

Tabla, 256-7; schools of playing, 264
Taj Mahal, 36, 206; calligraphy of, 109; cost, 16; distortion of history, 206, 207n. 58, 207n. 59
Talib Amuli, 95, 98
Tambur, 235
Tanka, 284, 285, 286, 288, 290; Jahangiri *tanka* of gold and silver, 296
Tansen, Miyan, 233, 236-8, 260; and Sufi saint Gwaliori, 65, 237
Tara Chand, 115
Tazkira Writing, 108-9, 131-3
Teg Bahadur, Sikh *Guru*, 74
Temples, 196-7, 202-3, 214, 223; Akbar, 197; Aurangzeb, 203, 216; in Delhi, 222; influence of Mughals on, 197, 203, 214, 225; Shahjahan, 204, 214
Terry, Edward, 27, 295
Thatta, 110; church, 72; population, 275; Shahjahani mosque, 81, 213, 310
Timur, Amir (Tamerlane), xi, 4, 10, 64, 84, 85n. 1, 103, 285, 292, 299; Aq Serai Palace, 184, 185, 191
Timurid culture/traditions: xi, 10, 64, 85n. 1, 103, 109, 146, 147, 152, 184, 200; architectural heritage, 184, 185-90 *passim*; coinage, 282-7 *passim*; musical heritage, 231-2
Tipu Sultan, 116
Todar Mal, 69, 70, 165
Trade, *also see* Commerce and Credit; 289, 293; Domestic, 16, 52, 200, 276-7; Foreign, 9, 17, 52-3, 274, 277-9; harassment by Portuguese, 33, 52, 80, 278
Tughluq, Muhammad, 230, 285
Tulsidas, 70
Turkish language, 66, 78, 120; as imperial family language, 31, 86-7
Turks, 61, 69, 76, 84, 236, 284
Tuzuk-i-Jahangiri, 87, 166, 173, 296, 297

U

Uch, 68
Udaipur, 214-5, 256
Udaipuri Begum, 37,
Urban population and employment, 274-5
Urdu poets: professions, origins, religions, gender, class, 132
Urdu, also see *Ghazal*; 64, 66, 68, 79, 102; colonial interventions and discontinuities in, 120, 124, 134; early history, 115-8; fiction about origins, 136-7; in Awadh, 262; love of poetry in all classes, 132; poetry, in 18th century, 117-31
Urfi, 96, 97
Ustad Ahmad Khan, architect, 210
Ustad/shagird, institution of, 131-5; secular, 133; women, 133

V

Vali (Aurangabadi), 116, 119, 133, 134; *Divan*, 118
Virgin Mary (Madonna), veneration in Islam, 28, 29n. 8, 72
Vrindavan, 197, 202-4 *passim*, 216

W

Wah Gardens, Pakistan, 196-7
Wajid Ali Shah, ruler of Awadh, 260; patronage of arts and culture, 262
Wazir Khan mosque, 210
Wazir Khan, 210
Women, Mughal: apartments, 41, 193, 195; as political advisers, 27, 37, 49, 51, 195; charity, 44, 213; diversity, 39; education and pastimes, 44-5, 68; financial resources, 43-4; patronage of: art and literature, 55, 66, 68, buildings, public works, gardens, 55-6, 200, 212-3, 221, music and dance, 55, 232, 238, 241, 244; pilgrimage to Mecca, 32, 47, 63, 81; pilgrimages, 47; poets, 55, 99, 132, 133; protection of, 41; religion, 47, 65; seclusion, 40; status of senior, 27, 40-1; trade, 49, 52

Y

Yakta, Ahad Ali Khan, 115
Yunus Khan, 31
Yusufzai, 5

Z

Zamindars, 10, 14-15, 17, 271, 273; increase in power of, 18; under British, 273
Zat, 12, 63
Zebunnisa, 37, 68, 79
Zinatunnisa, 37, 56, 68
Zoroastrians (Parsees), 62, 73, 292